The Kaiser and the Colonies

The Kaiser and the Colonies

Monarchy in the Age of Empire

MATTHEW P. FITZPATRICK

OXFORD
UNIVERSITY PRESS

OXFORD
UNIVERSITY PRESS

Great Clarendon Street, Oxford, OX2 6DP,
United Kingdom

Oxford University Press is a department of the University of Oxford.
It furthers the University's objective of excellence in research, scholarship,
and education by publishing worldwide. Oxford is a registered trade mark of
Oxford University Press in the UK and in certain other countries

First Edition published in 2022

Impression: 1

Published in the United States of America by Oxford University Press
198 Madison Avenue, New York, NY 10016, United States of America

British Library Cataloguing in Publication Data
Data available

Library of Congress Control Number: 2021949113

ISBN 978-0-19-289703-9

DOI: 10.1093/oso/9780192897039.001.0001

Printed and bound in Great Britain by
Clays Ltd, Elcograf S.p.A.

For Tash, for all the reasons

Acknowledgements

Much of this book was written in Tarndanya / Adelaide. In many ways it is a site where the concerns of this book loom large. Its European name commemorates the German royal Adelheid von Sachsen-Meiningen, later Queen Adelaide of the United Kingdom and Hanover, but its Indigenous name, Tarndanya, comes from the Kaurna people, the custodians of this land who never ceded their territory to the European settlers who effaced their culture and language as they built a European-style city. Without reference to their interests or views, the Kaurna people have seen their country knitted together with other British settler colonies to become part of the nation-state of Australia. My family and I, who live on Kaurna country, pay our respects to their Elders, past and present. Ngadlu tamp-inthi ngadlu Kaurna yartangka tikanthi. Ngadludlu tampinthi, parnaku tuwila yartangka.

This book is the product of an Australian Research Council Discovery Grant (DP180100118, 'Monarchy, Democracy and Empire: German Imperial Policy before 1914'). I would like to thank the ARC for its generosity. My home institution Flinders University was also helpful in allowing me to take study leave in 2018, so that I could take up a visiting fellowship at the Westphalian Wilhelms University in Münster to begin researching this project in earnest. I was kindly hosted in Münster by Thomas Großbölting and the scholars of the Excellence Cluster for Religion and Politics. In many ways this book is also a product of their intellectual and institutional generosity. My process blog for the research trip, https://monarchydemocracyempire.blogspot.com/, shows the joys and challenges of that year.

In Münster, Friday night *Stammtisch* with Felicity Jensz, Mark Padgham (and Ezra), as well as the treasured times spent with the Noël and Grüneberg families, Anke Lenzing, Peter Sobkowiak, Sandy Klein and Holger Winkler, meant that we were well looked after once we had transplanted ourselves to what has become a second home for us. Thanks too are due to Frederik Schulze and Silke Hensel for their hospitality in Münster. In Adelaide, our re-entry was greatly assisted by the Natalier-Kings, Kris, Alan, Luci and Xan, who helped us develop a local version of the *Stammtisch* tradition.

While writing this book I have benefited greatly from the assistance and advice of a large number of colleagues who kindly took an interest in parts of my work and commented or advised me on it. In no particular order, I would like to thank Susie Protschky, Felicity Jensz, Anja Schwarz, Cindy McCreery, Robert Aldrich, Michael Schubert, Peter Fäßler, Daniel Siemens, Peter Monteath, Romain Fathi,

Johanna Conterio, Andrekos Varnava, Jan Rüger, David Motadel, Ulf Morgenstern, Christine Winter, Andreas Eckl, Liu Wenming, Kate Bagnall, Clemens Büttner, Kate Fullagar, Alessandro Antonello, Benjamin Haas, Gerhard Keiper, Thomas Hermeling, David Pizzo, Andi Zimmerman, Michelle Moyd, Amrita Malhi, Clementine E. Burnley, Stefanie Michels, and Adam Blackler. Thank you, as well to the numerous area specialists with whom I spoke briefly at various talks and conferences who offered me precious advice and encouraged me to bring together these disparate case studies and show their interconnectedness. None of them should be held responsible for the errors I have made in doing so.

I would also like to thank Cathryn Steele, Shanmugasundaram Balasubramanian, Donald MacFarlane Watt, and the team at Oxford University Press for shepherding this project through to completion, as well as the archivists and librarians who were unfailingly helpful in my search for materials while I was hunting them down. Special thanks are due to Lisa Mudge and Paul Morisset for their assistance at various points throughout the project, and in particular Bodie Ashton, who read an initial draft of the entire manuscript and provided some timely advice. Some preliminary parts of the research presented here have also been published in different forms in *History Australia, International History Review,* and in two Manchester University Press collections edited by Robert Aldrich and Cindy McCreery, namely *Royals on Tour* and *Crowns and Colonies.* An attempt has been made to ensure that any websites footnoted here have been captured using the internet archive 'wayback machine.'

Finally, I would like to offer my deepest thanks to my wife, Natasha Grundy, who characteristically leapt at the opportunity to return to our Münster life, and to my children Ethan, Saskia, and Lily who only complained a little when riding their bikes to school through ankle deep snow while their friends at home were at the beach. Their healthy lack of interest in my work meant that I didn't entirely disappear into the world of the *Kaiserreich.*

MPF

Contents

List of Figures

Introduction

Royal Cosmopolitanism in the Age of Empire

In the first month of the First World War, German Cameroon's governor, Karl Ebermaier, announced that he had hanged an African king for treason:

> You people of Duala! I appeal to you and proclaim to you: Manga (Rudolf) Bell has been hanged today because he had proven himself to be a traitor to the Kaiser and the Empire…Those who do not wish to become criminals like Duala Manga and his assistant must tear themselves from every false leader that sits in the dark secretly brewing poison. Those that truly mean it are welcome. The government of the Kaiser will always be just and thankful towards true servants and true subjects…Manga himself had bid his people in his last hour that through his death the Duala would return in their hearts to loyalty to the Kaiser and obedience to the government.[1]

Significantly, some of the most damning evidence condemning King Rudolf Duala Manga Bell for his supposed conspiracy against the German Crown had come from another African king, namely, King Njoya of Bamum, whose seemingly ironclad evidence was sufficient to silence the Dualan king's supporters in the Reichstag.[2]

The hanging of Manga Bell lay at one extreme of relations between the German state and the monarchs of the extra-European world. At the other was Kaiser Wilhelm II's 1898 voyage to the Ottoman Empire, where he declared that he was very pleased to visit Sultan Abdulhamid II, a monarch who, in the wake of massacres against Christian minorities in his empire, was being treated by other European states as a pariah. The visit saw Wilhelm II stoutly defend the sultan's sovereign rights, not least in letters to Russia's Tsar Nicholas II, in which he

---

[1] Ebermaier, 8 August 1914, as quoted in Uwe Schulte-Varendorff, *Krieg in Kamerun* (Berlin: Ch. Links, 2011), 77. See too *Bundesarchiv* (BA) Berlin R1001/4430: 'Enteignung in Duala'.

[2] Adolf Rüger, 'Die Duala und die Kolonialmacht 1884–1914: Eine Studie über die historischen Ursprünge des afrikanischen Antikolonialismus', in Helmuth Stoecker (ed.), *Kamerun unter Deutscher Kolonialherrschaft* (Berlin: VEB Deutscher Verlag der Wissenschaften, 1968), 240–1, 248–9. Although the reasons for Njoya's accusations were complex, he claimed he feared that withholding evidence would lead the Germans to execute him 'because we broke our oath to the emperor'. Christoph Geprägs, Njoya to Krüger, 28 April 1914, in *Bundesarchiv* (BA) Berlin, R1001/4430, 184. See also Njoya to Krüger, 28 April 1914, in *Basler Missionsarchiv (BMA)* E-2, 42, 212.

The Kaiser and the Colonies: Monarchy in the Age of Empire. Matthew P. Fitzpatrick, Oxford University Press.
© Matthew P. Fitzpatrick 2022. DOI: 10.1093/oso/9780192897039.003.0001

warned that 'Turkey is very much alive and not a dying man. Beware of the Musulmen if you touch their national honour or their Khalif!'[3]

Between these two poles lay an intricate set of relations marked by occasions of summit diplomacy, royal visits, and the mutual exchange of gifts, letters, and treaties between the German emperor, his representatives and the monarchs of Africa, Asia, and the Pacific. By investigating these royal ties and the role of monarchy in Germany and in the wider world, the following chapters show how royal power was wielded and constrained within a global empire. They examine the varying modes and contexts of royal relations and illustrate how empire and monarchy—both structures based on inequality and social stratification—functioned via intersecting strategies of coercion, the negotiation of disparate interests, and the mobilization of carefully framed claims to sovereignty and legitimacy. Highlighting how questions of territorial, economic, and political sovereignty were addressed by different monarchs, this book makes clear when and why monarchs decided to embrace cooperation or conflict and what political, economic, and military effects their responses engendered. As a work of imperial history informed by postcolonial methods and insights, it pushes beyond earlier, one-dimensional stasis models of non-European polities and foregrounds how their histories of change, adaptation, and agency were structured by both domestic social pressures and the external strictures of German imperialism.

In part, understanding monarchical power in the global German Empire involves addressing the question of the actual role played by the German emperor in *Weltpolitik* and *Kolonialpolitik*. More importantly, however, it requires an explanation of how non-European monarchs sought to maximize their agency and express their authority as they navigated their way between the expectations of their subjects and German incursions into their sovereign domain. Without denying the clear structural inequalities of empire, the following chapters question the lopsided idea that only intra-European political relations are a matter for diplomatic history, while relations between Europe and the rest of the world are exclusively a matter for colonial history. By focusing on the global interactions between non-European monarchs and the German Empire, the following reminds European historians that Africa, Asia, and the Pacific have important histories of diplomacy and foreign relations that not only intersect with that of Europe but also profoundly affected it.

Wilhelm II's *Weltpolitik*?

While unveiling a monument in Bremen in 1905, Wilhelm II offered a detailed picture of his then current understanding of *Weltpolitik*. Reiterating the earlier

---

[3] Wilhelm II to Nicholas II, 20 October 1898; Wilhelm II to Nicholas II, 9 November 1898, in Isaac Don Levine (ed.), *Letters from the Kaiser to the Czar* (New York: Frederick A Stokes, 1920), 55–65.

sentiments of Bernhard von Bülow, who had argued that Germany did not wish to place anyone else in the shade as it sought its 'place in the sun',[4] the emperor claimed that:

> I have vowed, from the lessons learned from history never to strive for some-thing as tedious as global rule. For what has become of the so-called global empires? Alexander the Great, Napoleon I, all of the great military heroes have swum through blood and left behind suppressed nations that at the first chance have staged uprisings and brought the empires to ruin. The global empire of which I have dreamt should above all consist of a newly forged German Empire that enjoys absolute trust from all sides as a calm, honest, peaceful neighbour. If one day history should perhaps speak of a global German Empire or a global Hohenzollern Empire, its conquests would not be those won by the sword, but through mutual trust between nations striving after the same object—in short, as one great poet has expressed it, 'externally limited, internally unlimited'.[5]

At precisely the time this speech was delivered, however, Germany's military was locked in a genocidal war in German South West Africa, where suppressed African nations were fighting under under their paramount leaders Samuel Maharero and Hendrik Witbooi. Elsewhere in Africa, the first Moroccan crisis was in full swing, leading Wilhelm II to travel to Tangier to declare his full sup-port for the political sovereignty of Sultan Abdelaziz against the predations of France and Britain. Wilhelm II's vision of the German Empire as a calm, honest, and peaceful global power averting war and engendering trust between neigh-bouring nations was quite remote from global realities.

Whether the German Empire's expansionist military and diplomatic position across the world reflected the hopes and will of its sovereign is a question that many have sought to answer. Notwithstanding the long history of German imperialism that preceded his reign, 'the Kaiser's *Weltpolitik*' is a phrase often encountered in histories of the foreign and colonial policy of the *Kaiserreich*.[6] In 1965, Fritz Fischer could confidently (and erroneously) write that 'It is indisput-able that the turn towards new overseas acquisitions, colonies or spheres of influ-ence, was created in 1897/98 when *Weltpolitik* was created by Wilhelm II.'[7] Around the same time, William Henderson similarly declared that the advent of an imperialist foreign policy was directly attributable to the accession to the throne

---

[4] Bernhard von Bülow, in *Verhandlungen des Reichstages*, 6 December 1897, 60.
[5] Wilhelm II, 'Enthüllung eines Denkmals Kaiser Friedrichs ("Bremer Friedensrede"), Bremen, 22. März 1905', in Michael A Obst (ed.), *Die politischen Reden Kaiser Wilhelms II: Eine Auswahl* (Paderborn: Ferdinand Schöningh, 2011), 263–6.
[6] Alois Paul von Falkenegg, *Die Weltpolitik Kaiser Wilhelm's II: Zeitgemässe Betrachtungen* (Berlin: Boll und Pickardt, 1901), 79–87.
[7] Fritz Fischer, *Weltmacht oder Niedergang: Deutschland im ersten Weltkrieg* (Frankfurt: Europäische Verlagsanstalt, 1965), 80.

of 'the young Emperor Wilhelm II, who wanted Germany to have a place in the sun' and who had 'cast envious eyes' on Africa, the Ottoman Empire, China, and the Pacific.[8] A more recent adherent to this view has similarly argued that 'the adoption of *Weltpolitik* by Kaiser Wilhelm II' was a shift away from an 'earlier *Realpolitik*' and a 'fundamental shift in the empire's foreign policy'.[9]

For others, there is even a foundational date for this putatively royal push for empire, namely 18 January 1896, when the German emperor is said to have proclaimed a new era of *Weltpolitik* during a speech to parliamentarians.[10] Much has been made of this ostensibly landmark address, but the monarch's actual words are revealing. In his formal speech Wilhelm II made no mention of colonies, a naval programme, or anything regarding foreign policy at all. Only later at lunch did he allude to some of these themes obliquely, opining that:

> The German Empire has become a global empire. Thousands of our compatriots live everywhere, across the farthest reaches of the earth. German products, German ingenuity, and German energy travel over the ocean. The value of the materials that Germany has sent overseas numbers in the thousands of millions. The grave duty falls to you, gentlemen, to help me join this greater German Empire securely to ours.[11]

It was only with the assistance of the assembled parliamentarians, Wilhelm II admitted, that he could fulfil his duty 'not only to those Germans close to me, but also to the many thousands of compatriots abroad, that I protect them when I must'.[12]

This brief toast was hardly an announcement of a new direction in German foreign policy, nor did it herald a new naval plan (the so-called Tirpitz plan was a year and a half away).[13] Rather, apart from a frank admission of the emperor's inability to act on foreign policy matters without the Reichstag, his toast echoed

---

[8] William Otto Henderson, *Studies in German Colonial History* (London: Frank Cass, 1962), 8.

[9] Francesco Cerasani, 'Imperialism of Kaiser Wilhelm II: Perspectives and Historiography of German Südpolitik', in Antonello Biagini and Giovanna Motta (eds), *Empires and Nations from the Eighteenth to the Twentieth Century*, vol. 2 (Newcastle: Cambridge Scholars Publishing, 2014), 30–5.

[10] Geoff Eley, 'Empire by Land or Sea? Germany's Imperial Imaginary, 1840–1945', in Bradley Naranch and Geoff Eley, *German Colonialism in a Global Age* (Durham, NC: Duke University Press, 2014), 27; Holger W. Herwig, *'Luxury' Fleet: The Imperial German Navy 1888–1918* (London: Routledge, 2014), 18; Ekkehard Böhm, *Überseehandel und Flottenbau: Hanseatische Kaufmannschaft und deutsche Seerüstung 1879–1902* (Düsseldorf: Bertelsmann, 1972), 80; Ernst Hasse, *Weltpolitik, Imperialismus und Kolonialpolitik* (Munich: Lehmanns Verlag, 1908), 39.

[11] Wilhelm II, 18 January 1896, in Oskar Klaußmann (ed.), *Kaiserreden: Reden und Erlasse, Briefe und Telegramme Kaiser Wilhelms des Zweiten: Ein Charakterbild des Deutschen Kaisers* (Leipzig: J. J. Weber, 1902), 133.

[12] Wilhelm II, 18 January 1896, in Klaußmann (ed.), *Kaiserreden: Reden und Erlasse*, 133.

[13] Indeed, in January 1896, Tirpitz had not yet left for East Asia, where his understanding of Germany's naval requirements would crystallize. See Dirk Bönker, 'Global Politics and Germany's Destiny "from an East Asian Perspective": Alfred von Tirpitz and the Making of Wilhelmine Navalism', *Central European History* 46, no. 1 (2013), 61–96.

sentiments concerning overseas Germans (*Auslandsdeutsche*) that had been a commonplace in German public discourse since the 1840s: that the energies and wealth of emigrants had been lost to the nation and that it was in Germany's best interest to try and reintegrate them into the national community by protecting their interests.[14] His statement that since unification 'the German Empire has become a global empire' was no more than a statement of fact. In his lunchtime remarks, that is, Wilhelm II confirmed his acceptance of the tenets that had underwritten German foreign policy since its economy moved away from its earlier agricultural base towards the globally oriented mercantilism of the middle classes, who had long seen empire as a necessary part of their search for markets, resources, and the *embourgeoisement* of German society.[15]

The emperor certainly spoke on occasion of his pride in Germany's global empire. However even royalists seeking to represent Wilhelm II as a leading figure in the pro-colonial movement admitted that 'most colonial acquisitions had occurred under the reign of Wilhelm I', that is to say, under his grandfather. The most that colonial lobbyists felt they could argue was that Wilhelm II was not against colonialism in principle, even if he had shown a lack of interest in Germany's overseas possessions.[16]

If Wilhelm II was not the architect of empire, neither was the maintenance and administration of empire a domain for the royal prerogative, notwithstanding the enhanced powers that German law offered the emperor and his viceregal representatives in the colonies.[17] Despite this, a number of historians have viewed Wilhelm II as a strong monarch, either controlling or heavily influencing German foreign, military, and colonial policy.[18] Foremost amongst these is John C. G. Röhl, who in unsurpassable detail has argued steadfastly for four decades that 'the almost overwhelming personal power of Kaiser Wilhelm, who was able to determine the

[14] Bradley D. Naranch, 'Inventing the *Auslandsdeutsche*: Emigration, Colonial Fantasy and German National Identity, 1848–71', in Eric Ames, Marcia Klotz, and Lora Wildenthal (eds), *Germany's Colonial Pasts* (Lincoln, NE: University of Nebraska Press, 2005), 21–40; Matthew P. Fitzpatrick, *Liberal Imperialism in Germany: Expansionism and Nationalism, 1848–1884* (Oxford: Berghahn Books, 2008), 135–59, contra Böhm, *Überseehandel und Flottenbau*, 80–1.

[15] Fitzpatrick, *Liberal Imperialism in Germany*; Jens-Uwe Guettel, *German Expansionism, Imperial Liberalism, and the United States, 1776–1945* (Cambridge: Cambridge University Press, 2012); Arne Perras, 'Colonial Agitation and the Bismarckian State: The Case of Carl Peters', in Geoff Eley and James Retallack (eds), *Wilhelminism and Its Legacies: German Modernities, Imperialism, and the Meanings of Reform, 1890–1930* (New York: Berghahn Books, 2004); Frank Lorenz Müller, 'Imperialist Ambitions in Vormärz and Revolutionary Germany: The Agitation for German Settlement Colonies Overseas, 1840–1849', *German History* 17, no. 3 (1999), 346–68; Sebastian Conrad, *Globalisation and the Nation in Imperial Germany* (Cambridge: Cambridge University Press, 2010); Erik Grimmer-Solem, *Learning Empire: Globalization and the German Quest for World Status, 1875–1919* (Cambridge: Cambridge University Press, 2019).

[16] 'Die Kolonie unter Kaiser Wilhelm II', *Kolonie und Heimat* 6, no. 38 (January 1913) in BA Berlin, N 2146/86 Nachlass B von König.

[17] Matthew P. Fitzpatrick, *Purging the Empire: Mass Expulsions in Germany, 1871–1914* (Oxford: Oxford University Press, 2015), 230–3.

[18] Ernst-Wolfgang Böckenförde, *State, Society and Liberty: Studies in Political Theory and Constitutional Law*, trans. J. A. Underwood (New York: Berg, 1991), 87–114.

6 THE KAISER AND THE COLONIES

Reich's policy down to the smallest detail', was at the root of 'the global dimensions of German aims'.[19] Röhl, amongst others, has focused on what he has seen as the emperor's 'personal rule' or the 'kingship mechanism'.[20] To understand German military, naval, and foreign policies prior to the First World War, Röhl maintains, 'We could hardly do better than to adopt as our vantage point the view from the "mightiest throne in the world".'[21]

Abiding at the heart of this is a view of Germany's parliamentary constitutional monarchy that is out of step with recent studies which have shown how any lingering absolutist tendencies were receding. Historians such as Margaret Lavinia Anderson, Hedwig Richter, and Martin Kirsch have made clear that the increasingly liberal parliamentary political structures of Imperial Germany ensured that the reality of constitutional monarchy looked very different from Röhl's picture of an autocratic royal regime.[22] So too Christopher Clark, Martin Kohlrausch, and Alexander König have all (in differing ways) demonstrated the clear limits to Wilhelm II's power in both foreign and domestic politics, given the constraints imposed by the Reichstag, the media, the bureaucracy, the agitation of civil society groups, and their interpretation of the political and economic imperatives that drove the state.[23] As Wilhelm II's royal chamberlain Robert von Zedlitz-Trützschler argued, 'our government and the emperor himself are more

[19] John C. G. Röhl, *Wilhelm II: Into the Abyss of War and Exile, 1900–1941* (Cambridge: Cambridge University Press, 2014), 73.

[20] John C. G. Röhl, *Wilhelm II: The Kaiser's Personal Monarchy, 1888–1900* (Cambridge: Cambridge University Press, 2004); John C. G. Röhl, *Kaiser, Hof und Staat: Wilhelm II und die deutsche Politik* (Munich: C. H. Beck, 1988), 116–40; John C. G. Röhl, 'Introduction', in John C. G. Röhl and N. Sombart, *Kaiser Wilhelm II: New Interpretations* (Cambridge: Cambridge University Press, 1982), 1–22. On the inner circle of the Kaiser, see Isabel V. Hull, *The Entourage of Kaiser Wilhelm II, 1888–1918* (Cambridge: Cambridge University Press, 1982). For work reiterating Röhl's position, see Annika Mombauer and Wilhelm Deist (eds), *The Kaiser: New Research on Wilhelm's Role in Imperial Germany* (Cambridge: Cambridge University Press, 2003).

[21] Röhl, *Wilhelm II: Into the Abyss of War and Exile*, xvii.

[22] Margaret Lavinia Anderson, 'Ein Demokratiedefizit? Das deutsche Kaiserreich in vergleichender Perspektive', *Geschichte und Gesellschaft* 44 (2018), 367–98; Margaret Lavinia Anderson, 'Demokratie auf schwierigem Pflaster: Wie das deutsche Kaiserreich demokratisch wurde', in A. Briskina-Müller, A. Drost-Abarjan, and A. Meißner (eds), *Logos im Dialogos: Auf der Suche nach der Orthodoxie: Gedenkschrift für Hermann Goltz* (Berlin: Lit Verlag, 2011), 245–62; Margaret Lavinia Anderson, *Practising Democracy: Elections and Political Culture in Germany* (Princeton, NJ: Princeton University Press, 2000); Hedwig Richter, *Demokratie: Eine deutsche Affäre: Vom 18. Jahrhundert bis zur Gegenwart* (Munich: C. H. Beck, 2020); Martin Kirsch, *Monarch und Parlament im 19. Jahrhundert: Der monarchische Konstitutionalismus als europäische Verfassungsform: Frankreich im Vergleich* (Göttingen: Vandenhoeck & Ruprecht, 1999); Hans-Christof Kraus, 'Monarchischer Konstitutionalismus: Zu einer neuen Deutung der deutschen und europäischen Verfassungsentwicklung im 19. Jh.', *Der Staat* 43 (2004), 595–620.

[23] Christopher Clark, *Kaiser Wilhelm II: A Life* (London: Penguin, 2009); Martin Kohlrausch, *Der Monarch im Skandal: Die Logik der Massenmedien und die Transformation der wilhelminischen Monarchie* (Berlin: Akademie Verlag, 2005); Alexander König, *Wie mächtig war der Kaiser: Kaiser Wilhelm II zwischen Königsmechanismus und Polykratie von 1908 bis 1914* (Stuttgart: Franz Steiner Verlag, 2009). See also Oliver F. R. Haardt, 'The Kaiser in the Federal State, 1871–1918', *German History* 34, no. 4 (2016), 529–54.

influenced in important decisions by public opinion, the press, by assemblies and by parliament than they are aware.'[24]

Despite Wilhelm II's lofty claim that 'the king's will is the highest law,'[25] the constitutional parameters of the emperor's metropolitan authority were firmly spelt out in Articles 11–19 of the constitution. Here it was stipulated that the monarch was granted the power to declare war and to announce peace, to sign treaties, and to commission ambassadors. He was the ostensible chief commander of the navy, and all German army troops (including those of the semi-autonomous Bavarian army) were to obey his orders during times of war. Domestically, the emperor could call, open, and dissolve the popularly elected Reichstag and the Bundesrat. He was the final signatory to newly promulgated laws and he appointed state secretaries, the German equivalent of ministers, who were answerable to the chancellor.[26] Properly contextualized, the emperor's constitutional role extended to those aspects of statecraft where a single figurative executive head of the state was required: war and peace, and the formal promulgation of laws already passed by the bicameral legislature. Although significant military power was theoretically available to him, in most domestic matters the emperor was only one (and often the last) of several authorities who comprised a network of bodies that made decisions, ordinarily coming behind the bureaucracy, the chancellor, the Bundesrat, and the Reichstag.[27]

If Wilhelm II loudly proclaimed himself to be the ruler of his lands, this did not make it so.[28] As Hans Fenske has shown, in constitutional terms Germany was far from particularly authoritarian, but rather was (for better or worse) a 'normal member' of the European state system.[29] The perception that the personal will of the emperor drove state policy was, as Wolfgang J. Mommsen bluntly put it, a 'fiction'.[30] Wilhelm II was increasingly subject to close public scrutiny which routinely assessed and frequently condemned his performance.[31] Alongside other political and constitutional blockages, this scrutiny meant that Wilhelm II 'remained incapable of developing or realising a political programme of his own, or even of imposing his will on the executive in a consistent manner'. As Clark has

---

[24] Robert von Zedlitz-Trützschler, *Zwölf Jahre am deutschen Kaiserhof* (Stuttgart: Deutsche Verlags-Anstalt, 1925), 66.

[25] Robert K. Massie, *Dreadnought: Britain, Germany and the Coming of the Great War* (London: Vintage, 2007), 108–9.

[26] 'Gesetz, betreffend die Verfassung des Deutschen Reichs', 16 April 1871, *Deutsches Reichsgesetzblatt* 16 (1871), 63–85 (see especially §§11, 18, 64, and 68); Ernst Rudolf Huber, *Deutsche Verfassungsgeschichte seit 1879*, vol. 3: *Bismarck und das Reich* (Stuttgart: Kohlhammer Verlag, 1963), 931–2; Ernst Rudolf Huber (ed.), *Dokumente zur deutschen Verfassungsgeschichte*, vol. 2: *Deutsche Verfassungsdokumente, 1851–1900*, 3rd edn (Stuttgart: Kohlhammer Verlag, 1986).

[27] König, *Wie mächtig war der Kaiser?*, 267–75.   [28] König, *Wie mächtig war der Kaiser?*, 267.

[29] Hans Fenske, *Der moderne Verfassungsstaat: Eine vergleichende Geschichte von der Entstehung bis zum 20. Jahrhundert*, (Paderborn: Schöningh, 2001), 528.

[30] Wolfgang J. Mommsen, *War der Kaiser an allem Schuld? Wilhelm II und die preußisch-deutschen Machteliten* (Berlin: Ullstein 2005), 158.

[31] Kohlrausch, *Der Monarch im Skandal*, 461.

argued, Wilhelm II's significance 'lay less in the imposition of an autocratic will than in a chronic failure of leadership'.[32]

Despite the longevity and intensity of the debate over Wilhelm II's power in Germany, little research on the degree of his personal power over colonial sites has been undertaken. In terms of colonial warfare, Annika Mombauer has charted the emperor's clumsy role in garnering European support behind Alfred von Waldersee, his candidate for 'commander-in-chief' of the multinational force operating in China during the Boxer War.[33] Turning to Africa, others, most strenuously David Olusoga, Casper Erichsen, and Jeremy Sarkin, have claimed that the Herero-Nama Wars constituted the 'Kaiser's Holocaust'.[34] Assessing Wilhelm II's role in such colonial affairs certainly requires care, particularly as German law did in fact offer the emperor significantly enhanced formal legal latitude in the colonies. Given his public prominence and constitutional position, Wilhelm II was arguably not quite the spectral 'shadow Kaiser' that Hans-Ulrich Wehler described. Nonetheless, Wehler was certainly correct in pointing out that the emperor's role was far from decisive:

> Did the Kaiser himself direct the China, Pacific or Africa policies of German imperialism, or the unsuccessful informal expansion in the Near East with the help of the Baghdad railway? Or was he not simply one actor amongst many others…each pursuing different ends and able to claim varying degrees of agency in decision-making?[35]

Contemporaneous commentators support this judgement. Wilhelm II's chamberlain Zedlitz-Trützschler pointed out that the myth of royal power was no more evident than in 'the entirety of *Kolonialpolitik*', where the emperor thrust himself into the limelight, despite his lack of real influence, at the cost of making himself personally responsible for failures and policy reversals over which he had little effective control.[36] So too the emperor's Colonial Secretary, Wilhelm Solf, bluntly recalled that 'the Kaiser was extraordinarily uninterested in our colonies and colonial politics.'[37] According to Solf, the emperor saw *Kolonialpolitik* as a curiosity and, unlike committed liberal imperialists such as Solf, never considered

---

[32] Christopher Clark, 'How Powerful Was the Kaiser?', *London Review of Books* 37, no. 8, (2015).

[33] Annika Mombauer, 'Wilhelm, Waldersee and the Boxer Rebellion', in Annika Mombauer and Wilhelm Deist (eds), *The Kaiser: New Research on Wilhelm's Role in Imperial Germany* (Cambridge: Cambridge University Press, 2003), 91–119.

[34] David Olusoga and Casper Erichsen, *The Kaiser's Holocaust: Germany's Forgotten Genocide and the Colonial Roots of Nazism* (London: Faber, 2011); Jeremy Sarkin, *Germany's Genocide of the Herero: Kaiser Wilhelm II, His General, His Settlers, His Soldiers* (Cape Town: UCT Press, 2010).

[35] Hans Ulrich Wehler, *Deutsche Gesellschaftsgeschichte*, vol. 3: 1849–1914 (Munich: C. H. Beck, 2006).

[36] Zedlitz-Trützschler, *Zwölf Jahre am deutschen Kaiserhof*, 66.

[37] Solf to Geheimrat Eltester, 28 March 1930, Bundesarchiv Koblenz, N1053/81 Nachlaß Solf Amtliches und Politisches. Im Ruhestande Bd. 4, January–June 1930, 88–9.

colonies to be an essential part of Germany's global standing. This picture of Wilhelm II, incapable of or uninterested in wielding royal power in colonial affairs, has been borne out by decades of work on the emperor's theatrical but dilettantish approach to colonial matters displayed in such grave missteps as the 'Hun speech' and the *Daily Telegraph* interview—both of which point to a monarch who was ill informed and subsequently managed, corrected, and at times disowned by the chancellor, the Reichstag, and the bureaucracy, who all ensured that a more predictable (but no less assertive) form of *Weltpolitik* prevailed.[38] By focusing almost exclusively on the formal prerogatives of the Crown, accounts such as Röhl's have overemphasized the (in fact steadily receding) monarchical political tendencies of Germany. In doing so, they foreground a monarchical decisionism that goes beyond even the contemporaneous assessment of Carl Schmitt, who saw in the constitutional monarchy of the German Empire an attempted 'compromise and bridge' between the 'German soldier state and the liberal constitutional state' which, Schmitt believed, in the final analysis favoured parliamentarism.[39]

This is not to say that the emperor did not play a political role in Germany. As a constitutional monarch with clearly delineated political duties, Wilhelm II remained an important political presence. This was recognized several decades ago by Geoff Eley, who, while arguing that Wilhelm II was 'uninterested and uninvolved in the practice of governing in anything but the most sporadic, arbitrary and whimsical of ways', also recognized that any attempt to argue away the constitutional monarch's importance was as untenable as the 'kingship mechanism' as a historiographical paradigm.[40] Constitutionally and temperamentally incapable of implementing personal rule, Wilhelm II, nonetheless, played a political and symbolic role, including in foreign and colonial affairs, as the instantiation of the complex political, social, and economic relations that comprised the German Empire. As the royal embodiment of the state, the emperor's role in formal, set-piece diplomacy was particularly pronounced, not because he played a significant role in policy development, but rather because his actions and

---

[38] On the 'Hunnenrede', see Bernd Sösemann, 'Die sog. Hunnenrede Wilhelms II: Textkritische und interpretatorische Bemerkungen zur Ansprache des Kaisers vom 27 Juli 1900 in Bremerhaven', *Historische Zeitschrift* 222, no. 2 (1976), 342–58. See also Bülow, *Denkwürdigkeiten*, vol. 1, 358–61. On the Krüger telegram, see Paul Hoser, 'Die Krügerdepesche (1896)', in Jürgen Zimmerer (ed.), *Kein Platz an der Sonne: Erinnerungsorte der deutschen Kolonialgeschichte* (Frankfurt: Campus Verlag, 2013), 150–63. On the *Daily Telegraph* affair, see Peter Winzen, *Das Kaiserreich am Abgrund: Die Daily-Telegraph-Affäre und das Hale-Interview von 1908* (Stuttgart: Franz Steiner Verlag, 2002); Terence F. Cole, 'The Daily Telegraph Affair and Its Aftermath: The Kaiser, Bülow and the Reichstag, 1908–1909', in John C. G. Röhl and Nicolaus Sombart (eds), *Kaiser Wilhelm II: New Interpretations: The Corfu Papers* (Cambridge: Cambridge University Press, 1982), 249–68.
[39] Carl Schmitt, 'Die Logik der geistigen Unterwerfung', *Deutsches Volkstum* 16 (1934), 177.
[40] Geoff Eley, 'The View from the Throne: The Personal Rule of Kaiser Wilhelm II', *Historical Journal* 28, no. 2 (1985), 481–3.

presence in instances of summit diplomacy carried the full imprimatur and aegis of the German Empire.

As Fenske and Mommsen have pointed out, despite quite clear constitutional differences between Wilhelm II and other European monarchs, 'this is not to say that he was more powerful than the monarch in a country like Britain.'[41] In fact, as this book shows, Wilhelm II's role in Germany's colonial affairs was quite analogous to that of other constitutional monarchs such as Queen Victoria of Great Britain, or Queen Wilhelmina of the Netherlands, both of whom reigned over extensive overseas empires and found ways to have their presence felt in colonial affairs, particularly in diplomatic and ceremonial ways, without necessarily directing colonial policy or ruling as 'strong' monarchs.[42] When compared with that of King Leopold II of Belgium, a European monarch who really did play a vigorously independent role in the construction and maintenance of an overseas empire, Wilhelm II's role appears far more modest. While the Belgian king assumed an 'outsized' personal role in colonial affairs,[43] Wilhelm II was consistently led by his chancellors and senior ministers (in particular, Bernhard von Bülow), who in turn took their cues from a range of business leaders, Reichstag deputies, civic associations, diplomats, and media discussions. Almost without exception, Wilhelm II remained content to 'lead' Germany's foreign and colonial policy from behind, and to be positioned by his government as a useful, emblematic personification of more complex domestic political and economic dynamics.

Less welcome to him, but no less important, was his sporadic role as a convenient public scapegoat in times of foreign policy difficulty.[44] Despite his very modest role in policy formulation, Wilhelm II's public role in support of *Weltpolitik* meant that he was often held accountable for unwelcome developments or a perceived lack of progress. His frequent failure to achieve foreign policy successes on behalf of the nation in the empire's diplomatic and military endeavours engendered a growing cynicism towards his forays into foreign policy. The emperor also found himself open to sharp and very public criticism, with infamous incidents such as the *Daily Telegraph* affair, the Moroccan crises, and the Krüger telegramme bringing home to Wilhelm II exactly how dependent his position was on

---

[41] Wolfgang J. Mommsen, 'Kaiser Wilhelm II and German Politics', *Journal of Contemporary History* 25 (1990), 292; Fenske, *Der moderne Verfassungstaat*, 528.

[42] Miles Taylor, *Empress: Queen Victoria and India* (New Haven, CT: Yale University Press, 2018); Sarah Carter and Maria Nugent (eds), *Mistress of Everything: Queen Victoria in Indigenous Worlds* (Manchester: Manchester University Press, 2016); Miles Taylor, 'The British Royal Family and the Colonial Empire from the Georgians to Prince George', in Robert Aldrich and Cindy McCreery (eds), *Crowns and Colonies: European Monarchies and Overseas Empires* (Manchester: Manchester University Press, 2016), 27–50; Susie Protschky, *Photographic Subjects: Monarchy and Visual Culture in Colonial Indonesia* (Manchester: Manchester University Press, 2019), 1–25.

[43] Matthew G. Stanard, 'Violence and Empire: The Curious Case of Belgium and the Congo', in Robert Aldrich and Kirsten McKenzie (eds), *The Routledge History of Western Empires* (London: Routledge, 2014), 456.

[44] Mommsen, 'Kaiser Wilhelm II and German Politics', 301–4.

the public perception that he was a competent servant of the nation and its overseas empire.[45]

Crucially, this book illustrates that the same was often true for monarchs outside Europe. In an environment of shifting power relations and growing regional instability engendered by imperial disruptions, non-European monarchs also had to find a balance between the increasingly strident demands for concessions made by the Europeans in their midst and the protests of their people. As the following shows, while some African, Asian, and Pacific monarchs enjoyed broader discretionary domestic powers than the German emperor did in Germany, the legitimacy of non-European monarchs also often rested on the support of powerful notables and in many cases the (at least tacit) support of their people. Just as in Wilhelmine Germany, so too in Morocco, Hereroland, Zanzibar, China, and the Marshall Islands, the reign of an individual monarch, and even the stability of monarchy as an institution, relied on the monarch's performance as judged against well understood local criteria, including domestic security, prosperity, military competence, and adroitness in foreign relations. In almost all cases, the arrival of the Germans complicated this performance, enhancing the prospects of some monarchs who were able to profit by aligning themselves with the Germans, while others found themselves placed in an invidious and inescapable position of contradiction, torn between the demands of their new colonial rulers and the expectations of their people.

The Global Nature of Royal Cosmopolitanism

Given the remarkable durability of monarchy as an institution, no historical analysis of social stratification and its effects would be complete without an understanding of the position and role of monarchs. As Natalie Zemon Davis once remarked, any class analysis of history that only included the study of peasants would be intrinsically deficient.[46] David Graeber and Marshall Sahlins were quite correct when they argued that 'any theory of political life that…treats kingship as some sort of marginal, exceptional, or secondary phenomenon, is not a very good theory.'[47] More specifically with regard to European history, Frank Lorenz Müller has clearly shown that the nineteenth century was still at least formally 'an age of monarchy',[48] with almost all of the nations of Europe besides

---

[45] Kohlrausch, *Der Monarch im Skandal*, 243–63.

[46] Natalie Zemon Davis, 'Women's History in Transition: The European Case', *Feminist Studies* 3 (1975–6), 90.

[47] David Graeber and Marshall Sahlins, *On Kings*, (Chicago: Hau Books, 2017), 2.

[48] Frank Lorenz Müller, 'Stabilizing a "Great Historical System" in the nineteenth Century? Royal Heirs and Succession in an Age of Monarchy', in H. Mehrkens and F. L. Müller (eds), *Sons and Heirs: Succession and Political Culture in Nineteenth-Century Europe* (London: Palgrave, 2016), 2.

France boasting royal families. Indeed, until 1918 Germany alone had several royal houses, offering it the superficial appearance of a monarchical federation.[49]

To greater and lesser degrees, however, by the late nineteenth century many European monarchs had found that clear limits had been imposed upon their sovereign prerogatives by political changes resulting from the structural shift away from agrarian production and the manorial economy (which had privileged a landed nobility) towards industrialization and imperial globalization, which favoured geographically mobile, trade-oriented, urban elites. Germany was no exception to this structural change,[50] which saw the landowning nobility forced to accommodate increasingly liberal constitutional arrangements that reflected the strength of the newly ascendant industrial and trading bourgeoisie.[51]

Just as Germany's agrarian nobility were forced to navigate the shift into a liberal-bourgeois age by adapting their politics and transforming their economic practices and social roles,[52] so too Kaiser Wilhelm II was forced to come to terms with the new world that industrialists and merchants were building. This difficult process has been aptly described by Eva Giloi as an adjustment to the 'cults of monarchy in a bourgeois world' that saw royals like Wilhelm II become 'symbolic figureheads, rather than embodying an independently functioning form of *Herrschaft*'.[53] An important part of this shift in Germany was finding a role for the emperor in support of the nation's burgeoning global trade and colonial interests. This entailed refashioning Wilhelm II as an internationally connected royal metonym for the expansionist German nation, familiar with and connected to the affairs and rulers of kingdoms beyond his own.

Of course, monarchs had a long, pre-industrial history of 'the international dynastic game' which saw monarchs by turn jostling for position and cooperating transnationally to maintain or expand their sovereign prerogatives.[54] Yet, in a process that Johannes Paulmann has described as a shift from 'monarchical internationalism' to 'royal cosmopolitanism', by the late nineteenth century the royal

---

[49] Frank Lorenz Müller, 'The German Monarchies', in Matthew Jeffries (ed.), *The Ashgate Companion to Imperial Germany* (Abingdon: Routledge, 2015), 56.

[50] Brett Fairbairn, 'Economic and Social Developments', in James Retallack (ed.), *Imperial Germany, 1871–1918* (Oxford: Oxford University Press, 2010), 68–72.

[51] Geoff Eley, 'The Wilhelmine Right: How It Changed', in Richard J. Evans (ed.), *Society and Politics in Wilhelmine Germany* (London: Croom Helm, 1978), 126–8.

[52] Oliver Grant, '"Few Better Farmers in Europe"? Productivity Change, and Modernization in East-Elbian Agriculture, 1870–1913', in Geoff Eley and James Retallack (eds), *Wilhelminism and Its Legacies: German Modernity, Imperialism and the Meanings of Reform, 1890–1930* (New York: Berghahn, 2004), 51–72; Eley, 'The Wilhelmine Right: How It Changed', 126–8. Contra the *Sonderweg* narrative of 'feudalized' German elites, see Hans Ulrich Wehler, *The German Empire 1871–1918* (New York: Berg, 1985).

[53] Eva Giloi, *Monarchy, Myth, and Material Culture in Germany, 1750–1950*, (Cambridge: Cambridge University Press, 2011), 329–30; Johannes Paulmann, *Pomp und Politik: Monarchenbegegnungen in Europa zwischen Ancien Régime und Erstem Weltkrieg* (Paderborn: Ferdinand Schöningh, 2000), 331–2, *pace* Müller, 'The German Monarchies', 61.

[54] John H. Elliott, 'A Europe of Composite Monarchies', *Past and Present* 137, no. 1 (1992), 48–71.

houses of Europe, including Germany, were no longer able to act as representatives of narrow dynastic interests. Instead, monarchies were increasingly nationalized, in the sense that crowned heads were now expected to further the interests of their people in their international dealings, rather than their own or those of their fellow dynasts.[55] As Giloi has argued, 'the sovereign was expected to work for the people, not the other way around.'[56] While monarchs still drew upon the rich symbolic language of an earlier absolutist era in their displays of international royal connection, during the 'age of imperialism' royal summits, correspondence, and gifts between monarchs underlined not so much the enduring 'political role of dynasties'[57] as the congruence and even subservience of royal diplomacy to the new political imperatives of the nation state. This was as true of the 'Willy and Nicky' correspondence between Kaiser Wilhelm II and Tsar Nicholas II as it was of the exchanges between Wilhelm II and King Chulalongkorn of Siam.[58]

In this sense, not only is Paulmann absolutely correct to argue that, with the shift to royal cosmopolitanism, monarchy had been transformed so that 'its success was [now] linked to the national cause',[59] but his insight might also be applied profitably to global monarchical relations. Framing 'royal cosmopolitanism' and the concomitant domestication of monarchs by the nation state as exclusively affecting Europe unnecessarily limits its utility as an analytical framework. As the following chapters show, retooling Paulmann's concept of 'royal cosmopolitanism' for a global study of German *Weltpolitik* offers a fresh lens for examining pre-1914 conflicts over territorial and political sovereignty. It helps foreground the lively contests for political agency mounted by 'imperially literate' colonized rulers who understood both the local conditions of their power and their position in a broader imperial logic.[60] It also helps explains why virtually all of the European powers that colonized non-European lands in the nineteenth century, France notwithstanding, did so 'in the name of monarchs',[61] and why the territorial sovereignty of the monarchs of colonized kingdoms was declared to have been

[55] Johannes Paulmann, 'Searching for a "Royal International": The Mechanics of Monarchical Relations in Nineteenth-Century Europe', in Martin H. Geyer and Johannes Paulmann, *The Mechanics of Internationalism: Culture, Society and Politics from the 1840s to the First World War* (Oxford: Oxford University Press, 2001), 145–76.

[56] Giloi, *Monarchy, Myth and Material Culture*, 341.

[57] Robert Aldrich and Cindy McCreery, 'Empire Tours: Royal Travel between Colonies and Metropoles', in Robert Aldrich and Cindy McCreery (eds), *Royals on Tour: Politics, Pageantry and Colonialism* (Manchester: Manchester University Press, 2018), 6.

[58] Isaac Don Levin (ed.), *Letters from the Kaiser to the Czar* (New York: Frederick A. Stokes, 1920).

[59] Paulmann, 'Searching for a "Royal International"', 176.

[60] Tracey Banivanua Mar, 'Imperial Literacy and Indigenous Rights: Tracing Transoceanic Circuits of a Modern Discourse', *Aboriginal History* 37 (2013), 1–28.

[61] Robert Aldrich, *Banished Potentates: Dethroning and Exiling Indigenous Monarchs under British and French Colonial Rule, 1815–1955* (Manchester: Manchester University Press, 2018), 8–9. Private sector imperialism also existed alongside this state imperialism. See Steven Press, *Rogue Empires: Contracts and Conmen in Europe's Scramble for Africa* (Cambridge, MA: Harvard University Press, 2017); Matthew P. Fitzpatrick, 'Imperialism from Below: Informal Empire and the Private Sector in Nineteenth-Century Germany', *Australian Journal of Politics and History* 54, no. 3 (2008), 358–72.

extinguished and replaced with 'Crown land', transferred by viceregal representatives to European sovereigns.[62] It offers, that is, a sense of how royal diplomacy, transcontinental royal relations, and international monarchical exchanges both contributed to and complicated the material processes of imperialism.

Given the role of monarchy and monarchical concepts in the mechanics of empire, David Motadel is quite rightly surprised that 'encounters between European and non-European sovereigns have so far received little attention.'[63] As this book makes clear, however, these royal interactions were multidirectional and defy easy aggregation, something demonstrated by Robert Aldrich and Cindy McCreery, who have shown how royal relations between Europe and colonized kingdoms were marked by both 'cooperation and coercion'. While, in some sites, non-European monarchs were (willingly and unwillingly) transformed into 'loyal feudatories' and co-opted by the governing apparatus of the colonizing power,[64] other monarchs refused to be co-opted. Many of these were subsequently set aside through banishment, war, or assassination and replaced with more pliant local notables.[65]

In the German Empire, no example demonstrates this more clearly than the well-studied fate of Sultan Mkwawa of the Hehe in East Africa, who fought the Germans until he decided on suicide rather than capture, while the Germans ruled via Mkwawe's brother Mpangile, whom they styled as 'Sultan of Uhehe', until he too was seen by the Germans as a threat and executed.[66] Yet, even in this bitter conflict, the new circumstances created by empire had engendered new possibilities for agency for a number of other local monarchs. As David Pizzo has argued, these monarchs sought 'to position themselves within the emerging colonial system as beneficiaries and power brokers.' No mere victims, 'these leaders and their subordinates were active, self-interested participants in the process of colonization.'[67]

Elsewhere too, despite the implacable, structural nature of Europe's global imperial encroachments and the frequently evident power imbalance between the Germans and those whose lands they colonized, issues of sovereignty and political (including royal) agency in sites of colonization were not monolithically decided by a violent reordering of the societies they encountered. Rather,

---

[62] Lisa Ford, *Settler Sovereignty, Jurisdiction and Indigenous People in America and Australia, 1788–1836* (Cambridge, MA: Harvard University Press, 2010); Aldrich, *Banished Potentates*, 8–9.

[63] David Motadel, 'Qajar Shahs in Imperial Germany', *Past and Present* 213 (2011), 197.

[64] Robert Aldrich and Cindy McCreery, 'European Sovereigns and their Empires "beyond the Seas"', in Aldrich and McCreery (eds), *Crowns and Colonies*, 9.

[65] Aldrich, *Banished Potentates*.

[66] David Pizzo, *'To Devour the Land of Mkwawa': Colonial Violence and the German-Hehe War in East Africa, c.1884–1914* (Saarbrücken: Lambert Academic Publishing, 2010); Alison Redmayne, 'Mkwawa and the Hehe Wars', *Journal of African History* 9 no.3 (2968), 409–36.

[67] David J Pizzo, '"Cunning Tactic": Indigenous Responses to the Imposition of German Colonial Rule in East Africa', *History Research* 2, no.2 (2012), 75.

responses were calibrated in response to local conditions and demands.[68] Imperial rule was approached pragmatically, with monarchs on both sides of the frontier often striving to maintain a veneer of monarchical solidarity, or royal cosmopolitanism, often for domestic political reasons, in the face of the unfolding processes of dispossession and disempowerment. Part of this pragmatism included seeking a wary modus vivendi to avert armed conflict. As part of this, non-European monarchs frequently insisted upon 'their right to address Europeans as their equals (or inferiors)…and successfully played off one European group against another.'[69] Royals in Africa, Asia, and the Pacific, that is, frequently approached the colonizing Germans with adroitness, confidence, and, in many cases, defiance, in accordance with their perceived best interests, forcing the Germans to constantly reassess what was politically possible in any given territory.

As Sanjay Subrahmanyam has suggested, many of these global royal interactions reveal that courtly summit diplomacy could play a key role as an intercultural bridge, minimizing outright conflict and belying pseudo-anthropological claims that imperial friction between European and non-European monarchies mirrored a putatively innate 'cultural incommensurability'.[70] Far from being a setting for unbridgeable clashes of cultures, the meticulous cultural adjustments made by monarchs in set-piece diplomatic encounters such as royal visits[71] and the intricacy and fluency of diplomacy and courtly interactions between royals within the frame of empire illustrate quite clearly that European and non-European powers could choose to ignore, embrace, or weaponize perceived cultural differences in accordance with their own domestic and foreign policy interests.

These finely honed royal interactions often engendered, as Christian Windler has noted, 'polysemic' cultural exchanges between monarchs. By creatively and pragmatically deploying royal diplomacy, both colonizers and the colonized could maintain a productive range of diplomatic possibilities beyond warfare in often fraught imperial situations.[72] This potential for a productive ambiguity in royal relations has been confirmed by Natasha Eaton, who has argued that intercultural monarchical exchanges facilitated a 'colonial *hybridization*' which, she argues, along similar lines as Subrahmanyam, resists a reading of colonial exchanges as inherently beset by conflict 'between two pre-existing essences'.

[68] Charlotte Backerra, Milinda Banerjee, and Cathleen Sarti, 'The Royal Nation in Global Perspective', in Milinda Banerjee, Charlotte Backerra, and Cathleen Sarti (eds), *Transnational Histories of the 'Royal Nation'* (London: Palgrave, 2017), 1–3.

[69] Aldrich and McCreery, 'European Sovereigns and their Empires', 10.

[70] Sanjay Subrahmanyam, *Courtly Encounters: Translating Courtliness and Violence in Early Modern Eurasia* (Cambridge, MA: Harvard University Press, 2012), 1–8.

[71] As per David Motadel, 'The German Other: Nasir al-Din Shah's Perceptions of Difference and Gender during His Visits to Germany, 1873–89', *Iranian Studies* 44, no. 4 (2011), 563–79.

[72] Christian Windler, 'Tributes and Presents in Franco-Tunisian Diplomacy', *Journal of Early Modern History* 4, no. 2 (2000), 168–99.

Difference and alterity in colonial settings, that is, were strategically 'enacted and performed rather than scripted beforehand', in accordance with *raison d'état*.[73] Colonial conflict and warfare were not innate structural features of intercultural encounters or a 'clash of cultures'. Rather, they were a willed and calculated product of power in concrete material situations.

After Ornamentalism

Although this book's emphasis on the global dimension of royal cosmopolitanism recalls David Cannadine's notion of 'ornamentalism', it is in fact quite different from his conceptualization of the global bonds of royalty. While Cannadine's work usefully foregrounded the role of monarchs in the worldwide 'construction of affinities', other aspects of his theory oversimplified other imperial complexities.[74] His idiosyncratic claim, for example, that the global pressures of class solidarity and the maintenance of social hierarchies across the British Empire invalidated Edward Said's claim that empires encoded and reified racial and cultural alterity is simply unsustainable.[75] As Eley noted in 2002, 'Why should talking about *class* require silence about *race*, particularly when the returns are so rich on exploring them together?'[76]

What remains instructive, however, is Cannadine's attention to regal and vice-regal ceremony and ritual, and the symbolism of the monarch in concentrating, personifying, but also buffering and rationalizing the diffuse material effects of colonial penetration. As Edmund Burke once wistfully opined, royal ceremony could mask the blunter mechanics of structural inequality and dispossession with 'pleasing illusions which made power gentle'.[77] In the German case (but not only there), the stark imperial realities of asymmetrical relations between the colonizers and the colonized were indeed often cushioned and mediated by interpersonal connections between monarchs. These connections were manifested, for example, in royal visits, the mutual bestowal of high orders, and the strategic deployment of the imagery and ritual of courtly society. Naked force and the loss of sovereign rights were often obscured by grand metonymic conceptual obfuscations which mystified more material processes. As such, Jean Allman was not

---

[73] Natasha Eaton, 'Between Mimesis and Alterity: Art, Gift and Diplomacy in Colonial India, 1770–1800', *Comparative Studies in Society and History* 46, no. 4 (2004), 816–44 (emphasis in the original).

[74] David Cannadine, *Ornamentalism: How the British Saw Their Empire* (Oxford: Oxford University Press, 2001).

[75] Cannadine, *Ornamentalism*, xiv; Edward Said, *Orientalism* (London: Penguin, 2003).

[76] Geoff Eley, 'Beneath the Skin: Or How to Forget about the Empire without Really Trying' *Journal of Colonialism and Colonial History* 3, no. 1 (2002). doi: 10.1353/cch.2002.0008 (emphasis in original).

[77] Edmund Burke, *Select Works of Edmund Burke: A New Imprint of the Payne Edition*, vol. 2 (Indianapolis, IN: Liberty Fund, 1999), 171.

quite correct to disregard 'the chivalrous medals and plumed helmets of Cannadine's empire of make-believe'.[78] Even in domains where the symbols of royal power provided deliberate mystifications of material developments, they were not entirely fictive. As Eley has argued, the focus on the role of ritual and spectacle as a means of both expressing and sublimating systems of solidarity or subordination is perhaps the primary salvageable aspect of Cannadine's thesis, building, as it did, on his earlier, richer work that had illustrated how empires too could 'invent tradition'.[79]

Precisely because of the ways in which they obscured and mitigated the operation of state and economic power, courtly ceremonies and the performance of royal duties were socially, politically, and culturally important instantiations of monarchy, both in the sense of offering a public demonstration of constitutional and traditional royal duties that reinforced the affective ties of national belonging,[80] but also in the phenomenological sense that monarchs remained recognizably royal (to themselves and others) through their iterative performance of culturally identifiable royal acts. In the age of global royal cosmopolitanism, when European ruling dynasties had been nationalized and colonized, monarchs fought for the recognition of their sovereign rights and took very seriously their embodied performance of social scripts which reanimated and reinscribed collectively understood markers of monarchy.[81] In the case of Germany, the persistence of royal pageantry in an age of liberal imperialism not only helped stabilize the position of the emperor domestically but also offered an intelligible personification of the myriad strands of imperial power to the extra-European world. As both Paulmann and Giloi suggest for the domestic sphere, so too in the wider world the theatricality of monarchy was designed to confirm and naturalize unequal social relations and encourage political integration.[82]

In the context of globalized colonial politics, the monarch personified the state and could be invoked synecdochically by viceregal civilian and military officials across the world. In the colonies, 'Kaiser Wilhelm II' offered a simple and stable image of German power around which more complex assemblages of political,

[78] Jean Allman, "'England Swings like a Pendulum Do?...'" Africanist Reflections on Cannadine's Retro-Empire', *Journal of Colonialism and Colonial History* 3, no. 1 (2002). doi: 10.1353/cch.2002.0001.

[79] Eley, 'Beneath the Skin'; David Cannadine, 'The Context, Performance and Meaning of Ritual: The British Monarchy and the "Invention of Tradition", *c.*1820–1977', in Eric Hobsbawm and Terence Ranger (eds), *The Invention of Tradition* (Cambridge: Canto, 2000), 101–64.

[80] Andreas Biefang, Michael Epkenhans, and Klaus Tenfelde, 'Das politische Zeremoniell im Deutschen Kaiserreich 1871–1918: Zur Einführung', in Andreas Biefang, Michael Epkenhans, and Klaus Tenfelde (eds), *Das politische Zeremoniell im Deutschen Kaiserreich 1871–1918* (Düsseldorf: Droste Verlag, 2008), 20.

[81] As per Maurice Merleau-Ponty's notion that the experience of social class is constituted by 'institutions as I carry them within me and experience them...my way of being in the world within this institutional framework': Maurice Merleau-Ponty, *Phenomenology of Perception* (London: Routledge, 2002), 515.

[82] Paulmann, *Pomp und Politik*, 343; Eva Giloi, 'Royally Entertained: Visual Culture and the Experience of Monarchy in Wilhelmine Prussia', *Intellectual History Review* 17, no. 2 (2007), 204.

economic, and military interests could cluster, or behind which they could hide from scrutiny.[83] For their part, the royals of Africa, Asia, and the Pacific played a similar role for Germans unfamiliar with the internal workings of the sites they sought to control. Both Wilhelm II and the colonized monarchs with whom his subjects interacted offered a critical focal point for the negotiation of the extent and limits of imperial rule. With monarchs offering a mutually presumed direct route to the centre of state power, personal access to the monarch was highly prized on both sides of the frontier. Germans frequently sought the imprimatur of a local ruler in their dealings with the people their colonizing endeavours affected, while non-European monarchs often aimed their diplomacy directly at the German emperor in the mistaken hope that he dominated decision-making in Germany.

Worldwide royal interconnectedness was also a common feature of European empires beyond Germany. For some crown princes and other young royals, international travel, particularly to the colonies and to the courts of extra-European monarchies such as Qing China, Meiji Japan, and the royal houses of the Indian subcontinent formed part of their training in global politics.[84] Such journeys were not merely diplomatic and educational experiences, but, in the case of many young royals, life-changing trips that left a lifelong intellectual and even quite literally physical mark on the future crowned heads of Europe.[85] Many of these young travelling royals would return home with personal links to non-European royal houses, links that were confirmed in reciprocal visits to Europe by the monarchs and scions of ruling African, Asian, and Pacific families.[86] Some of these reciprocal royal visits to Europe were undertaken with the hope that positive foreign policy outcomes might result from them. Others were orchestrated with the intent of harvesting domestic and international prestige from appearing alongside fellow royals in European courts. As Motadel has shown, a 'royal reception in a European metropolis' offered some rulers who were threatened by both internal

---

[83] Susie Protschky, *Photographic Subjects: Monarchy and Visual Culture in Colonial Indonesia* (Manchester: Manchester University Press, 2019).

[84] Aldrich and McCreery (eds) *Royals on Tour*; Charles V. Reed, *Royal Tourists: Colonial Subjects and the Making of a British World, 1860–1911* (Manchester: Manchester University Press, 2016); Sophie Gordon, 'Travels with a Camera: The Prince of Wales, Photography and the Mobile Court', in Müller and Mehrkens (eds) *Sons and Heirs*, 92–108.

[85] Tsarevich Nicholas II, for example, not only got a tattoo but sustained a serious head wound which left him with headaches for the rest of his life after an assassination attempt whilst touring Meiji Japan in 1891. See George Alexander Lensen, 'The Attempt on the Life of Nicholas II in Japan', *Russian Review* 20, no. 3 (1961), 232–53.

[86] Cindy McCreery, 'Something Borrowed, Something Blue: Prince Alfred's Precedent in Overseas British Royal Tours, *c.*1860–1925', in Aldrich and McCreery (eds), *Royals on Tour*, 56–79; Filipa Lowndes Vicente and Inês Vieira Gomes, 'Tensions of Empire and Monarchy: The African Tour of the Portuguese Crown Prince in 1907', in Aldrich and McCreery (eds), *Royals on Tour*, 146–68.

dissenters and the predations of Europeans an opportunity 'to present themselves on the same level as European monarchs'.[87]

These transcontinental encounters led in some cases to closer ties between the reigning dynasts of Europe and the monarchs of their colonial possessions or with other politically and economically significant independent (or semi-independent) monarchies such China, Japan, and Siam. As Chapter 1 on King Chulalongkorn of Siam demonstrates, these ties could be renewed when members of an extra-European royal family visited Europe. When Chulalongkorn visited Nicholas II in Russia, he was treated as an old friend and someone deserving of the highest honours. In Germany too, pre-existing global ties between royals saw Prince and Princess Arisugawa of Meiji Japan and Prince Chow Fa Charaongse of Siam attend the wedding of Crown Prince Friedrich Wilhelm to Cecile Duchess of Mecklenburg-Schwerin in June 1905.[88] The experiences of non-European royals including Queen Kapiʻolani of the Hawaiian Islands, who attended the Golden Jubilee of her 'sister sovereign', Queen Victoria, in 1887 are also well attested.[89]

Unlike in the British case, where world tours by royals prior to their ascension to the throne helped forge a 'multi-centred imperial culture',[90] the relative immobility of Wilhelm II saw Germany rely more heavily on its viceregal governors and diplomats to impress upon the world the status of the German Kaiser. Although the emperor's brother Prince Heinrich was far more mobile,[91] it was only during his visits to the Ottoman sultan and one (deeply reluctant) visit to Morocco that Wilhelm II left Europe behind. Despite his reputation in Germany as the 'travelling Kaiser' (Reisekaiser),[92] the failure of Wilhelm II or his children to visit any of Germany's overseas colonies meant that German royal cosmopolitanism hinged on the rather one-sided form of welcoming travelling monarchs from around the globe to Berlin. Otherwise, it was left to Germany's viceregal governors bearing portraits of the German emperor or other royal gifts to instil a sense of

[87] David Motadel, 'Qajar Shahs in Imperial Germany', Past and Present 213 (2011), 194. See also Motadel, 'The German Other', 563–79.

[88] Daniel Schönpflug, 'Heirs before the Altar: Hohenzollern Marriages in a Bourgeois Age', in Müller and Mehrkens (eds), Sons and Heirs, 53–71.

[89] Lindsay Puawehiwa Wilhelm, 'A Meeting of "Sister Sovereigns": Hawaiian Royalty at Victoria's Golden Jubilee', in Richard Fulton, Stephen Hancock, Peter Hoffenberg, and Allison Paynter (eds), South Sea Encounters: Nineteenth-Century Oceania, Britain, and America (New York: Routledge, 2018), 63–86.

[90] Reed, Royal Tourists, xix–xx.

[91] Ernst Dietrich Mirbach, Prinz Heinrich von Preussen: Eine Biographie des Kaiserbruders (Köln: Böhlau, 2013), 72–123, 251–89.

[92] Wilhelm II's domestic voyages were monitored very closely by the French, particularly his numerous visits to Alsace-Lorraine. See Archives Nationales, Paris, Intérieur; Direction de la Sûreté générale. Fichier central: dossiers du coffre dit dossiers Panthéon (1880–1945), Guillaume II F/7/15965/3.

cosmopolitan royal solidarity between Wilhelm II and local elites in the German colonies.[93]

Alternatively, for many African, Asian, and Pacific monarchs, the mutual bestowal of ranks, orders, and distinctions became important substitutes for royal visits, a practice that paid appreciable domestic political dividends.[94] As they were in other empires, German royal portraits, gifts, and decorations proved to be diplomatically malleable tokens that allowed the monarchs of places as far apart as Cameroon in West Africa, Witu in East Africa, Siam in South East Asia, and Samoa in the Pacific to interact creatively with metropolitan symbols of German monarchical power and collect what Anne McClintock has called the 'fetishes' of European power in ways that could locally reframe German claims to pre-eminence.[95] As the following chapters show, despite the absence of British-style royal tours to the colonies, the manipulations and repurposing of the artefacts and gifts of German royalty across the world ensured that 'metropolitan society had no monopoly on the cultural construction of…imperial identities'.[96] Instead, the paramount leaders of Africa, Asia, and the Pacific worked hard to ensure that they too could shape their corner of the German Empire by narrating to domestic audiences their preferred meaning of their encounters with royal paraphernalia.[97]

As this book shows, however, any hopes harboured by extra-European monarchs that a personal relationship with Wilhelm II would alter the course of German foreign policy in their favour were routinely disappointed. Whether on questions of trade and investment, the direction of future colonizing endeavours, or the building of diplomatic or military alliances, the emperor could neither set nor alter the direction and consequences of German *Weltpolitik* and *Kolonialpolitik*. Even in those instances in which Wilhelm II forged cordial personal relations with non-European royals such as King Chulalongkorn of Siam or Prince Zaifeng of China, his cordiality neither implied nor led to a German commitment to closer relations or protective alliances. The clear reason for this was that there

---

[93] The same was true of the Dutch monarchy: Protschky, *Photographic Subjects*.

[94] On the role of gift-giving in colonial diplomacy more generally, see Birgit Tremml-Werner, Lisa Hellman, and Guido van Meersbergen, 'Introduction: Gift and Tribute in Early Modern Diplomacy: Afro-Eurasian Perspectives' *Diplomatica* 2, no.2 (2020), 185–200; Gazi Algazi, 'Introduction: Doing Things with Gifts', in Gazi Algazi, Valentin Groebner, and Bernhard Jussen (eds), *Negotiating the Gift: Pre-Modern Figurations of Exchange* (Göttingen: Vandenhoeck & Ruprecht, 2003), 9–10; Christian Windler, 'Tributes and Presents in Franco-Tunisian Diplomacy', *Journal of Early Modern History* 4, no. 2 (2000), 168–99; Eaton, 'Between Mimesis and Alterity', 816–44. In other settings where relations with the colonizing power were considered traitorous or simply indecorous, such gift-giving and the bestowal of orders could inflict reputational damage. See Karen Fox, 'Ornamentalism, Empire and Race: Indigenous Leaders and Honours in Australia and New Zealand', *Journal of Imperial and Commonwealth History* 42, no. 3 (2014), 499.

[95] Protschky, *Photographic Subjects*, 26–52, 118–53; Anne McClintock, *Imperial Leather: Race, Gender and Sexuality in the Colonial Contest* (New York: Routledge, 1995), 226–31.

[96] Reed, *Royal Tourists*, xxi.

[97] Windler, 'Tributes and Presents in Franco-Tunisian Diplomacy'; Eaton, 'Between Mimesis and Alterity'.

was no operative kingship mechanism that could alter the course of German *Weltpolitik* or forge decisive political bonds between monarchs. This led to frustration and disappointment for many monarchs who had made the trip to Berlin. Others more attuned to the political culture of Germany, like the German-educated King Rudolf Duala Manga Bell of Cameroon, understood that the German emperor might be bypassed in favour of more promising institutions such as the German Reichstag.

Least likely to succeed were the overtures of monarchs from within the German Empire, who were (at least according to German law) formally subordinate to the German emperor. As this book shows, this did not stop royals such as Kabua of the Marshall Islands, Tamasese of Samoa, Fumo Bakari of Witu, Njoya of Bamum, and Rudolf Duala Manga Bell of Duala from seeking to address Wilhelm II as a brother monarch, as well as loyal dependents. Although hopes that this strategy would offer tangible effects endured for the entirety of the colonial period, it uniformly failed to win meaningful concessions from the Germans, not only because the claims of these royals to formal equality were not accepted by the German Colonial Office if they contravened German interests but also because Wilhelm II played little to no role in overseeing these relationships or in guiding German colonial policy.

Monarchs and Empire

Focusing squarely on monarchy and its role in sustaining and disrupting German *Weltpolitik*, the following chapters make clear that Germany's expansion brought it into close contact with paramount rulers across the world, producing a global, German version of royal cosmopolitanism. They map how the agency and expressions of sovereignty of non-European monarchs complicated, challenged, but also accommodated Germany's claims to rule. Although cognizant of the problems involved in transferring the concept of 'monarchy' to contexts in which paramountcy took different forms, this book nonetheless argues that the term is appropriate for any polity in which sovereign power was concentrated (even if largely symbolically) in the hands of an individual ruler whose claim to be in a permanent position at the apex of that polity was (at least tacitly) acknowledged by those within it. With the differences in how this paramountcy was expressed and defended in mind, this book also seeks to understand how a global cross-fertilization of the forms of paramount leadership between periphery and metropole was enabled (and sometimes required) by the German Empire. It demonstrates that non-European 'monarchical' power quite often survived, albeit in different forms, under and alongside empire. In many instances, however, while the institution of monarchy persisted, individual monarchs were regularly displaced by German attempts to wrest control of their territory.

By studying different instances of monarchical relations, the following chapters reframe royal power in a way that foregrounds the variegated complexion of the entanglements between monarchs and the German state, civil society, and commerce. The personal role of Wilhelm II in these imperial encounters, it finds, was primarily a symbolic, diplomatic one, secondary to the imperatives of global commerce and settler colonialism that were managed by German firms and the colonial and military bureaucracies. As the constitutionally proclaimed embodiment of German state power, the emperor was most frequently a diplomatic tool in the hands of those pushing Germany towards a globalized industrial modernity. Only rarely, this book confirms, did Wilhelm II's role involve the application of his inexpert personal judgement, prerogative power, and royal authority.

With regard to the monarchs of Africa, Asia, and the Pacific, this book uncovers the nature of their responses to the encroachments of the German Empire upon their territorial and political sovereignty and examines how they sought to maintain, defend, and reinvent their power in the face of the growing economic, political, and legal predations of the Germans. It highlights the strategies of accommodation and resistance that assisted non-European monarchs in maintaining their positions wherever possible. This book also emphasizes the use by non-European monarchs of international diplomacy and statecraft as a means of inserting their priorities and projects into the mechanics of German imperialism. It uncovers the complex contestations for political power in colonial sites and the extent to which colonized elites could at times successfully make claims on the German Empire to enhance their domestic position or better the position of their people vis-à-vis Europe. It nonetheless illustrates that whenever the sovereignty of non-European monarchs brought German imperial power into question or became an alternative pole of political power, the diplomatic, political, and military apparatus of the German state moved quickly and decisively, either by deposing and replacing the monarch in question or, as in the case of King Rudolf Manga Bell, through judicial murder.

These royal interactions left clear traces in German memoirs, media, and archival records but also in the letters, recollections, interviews, memoirs, and public pronouncements of non-European royals themselves. An important part of this book, therefore, is the attempt to recover and foreground the perceptions, pronouncements, and calculations of non-European monarchs when they visited Berlin, after they returned home, or when they were confronted by the consequences of the claims to sovereignty made by Wilhelm II's viceregal representatives in their own lands. Following Dipesh Chakrabarty, it seeks to overcome the 'asymmetric ignorance' of the colonized displayed in earlier European histories of diplomacy and global politics and to dislodge the deficit framing of the extra-European world which reads non-European difference as politico-cultural lack.[98] It also seeks

[98] Dipesh Chakrabarty, *Provincializing Europe: Postcolonial Thought and Historical Difference* (Princeton, NJ: Princeton University Press, 2008), 28–35.

to move away from an earlier historiographical model that assesses the politics and diplomacy of Africa, Asia, and the Pacific in terms of its deviation from European models and norms.

While in some instances the voices from outside Europe that appear here are modulated or distorted by the colonial archive and the political contexts in which they appear, the first-hand accounts of the colonized presented here are, nonetheless, indicative of the outward-facing (and sometimes domestic) responses to imperial interactions with Germany that were made by political elites attempting to navigate the shifting terrain of global imperialism. By recovering the extant perspectives of colonized monarchs and their subjects and reinscribing their hitherto effaced presence and histories within the history of Germany, the following chapters seek to complicate imperial relations and offer some modest tools for decolonizing historians and activists seeking to assert their own histories of diplomacy and empire.[99]

In an attempt to adequately represent developments in both Europe and the extra-European world, this book is divided into two parts. Part I, 'Monarchy in the Metropole', scrutinizes the role of Wilhelm II in the creation and maintenance of empire and his interactions with the monarchs of Africa, Asia, and the Pacific. It assesses his contribution in both material and ceremonial terms and examines the ways in which his role at the apex of the German Empire was expressed through action and, just as importantly, inaction rather than simply in word. Following Chakrabarty's injunction that 'the first step in a critical effort must arise from a gesture of inversion,'[100] Part II of this book, 'Monarchy beyond the Metropole', then turns this picture inside out and examines how monarchs outside Europe interacted with and were affected by the German Empire, including the emperor and his viceregal representatives abroad. Making no claims to completeness (there are countless other interactions between Germany and the monarchies of the wider world that deserve close study), it demonstrates that the numerous individual contests for land and sovereignty within Germany's overseas empire rarely centred on Wilhelm II and almost always reflected commercial or strategic decisions that had been made elsewhere and which privileged interests other than those of the reigning monarch. Despite this, particularly given the central role of non-European monarchs in their negotiations with the *Kaiserreich*, the institution of monarchy emerges as having been integral to the mechanics of imperialism, even in states such as Germany where the monarch reigned but did not rule.

---

[99] For a longer theoretical discussion of the possibilities for academic decolonization, see Matthew P. Fitzpatrick, 'Indigenous Australians and German Anthropology in the Era of "Decolonization"', *Historical Journal* 63, no. 3 (2020), 686–709.

[100] Chakrabarty, *Provincializing Europe*, 34.

PART I

MONARCHY IN THE METROPOLE

1

A Siamese Charm Offensive

When King Chulalongkorn of Siam, 'the first sovereign ruler of an East Asian kingdom to visit the West', announced his plan to visit Kaiser Wilhelm II of Germany, an article in the illustrated family periodical *Die Gartenlaube* described his realm in lavishly orientalist terms:

There was once a king who lived in a fairy palace of beautiful marble and crystal. He had a thousand of the fairest ladies and two thousand slaves, all ready to fulfil his slightest wish. He lived in splendour and grandeur and his septuple crown shone and flashed with diamonds. His lavish garments were covered in rubies, and, like him, his young maidens possessed the most expensive jewellery. They were there to help him pass the time; they danced and sang and they ate with him from golden dishes and they sailed with him on golden boats on the great river. If he wanted to go on a trip, dozens of elephants, saddled and decorated with expensive hanging covers, were immediately ready for him and his radiant followers. A page fanned him with cooling ostrich feathers, while another held a ninefold silk parasol over him. A third carried his gold spittoon inlaid with rubies. His people loved him, and when they saw their king coming from afar, they threw themselves down before him. Hundreds of princes were at his palace, each with his own radiant household, including hundreds of beautiful princesses, who could not show their beauty and their riches, according to the customs of the palace. All of them—king, princes, and people—lived in a great city amidst marvellous palm groves, where enormous tropical trees and the large-leafed breadfruit, durian, mangrove, and other evergreen giants of the forest shaded the houses of the city. Wonderful exotic pagodas, towers, and pyramids lifted themselves above the palm leaf canopy of the people's homes, all bristling with gold or resplendent in the brightest colours.

According to the article's author, Ernst von Hesse-Wartegg, the Siamese king was sure to find the meagre attractions awaiting him in Europe disappointing in comparison with this fairy-tale city. Chulalongkorn's eyes, 'accustomed to the splendours of his residence will search here in vain for something that might compare in uniqueness, wealth, and colourfulness with the temple city of Bangkok!'[1]

---

[1] Ernst von Hesse-Wartegg, 'Eine Märchenstadt in Hinterindien', *Die Gartenlaube* 25 (1897), 416–20; Ernst von Hesse-Wartegg, *Siam: Das Reich des weißen Elefanten* (Leipzig: J. J. Weber, 1899), v.

The Kaiser and the Colonies: Monarchy in the Age of Empire. Matthew P. Fitzpatrick, Oxford University Press.
© Matthew P. Fitzpatrick 2022. DOI: 10.1093/oso/9780192897039.003.0002

King Chulalongkorn (Rama V) reigned over Siam during the period when the commercial penetration and (not unrelatedly) territorial losses inflicted upon Siam by Europeans were at their height. As Siam's predicament steadily worsened, he, like other dynasts outside of Europe,[2] felt that visiting European states such as Germany to make the personal acquaintance of fellow monarchs such as Kaiser Wilhelm II was necessary for the survival of his kingdom. Chulalongkorn's 1897 European tour was predicated on the assumption that summit diplomacy could facilitate a form of 'monarchical internationalism'[3] through which strong fraternal bonds of monarchy could be forged through personal visits and shared occasions of public pomp and splendour. These personal ties, it was hoped, could then be leveraged for political purposes, both at home and abroad. As Mustafa Serdar Palabıyık has argued, domestically it was important to Chulalongkorn that he be seen to be admitted to the 'exclusive club of "civilized" states'", while in international affairs it was vital that his sovereignty 'be recognized as being equal to that of European monarchs'.[4]

Despite the lavish public displays that marked his royal visit, the hoped-for fruits of an internationalist kingship mechanism failed to materialize. Instead, Chulalongkorn's visit exemplified what Johannes Paulmann has called 'royal cosmopolitanism', a display of pomp that obscured the extent to which European crowned heads such as Wilhelm II were no longer autonomous rulers but had been 'nationalized', in the sense that their elevated social position now relied upon the congruence of their actions with the interests of their state rather than the particularist class interests of their dynasty or their fellow monarchs.[5] Under these conditions, the public performance of close relations between monarchs that followed long-standing norms of courtly etiquette did not stymie the prosecution of a foreign policy that forthrightly eroded the interests of these royal visitors and their people.

For Hesse-Wartegg's 'close connections' to German colonial associations, see Andreas Dutz and Elisabeth Dutz, *Ernst von Hesse-Wartegg (1851–1918): Reiseschriftsteller, Wissenschaftler, Lebemann* (Vienna: Böhlau Verlag, 2017), 189–90. For the reception of his representation of Siam in contemporary Thailand, see Aratee Kaewsumrit, 'Die Darstellung Siams in Ernst von Hesse-Warteggs Siam: Das Reich des weissen Elefanten', *Journal of Humanities Periscope* 40, no. 1 (2018), 34–48.

[2] For visits by the similarly beleaguered Persian shahs, see Motadel, 'Qajar Shahs in Imperial Germany', 191–235; Motadel, 'The German Other', 563–79. Before leaving for Europe, Chulalongkorn had studied the travel diary of the Persian Shah. See Sud Chonchirdsin, 'The Ambivalent Attitudes of the Siamese Elite towards the West during the Reign of King Chulalongkorn, 1868–1910', *South East Asia Research* 17, no. 3 (2009), 442.

[3] Johannes Paulmann, 'Searching for a "Royal International": The Mechanics of Monarchical Relations in Nineteenth-Century Europe', in Martin H. Geyer and Johannes Paulmann, *The Mechanics of Internationalism: Culture, Society and Politics from the 1840s to the First World War*, (Oxford: Oxford University Press, 2001), 145–76.

[4] Mustafa Serdar Palabıyık, 'The Sultan, the Shah and the King in Europe: The Practice of Ottoman, Persian and Siamese Royal Travel and Travel Writing', *Journal of Asian History* 50, no. 2 (2016), 211–12.

[5] Paulmann, 'Searching for a "Royal International,"' 145–76.

As this chapter demonstrates, despite its success as a showcase for global royal relations, Chulalongkorn's visit to Wilhelm II in no way diverted Germany's expansionist foreign policy in South East Asia. Although Chulalongkorn's visit to some extent corroborates David Motadel's argument that the ceremonial aspects of royal tours by non-European monarchs could 'symbolically level asymmetric power relations',[6] the aftermath of Chulalongkorn's visit casts doubt on the extent to which his royal visit had any material effect on the structural elements and unfolding design, direction, and prosecution of German *Weltpolitik*.

The Reputation of Chulalongkorn

Despite not having visited Europe prior to 1897, European culture and its global empires were far from unknown to Chulalongkorn. The king had been educated by an English governess, Anna Leonowens, impressing her as a 'bright, ambitious scholar'.[7] After his coronation in 1868 (but before beginning to rule in his own right in 1873) he had also toured British Malaya, Burma, Singapore, and India, as well as Dutch Java, witnessing first-hand the application of imperial technologies and administrative systems to Europe's Asian colonies. As a result of what he saw, Chulalongkorn became a determined (and trenchantly absolutist) modernizer, introducing wide-ranging political and economic reforms upon ascending to the throne.[8] These reforms were carried out at the expense of Siam's landed nobility, and a subsequent power struggle known as the Wang Na or 'Front Palace' Crisis broke out in Bangkok in 1874–5. The crisis led Chulalongkorn to seek the assistance of the British governor of Singapore, Andrew Clarke. With his support, the young king overcame his rivals and pushed through his land and trade reforms, repositioning Siam as an exporting power with free labour and a regularized taxation system, at the cost of British informal oversight.[9]

In Germany these reforms were seen as evidence that Chulalongkorn was an Asian monarch who had 'recognized the value of Western culture as a civilizing

---

[6] Motadel, 'Qajar Shahs in Imperial Germany', 193–97, 232–5.

[7] Anna Harriette Leonowens, *The English Governess at the Siamese Court: Being Recollections of Six Years in the Royal Palace at Bangkok* (Boston, MA: James R. Osgood & Co, 1873), vi, 154–66.

[8] Patricia Lim Pui Huen, *Through the Eyes of the King: The Travels of King Chulalongkorn to Malaya* (Singapore: Institute of Southeast Asian Studies, 2009); Charnvit Kasetsiri, 'King Chulalongkorn's Grand Europe Tours with Special Reference to Germany', in Pornsan Watanangura (ed.), *The Visit of King Chulalongkorn to Europe in 1907: Reflecting on Siamese History* (Bangkok: Centre of European Studies at Chulalongkorn University, 2008), 18; Maurizio Peleggi, *Lord of Things* (Honolulu: University of Hawai'i Press, 2002), 5–7.

[9] Kullada Kesboonchoo Mead, *The Rise and Decline of Thai Absolutism* (London: Routledge, 2012), 60–5; Shunyu Xie, *Siam and the British, 1874–1875: Sir Andrew Clark and the Front Palace Crisis* (Bangkok: Thammasat University Press, 1988); Kullada Kesboonchoo-Mead, 'Thai-European Relations at the Beginning of King Chulalongkorn's Reign', in Charit Tingsabadh (ed.), *King Chulalongkorn's Visit to Europe: Reflections on Significance and Impacts* (Bangkok: Centre for European Studies, Chulalongkorn University, 2000), 21–9.

fo rafch wie möglich hinaus in die Großstadtstraße, wo er   Ambrosius, die Entschließung des Malesitantenrichters sinnli von Hildegards Nähe ein paar glückselige Stunden erhoffte.   hervorgerufen. Obgleich er also in seiner Wohnung nicht Ohnedies war er jetzt in der rosigsten Laune. Was ihm noch   mehr zu suchen hatte und recht sehr darauf brannte, d unflar vorschwebte, als er dem Laufmädchen den gewünschten   Veripätung im Geierhäuschen durch verdoppelte Eile weit z

Der König und die Königin von Siam.

Figure 1.1 The illustration of King Chulalongkorn and Queen Saovabha accompanying Hesse-Wartegg's article in *Die Gartenlaube*, August 1897

force'.[10] As his main German-language advocate Hesse-Wartegg maintained, given his Westernizing proclivities, Chulalongkorn could not be seen as the equivalent of the ostensibly 'minor' kings of Cambodia or Annam, or even the Shah of Persia. Rather, he was, Hesse-Wartegg insisted, 'unquestionably one of the greatest and most enlightened princes who has ever sat on an Asian throne, a man of European education and manners' (see Figure 1.1).[11]

Another sign of the king's guarded embrace of what was known in Siam as *siwilai* (civilization and 'being civilized'),[12] was that, beginning in the late 1880s, several Siamese princes were sent to study in Germany (as well as other European countries). Most prominently, Prince Paribatra trained for five years as a German military officer before being accepted into the Empress Augusta Grenadier

---

[10] Pornsan Watanangura, '"The Beginnings of a New Era in Thai-European Relations: King Chulalongkorn, the First "Honorary European"', *Journal of the Royal Institute of Thailand* 1 (2009), 9; Andreas Stoffers, *Thailand und Deutschland: Wirtschaft, Politik, Kultur* (Berlin: Springer, 2014), 99–100.

[11] Hesse-Wartegg, *Siam: Das Reich des weißen Elefanten*, vi.

[12] Thongchai Winichakul, 'The Quest for "Siwilai": A Geographical Discourse of Civilizational Thinking in the Late Nineteenth and Early Twentieth-Century Siam', *Journal of Asian Studies* 59, no. 3 (2000), 528–49. It is worth noting that Chulalongkorn was well aware of the shortcomings of Europe: Chonchirdsin, 'The Ambivalent Attitudes of the Siamese Elite'.

Regiment.[13] From Germany's perspective, the chance to train Siam's princes represented a welcome opportunity to inculcate pro-German attitudes in those who would be making military and economic decisions that would impact upon Germany's economic and political prospects in South East Asia.[14] Siam's auto-colonizing efforts were not unidirectional, however, with Chulalongkorn expressly warning Siamese princes studying abroad against behaving like Westerners upon their return.[15] For some the experience of studying in Europe was a mixed one, with one Siamese prince training in Potsdam embroiled in a duel with another cadet after an exchange of insults.[16] Nevertheless, many of these German-trained Siamese princes became immensely important ministers in Siam, with Paribatra becoming the Siamese naval minister and then defence minister, as well as an important adviser to Chulalongkorn's successors King Vajiravudh and King Prajadhipok.[17] Tellingly, the latent pro-German tendencies harboured by Paribatra (as well as other prominent German-educated princes such as Mahidol and Rangsit) were sufficient to keep Siam neutral during the First World War until 1917, when the kingdom sided with the Entente powers, confiscated German ships, and sent a small expeditionary force to fight in Europe.[18]

Beyond his personal facility with things European, Chulalongkorn was also acutely aware of the geopolitical realities of his region, which was the site of an imperial contest between Britain, France, and, to a lesser extent, Germany for control over South East Asian trade routes. With Britain controlling not only India but also Penang, Malacca, and Singapore, and having fought three wars to control and then overthrow the Burmese royal family (with Siamese assistance in the second of these wars), Britain's preponderance in the region between the 1820s and the 1880s was hardly a new geostrategic reality when Chulalongkorn visited Europe.[19]

British control was not absolute, however, and to many smaller neighbouring kingdoms and sultanates, the Kingdom of Siam was itself an unwelcome imperial power scarcely different from the British.[20] As Tamara Loos has made clear, viewing Siam one-sidedly as a simple victim of European imperialism is to ignore Siam's own expansionist and colonial characteristics during the nineteenth

---

[13] *Norddeutsche Allgemeine Zeitung*, 11 August 1907, in PAAA R 131804, 'Die Reise des Königs von Siam nach Europa bzw. Deutschland' (unnumbered).

[14] Stoffers, *Thailand und Deutschland*, 124–9.

[15] Chonchirdsin, 'The Ambivalent Attitudes of the Siamese Elite', 437, 452.

[16] August Bebel, *Verhandlungen des Reichstages*, Bd. 169 (22 February 1900), 4226.

[17] Stoffers, *Thailand und Deutschland*, 129.

[18] Stefan Hell, *Siam and World War I: An International History* (Bangkok: River Books, 2017).

[19] Eric Tagliacozzo, 'Ambiguous Commodities, Unstable Frontiers: The Case of Burma, Siam, and Imperial Britain, 1800–1900', *Comparative Studies in Society and History* 46, no. 2 (2004), 354–77; Victor G. Kiernan, 'Britain, Siam and Malaya: 1875–1885', *Journal of Modern History* 28, no. 1 (1956), 1–20.

[20] Amrita Malhi, 'Making Spaces, Making Subjects: Land, Enclosure and Islam in Colonial Malaya', *Journal of Peasant Studies* 38, no. 4 (2011), 727–47.

century.[21] At the same time as Siam was under 'semi-colonial' pressure from the Europeans,[22] it was exerting its own regional imperial pressure. The sovereignty of Siam under Chulalongkorn may have been 'qualified' by the British and the French, but Siam's monarch was also quite capable of enacting his own 'colonial measures domestically'.[23]

In terms of European threats to British hegemony over Siam, London was convinced in the 1880s and 1890s that Germany might seek to obtain a port for an eastern naval squadron on Siam's Malayan west coast in exchange for supporting Siam against the predations of the French.[24] For their part, the French had already colonized the mouth of the Mekong and declared a protectorate over Cambodia in the Franco-Siamese treaty of 1863, all at the expense of Siamese hegemony in the region. This pressure on Siam's northerly Mekong holdings was tightened in 1887 by the incorporation of the rest of Vietnam into French Indochina.[25]

As an Anglophile with a long tradition of requesting and receiving assistance from Britain, Chulalongkorn had predicated his diplomacy in the 1880s and early 1890s on the assumption that his kingdom's status as an independent state relied on British guarantees of Siamese territorial integrity in the face of French expansion.[26] As Kullada Kesboonchoo-Mead has argued, however, 'Siam was not significant enough for Britain to risk confrontation with the French'.[27] This became apparent when France moved into Siam's Mekong territory during the Paknam Incident of July 1893.[28] With the French looking to obtain Siamese territory thought to be under British protection, the preconditions for 'an Asiatic Fashoda' seemed to have developed half a decade before the famous stand-off in Africa.[29]

---

[21] Tamaro Loos, 'Competitive Colonialisms: Siam and the Malay Muslim South', in Rachel V Harrison and Peter A. Jackson (eds), *The Ambiguous Allure of the West: Traces of the Colonial in Thailand* (Hong Kong: Hong Kong University Press, 2010), 75–92.

[22] Peter A Jackson, 'The Ambiguities of Semicolonial Power in Thailand', in Harrison and Jackson (eds), *The Ambiguous Allure of the West*, 37–56.

[23] Loos, 'Competitive Colonialisms', 75–7.

[24] Eunice Thio, 'Britain's Search for Security in North Malaya, 1886–1897', *Journal of Southeast Asian History* 10, no. 2 (1969), 290–1; Kiernan, 'Britain, Siam and Malaya: 1875–1885', 13; Amrita Malhi, 'Like a Child with Two Parents: Race, Religion and Royalty on the Siam-Malaya Frontier, 1895–1902', *Muslim World* 105, no. 4 (2015), 480.

[25] Pierre Brocheux and Daniel Hémery, *Indochina: An Ambiguous Colonization, 1858–1954* (Berkeley, CA: University of California Press, 2009), 15–69; John Tully, *France on the Mekong: A History of the Protectorate in Cambodia, 1863–1953* (Lanham, MD: University Press of America, 2003); R. Stanley Thomson, 'Siam and France 1863–1870', *Journal of Asian Studies* 5, no. 1 (1945), 28–46; Junko Koizumi, 'The "Last" Friendship Exchanges between Siam and Vietnam, 1879–1882: Siam between Vietnam and France—and Beyond', *TRaNS: Trans-Regional and -National Studies of Southeast Asia* 4, no. 1 (2016), 131–64.

[26] Minton F. Goldman, 'Franco-British Rivalry over Siam, 1896–1904', *Journal of Southeast Asian Studies* 3, no. 2 (1972), 210.

[27] Kesboonchoo-Mead, 'Thai-European Relations', 27.

[28] Chandran Jeshurun, 'The Anglo-French Declaration of 1896 and the Independence of Siam', *Journal of the Siam Society* 58, no. 2 (1970), 105; Chompunut Nakirah, 'General Advisers and Siam's National Survival', in Tingsabadh (ed.), *King Chulalongkorn's Visit to Europe*, 65; Martin Stuart-Fox, 'The French in Laos, 1887–1945', *Modern Asian Studies* 29, no. 1 (1995), 111–39.

[29] Alfred Vagts, 'William II and the Siam Episode', *American Historical Review* 45, no. 4 (1940), 836.

Actual fighting broke out when Siamese troops, under the impression that the British would support them, tried to defend their territory against French gunboats.[30] War between France and Britain seemed almost certain to follow when the French demanded that the British remove their naval vessel *Linnet* from its Bangkok anchorage to a position outside the French cordon. Its commander refused and the situation was so serious that the British foreign minister, Archibald Primrose, Earl of Rosebery, asked Ambassador Edward Malet in Berlin to find out whether the Germans would consider fighting alongside Britain.[31] Queen Victoria followed this up by writing to Kaiser Wilhelm II on 30 July in search of German support against the French in any war for Siam.[32]

The queen's request deeply unsettled the German emperor, who received it from his 'deathly pale private secretary at midnight'.[33] The thought of war with France sent Wilhelm II into a panic which only subsided when his confidant, Philipp von Eulenburg told him that war could be avoided if he would just 'listen with a benevolent smile to what the English say and keep as quiet as possible'. This message was reiterated by Alfred von Kiderlen-Wächter and Paul Wolff-Metternich, who saw to it that, as the crisis unfolded, the emperor was effectively 'driven into a modest corner, and politically shut out'.[34] Despite Queen Victoria's personal appeal to Wilhelm II, the matter was managed by the German Foreign Office, which decided not to allow Germany to be dragged into any war unless Britain was already fighting, for fear of being left to shoulder the burden alone.[35] Indeed, Germany's Foreign Office was deeply pessimistic about Siam's future, with one of its sources opining that 'a long life can certainly not be prophesied for the Kingdom of Siam. Either in its entirety or divided, it will fall to one of the surrounding Great Powers.'[36] To Wilhelmstrasse, France's attempts to generate a *casus belli* on the Mekong appeared to be a prelude to the absorption of the entire kingdom into French Indochina, despite French assurances to the contrary.[37] Certainly, the absorption of Siam was known to feature prominently in the plans

[30] Nakirah, 'General Advisers and Siam's National Survival', 65.

[31] Hatzfeldt to the German Foreign Office, 26 July 1893, in J Lepsius, A Mendelssohn Bartholdy and F Thimme (eds.) *Die Grosse Politik der Europäischen Kabinette 1871–1914*, vol. 8 (Berlin: Deutsche Verlagsgesellschaft für Politik und Geschichte, 1924), 103–5; Rainer Lahme, *Deutsche Aussenpolitik 1890–1894: Von der Gleichgewichtspolitik Bismarcks zur Allianzstrategie Caprivis* (Göttingen: Vandenhoeck & Ruprecht, 1990), 398–9. Later accounts suggest that there were in fact three British naval vessels in Bangkok that had been told to move (ibid., 407).

[32] Kiderlen to the Foreign Office, in *Grosse Politik*, vol. 8, 107–8.

[33] Marginal note by Wilhelm II on Hatzfeldt to the German Foreign Office, 3 November 1893, in *Grosse Politik*, vol. 8, 107.

[34] Röhl, *Wilhelm II: The Kaiser's Personal Monarchy*, 485–6. For the British perspective on the threat of war, see Vagts, 'William II and the Siam Episode', 837–9.

[35] Norman Rich, *Friedrich von Holstein. Politics and Diplomacy in the Era of Bismarck and Wilhelm II* (Cambridge: Cambridge University Press, 1965), 350–4; Hatzfeldt to the German Foreign Office, 31 July 1893, in *Grosse Politik*, vol. 8, 108–10; Marschall to Hatzfeldt, 4 August 1893, in *Grosse Politik*, vol. 8, 115–16; Lahme, *Deutsche Aussenpolitik 1890–1894*, 407.

[36] Paul Jaeschke to Naval Secretary Hollmann, 18 June 1896, in BA Freiburg RM3/6692, 226–7.

[37] Lahme, *Deutsche Aussenpolitik 1890–1894*, 396.

of colonial enthusiasts in France who saw Siam as a foundation for a southern route to lucrative Chinese markets.[38]

Wilhelm II's inability to respond at a crucial political and military juncture proved inconsequential once the demand to remove the British gunboat from Bangkok was declared by the French to have been a 'misunderstanding' and Britain's foreign secretary, Rosebery, signalled to the French that they would not intervene in a Franco-Siamese dispute over the River Mekong.[39] The British also advised the Siamese to give up a 25-kilometre-wide strip of land on the Mekong's west bank to the French so as to 'save the rest',[40] bluntly warning the Siamese that they must 'recognize Britain's claim to advise them on their foreign policy', as a failure to do so would 'result at no distant date in the more or less complete extinction of Siamese national existence'.[41] Chulalongkorn, who was said to have suffered a breakdown under the strain, had little choice but to accept the territorial losses to save his kingdom.[42]

The Anglo-French Declaration of 1896 did very little to assuage Siamese fears about European designs on their kingdom, given that it privileged British and French imperial considerations over Siamese sovereignty.[43] The declaration also did nothing to halt French economic and political inroads into eastern Siam, while the secret Anglo-Siamese treaty of 1897, signed the day before Chulalongkorn left for Europe, left the door open for the British to peel away Siam's southern tributaries.[44] With the illusion that the British would protect Siam shattered, Chulalongkorn came to Europe seeking 'alternatives to Siam's earlier diplomacy and policies', which had transparently failed to keep the kingdom safe.[45] Despairing at the calibre of Siamese diplomats working in Europe,[46]

---

[38] Hesse-Wartegg, *Siam: Das Reich des weißen Elefanten*, 243; Stuart-Fox, 'The French in Laos, 1887–1945', 114–15. On the French *parti colonial* designs of a Greater Indochina including Siam, see C. M. Andrew and A. S. Kanya-Forstner, 'The French "Colonial Party": Its Composition, Aims and Influence, 1885–1914' *Historical Journal* 14, no. 1 (1971), 117–18; Louis Pinchon, *Notes sur la question siamoise* (Paris: Nourrit, 1893); *Journal officiel de la République française: Débats parlementaires: Chambre des députés*, 5 February 1893.

[39] Metternich to the German Foreign Office, 31 July 1893, in *Grosse Politik*, vol. 8, 110–11.

[40] Jeshurun, 'The Anglo-French Declaration of 1896', 110.

[41] Kimberly to De Bunsen, 27 October 1894, quoted in Jeshurun, 'The Anglo-French Declaration of 1896', 117.

[42] Ira Klein, 'Britain, Siam and the Malay Peninsula 1906–1909', *Historical Journal* 12, no. 1 (1969), 134.

[43] Jeshurun, 'The Anglo-French Declaration of 1896', 106.

[44] Goldman, 'Franco-British Rivalry over Siam', 213–16. Chulalongkorn's preference had been to discuss the terms of the agreement in London before signing, so as to extract a deal that he could use as leverage against the French when he visited Paris: Thio, 'Britain's Search for Security in North Malaya', 300–3.

[45] Kesboonchoo-Mead, 'Thai-European Relations', 27.

[46] Chulalongkorn to Saovabha Phongsri, 5 September 1897, in Pornsan Watanangura, Naruemit Sodsuk, and Khanitta Boonpan (eds), *Die erste Europareise des Königs Chulalongkorn 1897: Persönliche Briefe und Dokumente aus der ersten Europareise des Königs Chulalongkorn 1897* (Bangkok: Centre for European Studies Chulalongkorn University, 2003), 265–6.

King Chulalongkorn turned to summit diplomacy[47] in the hope that he could negotiate directly with Europe's heads of state to find a diplomatic solution that would stymie the Parisian colonial lobby.[48]

Chulalongkorn's 1897 Visit

On 2 February 1897, the German minister resident in Bangkok, Baron von Hartmann, wrote to the German Foreign Office on two matters. The first was the 'renewed urging' of the King of Siam on whether a decision had been made to accept his son Prince Paribatra into the Prussian military academy. The second was the intention of the Siamese king to travel to Europe for six months with his ministers to visit the royal houses of Britain, Germany, Russia, and Austria, before travelling home via America and Japan.[49] After initial difficulties finding a time that would fit in with the pre-existing travel plans of Germany's *Reisekaiser*, the Germans confirmed a slot in the final third of August, allowing King Chulalongkorn to accompany Wilhelm II to the autumn military parade on 28 August.[50]

The king had made it clear that his voyage was 'not a pleasure cruise,' but that it should 'serve to instruct him and to promote the interests of the country'.[51] Intertwined with the diplomatic importance of Chulalongkorn's visit was its economic dimension. The king was deeply interested in the rapid economic development of Germany and what lessons he might draw for the development of Siam. Accordingly, he made time in his itinerary to visit mines, factories, and foundries, as well as the harbour city of Hamburg, offering German industrialists the opportunity to showcase their capacity to assist with the reform of Siam's economic infrastructure. Chulalongkorn also stayed as an honoured guest of the Krupp family after surveying their industrial precinct and the world-famous Krupp arms bazaar in Essen (see Figure 1.2).[52]

Many of these trade-minded Germans saw themselves and Germany as a 'counterweight' to Anglo-French power in Asia and a third force in Siam with a rapidly growing economic role that meant they could no longer be ignored in

[47] Watanangura, 'The Beginnings of a New Era', 2.

[48] Niels P. Petersson, 'König Chulalongkorns Europareise 1897: Europäischer Imperialismus, symbolische Politik und monarchisch-bürokratische Modernisierung', *Saeculum* 52, no. 2 (2001), 298.

[49] Hartmann to Foreign Office, 2 February 1897, Hartmann to Chancellor Hohenlohe, 5 March, 1897, in PAAA R 251052, Die Reise des Königs von Siam nach Europa bzw Deutschland (unnumbered).

[50] Kiderlen to Foreign Office, 21 April 1897, 23 April 1897, in PAAA R 251052. It was also confirmed that Paribatra had been accepted into the cadet training academy in Potsdam.

[51] Hartmann to Foreign Office, 10 April 1897, in PAAA R 251052.

[52] Stoffers, *Thailand und Deutschland*, 98, 102. The visit left Chulalongkorn overwhelmed by the scale of the task of industrialization. See Petersson, 'König Chulalongkorns Europareise 1897', 315–16.

Figure 1.2 King Chulalongkorn inspecting artillery for sale while visiting the Krupp family in Essen
Source: Photo courtesy of the Historisches Archiv Krupp.

South East Asian affairs.[53] German railway interests in Siam had blossomed in the 1880s (despite British opposition), after the Siamese Prince Thewawong had visited Krupp in Germany and appointed Krupp's China agent, Karl Bethge, director general of Siam's new Royal Railways department. Backed by three German banks, Bethge had been tasked with building the Bangkok to Khorat railway line.[54] By 1896, the German consul in Bangkok was looking for ways to ensure that it was German banks that financed Siam's growing debt and in this way 'stake a place in the centre of Siamese interests, and establish a foundation for the further spread of our role in the opening up of this rich and very promising land'.[55]

---

[53] Volker Grabowsky, 'Deutschland 1899 im Spiegel des zeitgenössischen Siam', *Thailand-Rundschau* 16, no. 2 (2003), 74.

[54] Hesse-Wartegg, *Siam: Das Reich des weißen Elefanten*, 237–41. Hesse-Wartegg was particularly keen to see more German capital flow into Siam and Bethge assisted Hesse-Wartegg in preparing his manuscript, See ibid., vi. See also Nigel Brailey, 'The Scramble for Concessions in 1880s Siam', *Modern Asian Studies* 33, no. 3 (1999), 529, 534–5; for the period thereafter, see Chandran Jeshurun, 'Lord Lansdowne and the "Anti-German Clique" at the Foreign Office: Their Role in the Making of the Anglo-Siamese Agreement of 1902', *Journal of Southeast Asian Studies* 3, no. 2 (1972), 229–46. On German leadership of Siam's railway construction, see Luis Weiler, *Anfänge der Eisenbahn in Thailand* (Bangkok: Chalermnit, 1979); Volker Grabowsky, 'Thai-German Relations from King Chulalongkorn's First Visit to Europe until World War II', in Watanangura (ed.), *The Visit of King Chulalongkorn to Europe*, 58–60.

[55] Hartmann to Hohenlohe, 26 August 1896, in PAAA R19237, 'Allgemeine Angelegenheiten Siams', 88–91.

This status as a looming third power was directly targeted by the Anglo-French Agreement, which insisted that Chulalongkorn not enter 'into any agreement with a third Power to intervene within this area'.[56] Even after this preventative anti-German measure, the British worried that the vague terms of the 1896 agreement might allow the Germans to make colonial claims over Siamese territory.[57] Accordingly, the Anglo-Siamese agreement of 1897 further targeted any German plans for empire on Siamese soil, including any naval presence on the strategically sensitive west coast of Siam.[58]

Chulalongkorn's crowded list of geostrategic, diplomatic, and economic goals makes it unlikely that the political tasks of the visit were subordinate to what Winichakul has called the 'quest to experience the source of *siwilai* [civilization] firsthand',[59] or simple eagerness to 'experience Western civilisation in its birthplace'.[60] Although elements of an 'autocolonizing quest for *siwilai*' are present in Chulalongkorn's 1897 royal tour, these personal grounds seem to have been second-order considerations, given his clear sense that the empires of Europe were in a position to preserve or carve up his kingdom and his belief that his personal intervention might prove decisive.[61] The king's correspondence with the Siamese queen, Saovabha Phongsri, who ruled Siam during his extended absence, makes this abundantly clear. From Florence in mid-June 1897, he wrote to the queen confessing that 'I see my visit could be a chance for the survival of our country. I am greatly worried and feel myself burdened.'[62] Queen Saovabha shared his concerns, disparaging the 'exceptionally treacherous' French and pointing out that the asymmetries of power between the empires of Europe and Siam were simply too great to be overcome without a powerful European ally.[63]

While the king's visit to Paris was scheduled for 11 June, the animosity of the French was so pronounced that Chulalongkorn decided to visit Russia first.[64] Nicholas II's welcome did not disappoint the Siamese king.[65] Tsar Nicholas II sent ten thousand troops to accompany him from the border in a flourish of pomp

[56] Jeshurun, 'The Anglo-French Declaration of 1896', 106; Hesse-Wartegg, *Siam: Das Reich des weißen Elefanten*, 249. See also Grabowsky, 'Deutschland 1899 im Spiegel', 74.

[57] Chandran Jeshurun, 'The Anglo-French Declaration of 1896', 124.

[58] Thio, 'Britain's Search for Security in North Malaya', 298–9.

[59] Winichakul, 'The Quest for "Siwilai"', 539, 542.

[60] Palabıyık, 'The Sultan, the Shah and the King in Europe', 211–12.

[61] Rachel V. Harrison, 'The Allure of Ambiguity: The "West" and the Making of Thai Identities', in Harrison and Jackson (eds), *The Ambiguous Allure of the West*, 18. For Chulalongkorn's wry self-awareness of the paradoxes of autocolonization, see Chulalongkorn to Saovabha Phongsri, 30 July 1897 and 8 August 1897, in Watanangura, Sodsuk, and Boonpan (eds), *Die erste Europareise des Königs Chulalongkorn 1897*, 253, 255.

[62] Chulalongkorn to Saovabha Phongsri, 13 June 1897, in Watanangura, Sodsuk, and Boonpan (eds), *Die erste Europareise des Königs Chulalongkorn 1897*, 80–1.

[63] Saovabha Phongsri to Chulalongkorn (undated), in Watanangura, Sodsuk, and Boonpan (eds), *Die erste Europareise des Königs Chulalongkorn 1897*, 83.

[64] Hartmann to Foreign Office, 10 April 1897, in PAAA R 251052.

[65] Karen Snow, 'St. Petersburg's Man in Siam: A. E. Olarovskii and Russia's Asian Mission, 1898–1905', *Cahiers du Monde Russe*, 48, no. 4 (2007), 613–14, 617–19.

and circumstance.[66] This effusive welcome was utterly consistent with Russia's policy of deep engagement with Asia, but was also an expression of gratitude for the hospitality shown to him when, as tsarevich in 1891, he had visited Chulalongkorn in Bangkok. This Russian welcome, the Siamese king hoped, would put pressure on the French to be more hospitable, a hope that was fulfilled not only in Paris but throughout Continental Europe.[67] The treatment of Chulalongkorn as a monarch of full rank soon became pan-European, infuriating the French foreign minister, Gabriel Hanotaux, who complained that 'insolence which could not be tolerated from a South American Republic, could certainly not be borne from Siam...this petty oriental Kingdom'. Although it was not exactly true that Chulalongkorn was treated everywhere as 'a monarch and not an Asian',[68] he was certainly treated by the crowned heads of Europe as a monarch who was 'different but not exceedingly so',[69] personifying what Thongchai Winichakul has termed 'hybrid *siwilai*',[70] resplendent in a carefully chosen European uniform and fully conversant with European courtly etiquette.[71]

Chulalongkorn was at first heartened by his foreign policy discussions in Russia. Falling well short of a promise to intervene on Siam's behalf on outstanding territorial questions, the tsar nonetheless offered to smooth the way for the king to visit France, acting as 'a friend who tries to mediate between both their friends'.[72] The British leg of the tour, on the other hand, proved disappointing to Chulalongkorn, if not the Germans.[73] It was known that the king had come to London to seek a firm commitment to defend the territorial integrity and independence of Siam.[74] The London visit had been marked as crucial by the German envoy in Bangkok. If Chulalongkorn had left with a firm agreement, then 'all the offers of friendship offered him' in Germany might have been seen as 'simply due courtesies' for a British-aligned monarch. If, however, the king came away from Britain empty-handed, then this might 'increase his respect for Germany and instil a better opinion of the worth of its friendship'.[75] When the news of Britain's

[66] Petersson, 'König Chulalongkorns Europareise 1897', 305–8, 310.

[67] David Malitz, 'The Monarch's New Clothes: Transnational Flows and the Fashioning of the Modern Japanese and Siamese Monarchies' in Milinda Banerjee, Charlotte Backerra, and Cathleen Sarti (eds.), *Transnational Histories of the 'Royal Nation'* (New York: Palgrave, 2017), 164–5. While no concrete proposals were agreed upon, a guarded spirit of détente marked the visit. See Petersson, 'König Chulalongkorns Europareise 1897', 316–18.

[68] Petersson, 'König Chulalongkorns Europareise 1897', 308, 312.

[69] Watanangura, 'The Beginnings of a New Era', 9.

[70] Winichakul, 'The Quest for "Siwilai"', 539.

[71] Malitz, 'The Monarch's New Clothes', 164–5.

[72] Chulalongkorn to Devawongse, 5 July 1897, in Watanangura, Sodsuk, and Boonpan (eds), *Die erste Europareise des Königs Chulalongkorn 1897*, 202.

[73] Chulalongkorn to Saovabha Phongsri, 30 July 1897 and 8 August 1897, in Watanangura, Sodsuk, and Boonpan (eds.), *Die erste Europareise des Königs Chulalongkorn 1897*, 80–1, 253–5.

[74] Stoffers, *Thailand und Deutschland*, 99; Neil A. Englehart, 'Representing Civilization: Solidarism, Ornamentalism, and Siam's Entry into International Society', *European Journal of International Relations* 16, no. 3 (2010), 430–1.

[75] Hartmann to Foreign Office, 10 April 1897, in in PAAA R 251052.

lacklustre reception was reported to Wilhelm II, he remarked, 'Very pleasing. We will treat him better.'[76]

Part of the charm offensive orchestrated by the German Foreign Office and performed by the emperor was the bestowal of prestigious royal orders, a seemingly significant ceremonial action which, nonetheless, did not imply any concrete future foreign policy obligations. While Germany did not have a national set of orders and decorations, Wilhelm II could offer Prussian orders such as the Black Eagle and the Red Eagle.[77] That these royal orders and decorations would be bestowed upon a non-European monarch under such clear territorial and political pressure as the King of Siam was not entirely self-evident and in offering some of Prussia's highest honours, Wilhelm II publicly confirmed the Siamese king's status as a brother monarch. In doing so, however, he was also closely following the instructions of Chancellor Hohenlohe and State Secretary Bülow, who in turn had been advised by Hartmann in Bangkok of the various ranks of the king's retinue,[78] and by German embassies around Europe, that had noted the orders other monarchs had bestowed upon the Siamese contingent.[79] Strikingly, as Chulalongkorn had already been awarded the highly prestigious Order of the Black Eagle in 1873, he received the Chain of the Order of the Red Eagle, an honour that, Wilhelm II impressed upon the king, was only conferred upon very few people, including Otto von Bismarck.[80] Alongside these Prussian honours, Chulalongkorn was also given the Order of the Red Crown by the King of Saxony.[81]

Despite, or perhaps because of, the ambiguity of the commitment they signalled, these decorations mattered greatly to the Siamese delegation because they at the very least formally implied a notional equivalency in Europe at a time when any sign of international legitimacy could help raise the status of their kingdom and thereby assist in salvaging it. No mere recipients, the Siamese delegation also sought to offer Siamese honours including the Order of the Crown of Siam and the Order of the White Elephant to 127 recipients, which the German Foreign Office helped the Siamese envoy to Berlin, Nond Buri, cull back to 83 eventual

[76] Wilhelm II, margin note on Hatzfeldt to Hohenlohe, 18 August 1897, in PAAA R19239 'Allgemeine Angelegenheiten Siams', 6.

[77] Otto Lackmann, *Das Kaisertum in den Verfassungen des Deutschen Reiches vom 28. März 1849 und vom 16. April 1871* (Bonn: Carl Georgi, 1903), 14; Richard Fischer, *Das Recht des Deutschen Kaisers* (Berlin: W. Moeser Hofbuchhandlung, 1895), 60.

[78] Hartmann to Hohenlohe, 26 April 1897, in in PAAA R 251052, Bülow to Wilhelm II, 20 August 1897, Eulenburg to the Prussian Ministry of Foreign Affairs, 22 August 1897, in PAAA R 251053, 'Die Reise des Königs von Siam nach Europa bzw Deutschland.'

[79] Lichnowsky to Hohenlohe, 9 July 1897; Radolin to Hohenlohe, 16 July 1897, in PAAA R 251052.

[80] Chulalongkorn to Saovabha Phongsri, 28 August 1897, in Watanangura, Sodsuk, and Boonpan (eds), *Die erste Europareise des Königs Chulalongkorn 1897*, 260.

[81] Chulalongkorn to Saovabha Phongsri, 24 August 1897, in Watanangura, Sodsuk, and Boonpan (eds), *Die erste Europareise des Königs Chulalongkorn 1897*, 257.

recipients.[82] Chulalongkorn also laid wreaths upon the graves of both Kaiser Friedrich and Wilhelm I, diplomatic ceremonies that offered Siam further 'symbolic capital' within Germany.[83]

A public display of mutual regard was also evident at a banquet on 27 August 1897, at which Wilhelm II offered an after-dinner toast in English to King Chulalongkorn and Siam. He wished the king good luck with all of his 'great endeavours' and expressed the hope that the 'bonds of friendship and trade' between the two states would grow. Chulalongkorn replied by speaking warmly of the future of German interests in Siam, noting approvingly the German offers of material assistance with 'the establishment of post and telegraph and the building of railways'. With perhaps a veiled reference to the desire for deeper diplomatic as well as economic engagement, the king ended by expressing the hope 'that I may always count on attracting such help in all of the affairs of my country'.[84]

What Chulalongkorn did not know when he was toasting Siamese-German relations is that Bülow's Foreign Office had explicitly cautioned Wilhelm II against going any further than encouraging a general mood of bonhomie, forbidding him from discussing Germany's affairs in and position towards Siam. While rumours later circulated in Britain that the emperor had raised the possibility of a 'collective guarantee of the great powers for the independence of Siam',[85] such musings fell far outside the emperor's actual scope for action. Without the approval of the Foreign Office, the state secretary, and the chancellor, no guarantees of any kind could be supported, much less any spontaneously initiated by Wilhelm II. Chulalongkorn might have been able to directly intervene in Siamese foreign policy, but the German emperor studiously followed the directions of his advisers.

[82] Nond Buri to Foreign Office, 27 March 1899, 11 April 1899, in PAAA R 131804, 'Die Reise des Königs von Siam nach Europa bezw. Deutschland.' These orders were not always without controversy, with two officials refusing theirs, as they had also been given to officials of an inferior rank. The Siamese Legation responded by upgrading the two honours in question. See Reichspostamt to Schoen, 8 January 1908, Phya Sridhamasasana to Schoen, 2 May 1908, in PAAA R 131805, 'Die Reise des Königs von Siam nach Europa bezw. Deutschland.'

[83] Chulalongkorn to Saovabha Phongsri, 28 August 1897, in Watanangura, Sodsuk, and Boonpan (eds), *Die erste Europareise des Königs Chulalongkorn 1897*, 260; Petersson, 'König Chulalongkorns Europareise 1897', 325.

[84] *Deutscher Reichsanzeiger*, 28 August 1897, in PAAA R 251053. At the same dinner, Wilhelm II introduced the king to Germany's new Minister Resident to Siam. Chulalongkorn used the opportunity to disparage the behaviour of the current minister resident, who was part of the reason why 'difficulties arise' with Germany. Chulalongkorn to Saovabha Phongsri, 28 August 1897 and 5 September 1897, in Watanangura, Sodsuk, and Boonpan (eds), *Die erste Europareise des Königs Chulalongkorn 1897*, 260, 271. Presumably alluded to here was Hartmann's 1897 brush with the Siamese authorities after he had drunkenly run his cart over an ice-cream vendor in Bangkok. See Hong Lysa, '"Stranger within the Gates": Knowing Semi-Colonial Siam as Extraterritorials', *Modern Asian Studies* 38, no. 2 (2004), 327–54.

[85] Petersson, 'König Chulalongkorns Europareise 1897', 315.

Before leaving Germany for France, Chulalongkorn drew some conclusions about the usefulness of summit diplomacy with Wilhelm II and the other monarchs of Europe. Chulalongkorn realized that even cordial relations with European monarchs would bring Siam precious little, unless the material and geostrategic interests of those states coincided with Siam's. Accordingly, Chulalongkorn vacillated between hope and pessimism:

> I ponder night and day what assistance this trip should bring. I can only think that I am like a dreamer that dreamed of springs of gold and silver…The foreign governments consider us to be completely unimportant…Regarding the expectation of support from other countries, as I understood it after I spoke with the tsar of Russia, Count Muravyov, Lord Salisbury, Mister Curzon and the German Kaiser, I believe I have no choice but to trust their words. If our independence is threatened, they will certainly have a say and not allow anyone to do anything to us. This could under some conditions lead to war. Hopefully that will not happen. We cannot expect any further help. No one will speak or think for us if we fall into trouble. Don't dream that someone will take up all our affairs for us…As an independent state, we must look after ourselves.[86]

Chulalongkorn was particularly sceptical about Wilhelm II, understanding that German foreign policy towards Siam was largely guided by how German actions in Asia would be received in Europe. 'Regarding the German emperor', he wrote to Saovabha Phongsri, 'his character and his position towards the affairs of our country…[show] that he is not entirely committed…He shares the protests for our affairs only because he wishes to satisfy the Tsar'—a basis for foreign policy, Bismarck had warned him, that was not 'stable and enduring'.[87]

The German emperor, nonetheless, publicly offered Chulalongkorn the hospitality befitting a brother monarch and in so doing momentarily bridged the perceived divide between Europe and Asia, if only at the level of royal courtesy.[88] The display of mutual respect between the monarchs extended as far as an exchange of letters after Chulalongkorn's departure. His visit, the king wrote, had taught him 'to fully appreciate the greatness of the German Empire with its excellent and wise administration'. Having travelled all over Germany, he opined that 'everything one sees tends to show the immense progress of arts, sciences, and industry. I cannot help congratulating Your Majesty for being the ruler of so great a nation'.[89] Wilhelm II's warm reply thanked Chulalongkorn for his 'friendship and cordial

---

[86] Chulalongkorn to Saovabha Phongsri, 5 September 1897, in Watanangura, Sodsuk, and Boonpan (eds), *Die erste Europareise des Königs Chulalongkorn 1897*, 265–6.

[87] Chulalongkorn to Saovabha Phongsri, 5 September 1897, in Watanangura, Sodsuk, and Boonpan (eds), *Die erste Europareise des Königs Chulalongkorn 1897*, 271–2.

[88] Palabıyık, 'The Sultan, the Shah and the King in Europe', 228.

[89] Chulalongkorn to Wilhelm II, 20 March 1898, in PAAA R 251053.

feelings', and he declared that 'I take no less interest in all that concerns you and your country and...I cherish the most heartfelt wishes for Your Majesty's welfare and the increasing prosperity of the Siamese Kingdom.'[90] The mutual courtesies even extended to Queen Saovabha Phongsri, who also thanked Wilhelm II for his gift and his hospitality to the king, signing her telegram 'from your Asiatic sister'[91] The emperor answered her telegram too, thanking her for her good wishes.[92] Nonetheless, Chulalongkorn came and went from Germany without any foreign policy guarantees for his beleaguered kingdom. Indeed, that the visit changed German attitudes towards Chulalongkorn's sovereign rights is highly unlikely, given German naval developments on the west coast of Siamese Malaya in the coming years.

The Push for a German Langkawi

After Chulalongkorn's royal visit there were some firm signs of improved economic cooperation between Siam and Germany.[93] German capital's control over Siam's railway construction tightened, with Hesse-Wartegg commenting in 1899 that 'the operation of the railway is under German leadership, as is the entire railway business.'[94] As Andreas Stoffers has argued, the Germans were increasingly viewed as safer, less predatory partners for the construction of sensitive infrastructure projects like railway, telegraph, and postal communications networks than either British or French firms. For German industry, the Siamese king's modernization project continued to be a lucrative opportunity, albeit one that came at the cost of increasingly antagonizing the French and the British, who were both keen to divide Siamese commercial opportunities between themselves.[95]

If Chulalongkorn was recognized as a visiting monarch and received a corresponding level of treatment while in Europe, the visit was far less successful in arousing compunction regarding the erosion of Siamese sovereignty. Despite Wilhelm II's professed warm wishes for the security and prosperity of Siam, and despite the foreign office's theoretical preference for simply maintaining the 'open door' to German trade in Siam rather than undertaking any imperial adventures,[96] consideration of colonial opportunities in Siam was not stymied in other German ministries by Chulalongkorn's visit. Less than a year after the Siamese king had

---

[90]   Wilhelm II to Chulalongkorn, 31 March 1898, in PAAA R 251053.
[91]   Saovabha Phongsri to Wilhelm II, 30 August 1897, in PAAA R 251053.
[92]   Wilhelm II to Saovabha Phongsri, 2 September 1897, in PAAA R 251053.
[93]   Stoffers, *Thailand und Deutschland*, 99.
[94]   Hesse-Wartegg, *Siam: Das Reich des weißen Elephanten*, 239.
[95]   Stoffers, *Thailand und Deutschland*, 107–20.
[96]   Volker Schult, *Wunsch und Wirklichkeit: Deutsch-philippinische Beziehungen im Kontext globaler Verflechtungen 1860–1945* (Berlin: Logos Verlag, 2008), 149–50.

left Berlin, Hamburg traders Arnold Otto Meyer and his son Eduard Lorenz Meyer proposed to the naval secretary, Alfred von Tirpitz that Germany should establish a naval presence on the west coast of Siam. According to Lorenz Meyer, Vizier Wan Mohammed Saman from the northern Malay Sultanate of Kedah, a subject state of Siam, had informed him that 'Siam would without doubt be glad to see a German colony established on the west coast of the Malay Peninsula' and that the island cluster of Langkawi, as fertile and large as Penang, would be ideal for this purpose.[97]

The proposal was sent from the Admiralty to Bülow in the Foreign Office in early September 1898.[98] Without expressing any concerns about Siam's territorial sovereignty, the foreign secretary replied that 'for his part he would not be averse to considering more carefully the question of the future establishment of a coaling station in the region of the Strait of Malacca' if it was deemed desirable by the navy. To that end, he left it to Tirpitz's discretion whether he wished to send a ship to inspect Langkawi. Were he to do so, Bülow wrote, the nature of the mission should be kept absolutely secret so as not to arouse the suspicion of the other powers.[99]

With Bülow having given the green light, Tirpitz ordered Admiral Knorr to investigate the possibility of establishing a German naval base on Siam's west coast by sending a German naval vessel (SMS *Iltis*) to secretly study Langkawi's suitability for German purposes.[100] An initial telegram from the *Iltis* in mid-April 1899 described Langkawi as 'very suitable'.[101] The full report from corvette captain Wilhelm Lans was even more enthusiastic, describing Langkawi as 'exceptionally usable', with an 'economic worth so great that the acquisition of the island group can only be warmly recommended'.[102] Including a closely detailed map, the report argued that Langkawi possessed a perfectly formed natural harbour with sufficiently deep water for ships of any size. The harbour was also sheltered from wind from all directions and had three entrances. Its mountains were covered in

[97] Meyer to Tirpitz, 27 July 1898, in BA Freiburg, RM3/4353 'Erforschung und Erwerbung von Ländern in Ostasien', 115–16. Simultaneously under consideration in South East Asia were Batam Island, Redang Island, St John Island, and Mindoro. Kedah's actions fit in with broader attempts by Malay monarchs to protect their sovereignty against the predations of both Britain and Siam by granting land to private interests from places such as Germany, Denmark, and Japan so as to forestall their wholesale absorption. See Malhi, 'Making Spaces, Making Subjects', 727–47.
[98] BA Freiburg, RM3/4353, 118.
[99] Bülow to Tirpitz, 11 October 1898, in BA Freiburg, RM3/4353, 123, reproduced in PAAA RZ201/2534, 'Kolonien und Flottenstationen', 21–2. See also Ekkehard Böhm, *Überseehandel und Flottenbau: Hanseatische Kaufmannschaft und deutsche Seerüstung 1879-1902* (Gütersloh: Bertelsmann Universitätsverlag, 1972), 114–15.
[100] Tirpitz, 11 October 1898, in BA Freiburg, RM3/4353, 124–5; Tirpitz to Bülow, 19 January 1899, in PAAA RZ201/2534, 72; Peter Overlack, 'Asia in German Naval Planning before the First World War: The Strategic Imperative', *War and Society* 17, no. 1 (1999), 5–7; Schult, *Wunsch und Wirklichkeit*, 149–50.
[101] Breusing to Tirpitz, 26 April 1899, in BA Freiburg RM3/4354 'Erforschung und Erwerbung von Ländern in Ostasien', 10; Tirpitz to Bülow, 9 May 1899, in PAAA RZ201/2534, 149.
[102] Lans to Prince Heinrich, 6 May 1899, in PAAA RZ201/2534, 183. Also to be found in BA Freiburg RM3/4354, 77–82.

useable timber and its valleys were 'exceptionally fertile', with a good supply of fresh water. Rice, coconuts, and sugar could all be grown there. Importantly, no other European power could entrench itself in the area and Langkawi could, Lans argued, offer Germany not only a coaling station but also an important trading post that might spread across neighbouring islands as well.[103] Conceivably, the report continued, Germany could buy it from its ruler, the 'indebted' Sultan of Kedah, a dependent monarch of King Chulalongkorn, for a 'not too high price'. A long-term lease was another possibility. Lans pressed the navy to act, concluding that Langkawi was 'extraordinarily viable'.[104] From the ministries, Lans's report made its way to Wilhelm II, who, without recalling his pledges of friendship to Chulalongkorn, asked Bülow to advise him on the steps he would like to see taken regarding this freshly reconnoitred Siamese colonial site.[105]

Despite Lans's and subsequently Tirpitz's enthusiasm, not everyone was enamoured of the proposal for a German colony in Siam, with the Foreign Office reminding Tirpitz of the complexities associated with interfering with Siamese territory. The undersecretary of foreign affairs, Oswald von Richthofen, wrote to Tirpitz before briefing a naval cabinet meeting at which Wilhelm II would be present. Richthofen warned Tirpitz that the 'rajah of Kedah' was, in fact, a subordinate ruler in a feudal relation with Siam and that the Siamese government could not be ignored in any decision regarding the partition of its territory. Furthermore, Richthofen reminded Tirpitz that Germany had stayed well away from South East Asia for good reason, namely because the Foreign Office saw it as undesirable to become embroiled in 'the extremely acute Anglo-French antagonism on the Malay peninsula'. Prior to speaking to the emperor, Richthofen wanted to make sure he fully understood what worth the navy placed on the rapid acquisition of Langkawi and whether it was worth antagonizing the British, given the recent German acquisition of the Caroline, Mariana, and Palau Islands.[106]

In his marginal comments to Richthofen's letter, Tirpitz expressed his strong disagreement with the undersecretary's caution, writing that such an outpost was 'very important' for the navy and exclaiming that 'We cannot let ourselves miss out.'[107] These sentiments were relayed back to the Foreign Office in a lengthy reply in which Tirpitz declared that he saw the 'imminent acquisition' of the Langkawi Islands as 'extremely desirable' for expanding Germany's global naval

---

[103] Lans to Prince Heinrich, 6 May 1899, in PAAA RZ201/2534, 183. Also to be found in BA Freiburg RM3/4354, 77–82; See also Böhm, *Überseehandel und Flottenbau*, 115.

[104] Lans to Prince Heinrich, 6 May 1899, in BA Freiburg RM3/4354, 77–82; Schult, *Wunsch und Wirklichkeit*, 152–3. For the Sultan of Kedah, Siam, and the British in this period, see Malhi, 'Like a Child with Two Parents'.

[105] Wilhelm II to Bülow, 27 July 1899, in PAAA RZ201/2534, 182.

[106] Richthofen to Tirpitz, 2 August 1899, in BA Freiburg RM3/4354, 90–1. Also reproduced in PAAA RZ201/2534, 194–7.

[107] Tirpitz, Marginal notes to Richthofen to Tirpitz, 2 August 1899, in BA Freiburg RM3/4354, 90.

reach.[108] Recent acquisitions in the Pacific had not changed this. Langkawi's position in the Strait of Malacca meant it was an ideal staging point for East Asia, offering Germany independence from British possessions such as Penang and Singapore, as well as promising conditions for economic development as a German trading and shipping entrepôt. It was also a convenient midpoint for ships moving between German East Africa and Kiautschou.[109] Politically speaking, the indebtedness of Kedah's sultan was also in Germany's favour. With Prince Heinrich of Prussia already in Asia, high-level negotiations with the Siamese government could also get under way quickly.[110]

News from the *Iltis* in August 1899 had confirmed that haste would be required if Germany wished to acquire Langkawi. According to Lans, Sultan Abdul Hamid Halim of Kedah (whom the Germans dealt with via the crown prince, the 'Rajah Mudah') was known to be a thorn in the side of the British, and it was highly likely that they would move to seize his territory upon his death, assimilating Kedah as they had Perak.[111] Richthofen wrote to the German minister resident in Bangkok, Conrad von Saldern, asking whether in his opinion the acquisition would cause any difficulties with Siam or Britain and whether Germany should begin negotiations straight away.[112] Saldern replied in a telegram that 'Siam jealously guards its sovereignty and rights' over its vassals in the Malay peninsula such as the Sultan of Kedah. If Chulalongkorn would not accept financial incentives (which he assumed he would not), Saldern suggested that the king might accept Germany acquiring Langkawi in return for Germany offering Siam support against any British attempts to annex northern Malaya.[113]

In his longer report to Chancellor Hohenlohe-Schillingsfürst, however, Saldern was more pessimistic. Ruling out the possibility that direct negotiations with Kedah would be successful, Saldern reported that most of Chulalongkorn's Malay vassals had been either subdued or removed, and that Kedah was now too firmly attached to Siam for Langkawi to be simply acquired without reference to Bangkok. Any incentives, he argued, would have to be offered to Chulalongkorn, not his vassal in Kedah. Casting doubt on Langkawi's commercial worth and pointing out that a German seizure of Langkawi might embolden Britain and France to begin the dismemberment of Siam, Saldern suggested that the only chance of success lay in presenting the other powers with a fait accompli, claiming the island, and pressuring Chulalongkorn to concede while leaving Britain to

---

[108] Tirpitz to Foreign Office, 12 September 1899, in BA Freiburg RM3/4354, 92–5 and PAAA RZ201/2534, 242–6; Böhm, *Überseehandel und Flottenbau*, 116.

[109] Tirpitz to Foreign Office, 12 September 1899, in BA Freiburg RM3/4354, 92–5.

[110] Tirpitz to Foreign Office, 12 September 1899, in BA Freiburg RM3/4354, 92–5.

[111] Lans to Heinrich, 4 August 1899, in BA Freiburg RM3/4354, 112–113, reproduced in PAAA RZ201/2534, 267–8.

[112] Richthofen to Saldern, 21 September 1899, in PAAA RZ201/2534, 250–1.

[113] Saldern to German Foreign Office, 27 September 1899, in PAAA RZ201/2534, 254–5.

simply come to terms with a German naval presence just north of Penang in the Malacca Strait.[114]

Even before Saldern's cautious appraisal arrived in Berlin, Richthofen had quietly rejected any state-led plan that would set a deliberate collision course with Britain and suggested instead a private sector solution, making use of a business-man already in the region recommended by Tirpitz, namely Sholto Douglas, to undertake direct negotiations with the Sultan of Kedah for a commercial monopoly over Langkawi.[115] After promising initial discussions, Douglas met with Foreign Minister Bülow in mid-October 1899, informing him that he had been able to negotiate an economic and development monopoly over Langkawi with Kedah and that the contract only required the ratification of King Chulalongkorn. His only other concern was that the British might raise objections.[116]

With Saldern's pessimistic assessment now circulating in Berlin, by the end of 1899, Bülow had also gone cool on an obviously state-led initiative. In a letter to Wilhelm II on 8 December, the foreign secretary made clear his doubts about a naval seizure of Langkawi. Any opposition from the Siamese, he argued, would be supported by Britain, which would be keen to preserve its dominance over the Malacca Strait and the Malay Peninsula. Seizing Langkawi militarily in the manner of Kiautschou would risk provoking serious conflict with Britain. Bülow instead threw his weight behind the bid for company control of Langkawi by Douglas' newly established private sector entity, the *Deutsche Übersee Gesellschaft*, which promised Germany a back-door, private sector path to effective control over the island, as colonial company leases had elsewhere.[117] Indeed, the private sector plan appeared to be already showing signs of success, with Douglas already having signed a twenty-year monopoly contract for infrastructure development in Langkawi with Kedah's sultan, pending the approval of King Chulalongkorn.[118] Wilhelm II agreed with Bülow, scribbling 'no' next to the question of whether it made sense to court a disastrous conflict with Britain for the sake of Langkawi and 'yes' next to the suggestion of a quiet and gradual takeover under the guise of

[114] Saldern to Hohenlohe-Schillingsfürst, 29 September 1899, in PAAA RZ201/2535, 22–39. See also Böhm, *Überseehandel und Flottenbau*, 116.

[115] Richthofen, 1 October 1899, in PAAA RZ201/2534, 256–8.

[116] Douglas to Bülow, 16 October 1899, in PAAA RZ201/2534, 275.

[117] Bülow to Wilhelm II, 8 December 1899, in PAAA RZ201/2535, 'Kolonien und Flottenstationen', 75–85; Böhm, *Überseehandel und Flottenbau*, 116–17. Bülow also informed Tirpitz of his strong advice to avoid conflict with Britain. See Bülow to Tirpitz, 22 December 1899, in BA Freiburg RM3/4354, 127–8. For the global structure and ambition of the *Deutsche Übersee Gesellschaft*, see PAAA RZ201/2535, 'Kolonien und Flottenstationen', 14–19. For a rival private sector group with a similar plan, the *Malacca-Syndikat*, headed by Gustav Meinecke, see PAAA RZ201/2535, 141–3.

[118] Douglas to Tirpitz, 25 November 1899, in BA Freiburg RM3/4354, 133; Douglas to Richthofen, 25 November 1899, in PAAA RZ201/2535, 59. The deal was formally for a loan with rights over tariffs, railways, mines, and trade concessions as collateral. See PAAA RZ201/2535, 168.

private enterprise. The emperor also accepted Bülow's strong advice not to discuss Langkawi with the British.[119]

These German hopes for private sector imperialism in Siam were dashed, however, when Chulalongkorn refused to ratify the company monopoly of the *Deutsche Übersee Gesellschaft*, despite Kedah's crown prince personally travelling to Bangkok to try and convince Chulalongkorn.[120] Behind the scenes in Bangkok, the plan was also leaked to the *London and China Express* and *Bangkok Times* newspapers by J. G. Scott, Siam's mining minister and a British agent who was also putting considerable pressure on Chulalongkorn.[121] A *Bangkok Times* article declared that a German Langkawi would be 'a menace to British interests' and reminded the Siamese government of the 1896 Anglo-French Agreement, as well as the probable 'disquiet' of the Dutch. Two days later, the same newspaper revisited the issue, declaring that it had 'authority for stating' that 'no such proposal...would be listened to for a moment by the Siamese government' because it would signal the end of Siamese sovereignty over Langkawi, and 'Siam very rightly shows herself exceedingly jealous lest any of her sovereign rights be impaired.'[122]

The British and Siamese governments refused to accept a German private sector monopoly over Langkawi. For his part, Douglas shied away from the risk of quietly buying parcels of land on the island from the Sultan of Kedah without reference to Bangkok.[123] Despite Otto Meyer of the *Deutsche Übersee Gesellschaft* declaring that King Chulalongkorn's refusal to ratify the treaty the company had signed with Kedah was a 'clear breach of contract' that could only be answered by 'the seizure of Langkawi',[124] German Foreign Office concerns about British and French reactions saw enthusiasm for the plans for a German colony in Langkawi gradually wane.

From the British perspective, this was far from a principled decision to preserve Chulalongkorn's claims to sovereignty over north-western Malaya. Rather, it was merely an attempt to displace its German competitor and thereby enable its own expansionist plans. On 6 August 1909, Langkawi was formally seized by the British as a consequence of the Anglo-Siamese treaty of 10 March 1909.[125]

[119] Bülow to Wilhelm II, 8 December 1899, in PAAA RZ201/2535, 107–9.
[120] Douglas 2 January 1900, Meyer 26 January 1900 in PAAA RZ201/2535, 132, 174.
[121] Saldern to German Foreign Office, 27 January 1900, in PAAA RZ201/2535, 137; Douglas to Tirpitz, 2 February 1900, 28 February 1900, in BA Freiburg RM3/4354, 148–50, 160–1.
[122] 'Is It for a Coaling Station?' *Bangkok Times*, 25 January 1900, in PAAA RZ201/2535, 179.
[123] Douglas to Richthofen, 28 February 1900, in BA Freiburg RM3/4354, 188–90, reproduced in PAAA RZ201/2535, 172–3.
[124] Meyer to Douglas, 27 June 1900, in PAAA RZ201/2536, 129.
[125] Böhm, *Überseehandel und Flottenbau*, 120; Overlack, 'Asia in German Naval Planning', 6–9; Schult, *Wunsch und Wirklichkeit*, 173.

Post-Tour Disappointments

Enthusiastic claims have been made about the diplomatic efficacy of Chulalongkorn's royal tour. Pornsan Watanangura, for example, has argued that the visit had profound long-term effects on Siam's position in the Europe-dominated international system of the late nineteenth and early twentieth centuries. 'King Chulalongkorn's trips to Europe in 1897 and 1907,' he has argued, 'set the stage for a new era in Siamese-European relations.' These enhanced relations, he has claimed, were largely a product of the monarch being 'received as an "equal" by the crowned heads and leaders of Europe'.[126]

It is difficult to sustain this sanguine view. The Siamese king was disappointed that no formal diplomatic offers to assist with Siam's struggle for independence were forthcoming from European royals such as Wilhelm II, who, as a constitutional monarch, was controlled by the German Foreign Office, which had explicitly warned him against intervening in sensitive South East Asian affairs. For all the courtesy he was shown by his European royal peers, Chulalongkorn remained isolated and, in diplomatic terms, largely friendless in Europe. His tour of Germany had done nothing to forestall the German Naval Office's search for a South East Asian naval colony. Although Chulalongkorn's formal claims to be treated as the monarch of a modernizing Asian nation were clearly accepted while he was in Europe, the fate of his kingdom was still decided by European imperial calculations.

Predictably, German pro-colonial and pro-Siamese figures such as Hesse-Wartegg demanded more. Warning of the possibility that France might simply absorb Siam, Hesse-Wartegg noted that this could not be halted 'by notes of protest from England', but rather by German diplomatic and potentially even military action:

> Germany has every reason to have its say forthrightly, and it also has the power, if it comes to that, to support its words. The independence of Siam lies in the interests of the German Empire, and if these interests are correctly recognized by those in authority, then Siam will have no better friend in Europe than Germany. Siam cannot defend itself with its own strength against the tentacles of the Gallic octopus.[127]

Notwithstanding Germany's naval adventurism in Langkawi, however, Germany's role in Siam remained strictly economic. This was not a product of any deference to the sovereign rights of Chulalongkorn, but was a product of the threat of provoking a conflict with Britain. Significantly, Hesse-Wartegg's desire to meet with

---

[126] Watanangura, 'The Beginnings of a New Era', 2.
[127] Hesse-Wartegg, *Siam: Das Reich des weißen Elefanten*, 248–9.

Bülow in 1899 to discuss his plans for a German role in Siam were rebuffed.[128] Having just decided on private sector imperialism rather than state power for furthering German geostrategic interests in the Malacca Strait, Bülow was in no mood to entertain Hesse-Wartegg's suggestion that Prince Heinrich negotiate the acquisition of Langkawi with Chulalongkorn.[129]

Chulalongkorn had left Europe in 1897 somewhat reassured by 'the phrase Siam's independence would never be destroyed' that he had heard while there.[130] He had certainly delivered the message to Europe's political leaders that foreign policy decisions concerning Siam should be formulated in consultation with the Siamese. Despite this, his trip to Europe did not alter the imperial policies of Europe's major powers regarding Siam.[131] Although the trip redoubled the king's resolve to continue his economic and political reforms and saw Germany rewarded with a significant increase in the volume of its trade with Siam,[132] there are no grounds to suggest, as Neil Englehart has, that 'King Chulalongkorn's foreign travels were crucial for advancing Siam's diplomatic agenda.'[133] As Grabowsky has argued, 'in the sphere of *Realpolitik* the "German card" was never a real option' for Siam.[134]

In the coming two decades, both Britain and France would extract further territories from Siam without a murmur from the Germans, who were only annoyed at having been beaten to Langkawi by the British.[135] While in the Draft Treaty of 1902 the British would confirm Siam's claim on Kedah, this was negated by the treaty of 1909.[136] Later, despite having instructed his envoy to Bangkok to offer Siam 'the necessary moral support in the unequal struggle with her mighty neighbours',[137] Tsar Nicholas II would side with the French in crucial diplomatic negotiations surrounding Siam's territorial sovereignty.[138] For all the splendour of his 1897 visit to Europe, Chulalongkorn had found himself without reliable European allies when it counted.

With no respite having been won from further attacks on Siam's territorial integrity, it is little wonder that Chulalongkorn's 1907 return visit to Germany was

---

[128] Bülow to Hesse-Wartegg, 8 December 1899, in PAAA RZ201/2535, 110–11.

[129] Richthofen to Bülow, 12 December 1899, in PAAA RZ201/2535, 113–15.

[130] Chulalongkorn, quoted in Pornsan Watanangura, 'Europe, King Chulalongkorn and the Kingdom of Siam', in Watanangura (ed.) *The Visit of King Chulalongkorn to Europe*, 30.

[131] Contra Winichakul, 'The Quest for "Siwilai"', 538.

[132] Kittisak Prokati, 'King Rama V and Constitutionalism in Thailand', in Watanangura (ed.) *The Visit of King Chulalongkorn to Europe*, 128.

[133] Englehart, 'Representing civilization', 424.   [134] Grabowsky, 'Thai-German Relations', 61.

[135] Goldman, 'Franco-British Rivalry over Siam', 216–28; Chandran Jeschurun, 'The British Foreign Office and the Siamese Malay States, 1890–97', *Modern Asian Studies*, 5, no.2 (1971), 143–59; Klein, 'Britain, Siam and the Malay Peninsula', 119–36.

[136] Malhi, 'Like a Child with Two Parents', 474.

[137] Yevgeny D. Ostrovenko, 'Russian-Thai Relations: Historical and Cultural Aspects', *Journal of the Siam Society* 92 (2004), 121.

[138] Snow, 'St. Petersburg's Man in Siam', 630–3.

made incognito.[139] On this visit, Chulalongkorn spent only a single night visiting Wilhelm II—9 August 1907—when, apart from a short discussion about the possibility of raising import duties in Siam, the conversation remained fixed on art and the possibility of another of Chulalongkorn's sons training at the Potsdam officer cadet academy.[140] By far the most enduring legacy of the 1907 visit was the modest Siamese pavilion built in the Bad Homburg gardens, and even this had arrived in broken pieces.[141]

In the wake of the failure of his summit diplomacy, Chulalongkorn came to have a firm grasp of the structural, material engine of European imperialism and its imperviousness to ad hoc royal negotiations. He now saw Europe as a continent whose way of life was predicated on the ceaseless acquisition of the land and resources of the rest of the world, including Siam. In Europe, he wrote:

> All of the arable land is under cultivation. Not a single square inch of unused land remains. There is no more room for further expansion...All available farmland is already under cultivation. Mineral resources such as coal have also been fully exploited...The people must eat, and the countries of Europe are already producing as much food as they can. There is enough food for people today, but in the future, as the population grows, there will not be enough land to support them as all the available farmland in Europe is already under cultivation. It will be necessary to expand trade to find enough food to eat, or it will be necessary to make money from other countries with which to purchase food. The Europeans have already settled the Americas, and taken control of almost all of Africa. They have settled across the entire continent of Australia as well, and colonised large portions of Asia. The reason for this is there are no more available resources in Europe, and this has made it necessary for them to look elsewhere.[142]

---

[139] Chulanlongkorn, *King Chulalongkorns Reisetagebuch 'Glai Baan' (Fern von Zuhause)*, trans. Ampha Otrakul, (Bonn: Deutsch-Thailändische Gesellschaft, 2001).

[140] Barend Jan Terwiel, 'King Chulalongkorn as Diplomat: Three Accounts of the Dinner with the German Kaiser on 9 August 1907', in Watanangura (ed.), *The Visit of King Chulalongkorn to Europe*, 81–102. For the preparations for this visit, see PAAA R 131804, PAAA R 131805, 'Die Reise des Königs von Siam nach Europa bezw. Deutschland'.

[141] For problems surrounding the building of this expensive gift from Chulalongkorn (9,000 of the 15,000 pieces sent from Siam were broken, and German builders had no idea how to build it), see PAAA R 131805.

[142] Chulalongkorn, *Glai Baan*, as cited in Watanangura, 'The Beginnings of a New Era', 18.

2

In Search of a German Hong Kong

As the European powers consolidated their presence in China in the 1860s and 1870s, important sections of Chinese public opinion became increasingly anti-Western. Decades of conquests, humiliating treaty concessions, and the insinuation of European missionaries into the provinces had led to a sense among many Chinese that the Middle Kingdom was under siege from a relentless tide of Western barbarians (*yi*).[1] The most obvious sign of Europe's barbarism in the capital had been the destruction and looting of the Xianfeng emperor's Summer Palace in 1860.[2] The ongoing effects of European infiltration were felt and resented most acutely far away from the Chinese royal court, however, and rumours regarding the predations of the Europeans were spread among ordinary people by word of mouth or even appeared in Chinese tabloid newspapers. One rumour, which claimed that Christian missionary orphanages were harvesting the body parts of children to make medicine, led to a massacre of missionaries in 1870.[3] Despite attempts by Qing authorities to allay such fears, almost twenty years later a Chinese newspaper was still suggesting that Europeans were boiling down Chinese corpses to make soap.[4]

The continued signs of grassroots rancour surrounding Europe's penetration of China led Germany's ambassador Max von Brandt to discuss the issue with China's foreign affairs bureau, the Zongli Yamen. Brandt protested that anti-Western sentiment (rather than the disruptive expansion of missionary outposts in provincial China) was leading to 'murderous attacks upon innocent men and women'.[5] Brandt's sense that European settlers were vulnerable to attack was not without foundation. In November 1897, one such 'murderous attack' saw two

---

[1] On the debate over the meaning of the term *yi*, see Fang Weigui, '*Yi, Yang, Xi, Wai* and Other Terms: The Transition from "Barbarian" to "Foreigner" in Nineteenth-Century China', in Michael Lackner, Iwo Amelung, and Joachim Kurtz (eds), *New Terms for New Ideas: Western Knowledge and Lexical Change in Late Imperial China* (Leiden: Brill, 2001), 96; Dilip K. Basu, 'Chinese Xenology and the Opium War: Reflections on Sinocentrism', *Journal of Asian Studies* 73, no. 4 (2014), 927–40; contra Lydia Liu, *The Clash of Empires: The Invention of China in Modern World Making* (Cambridge, MA: Harvard University Press, 2004), 31–69.
[2] Erik Ringmar, 'Liberal Barbarism and the Oriental Sublime: The European Destruction of the Emperor's Summer Palace', *Millennium*, 34 no.3 (2006), 917–33.
[3] Robert Bickers, *The Scramble for China: Foreign Devils in the Qing Empire, 1832–1914* (London: Penguin, 2016), 230–1.
[4] *Illustrated News*, January 1889, in PAAA R18060, 'Die chinesische Presse', 51.
[5] Brandt to Prince Ching, 14 January 1889, in PAAA R18060, 51. For German reports on attacks on their citizens, see PAAA R17666, 'Innere Angelegenheiten Chinas', 125–9, 208, 260, 307–8.

The Kaiser and the Colonies: Monarchy in the Age of Empire. Matthew P. Fitzpatrick, Oxford University Press.

German Catholic missionaries killed. As their fellow missionary Georg Stenz later recounted, Richard Henle and Francis Xavier Nies died when a group of Chinese burst into their compound and repeatedly stabbed them, with Stenz narrowly escaping after a group of local Chinese Christians came to defend the settlement.[6]

When news of the killings reached Germany, Kaiser Wilhelm II expressed his outrage by issuing a spontaneous, personal order for the seizure of Kiautschou Bay [Jiaozhou Bay] by the German navy. This independent royal military order, seemingly suggestive of a functioning 'kingship mechanism' in Wilhelmine Germany, saw Kiautschou remain a German colony until the First World War. The genesis of the occupation, however, is far more complicated than this apparently impulsive order would suggest. Without doubt, Wilhelm II acted within the scope of his constitutional powers as supreme commander of the navy.[7] The order was, however, without parallel throughout the rest of Wilhelm II's reign. Indeed, as Klaus Mühlhahn has made clear, the royal order came very close to being rescinded by his government and was openly disapproved of by both the naval secretary, Alfred von Tirpitz, and Chancellor Hohenlohe-Schillingsfürst, who saw it as hindering rather than helping Germany's penetration of China and Chinese trade.[8] This opposition was not, however, a principled stand against the annexation of a Chinese harbour, which had already been carefully planned for by the Foreign Office and the Naval Office, but a reflection of the fact that the undue haste of the emperor's order engendered precisely the kind of diplomatic and foreign policy difficulties that the preceding period of careful planning had sought to avoid. It was the haphazard execution of the annexation, not the annexation itself, that was Wilhelm II's primary contribution. Believing himself to be acting in the spirit of advice given to him by the foreign secretary, Bernhard von Bülow, the German Kaiser seized on an incident in China as a pretext for annexing a long-coveted harbour. By crashing through the norms of diplomacy and rushing to embrace a naval solution, he had created an international furore in precisely the way his state secretaries had foreseen.

The Search for an Economically Useful Harbour

Wilhelm II had certainly hastened the pace of Germany's seizure of a naval harbour on Chinese territory. Yet, as his correspondence with Bülow reveals, the push was scarcely a bolt from the blue, with the German Foreign Office well aware

---

[6]   Georg M Stenz, *Erlebnisse eines Missionars in China* (Trier, Paulinus Druckerei, 1899), 70–7.

[7]   Oliver F. R. Haardt, 'The Kaiser in the Federal State, 1871–1918', *German History* 34 no.4 (2016), 534, 537.

[8]   Klaus Mühlhahn, *Herrschaft und Widerstand in der 'Musterkolonie' Kiautschou: Interaktionen zwischen China und Deutschland, 1897–1914* (Munich: Oldenbourg, 2000), 95–6.

that the navy had been arguing for the better part of thirty years about which Chinese harbour Germany should occupy.[9] For their part, the Chinese were also well aware of Germany's desire for a position in China and had, at German prompting, already offered Germany two small Crown concessions in Hankow [Hankou] and Tientsin [Tianjin] in October 1895 as thanks for their diplomatic support against Japanese territorial claims in the wake of the Sino-Japanese War.[10]

The navy's protracted discussions and hesitancy to settle definitively on Kiautschou before 1897 had not been a product of any reticence about undermining the territorial integrity of China or the political sovereignty of the Guangxu emperor and the Empress Dowager Cixi. Rather, the cautious approach reflected broader concerns about how other powers, in particular the British, would react to the seizure of desirable harbours that would facilitate access to the most important commercial sea lanes in East Asia and offer an important centre for Germany's economic expansion into East Asia.

Earlier attempts by Wilhelm II to set the pace of a Chinese acquisition had failed spectacularly. In the wake of the Sino-Japanese War, he had written to Chancellor Hohenlohe, advising that Germany should side with Japan in the peace negotiations. Germany's price, he reasoned, would be Formosa, which would ensure that Germany was not locked out of China.[11] The result of his intervention was that precisely the opposite occurred. As Fu-teh Huang has argued, 'All of the Kaiser's spontaneous suggestions were blocked by the German Foreign Office and the navy.'[12] On the advice of the Foreign Office, and in particular, embassy officials in China, Germany instead sided with Russia and France against Japan and in support of China in the peace negotiations that led to the revision of the 1895 Treaty of Shimonoseki a week after it had been signed. It was left to the chancellor to explain to Wilhelm II why his scheme to annex Formosa was simply not an option for the Germans.[13]

---

[9] Marschall to Hatzfeldt, 1 February 1895; Reinhold Klehmet, 'Promemoria', 20 February 1895, in *Grosse Politik*, vol. 9, 249, 255. For earlier discussions of these deliberations, see Sang Su Jung, *Deutschland und das Gelbe Meer: Die deutsche Weltpolitik in Ostasien 1897–1902* (Frankfurt am Main: Peter Lang, 1996), 27–53; Rolf-Harald Wippich, *Japan und die deutsche Fernostpolitik 1894–1898: Vom Ausbruch des Chinesisch-Japanischen Krieges bis zur Besetzung der Kiautschou-Bucht: Ein Beitrag zur Wilhelminischen Weltpolitik* (Stuttgart: Steiner, 1987), 273–97, 325–46; Klaus Mühlhahn, *Herrschaft und Widerstand in der 'Musterkolonie' Kiautschou: Interaktionen zwischen China und Deutschland, 1897–1914* (Munich: Oldenbourg Verlag, 2000), 65–111.

[10] John V. A, MacMurray, *Treaties and Agreements with and concerning China, 1894–1919* (Leiden: Brill, 2007), 42–50.

[11] Hohenlohe to Marschall, 17 November 1894, in *Grosse Politik*, vol. 9, 245–6; Hohenlohe to Marschall, 17 November 1894, in Mechthild Leutner (ed.), *'Musterkolonie Kiautschou': Die Expansion des Deutschen Reiches in China: Deutsch-chinesische Beziehungen 1897–1914: Eine Quellensammlung* (Berlin: Akademie Verlag, 1997), 80.

[12] Fu-teh Huang, *Qingdao: Chinesen unter deutscher Herrschaft 1897–1914* (Bochum: Projekt Verlag, 1999), 25.

[13] Hohenlohe to Wilhelm II, 19 March 1895, in *Grosse Politik*, vol. 9, 253–8.

The initial decision to push for some Crown concessions by siding with China over Japan had come from Germany's ambassador in Peking [Beijing], Gustav Schenck zu Schweinsberg. Schenck had written to Hohenlohe in late 1894 to suggest that, with Japan's territorial claims having opened the door to an internationalization of the question of access to Chinese harbours, the time was ripe for Germany to take the next step in its globalization of its trade and naval capacity by seeking a concession for Kiautschou Bay.[14] The Foreign Office secretary, Adolf Marschall von Bieberstein, however, was pessimistic about the suggestion, arguing that Kiautschou was too far north to bring any real commercial advantage and could risk triggering a war.[15] Three months later, Schenck returned with a different suggestion, that Germany push for Crown concessions along the Yangtze River. Despite his opinion that 'Free or international settlements are the most desirable regime,' Schenck nonetheless reminded Hohenlohe that in a number of Yangtze harbours there were 'so-called Crown concessions' under British administration in which the British enjoyed special rights that other Europeans did not. This was a model, Schenck argued, that might profit German commerce:

> In case in the future Germans want to take part in the river shipping on the Yangtze, this type of concession, for example in Hankow, Chinkiang [Zhenjiang], and Chunking [Chongqing] might perhaps prove desirable, even necessary, if it is not possible to win equal rights for all in the existing concessions.[16]

Tellingly, this initial search for a riparian foothold in China was predicated on diplomacy and negotiations with the Chinese themselves rather than naval pressure. Against the background of the Deutsch-Asiatische Bank competing for a share of the loans that China needed to raise to pay off its war indemnity with Japan, in April 1895, Consul Albert von Seckendorff reported that he had discussed the issue of a German concession in China with Grand Secretary Li Hongzhang, suggesting that, in view of their trade relations, it might be appropriate for China to grant Germany a settlement in Tientsin. The reply he was given was that an agreement for a German settlement might be reached if Germany supported China against Japan's territorial ambitions. According to Seckendorff, Li Hongzhang left him with the foundations for a deal: 'Help us to keep the Liaotung Peninsula [Liaodong Peninsula] for the Chinese Empire, and we would be very happy to offer you settlements in the most important treaty ports.'[17]

Accordingly, against the advice of Wilhelm II but in concert with Russia and France, the German government lent China support to force Japan to rescind its

---

[14]   Schenck to Hohenlohe, 23 November 1894, in *Grosse Politik*, vol. 9, 248.

[15]   Marschall to Hatzfeldt, 1 February 1895, in *Grosse Politik*, vol. 9, 248–50.

[16]   Schenck to Hohenlohe, 7 March 1895, in PAAA R18553, 'Die Fremden Niederlassungen in China', 7–10.

[17]   Seckendorff to Hohenlohe, 25 April 1895, in PAAA R18553, 16–17.

control over the Liaotung Peninsula.[18] In June 1895, Schenck checked with the German Foreign Office whether he should raise the settlement idea once more with the Chinese. The Foreign Office instructed him to go ahead and report back on his success. By 6 July 1895, Schenck could report that he had been successful. After the approval of both Li Hongzhang and the Zongli Yamen was forthcoming, Germany was offered settlements in Hankow and thereafter Tientsin.[19] Settlement treaties for the two concessions were signed in October 1895.[20]

The response in Germany to the acquisition of these modest territorial concessions was positive and taken as a sign of Germany's diplomatic prowess and ever-growing status on the world stage. The *National-Zeitung* boasted that Germany had secured a place on 'one of the most important harbours to have been opened to shipping through negotiations with the Chinese government'.[21] In Hamburg, one newspaper quoted the British press as having remarked that 'Two years ago, the surrender of a piece of the Chinese mainland to Germany would have greatly inflamed public opinion and led to diplomatic complications...Today it is seen as taken for granted and is barely noticed'.[22] Out of an abundance of caution, Foreign Affairs Secretary Marschall would wait until February 1896 to explain to Kaiser Wilhelm II what the concessions meant.[23]

Even before these modest concessions—won through careful diplomatic exchanges with the Chinese—were formalized, consideration turned to negotiations for a major German coaling and naval harbour. Foreign Office Secretary Marschall wrote to the navy in March 1895 to rule out Wilhelm II's first preference of Formosa and to demand that the German navy make clear what it considered to be the best sites for a naval base. Acknowledging that Ferdinand von Richthofen had already made some suggestions in the 1870s, the Foreign Office needed to know what the navy's current thinking was, so that it could enter into meaningful negotiations with the Chinese.[24]

Germany's naval secretary, Friedrich von Hollmann, asked his subordinates to look into the matter, and offered the provisional reply that both Kiautschou and Amoy [Xiamen] were the best two candidates.[25] A series of reports made it clear,

---

[18] Urs Matthias Zachmann, 'Imperialism in a Nutshell: Conflict and the "Concert of Powers" in the Tripartite Intervention, 1895', *Japanstudien* 17, no. 1 (2006), 57–82.

[19] Schenck to German Foreign Office, 11 June 1895, German Foreign Office to Schenck, 12 June 1895, Schenck to German Foreign Office, 6 July 1895, Schenck to Hohenlohe, 9 July 1895, Hildebrand to Stuebel, 18 August 1895, in PAAA R18553, 18–21, 103–4.

[20] The settlement treaty for Hankow was signed on 3 October 1895, and for Tientsin on 30 October 1895. See PAAA R18553, 274–82.

[21] 'Asien', *National Zeitung*, 9 October 1895.

[22] *Hamburgischer Correspondent*, quoting the British *Mercury*, 13 January 1896.

[23] Marschall to Wilhelm II, 21 February 1896, in PAAA R18553, 158.

[24] Marschall to Hollmann, 11 March 1895, in BA Freiburg RM3/6692, 'Erforschung Erwerbung pp von Ländern in Ostasien', 1–5.

[25] Hollmann to Marschall, 17 April 1895, Knorr to Hollmann, 25 March 1895, in BA Freiburg RM3/6692, 7–14.

however, that opinion remained divided. Tellingly, the basis for the navy's delib-erations was that purely military considerations were insufficient for any decision and that an 'incorporation of economic factors is to be sought' and industry, trade and communications had to be considered. On this basis, for example, Weihaiwei [Weihai] was ruled out as completely unsatisfactory, much to the disappointment of Wilhelm II, who accepted the judgement of his subordinates but wanted to know what other harbours they had in mind.[26]

One that Wilhelm II had already heard about was Kiautschou Bay. In September 1895, Under State Secretary Wolfram von Rotenhan penned a memo-randum in which he argued against a number of sites, but noted that the well-protected harbour of Kiautschou was the most likely candidate for German success, given that other harbours such as Amoy would be contested by the other powers. Its main problem was, however, that it was not always free of ice in win-ter. While this prompted Hollmann (who preferred Amoy) to question the suit-ability of Kiautschou, it did not dissuade the emperor, who read the report and made a note to himself in the margin about Kiautschou's possible suitability.[27]

As a means of hastening the process, Chancellor Hohenlohe requested that the navy reconnoitre the coastline, in particular Kiautschou Bay and Swatow [Shantou], on the pretext of sending naval vessels to support German missionar-ies being threatened in the interior of China.[28] The move alarmed the port super-intendent (*tao tai*) of Quemoy [Kinmen], who demanded an explanation as to why two German steamers were measuring water depths in the region.[29] The Chinese ambassador in Berlin was similarly alarmed when Foreign Secretary Marschall pressed him on the question of when Germany could expect permis-sion for a large naval base in China like those of Britain and France. Fearing for the consequences for the territorial sovereignty of China, the ambassador warned the Zongli Yamen.[30] The Chinese were put under further pressure by Marschall in August 1896, when he pressed Li Hongzhang for a naval base. Although Li Hongzhang agreed to explore the idea, it was stymied by the Zongli Yamen, which feared that it would unleash counterclaims by the other European powers.[31]

[26] Hollmann, 'Denkschrift: Welche Gesichtspunkte sind für die Wahl eines maritimen Stützpunktes in Ostasien bestimmend und wie entspricht denselben der Hafen von Wie-hai-wei', 25 October 1895; Senden to Hollmann, 30 October 1895; Senden to Knorr, 30 October 1895, in BA Freiburg RM3/6692, 47–65, 99–100.

[27] Rotenhan, 'Aufzeichung betreffend die für eine auf friedliche Wege zu erwerbende Flotten und Kohlenstation in China in Betracht kommenden Punkte', 9 September 1895; Hollmann to Marschall, 25 September 1895, in BA Freiburg RM3/6692, 18–21.

[28] Rotenhan to Knorr, 21 September 1895; Hollmann to Knorr, 5 October 1895, in BA Freiburg RM3/6692, 25–7.

[29] Yieh, 'Schreiben des Taotai an das Kaiserliche Konsulat', in BA Freiburg RM3/6692, 168.

[30] Xu Jingcheng to the Zongli Yamen, 30 December 1895, in Leutner (ed.), '*Musterkolonie Kiautschou*', 89–90.

[31] Heyking to Tirpitz, 10 August 1896, in BA Freiburg N253/43, 8–13, 53–5.

In the German Naval Office's internal discussions, Hollmann made clear his scepticism about the position of Kiautschou and his preference for the more commercially useful Amoy. He warned Admiral Eduard von Knorr to couch any future recommendations to the chancellor with this in mind.[32] Accordingly, Knorr suggested that Kiautschou Bay was 'just as unsuitable as Weihaiwei as a naval post for our fleet in East Asia'. Accumulating worthless territorial possessions, he warned, would simply damage Germany's standing in the region. Any possession must be suitable for Germany's navy to defend its sharply growing mercantile and shipping interests in the region, and it should be as close to the major shipping lanes as possible. 'Everything', he argued, 'depends on us establishing a German Hong Kong.' That meant choosing a location close to the trading hubs of the Yangtze River in a location such as Chusan Island [Zhoushan Island], a territory that could compete not only with Hong Kong but also Shanghai. The problem with Chusan Island, he admitted, was that the Chinese had already signed a treaty with the British not to allow a third power to possess the island. Nevertheless, Knorr argued, the British had not activated any claim to the island for fifty years. If Germany could successfully fabricate a crisis in Chusan, as the British had in Egypt and Cyprus, and in doing so let the British know that they would be willing to trade their claim to Samoa for possession of Chusan, perhaps a deal could be struck. 'Samoa is only Samoa', he argued. 'Chusan, however, represents for us taking a worthwhile part in the economic conquest of China.' In comparison to this potential trading hub, he concluded, Kiautschou was both militarily and economic inconsequential.[33]

The admiral of the East Asia Cruiser Division, Paul Hoffmann, concurred. For Hoffmann, the principle of 'the inviolability of the Chinese mainland' was difficult to combine with the desire for a German harbour. Furthermore, alienating the Zongli Yamen would jeopardize important economic endeavours such as brokering German loans to the Chinese government for its Japanese war indemnity payments and enhancing the status of Germany's existing concessions. The occupation of any harbour would also need to be carefully discussed with the other powers, who were unlikely to agree to Germany taking possession of a treaty port. Indeed, Hoffmann ruled out Chusan Island because it would unnecessarily create conflict with the British. He also considered Kiautschou and the Shantung Peninsula [Shandong Peninsula] to be politically difficult, adding that he had received advice that Kiautschou Bay was simply too shallow for anything other than a temporary anchorage. From his perspective, Amoy was probably of most use to Germany, as it was close enough to the new German concessions of

---

[32] Rotenhan to Knorr, 21 September 1895; Hollmann to Knorr, 5 October 1895, in BA Freiburg RM3/6692, 25–8.
[33] Knorr, 'Denkschrift betreffend den Stützpunkt in Ostasien', 8 November 1895, in BA Freiburg RM3/6692, 115–28.

Tientsin and Hankow to be of use. While its status as a treaty port made it diplomatically difficult to achieve, and significant investment would be required to establish a worthwhile German presence, only Amoy, or perhaps Quemoy or Samsah [Sansha Wan], made sense both militarily and economically, offering Germany the opportunity to engage with Yangtze region trade.[34]

Reporting back to Marschall in the Foreign Office in May 1896, Knorr relayed Hoffmann's strong preference for Amoy as Germany's best option for a naval base, repeating too his earlier suggestion of following the British example in Egypt and Cyprus and simply using the navy to secure the site.[35] The Foreign Office instead opted for heightened diplomatic pressure, broaching the subject with Li Hongzhang when he visited Berlin in June 1896. At this meeting Marshall made the veiled threat that Germany might not assist China in future regional disputes as it had when Japan had laid claim to Chinese territory. Li Hongzhang informed the foreign secretary that, despite China's gratitude towards Germany for its diplomatic intervention against Japan, it could not grant Germany a harbour for a naval base without encouraging claims from the other European powers. He nonetheless promised to do what he could upon returning to China, hinting that there might be scope for Germany to lease a harbour for fifty years.[36]

No offer for a lease was forthcoming, however, and in September 1896, Under State Secretary Rotenhan at the Foreign Office reported to Naval Secretary Hollmann that German merchants and financiers in East Asia were lobbying strenuously for Germany to build a port in Amoy.[37] The German ambassador, Edmund von Heyking, also spoke in favour of Amoy over Kiautschou.[38] In a fit of circular reasoning, Heyking also warned that Germany needed to keep its East Asian squadron in China to project the idea that Germany required a naval port there. For slightly different reasons, Foreign Secretary Marschall agreed, opining that 'if we do not consistently demonstrate to the Chinese a respectable degree of naval power on hand, following the example of other nations, then all of our more important diplomatic efforts in China cannot count on success.'[39]

Dissenting voices were in evidence, however, with Captain Paul Jaeschke (who would later become governor of Germany's Chinese territory) writing to Naval Secretary Hollmann to argue that Shantung (particularly Kiautschou) would be a

---

[34] Hoffmann to Knorr, 26 August 1895; Hoffmann to Knorr, 12 November 1895; Hoffmann to Knorr, 20 October 1895; Hoffmann to Knorr, 15 October 1895; Hoffmann to Knorr, 29 November 1895; Hoffmann to Knorr, 24 March 1896; Hoffmann to Knorr, 2 May 1896 BA Freiburg RM3/6692, 34–41, 131–133, 135–144, 152–154, 199–201, 277.

[35] Knorr to Marschall, 21 May 1896, in BA Freiburg RM3/6692, 200–201, 277.

[36] Marschall, 'Aufzeichnung des Staatssekretärs des Auswärtigen Amtes', 19 June 1896, in *Grosse Politik*, vol. 14, 27–34.

[37] Rotenhan to Hollmann, 10 September 1896, in BA Freiburg RM3/6692, 299.

[38] Tirpitz, 'Abmachung mit Herrn von Heyking', 6 August 1896, in BA Freiburg N253/43, Nachlass Tirpitz, 6–7.

[39] Marschall to Hollmann, 27 August 1896, in BA Freiburg, RM3/6692, 290–5.

fitting place for furthering German *Weltpolitik*, a point refuted by Hoffmann in the margins before it reached Hollmann. Mediating between Jaeschke and Hollmann, Hoffmann reiterated his view that Shantung was too far away from China's economic hub in the south and that its mountainous hinterland was 'worthless and politically unfavourable, stuck between the sphere of conflict between Russia and China'.[40] Schenck's letter to both Hollmann and Chancellor Hohenlohe in May 1896 had a greater impact, driving home the message that Kiautschou would be suitable for a naval base and reporting that the Russians had been anchoring there, albeit without leaving behind any indication that they had formally claimed the bay.[41]

From Amoy to Kiautschou

Perhaps the most important voice to emerge against Amoy was Admiral Alfred von Tirpitz. This came as something of a surprise to Heyking in Peking, who had thought that Tirpitz had completely agreed with him regarding the suitability of Amoy in August 1896. Initially, Tirpitz had not only given Heyking that impression but also written to Knorr intimating that Germany would in all probability meet no resistance from the British if they took Amoy. The British would be relieved, he argued, if German demands in the region could be so easily met as by the possession of Amoy. The bulk of his report, however, was dedicated to Kiautschou, which he saw as favourable for a number of reasons: it lay outside the typhoon zone, it possessed potable water, and it was well situated for trade and for future rail links with Tientsin, Peking and China's coalfields. For Tirpitz, Kiautschou was worth serious consideration.[42]

Tirpitz's endorsement of Kiautschou as a site for a German naval base was a direct challenge to Heyking's rejection of the northern harbour. Ironically, however, it was Heyking's 1896 complaint about this that revived Wilhelm II's interest in the harbour. When Heyking had written to the chancellor in August warning him of Tirpitz's freelancing on the subject of Kiautschou, Wilhelm II also read the letter. Heyking prefaced his remarks by saying that he had met Tirpitz, who had spoken to him of the advantages of Kiautschou. To this, the emperor wrote in the margin, 'Perhaps after all!' When Heyking recounted that he had warned Tirpitz that the Russians considered the bay to be part of their sphere of interest, but that Tirpitz had replied that the Russians had enough with Korea and Liaotung, Wilhelm II expressed his disappointment that no one had acted earlier, arguing

---

[40] Jaeschke to Hollmann, 18 June 1896 in BA Freiburg, RM3/6692, 212–75.
[41] Schenck to Hollmann and Hohenlohe, 23 May 1896; Lenz to Schenck, 23 May 1896, in BA Freiburg RM3/6692, 282–8.
[42] Tirpitz to Knorr, 5 September 1896, in BA Freiburg N253/45, Nachlass Tirpitz, 21–38.

that 'We could have had the bay last summer, but the navy didn't want it. I was definitely for it!'[43] Despite Heyking's message that the Russian ambassador in China had made it very clear to him that the Russians considered Kiautschou to be all but theirs, Wilhelm II preferred Tirpitz's more sanguine (and in the event incorrect) estimation that Russia would not pose a problem.

Tirpitz was supported in his suggestion of seizing Kiautschou by a German ex-colleague of Li Hongzhang, Gustav Detring. Kiautschou Bay, Detring argued, lay on a strategically important point of the shipping lanes of North China, and possessed a hinterland rich with raw materials. Dredging the bay to improve its depth would cause no insurmountable difficulties. In addition, it offered the possibility of a railway link to Peking, a good climate for Europeans, and, he suggested, the 'physically and mentally' best population in China. Although he admitted that the Russians anchored there and 'play the part of masters of the bay', Detring was convinced that 'there could be no talk of it having been surrendered to Russia.'[44] Unsurprisingly, when the Chinese later suggested that Detring supported their view that Germany did not need a naval base in China, Wilhelm II was surprised, writing on the report, 'He just said the opposite to me,' before complaining that he had 'tried for two years completely without success' to convince the Foreign Office that Germany's prestige in East Asia relied on the acquisition of a naval base in China.[45]

Wilhelm II's desire for a naval base was, however, far from fixed on a single target. At the same time as his interest in Kiautschou was growing, he was also demanding that Germany act 'boldly and decisively' elsewhere. Pointing out (quite correctly) that his East Asian policy had been completely ignored by his government for two years, Wilhelm II insisted in November 1896 that Germany strike, issuing a 'strictly secret' order to the chancellor that 'Amoy must be immediately occupied.'[46] The next day, however, the Foreign Office came to precisely the opposite conclusion, ignoring the royal order and insisting that both Chinese and British resistance to such an unheralded occupation meant that it was simply impractical. Reinhold Klehmet in the Foreign Office opined that 'the irretrievable compromise of our politics by a naked breach of law would not be made up for even by winning a coal station.' Germany's best course of action, Klehmet argued in accord with others who had championed the Egypt or Cyprus option, was to wait for a Chinese atrocity and to use it to intervene in the region and in the process claim a more modest port like Samsah:

---

[43] Heyking to Hohenlohe, 22 August 1896, in BA Freiburg, RM3/6693, 'Erforschung, Erwerbung pp von Ländern in Ostasien', 27–9.

[44] Barandon, 'Denkschrift zum Immediatvortrage, betreffend Kiautschou-Bucht', 5 November 1895, in BA Freiburg, RM3/6693, 'Erforschung, Erwerbung pp von Ländern in Ostasien', 66–71.

[45] Radolin to Hohenlohe, 19 November 1896, in Grosse Politik, vol. 14, 39–42.

[46] Wilhelm II to Hohenlohe, 27 November 1896, in Grosse Politik, vol. 14, 43.

The only way is to watch out until the Chinese give us a reason for reprisal, and then to occupy Samsah immediately, to keep it as a security and then to negoti- ate with the Chinese to obtain an initially leased surrender of the place. We will most likely not have to wait too long for pretexts. In the last two years there have been several occasions, for example in the circumstances of our missionaries or German instructors, where we might have found reasons to proceed.[47]

With this, the Foreign Office had an almost an exact blueprint for the circum- stances that arose in late 1897.

Not only was Wilhelm II's insistence on an immediate occupation of Amoy rejected by the Foreign Office, but both Knorr and Tirpitz came out strongly against it. In late November 1896, Knorr wrote to the emperor arguing that Chusan and Amoy would attract strong British opposition and that Samsah was economically unviable, while Kiautschou Bay might be preferable, if the Russians did not have a current claim to it.[48] A week later Tirpitz submitted a detailed report that made clear his staunch opposition to taking Amoy. While Amoy made sense in terms of its proximity to Yangtze trade, it would be almost impossible to defend. Instead, if the Yangtze region was important to the Germans, then Wusung or perhaps Samsah was preferable. In any case, he wrote, anywhere in the Yangtse region would fall foul of the British. With regard to Kiautschou, Tirpitz admitted that it looked like the Russians were moving towards annexing it, although in his opinion, the Russian sphere of interest in North China was already overextended. 'I am', he argued, 'freely of the opinion, that Russia has taken too much here, more than can be tolerated.'[49]

With the navy now leaning towards Kiautschou Bay, the emperor asked the Admiralty in December 1896 whether it had any plans for taking it.[50] A detailed description of the logistical preparations was dutifully forwarded (which made no mention of any Russian protests),[51] and the emperor immediately called for a partial mobilization of the navy and an occupation to take place 'without delay'.[52] Once again, this royal activism was stymied, and no occupation force was launched. The navy sent word to Wilhelm II that there would be no precipitous action, that it was logistically imprudent to occupy the bay now, and that a partial mobilization of the navy did not make any military sense. In addition to this, Knorr argued that 'It is of the greatest worth to know whether the Russians have laid their hands on Kiautschou Bay in such a way as to rule it out for us.'[53]

[47] Klehmet, 28 November 1896, in *Grosse Politik*, vol. 14, 43–6.
[48] Knorr to Wilhelm II, 28 November 1896, in BA Freiburg, RM3/6693, 72–9.
[49] Tirpitz to Knorr, 7 December 1896, in BA Freiburg N 253/45, Nachlass Tirpitz, 67–82.
[50] Marschall to Hollmann, 15 December 1896, in BA Freiburg RM3/6693, 9, 12.
[51] Knorr to Wilhelm II, 15 December 1896, in BA Freiburg RM3/6693, 31–44.
[52] Senden to Knorr, 23 December 1896, in BA Freiburg RM3/6693, 45–6.
[53] Knorr to Wilhelm II, 6 January 1897; Knorr to Hollmann, 12 January 1897, in BA Freiburg RM3/6693, 72–79, 92–3.

Despite this third direct rebuff to his various plans for China, Wilhelm II began suggesting plans for training colonial troops for Kiautschou Bay.[54] Meanwhile the Foreign Office and the Naval Office continued to seek a negotiated outcome with the Zongli Yamen, infuriating Wilhelm II, who denounced such negotiations as a 'humiliation' and insisted that there be 'no more requests'. Despite his increasingly shrill demands that as soon as a place was agreed upon, it should be immediately occupied, he was quietly ignored.[55] As Elisabeth von Heyking, wife of the German ambassador remarked, the appearance was that 'the government, and in particular the Foreign Office, was actually only there to block His Majesty on everything'.[56]

When Edmund von Heyking suggested to the Zongli Yamen in January 1897 that Germany might find its Hong Kong in Kiautschou Bay, the council of Chinese princes immediately sought a strategy to combat a seemingly imminent German occupation. The plan they decided upon was to declare that Kiautschou Bay was earmarked for their own naval purposes.[57] Accordingly, in March 1897, the Chinese publicly announced that they would construct their own naval base in the northern harbour, Russia's protests notwithstanding.[58] Despite this announcement, as Elisabeth von Heyking recorded in her diary, now that Tirpitz had taken over as naval secretary, Kiautschou remained the preferred site for a German naval outpost.[59]

In the time it had taken for the German navy to coalesce around the suitability of Kiautschou, the politics of simply occupying the bay had become more diffi-cult, with both China and Russia having declared a pre-existing interest in it.[60] While a glimmer of hope emerged when the Russians feigned their lack of inter-est in occupying Kiautschou in light of China's declaration of interest, it quickly became apparent that Russia's influence over the region could not be ignored and that it still intended to use the bay as a winter port.[61] Accordingly, Chancellor Hohenlohe determined that he would raise the issue when he and Wilhelm II visited St Petersburg in August.[62]

[54] Knorr to Hollmann, 3 February 1897; Hollmann to Marschall, 17 February 1897, in BA Freiburg RM3/6693, 145, 147.
[55] Marschall to Wilhelm II, 19 February 1897, in *Grosse Politik*, vol. 14, 49–50.
[56] Elisabeth von Heyking, *Tagebücher aus vier Weltteilen 1886/1904* (Leipzig: Koehler & Amelang, 1926), 223.
[57] 'Memorandum der Prinzen und Minister des Zongli Yamen', 13 February 1897, in Leutner (ed.), *'Musterkolonie Kiautschou'*, 100–1.
[58] Knorr to Büchsel, 24 April 1897; Heyking to Marschall, 25 March 1897, in BA Freiburg RM3/6693, 177.
[59] Elisabeth von Heyking, *Tagebücher aus vier Weltteilen*, 215–16.
[60] Zeye to Knorr, 10 June 1897, in BA Freiburg RM3/6693, 183–212.
[61] Heyking to Hohenlohe, 5 May 1897; Radolin to Hohenlohe, 3 July 1897; Radolin to Hohenlohe, 8 July 1897, in *Grosse Politik*, vol. 14, 50–54, 56–7.
[62] Hohenlohe to Rotenhan, 12 July 1897, in *Grosse Politik*, vol. 14, 57.

The issue of Kiautschou Bay was indeed raised, if inelegantly, during the visit, when the emperor bluntly asked the tsar whether he had any reservations about 'German warships, which lack a German naval base, anchoring in Kiautschou Bay if they needed to after gaining permission from Russian naval authorities'. The tsar answered that this seemed fair, and the matter was formalized in what became known as the Peterhof Agreement:

> His Majesty the Emperor of Germany, having asked His Majesty the Emperor of Russia, if Russia had views on Kiautschou Bay, His Majesty replied that indeed Russia had an interest in securing the access of said bay until it obtained a port more northern than that she had in sight. The Emperor of Germany asked if Emperor Nicholas saw any difficulties with German ships, in case of need and after having received the consent of the Russian naval authorities, anchoring in Kiautschou Bay. His Majesty the Emperor of Russia replied negatively.[63]

This agreement fundamentally changed Germany's behaviour in northern China in the sense that thereafter Germany behaved as if it was only with Russia that they had to discuss matters pertaining to Kiautschou Bay, even though China had made its own claims to exclusive naval rights there. As Li Hongzhang pointed out to Heyking in Peking in October 1897, decisions about the bay had 'nothing to do with the Russians', because 'Kiautschou is Chinese territory.'[64] From the German navy's perspective, Wilhelm II had also complicated Germany's path to acquiring Kiautschou Bay because he had committed Germany to asking in advance for Russian permission before even entering Kiautschou Bay, let alone occupying it with a view to permanent possession. Understandably, the navy found the new regulations, which seemed to concede Russian primacy, somewhat 'odd'.[65]

In addition, the Germans, primary amongst them Wilhelm II and the new Foreign Office secretary, Bülow, fundamentally or perhaps wilfully misunderstood the Russian foreign minister, Mikhail Muraviev, when he offhandedly remarked that it was not Russia's intention to possess Kiautschou Bay permanently, but that when they eventually decamped (and he professed to not knowing when that would be), Germany might return to it, if only to keep out the British.[66] In the age of Britain's 'temporary' occupation of Egypt, any sense that Muraviev had thereby promised to evacuate Kiautschou in favour of the Germans was utterly misplaced. As Elisabeth von Heyking wryly commented, the Russian

---

[63] Bülow to Foreign Office, 11 August 1897, in *Grosse Politik*, vol. 14, 58–9; Bülow to Tirpitz, 10 September 1897, in BA Freiburg RM3/6693, 211–12.

[64] Heyking to Foreign Office, 3 October 1897, in *Grosse Politik*, vol. 14, 61–2.

[65] Bülow to Knorr, 12 October 1897; Knorr to Bülow, 13 October 1897, in BA Freiburg RM3/6693, 347–8.

[66] Bülow to Foreign Office, 11 August 1897, in *Grosse Politik*, vol. 14, 58–9.

evacuation of their 'temporary' position in Kiautschou might never come: '*ad calendas graecas*'.[67]

By September, this premonition had been confirmed, when Edmund von Heyking received the text of an agreement between Russia and China concluded in late 1896 that allowed Russia a fifteen-year lease over Kiautschou Bay, camouflaged by the fiction that it was the Chinese who were developing a naval facility there.[68] Despite this, when the Heykings personally visited Kiautschou Bay onboard the *Prinzeß Wilhelm* on 10 October 1897 and there was no sign of any construction, they decided that the Russo-Chinese agreement could be ignored and that the Russian occupation was 'an occupation on paper only, that we should not let deter us from seizing it'. That there was a Chinese warship in the bay indicated to them only that the Chinese had been informed of their visit.[69]

Pretext for Occupation

Since November 1895, the advice of the Admiralty and Foreign Office had been that Germany might be able to leverage a crisis in China into a long-lasting occupation in the same way that Britain had in Egypt and Cyprus. In that time, Wilhelm II had consistently been shepherded away from any pre-emptive action without a passable pretext. At the end of October and the first week of November 1897, two incidents that occurred in quick succession offered Germany just such a pretext, one that Wilhelm II used to order the occupation of Kiautschou Bay.

The first incident involved the *Cormoran*, the light cruiser that took the Heykings up the Yangtze River from Wuchang. On 30 October, Captain Brussatis had taken a small steam cutter attached to the *Cormoran* to Wuchang, where he was attacked with stones by a Chinese mob. The cutter, which was flying the German flag, was also attacked. In the wake of the incident, Heyking sent telegrams to Berlin and to the admiral of the East Asian Squadron. The Foreign Office ordered Heyking to coordinate with the admiral, but not to undertake any military action without contacting Berlin first.[70] The acting admiral of the East Asia squadron, Hans von Koester, was advised by Wilhelm II to 'agree to further measures with the Foreign Office', which, he suggested, could 'exploit the incident to further our interests in China'.[71]

It was while Heyking and Koester were still discussing how best to proceed on the Wuchang incident that Heyking received the news that two German

[67] Elisabeth von Heyking, *Tagebücher aus vier Weltteilen*, 223.
[68] Elisabeth von Heyking, *Tagebücher aus vier Weltteilen*, 224; 'Text of the Russo-Chinese Treaty', *The Times*, 7 December 1897, in BA Freiburg RM3/6693, 10.
[69] Elisabeth von Heyking, *Tagebücher aus vier Weltteilen*, 228.
[70] Elisabeth von Heyking, *Tagebücher aus vier Weltteilen*, 232–4.
[71] Koester to Tirpitz, 2 November 1897, in BA Freiburg RM3/6694, 'Erforschung Erwerbung pp von Ländern in Ostasien', 1.

missionaries in Shantung had been attacked, with one missionary dead and another feared dead. At this point, a crucial difference emerged between Heyking, who initially attempted to deal with the incidents separately, and Berlin, where they were treated cumulatively. Heyking decided to 'deal with the issue in Wuchang as quickly as possible' so as to rush back to Peking to deal with the more serious attack on the missionaries. What Heyking did not know, however, was that the German Foreign Office, Bülow, and ultimately Wilhelm II had already discussed and been waiting for just such an incident as a pretext for naval action. Consequently, while hurrying back, and still under the assumption that he was responsible for formulating a response to the incidents, Heyking put into action his own plan to deal with the murder of the German missionaries. He sent the Zongli Yamen a list of demands, including a stiff reparations bill, severe punishment for the attackers, the removal of the Chinese Governor of Shantung and payment for the erection of a new Catholic cathedral, while the entire Zongli Yamen should also personally apologize to the German ambassador. The next day, both Heyking and the Zongli Yamen were surprised to be told that the German Kaiser had instead personally ordered the occupation of Kiautschou Bay.[72]

In Berlin the emperor had indeed reacted violently to the news of the killings and sent a telegram at 2:17 p.m. on 6 November 1897 to the German Foreign Office, arguing that, in light of the murders, Germany should occupy Kiautschou Bay, ostensibly as a means of extracting territorial compensation:

I have just read in the press the news of the attack on the German-Catholic mission in Shantung under my protectorate. For this purpose, far-reaching atonement must be extracted through the energetic intervention of the fleet. The squadron must go to Kiauchou immediately and occupy the Chinese town and threaten the most serious reprisals, unless the Chinese government immediately pays a large sum in compensation, and the prosecution and punishment of the criminals is *actually effected*. I am absolutely determined to give up our hyper-cautionary policy, which is already regarded as weak in the whole of East Asia, and to show the Chinese, if necessary with the most brutal ruthlessness, that the German emperor does not allow himself to be trifled with and that it is terrible to have him as an enemy. Please send a prompt telegraphic reply of agreement, so I can instantly telegraph the admiral. The energetic demeanour is all the more necessary given that I can thereby prove to my Catholic subjects, including the ultramontanes of late, that their well-being is close to my heart and they can count on my protection as greatly as my other subjects. Wilhelm IR.[73]

---

[72] Elisabeth von Heyking, *Tagebücher aus vier Weltteilen*, 232–4.
[73] Wilhelm II to Foreign Office, 6 November 1897, in PAAA R18232, 'Erwerbungen der Großmächte in China', 5–7. Bülow would later call it a 'highly rhetorical , quite agitated telegram'. See Bernhard von Bülow, *Denkwürdigkeiten*, vol. 1: *Vom Staatssekretär bis zur Marokko-Krise* (Berlin: Ullstein, 1930), 184.

Less than two hours after this appraisal of the domestic and foreign policy implications, word came from the palace that the emperor had not waited for Bülow to
respond and had already sent his orders for a naval occupation to Admiral
Diedrichs in Wusung:

> Proceed immediately with the entire squadron to Kiautschou, occupy suitable
> positions and towns there and compel complete atonement from there in the
> manner you see as most suitable. Greatest vigour is required.[74]

The emperor's order seems to offer a clear example of the exercise of an unfettered
royal prerogative in military and foreign policy matters. Not only the degree of
earlier planning for just such a crisis[75] but his further correspondence with his
Foreign Secretary suggest otherwise. In his telegrams to Foreign Secretary
Bernhard von Bülow (then in Rome), Wilhelm II made it clear that he had got the
idea of a decisive territorial move in China from Bülow himself.[76]

As the imputed author of the emperor's actions, Bülow unsurprisingly congratulated Wilhelm II for bolstering Germany's position in East Asia.[77] Chancellor
Hohenlohe, however, was less impressed when he wrote to Wilhelm II on 6
November to inform the emperor that he was already in the process of dealing
with the situation and that the emperor need do nothing. The chancellor pointed
out that a hasty decision to use the crisis to bring about a naval occupation would
directly contradict the recent Peterhof Agreement struck between Wilhelm II and
Nicholas II and significantly worsen Germany's already deteriorating relations
with Russia. The agreement with Russia had been struck precisely to de-escalate
tensions between the two powers that had arisen as Russia carved out a sphere of
influence over northern China and Germany sought a secure and economically
profitable harbour outside the British sphere in southern China. In effect,
Wilhelm II had decided on a course of action that Hohenlohe warned him would
precipitate exactly the kind of difficulties with Russia the agreement had been
struck to avoid.

The chancellor informed the emperor that a telegram had already been sent to
Germany's ambassador instructing him to 'present the Chinese government with

---

For the emperor's own erroneous version of events, see Wilhelm II, *Ereignisse und Gestalten 1878–1919*
(Leipzig: Koehler Verlag, 1922), 55–8.

   [74] Franceson to German Foreign Office, 6 November 1897, in PAAA R18232, 8–9.

   [75] See Klehmet, 28 November 1896, in *Grosse Politik*, vol. 14 (i), 43–6.

   [76] Wilhelm II to Bülow, 7 November 1897, in PAAA R18232, 13–19.

   [77] Bülow to Wilhelm II, 8 Nov 1897, in PAAA R18232, 24–5. If Bülow felt that his support would
earn him recognition from the emperor, he was mistaken. By 1906, Wilhelm II was reported in the
French press as having said that he and Hohenlohe had been responsible for Germany's 'success' in
China, while Bülow's Foreign Office had 'soiled their pants'. Both the sentiment and the sharp language led Bülow to confront the emperor to correct the record: Bernhard von Bülow, *Denkwürdigkeiten*,
vol. 1, 210–11.

strict conditions for reparations'. If the emperor wished to proceed militarily, then, Hohenlohe continued, he should choose somewhere else, or at least notify the Russians to avoid any misunderstandings:

> In the event that Your Majesty wishes to give the squadron commander the order for immediate action without waiting for the answer, it might be necessary to take a different place than Kiautschou, as in accordance with the agreement struck at Peterhof between Your Majesty and the Emperor of Russia, the agreement of Russia would need to be sought for the possession of Kiautschou.[78]

With Hohenlohe less than impressed by his emperor's hasty embrace of naval action, an unsettled Wilhelm II turned once again to Bülow in Rome for reassurance, confiding in him that he had only done what the foreign secretary had recently suggested to him, that is, wait for a pretext that would allow Germany to take decisive action and seize a Chinese harbour. Now under pressure from several quarters, Wilhelm II protested that the idea of reorienting Germany's China policy had not been his idea but Bülow's. The monarch wrote to Bülow, reporting that:

> Our conversation about Kiautschou…at the end of which you emphasized that it was high time to prosecute our faltering and tepid politics in East Asia more energetically, has had a rapid sequel far more quickly than we had thought. Yesterday I received the official report of the attack and murder and plunder of a German mission station…Finally the Chinese have offered us the so long desired grounds and incident. I resolved to seize it immediately, as, according to all reports, whether written officially or privately or oral reports from travellers who have returned from East Asia, there is no doubt that we stand at a turning point for our entire prestige, influence, and prospects of commercial development. All eyes, both those of the Asians and those of the Europeans living there, are upon us, and all are asking themselves whether we will allow this to be done to us or not.[79]

The emperor also admitted that Hohenlohe had instructed him to consult Russia, given the Peterhof Agreement regarding relations in northern China. Although he professed to find it somewhat demeaning to have to ask St Petersburg before taking action to 'defend German lives' in China, Wilhelm II told Bülow that he had followed Hohenlohe's instructions and sent the tsar the following telegram:

---

[78] Hohenlohe to Wilhelm II, 6 November 1897, in PAAA R18232, 10–12.
[79] Wilhelm II to Bülow, 7 November 1897, in PAAA R18232, 13–19.

Chinese attacked German missions Shantung, inflicting loss of life and property. I trust you approve according to our conversation Peterhof my sending German squadron to Kiaochou, as it is the only port available to operate from as a base against marauders. I am under obligations to Catholic party in Germany to show that their missions are really safe under My protectorate.[80]

The tsar answered Wilhelm II to the effect that he was grateful to have been personally advised of German action and that he regretted the attack on German Catholic missionaries, but that he 'could neither allow nor hinder your sending of the German squadron to Kiautschou, as I have recently learned that this harbour had only temporarily been ours from 1895 to 1896'. He went on to express his grave concerns, however, that any action regarding the harbour would only 'increase instability and widen the gulf between the Chinese and Christians'.[81] Failing to read the tsar's subtextual warning against precipitous action, Wilhelm II told Bülow that he did not share this view. 'Thousands of German Christians', the emperor argued, would be relieved to know that his ships were nearby, while 'hundreds of German merchants would shout for joy in the knowledge that the German Empire has finally won a firm foothold in Asia.' Henceforth, the emperor's motto in East Asia would be *'nemo me impune lacessit'* (no one attacks me with impunity).[82] If he had any misgivings, Bülow did not make them known. Instead, he congratulated the emperor for having exploited a suitable moment 'powerfully and decisively'.[83]

The Aftermath of Occupation

Wilhelm II's decision to take it upon himself to follow Bülow's advice and implement the Naval office's long-mooted plan to use a crisis to seize a Chinese port, without first seeking guidance from the chancellor and in the absence of the foreign secretary, caused the difficulties with Russia that Hohenlohe predicted it would. With Bülow still in Rome, it was left to the chancellor to try and steer the emperor towards securing a Russian agreement that amounted to more than a short, ambiguous note from the tsar, who had only a limited grasp of the finer points of Russia's China strategy. Such inter-royal correspondence was, Hohenlohe implied, entirely insufficient for the prosecution of foreign policy. Instead, what was required was clarity from the Russian foreign minister, Mikhail Muraviev,

---

[80] Wilhelm II to Bülow, 7 November 1897, in PAAA R18232, 13–19.
[81] Wilhelm II to Bülow, 7 November 1897, in PAAA R18232, 13–19.
[82] Wilhelm II to Bülow, 7 November 1897, in PAAA R18232, 13–19.
[83] Bülow to Wilhelm II, 8 November 1897, in PAAA R18232, 24–5.

who would be in a better position to advise the Germans of the contents of any secret treaty between Russia and China regarding Kiautschou Bay.[84]

It did not take long for the Russian government to respond, with Muraviev expressing regret at the German decision, and speculating that 'the consequences might well be that the English and perhaps the French will send their ships to Kiautschou Bay.' Muraviev argued that this was in no one's best interests.[85] As Rotenhan explained to Wilhelm II, regardless of what the tsar might have said to him in his short note, 'The Russian minister explained clearly, that the government of Emperor Nicholas does not intend to allow possession of Kiautschou Bay, in the event that China should lose it, to fall to another power. Rather that they want to take it for themselves.'[86] Upset that royal diplomacy had been exposed as lacking any real standing, the emperor responded with a long and personal diatribe against 'this lying man' Muraviev.[87]

To his dismay, Wilhelm II also found that he did not have the support of Naval Secretary Tirpitz, who told the chancellor privately that the occupation would in all likelihood start a war with China.[88] Publicly, however, he argued that he held 'the action against China to be unfavourable given the Naval Bill, and dubious in its present form'.[89] It was on this front, the manner of Wilhelm II's intervention, that Hohenlohe now moved, attempting to limit the damage caused by the emperor's hasty order. On 11 November, Hohenlohe wrote to Wilhelm II looking for a choice of words that would allow a respectable volte-face. He argued that surely the intention of His Majesty's order to Diedrichs was to occupy the bay 'if the Chinese response was unsatisfactory'. Should the admiral have already occupied Kiautschou Bay, then he should be reminded to deport himself in such a way as 'not to prejudice any later diplomatic negotiations'. To this, the emperor meekly replied, 'Agreed.'[90] Against the backdrop of Muraviev once again strongly reiterating Russia's rights of first anchorage, Hohenlohe belatedly added to Wilhelm II's orders to Diedrichs the advice that 'the Russians have retrospectively asserted their prior rights over Kiautschou Bay, which must be negotiated.' The final version added that even if the occupation had taken place, it should be seen as temporary 'until sufficient reparations have been made.'[91]

---

[84] Hohenlohe to Wilhelm II, 7 November 1897, in *Grosse Politik*, vol. 14, 71.

[85] Tschirschky to Foreign Office, 9 November 1897, in PAAA R18232, 32–5.

[86] Rotenhan to Wilhelm II, 10 November 1897, in *Grosse Politik*, vol. 14, 73–4.

[87] Wilhelm II to Foreign Office, 10 November 1897, in PAAA R18232, 42–5. Even before the seizure of Kiautschou Bay Muraviev was seen as not only anti-German, but as harbouring a personal animosity towards Wilhelm II. See Holstein to Radolin, 10 January 1897, in N. Rich and M. H. Fisher (eds), *Die geheimen Papiere Friedrich von Holsteins*, vol. 4 (Göttingen: Musterschmidt Verlag, 1963), 1.

[88] Holstein to Hatzfeldt, 13 November 1897, in Rich and Fisher (eds), *Die geheimen Papiere Friedrich von Holsteins*, vol. 4, 43–6.

[89] Tirpitz to Hohenlohe, 10 November 1897, in BA Freiburg RM 3/6694, 9.

[90] Hohenlohe to Wilhelm II, 11 November 1897, in *Grosse Politik*, vol. 14, 78–9.

[91] Hohenlohe, 'Unterredung mit dem russischen Botschafter', 12 November 1897, in PAAA R18232, 61–5; Rotenhan to Tirpitz, 12 November 1897; Knorr to Bülow, 12 November 1897, in BA Freiburg RM 3/6694, 12, 14.

In China, however, events on the ground had already overtaken Hohenlohe's domestic success in reining in his emperor. By 15 November word from China had returned that Diedrichs had indeed already taken Kiautschou Bay and had issued a proclamation declaring German sovereignty over it before the rewritten order of 12 November had reached him.[92] The news that Kiautschou had been unequivocally declared German territory necessitated a meeting between the emperor, Hohenlohe, and naval and foreign office officials, in which a plan was hatched to stabilize the increasingly chaotic situation by trying to keep the Chinese territory while brazening out the protests of Russia. Despite Tirpitz's earlier pessimistic assessment, those at the meeting now concluded that they did not expect the Chinese to attack. Even as Chinese newspapers optimistically reported their expectation that the crisis would be short-lived and that the Germans would not allow this 'small matter' to sour Germany's 'traditionally good relations' with China, the Berlin meeting determined that Germany's demands to the Zongli Yamen would be sufficiently unacceptable to ensure that China would refuse them, and the occupation could then quietly be turned into a long-term lease. Confident too that Russia would eventually capitulate and that the German public, including German Catholics, would endorse the emperor's peremptory action in apparent defence of their missionaries, Wilhelm II authorized the creation of an occupation force.[93]

Russia's stiff opposition to the occupation, however, did not waver. Muraviev argued that Wilhelm II had improperly extracted a statement from the tsar over the heads of his ministers under pressure, and had used this personal correspondence to imply that the Nicholas II had waived Russia's rights in China in a way that the tsar had never intended.[94] So too, Russia's finance minister, Sergei Witte, insisted that Germany should settle for the death penalty for the missionaries' murderers and financial compensation. Witte, the architect of Russia's China policy, added callously that 'the Chinese government will hang as many as the Germans demand.' If Germany remained in Kiautschou, however, it could have 'dangerous consequences', including unleashing a large, general war involving Britain and Japan for territory in China.[95] Although self-evidently an attempt to sustain Muraviev's objections via different arguments, Witte's warning was not

---

[92] Knorr to Tirpitz, 15 November 1897; Knorr to Tirpitz, 17 November 1897, in BA Freiburg RM 3/6694, 15–17.

[93] Abschrift, 15 November 1897, PAAA R18232, 67–72. In the Naval Ministry, complaints soon arose about Wilhelm II's ham-fisted attempts to meddle in the training and arming of this force. Knorr to Tirpitz, 29 November 1897, in BA Freiburg RM3/6696, 'Besetzung der Station in China', 10; 'Kommentar der Guowen Bao', 20 November 1897, in Leutner (ed.), *Musterkolonie Kiautschou*', 134–6.

[94] Hohenlohe to Wilhelm II, 18 November 1897, in PAAA R18232, 91–3.

[95] Muraviev to German Foreign Office, 16 November 1897; Tschirschky to German Foreign Office, 17 November 1897; Tschirschky to German Foreign Office, 26 November 1897, in PAAA R18232, 90–94, 125–31. In China, the German ambassador, Heyking, was made aware of Russia's misgivings on 17 November. See Elisabeth von Heyking, *Tagebücher aus vier Weltteilen*, 237.

without substance, with the Japanese press urging further naval armaments that would allow them to act in a similarly unilateral fashion.[96]

By 21 December, the British East Asian fleet had also reached Waiheiwai just to the north of Kiautschou, a move they were careful to portray as an anti-Russian rather than anti-German naval display.[97] The French too were closely monitoring the situation, with Ambassador Georges Dubail writing to his foreign minister, Gabriel Hanotaux, that the Zongli Yamen was extremely worried about what measures the German government might resort to, including 'the surrender of a place long coveted by Kaiser Wilhelm', namely Kiautschou, which France knew had recently been visited by a German warship, which had caused the Chinese 'some apprehension'. The Zongli Yamen, Dubail concluded, was 'very determined to resist restitution of this nature, so much so that it hopes to gain some support, even if latent, from other European powers'.[98] As the power with the most to lose, however, it was the Russians who gave the greatest amount of diplomatic support to the enraged Zongli Yamen, which had indeed decided to resist the German occupation diplomatically, as well as to send a warship to Kiautschou Bay. Chinese troops moved to a position fifteen kilometres away from the German occupying forces awaiting orders, while the Zongli Yamen refused to discuss any further reparations while the harbour remained occupied.[99]

Hohenlohe bluntly informed Wilhelm II just how much he had damaged relations with Russia by embarrassing the tsar internationally and occupying what Russia considered to be territory within their sphere of influence. The chancellor also requested that the emperor make good his mistake and try to strike a conciliatory tone by contacting Nicholas II to assure him that Russian vessels would always be welcome to anchor in Kiautschou Bay. Wilhelm II agreed, but stubbornly maintained that he had only acted in Germany's interests to secure a harbour on the eve of what he saw as the imminent fall of the Qing dynasty.[100]

In China, Heyking made a last-ditch attempt both to help the Chinese save face and bring his longstanding plan for a German naval station in Amoy to fruition by suggesting the Chinese emperor offer a southern harbour to Wilhelm II's

[96] Bülow to Tirpitz, 29 January 1898, in BA Freiburg RM3/6695, 'Erforschung. Erwerbung pp von Ländern in Ostasien', 21.

[97] Bülow to Tirpitz, 21 December 1897, in BA Freiburg RM3/6694, 149; Hosea Ballou Morse, *The International Relations of the Chinese Empire*, vol. 3: *The Period of Subjugation 1894–1911* (London: Longman, Green & Co., 1918), 118–19.

[98] Georges Dubail to Gabriel Hanotaux, 10 November 1897, in Archives diplomatiques (AD) NS 149 'Chine: Politique étrangère: Relations avec l'Allemagne 1896–1897', 67.

[99] Elisabeth von Heyking, *Tagebücher aus vier Weltteilen*, 238–43; Heyking to German Foreign Office, 19 November 1897; Heyking to German Foreign Office, 21 November 1897; Heyking to German Foreign Office, 22 November 1897; Hsü to Bülow, 24 November 1897, in BA Freiburg RM 3/6694, 64–5, 67, 92; Dubail to Hanotaux, 18 November 1897; Dubail to Hanotaux, 25 November 1897, in AD NS 149, 91–3, 137–8.

[100] Hohenlohe to Wilhelm II, 18 November 1897; Wilhelm II to Foreign Office, 17 November 1897, in PAAA R18232, 91–3; Wilhelm II to Foreign Office, 17 November 1897, in PAAA R18232, 106–12.

brother, Prince Heinrich, in exchange for ending the occupation of Kiautschou. With Germany's (and Wilhelm II's) international prestige now so publicly entwined with the occupation of Kiautschou, the plan met with an emphatic no from both Bülow and Wilhelm II.[101] Despite quiet Russian support for the Zongli Yamen's position that the bay be evacuated before discussions could begin on the terms under which Germany might receive territorial compensation in China, by December 1897 Russia's overt expressions of outrage had cooled, particularly once the Russians had moved to occupy Port Arthur. The Germans expressed their delighted agreement with this development and vowed they would forever after support Russia against Japan or even Britain and France if ever there was a serious conflict in the region.[102] Making what they could of the situation, the Russians formally argued that Kiautschou Bay should not become a treaty harbour, as that would make defending China from Japan difficult and extinguish any hope China might have of the harbour one day returning to their possession. For the time being, however, they conceded that the Germans might remain there.[103]

In mid-December 1897, Wilhelm II agreed to send Prince Heinrich to China to meet with the Chinese emperor and assist in the formal handover of Germany's newest colonial acquisition (Figure 2.1).[104] Careful to keep the Russians informed, the emperor wrote in English to Nicholas II declaring that Heinrich was 'happy to meet your officers and ships out in the East, on whose side he has my orders to place himself if ever serious danger threatens them or your interests'. Nicholas II replied that he was 'especially thankful' that Wilhelm II had given 'such clear instructions to Henry'. The tsar's cool but cordial reply was enough to leave Wilhelm II waxing lyrical about the unshakeable bonds of the Germans and the Russians in the Far East:

> Please accept my congratulations at the arrival of your squadron at Port Arthur. Russia and Germany at the entrance of the Yellow Sea may be taken as representing St George and St Michael shielding the Holy Cross in the Far East and guarding the gates to the Continent of Asia. May You be able fully to realize the plans You often unrolled [sic] to me. My sympathy and help shall not fail in case of need.[105]

---

[101] Elisabeth von Heyking, *Tagebücher aus vier Weltteilen*, 246; Heyking to German Foreign Office, 7 December 1897; Abschrift, 8 December 1897; Bülow to Heyking, 12 December 1897, in PAAA R18232, 173–6.

[102] Heyking to Foreign Office, 7 December 1897; Heyking to Foreign Office, 11 December 1897; Bülow to Tschirschky, 28 November 1897; Bülow, Abschrift, 30 November 1897; Radolin to German Foreign Office, 6 December 1897; Heyking to German Foreign Office, 6 December 1897, in PAAA R18232, 132–49, 173–6, 193.

[103] Heyking to German Foreign Office, 24 December 1897, in PAAA R18232, 'Erwerbungen der Großmächte in China', 29–31.

[104] Ferdinand von Richthofen, *Schantung und seine Eingangspforte Kiautschou* (Berlin: Dietrich Reimer, 1898), 309.

[105] Wilhelm II to Nicholas II, 16 December 1897; Nicholas II to Wilhelm II, 16 December 1897; Wilhelm II, 18 December 1897, in PAAA R18232, 261–3.

Figure 2.1 Prince Heinrich and entourage visit the Temple of Heaven, Peking, 1898
Source: Courtesy of the Bundesarchiv.

At the same time as Wilhelm II was pledging Germany's unstinting support for Russia's interests in China, however, Foreign Secretary Bülow was looking for ways to accommodate Russia's rival, Japan, so as to forestall a naval conflict with what was recognized to be a superior, British-aligned naval force in the region.[106] The scale of the disingenuousness and unreliability of Wilhelm II's declarations of unfailing assistance to Russia in Asia only became truly evident during the Russo-Japanese War, in which Germany offered no significant military assistance to the tsar.

Germany's Unravelling of China

'The abasement of China', Hosea Ballou Morse haughtily wrote in 1918, 'was perhaps scarcely felt by the toiling millions.'[107] Nonetheless, the seizure of Kiautschou Bay, the first section of the Chinese mainland to be alienated from Chinese control, significantly impacted upon the political development of China and the future of its people thereafter. The Zongli Yamen was deeply shaken by the

---

[106] Bülow to Wilhelm II, 13 December 1897, in PAAA R18232, 207–8.
[107] Morse, *The International Relations of the Chinese Empire*, vol. 3, 128.

concession, which it reluctantly ratified on the afternoon of 4 January 1898.[108] The occupation unleashed a litany of other European and Japanese claims to Chinese territory, while Han Chinese reportedly saw the territorial loss as a sign that all of Manchuria might be lost to the Europeans and that a Han Chinese dynasty might be refounded with its capital in Nanking.[109]

For his part, the Guangxu emperor was shocked into moving closer to Britain and undertaking an ambitious reform project designed to strengthen China against future external threats. As Klaus Mühlhahn has argued, the German occupation of Kiautschou and the scramble for concessions it unleashed were the 'single most important factor' prompting the One Hundred Days reform agenda.[110] In his foundational reformist edict, the Guangxu emperor made clear that it was the threat posed by militarily stronger external enemies that had necessitated the changes he proposed.[111] The course of action announced by the edict owed much to reformists close to the emperor who agreed with the modernization agenda proposed by the political radical Kang Youwei, who was convinced that rapid and transformative change was necessary if China was to address the crisis of sovereignty precipitated by the 'German menace'.[112] Writing in December 1897, Kang Youwei argued in his 'Fifth Memorial' that the occupation of Kiautschou and acceding to German demands was 'the start of a chain reaction' that would prove to be China's undoing. It showed that China had sunk in European estimations from the status of a 'half-civilized nation' to that of 'negro slaves in Africa'—an alarming shift in Kang Youwei's estimation, given that the history of European imperialism demonstrated that 'according to their treaties only civilized nations have a right to protection. Barbarian peoples shall be eradicated'.[113] The obvious strength of the foreigners meant that if it wanted to survive intact, China needed to learn from and imitate their approach to economic, political, and military matters.[114]

The reforms greatly alarmed Chinese conservatives, who saw its westernizing thrust as directly endangering their interests and the independence of China. These fears led to a palace coup aimed at reversing the changes heralded by the

---

[108] Heyking to German Foreign Office, 4 January 1898, in PAAA R18232, 'Erwerbungen der Großmächte in China', 144. For the text of the treaty, see 'Abkommen zwischen dem Deutschen Reich und der Qing-Dynastie', 6 March 1898, in Leutner (ed.), 'Musterkolonie Kiautschou', 164–8.

[109] Vossische Zeitung, 17 January 1898, in PAAA R17669, 'Innere Angelegenheiten Chinas', 119.

[110] Klaus Mühlhahn, 'Negotiating the Nation: German Colonialism and Chinese Nationalism in Qingdao, 1897–1914', in Bryna Goodman and David S. G. Goodman (eds), Twentieth-Century Colonialism and China: Localities, the Everyday and the World (London: Routledge, 2012), 45.

[111] Luke S. K. Kwong, 'Chinese Politics at the Crossroads: Reflections on the Hundred Days Reform of 1898', Modern Asian Studies 34, no. 3 (2000), 667.

[112] Young-Tsu Wong, 'Revisionism Reconsidered: Kang Youwei and the Reform Movement of 1898', Journal of Asian Studies 51, no. 3 (1992), 519–20.

[113] Kang Youwei, as quoted in Mühlhahn, 'Negotiating the Nation', 44. See also 'Memorandum des Philosophen Kang Youwei an den Thron', in Leutner (ed.), 'Musterkolonie Kiautschou', 151–3.

[114] Yunzhi Geng, An Introductory Study on China's Cultural Transformation in Recent Times (Heidelberg: Springer, 2015), 180.

Guangxu emperor and reinstating Empress Dowager Cixi as the ruler of China. Although Cixi was not initially inclined to dispute the need for change, once she became convinced that the reforms were the result of external influence (in particular Japanese influence), she was persuaded that the emperor needed to accept her 'close supervision' of his rule.[115] By mid-June 1898, Cixi was actively working to reverse the reforms and to remove key personnel involved in their implementation. By 21 September 1898, Cixi felt sufficiently emboldened to have the emperor arrested and imprisoned on Yingtai Island. Incorrect rumours came back to Europe that the emperor had been murdered.[116] The nine gates of Peking were closed, and the order was given to arrest reformers such as Kang Youwei. Although he escaped to Hong Kong with the help of the British, others were not so lucky.[117]

If the Guangxu emperor had attempted to initiate his reforms under the influence of the British, the palace coup was seen by many as a Russian success. Certainly, Germany's ambassadorial couple, the Heykings, saw the coup as fitting suspiciously well with Russian interests in China. The Russians, they wrote, had complained about the Chinese emperor's sidelining of Li Hongzhang at the request of the British in the aftermath of the territorial losses inflicted by the Russians and the Germans in the north. Even the representatives of St Petersburg forthrightly proclaimed the palace coup to be a Russian victory over Anglo-Japanese attempts to bring China into their orbit.[118]

It was not only the Heykings who saw a lurch towards the Russians in the palace coup.[119] British papers like the *Morning Post* and the *Daily Chronicle* noted it as well. To their Anglophone eyes, Cixi's coup represented a recklessly retrograde step by anachronistic elements of the Qing court, as well as an acknowledgement of the revolutionary potential of broader anti-Western sentiment in China. The anti-British and anti-Japanese hues of the palace coup and the re-establishment of Russian influence at court were also clearly recognized. The reinstatement of Li Hongzhang and the banishment of his pro-British 'Cantonese enemy' Chang Yin Huan to Turkestan were as much remarked upon as the removal of the reformist emperor. 'In the cause of Civilisation', one editor opined about the Guangxu emperor, 'it is much to be regretted that his attempt to reform China has not been

[115] Kwong, 'Chinese Politics at the Crossroads', 674–5.

[116] *Morning Post*, 23 September 1898; *The Standard*, 23 September 1898, in PAAA R 17997, 'Die kaiserliche Familie von China', 26–8.

[117] Hao Ping, *Peking University and the Origins of Higher Education in China* (Los Angeles: Bridge 21 Publications, 2013), 140–64.

[118] Heyking to Foreign Office, 12 September 1898; Heyking to Foreign Office, 26 September 1898, in R17669, 'Innere Angelegenheiten Chinas', 192, 203. See also Elisabeth von Heyking, *Tagebücher aus vier Weltteilen*, 271–5.

[119] Heyking to Foreign Office, 26 September 1898, in PAAA R17997, 'Die kaiserliche Familie von China', 33–4.

received with the enthusiasm it deserved.'[120] For its part, *The Times* lamented that the 'virtual restoration of the regency' had halted 'the sincere desire of the Emperor to introduce energetic measures of administrative, financial and industrial reform'.[121] The paper also accused Li Hongzhang and Cixi of being in cahoots, but nonetheless recognized the popularity of the coup among many Chinese.[122] It had to be admitted, *The Times* reported, that the conservative court faction might have been moved to action in order to stave off brewing 'anti-foreign riots and anti-dynastic rebellion'.[123]

Cixi's palace coup ending the reforms of the One Hundred Days has been seen by some Chinese historians as the moment when China and its monarchy reached its historical turning point and failed to turn.[124] Such teleological ascriptions are certainly in line with the views of the British press at the time but overlook both the external barriers to Chinese autonomous self-development posed by the predations of the imperial powers, particularly Germany, and the internal ructions these attacks on Chinese sovereignty unleashed both on those proposing and those opposing reforms. With Cixi in power in the palace and Li Hongzhang restored to his earlier key position, the palace-led route to reform continued, but at a far slower pace.

Although Wilhelm II had foreseen that the Guangxu emperor, indeed the entire Qing dynasty, would encounter difficulties holding onto the throne, in particular in keeping up with Chinese public opinion,[125] there is no evidence to suggest that he grasped the connection between his own clumsy execution of the Foreign and Naval Offices' existing plan to acquire a harbour on the Chinese mainland and the political turmoil that beset China thereafter. Rather, in later years the German emperor saw in Kiautschou only a 'blooming German trading colony, prized and admired by the Chinese'.[126] His admiration for the forced westernization of Chinese territory was not shared, however, by the Chinese Boxer movement, nor by their royal patron, Empress Dowager Cixi.[127] It came as no surprise to European observers that Cixi, firmly anti-imperialist in her political bearing, would come to support the Boxer Rebellion, when it broke out in 1900.[128]

---

[120] *Morning Post*, 23 September 1898; *Daily Chronicle*, 23 September 1898, in PAAA R17997, 'Die kaiserliche Familie von China', 26, 29; *Morning Post*, 27 September 1898, in PAAA R17669, 'Innere Angelegenheiten Chinas', 217.

[121] *The Times*, 22 September 1898, in PAAA R17997, 'Die kaiserliche Familie von China', 19.

[122] *The Times*, 22 September 1898, in PAAA R17997, 20–1.

[123] *The Times*, 22 September 1898, in PAAA R17997, 20–1.

[124] Cheng Jie, 'Why Late Qing Constitutional Reform Failed: An Examination from the Comparative Institutional Perspective', *Tsinghua China Law Review* 10, no. 107 (2017), 108–9.

[125] Wilhelm II to Foreign Office, 17 November 1897, in PAAA R18232, 106–12.

[126] Wilhelm II, *Ereignisse und Gestalten*, 65.

[127] David Schimmelpenninck van der Oye, 'Russia's Ambivalent Response to the Boxers', *Cahiers du monde russe* 41 no. 1 (2000), 66–7.

[128] Li Yuhang and Harriet T. Zurndorfer, 'Rethinking Empress Dowager Cixi through the Production of Art', *Nan Nü* 14, no. 1 (2012), 6.

3

A Pilgrim to the Holy Land

Emperor Wilhelm II was often mocked in Germany as the 'travelling Kaiser' (*Reisekaiser*). Indeed, he travelled so much (up to three-quarters of the year by one estimate) that some Germans joked that the German Empire's national anthem should be changed from 'Hail to Thee in Victor's Crown' to 'Hail to Thee in Private Train'. Yet, despite reigning over colonies in Africa, the Pacific, and China, Wilhelm II never set foot in any of them. Instead, he preferred to spend his time in aimless travel to Mediterranean destinations such as Italy and Corfu or on scenic tours of the fjords of Scandinavia. When he returned from his overseas sojourns on his royal yacht, it was to criss-cross Germany in his personal train.[1]

Although he never travelled as far as the German colonies, Wilhelm II did make three separate journeys to the Ottoman Empire. The first and the last trips (in 1889 and 1917) were relatively quiet affairs, however his second voyage, undertaken in the autumn of 1898 with Empress Augusta Victoria, was occasioned by a hitherto unprecedented level of pomp and ceremony. It was organized down to the last detail by the British commercial travel agency Thomas Cook and was accompanied by an enormous entourage of eminent Germans, as well as 1,430 horses and pack animals, 116 coaches and wagons, 800 muleteers, and 290 servants.[2] 'Cook's crusader', as London's satirical *Punch* magazine labelled him,[3] even commissioned bespoke tropical uniforms for the occasion, a source of great mirth amongst those dragooned into accompanying the royal pair.[4] The emperor's voyage was also shadowed by a steam liner filled with well-heeled tourists who had timed their pilgrimages to coincide with the royal visit. The total cost of the voyage on the German side was 1.26 million marks.[5]

---

[1] Martin Kohlrausch, 'Der Mann mit dem Adlerhelm: Wilhelm II: Medienstar um 1900', in Paul Gerhard (ed.), *Das Jahrhundert der Bilder: 1900 bis 1949* (Göttingen: Vandenhoeck & Ruprecht, 2009), 72; Bettina Vaupel, 'Allerhöchste Eisenbahn', *Monumente* 23 (2013), 13; Marco Althaus, 'Heil Dir im Sonderzug', *Politik und Kommunikation* 12, no. 4 (2012), 36–7.

[2] Obituary of James Cook, *Frankfurter Zeitung*, in GStAPK BPH Rep113 Nr 1099, 'Acta betreffend Orient-Reise 1898', 224–5.

[3] *Punch*, 15 October 1898, 170.

[4] For the order of 23 August 1898 of two tropical uniforms for each participant, see GStAPK BPH Rep 113 Nr 1094, 'Acta betreffend Orient-Reise 1898', 23. For the army's refusal to pay for the ornamental uniforms and its demand that Wilhelm II pay for them, see BPH Rep 113 Nr 1095, 'Acta betreffend Orient-Reise 1898', 163.

[5] GStAPK BPH Rep 113 Nr 1103, 'Acta betreffend Orientreise 1898', 2. For the logistical minutiae of the trip, see GStAPK BPH Rep 113 Nr 1097, 'Acta betreffend Orient-Reise, Jerusalem 1898', BPH Rep 113 Nr 1095, BPH Rep 113 Nr 1092 1898, 'Acta betreffend Orient-Reise 1898'.

The Kaiser and the Colonies: Monarchy in the Age of Empire. Matthew P. Fitzpatrick, Oxford University Press.
© Matthew P. Fitzpatrick 2022. DOI: 10.1093/oso/9780192897039.003.0004

On the Ottoman side, not only did Sultan Abdulhamid II spend liberally on sprucing up the cities and towns along the Germans' route, but he also built a new wharf at Haifa which would allow Wilhelm II's private yacht to berth there.[6] The sultan also ordered that a section of the wall of Jerusalem's old city abutting Jaffa Gate be demolished so as to allow Wilhelm II to ride into the city on horseback. News of the demolition horrified the German emperor, who, upon hearing about, it exclaimed, 'This must be stopped! I hope that such barbarism has not been committed.' In Germany, the dramaturgical question of which gate Wilhelm II should use to enter the city was not yet settled, with some recommending that he use the Damascus Gate, reputedly the same gate used by Kaiser Friedrich II in the thirteenth century.[7]

The announced reason for the tour was the opening and dedication of the Church of Christ the Redeemer, built in Jerusalem with a royal bequest and donations from German Protestants on land given to Wilhelm II's father, Crown Prince Friedrich Wilhelm, by Sultan Abdulaziz in 1869.[8] Once it was confirmed that work had finished on the church, the German ambassador, Adolf Marschall von Bieberstein, had contacted the sultan in November 1897 to plan Wilhelm II's trip. Given that the planned visit had been the subject of a lengthy article in the German press in the preceding September, it is likely that word had already reached the Ottoman monarch.[9]

The contours of the trip are easily reconstructed. Once the exhaustive arrangements had been finalized, the royal party set out from the palace in Potsdam on 11 October 1898. They boarded the royal yacht, the *Hohenzollern*, on 13 October 1898 in Venice and sailed for five days to reach Constantinople. Here they spent several days (including the empress's birthday) as Sultan Abdulhamid II's personal guests. The German royals left Constantinople late on 22 October for Haifa and Jaffa, before journeying on to Jerusalem, arriving there on 29 October. The next day saw them visit the Church of the Nativity in Bethlehem, prior to the dedication of the Church of the Redeemer in Jerusalem on 31 October. The royal party stayed in and around Jerusalem until 3 November (see Figure 3.1), after which they travelled north via Beirut (5–6 November) to Damascus, where they stayed between 7 and 9 November. On 11 November, Wilhelm II visited the ruins of Baalbek, which impressed him so much that he decided to pay for them to be systematically excavated, before returning to Beirut for a leisurely sea voyage

[6] GStAPK BPH Rep 113 Nr 1092 1898, 257.
[7] *Le Gaulois*, 26 September 1898, PAAA IA, 'Preussen 1 (Personalia)', Nr1 Nr 4v R3730-3 Bd 5, 241. Barkhausen to Eulenburg, 20 September 1898, in GStAPK BPH Rep 113 Nr 1092 1898, 169.
[8] Barkhausen to Bülow, 27 August 1897, in PAAA R3729-1 Bd 4, 'Reise Seiner Majestät des Kaisers nach Athen und Konstantinopel', 37–9.
[9] Marschall to Chancellor Hohenlohe-Schillingsfürst, 20 November 1897, in PAAA R3729-1 Bd 4, 42–8; *Berliner Neueste Nachrichten*, 3 September 1897, in PAAA R3729-1 Bd 4, 40.

Figure 3.1 Wilhelm II and his entourage in Jerusalem in 1898

home.[10] The royal tour ended with Wilhelm II's arrival back in Berlin on 26 November, just in time for him to reopen the Reichstag on 6 December 1898.[11]

Given his predilection for travelling, many Germans saw the voyage as yet another personal excursion by a monarch suffering excessive wanderlust. The cover illustration of the special Palestine issue of the satirical magazine *Simplicissimus* spoke for many Germans when it showed the leader of the First Crusade, Godfrey of Bouillon, advising a hysterically laughing Frederick Barbarossa (who had died while leading the Third Crusade) not to laugh too heartily at Wilhelm II's journey, given that 'our Crusades were also pointless.'[12]

If German satirists felt that the voyage was pointless, others were less dismissive. Indeed, many were convinced that the voyage was being planned with deeper political motivations in mind. One early German press report in 1897 speculated that the opening of the church was only part of the story. Endemic conflict between the Latin and Orthodox churches in Jerusalem, the article opined, had seen the prestige of Christians sink in the eyes of Muslims and Jews in the region. Despite both Russians and the French claiming to be the protectors of

[10] Thomas Scheffler, 'The Kaiser in Baalbek: Tourism, Archaeology, and the Politics of Imagination', in Hélène Sader, Thomas Scheffler, and Angelika Neuwirth (eds), *Baalbek: Image and Monument 1898–1998* (Beirut: Orient-Institut der Deutschen Morgenländischen Gesellschaft, 1998), 15–16.

[11] For the details of the itinerary, see Ernst von Mirbach, *Die Reise des Kaisers und der Kaiserin nach Palästina* (Berlin: Ernst Siegfried Mittler und Sohn, 1899).

[12] *Simplicissimus* 3, no. 31 (1898), 241.

Christendom in the Holy Lands, neither had effectively fulfilled this role. Now perhaps Wilhelm II could show the world that Germany was able to protect its own Catholic and Lutheran citizens without recourse to intermediary powers, thereby demonstrating to the region's Muslims that 'at least one of the powers of Western Europe concerns itself with the preservation of Christianity in the Holy Lands.'[13]

Such speculation was not isolated, and senior representatives of the Christian denominations, as well as German colonists, European Zionists, and the governments of Britain, France, and Russia all watched—some with fear, some with hope—to see what the German emperor might do while visiting the Ottoman Empire. Europe's great powers were particularly watchful, given that the trip came so soon after the Germans' pointed diplomatic silence on the Armenian massacres of 1894–6 in the Ottoman Empire and Germany's logistical assistance in the Ottoman victory over the Greeks in 1897. Wilhelm II's visit was also seen as knowingly undermining the pan-European pressure being applied to the sultan in Crete.[14] Seemingly in defiance of the rest of Europe, the emperor was visiting the 'Red Sultan', and in doing so, rehabilitating him in the eyes of the world.[15]

There was also a degree of consternation amongst European royals, with Queen Victoria agreeing with Frank Lascelles in Berlin that 'The visits to Constantinople & Jerusalem were much to be regretted.'[16] Even Wilhelm II's own mother, who deplored Germany's show of support for the sultan, admitted that 'all liberal-minded men and thinking in Germany deplored' Germany's policies towards the Ottoman Empire, and that she 'looked forward with great anxiety to the Emperor's journey to Jerusalem'. Although she professed to understand that he might wish to visit the Holy Land, she was horrified to think that he would do so as 'the guest and personal friend of the sultan.'[17]

Perhaps most alarming for the other European powers were the rumours that Wilhelm II would use the trip to announce the establishment of a German colony

[13] *Berliner Neueste Nachrichten*, 3 September 1897, in PAAA R3729-1 Bd 4, 40. For the diplomatic manoeuvring between the Christian powers regarding Jerusalem, see Johannes Lepsius, Albrecht Mendelssohn Bartholdy, and Friedrich Thimme (eds), *Die grosse Politik der europäischen Kabinette 1871–1914*, vol. 12 (2) (Berlin: Deutsche Verlagsgesellschaft für Politik und Geschichte, 1924), 589–638.

[14] PAAA IA, 'Preussen 1 (Personalia)', Nr 1 Nr 4v R 3731-3 Bd 6, 193. See also *Pall Mall Gazette*, 6 October 1898, PAAA IA, 'Preussen 1 (Personalia)', Nr 1 Nr 4v R 3731-3 Bd 6, 137.

[15] Thomas Benner, *Die Strahlen der Krone: Die religiöse Dimension des Kaisertums unter Wilhelm II vor dem Hintergrund der Orientreise 1898* (Marburg: Tectum Verlag, 2001), 159–65; Abdel-Raouf Sinno, 'The Emperor's Visit to the East as Reflected in Contemporary Arabic Journalism', in Sader, Scheffler, and Neuwirth (eds), *Baalbek*, 115–16. See also, however, 'Berlin and Constantinople', *The Spectator*, 22 October 1898, in PAAA IA, 'Preussen 1 (Personalia)', Nr 1 Nr 4v R3732-2 Bd 7, 71, which argued that Britain could not lecture the Germans after the British put their own interests before those of the Bulgarians when they too were massacred. See also *The Daily Telegraph*, 11 October 1898, PAAA IA, 'Preussen 1 (Personalia)', Nr 1 Nr 4v R 3731-3 Bd 6, 222.

[16] Victoria, 28 October 1898 in *Queen Victoria's Journals*, vol. 108, 151.

[17] Lascelles to Victoria, 19 October 1898, in National Archives FO 800/17, 153–4; Lascelles to Salisbury, 18 February 1898, in National Archive FO 800/17, 123.

on Ottoman territory, a move that threatened to unleash a dangerous and destabilizing scramble between the Germans and Britain, Russia, France, and Austria
for Ottoman territory in Anatolia. With fears of a general European conflict over
the 'Eastern question' having informed European politics since 1878, the great
worry of many Europeans was not that the emperor was indulging in a pointless
and expensive voyage, but that it would be the occasion for a disastrous personal
sally into an internationally fraught domain of foreign policy.

Guessing the Emperor's Intentions

Although Bismarck famously declared that he never bothered opening any diplomatic correspondence from Constantinople, Wilhelm II was not the first German
ruler to treat the Ottoman Empire seriously. In fact, Bismarck had spent a great
deal of his time dealing with issues surrounding the Ottoman Empire, with the
so-called 'Eastern question' and the fate of Ottoman territorial sovereignty one of
the most pressing issues in German foreign policy after 1875.[18] Bismarck's mock
lack of interest in eastern affairs has led many historians to believe that the
Ottoman Empire only entered into German imperial calculations after Wilhelm
II had ascended the throne and ostensibly instigated a new era of *Weltpolitik*.[19]
Far from heralding Germany's discovery of the Ottoman Empire, however,
Wilhelm II's visit was observed so keenly precisely because of the scale of
Germany's pre-existing interests in the region. By the 1890s the rapid globaliza-
tion of German trade had seen German banking and industrial interests seek out
contracts from the Ottoman Porte for a system of railways that would traverse
Asiatic Turkey and terminate at Basra on the Persian Gulf. This plan for a so-
called 'Baghdad Railway' had always necessitated strong commercial and economic ties with the sultan.[20] It also required the avoidance of any agreements
between the other powers to partition the Ottoman Empire to the disadvantage of
Germany.

If Wilhelm II was not the originator of German interest in the Ottoman
Empire, he was, nonetheless, certainly capable of upsetting the delicate status quo

---

[18] Friedrich Scherer, *Adler und Halbmond: Bismarck und der Orient, 1878–1890* (Paderborn:
Ferdinand Schöningh, 2001), xii.
[19] See for example Klaus Jaschinski, 'Des Kaisers Reise in den Vorderen Orient 1898, ihr his-
torischer Platz und ihre Dimensionen', in Klaus Jaschinski and Julius Waldschmidt (Eds), *Des Kaisers
Reise in den Orient 1898* (Berlin: Trafo Verlag, 2002), 19; Sean McMeekin, *The Berlin-Baghdad Express:
The Ottoman Empire and Germany's Bid for World Power* (Cambridge, MA: Harvard University Press,
2010), 11; Francesco Cerasani, 'Imperialism of Kaiser Wilhelm II: Perspectives and Historiography of
German Südpolitik', in Antonello Biagini and Giovanna Motta (Eds), *Empires and Nations from the
Eighteenth Century to the Twentieth Century*, vol. 2 (Newcastle: Cambridge Scholars Press, 2014), 30.
[20] Murat Özyüksel, *The Berlin–Baghdad Railway and the Ottoman Empire: Industrialization,
Imperial Germany and the Middle East* (London: I. B. Tauris, 2016).

there. Across Europe, speculation grew regarding the German emperor's motives and what interests lurked behind the trip. With virtually no mention of Sultan Abdulhamid II and his capacity to forestall any German expansionist plans that did not suit his purposes, reports focused squarely on what Wilhelm II would do and what that would mean for the balance of power in the region. During the planning phase for the voyage, the nationalist press in France expressed its fears that France's historic (and strategically important) rights as protector of Christians in the Holy Lands must inevitably suffer as a result of Wilhelm II's personal visit as a guest of the sultan.[21] The royalist *Le Soleil* saw the trip as part of a calculated German foreign policy aimed at 'substituting German influence for ours in the Orient'. The newspaper also warned that German newspapers were boasting that 'Germany will take on France in the land of Syria which hitherto has morally been ours'. Such designs were seen by French nationalists as a serious affront. 'Why not just take the opportunity to be crowned king of Jerusalem?', the paper asked sardonically, just as Friedrich II had been crowned King of Jerusalem in 1228.[22] Similarly, the arch-nationalist *Le Matin* opined that the trip 'directly threatens our secular authority in the Christian Levant'.[23] The Belgian Catholic-conservative *Le Vingtième Siècle* concurred, arguing that the ostensible 'pilgrimage' would use the issue of protecting German Catholics in Jerusalem as a means to bring into question the historic rights of France as protector of Christians in the Orient. No mere religious question, this would 'offer Germany strong moral backing for its influential material position of power'. On reading this report, Wilhelm II wrote in the margin that there was nothing new here: whatever the French might have thought, German Christians of all denominations in the Holy Land had been under the protection of the Hohenzollerns ever since German unification in 1871.[24]

Russia also saw itself as the traditional protector of Christians in Palestine, and had grown accustomed to jostling only with France for this right. With Wilhelm II poised to enter Jerusalem, however, this looked set to change. With Germany's wresting of Kiautschou from Russia still fresh in the minds of nationalists, the tsarist organ *Novoye Vremya* expressed its displeasure, declaring Wilhelm II's trip to be a transparent 'continuation of the comprehensively planned action of Germany in East Asia and Asia Minor'. Putting aside long-standing Franco-Russian rivalry in the Holy Land, the newspaper argued that Germany was beginning to displace France in the Levant and urged the French to work with Russia to

---

[21] Münster to Chancellor Hohenlohe, Paris, 10 June 1898, in PAAA R3729-2 Bd 4, 'Reise Seiner Majestät des Kaisers nach Athen und Konstantinopel', 156; IA, 'Preussen 1 (Personalia)', Nr 1 Nr 4v R 3731-3 Bd 6, 237. See Benner, *Die Strahlen der Krone*, 189–95.

[22] *Le Soleil*, 24 August 1898, in PAAA IA, 'Preussen I (Personalia)', Nr 1 Nr 4v R3730-1 Bd 5, 75.

[23] *Le Matin*, 17 October 1898, in PAAA IA, 'Preussen 1 (Personalia)', Nr 1 Nr 4v R 3731-3 Bd 6, 241.

[24] *XXe Siècle*, September 1898, in PAAA IA, 'Preussen 1 (Personalia)', Nr1 Nr 4v R3730-2 Bd 5, 119–20.

bring German intrigues to a halt. 'Russia', the paper warned, 'will hardly be able to remain indifferent to the plans of the German government... Complete unity with France on this question appears highly desirable.' Only this could stop any 'secret agreement between Germany, Turkey, and the Vatican'.[25]

The conspiracy theory that the Vatican might secretly be involved in the royal visit formed the basis of perhaps the most outlandish rumour, which came from London's *Daily Chronicle*. According to this report, the emperor was travelling 'to Palestine as a crusader... who by his mailed fist, hidden or displayed, will win back the Holy Places from the Infidel'. The sultan, the newspaper opined, would be forced to relinquish Jerusalem to the Emperor of Germany, as the price for German support in Europe. Having secured the Holy City, the article concluded, Wilhelm II would hand it over 'as a solemn gift to the Pope'. Thereafter, the seat of the papacy would be moved 'from the Janiculum to Mount Zion'.[26] This rumour was reported elsewhere, although the *Strassburger Post* predicted that any such plan to move the seat of the papacy to Jerusalem would fail due to the resistance of the Russian Orthodox Church.[27]

Far more sober in its analysis, *The Times* in London discounted Russian fears of any pending surprise colonial announcement by Wilhelm II in Palestine. 'The Russian press', the *Times* assured it readers, 'need not be afraid that he is going to declare himself a sort of Lord Paramount of Asiatic Turkey.' The British newspaper argued instead that the voyage would aim at rekindling the nationalist sensibilities of German Catholics alienated by the anti-Catholic *Kulturkampf* by affirming that Germany rather than France was best positioned to defend their interests in the Levant.[28] This suggestion proved prescient, and the sense that Wilhelm II would in some way demonstrate the capacity of Germany to defend the interests of German Catholics in Palestine was applauded by even the most ultramontane elements of the German Catholic community, which professed their preference for the protection of the German Empire to French claims to be their rightful protector.[29] This stance was at odds with the formal position of the Vatican, which maintained its support for France's historic claims to be the protector of all Catholics in the Holy Lands rather than the division of Catholics according to nationality.[30]

---

[25] *St Petersburger Zeitung*, 5 July 1898, reporting on *Novoye Vremya* in PAAA R3729-2 Bd 4, 181.

[26] *The Daily Chronicle*, 6 October 1898 in PAAA IA, 'Preussen 1 (Personalia)', Nr 1 Nr 4v R 3731-2 Bd 6, 135.

[27] 'An heilige Stätte', *Strassburger Post*, 10 October 1898. BPH Rep113 Nr 1099, 12.

[28] *The Times*, 8 October 1898, in PAAA IA, 'Preussen 1 (Personalia)', Nr 1 Nr 4v R 3731-2 Bd 6, 148–9.

[29] See Vienna's *Fremden-Blatt*, 11 October 1898, in PAAA IA, 'Preussen 1 (Personalia)', Nr 1 Nr 4v R 3731-3 Bd 6, 203.

[30] 'Germany and the Vatican', *The Times*, 12 October 1898, in PAAA IA, 'Preussen 1 (Personalia)' Nr 1 Nr 4v R 3731-3 Bd 6, 220.

The historic struggle for religious primacy in Palestine remained central to the planning of the royal visit. In the lead-up to the voyage, the very staging of the emperor's arrival at various sites was planned with a close eye to the political implications on the Orthodox/Catholic contest for control over the holy sites. The detailed plans for Wilhelm II's visit to the Church of the Nativity in Bethlehem, for example, make clear that simply deciding which door he would use to enter the church would determine whether Germany would be seen as supporting Orthodox Russian or Catholic French claims to supremacy:

> If the entrance through the Franciscan Church of St Catherine is taken, the Orthodox clerics will be thrust into the background, while it is also likely that initial entry through the Orthodox occupied basilica will see the Latins over-shadowed. Whether one is to be preferred over the other can only be decided on political grounds, on which it might be advisable to give the Foreign Office the opportunity to offer advice.[31]

Further complicating matters was the presence of Armenian clerics, whose noticeable proximity to Wilhelm II so soon after the Hamidian massacres was considered by staff at the German Foreign Office to be potentially embarrassing, particularly given the rumours that Armenian protestors might seek to disrupt the royal visit.[32] Given the opportunity to reinforce the nationalist sentiments of Germany's Catholic population, which still remembered the *Kulturkampf*, the German Foreign Office offered the advice that in all doubtful situations Catholic clerics were to be prioritized over Orthodox ones.[33]

An Egyptian Interlude

By mid-March of 1898, the keen amateur archaeologist Wilhelm II had decided to add a visit to Egypt to his itinerary. The surprise plan to visit British-occupied Egypt was revealed to Britain's ambassador to Berlin, Frank Lascelles, during a dinner conversation with the German emperor.[34] His intention was to visit Alexandria, Cairo, the pyramids at Giza, and then make his way south to Luxor to

---

[31] Barkhausen to Eulenburg, 20 September 1898, GStAPK BPH Rep 113 Nr 1092 1898, 'Acta betreffend Orient-Reise 1898', 164–5. See also Barkhausen's Abschrift of 23 March 1898 to Eulenburg, in GStAPK BPH Rep113 Nr 1098, 'Acta betreffend Orient-Reise Jerusalem, 1898', 7–8.

[32] Consul in Sinaia to chancellor, 5 October 1898, in PAAA IA, 'Preussen 1 (Personalia)', Nr 1 Nr 4v R 3731-2 Bd 6, 108.

[33] Derenthal to Eulenburg, 28 September 1898, in GStAPK BPH Rep 113 Nr 1092 1898, 207.

[34] Lascelles to Sanderson, 19 March 1898, National Archives FO 800/17, 132. The political importance of a German visit to British-occupied Egypt is curiously downplayed in Martin Kröger, 'Le Baton égyptien'—Der ägyptische Knüppel: Die Rolle der 'ägyptischen Frage' in der deutschen Außenpolitik von 1875/6 bis zur 'Entente Cordiale' (Frankfurt am Main: Peter Lang, 1991), 168–71.

visit the Temple of Karnak, before returning to Cairo and departing from Alexandria.[35]

The proposed visit to Egypt added yet another political complication to a voyage that had already strained European relations. It would be the first by a head of state since the beginning of the British occupation (indeed, since the opening of the Suez Canal), and, from the position of Russia and particularly an outraged France, this seemed to be Germany's way of confirming their acceptance of British claims there—a particularly divisive stance during the ongoing Sudan campaign. France's alarm was palpable in the press, with articles in the nationalist *L'Éclair* and conservative *Le Figaro* convinced that this visit could only damage France's position vis-à-vis Britain in Egypt.[36] The tsarist media in Russia too expressed its fears that the German visit might confirm Britain's hold over Egypt, with *Novoye Vremya* reminding Germany that, as a signatory to the 1878 Treaty of Berlin, it had a responsibility to maintain the status quo in the East and that by 'accepting English hospitality' Wilhelm II was in fact placing himself 'on the side of those who have damaged the Berlin Treaty and those who are Germany's competition in Africa'. This seemed at odds, the Russian paper concluded, not only with Germany's treaty obligations but also with the 'complicated and hitherto unexplained plans of German colonial policy.[37]

For his part, Lascelles immediately apprehended the public relations potential of having the German emperor 'see with His own eyes how British administration can deal successfully with an Oriental country'. The prime minister (and foreign minister of long standing), Salisbury, agreed. In Cairo, however, the consul general, Evelyn Baring, Earl of Cromer, was more ambivalent, pointing out that there was no way of knowing what the effect would be of 'launching such an extremely erratic comet as the German Emperor on the political firmament of Egypt. He may do much harm or good.' While agreeing that Wilhelm II should be made welcome in Egypt, Cromer feared that Wilhelm II would make it more difficult to deal with the Khedive of Egypt, Abbas II, particularly if the emperor hinted at Germany's support for him against Britain.[38]

As part of their careful attempt to maintain the charade of Egyptian authority, the British made a great show of ensuring that the formal invitation to Wilhelm II came not from London or Cromer but from the Egyptian Khedive.[39] To their

[35] PAAA R19719, 'Programme für die Reisen Sr Majestät des Kaisers und Königs'.

[36] Below to Hohenlohe, 27 August 1898, in PAAA IA, 'Preussen I (Personalia)', Nr 1 Nr 4v R3730-1 Bd 5, 70–9.

[37] *St Petersburger Zeitung*, quoting *Novoye Vremya*, 23 August 1898, in PAAA IA, 'Preussen I (Personalia)', Nr 1 Nr 4v R3730-1 Bd 5, 44.

[38] Lascelles to Bertie, 19 March 1898, National Archives FO 800/17, 133; Sanderson to Lascelles, 23 March 1898, in National Archives FO 800/8(3), 279; Cromer to Sanderson, 24 March 1898, in National Archives FO 800/8(3), 287–9.

[39] Bülow to the Kaiser, 25 March 1898; Bülow to the Kaiser, 2 April 1898, in PAAA R3729-1 Bd 4, 62–5, 74–5.

annoyance, however, it became clear to the British that Abbas II had taken the opportunity to insist upon accompanying Wilhelm II on his travels south. The Germans informed Thomas Cook that 'the emperor and king must accept the hospitality of the Khedive', which at least came with the additional bonus of five steamers to be placed at their disposal for their journey up the Nile.[40]

The British press made clear that it was not the Khedive, but the British occupation that would benefit from Wilhelm II's visit. *The Times* lauded the German monarch's farsightedness in seemingly accepting and supporting British rule in Egypt, portraying Wilhelm II as Britain's great friend, who had 'always manifested a lively and intelligent interest in the work performed by England in Egypt'. The London paper assured its readers that the emperor would inevitably be impressed by what he would see in Egypt, just as he had been by the reports of Herbert Kitchener's recent victories in the Sudan. As the first European monarch to visit Egypt since the British had arrived, the emperor was to be welcomed as a 'friendly Monarch who has energy to see and intelligence to appreciate the fruits of the great reformation that has been effected since the days of Ismail's transient splendour'.[41]

Wilhelm II's British hunting friend, Lord Lonsdale (Hugh Lowther), was similarly enthusiastic about the trip, pointing out the potential geostrategic and commercial benefits that might accrue, should he visit there. He had learned, he said, that Germany was already enmeshed in some of the most important British plans for Egypt, and he believed that the royal tour would boost Germany's role in 'the three greatest undertakings in Egypt—the National Bank, the Daira Sanieh Properties and the great Irrigation Scheme'. Anglo-German cooperation in Egypt would point the way, he believed, towards establishing 'the most solid alliance in the world', between Britain and Germany.[42]

In the end, however, a plot by several Italian anarchists to assassinate Wilhelm II while he was in Egypt was uncovered in late September 1898.[43] Given the 10 September assassination of the Austrian empress, Elisabeth, by an Italian anarchist, the threat was taken very seriously and had immediate consequences for the German emperor's voyage. The sultan expelled all Italians from Western Anatolia for the duration of the German emperor's trip,[44] and the Egyptian leg of the tour was cancelled. Wilhelm II was 'bitterly disappointed' about having to give up the trip to Egypt, and the German officials who had been dragooned into

[40] Telegram Eulenburg to Thomas Cook, 25 August 1898, in GStAPK BPH Rep 113 Nr 1096, 'Acta betreffend Orient-Reise 1898 (Egypten)', 49. See also BPH Rep 113 Nr 1096, 96–7; Metternich to the German Foreign Office BPH Rep 113 Nr 1096, 42.

[41] *The Times*, 16 June 1898, in PAAA R3729-2 Bd 4, 167–8.

[42] Lonsdale to the Kaiser, 4 August 1898, in GStAPK BPH Rep 53 7 Lit L Nr 12, 23–9.

[43] Bülow, *Denkwürdigkeiten*, vol. 1, 242.

[44] Marschall to Foreign Office, 9 October 1898, in PAAA IA, 'Preussen 1 (Personalia)', Nr 1 Nr 4v R 3731-2 Bd 6, 126–8. For more on the anarchist plot in Egypt, see GStAPK BPH Rep 113 Nr 1096, 'Acta betreffend Orient-Reise 1898', 103–19.

accompanying the emperor on his voyage were similarly disappointed by the axing of what seemed to them to be the most interesting part of the trip. Nonetheless, the emperor reluctantly agreed in early October 1898, just two days after he had signed off on the Khedive's proposed itinerary, that the trip was too risky and that he should skip the Egyptian leg of his voyage and embark for Europe directly from Beirut. Officially, the cancellation was blamed on the seriousness of the Fashoda Incident, which saw Britain and France at daggers drawn in the Sudan, and the pressing need to return home to Germany to open the new Reichstag.[45]

In Britain, regret that the Egyptian leg of the emperor's trip had been cancelled was expressed in the same nationalist tones as the original announcement had been made. Not only had the emperor forgone the opportunity for a 'complete holiday', but he had also missed the chance to 'observe on the spot the stimulus to prosperity which most accounts attribute to the British occupation'.[46]

European Media Fears and Speculation

With the distraction of a side trip to Egypt now ruled out, attention returned to precisely what Wilhelm II had planned for his visit to the Ottoman Empire. Throughout Europe, and particularly in France and Russia, the fear that the German emperor would make a major colonial announcement while visiting Palestine had not abated. The French consul general in Syria reported to Paris that it was expected that Wilhelm II would ask for a territorial concession for a German colony in the vicinity of Homs.[47] So too, the ambassador in St Petersburg, Hugo von Radolin, noted in his correspondence with Chancellor Hohenlohe-Schillingsfürst (a copy of which was sent to Wilhelm II) that the Russian press was circulating the view that Wilhelm II's voyage was intimately connected with German colonization in the Ottoman Empire. The Russians had also made it clear that any major colonial announcement in favour of Germany in Asiatic Turkey would raise the ire of Russia and put the sultan in a very difficult position.[48]

---

[45] Lascelles to Victoria, 19 October 1898, in National Archives FO 800/17, 153; Lascelles to Sanderson, 8 October 1898, National Archives FO 800/17, 153; Kaiser to Marschall, 7 October 1898, in PAAA IA, 'Preussen 1 (Personalia)', Nr 1 Nr 4v R 3731-2 Bd 6, 110; Foreign Office to Ministry of the Interior, 23 September 1898, in PAAA IHA Rep 77 Tit 96 Nr 2 Adh 1 Bd 1, 'Orientreise 1898', 15; Bülow to the Kaiser, 7 October 1898, IA, 'Preussen 1 (Personalia)', Nr 1 Nr 4v R 3731-1 Bd 6, 77–82; Rudolf Vierhaus (ed.), *Das Tagebuch der Baronin Spitzemberg geb. Freiin v. Varnbüler: Aufzeichnungen aus der Hofgesellschaft des Hohenzollernreiches* (Göttingen: Vandenhoeck & Ruprecht, 1976), 377–88; *Norddeutsche Allgemeine Zeitung*, 14 October 1898.

[46] *The Morning Post* (London), 11 October 1898, in PAAA IA, 'Preussen 1 (Personalia)', Nr 1 Nr 4v R 3731-3 Bd 6, 219.

[47] Consul General to Delcassé, 12 August 1898, in Archives diplomatiques NS 166, 'Turquie: politique étrangère', 154–6.

[48] Radolin in St Petersburg to Hohenlohe, 27 August 1898, IA, 'Preussen I (Personalia)', Nr 1 Nr 4v R3730-1 Bd 5, 91.

Indeed, the tsarist press forthrightly warned the sultan that if Germany was granted territorial concessions by the Sublime Porte, Russia and France could rightfully expect the same.[49]

Such warnings were positively mild in comparison with the strident claims made by Vissarion Komarov's popular pan-Slavist organ *Svet*, which argued that Germany was 'openly seeking hegemony in Europe' and in the first instance was looking to annex Ottoman Thessaloniki. Thereafter, the paper maintained, Germany would seek to establish a beachhead in Asia Minor for a 'major route to the Persian Gulf'. This would entail knocking out Orthodox interests in Jerusalem while insinuating the Lutherans and replacing France as the protector of the Catholics. Russia, the pan-Slavist organ insisted, could not allow this to happen, because, if Russia was 'weak in the West', it would lose the 'West Slavic world, the solitary defence against pan-Germanism'. This would see the loss of Russian influence in the Balkan peninsula and German control over the Black Sea, 'directly threatening the interior of Russia itself'.[50]

Alarmed at the virulence of the debate in Russia, Wilhelm II wrote directly to Tsar Nicholas II to smooth the waters. In this 1898 instalment of the Willy/Nicky correspondence he admonished the press and politicians of Europe for indulging in such wild speculation and impressed upon the tsar that the voyage was an expression of personal piety and nothing more:

> I am most astonished at the amount of bosh and blarney that is being ventilated in the newspapers of Europe about my visit to Jerusalem! It is most discouraging to note that the sentiment of real faith which propels a Christian to seek the country in which our Saviour lived and suffered is nearly quite extinct in the so-called better classes of the nineteenth century, so that they must explain the pilgrimage forcibly by political motives. What is right for thousands even of your lowest peasants is right for me too![51]

British reports expressing their belief that Germany was pursuing colonial objectives in the Ottoman Empire were no less plentiful than Russian ones. To British eyes, however, the prospect was less distressing, notwithstanding the expected impact it would have on the European balance of power in Anatolia and the Levant. As one newspaper saw it:

> Everyone knows that to Asia Minor German eyes have long turned as a field for expansion and commerce. Asia Minor has a long Mediterranean littoral; it is the

[49] *St Petersburger Zeitung*, 20 October 1898, IA, 'Preussen 1 (Personalia)', Nr 1 Nr 4v R3732-2 Bd 7, 99.

[50] Radolin in St Petersburg to Chancellor Hohenlohe, 1 July 1898, in PAAA R3729-2 Bd 4, 173.

[51] Kaiser to Tsar, 18 August 1898, in Isaac Don Levine (ed.), *Letters from the Kaiser to the Czar* (New York: Frederick A. Stokes, 1920), 53.

buffer state between Europe and Asia; it is the Western land-gate to the East; it will not remain much longer under the rule of its present suzerain. England has Egypt in that part of the world, France has Tunis, Russia will succeed to at least part of Turkey. The new German Welt-Politik may well foresee the need of a German possession in the Eastern end of the great European midland sea, and the Western end of the continent of Asia. We shall be astonished if the Kaiser's journey is concluded without some indication on his part that such a result is in view... Our own position in that part is practically, if not nominally, secured, and we should welcome any substitution, direct or indirect, of German influence for Turkish misgovernment. France will not view the matter with so much equanimity.[52]

Such optimism about German influence in the region was not isolated, with another British pundit arguing against the prevailing stereotype of Prussian militarism, commenting that 'the Germans are not an aggressive military race; they are now essentially a commercial people, and while our rivals, they have numberless points in common and in sympathy with us English.' All that was needed, it seemed, was a little 'practical common-sense', and the imperial cooperation of the two powers could become permanent, to the benefit of both empires.[53]

Others were less sanguine. In rather more florid terms, *The Spectator* insisted that Wilhelm II's trip to Jerusalem was the beginnings of the emperor's personal plan for mastery of Asia Minor and the first step towards making Constantinople German. The desire to visit the holy sites of Jerusalem was, according to this report, simply a cover for the establishment of the next phase of German colonialism after its African phase. 'Asia Minor, the land between the Tigris and the Euphrates, and Syria...these are the places which the Emperor thinks should someday be claimed by Germany.' This plan, it was warned, would plunge Europe into tumult, given that France and Russia would inevitably contest Germany's Eastern Mediterranean designs.[54] On what the Ottoman sultan might do about this supposed existential threat to his territorial sovereignty the *Spectator* was silent.

For its part, the *Pall Mall Gazette* eschewed such predictions of a coming Eastern crisis, correctly pointing out that Wilhelm II's frequent voyages had never yet resulted in colonial enterprises. Somewhat disingenuously, it pointed out that he often went to Norway, 'restoring cathedrals and in search of scenery and

---

[52] *Daily Chronicle*, 13 October 1898, PAAA IA, 'Preussen 1 (Personalia)', Nr 1 Nr 4v R 3731-3 Bd 6, 228.

[53] 'The German Emperor and Palestine', *The Fortnightly Review*, October 1898, PAAA IA, 'Preussen 1 (Personalia)', Nr 1 Nr 4v R 3731-1 Bd 6, 32.

[54] *The Spectator*, 20 August 1898, clipped in Hatzfeldt to Foreign Office, 21 August 1898, in PAAA IA, 'Preussen I (Personalia)', Nr 1 Nr 4v R3730-1 Bd 5, 45–55. See also the same sentiments in 'Berlin and Constantinople', *The Spectator*, 22 October 1898, PAAA IA, 'Preussen 1 (Personalia)', Nr 1 Nr 4v R3732-2 Bd 7, 71.

whales, without being suspected of designs on the Hardanger Fjord or the whaling stations at Skaarö'. The paper admitted that 'the Palestine jaunt is by no means a Norwegian pleasure cruise' but argued that it was also hardly likely to be the occasion of an ostentatious display of Wilhelmine expansionism. Without denying the prospects for future Great Power disagreement over the partition of the Ottoman Empire—a 'big European fuss', as the author termed it—it was doubtful that the German emperor would initiate it in such a way as to ensure that all of Europe was arrayed against him. Instead, Wilhelm II's trip would simply show that 'even Protestantism has an interest in the Holy Places', while doing 'no harm to German business'. At most, the tour was a 'strategic walk', sizing up the lie of the land, perhaps for long-term military purposes that might be required against an expansionist Russia. It was clear, the report concluded, that the emperor did not want Constantinople for himself, but, to British eyes, he was 'quite right to do everything to strengthen it against the chance of any other Emperor getting it'. And it was certainly in Germany's interests to try and court the 'assistance of the magnificent soldiers of the Turkish army', which would be 'very valuable to whoever has it when Armageddon comes'.[55] It was not surprising, the *Pall Mall Gazette* commented, that the sultan was more amenable towards the German emperor and German interests more generally than towards other European heads of state and business concerns, given the diplomatic support Wilhelm II had given him 'at a time when the whole of Europe was denouncing Abdulhamid, and demanding his deposition'. As long as it remained the case that it was in German interests to preserve the territorial integrity of the Ottoman Empire, Germany would continue to receive preferential treatment. In terms of what the deeper significance of the present voyage was, it was as simple as the fact that the emperor 'is fond of travel' and had long cherished a desire to visit the Holy Land.[56]

Liberal British outlets such as the *Daily Telegraph* and *Daily News* similarly rejected the fears that the emperor was leading a colonial crusade to Jerusalem, seeing instead proof only of the innate wanderlust of the 'distinguished holiday makers' who had, like so many other tourists, booked their trip with the British travel agency Thomas Cook.[57] If he had any colonial aspirations, they were gradualist ones and not unlike those of the rest of Europe's powers, who recognized that 'Turkey is one of those "dying States"...whose remains will one day be divided.' When that day of division came, the *Daily News* opined, it was unsurprising that Germany too might seek to claim a share. Such things, however, lay

---

[55] *Pall Mall Gazette*, 18 August 1898, in PAAA IA, 'Preussen I (Personalia)', Nr 1 Nr 4v R3730-1 Bd 5, 53–4.

[56] 'The Kaiser, the Caliph and the Khedive', *Pall Mall Gazette*, in Hatzfeldt to Hohenlohe, 31 August 1898, in PAAA IA, 'Preussen 1 (Personalia)', Nr1 Nr 4v R3730-2 Bd 5, 102–3.

[57] *The Daily Telegraph*, 20 August 1898, in PAAA IA, 'Preussen I (Personalia)', Nr 1 Nr 4v R3730-1 Bd 5, 55. Using Thomas Cook had put the Kaiser in a difficult position when he was accused of ignoring Germany's oldest travel agent, Carl Stangen Reise-Bureau. See GStAPK BPH Rep113 Nr 1099, 84–103, esp. 89.

in the future, and Britain could watch both Wilhelm II's current journey and Germany's growing relations with the Ottoman Empire 'without jealousy'.[58]

Nonetheless, in some quarters, the view that the German emperor's visit heralded the opening salvo in Germany's colonial march on Palestine remained unshakeable. According to this view, Russia too might be accommodated: 'A slice of Asia Minor from the Aegean to Arabia would suit Germany very well, and would yet leave broad and fertile provinces to satisfy the Russian thirst for acquisition.' Such a German colony would, it was speculated, hold room for ten million Germans, who, in contrast to the current population, would know how to cultivate the land. Only Russian and French claims to Jerusalem could stymie such a plan, and the trickle of Jewish immigration to the region was no impediment. This German colonial plan could not be objected to, it was admitted, by the British. It was simply 'too absurd' for London to 'annex an area equal to France every year or two, and then grumble about the "land hunger" of any other civilized power'. The British could not expect 'a mighty people like the Germans to abstain from asking their share in the great Distribution, or to refrain from anger when their asking is so persistently denied'.[59]

Despite the relaxed attitude of much of the British press towards Wilhelm II's voyage, the same was certainly not true of the nationalist press of Catholic France and Orthodox Russia, states which had long-standing religious rights and imperial aspirations in the Ottoman Empire. Wilhelm II was aware of this, assiduously reading the press clippings sent to him that discussed the impact German penetration of the Ottoman Empire might have, as well as the effects that this might have on European politics. Although not harbouring any concrete plans for a colonial announcement, the emperor was also not opposed to seeing the other empires of Europe take German power in the region seriously. When his London-based ambassador, Paul von Hatzfeldt, drew his attention to a British report which opined that 'a Germanized Turkey would prove a dangerous antagonist to the Russian bear, and equally so to the British lion in Egypt', Wilhelm II enthusiastically wrote 'Yes!' in the report's margin.[60]

Settler Colonialism in the Holy Land: Templers and Zionists

The wild speculation of the British, French, and Russian press did not abate until Wilhelm II had returned to Germany. Indeed, the French were worried enough to

[58] *The Daily News*, 8 October 1898, in PAAA IA, 'Preussen 1 (Personalia)', Nr 1 Nr 4v R 3731-2 Bd 6, 153.

[59] 'The German Emperor's Fixed Idea', *The Spectator*, 8 October 1898 in PAAA IA, 'Preussen 1 (Personalia)', Nr 1 Nr 4v R 3731-2 Bd 6, 152.

[60] Hatzfeldt to Hohenlohe, 30 September 1898, in PAAA IA, 'Preussen 1 (Personalia)', Nr 1 Nr 4v R 3731-1 Bd 6, 17.

dedicate some high-ranking military and foreign office officials to monitor the trip.[61] Although this Europe-wide conjecture was often spectacularly wrong-headed, it was not entirely misplaced, given that there were a number of attempts to entice the German emperor to support colonial plans for the Ottoman Empire. At least one of these plans gained his early support.

Beyond the trade-related infiltration of Asia Minor desired by those hoping to win infrastructure contracts, the most prominent German plan for settler coloni-alism in the Holy Land came from the Württemberg Templers. The Templers had arrived in Palestine in 1869 as a radical Pietist movement that had decided to occupy the Holy Land in preparation for the Second Coming.[62] Having gradually moved away from their millenarian beginnings towards a more secular form of settler colonialism, the Templers saw the emperor's visit as an opportunity to gar-ner royal support for their plans to expand their Palestinian colonies in places such as Sarona and Jaffa. Some months before the tour, the Templer leadership petitioned the emperor for an audience at one of their colonies where they might present him with a proposal.[63] To their great delight, Wilhelm II assented to a meeting.[64] Despite their joy at the prospects of a royal visit, the Templers remained cautious, conceding that the emperor's impending tour might be a sign of his benevolence and goodwill towards Germany's expatriate colonists,[65] but that the real purpose of his visit to Palestine centred around the dedication of the evangelical Church of the Redeemer in Jerusalem.[66]

In Germany, where private sector settler colonies had long been seen by liberal imperialists as a means of expanding German territory,[67] expectations for the meeting with the Templers were high. The national-liberal press in particular wrote warmly of the Templers' colonial endeavours in Palestine, expressing the hope that Wilhelm II's visit would offer them the help they needed. The Templers were the vanguard of German colonialism, it was argued, who were maintaining and strengthening 'the dominant position of Germandom in Palestine'. To ensure that this dominance was not threatened, new German farmers and pastoralists

---

[61] Eulenberg to Bülow, 11 October 1898, in PAAA IA, 'Preussen 1 (Personalia)', Nr 1 Nr 4v R 3731-2 Bd 6, 184.

[62] Matthew P. Fitzpatrick and Felicity Jensz, 'Between Heaven and Earth: The German Templer Colonies in Palestine', in Andrekos Varnava (ed.), *Imperial Expectations and Realities: El Dorados, Utopias and Dystopias* (Manchester: Manchester University Press, 2015), 144–65.

[63] Letter to Kaiser's Ober-Hofmarshallamt from Chr Hoffmann, Vorsteher der Templegemeinde Jerusalem, July 1898, in GStAPK BPH Rep113 Nr 1098, 102. See also Alex Carmel and Ejal Jakob Eisler, *Der Kaiser reist ins Heilige Land: Die Palästinareise Wilhelms II: 1898* (Stuttgart: Kohlhammer, 1999), 52.

[64] Reply from Wilhelmshöhe, 7 Aug 1898 in GStAPK BPH Rep113 Nr 1098, 1898', 103.

[65] 'Orientpost', *Die Warte*, 17 February 1898, in Alex Carmel, *Palästina-Chronik 1883–1914* (Langenau-Ulm: Vaas, 1983), 200–1.

[66] Paul Sauer, *Uns rief das Heilige Land: Die Tempelgesellschaft im Wandel der Zeit* (Stuttgart: Theiss, 1985), 85.

[67] Matthew P. Fitzpatrick, 'Imperialism from Below: Informal Empire and the Private Sector in Nineteenth-Century Germany', *Australian Journal of Politics and History*, 54 no.3 (2008), 358–72.

needed to join them, and this required a coordinated government approach and the unambiguous support of the German state. 'It would be excellent', one newspaper enthused, 'if a concrete decision in this direction could be made by the time of the Kaiser's arrival.'[68] No matter how energetic the Templers were, and no matter how exciting the emperor's visit to them was, the success of his journey for the nation could only be measured by its success in strengthening and expanding these colonies. A passing royal visit could do nothing alone. Germany also had to 'declare the goal of establishing new colonies under the protection of our Kaiser'.[69]

Other liberal newspapers also came out strongly in favour of expanding Germany's colonial presence in Palestine, described as a site where German colonists could maintain their characteristic 'Germanness'. The Templers were commended for their perseverance in the face of ongoing land disputes with the Ottoman authorities and their hard work, which had transformed 'the desert into an orchard'. With the emperor's visit heightening interest in these endeavours, it continued, the chances of a truly German colony in Palestine had greatly increased, with sites such as Haifa ready for planned German emigration.[70] The Templers were also presented as model colonists by liberal British commentators, who professed admiration for 'their neat dwellings and well-ordered institutions', which they contrasted in Orientalist terms with the 'squalor and misrule existing around'. Whether the emperor's visit would do them any good, however, was less clear, although it seemed to be the case, one report noted, that Wilhelm II saw them as 'a sort of vanguard for a German movement in Asia'.[71]

The Templers in Haifa spent the time before the emperor's arrival busily discussing their plans for maximizing the advantages that their colony and the city of Haifa might gain through 'the presence of the Kaiser'. In particular, the colonists hoped that Wilhelm II's visit might add impetus to the long-mooted Jezreel Valley railway between Haifa and Damascus which the British had begun, but then halted when its British backer had been declared bankrupt. The Templers dared to hope that, with the emperor's assistance, a German company might be granted the concession to finish the railway, so that the 'German colony can maintain its dominance and not too many foreign elements can insinuate themselves there'.[72]

Beyond their hopes for colonial expansion, Wilhelm II's visit was viewed as an important opportunity for the Templers to resolve in their favour a serious land

[68] *National-Zeitung*, 3 July 1898.
[69] 'Zur Reise des Kaisers nach Palästina', *National-Zeitung*, 13 September 1898, in GStAPK BPH Rep 113 Nr 1092 1898, 138–9.
[70] *Hamburger Nachrichten*, 21 October 1898.
[71] *Daily Telegraph*, 29 September 1898, in GStAPK BPH Rep 113 Nr 1092 1898, 'Acta betreffend Orient-Reise 1898', 199–202; *Daily Telegraph*, 18 October 1898, in PAAA IA, 'Preussen 1 (Personalia)' Nr 1 Nr 4v R 3731-3 Bd 6, 265–6.
[72] 'Vorbereitung für den Kaiserbesuch in Palästina', *Deutsche Warte*, 29 June 1898 (read by Kaiser, 2 July), in PAAA R3729-2 Bd 4, 171.

dispute they had been experiencing with the Ottoman authorities for more than half a decade. According to the Templers, local Ottoman officials had summarily changed their land title from freehold to a lifetime lease potentially extinguishable upon the death of the leaseholder.[73] With the ability of settlers to bequeath their property in perpetuity to their children apparently now lost, the dispute jeopardized the long-term prospects of the Templer colonies. The issue had been followed closely in the German press, and Wilhelm II's visit was also seen in Germany as an opportunity to settle the matter.[74]

In this matter, perhaps as a result of the goodwill generated by the royal visit, the Templers had some success. Notwithstanding the dangerous precedent it might potentially set for those seeking to colonize Ottoman territory, at the end of 1898, the land issue was suddenly resolved in the Templer's favour, with the sultan decreeing that the Templers be issued with title deeds to all non-state land in their possession.[75] This, however, is as far as their success extended during the royal visit. During his visit Wilhelm II did not offer any public support for German colonial plans in the Levant and was deliberately evasive about the type of support Germany might offer the Templers. No promise of state assistance for expanding the colonies appeared in his multiple speeches directed towards the Templers. Instead, the emperor offered blandishments in praise of the Templers' cultural role in assisting the sultan in raising the standard of living of his subjects.[76] Wilhelm II assured the Templers that he was 'greatly pleased' by the good example they had set their Arab neighbours, which had earned them and Germany a good reputation. He also offered them the vague promise of his protection 'irrespective of confession' as part of Germany's broader commitment to offer 'its enduring protection to its citizens abroad'.[77] There was, however, no indication that Wilhelm II supported the nationalization or an increase in the extent of the German colonies already in Palestine.

With no progress made during the emperor's visit, the following year German civil society again took matters into its own hands, establishing the Society for the Assistance of German Settlers in Palestine in Stuttgart, with the aim of assisting the 'vanguard of German work in the Orient'. Wilhelm II even offered the

---

[73] For an extended discussion of this issue, see Fitzpatrick and Jensz, 'Between Heaven and Earth', 144–65.

[74] *Berliner Neueste Nachrichten*, 6 March 1898. See also articles from 31 May 1898 and 6 July 1898, and the *Münchener Allgemeine Zeitung*, 4 June 1898.

[75] Helmut Glenk, *From Desert Sands to Golden Oranges: The History of the German Templer Settlement of Sarona in Palestine 1871–1947* (Victoria, BC: Trafford, 2005), 30.

[76] 'Die Kaisertage in Palästina', *Die Warte*, 1 December 1898, in Carmel, *Palästina-Chronik 1883–1914*, 206–8; 'Die Kaisertage in Palästina (Fortsetzung II)', *Die Warte*, 8 December 1898, in Carmel, *Palästina-Chronik 1883–1914*, 213–14.

[77] *Norddeutsche Allgemeine Zeitung*, 3 November 1898; also reproduced in the Templer periodical, *Die Warte*: see 'Die Kaisertage in Palästina (Fortsetzung II)', *Die Warte*, 8 December 1898, in Carmel, *Palästina-Chronik 1883–1914*, 213–14.

association a modest amount of seed funding.[78] The German Colonial Society also continued to lobby for support for the Templers after the emperor's visit, arguing that, as a result of the royal visit, the German people had been alerted to the importance of the Templers to the future of German influence in the Orient.[79] In the Reichstag, Wilhelm II's visit also framed the 1899 appeal of the Württemberg National Liberal Johannes Hieber to the foreign secretary, Bernhard von Bülow, that he ensure the property rights of the 'Swabian' Templers would be protected. This protection, Hieber argued, would represent 'a welcome service to one of the best and oldest German colonizing endeavours'.[80] Bülow responded in the same Delphic manner as the monarch had while in Palestine, replying that he had visited the Templer colonies himself the previous year and that Germany would 'continue to support the interests of these colonies in the future where possible, and those particular matters raised by the previous speaker will receive careful and sympathetic scrutiny'.[81] Neither the emperor nor his government, however, saw the visit as an opportunity to expand German settler colonies in the Ottoman Empire.

It was not only Christian colonists who sought out the emperor's help in convincing Sultan Abdulhamid II to allow a protectorate in Palestine. Theodor Herzl, the intellectual leader of Europe's Zionist movement, had also sought to enlist the assistance of Wilhelm II for his plan for a Jewish settler colony there. The Zionists' plan to colonize Palestine was hardly a secret, having been the focus of high-profile congresses in Basel in August 1897 and 1898, and the European press had reacted with interest to Wilhelm II's seeming desire to assist the project to establish a settler colonial Jewish state in the Levant. To some commentators, it was seen as self-evident that, with so many Zionists being German, Wilhelm II could not be an 'indifferent spectator' to their cause. Indeed, by October 1898 some British newspapers, such as *The Globe* in London, were seemingly already resigned to the idea that the sultan would inevitably lose Jerusalem, 'just as he had lost Egypt'. The main question was whether a future German-sponsored Zionist colony would close its doors to British trade, locking it out of the Levant. Irrespective of who ultimately took the city and its surrounds, the British paper demanded that 'The open door must be preserved.'[82]

These concerns about the future tariff policies of a German-Jewish state in Ottoman Palestine were spectacularly premature. While Wilhelm II harboured a primarily antisemitic interest and even enthusiasm for the idea of assisting

[78] 'Aufruf zur Förderung der deutschen Ansiedlungen in Palästina', October 1899, in *BA* Berlin R901/31731. The appeal was repeated in 1904. See also Sauer, *Uns rief das Heilige Land*, 89.

[79] Erwin von Rupp to (Foreign Office), 3 February 1899, *BA* Berlin R901/30185.

[80] Johannes Hieber, 11 March 1899, in *Verhandlungen des Reichstages*, vol. 166: *1898/1900*, 1497–8.

[81] Bernhard von Bülow, 11 March 1899, in *Verhandlungen des Reichstages*, vol. 166: *1898/1900*, 1498.

[82] *The Globe*, 17 October 1898, in PAAA IA, 'Preussen 1 (Personalia)' Nr 1 Nr 4v R 3731-3 Bd 6, 264.

German Jews emigrate to far-off Palestine, he was in no position to demand that the sultan sacrifice his territory to the Zionists or to instruct his Foreign Office to assist such a brazenly anti-Ottoman venture. Despite Wilhelm II's declaration that he was 'convinced that the settlement of the Holy Land through the capital-rich and hard-working nation of Israel' would benefit Palestine with 'unimaginable blossoming and blessings', his enthusiasm carried no weight in the real world of politics.[83]

That the emperor was not the author of German foreign policy was, however, something that Theodor Herzl learned too late. For much of the second half of 1898 it was clear that Herzl laboured under the misapprehension that the emperor enjoyed untrammelled freedom in directing Germany's foreign affairs. When he was told in early October 1898 that Wilhelm II was not only interested but very enthusiastic about a Zionist colony under German protection and that Wilhelm II was keen to meet a deputation of Zionists in Jerusalem, he allowed himself to imagine that the foundation of a Jewish colony in Jerusalem under royal German protection was a fait accompli.[84]

Had he been looking, there were early warning signs that might have given Herzl pause for thought. When Herzl met with Foreign Secretary Bülow, first in Vienna in September 1898 and then again with Chancellor Hohenlohe in Berlin in October, it was made very clear to him that not only were they unimpressed by his plans for a Jewish state in the heart of the Ottoman Empire but also they did not believe that the Turks were remotely interested in giving up such a vitally important region either. Having met them without Wilhelm II present, Herzl was left to wonder how their attitude could be so 'depressingly cool' towards his plans when the emperor was so positively engaged. In a moment of political clarity, Herzl permitted himself the private worry in his diary that convincing the German monarch might not be enough to ensure the success of Zionism's settler colonial plans. He reminded himself that 'the most glittering intentions of this inspired Kaiser are often subsequently corrected, disclaimed and altered by his advisers.' Quite often, Herzl mused, the emperor 'has not been able to carry out his best decisions. So careful!'[85]

Herzl's doubts about the limitations of the royal prerogative were, however, short lived. Despite being vaguely aware of the emperor's inability to dictate German foreign policy (or indeed the attitude of his ministers towards it), Herzl cast his doubts aside when he met Wilhelm II in Constantinople on 18 October 1898. The Zionist leader was entirely star-struck as the monarch greeted him for a personal audience (with Bülow also in attendance) to discuss the Zionists' colonizing objectives. Herzl remained undeterred as the emperor jibed at him in a

---

[83] Wilhelm II, 29 September 1898, in Benner, *Die Strahlen der Krone*, 219.
[84] Theodor Herzl, *Tagebücher*, vol. 2 (Berlin: Jüdischer Verlag, 1923), 145–55.
[85] Herzl, *Tagebücher*, vol. 2, 160–4. See also Benner, *Die Strahlen der Krone*, 224–5.

distinctly antisemitic vein, expressing his support for ridding Germany of Jewish usurers and socialists and observing that the Jews would not be short of money or numbers for the successful colonization of Palestine. Herzl also ploughed on through the monarch's bewildering asides about the Dreyfus affair in France. Eventually, he managed to bring the emperor's attention back to the details of his plan.[86]

After a long and detailed explanation of Zionism's objectives, Wilhelm II expressed his certainty that the Ottoman Sultan would listen to him, given that he was the only ruler to have supported him, and that German Jews would enthusiastically embrace Herzl's colonial plans if they knew that 'they were under his protection, that they were not, so to speak, leaving Germany'. Despite Bülow's continual attempts to point out the deficiencies in Herzl's plans, the Zionist leader felt that Wilhelm II remained enthusiastic, with the monarch commenting that the plan made great sense to him and that it would certainly make 'an impression, if the German Kaiser looked after this and showed an interest in it'. Checking the clock and getting up to leave, the emperor promised to 'work through' Herzl's proposal for a Jewish 'chartered company under German protection'. Herzl left the meeting with the impression that Wilhelm II was prepared to support his plan for a Zionist colony when he discussed the matter with Abdulhamid II.[87]

Once again, however, when Herzl moved beyond the heated enthusiasm of the emperor, the 'icy winds of the reasons of state' blew.[88] As soon as the monarch had left them, Bülow flatly informed Herzl that 'the Turks are currently unfavourably disposed' towards a German-Jewish colony in Palestine.[89] While Wilhelm II might enthusiastically entertain supporting a plan he could not enact, Herzl was given a clear warning by Bülow that a Zionist colony under German protection was simply not a viable direction for German policy, given the material fact of Ottoman antipathy towards the plan.

Unsurprisingly, given Wilhelm II's seeming early enthusiasm, Herzl was deeply disappointed by his second and third meetings with Wilhelm II in Jerusalem. The second was a short, roadside exchange of pleasantries on 29 October, a meeting later commemorated in a famous photomontage of the meeting (see Figure 3.2). However, the third was a more formal meeting at the royal tent on 2 November.[90] At this meeting, Herzl was left confused by Wilhelm II's guarded statement that the Zionists' proposal was very interesting but required further study and debate. Stopping well short of endorsing Herzl's plan, the emperor now commented that both the Templer colonies and the Jewish settlements had shown how the land might be developed, including by the existing population, before he lapsed into

---

[86] Herzl, *Tagebücher*, vol. 2, 189–98.   [87] Herzl, *Tagebücher*, vol. 2, 189–98.

[88] John C. G. Röhl, *Wilhelm II: Der Aufbau der persönlichen Monarchie 1888–1900* (Munich: C. H. Beck, 2001), 1056.

[89] Herzl, *Tagebücher*, vol. 2, 183–99.   [90] Herzl, *Tagebücher*, vol. 2, 209–10.

Figure 3.2 Photomontage of two images created to replicate the meeting of Herzl and Wilhelm II in Jerusalem, 1898

another antisemitic aside that the plan appeared expensive but that the Jews must certainly have enough money, 'more money than us all'. Thereafter, Herzl had scarcely enough time to blurt out his plans to rebuild Jerusalem before Wilhelm II stuck out his hand and wished him good day. The audience was at an end.[91]

The brevity of the November Jerusalem meeting and the emperor's evasiveness were better understood by Herzl once he read Wilhelm II's comments to the European press at the time in which he stated (in accordance with Ottoman policy on foreign settlements) that he could only support endeavours 'that were aimed at improving the agriculture of Palestine so as to maximize the benefit to the Turkish Empire, with full respect for the sovereignty of the sultan'. There was to be no German protectorate in Palestine or a Jewish colony under the German emperor's royal protection. This swift reversal in the fortunes of the Zionist movement, Herzl surmised, could only be the work of Foreign Secretary Bülow.[92]

---

[91] Herzl *Tagebücher*, vol. 2, 222–6.
[92] Herzl, *Tagebücher*, vol. 2, 237–8. See also Anon., *Das deutsche Kaiserpaar im heiligen Lande im Herbst 1898* (Berlin: Ernst Siegfried Mittler und Sohn, 1899), 287–8.

It is true that Bülow had made clear to Herzl and Wilhelm II wherever possible that he simply did not believe that the Zionists' plans could be realized. To blame Bülow personally for Herzl's lack of success, however, is misleading. Wilhelm II had never been in a position to make such a drastic foreign policy decision on Germany's behalf, and the real resistance to the plan rested with those it affected the most, namely the Ottoman government. In reality, Bülow had only given him forewarning of the firm position of Sultan Abdulhamid II and his Foreign Ministry. As Mim Kemal Öke has argued, 'It was Abdulhamid II himself who laid the cornerstone of the Ottoman reaction toward the Zionists.'[93] Bülow made this clear in his later memoirs, where he described the abrupt end to Wilhelm II's interest in Zionism once he was confronted by the sultan with the reality that Palestine was not the German monarch's to offer. As Bülow later wrote, 'Wilhelm II was initially fire and flame in favour of the Zionist idea, because he hoped in this way to rid his country of several elements that were not particularly sympathetic towards him.' Once it was made clear to him by the Turks that 'the sultan did not want to hear about Zionism or about an independent Jewish state, he dropped the Zionist notion.'[94]

It was the sultan, and not Bülow, who ended the late nineteenth-century attempt to found a Zionist colony in Palestine under German auspices. Abdulhamid II dealt brusquely with the suggestion that he should carve out a colony for Herzl's imperial dream, arguing that he would not and could not sell 'a single foot of land, because it belongs not to me but to my people'. To this he added the parting jibe that 'If my empire is one day partitioned, they might get Palestine for nothing. Our corpse might be stripped, but I will never agree to vivisection.'[95]

Throughout his dalliance with Zionism, Wilhelm II had exhibited no real affection for either Germany's Jews or the Jewish *Yishuv* in Palestine. Apart from his continual insinuations that the appeal of Zionism was its capacity to rid him of unwanted elements of the German population, his private letters home from the Holy Land made clear his visceral dislike of the Jews he had encountered there. In a letter home to his mother on 20 November 1898 that dripped with antisemitism, he complained of 6,000 Jews 'greasy and squalid, cringing and abject, doing nothing but making themselves obnoxious to Christian and Muslims alike by trying to fleece these neighbours of every farthing they manage to earn'. Of the people on whose behalf he had promised to intercede to help build a settler

[93] Mim Kemal Öke, 'The Ottoman Empire, Zionism, and the Question of Palestine (1880–1908)', *International Journal of Middle East Studies* 14, No. 3 (1982), 329–41, Bülent Kemal Öke, 'Zionists and the Ottoman Foreign Ministry during the Reign of Abdulhamid II (1876–1909)', *Arab Studies Quarterly* 2 no.4 (1980), 364–74.

[94] Bülow, *Denkwürdigkeiten*, vol. 1, 254.

[95] Röhl, *Wilhelm II: Der Aufbau der persönlichen Monarchie*, 1057.

colony, he remarked 'Shylocks by the score!'[96] Wilhelm II's Zionism was a product of his antisemitic interest in the idea of Jews leaving Germany for Palestine. As his chancellor and foreign secretary knew perfectly well, however, this plan had no chance of success, given Abdulhamid II's determination to safeguard his territorial sovereignty.

German Catholicism and Capital

If Wilhelm II had initially wished to support the creation of a Jewish state under German protection in Palestine, he was far more circumspect in his approach to the question of assisting German Catholics to acquire a piece of vacant land in Jerusalem reputed to be where the Virgin Mary had lived and died. The site, long coveted by the French, was known as *Dormitio Sanctae Mariae Virginis*, and a Catholic organization, the German Association in the Holy Land, was hoping that the emperor's visit would help it secure the site so that they could build a chapel on it.[97] In a direct inversion of the situation regarding Zionism, this was not a royal plan: rather, it originated with Bülow and the Foreign Office, who had to push Wilhelm II very hard to approach the sultan for the purchase of the vacant land. Contrasting with his stance on Herzl's settler colonial plans, the emperor was against approaching Abdulhamid II, citing the sensitivities of the Turks to suggestions that they relinquish their land in Germany's favour. Eventually, however, he followed Bülow's lead and agreed to bring up the issue, on the proviso that 'the Mohammedans have absolutely nothing against it; otherwise under no circumstances'.[98]

The emperor may have been uninterested in this small plot of land, but Bülow ardently wanted to procure it as a sign to German Catholics (and indeed to France) of Germany's ability to champion the interests of its Catholic subjects in the Holy Land. In this domestically charged piece of foreign policy, Bülow found a willing accomplice in Marschall, who shared his foreign secretary's commitment to pricking French pretensions in the region. It was Marschall who duly presented the sultan with the request to purchase the land so that it might be given as a gift by him to Wilhelm II, who in turn would give the land to the German Catholic Association in Jerusalem.[99] In many ways, the plan was designed to echo the circumstances surrounding the gift of land made to Prince

---

[96] Carmel and Eisler, *Der Kaiser reist ins Heilige Land*, 173–4.

[97] On this and the consequences for Franco-German rivalry in the Ottoman Empire, see Naci Yorulmaz, *Arming the Sultan: German Arms Trade and Personal Diplomacy in the Ottoman Empire before World War I* (London: I. B. Tauris, 2014), 135–7.

[98] Benner, *Die Strahlen der Krone*, 200.

[99] Anon., *Das deutsche Kaiserpaar im Heiligen Lande*, 261–2. For Bülow and Marschall's careful management of the issue of German Catholics in Palestine, see Benner, *Die Strahlen der Krone*, 190–205.

Friedrich Wilhelm in 1869, which had also been suggested by the German side and facilitated by Prussia's diplomatic representative to the Porte.[100]

Unlike the settler colonial plans of the Templers and Herzl, the gift of a small plot of land for religious purposes did not injure the sovereign rights of the Ottoman Empire and the sultan duly assented to the gift. At 4 p.m. on 31 October, the formal transfer was made in a ceremony attended by Wilhelm II, his retinue, the Catholic Patriarch Piavi, the leadership of the German hospice in Jerusalem, and German Franciscans, along with a large number of Turkish officials. In his speech during the ceremony, Wilhelm II overtly compared the sultan's gift of this land with that to his father twenty-nine years earlier which had enabled the building of the Church of the Redeemer which he had opened that morning. Transferring this new gift to German Catholics, he hoped, would be a 'blessing' for his 'Catholic subjects, especially for their endeavours in the Holy Land'.[101] The Prussian anthem was played, and the senior German Catholic cleric in Jerusalem, Father Schmidt, 'gave thanks in a warm-hearted, patriotic, truly German speech' that made clear the domestic political capital that the gift of land had earned for the emperor.[102] As a result of this gift, Schmidt proclaimed, 'The loyalty of your Catholic subjects shall remain strong forever and ever.'[103] As another eyewitness later wrote, the gift had demonstrated not only the emperor's dedication to his Catholic subjects but that the Protestant emperor could assist all of the Catholics of the world in securing a holy site for Catholicism that the French, despite their much vaunted protectorate rights, could not.[104] Securing the land had been a modest domestic and foreign policy coup for Bülow and Marschall. Characteristically, however, it was the emperor, who had doubted the wisdom of the undertaking, who was lauded.

Religious matters aside, perhaps the most often remarked upon 'success' of Wilhelm II's visit to the Holy Land was that it facilitated increased access for German capital to the Ottoman Empire. Indeed, many historians assume that Wilhelm's tour was conceived with vigorous lobbying for German control over the Baghdad Railway in mind, with the royal visit a Trojan horse campaign enabling the extension of German commercial control over Asia Minor. According to this view, the summit diplomacy of the emperor was crucial to delivering the contract to German investors, and 'Wilhelm II was, so to speak, the highest lobbyist

---

[100] For Friedrich Wilhelm's account of the acquisition of the land, see Hans Rothfels (ed.), *Tagebuch meiner Reise nach dem Morgenlande 1869* (Frankfurt am Main: Propyläen, 1971), 36–7.

[101] Anon., *Das deutsche Kaiserpaar im Heiligen Lande*, 258.

[102] Ernst von Mirbach, *Die Reise des Kaisers und der Kaiserin nach Palästina* (Berlin: Ernst Siegfried Mittler und Sohn, 1899), 57–8.

[103] Anon., *Das deutsche Kaiserpaar im Heiligen Lande*, 259.

[104] Ludwig Schneller, *Das Kaiserfahrt durch's heilige Land* (Leipzig: Kommissionsverlag von Wallmann, 1899), 142–6.

for German capital.'[105] The British were certainly aware that the project's financier, Georg von Siemens, and Wilhelm II would be in the same place at the same time and surmised that this was no accident.[106] In a strange inversion of the political and economic order of things in the German Empire, this view contends that 'the Kaiser and his ambassador were the driving force, with Georg von Siemens and the Deutsche Bank the driven.'[107]

There is very little evidence to suggest, however, that the emperor played any role in negotiations between German business interests and the Sublime Porte. While the long-desired concession to the Haydarpasha Port was granted to the Anatolian Railway Company upon the occasion (but not because) of Wilhelm II's visit, more than a year of hard-fought diplomacy would still be needed before Georg von Siemens's Deutsche Bank consortium (not 'Germany') would be granted a preliminary agreement—and this only after it had loaned the Ottoman Empire 3.5 million marks. In fact, a final concession would not be granted to the bank until 5 March 1903.[108] To the extent that German officials were involved, it was Ambassador Marschall and Chancellor Hohenlohe who had been coordinating their actions in support of a solely German Baghdad Railway since April 1898,[109] but even their concerted efforts had not brought definitive success, again because the sultan was under pressure from his own ministers not to offer any concessions to the Germans. As the French ambassador's reports to Paris made clear, although the sultan had raised the matter of railways in a private meeting with Wilhelm II, who promised to inform German financiers of the sultan's interest,[110] the stiff opposition of the Council of Ministers (particularly the Ministry of War) ensured that the sultan did not go any further.[111]

Most German accounts from the time that covered the voyage were steadfastly uninterested in the role of the railway in the visit. One semi-official account of the

---

[105] Klaus Polkehn, 'Wilhelm II. in Konstaninopel: Der politische Startschuß zum Bau der Bagdadbahn', in Jaschinski and Waldschmidt (eds), *Des Kaisers Reise in den Orient 1898*, 62. See also Röhl, *Wilhelm II: Der Aufbau der persönlichen Monarchie*, 73. For a useful corrective to this, see Florian Krobb, '"Welch unbebautes und riesengroßes Feld": Turkey as Colonial Space in German World War I Writings', *German Studies Review* 37, no. 1 (2014), 1.

[106] *National-Zeitung*, 20 October 1898, in PAAA IA, 'Preussen 1 (Personalia)', Nr 1 Nr 4v R 3731-3 Bd 6, 269.

[107] Alexander Honold, 'Nach Bagdad und Jerusalem: Die Wege des wilhelminischen Orientalismus', in Alexander Honold and Oliver Simons (eds), *Kolonialismus als Kultur: Literatur, Medien, Wissenschaft in der deutschen Gründerzeit des Fremden* (Tübingen: Francke, 2002), 151.

[108] Murat Özyüksel, *The Hejaz Railway and the Ottoman Empire: Modernity, Industrialisation and Ottoman Decline* (London: I. B. Tauris, 2014), 23–4.

[109] Jonathon McMurray, *Distant Ties: Germany, the Ottoman Empire, and the Construction of the Baghdad Railway* (Westport, CT: Praeger, 2001), 30–1. As Robert J. Kerner once wrote, 'Marschall von Bieberstein created the Bagdad Railway.' See Robert J. Kerner, 'The Mission of Liman von Sanders: I: Its Origin', *Slavonic Review* 6, no.16 (1927), 27.

[110] Cambon to Delcassé, 25 October 1898, in Archives diplomatiques, Paris, NS 166, 'Turquie: Politique étrangère', 175.

[111] Cambon to Delcassé, 26 October 1898, in Archives diplomatiques, Paris, NS 166, 'Turquie: Politique étrangère', 178–85.

visit mentioned the monarch's short one-way trip on the 'under German management Anatolian Railway' to open the end station of Haydarpasha, but no mention was made of any plans for any extension.[112] Another noted only that the royals took an 'interesting trip on the Anatolian Railway', and only then because Bülow had personally written to the author reminding him of it.[113] A third travelogue completely ignored anything that happened before Wilhelm II reached Palestine.[114]

While the royal visit may have assisted in improving the atmospherics surrounding the negotiations for the railway, Wilhelm II only briefly came into contact with the Anatolian Railway and did not give any impression of being particularly interested in it. The closest the emperor came to railway politics was presiding over a short ceremony in Constantinople to award Siemens a minor German honour.[115] Others, however, were far more interested in making use of the visit to assist German commerce. Ambassador Marschall, Chancellor Hohenlohe, and Foreign Secretary Bülow had been closely coordinating their actions since April 1898 in support of those mounting a bid for the Baghdad Railway contract.[116] It was Bülow who met with Georg von Siemens during their time in Constantinople and, during the trip on the Anatolian Railway, Siemens spoke with Bülow once again. With his own work in mind, Bülow's correspondence from the time dared to hope that 'the repercussions of the royal voyage will hopefully make themselves felt on the banks of the Euphrates.'[117]

It is clear that Wilhelm II was not involved in the discussions in which Siemens outlined what he required from the German government for the Baghdad Railway to be made feasible for the sultan and for German investors.[118] Not only was the German Kaiser not involved in the negotiations, but when asked point-blank by Bülow to intervene on behalf of Siemens, Wilhelm II flatly refused, citing strict instructions from the Prussian finance minister, Johannes von Miquel, that he was not to do so.[119] Tellingly, the idea of showcasing German railway interests during the royal visit came extremely late. It was not until August 1898 that Siemens made contact with Eulenburg to enquire whether Wilhelm II might like to visit the German enterprise's rail line and take a brief trip on the Anatolian

---

[112] Anon., *Das deutsche Kaiserpaar im Heiligen Lande*, 69.
[113] Mirbach, *Die Reise des Kaisers und der Kaiserin*, 14; Bülow to Mirbach, 26 March 1899, in Lepsius, Mendelssohn Bartholdy, and Thimme (eds), *Die Grosse Politik der Europäischen Kabinette1871–1914*, vol. 12 (2), 579–80.
[114] Schneller, *Die Kaiserfahrt durch's heilige Land*.
[115] PAAA IA, 'Preussen I (Personalia)', Nr 1 Nr 4v R3732-1 Bd 7, 18.
[116] Jonathon McMurray, *Distant Ties*, 30–1.
[117] Bülow to Müller, 15 November 1898, in Lepsius, Mendelssohn Bartholdy and Thimme (eds), *Die Grosse Politik der Europäischen Kabinette 1871–1914*, vol. 12 (2), 579.
[118] Bülow, *Denkwürdigkeiten*, vol. 1, 253.
[119] Karl Helfferich, *Georg von Siemens: Ein Lebensbild aus Deutschlands großer Zeit*, vol. 3 (Berlin: Springer, 1923), 87–8; Bülow, *Denkwürdigkeiten*, vol. 1, 253.

Railway.[120] With real control over the project resting largely with the sultan and his ministers, the only partially successful push for German interests to gain the contract to build the Baghdad Railway was driven at the German end by the combined energies of German capital and the Bülow-led Foreign Office, and not by the emperor, who had been expressly forbidden to do so by his finance minister.[121]

Champion of Christianity and Islam

With the Redeemer Church formally opened and a new plot of religiously significant land secured for German Catholics, Wilhelm II's Jerusalem visit had demonstrated royal support for the two main Christian denominations of Germany. To this extent, the emperor's voyage had some salutary effects on the religious sensibilities of his subjects and demonstrated the monarch's apparent willingness to take concrete steps to support German Catholics, an important gesture two decades after the *Kulturkampf*. Prior to leaving Germany, the emperor had insisted that his trip was purely religious in nature, and it was certainly religion and the politics of religion that had stood in the foreground during the royal tour.

Yet, far from deepening his Christian faith, Wilhelm II left the Ottoman Empire far more impressed with Islam than with the squabbling factions of Christianity. Very famously, in Damascus on 8 December he offered a toast to Sultan Abdulhamid II in which he spontaneously proclaimed that the world's 300 million Muslims had an eternal friend in the German emperor—a speech that sent a shiver down the imperial spines of Britain and France, which ruled over so many of them.[122] In the Islamic world, this professed appreciation of Islam even saw rumours abound that Wilhelm II had become a Muslim who had undertaken the hajj *incognito*.[123] Less well known, however, is the emperor's letter to the tsar from Damascus in which he confirmed his personal admiration for Islam:

> My personal feeling in leaving the Holy City was that I felt profoundly ashamed before the Moslems and that if I had come there without any Religion at all I certainly would have turned Mahommetan! The way religion is understood in Jerusalem, it will never lead to the conversion of a single Moslem...I am afraid that religion in Jerusalem is often used by the clergies as a cover for political devices and designs and that it is very wrong and does Christianity a very great

---

[120] Siemens to Eulenburg, 30 August 1898, in GStAPK, BPH Rep113 Nr 1102, 'Acta betreffend Orientreise 1898', 13–15. Eulenburg to Siemens, 31 August 1898, in GStAPK BPH Rep113 Nr 1102, 16.

[121] Yorulmaz, *Arming the Sultan*, 141–2.

[122] Fritz Fischer erroneously saw this as a calculated move inspired by Max von Oppenheim to spark a pan-Islamic revolt against France, Russia, and Britain: Fritz Fischer, *Griff nach der Weltmacht* (Düsseldorf: Droste Verlag, 1961), 142–3.

[123] Peter Hopkirk, *On Secret Service East of Constantinople: The Plot to Bring Down the British Empire* (New York: Oxford University Press, 1994), 4, 23–4.

harm as the Moslems have long ago perceived this and treat us accordingly. I return home with feelings of great disillusion.[124]

While religion stood at the centre of the voyage, the settler colonial announcement feared by the other European powers as constituting the real reason for the journey failed to materialize. Even the informal imperialism of German railway and finance interests was studiously avoided by the monarch, despite the prompting of the sultan and Bülow and Marschall's work with Siemens behind the scenes during the royal tour. As the French ambassador to Constantinople, Paul Cambon, noted with satisfaction, Wilhelm II was returning to Germany empty-handed, 'without having obtained a concession or any new order'.[125]

That Cambon saw this as a failure rather than the intent of the voyage illustrates just how convinced many outside Germany were of an underlying colonial intent to the trip. As Herzl and the Templer colonists learned (to their cost) during the voyage, however, irrespective of the extent of Wilhelm II's personal enthusiasm, he was neither in control of German *Weltpolitik* nor in a position to foist a new German colonial plan on an unwilling Sultan Abdulhamid II. In the end, Wilhelm II's trip to the Ottoman Empire reflected nothing more than the duties of a constitutional monarch invited to open a church in Jerusalem on behalf of his Christian subjects.

Whether in regard to the expansion of colonies in the area, the fate of the Baghdad Railway, the French and Russian claims to primacy in Jerusalem, or Europe's concerns for the preservation of the Ottoman Empire, depictions of Wilhelm II's *Orientreise* by his contemporaries as an expression of German foreign policy were entirely mistaken. While the emperor felt at liberty to imply to eager lobbyists that he had the power to grant the most outlandish of colonial plans, Wilhelm II was in fact unable to choose which door to use when entering a church without deferring to the Foreign Office. The royal tour to the Ottoman Empire was so ineffectual that the Reichstag initially refused to contribute to any of the costs for it on the grounds that it had not fulfilled any political purpose. Many in the parliament saw the voyage as a personal visit without political use or meaning for the nation. Only after months of jostling could any funds be prised from a parliament which, for good reason, baulked at the notion that it should pay for the overseas jaunts of the *Reisekaiser*.[126]

[124] Kaiser to Tsar, 9 November 1898, in Levine (ed.), *Letters from the Kaiser to the Czar*, 61.

[125] Cambon to Delcassé, 30 October 1898, in Archives diplomatiques, Paris, NS 166, 'Turquie: Politique étrangère', 192.

[126] Paul Singer, *Verhandlungen des Reichstages*, 22 March 1900, 4896; *VdR*, 16 May 1900, 5533–41; *VdR*, 18 May 1900, 5587–8.

4

Kowtowing before the Kaiser

The German seizure of Kiautschou in 1897 had alerted the Chinese court to the seriousness of the threat posed by the Europeans to China's territorial sovereignty. At the palace, this threat had been answered by the Guangxu emperor's rapid modernization undertaking, known as the 'One Hundred Days', that was subsequently overturned by a palace coup which effectively reinstated the Empress Dowager Cixi.[1] Outside the palace, a violent challenge to expansionist Christian outsiders was mounted by the Yihetuan Movement, commonly referred to as the Boxers. The anti-imperialism of the Boxers, who had gained the approval of Cixi, burst its banks in early 1900, when they launched a full-scale assault on the diplomatic legations in Peking (Beijing). This, and the murder of Germany's ambassador, Clemens von Ketteler, while he was en route to confront the Zongli Yamen, sparked an international military campaign and the subsequent occupation of Peking.[2] The international military campaign was, at least in name, led by Germany's Field Marshal Alfred von Waldersee, in recognition of the centrality of German grievances to the campaign.[3] The German troops that Waldersee led, however, missed the bulk of the fighting.[4]

The formally preponderant position of Germany was also signalled in the peace treaty, which foregrounded both Germany's grievances against the Chinese and the internationally agreed-upon steps to be taken by the Chinese imperial government to address them. Having arrived too late for much of the war, Germany now dominated the peace, with the first article of the Boxer Protocol, signed on 7 September 1901, stating:

ARTICLE Ia. By an Imperial Edict of the 9th of June last (Annex No.2), Tsai Feng, Prince of the First Rank Ch'ün, was appointed Ambassador of His Majesty the

---

[1] Klaus Mühlhahn, 'Negotiating the Nation: German Colonialism and Chinese Nationalism in Qingdao, 1897–1914', in Bryna Goodman and David S. G. Goodman (eds), *Twentieth-Century Colonialism and China: Localities, the Everyday and the World* (London: Routledge, 2012), 45.

[2] On the Boxer War, see, e.g., Robert Bickers and Rolf G. Tiedemann (eds.), *The Boxers, China and the World*, (Plymouth: Rowman & Littlefield, 2007); Paul Cohen, *History in Three Keys: The Boxers as Event, Experience, and Myth* (New York: Columbia University Press, 1997).

[3] On Wilhelm II's role and the subsequent international difficulties and confusion surrounding Waldersee's appointment, see Annika Mombauer, 'Wilhelm, Waldersee, and the Boxer Rebellion', in Annika Mombauer and Wilhelm Deist (eds), *The Kaiser: New Research on Wilhelm II's Role in Imperial Germany* (Cambridge: Cambridge University Press, 2004), 91–118.

[4] For the coverage of the Boxer War in the German media, see Yixu Lü, 'Germany's War in China: Media Coverage and Political Myth', *German Life and Letters* 61 no. 2 (2008), 202–14.

The Kaiser and the Colonies: Monarchy in the Age of Empire. Matthew P. Fitzpatrick, Oxford University Press.
© Matthew P. Fitzpatrick 2022. DOI: 10.1093/oso/9780192897039.003.0005

Emperor of China, and directed in that capacity to convey to His Majesty the German Emperor the expression of the regrets of His Majesty the Emperor of China and of the Chinese Government for the assassination of His Excellency the late Baron von Ketteler, German Minister. Prince Ch'ün left Peking the 12th of July last to carry out the orders which had been given him.

ARTICLE Ib. The Chinese Government has stated that it will erect on the spot of the assassination of His Excellency the late Baron von Ketteler a commemorative monument, worthy of the rank of the deceased, and bearing an inscription in the Latin, German, and Chinese languages, which shall express the regrets of His Majesty the Emperor of China for the murder committed. Their Excellencies the Chinese Plenipotentiaries have informed His Excellency the German Plenipotentiary, in a letter dated the 22nd of July last... that an arch of the whole width of the street would be erected on the said spot and that work on it was begun the 25th of June last.[5]

Zaifeng (Tsai Feng), or Prince Chun, as he was known to the European press, did indeed visit Germany in 1901 on what was dubbed a 'mission of atonement' (*Sühnemission*).[6] Conceived as a set-piece form of summit diplomacy, the royal visit was unlike other diplomatic tours by foreign dignitaries in that it fulfilled an obligation established by the peace settlement that ended the war in China. Legally a product of international diplomacy, it was symbolically designed to assert the formal dominance of Germany (and by extension Europe) over China and the Chinese imperial family. What occurred, however, was quite different. Rather than an assertion of German supremacy over the dynasts of the Far East, Zaifeng's tour of Germany was viewed throughout Germany and Europe as an assertion of Chinese dignity and a triumph of Chinese diplomacy at the expense of the German emperor who was, it was reported, seemingly thwarted at every turn. The Chinese Empire transformed a publicly staged act of ritual abasement into an assertion of Chinese defiance that succeeded in embarrassing the Kaiser in the eyes of Europe and formally inverting Germany's claim to be upholding the norms of civilized behaviour. While the overall dynamics of military and imperial power in East Asia remained firmly in favour of the West after Zaifeng's mission

---

[5] 'Settlement of Matters Growing out of the Boxer Uprisings (Boxer Protocol)', in Charles I. Bevans (ed), *Treaties and Other International Agreements of the United States of America, 1776-1949*, vol. 1 (Washington DC: US Government Printing Office, 1968), 302.

[6] For a short but very useful German-language discussion of this mission, see Klaus Mühlhahn, 'Kotau vor dem deutschen Kaiser? Die Sühnemission des Prinzen Chun', in Mechthild Leutner and Klaus Mühlhahn (eds), *Kolonialkrieg in China: Die Niederschlagung der Boxerbewegung 1900-1901* (Berlin: Ch. Links, 2007), 204-9. For Chinese-language accounts, see Xuetong Li, 'Chun Qinwang Zaifeng Shide Shishikao' ['An Investigation of the Historical Facts of Zaifeng, Prince Chun's Envoy to Germany'], *Lishi Dang'an* [*Historical Archives*] 2 (1990), 134-6; Kaixi Wang, 'Zaifeng Shide Qijian De Liyi Zhizheng' ['The Disputes on Propriety Issues during Prince Zaifeng's Envoy to Germany'], *Zi Jin Cheng* [*The Forbidden City*] 1 (2002), 23-7; Zhiwu Li, 'Zaifeng Shide Shulun' ['On Zaifeng's Mission to Germany'], *Journal of South China Agricultural University* 2, no. 1 (2003), 86-92.

to Germany, China was still able to signal its independence, even in the heart of Europe, at the moment of China's greatest weakness.

The Mission of Atonement

Although not formalized in a treaty until a year later, the 'sending of a Chinese delegation of apology including an Imperial Prince to Berlin' was one of the German Foreign Office's initial surrender conditions for the Chinese in September 1900.[7] Just days after this condition was made known, Ketteler's replacement as German ambassador to China, Alfons Mumm von Schwarzenstein, could report that the Chinese had agreed to this demand.[8] By January 1901, Mumm was able to confirm that the 18-year-old prince, Zaifeng, was the most suitable candidate for the royal mission. Indeed, Zaifeng had personally visited Mumm with a view to demonstrating his suitability for an audience with the Kaiser, 'an event that', Mumm argued, 'even a year ago would have been unthinkable according to Chinese custom, and might be considered as a symptom of the Chinese wish to end the crisis'.[9] The ambassador also confirmed that Zaifeng was a prince of the first rank and was the most suitable candidate, with others being too old, too young, or viewed as too sympathetic to the Boxer movement. Mumm confirmed that the prince 'had left a good impression' on him, and this glowing recommendation was sent to the Kaiser, who wrote in its margins, 'He should come'.[10] The German Foreign Office also agreed that China's German-speaking ex-ambassador to Germany, General Yin Chang, would also accompany the prince.[11] In total, a delegation of forty-three Chinese dignitaries and servants were chosen to make the journey to Berlin.[12]

In issuing his invitation, the ex-foreign secretary and recently appointed chancellor, Bernhard von Bülow, made it clear that the mission was to be treated as part of the broader peace agreement and that the timing of it was dependent upon the agreement of all of the powers which would become signatories to (and

---

[7] Richthofen to Mumm (in Peking), 5 September 1900, in PAAA R/18506, 'Akten betreffend den Aufstand in China: Chinesische Sühnemission nach Berlin', 14, 24.

[8] Mumm to German Foreign Office (AA), 17 September 1900, in PAAA R/18506, 18.

[9] Mumm to AA, 10 January 1901, in PAAA R18506, 38–9. Xuetong Li has argued that, once Mumm had recommended Zaifeng, the Qing court 'did not dare to differ' Xuetong Li, 'Chun Qinwang Zaifeng Shide Shishikao', 134).

[10] Mumm to AA, 14 January 1901, in PAAA R/18506, 53–63.

[11] Mumm to Richthofen, 14 June 1901, in PAAA R/18506, 103. See also the Qing Imperial Edict of 9 June 1901 in Bevan (ed), *Treaties and Other International Agreements of the United States of America, 1776–1949*, vol. 1, 310.

[12] Mumm to Bülow, 27 June 1901, in PAAA R/131819, 'Die Chinesische Sühnegesandschaft aus Anlaß der Ermordung des deutschen Gesandten in Peking, Freiherrn von Ketteler', unnumbered. These included a legation councillor, five legation secretaries (including a doctor), five translators, four attachés, eleven bodyguards, two eunuchs, eleven craftsmen, and other assorted servants.

therefore guarantors of) the peace treaty. For Bülow, it was important that the young prince should only come 'after China had conformed to the collective demands of the Powers, that is, had either carried them out or ensured that they will be carried out'. Zaifeng would be granted an audience, he wrote, as soon as 'the now provisional negotiations have come to an end through the signing of the required agreements'.[13]

The Chinese prince left Peking in mid-July 1901, almost two months before the Boxer Protocol would be signed. In Germany, the press hailed his impending arrival as striking an important blow for Europe against China's ostensible cultural chauvinism. Describing Zaifeng's voyage, one newspaper argued without the slightest trace of self-awareness that:

> With the courage of youth, he steps out into what is slandered as the barbaric and bedevilled European world of culture so as to…fulfil a great mission, to be placed in the vanguard against the pernicious racial prejudice of his homeland's people regarding the peoples, culture, and civilization of the Western world. With this he can only contribute to waking China from its thousand-year-long cultural slumber.[14]

While Zaifeng was on his way to Germany, however, a controversy broke out about the particulars of the court ceremony that would see him apologize to the Kaiser. As a result of a last-minute personal order from Wilhelm II, the Chinese party of dignitaries accompanying the prince was instructed not merely to bow but to kowtow in front of the German emperor as a sign of their complete abasement.[15] This demand caused instant consternation among the Chinese, with the Chinese ambassador in Berlin expressing to the German Foreign Office the Chinese Emperor's firm wish to avoid this gesture of ritual humiliation. Mühlberg in the Foreign Office replied that this refusal would have to be presented to Wilhelm II. He advised the Chinese ambassador, however, that from his position, given that it was a royal order, 'there is nothing to haggle and argue over.' The German official also attempted to impress upon the Chinese envoy the gravity of the occasion, reminding him that 'the mission of Prince Chun is to represent an act of expiation for a crime committed against our ambassador, the like of which is unheard of in the annals of history.' Given its historical uniqueness, Mühlberg argued, it could not be compared with other diplomatic missions. When the Chinese envoy asked whether at the very least Yin Chang, the former diplomat to

---

[13] Bülow to Mumm, 16 January 1901, in PAAA R/18506, 40–1.
[14] *Berliner Lokal-Anzeiger* (quoting the *Ostasiatische Correspondenz*), 21 July 1901, in PAAA R 131819.
[15] Conrad Bornhak's 1929 account specified that what was asked of the delegation was to 'to press their foreheads to the floor nine times': Conrad Bornhak, *Die Kriegschuld, Deutschlands Weltpolitik 1890–1914* (Berlin: Verlag Tradition, 1929), 233.

Germany who had been decorated with the German Crown Order (Second Class with star), might be exempt from this demand, Mühlberg remained non-committal. As an exercise touching not only on the forms of international summit diplomacy but also on courtly protocol (one of the few things over which the emperor exercised immediate influence) Wilhelm II's input was unavoidable. Seeking to put the issue to rest, Mühlberg asked Heinrich von Tschirschky, a career diplomat close to Wilhelm II, to enquire of the emperor as to how he wanted to proceed.[16]

Three days later, formal word from Peking arrived that the Imperial Court was not willing to accede to Wilhelm II's demand that the Chinese delegation kowtow before him. In their response, the Chinese inverted the civilizationary assumptions of the Germans by arguing that the Germans were acting contrary to the norms of modern civilized behaviour by insisting upon the kowtow. Establishing themselves as arbiters of civilized political conduct, the Chinese appropriated for themselves a role forestalling potentially barbarous German behaviour:

> Prince Chun entreated me to ask you in his name to submit to the Imperial Chancellor the desire of the delegation accompanying Prince Chun to refrain from the required kowtow before His Majesty the Kaiser and King which was relayed by the Chinese ambassador in Berlin, as this ceremony has hitherto not been customarily required of Chinese delegations in Europe and does not accord with European regional and civilized customs, and in China itself, where reforms are currently being carried out, the kowtow is considered an anachronism to be abolished.[17]

On the same day, however, Wilhelm II, ruled out any alterations to the formalities. On 23 August, the Foreign Office received word from Tschirschky that the emperor was continuing to insist on the kowtow and that from the monarch's perspective 'there could be no talk of altering the ceremony now that it had been established'.[18] The intransigence of Wilhelm II's demand for a ceremony including the kowtow caught the German government off guard, with Holstein hastily cabling Chancellor Bülow for guidance while the latter was on summer holiday on the island of Nordeney. Holstein was well aware that Germany could expect no support from the other powers active in China for such an extravagant demand. He also knew that if the Chinese refused to continue to Berlin on these grounds, there was very little that they could do about it. Given this broader European context, Holstein asked Bülow what the emperor would do if the Chinese delegation

---

[16]   Mühlberg to Tschirschky, 20 August 1901, in PAAA R18506, 161–5.

[17]   Mumm to AA, 23 August 1901, PAAA R/18506, 172. Duplicate in PAAA R 131819.

[18]   Tschirschky to Mühlberg, 23 August 1901, in PAAA R/18506, 181. The Kaiser couched this intransigence as support for Mühlberg's earlier approach. This was sent to Bülow on the same day; see PAAA R18506, 183.

refused to continue on because of his insistence that the members of the delegation ritually abase themselves before him.[19]

Despite attempts by Ambassador Mumm to argue for the reasonableness of the
kowtow in Peking,[20] the Chinese delegation was indeed moving towards just such
a refusal. Having found out about the ceremonial expectations imposed by
Wilhelm II for the planned meeting while travelling to Basel in Switzerland after
disembarking in Genoa, the Chinese mission simply refused to cross the border
into Germany until the emperor reversed his decision. Zaifeng's travelogue of his
time in Europe offers some coy hints of the behind-the-scenes discussions of the
Chinese delegation:

August 28, 1901: Envoy Lu Haihuan has come from Germany via Lucerne to discuss protocol. [We] deliberate over sending a telegram.

August 31, 1901: Evening. [I] ordered Envoy Lu to return to Berlin and ordered
assistant minister Yin Chang to prepare a letter in the German language to give to
the German Embassy's attaché to forward to the German Foreign Office to tact-
fully consult on [how to] present [myself] before the [German sovereign].[21]

The German consul in Basel, Rudolf Eiswaldt (who had also served previously in
China), reported on the reasoning of the Chinese, in particular Yin Chang, who
argued that, as a representative of the Qing court, his body was not his own to do
with as he pleased during the meeting:

Yingchang repeatedly asserted that personally he would not waste a second
hesitating to kneel before His Majesty the Kaiser, but for him as a designated
diplomatic representative of the Chinese Emperor, as a designated diplomatic
representative of China to His Majesty, it was not the individual but the official
position that came in question for him.

Yin Chang also pointed out the religious connotations of the kowtow, grounded
in an earlier, traditional view of the Chinese emperor as the 'Son of Heaven',
which, he argued, did not make sense in a German context. When reminded of
the extraordinary nature of the mission of atonement, Yin Chang replied that the
gravity of the mission to atone for the murdered ambassador was not lost on the
delegation, but that this did not mean that they should be required to submit to
unreasonable requests contrary to international diplomatic custom. On balance,
Eiswaldt advised the Germans to show a willingness to compromise on the question of kowtowing.[22]

---

[19] Holstein to Bülow, 23 August 1901, in PAAA R/18506, 174.
[20] Mumm to AA, 26 August 1901, PAAA R/18506, 258.
[21] Zaifeng, 'Chun Qingwang shi-De riji', *Jindaishi ziliao*, 73 (1989), 153.
[22] Eiswaldt to Bülow, 26 August 1901, PAAA R18506, 272–8.

Kowtowing and the Diplomatic Body

Yin Chang's reference to his position draws attention to what was physically, that is corporeally, required of him as a representative of the Chinese emperor. Although historians have been slow to incorporate embodiment theory into diplomatic history, there is a growing political science and sociological literature that foregrounds the diplomatic body and its role in conveying important political signals across linguistic and cultural lines.[23] The role of the body and the etiquette and ritual that govern its posture and movements in international diplomacy is key to understanding diplomatic history. As Christer Jönsson has made clear, diplomatic body language, which 'encompasses everything from personal gestures and the shape of a negotiating table to the mobilization and movement of military troops,' is too important to be ignored.[24] So too Alisher Faizullaev has pointed to the importance of symbolism and ritual in the actions of the diplomat, arguing that in their physicality, diplomatic agents serve as 'sensible "evidences" of the state'. They are, he argues, 'organic parts of the symbolic construction of inter-state relations and international politics'. This is nowhere clearer, Faizullaev maintains, than in the case of extraordinary political events such as formal state apologies, where the ways in which the symbolism and rituals of a state occasion are physically negotiated by the embodied diplomat have practical consequences for the interests of the state itself.[25] In such situations, the 'diplomatic self' comes to the fore, self-consciously embodying and expressing not merely their own subjectivity, but also their role as a corporeal expression of the status of the state they represent.[26]

The importance of bodily movements and rituals in the delivery and acceptance of state apologies has also been noted by others, with Michel-André Horelt arguing that too often 'in the literature of public apologies, observers... tend to reduce the concept of "ritual" to an insignificant, residual category'. Rather than an extraneous element to the delivery of the text of a state apology, Horelt maintains, 'Rituals have the potential to create changes through their very enactment'.[27] Crucially, the incorporation of movements and symbolically laden bodily performances can either reinforce or subvert the politics of a diplomatic encounter.

---

[23] Raymond Cohen, *Theatre of Power: The Art of Diplomatic Signalling* (London: Longman, 1987); Christer Jönsson and Karin Aggestam, 'Trends in Diplomatic Signalling', in Jan Melissen (ed), *Innovation in Diplomatic Practice* (New York: Palgrave, 1999), 151–70.

[24] Christer Jönsson, 'Diplomatic Signalling in the Television Age', *International Journal of Press/Politics* 1, no. 3 (1996), 25–6.

[25] Alisher Faizullaev 'Diplomacy and Symbolism', *Hague Journal of Diplomacy* 8 (2013), 94.

[26] Alisher Faizullaev 'Diplomacy and Self', *Diplomacy and Statecraft* 17, no. 3 (2006), 501, 517.

[27] Michel-André Horelt, 'The Power of Ritual Ceremonies in State Apologies: An Empirical Analysis of the Bilateral Polish-Russian Commemoration Ceremony in Katyn in 2010', in Mihaela Mihai and Mathias Thaler (eds), *On the Use and Abuse of Political Apologies* (London: Palgrave, 2014), 76.

In the case of the state apology, as Hiro Saito has argued, state representatives are engaged in a 'social performance' in which:

> power relations…permeate the entire performance; for example, which collect-
> ive representations are dominant, who is authorized to act, whether the audi-
> ence is able to disrupt the performance, which means of symbolic production
> are selected, and which version of *mis-en-scène* is adopted, are all dependent on
> political struggles.[28]

That the politics of corporeal position was intelligible to both German and Chinese officials was clearly the case in the dispute about the suitability and acceptability of the kowtow to a royal Chinese delegation meeting the German emperor. In effect, Wilhelm II had insisted that the delegation not only abase itself before him but also perform decontextualized and anachronistic bodily acts of Chinese subjecthood. The kowtow ritual was insisted upon by the German monarch as a flamboyant marker of excessive and exotic domination. At stake here was not merely the question of the exact depth of contrition the delegation should show for the murder of the German ambassador, but what the political and military consequences for refusing to assume this submissive position might be. Given that the formal apology was written into the text of the multilateral peace agreement ending the war in China, had Wilhelm II insisted upon the per-formance of the kowtow, the consequences could have included precipitating a split in the pan-European alliance that had been forged to fight the Boxer War. Alternatively, if pan-European solidarity was maintained despite Wilhelm II's excessive demands, the refusal of the members of the delegation to bend their bodies before the emperor might have led to the resumption of the war in China, on the grounds that the Chinese had failed to satisfactorily meet the conditions of the peace accord.

The body politics of the kowtow had previously stymied diplomatic relations between the two hemispheres in the eighteenth and nineteenth centuries, when European embassies had sought to establish diplomatic relations with China. In particular, two well-reported incidents had shaped European understandings of the significance of the kowtow, when the British embassies to China in 1795 and 1816, led by George Macartney and William Pitt Amherst, refused to kowtow before the Qianlong and Jiaqing emperors. Their justification for refusing the gesture was that they viewed it to be an undignified and inappropriate form of abasement for a royal representative before a foreign monarch. At the time of Macartney's failed embassy, he was rebuked in the press for his 'nonsensical

---

[28] Hiro Saito, 'The Cultural Pragmatics of Political Apology', *Cultural Sociology* 10, no. 4 (2016), 450–1.

scrupulousness', which was said to have had brought about the failure of the mission.[29] By the time of the Amherst delegation, however, British attitudes had shifted from viewing the kowtow as an unimportant local custom that might be accommodated to seeing it as a barbaric expression of the will of a 'capricious despot'.[30] The British were not alone in their objections. Although the late eighteenth-century Dutch ambassador to China and Japan, Isaac Titsingh, showed no compunction when kowtowing before East Asian monarchs,[31] the Russian envoy Yurii Golovkin had scarcely begun his mission to China in 1805 before a 'dispute over kowtow protocol' saw him sent back to Russia by Chinese officials.[32] A century later, despite its clearly divisive history and status in international affairs, Wilhelm II not only demanded the resurrection of the kowtow but demanded its use at his own court, where it had no cultural logic or history. It was a gesture deliberately calibrated to demean and degrade the Chinese delegation.

The refusal of the Chinese delegation to submit to the request for ritual humiliation before the German emperor sent German foreign policy experts and Sinologists scrambling to try and understand the cultural meaning of kowtowing and to divine whether or not the Chinese delegation's objections were genuine or a form of diplomatic intransigence designed to improve China's standing in the post-Boxer era. In Peking, Mumm rushed to learn the history of the Macartney embassy, asking the British ambassador, Ernest Satow, what he knew about it.[33] In Berlin, the Foreign Office reached the preliminary judgement that the kowtow was a Chinese religious rather than secular gesture, pointing to the judgement of the American Sinologist Wells Williams, who, in his book *The Middle Kingdom*, argued that:

> the emperor, considering himself as the representative of divine power exacts the same prostration which is paid the gods; and the ceremonies which are performed in his presence partake therefore of a religious character and are

[29] Laurence Williams, 'British Government under the Qianlong Emperor's Gaze: Satire, Imperialism, and the Macartney Embassy to China, 1792–1804', *Lumen* 32 (2013), 99–100. Most recently, Henrietta Harrison has cast doubt on the centrality of the issue of the kowtow for the Chinese emperor, who in his reply to George III's overtures for closer ties focused on trade and military matters. In Europe, however, the issue of the kowtow remained central: Henrietta Harrison, 'The Qianlong Emperor's Letter to George III and the Early-Twentieth-Century Origins of Ideas about Traditional China's Foreign Relations', *American Historical Review* 122, no. 3 (2017), 684.

[30] Hao Gao, 'The "Inner Kowtow Controversy" during the Amherst Embassy to China, 1816–1817', *Diplomacy and Statecraft* 27, no. 4 (2016), 606–7; Hao Gao, 'The Amherst Embassy and British Discoveries in China', *History* 99, no. 337 (2014), 569.

[31] Leonard Blussé, 'Peeking into Empires: Dutch Embassies to the Courts of China and Japan', *Itinerario* 37, no. 3 (2013), 18.

[32] Golovkin had apparently refused a 'trial kowtow' before a tablet representing the emperor: Gregory Afinogenov, 'Jesuit Conspirators and Russia's East Asian Fur Trade, 1791–1807', *Journal of Jesuit Studies* 2 (2015), 71; Rosemary Quested, *Sino-Russian Relations: A Short History* (London: Routledge, 1984), 65–6.

[33] Ernest M. Satow, *The Diaries of Sir Ernest Satow, British Envoy in Peking (1900–1906)*, vol. 1 (Morrisville, NC: Lulu Press, 2006), 134.

not merely particular forms of etiquette, which may be altered according to circumstances.[34]

Unwilling to rely solely on this judgement, however, the German Foreign Office asked Carl Arendt at the Seminar for Oriental Languages in Berlin for further expert guidance on the cultural resonances of the kowtow and its position in Chinese courtly culture.[35] In his report, Arendt, who had earlier worked as a translator for German delegations in Peking, argued against Williams's assessment, asserting that the Chinese protest was disingenuous and politically motivated. For Arendt, it was 'an absolutely untrue description, and can only be understood as subterfuge on the side of the Chinese, when it is claimed that the kowtow always and in every form represents a type of religious ceremony'. There were, he argued, numerous forms and meanings of the kowtow, and he suggested as a compromise that the delegation be asked to fall to one knee rather than perform the full kowtow, given that this form was, in his estimation, less demeaning.[36] At the same time, yet another passage culled from Williams's *The Middle Kingdom* was being passed around the Foreign Office, this time from a section which many saw as lending support to Wilhelm II's demand for a strong corporeal signal of abasement. In this passage, 'eight gradations of obeisance' were described, including one ostensibly 'expressing in the strongest measure the submission and homage of one state to another'.[37]

The forthright advice of ex-Vice Consul Albert von Seckendorff to Chancellor Bülow, however, contradicted Arendt's support for the emperor's demand. In his submission, Seckendorff professed his confidence 'on the basis of his long experience in China that the kowtow has a religious origin'. It was performed, he argued, 'in ancient times only in holy places and at the graves of the deceased by devotees or mourners'. If Wilhelm II insisted that the Chinese perform it before him, Seckendorff argued, it would be 'viewed as absolutely beneath their human dignity'.[38] In Peking, Ambassador Mumm also reported back to the Foreign Office that 'the kowtow offered to the Emperor of China does indeed, in the opinion of canvassed experts, have a religious significance, insofar as the Emperor of China is viewed as the Son of Heaven and the Representative of Godhead on Earth'. Urging some measure of flexibility and understanding of cultural difference, Mumm reminded the Foreign Office of the enormous concession to Germany already made by the Chinese, and that 'the sending of a mission of atonement led by one of the Imperial Princes and brother of the Chinese Emperor is in itself a

---

[34] PAAA R/18506, 281–7.
[35] On Carl Arendt, see Mechthild Leutner, *Kolonialpolitik und Wissensproduktion: Carl Arendt (1838–1902) und die Entwicklung der Chinawissenschaft* (Münster: Lit Verlag, 2016).
[36] PAAA R/18506, 323–6.   [37] PAAA R/18506, 329.
[38] Seckendorff to Bülow, 31 August 1901, in PAAA R/18506, 342–8.

success demonstrating the rising power of Germany in the Far East.'[39] Any attempt to enforce the kowtow risked the substantial political gains that Germany had made through the mission of atonement.

Recent Chinese scholarship on the social semiotics of the kowtow has confirmed that the transferal of the kowtow to a European context was viewed by the Chinese delegation as a calculated insult. For Kaixi Wang, the demand for a Chinese royal delegation to kowtow before Wilhelm II, who was to remain seated upon a raised dais, was simply inadmissible to the Qing court. Any kneeling or kowtowing before Chinese emperors by Europeans in the past had been a simple matter of adapting to local practices, and many Europeans had refused to comply. Yet Zaifeng's delegation was supposed to perform the ritual in Germany, where it had no historical precedent or semiotic function in courtly or diplomatic ceremony. In addition, kowtowing in China had never been enforced by the threat of military action in the case of its refusal, as Germany threatened China in 1901.[40]

Beyond this, when Wilhelm II's brother, Prince Heinrich, had visited Peking three years earlier, diplomatic protocols had been shifted in ways that had emphasized the desire for friendship between the two nations, despite the fact that Germany had recently seized Chinese territory. The Chinese emperor had not only left his throne to welcome his royal guest but also allowed the Prussian prince to be seated during the audience, a highly exceptional state of affairs in the context of Chinese court protocols. By contrast, in 1901, the Chinese felt that, despite the Boxer War having ended, they were being placed in a position where a deliberately demeaning insult to the majesty of the Guangxu emperor was being foisted upon them.[41] The proposed ostentatious display of German power and Chinese subservience was carefully designed, it was felt, to bolster Germany's imperial credentials in the eyes of Europe at the expense of the dignity of the Chinese emperor. As Zhiwu Li has made clear, the impact of Wilhelm II's ritualized insult was exacerbated by the fact that he was demanding a bodily signal of submission from a prince he believed would in time become the next Chinese emperor.[42]

Negotiating the Ritual of Atonement

Unsurprisingly, the Chinese delegation's sudden unscheduled halt in Basel attracted the attention of the international press. Initially, the Swiss *Allgemeine*

[39] Mumm to AA, 31 August 1901, PAAA R/18506, 353–6. This view that the mission itself represented an enormous concession by China to Germany is also largely in accord with the analysis of Kaixi Wang, 'Zaifeng Shide Qijian De Liyi Zhizheng', 25–6.

[40] Kaixi Wang, 'Zaifeng Shide Qijian De Liyi Zhizheng', 23–7.

[41] Kaixi Wang, 'Zaifeng Shide Qijian De Liyi Zhizheng', 23–7.

[42] Zhiwu Li, 'Zaifeng Shide Shulun', 87.

Schweizer-Zeitung dutifully reported the Chinese delegation's public position that Zaifeng was staying in Basel because of an undisclosed illness. At the same time, however, it speculated that the prince's illness might not have been the root cause of the extended stay in Switzerland:

> This illness occurred directly before crossing the German border, that is, at the last moment where one might still present further conditions regarding the reception in Berlin which, if not agreed upon, might still allow for their depart-ure, at least assuming that the unity of civilized states does not extend so far as to close off any other path for the Imperial Prince other than that to Germany. One can hardly hope for this unity, no matter how desirable it might be in the name of European civilization.

When the suspicion that the delegation's halt on the Swiss side of the German border was not a product of Zaifeng's ill health was put to Yin Chang by the Swiss reporter, Yin Chang conceded that 'Prince Chun was in fact unwell, but in add-ition there came news from Berlin that prompted him to temporarily remain here, as he cannot comply with the requirements that those in Berlin would place upon him without specific authorization from China.'[43]

Behind the scenes, Germany's consul in Genoa, Georg Irmer, opined to the German Foreign Office know that 'peevishness and anger are the real grounds of his illness.'[44] Less diplomatically, a cartoon in the satirical periodical *Kladderadatsch* on 1 September 1901 implied that the prince's illness was in fact a result of him soiling himself ahead of his meeting with Wilhelm II (see Figure 4.1).[45]

A few days later, the *Basler Nachrichten* attempted to downplay the escalating disagreement, arguing that the halt in Basel was not related to 'any principles and the points directly related to the peace agreement, rather simply regarding merely formal, incidental difficulties that have suddenly got in the way and are as good as overcome'. The newspaper's optimism was nonetheless undermined by the admis-sion that exceedingly lengthy (and costly) telegrams were being sent between Basel and Peking in an attempt to coordinate a formal Chinese response to the crisis. The same paper, however, rejected the (incorrect) claims made by the German press that the delay was due to the German government asking the dele-gation to wait until the peace treaty had officially been signed.[46] The delay, the

---

[43] *Allgemeine Schweizer Zeitung*, 27 August 1907, in PAAA R/18506, 289. The last paragraph of this article stating that Prince Chun could not go any further without the express permission of Peking was telegraphed directly from Basel to the Kaiser's military cabinet in Berlin. PAAA R/18506, 296.

[44] Irmer to AA, 23 August 1901, in PAAA R 131819.

[45] 'Die Krankheit Tschuns', *Beiblatt zum Kladderadatsch*, 1 September 1901 (unnumbered).

[46] The treaty was formally signed by the Chinese only once the formal apology had been com-pleted: Zhiwu Li, 'Zaifeng Shide Shulun', 89.

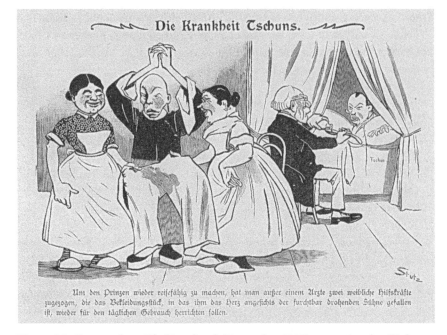

Figure 4.1 Cartoon from *Kladderadatsch* (September 1901) suggesting that Ziefang had soiled himself in fear prior to meeting Wilhelm II

paper asserted, had clearly been caused by misgivings harboured by the Chinese. Whether this was because the ceremonial programme for the audience with Wilhelm II did not meet with their approval or whether there were other grounds, the paper claimed it could not comment. In any case, the paper argued, 'the situation is in no way a comfortable one for German diplomacy and is nothing less than tragicomic when one brings to mind that this is the finale of the great Chinese expedition and Count Waldersee's glittering epilogue.'[47]

Interestingly, once the *Basler Nachrichten* learned from Berlin newspapers such as the *Berliner Lokal-Anzeiger* that the reason for the non-appearance of the Chinese atonement delegation was Wilhelm II's insistence that they perform the kowtow, the Swiss newspaper offered some support to the emperor. The newspaper declared that there were strong historical grounds for the demand, given the past experiences of European delegations seeking access to the Chinese emperor. 'Until the beginning of this century', the paper reasoned, 'it is well known that the Chinese required representatives of European rulers to kowtow before the Chinese emperor, that is, touch the ground with their forehead three times and then to bow nine times.' Offering a somewhat embellished version of the history of the Amherst delegation, the newspaper argued that the requirement

---

[47] *Basler Nachrichten*, 29 August 1901, in PAAA R/18506, 317–18.

had only been abandoned when the British refused to submit to the practice. Given the nature of the atonement mission, the newspaper continued, Kaiser Wilhelm II's stipulation was 'absolutely appropriate'. This support was not, however, unconditional, and the paper conceded that the spectacle of Yin Chang, a decorated Knight of the Order of the Crown, being forced to kowtow before the emperor would be 'disconcerting'. Summing up what it saw as a strange conclusion to the 'turmoil in China', the newspaper declared that they were now experiencing 'a tragedy ending as a burlesque'.[48]

The *Berliner Lokal-Anzeiger* also continued to report on the kowtow question, acknowledging the seriousness of the disagreement. It reported that 'the difficulties raised in Basel by Prince Chun, generally seen as easily resolved, appear to be intensifying in a fashion that could be of far-reaching consequence. As the matter now stands, it has become highly doubtful whether Prince Chun will come to Berlin at all.' According to the Berlin daily, the Chinese understood that this decision placed them and (still occupied) China in a precarious position. Nonetheless, the delegation had apparently made it clear that 'under the present conditions we could never ever travel to Berlin; we would prefer to sacrifice our lives rather than submit to these conditions.'[49]

In an attempt to defend the German emperor and to explain the seeming intransigence of the Chinese on a question of bodily deportment, the paper inverted the apparent causal nexus by arguing that, rather than the issue being a matter of Germany imposing excessive demands upon an already extraordinary mission of atonement, the dispute was symptomatic of precisely the type of Chinese cultural chauvinism that had caused the Boxer conflict in the first place. Europe, the paper argued, needed to resist China's refusal to submit to the conditions imposed upon it by the victorious powers:

> The refusal of the Chinese dignitaries to perform the kowtow in Berlin is actually not easy to assess from a European way of thinking. The refusal is related to the idea that the "Son of Heaven" is something completely different, something far loftier than other monarchs. Doubtless, however, the entire non-Asian political world has an interest in the Chinese discarding this idea, which is perhaps the root cause of many of the difficulties between the European powers and China.[50]

The Chinese, the newspaper argued, were poised to exploit the differences of opinion that might arise between the various European powers on the issue and

---

[48] *Basler Nachrichten*, 31 August 1901, in PAAA R/18506, 350-1.

[49] 'Tschuns Reise nach Berlin in Frage gestellt', *Berliner Lokal-Anzeiger*, 1 September 1901, in PAAA R/18507.

[50] 'Tschuns Reise nach Berlin in Frage gestellt', *Berliner Lokal-Anzeiger*, 1 September 1901, in PAAA R/18507.

that this might further complicate what was becoming an increasingly problematic diplomatic mission. Noting that several members of the Chinese delegation had honorary orders from Britain, France, and Russia, the paper conceded that political difficulties could erupt in Europe if, for example, the British were to veto the kowtowing of a British knight (such as Sir Liang Cheng, who had been knighted by Queen Victoria and was accompanying Zaifeng) before Wilhelm II.[51]

In the event, the worst potential consequences of the crisis were averted by an eleventh-hour concession from the German monarch that ended the impasse. On 1 September 1901, Eiswaldt wrote to the Foreign Office from Basel to try and break the deadlock, asking 'whether perhaps His Majesty might not *out of mercy and sympathy for the young and helpless Prince* most graciously rescind the order regarding the ceremony'.[52] With Bülow quietly building the case that the demand was unsustainable, given the international attention being drawn to the case, Wilhelm II relented, and the next day Eiswaldt had his reply from Berlin:

> In order that the ceremonial question might be dealt with, His Majesty has deigned to rule that Prince Chun, alone with Yin Chang as a translator, will appear in the His Highness' presence while the Prince's party remains in the antechamber.[53]

At the same time, it was requested of Mumm in Peking that he relay to the Chinese court that Yin Chang would only be required to bow (rather than kowtow) 'in the same manner as the prince himself'.[54] This decision took Mumm by surprise, who had informed Ernest Satow, Britain's envoy to Peking, as late as 2 September that 'The *ko-tóu* was a *sine qua non*,' despite Mumm's best efforts to convince Berlin 'six weeks ago... against any Oriental ceremonies being adopted'. By 4 September, Satow had been informed that 'The Emperor William has given way and will receive Prince Chun and the German-speaking member of the suite according to European ceremonial.' According to, Satow, upon hearing the news, 'the Chinese [were] jubilant'.[55]

In Switzerland, Zaifeng also recorded the news of the German change of heart in his travelogue:

> September 2, 1901: Received a telegram from envoy Lu saying that the German emperor had dispensed with the [demand that those] who come must kowtow.

---

[51] 'Tschuns Reise nach Berlin in Frage gestellt'. Liang Cheng was decorated by Queen Victoria in 1897 as a Knight Commander of the Order of St Michael and St George. See Edward J. M. Rhoads, *Stepping Forth into the World: The Chinese Educational Mission to the United States, 1872–1881* (Hong Kong: Hong Kong University Press, 2011), 208–9.

[52] Eiswaldt to AA, 1 September 1901, in PAAA R/18507, 36. Emphasis in the original.

[53] AA to Eiswaldt, 2 September 1901, in PAAA R/18507, 43.

[54] AA to Mumm, 2 September 1901, in PAAA R/18507, 53.

[55] Satow, *The Diaries of Sir Ernest Satow*, 134–5. The Kaiser's capitulation on the issue was sudden.

In the afternoon, the German consul in Basel, came to say that he received a telegram from his Foreign Office that also said that the German emperor will go on a tour of inspection on the sixth, and requesting that I quickly come to Germany. The German emperor would certainly receive me. The [demand that those] who come to kowtow had already been dispensed with. Therefore, at night, [we] caught our train for Potsdam.[56]

By having only the prince and his interpreter come before the German Kaiser, the Germans were able to retrieve the situation as the issue increasingly took on an international dimension. Although Haihuan Lü, the Chinese ambassador to Germany, tried to convince the Qing court that he had personally managed Wilhelm II's change of mind by convincing German court priests that it would have been idolatrous of the emperor to have someone kneel before him, the far more pressing concerns for the German Foreign Office were, as Zhiwu Li has argued, that China was refusing to sign the peace protocol for the Boxer Rebellion until it had been made clear that there would be no kowtow.[57] Given the grounds for China's refusal, the German Foreign Office could hardly expect any support from the other European powers to force the Chinese to sign and accept the kowtow.

With the kowtow demand having been dropped, events moved rapidly. Eiswaldt conveyed Zaifeng's message to the Foreign Office that 'the Prince begs leave to most humbly thank His Majesty the Kaiser for the exceedingly gracious Highest decision and will continue his journey this evening at 11 p.m. with a special train.' The prince arrived in Potsdam at 3.38 p.m. on 3 September, ready to be received by Wilhelm II at 12.30 p.m. on 4 September at Sanssouci.[58] The meeting itself was a stately one, with the *mise en scène* and corporeal deportment of the participants described in detail by the *Neue Preußische Zeitung*:

Shortly before 12.30 His Majesty the Kaiser and King appeared in the uniform of his regiment of the Gardes du Corps, with a Field Marshal's baton in his hand, and greeted those gathered, in particular the attending princes of the royal house. At the appointed time, Lord Marshal Eulenburg gave the signal that the atoning envoy was approaching. The State Secretary of the Foreign Office and Royal Consul Baron von Seckendorff was to the right, before the throne. The Kaiser, without removing his helmet, placed himself upon the throne with the

---

[56] Zaifeng, 'Chun Qingwang shi-De riji', 153.

[57] Zhiwu Li, 'Zaifeng Shide Shulun', 87. Three days after the apology was delivered, the Chinese signed the peace. This is corroborated by Ernest Satow's diary entry for 1 September 1901, which states that 'The edicts have been recd. some days ago, and are being held back solely in order that the question of ceremonial can be settled before signature' (Satow, *The Diaries of Sir Ernest Satow*, 134–5).

[58] Eiswaldt to AA, 1 September 1901; AA to Eiswaldt, 2 August 1901; Eiswaldt to AA, 2 September 1901; AA to Mumm, 2 September 1901; PAAA R/18507, 36, 43, 46, 53, 59, 61–2.

Field Marshal's baton in his hand and gazed with a grave expression at the young prince who had appeared with a deep bow at the door of the hall. With slow and solemn steps, in accordance with Chinese custom, Prince Chun approached…With another deep bow towards the throne, he offered with both hands the handwritten message from the Emperor of China, bound in yellow silk embroidered with the golden dragon.[59]

Zaifeng's own account of the meeting was, given the gravity of the occasion, surprisingly brief, even dismissive, with his description of the day in his travelogue only briefly mentioning the royal audience, sandwiched between a description of a visit to the grave of the German empress dowager, an extended discussion of the decor of the imperial residence, and a description of a boat trip:

12.00 to 13.00: [I] led assistant minister Yin Chang and the other participating members [of the mission] to the *Neues Palais* to present our credentials and to pay respects to the German emperor. The *Neues Palais* is merely half a kilometre from the Orangerie. I bowed three times, handed the credentials over and read the prepared speech. The German emperor made a speech in response, [and then] the ceremony was finished. The German emperor dispatched a cavalry company of 200 men to take us back to the Orangerie.[60]

The Chinese prince read the text of the emperor's message to the Kaiser, which avoided a direct apology and statement of guilt, a remarkable feat, given that the entire visit was ostensibly a mission of atonement. It expressed 'regret for these events', but accepted no responsibility for the murder of the German ambassador, Ketteler, and moved quickly on to the hope that the German emperor would renew the friendly relations they had once enjoyed. Wilhelm II replied by remarking upon the gravity and high seriousness of the occasion, before ending with the hope that now that this 'deeply sad and highly serious deterioration' had been dealt with, there could be a return to the 'earlier enduring, friendly, and peaceful relations between Germany and China that had been a blessing to both peoples and the entirety of human civilization'.[61] The prince then withdrew, walking backwards and bowing as he left. No kowtow was performed by Zaifeng or any of his attendants.[62] As *Kladderadatsch* wryly put it:

---

[59] *Neue Preußische Zeitung*, 6 September 1901, in PAAA R/18507, 132. Rockhill offers a similarly vivid account, stressing the significance of the relative bodily movements of Zaifeng, the Kaiser, and the palace guards. See William Woodville Rockhill, *Diplomatic Audiences at the Court of China* (London: Luzac, 1905), 52–4.

[60] Zaifeng, 'Chun Qingwang shi-De riji', 154.

[61] PAAA R/18507, 89, 91, 94.

[62] For a translation of Prince Chun's speech, see PAAA R/18507, 89. For the Kaiser's reply, see PAAA R/18507, 91.

What once began as tragedy
With murderous flowing blood
Has ended as comedy,
And now everything's all right again.
The atoning prince has come
But not quite exactly
As originally intended,
With the wretched kowtow.
He was allowed to leave undone
Anything embarrassing to him.[63]

More overtly demonstrating an awareness of what the Chinese delegation's refusal to comply with the Kaiser's demands for bodily abasement meant for Germany's claims of cultural superiority over the Chinese was a cartoon which dominated the cover of the satirical periodical *Simplicissimus* on 24 September 1901. The cartoon, 'The Atoning Prince' drawn by Thomas Theodor Heine, depicted Zaifeng literally thumbing his nose at the German military, with the image's ironic subtitle reading 'Translator: The Chinese hand movement means something like, "I beg most humbly for forgiveness"' (see Figure 4.2).[64]

International Reactions

The German press remained coy about explaining to the public Wilhelm II's decision to relent on the issue of the kowtow. When the *Berliner Tageblatt* reported that the prince was finally on his way from Switzerland, no mention was made of the nature of the sensitive negotiations between Berlin and Peking. Instead, it was only reported that 'the awaited telegram to Prince Chun from Peking has arrived.' Abroad, the kowtow affair was used to attack the German government, in particular the emperor, for his hubris. In the absence of solid information, newspapers in Britain and even New York ridiculed Wilhelm II for his insistence that the Chinese kowtow before him.[65] The *New York Times*, reporting on what it called 'this barbarous ceremony', argued that Zaifeng 'would rather die than kowtow to the Kaiser, and thus recognize him as the suzerain of their own Emperor.'[66] A few days later, after Wilhelm II had conceded the point, the paper reported that 'the Chinese are chuckling over the result of the Chun affair,' while pointing out that

[63] 'Der Sühneact', *Kladderadatsch*, 8 September, 1901, 137.
[64] 'Der Sühneprinz', *Simplicissimus* 6, no. 27 (1901), 209. Also reproduced in Klaus Mühlhahn, 'Kotau vor dem deutschen Kaiser?', 207.
[65] PAAA R/18508, 45–7.   [66] 'Prince Chun's Dilemma', *New York Times*, 2 September 1901.

Figure 4.2 Cover of *Simplicissimus* (1901) suggesting that Zaifeng was thumbing his nose at the Germans

Russian influence in Peking had greatly profited from Germany's capitulation, with their envoy in Peking having advised the Chinese 'to remain firm' against the Kaiser's demand.[67] The French paper *Le Matin* roundly criticized the German

---

[67] 'Chinese in Peking Please', *New York Times*, 5 September 1901.

plan to force the prince to prostrate himself bodily before Wilhelm II, which it argued effectively 'made the Chinese emperor seem a slave of the German Kaiser'.[68]

In Britain, opinions were split between a somewhat anodyne relief that peace between Germany and China had been formally re-established and an interest in what the kowtow episode had shown about the respective nations.[69] One report claimed that Wilhelm II had in fact already been rebuffed once before, when he had initially demanded that the prince too kowtow. When he refused, the article stated, Wilhelm II had then insisted that the prince's party perform the ceremony. In spite of its questionable provenance, the story gained traction in diplomatic circles, which led Mumm to lament that even the Japanese had believed this 'false report'.[70]

The Times, which was sympathetic towards the Germans on the question of the need for a diplomatic mission of atonement, found the entire story beyond belief. While understanding that the Germans wanted to ensure that the gravity of the diplomatic mission was recognized by the Chinese, they could scarcely credit the idea that the Germans would demand that Chinese royalty kowtow before the German Kaiser. In the city in which 'Voltaire was the guest of Frederick the Great', the paper argued, it seemed unlikely that the Chinese would 'be called upon to go through a ceremony which European envoys in China have resolutely refused to submit to for a hundred years':

> Excessive as is the importance attached to Court ceremonials in Berlin, it seems hardly conceivably that the Government of an enlightened people, with a strong sense of the ludicrous, should seriously propose to offer them the edifying spectacle of beholding their Sovereign made the principal in an extravagant rite borrowed from the servile etiquette of the Far East. The Berlin public, we hear, are already remarking that the mission would be an excellent subject for a comic opera.[71]

On the question of the matter being an inspiration for German satirists, the *Times* was correct. In several articles, *Kladderadatsch* had made clear just how the kowtow issue and Wilhelm II's inability to calibrate his courtly ritual in keeping with the interests of the nation had seen the solemn mission of atonement descend into farce. In one issue that assumed it was the Chinese prince who had been ordered to kowtow, it joked that Zaifeng's hesitancy to put his head on the ground

---

[68] 'La Mission du Prince Tchoun: Pourquoi elle reste en panne à Bâle', *Le Matin*, 1 September 1901, in PAAA R/18507, 124–6.
[69] Foreign Office to Bülow, 11 September 1901, in PAAA R 18508, 45–7.
[70] Mumm to AA, 2 September 1901, PAAA R/18507, 45, 57. The claim that Zaifeng had initially been instructed to kowtow was also made by Satow in Peking: Satow, *The Diaries of Sir Ernest Satow*, 135.
[71] *The Times*, 2 September 1901, in PAAA R/18507, 110.

was because China had sent a clockwork model of him to Germany that would be split in two if it hit the floor with its head.[72] In another, the periodical wondered aloud why the Chinese visitors were so upset about putting their foreheads to the floor, given that 'in the German Empire, many crawl on their bellies their entire lives.'[73] A third report joked that a privy counsellor had heard a rumour that the kowtow was to be introduced as standard practice at Wilhelm II's court and had then rushed to kowtow before the Chinese delegation in an attempt to perfect his technique. The bemused Chinese officials, the satirical article concluded, applauded his efforts, but confessed to being unfamiliar with the old-fashioned gesture that they had 'neither carried out, nor seen carried out by others' in China.[74]

On 3 September, *The Daily News* in London also picked up on the growing sense of farce evident in what it called 'The Kotow Comedy'. Incorrectly assuming that the demand for the kowtow was the product of pressure from the German press, it (correctly) reported that Zaifeng had been in close contact with Peking when deciding whether or not to comply with the performance demanded of him by Berlin. Its assessment of the incident and the German role in it was scathing; from beginning to end Wilhelm II had mismanaged both the politics and the staging of this highly significant royal visit from China in a way that was both completely characteristic of his style of misrule and inconsistent with the norms of European diplomatic behaviour:

> The whole affair is a singularly characteristic illustration of Kaiser Wilhelm's temperament. The Kaiser is a romanticist without a gleam of humour. In this business of the 'kowtow' he reveals as little sense of the ridiculous as he did when in his long boots and spurs he knelt on the Mount of Olives, and prayed with his faced turned to Jerusalem, while hordes of Cook's and Gaze's tourists looked on... It would be a whimsical reversal of the progress of ideas if a rite abandoned in Peking had been exacted in Berlin.[75]

In the wake of this international criticism, which had been met with glee by German progressives, the conservative German paper *Die Post* sought to maintain a royalist line, by reminding both internal and external critics that this was no laughing matter and that should the Chinese have decided not to proceed with the mission of atonement, 'all parties that had signed the peace agreement would be duty bound to apply sufficient pressure on China so that they recognize the importance of performing the atonement placed upon them'.[76] This was

---

[72] 'Die Wahrheit über Tschun', *Kladderadatsch*, 8 September 1901, 138.
[73] 'Kotau', *Kladderadatsch* 8 September 1901, 139.
[74] 'Das unverwerthbare Talent', *Kladderadatsch*. 15 September 1901, 142.
[75] 'The Kotow Comedy', *Daily News*, 3 September 1901, in PAAA R/18507, 102–3.
[76] *Die Post*, 5 September 1901, in PAAA R/18507, 121.

technically true, and the fact that it was Wilhelm II rather than the Chinese emperor who was forced to back down suggests that the Foreign Office was correct in its estimation that the German monarch's excessive demands for ritual abasement were simply not supported by the other signatories of the peace treaty.

For his part, in a marginal comment Wilhelm II blamed the failure of the Foreign Office rather than his own actions for the reactions of the other European powers. Unsurprisingly, he agreed with the paper's view that the other powers should have immediately supported his demands when the Chinese threatened not to proceed with the mission.[77] The emperor's criticism elicited a defence of the Foreign Office from State Secretary Oswald von Richthofen, who argued that the emperor's intention to demand a kowtow from the delegation had come to it as a complete surprise. Not only was the stipulation unknown to the Chinese until they arrived in Genoa, but, prior to that, the Foreign Office knew only that Wilhelm II would meet Zaifeng as an envoy, with no other conditions specified.[78]

The apology ceremony itself was watched with doubt from afar as well. In Britain, *The Times* was critical of the ceremony, arguing that the Chinese emperor's message amounted to a lukewarm apology that failed to even name the act of murder that had necessitated it, while suggesting that the reputedly anti-Western Empress Dowager Cixi had played an as yet undetected role in events from behind the throne. The paper expressed the hope that the Chinese had been suitably chastened, but worried that China had in fact been emboldened by the support of Russia. Reflecting on Wilhelm II's remarks, *The Times* mused:

> The Emperor spoke with truth, with force, and with dignity; but it is to be feared that the supposed diplomatic victory as regards the kotow on which the Chinese are pluming themselves may detract from the weight of his words. At Peking they are openly chuckling at their success, and our Correspondent tells us that the Russian Legation, with characteristic audacity, are ingeniously seeking to take credit to themselves for the result. They foresaw that Germany would give way, and accordingly they urged China to keep firm.[79]

Similarly sensing a Chinese diplomatic victory, an editorial in *The Standard* expressed its relief that the Germans had not forced the Chinese to kowtow in a way that might have demeaned all of the powers of Europe. Appealing to a racialized sense of a pan-European, civilizationary solidarity in the face of China, it expressed its concerns about the broader effects the incident might have had on the reputation of Europe:

---

[77] *Die Post*, 5 September 1901, in PAAA R/18507, 121.
[78] Richthofen to Wilhelm II, 10 September 1901, in PAAA R/18507, 165–8.
[79] *The Times*, 5 September 1901, in PAAA R/18507, 140.

The German Emperor received the Chinese Mission yesterday with dignified ceremonial, and some very plain speaking. We may congratulate ourselves, as members of the civilised world, that there were not exacted from the Celestial Envoy any of the grovelling forms of Asiatic respect.... Assurances are given on the part of the German authorities that there never was an intention to insist on an abject form of ceremonial abasement. We entertain no doubt that this is a correct version of the facts; but since the mistake of adopting one of the worst of Oriental models was not to be made, it is a pity that the officious persons who spread the report were not silenced sooner by an explicit statement of the Emperor's will. As it is, a good many people will remain persuaded that demands were made to which Prince Chun declined to agree, and only withdrawn in consequence of his refusal. The imaginary concession will continue to be quoted as a Diplomatic victory for the Chinese.[80]

In a more telling and bellicose vein, the same report drew the moral that Germany needed to learn the imperial lesson it said the British had learned in their dealings with India, namely that only violence or the threat of violence could subdue the hitherto independent kingdoms of the Far East:

The history of the British Empire in India shows that escape from immediate destruction frequently has no effect on wrong-headed Oriental dynasties and their servants except to encourage them to return, after an interval of cringing, to the very courses which have already proved disastrous. Yet the intelligence of the Chinese is said, by good authorities, to be rather greater than that of most Eastern peoples... It would be a delusion to suppose that the high Mandarins are reconciled to having to treat Europeans fairly, but they have learned to fear the power of the foreigners, and this wholesome dread must have some restraining influence.[81]

An even more frankly chauvinistic article which openly questioned the civilizationary level of the Chinese was published by the *Morning Post*, which praised the Kaiser and expressed its regret that the kowtow had not, in fact, been insisted upon as a means of educating the Chinese about the realities of imperialism:

The German Emperor was yesterday the representative of Europe, and, in a large sense, of civilisation. He might well doubt if the mission of apology which came before him was sent by a civilised nation, for how can a nation be admitted to the comity of the Great Powers which is openly disrespectful of the primary rules of international intercourse... It is not for us to criticise the decision of the

---

[80] *The Standard*, 5 September 1901, in PAAA R/18507, 141.
[81] *The Standard*, 5 September 1901, in PAAA R/18507, 141.

Emperor William and his advisers in dispensing with certain formalities which would have rendered the apology of Prince Tchun more formal, and would have brought the sense of shame more truly home to the Oriental mind... Few of us can claim to understand the Oriental temperament. None of us is master of even one-tenth of the difficulties which will present themselves as the full dimensions of the great task of civilising the East becomes apparent. But whatever may be the idiosyncrasies of the Celestial, and however he may object to Western expansion, he must learn that he has to treat Europeans with human kindness and human respect. If Prince Tchun carries homes this lesson to China his mission will not have been in vain.[82]

In a rare example of a paper attempting to grapple with Chinese conceptualizations of the apology, the liberal *Daily News* declared itself to be more sympathetic to the efforts made by the Chinese emperor, suggesting that the high-level delegation had been a risk for an emperor who was 'too liberal, by all accounts for the high and dry Tories of the Mandarinate'. The apology, it argued, had been 'straightforward and uncompromising', and the gravity of the situation had certainly been impressed upon the 'terribly nervous' young prince, who would, the paper asserted, 'remember as long as he lives the stern face and the sharp manner of the Kaiser during the apologetic stage of the ceremony'.[83]

In colonized India, reactions were also strong. The English-language newspaper *The Pioneer* vacillated between noting the air of farce that had come to surround the affair and criticizing the Germans for their high-handed treatment of the Chinese delegation. Noting that 'the German authorities have imposed upon him too many obeisances for a man of noble Chinese birth,'[84] it then went on to comment on the kowtow issue in detail:

To the intense relief of all sensible persons the great kowtow question has ended, if not satisfactorily, at all events less unsatisfactorily than many had feared. It would be a task of some nicety to strike a balance between Kaiser Wilhelm and Prince Chun, and say which has gained the advantage. In the language of whist the honours are even; but if either of the parties can be said to have got the better of the other, it is the heathen Chinee who has scored off the Christian Teuton. Prince Chun vowed he would not kowtow, and he has not kowtowed. He protested that neither should his suite kowtow, and they have not kowtowed. The Kaiser consented to waive the kowtow as regards Prince Chun, but insisted upon it in the case of the suite. A deadlock appeared to have been reached, and while

---

[82] *Morning Post*, 5 September 1901, in PAAA R/18507, 142.

[83] 'The Chinese Emperor's Letter', *Daily News*, 5 September 1901, in PAAA R/18507, 143.

[84] *The Pioneer*, 20 September 1901, in PAAA R 18508, 'Akten betreffend den Aufstand in China: Chinesische Sühnemission nach Berlin', 164.

Europe, holding both its sides and shaking with laughter, was waiting to see what would come next, the mind of an ingenious diplomat was struck with a brilliant idea. The Kaiser reiterated that if the suite came, they should kowtow; Prince Chun repeated that they should not. Let the difficulty be solved, therefore, by the suite stopping away. The simple suggestion met with the approval of all parties…The Kaiser found himself in a cleft stick. He must either give way, or see himself become more and more the laughing stock of the world. If he insisted on the kowtow, the Mission would return to China without coming to Berlin; and he would have quietly to pocket an additional affront to his outraged Majesty…He took the sensible alternative and consented to abate his demands and admit the Mission on their own terms.[85]

The *Times of India* went so far as to argue that Zaifeng had threatened to kill himself in the event that he was forced to kowtow before Wilhelm II, and thereby had won a diplomatic victory over Europe. 'Prince Chun's paltering sad threats of suicide', the paper argued, 'were so far successful that he performed his expiatory mission without prostrating himself at the German Emperor's feet.' This ruse had, it was reported, left the Chinese in Peking 'chuckling over the withdrawal of the German Emperor's demand of kowtow from Prince Chun'.[86] These sentiments were shared by the German consul general to India, Hermann Speck von Sternburg, who reported that the overall reaction was that the mission of atonement had, in fact, become a 'political success for China that must contribute to damaging not only the prestige of Germany but all of Europe in China'.[87] To this he added the complication that Russia had been able to insinuate itself into the good graces of the Chinese by supporting them on the kowtow issue,[88] offering the potential for a further wedge between Germany and the Russian Empire. As *The Pioneer* put it, 'The general feeling is that the whole affair has been bungled over in the same way as everything else connected with the unfortunate Chinese business.'[89]

The Rehabilitation of the Royal Penitent

As part of the royally ordered court ceremony, Wilhelm II's palace guards had pointedly ignored Zaifeng on his way into his audience with the Kaiser, treating him as an 'unpardoned penitent'.[90] Once Zaifeng had offered China's expression of regret, however, the palace guards had sprung to attention, signalling an

---

[85] *The Pioneer*, 25 September 1901, in PAAA R 18508, 165.
[86] *The Times of India*, in PAAA R 18508, 167.
[87] Sternburg to AA, 3 October 1901, in PAAA R/18507, 160–71.
[88] Sternburg to Foreign Office, 3 October 1901, in PAAA R 18508, 160–71.
[89] *The Pioneer*, 25 September 1901, in PAAA R 18508, 165.
[90] *Daily Chronicle*, 5 September 1901, in PAAA R/18507, 143.

immediate recognition of his new position as a royal guest once his 'apology' had been delivered.[91] This immediate shift in the mode of the treatment of the Chinese royal delegation baffled some overseas commentators and amused others. As London's *Daily Chronicle* archly opined, 'Prince Chun, we daresay, had a bad quarter of an hour in the discharge of the first part of the mission.'[92]

The question of how to act towards the prince and the Chinese delegation after the formal ceremony of atonement had been performed was a delicate one, and one that had been publicly discussed in Germany prior to Zaifeng's arrival. On 1 September, while the Chinese prince was still in Basel, *Kladderadatsch* had critiqued the honoured position that Zaifeng was to be afforded, with a full-page comic that disparaged the gap between what the magazine thought real atonement should look like and what it thought it would look like in reality. In a series of racialized panels, the comic emphasized that real penitence should involve bodily discomfort; the pulling of hair, the deprivation of liberty, meagre food allocations and being beaten, none of which, the image showed, would be inflicted upon the Chinese prince (see Figure 4.3).[93]

Despite the crudity of its fantasies of violence against a Chinese royal, *Kladderadatsch* was to some degree correct. Not only had Zaifeng withstood the German emperor's pressure to kowtow before him, but he was also spared any other bodily or social mortifications to signal China's remorse for the killing of Ketteler. Once the formal statement of regret had been offered, the German government immediately shifted to treating the members of the delegation as honoured royal guests. Despite the fact that Wilhelm II had forbidden palace staff and servants to accept gifts of appreciation from the Chinese prince,[94] in most other respects, the prince was feted by the German royal family. The prince toured Germany, not least of all visiting the naval manoeuvres in Danzig as an honoured guest of the emperor and empress, where he presented them with valuable gifts from the Guangxu emperor.[95] In a return to the forms of diplomacy used during King Chulalongkorn of Siam's visit in 1897, Prussia's second highest order, the Great Cross of the Order of the Red Eagle, was bestowed on Zaifeng, which left London's *Daily News*, already disgruntled by the fact that the prince was touring the industrial powerhouses of the German economy, to remark that 'the real object of his coming to Europe was pushed quite into the background. In the Celestial Empire they have every reason to be satisfied with the result of the

[91] *Daily Mail*, 5 September 1901, in PAAA R/18507, 145.
[92] *Daily Chronicle*, 5 September 1901, in PAAA R/18507, 143.
[93] 'Die Sühne, oder Ideal und Wirklichkeit', *Kladderadatsch*, 1 September 1901, 136.
[94] *Staatsbürger Zeitung*, 9 September 1901, in PAAA R/18507, 158.
[95] 'Chinesische Geschenke', *Das kleine Journal*, 10 September 1901, in PAAA R/18507, 178. These gifts were distributed to Berlin's art and ethnographic museums: PAAA R 18508, 183, 235–7. Even this met with protest, with Baden's envoy complaining that their museum would not receive any Chinese pieces: PAAA R 18508, 263.

Figure 4.3 Cartoon in *Kladderadatsch* (1901) suggesting that Zaifeng had been treated too well while in Germany

mission.'[96] The *Daily Chronicle* too had its doubts about the efficacy of the German treatment of the prince after his act of atonement, warning that 'we cannot avoid the suspicion which we have already expressed that all this sequel to the act of expiation will destroy its effect.'[97]

Nor did all Germans appreciate this all too rapid rehabilitation. The mother of the murdered German consul, Ketteler, bluntly refused the prince's request to visit her, replying to his letter that 'It is not my wish to receive his visit. We forgive as Christians the serious crimes that a misguided nation has committed against my son and human rights. However, we do not wish to come into contact with a representative of that nation.'[98] Yet even this potentially prickly incident was treated gently by the nationalist press, with the National-Liberal *Tägliche Rundschau* remarking that the prince's offer of a meeting should be seen sympathetically as a well-meaning gesture that originated not with any German instruction, but the prince's own desire to speak personally with the family.[99]

The views of others in Germany who were against the 'lenient' treatment of the Chinese prince were laid bare by Munich's *Allgemeine Zeitung*, which acknowledged that some expert and public opinion felt that bestowing high decorations on Zaifeng not only obscured the character of the mission of atonement but also handed yet another diplomatic victory to the Chinese court, still celebrating Germany's capitulation on the question of the kowtow. The paper quickly sought to assuage such concerns, however, arguing that when Wilhelm II's brother Prince Heinrich had visited China, he too had been awarded China's second highest order, namely Class One Level Two of the Double Dragon. It was only fitting, the paper maintained, that Zaifeng should receive an order of corresponding worth.[100]

More prosaically, the prince's mission of atonement was also viewed as an opportunity to showcase Germany's industrial capacity to the Chinese delegation in the hope of winning Zaifeng's royal patronage for future German commercial contracts in China.[101] To this end, Zaifeng visited the Krupp Villa Hügel as an esteemed guest on 24 September 1901 (see Figure 4.4).[102] Given the sensitive occasion of the royal visit to Germany, this commercial dimension of the visit was handled discreetly, with economic issues discussed out of public sight. As one

[96] *Daily News*, 29 September 1901, in PAAA R/18507, 270.
[97] *Daily Chronicle* 5 September 1901, in PAAA R/18507, 143.
[98] Letter to Münster, 9 September 1901, PAAA R/18507, 185.
[99] *Tägliche Rundschau*, 13 September 1901, in PAAA R/18507, 217.
[100] *Allgemeine Zeitung*, 25 September 1901, in PAAA R 18508, 'Akten betreffend den Aufstand in China: Chinesische Sühnemission nach Berlin', 33. For the Kaiser's formal report on the bestowal of this order, see his confirmation, 11 November 1901, in PAAA R 131819.
[101] For the place of China more broadly in Imperial German understandings of globalization, see Sebastian Conrad, *Globalisation and the Nation in Imperial Germany*, trans. S. O'Hagan (Cambridge: Cambridge University Press, 2010), 203–74.
[102] Historisches Archiv Krupp FAH 22/FAH3 H 33.1.

AUF DEM HÜGEL, DEN 24. SEPT. 1901

Figure 4.4 Zaifeng (centre) at Krupp's Villa Hügel, 24 September 1901
Source: Photo courtesy of the Historisches Archiv Krupp.

paper knowingly described the situation, 'Discussions regarding trade issues are not scheduled. However, it is highly likely that trade issues will be discussed.'[103]

In an era of competitive and rapid globalization, the economic potential of the Chinese royal visit was well understood by other European powers, with the British, Belgians, and Italians all asking the German Foreign Office whether Germany was opposed to Zaifeng touring their respective countries once the formalities of his visit had been finished. The Russians went so far as to express their hope that the prince might use the trans-Siberian railway to travel to Germany, to show him their railway network and capacity for building railway infrastructure. Claiming that the solemn nature of the voyage precluded any such side trips before the royal apology, the Germans told the other European powers that Zaifeng should travel more or less directly by German steamer to Germany to fulfil his mission. Thereafter, the German Foreign Office replied, 'once the mission

---

[103] *Berliner Lokal_Anzeiger*, 18 July 1901, in PAAA R 131819, 'Die Chinesische Sühnegesandschaft aus Anlaß der Ermordung des deutschen Gesandten in Peking, Freiherrn von Ketteler'.

of atonement had been completed, the German government considered Prince Chun free in all his further movements.'[104]

Nevertheless, while Zaifeng toured German factories and harbours, he did not tour any other European states. The Belgian press blamed Wilhelm II for forbidding the Chinese prince from visiting Belgium prior to leaving Europe.[105] The British press too bemoaned a commercial opportunity lost, with the *Daily News* complaining that the Chinese prince would not see British industry and reporting that, while in Germany, Zaifeng had 'promised orders' to German firms which might otherwise have flowed to British concerns. This loss of economic opportunity led the newspaper to remark rather sourly:

> One will not be far wrong in attributing this latest step of the government to Count von Bülow's interference. The independent press has throughout criticised the treatment of the Prince. After he had been made to feel that he had come as a penitent, he was invited to Danzig, and received a high Order, so that the real object of his coming to Europe was quite pushed into the background.[106]

In the end, with the prince departing Europe in late September without having left Germany while there, the German *Münchener Neueste Nachrichten* could report to its satisfaction that 'Prince Chun is...departing on 29 September without visiting another European country or America. He is in this way following an explicit order of his brother, the Emperor.' This, the paper continued, was yet further evidence of China's clever diplomacy.[107] Recent Chinese scholarship has suggested, however, that, far from this reflecting diplomatic statecraft directed from Peking, the Germans did, in fact, block Zaifeng from making other state visits outside Germany. Xuetong Li has argued that Germany had stressed that 'visiting other European countries like Great Britain, Italy, and Belgium would suggest a lack of sincerity, given that the trip was supposed to be a special one for an apology.'[108] These objections, Zhiwu Li too has argued, were deliberately calibrated to further embarrass the Qing court, which had already accepted some of these invitations.[109]

In the aftermath of Zaifeng's royal tour, the sense that China had come out of the visit looking somewhat better than Germany was widespread. Some Sinologists and sections of the German press argued that offering the Chinese

---

[104] Mumm to Foreign Office, 28 June 1901; Richthofen to Bülow, 1 July 1901; Foreign Office to Wedel, 11 July 1901 in PAAA Berlin R 18506, 119, 123, 133, 136, 142. See also German expressions of indignation over rumours of plans for the Chinese to travel via Britain's Asian colonies en route to Germany: *Deutsche-Asiatische Warte*, 24 July 1901, in PAAA Berlin R 18506, 147.

[105] *Le Soir*, 10 October 1901, in PAAA R 18508, 152.

[106] PAAA Berlin R 18507, *Daily News*, 29 September 1901, 270.

[107] PAAA Berlin R 18507; *Münchener Neueste Nachrichten*, 29 September 1901, 271.

[108] Xuetong Li, 'Chun Qinwang Zaifeng Shide Shishikao', 135–6.

[109] Zhiwu Li, 'Zaifeng Shide Shulun', 87.

prince the Great Cross of the Order of the Red Eagle had been a mistake that had betrayed the original solemn intention behind the mission. Others argued on the contrary that it was a visible sign that the actual mission of atonement had formally ended with the palace visit and that a new German-Chinese relationship had begun. Complaints about the cost of the trip were raised by some Germans, on the assumption that the German Empire had paid for the expenses of the Chinese delegation. These rumours were firmly batted away, with the German government emphasizing that China had paid for all of the prince's costs, apart from the free rail travel that was traditionally extended as a courtesy to other dignitaries visiting Germany and the small amount spent on Zaifeng while he was Wilhelm II's personal guest in Danzig (Figure 4.5).[110] This did not stop *Kladderadatsch* from publishing a mischievous, satirical poem depicting Zaifeng's tearful leave-taking from Germany as a product of his regret at leaving behind the unparalleled luxury he had lived in for three months at the expense of the German government.[111]

Figure 4.5 Zaifeng, Wilhelm II, and German army and naval officers, 1901
Source: Photo courtesy of the Bundesarchiv.

---

[110] 'Die Reisekosten des Prinzen Tschun', *Berliner Neueste Nachrichten*, 8 October 1901, in PAAA R 18508, 150.
[111] 'Das Sühneprinzen Zeche', *Kladderadatsch*, 13 October 1901, 159.

That China was able to make diplomatic capital from Zaifeng's visit, largely at the expense of Wilhelm II and the international reputation of the German Empire, seems a remarkable inversion of the intended consequences of the 'mission of atonement'. Instead of showcasing a spectacle of complete Chinese abasement before the might of the German Kaiser, Zaifeng left having delivered a non-apology according to ceremonial forms of China's choosing. For this the Chinese prince was seemingly rewarded by being feted throughout Germany, and receiving the second highest honour the empire had to offer. By successfully refusing the royally imposed kowtow, the Chinese diplomatic body had maintained its integrity, and remained, in a sense, an uncolonized site of China's imperial prestige, offering the Qing court an avenue to express its unconquered dignity in the wake of a military disaster. The diplomatic mission, that is, was part of the 'sharp check' to European imperialism in China heralded by the Boxer War.[112]

For many within Germany and throughout the world, far from having demonstrably punished China, the royal visit to Germany had increased the Asian kingdom's reputation throughout Europe at the expense of Kaiser Wilhelm II and Germany. Through the clamour over Zaifeng's inspection of German sites of industrial production, the visit had also increased China's attractiveness as an economic partner. And through the successful avoidance of bodily signs of abasement, the princely delegation had encouraged the Qing court's view that it was still possible for the Chinese to conduct diplomacy with European powers in Europe as equals. Rather than further quashing Chinese intransigence in the wake of the Boxer War, for many around the world, the atonement mission of Zaifeng and his Chinese delegation had left China emboldened in its dealings with the European powers.[113]

In Germany, the visit underlined two important issues related to Wilhelm II's role in German foreign affairs. On the one hand, it illustrated the important diplomatic and ceremonial role required of the German emperor, as a constitutional monarch and as the embodiment of the German nation. On the other, however, it illustrated the extent to which Wilhelm II's personal inability to satisfactorily play this metonymic role as a national figurehead, and his predilection for inappropriate and unsubtle grandiosity, had domestic and international consequences for the reputation of Germany as a power capable of projecting itself as a global empire. The emperor's personal overreach in the kowtow affair had made clear that it was risky for the German government to involve its constitutional monarch even in ceremonial displays of power.

---

[112] Robert Bickers, 'Introduction', in Bickers and Tiedemann (eds.), *The Boxers, China and the World*, xi.

[113] For this sentiment, that China had learned the wrong lessons from the royal visit, see, e.g., 'Tschuns Abschied', *Kladderadatsch*, 6 October 1901, 154: 'Confucius says, that just as soon / As the Boxers slaughter / Several thousand Christians violently / Then, hopefully we'll see each other again!'

5

The 'Kaiser's Holocaust' in Africa?

Upon arriving back in Berlin in late December 1905 after commanding the German army during the Herero-Nama Wars, the genocidaire Lieutenant General Lothar von Trotha was invited to a royal dinner in Potsdam with, among others, Kaiser Wilhelm II and Chancellor Bernhard von Bülow.[1] Also invited to the dinner was Major Victor Franke, who had been presented in the German press as a military hero of the Herero War, but was better known amongst the Herero as a rapist of African women.[2]

The public honour associated with an invitation from the emperor was usually a strong and rare signal of royal favour, and the ostensible purpose of the dinner was to honour the commander for his military success in South West Africa. If Trotha had expected to be feted by the monarch and the chancellor during the evening, however, he was sorely disappointed. It was already cause for scandal in arch-conservative court circles that Chancellor Bülow had refused to meet or speak with Trotha since his return from Africa, particularly given the high number of German casualties and the fact that the lieutenant general had been accused in the Reichstag of having brought dishonour on the German nation.[3] When Bülow was finally forced to meet with Trotha, as they travelled together to the royal dinner, they sat in virtual silence, with the chancellor's only comment being that he was glad to see that he had returned from Africa in good health.[4]

Things did not improve for Trotha when he arrived at the palace. During the dinner at which he was supposed to be the guest of honour, Trotha was 'pointedly ignored' by Wilhelm II, who was sitting next to him. The emperor said 'not a single word' about Africa or the war and offered his guests instead a loose and one-sided diatribe on Russia, hunting, and art which completely blocked Trotha from speaking. When the emperor had finished his monologue and spoke briefly with Franke, he brushed them off with the phrase 'Anyway, the war is over now,' and

---

[1] Vierhaus (ed), *Das Tagebuch der Baronin Spitzemberg*, 452–3.
[2] See Wolfram Hartmann, 'Urges in the Colony: Men and Women in Colonial Windhoek, 1890–1905', *Journal of Namibian History* 1 (2007), 42; Jan-Bart Gewald, 'The Herero Genocide: German Unity, Settlers, Soldiers and Ideas', in M. Bechhaus-Gerst and R. Klein-Arendt (eds), *Die (koloniale) Begegnung Afrikanerinnen in Deutschland 1880–1945: Deutsche in Afrika (1880–1918)* (Frankfurt am Main: Peter Lang, 2003), 118–19.
[3] Georg Ledebour, in *Verhandlungen des Reichstages*, 2 December 1905, 91; Vierhaus (ed), *Das Tagebuch der Baronin Spitzemberg*, 452–3.
[4] Vierhaus (ed), *Das Tagebuch der Baronin Spitzemberg*, 452–3.

The Kaiser and the Colonies: Monarchy in the Age of Empire. Matthew P. Fitzpatrick, Oxford University Press.
© Matthew P. Fitzpatrick 2022. DOI: 10.1093/oso/9780192897039.003.0006

summarily dismissed them, to the embarrassment of everyone else in the room.[5] Shortly thereafter, Trotha was quietly retired from active military service.

As the appointed commander of German troops during the Herero-Nama Wars in South West Africa, Germany's only settler colony, Trotha was viewed by the chancellor as bearing the primary responsibility for the shocking conduct of the war and the brutal treatment of both combatants and civilians.[6] Besides Trotha, however, other important German figures had played pivotal roles in the conflict, if not in the genocide. Most notable amongst these were Alfred von Schlieffen, the chief of the German General Staff and Governor Theodor von Leutwein, who was in charge of the colony when the war broke out, as well as Chancellor Bülow and, indeed, Kaiser Wilhelm II, the constitutionally appointed supreme commander of the German army, who had selected Trotha as commander. On the other side of the frontier, crucial decisions taken by Samuel Maharero, the Paramount Leader of the Herero, and Hendrik Witbooi, the Paramount Leader of the Nama, had deeply influenced the course of the war, without in any way somehow causing Trotha's turn to genocide.

As the following demonstrates, the colonial genocide at the heart of the war in South West Africa was purposively unleashed by Trotha. To that extent, the genocide was an expression of German state power and a consequence of the commander's formally enunciated military tactics. It was a strategy that was never formally disavowed by the metropolitan authorities, even after they worked for its discontinuation behind the scenes. An examination of the conduct of the German leadership both in Africa and in Berlin during the war makes this clear, as does as the nature of the relationship between the monarch, Germany's civilian and military authorities, and frontier actors during the war. It also clarifies the personal role of Kaiser Wilhelm II and offers a means of testing the veracity of Jeremy Sarkin's charge that the genocide was a product of the emperor's personal intent.[7] By examining the role of the emperor and other leaders in the conflict, this chapter

[5] Vierhaus (ed), *Das Tagebuch der Baronin Spitzemberg*, 452–3.

[6] This is not to deny settler colonialism's broader structural propensity for violence. See Patrick Wolfe, 'Settler Colonialism and the Elimination of the Native', *Journal of Genocide Research* 8, no. 4 (2006), 387–409; J. Kēhaulani Kauanui, '"A Structure, Not an Event": Settler Colonialism and Enduring Indigeneity', *Lateral* 5, no. 1 (2006), doi: 10.25158/L5.1.7; Lorenzo Veracini, *Settler Colonialism: A Theoretical Overview* (Basingstoke: Palgrave Macmillan, 2010). For concerns about the settler colonial analytical paradigm's propensity to flatten complex historical terrain and underplay the agency of the colonized, see Shino Kinoshi, 'First Nations Scholars, Settler Colonial Studies, and Indigenous History', *Australian Historical Studies* 50, no. 3 (2019), 304; Corey Snelgrove, Rita Kaur Dhamoon, and Jeff Corntassel, 'Unsettling Settler Colonialism: The Discourse and Politics of Settlers, and Solidarity with Indigenous Nations', *Decolonization, Indigeneity, Education and Society* 3, no. 2 (2014), 26–7; Miranda Johnson, 'Writing Indigenous Histories Now', *Australian Historical Studies* 45, no. 3 (2014), 317; Tim Rowse, 'Indigenous Heterogeneity'. *Australian Historical Studies* 45, no. 3 (2014), 310.

[7] Jeremy Sarkin, *Germany's Genocide of the Herero: Kaiser Wilhelm II, His Generals, His Settlers, His Soldiers* (Cape Town: UCT Press, 2011).

evaluates the claim that the war in South West Africa was, in the words of Casper Erichsen and David Olusoga, 'the Kaiser's Holocaust'.[8]

Military Power in South West Africa

Kaiser Wilhelm II had never shied away from the suggestion that Germany's wars for empire should be fought in a manner that saw non-European populations terrorized. Prior to German troops embarking for the Boxer War in China, for example, Wilhelm II had given his infamous *Hunnenrede*, later singled out by Chancellor Bülow as 'perhaps the most damaging speech Wilhelm II ever gave'.[9] The speech has often been seen as indicative of Kaiser Wilhelm II's views on the necessity of uncompromising brutality in the conduct of colonial warfare and his understanding of the 'virtues' embodied by the German military.[10] In it the monarch exhorted his troops to radical violence against the Chinese:

> Pardon will not be given! Prisoners will not be taken! Those who should fall into your hands will be lost! Just as a thousand years ago the Huns under their king Attila made a name for themselves that is still renowned in tales and fables, so may the name 'German' be established by you in China for a thousand years, so that never again should a Chinese look askance at a German.[11]

What looked like an outrageous royal order for the application of unlimited violence, however, was in fact an unscripted and thoughtlessly cruel flourish that carried no weight beyond the monarch's own febrile imagination. Meant to inspire the martial spirit of the departing troops, the speech horrified the chancellor (who sought to have reports of it suppressed) and much of German civil society.[12] More importantly, however, the speech played no role in directing the conduct of German troops in China, troops who, in the event, missed the war by some weeks and were left to conduct occupation and anti-Boxer mopping-up operations in occupied Peking.[13] Not only did Wilhelm II's speech not set the

---

[8] Casper W. Erichsen and David Olusoga, *The Kaiser's Holocaust: Germany's Forgotten Genocide and the Colonial Roots of Nazism* (London: Faber and Faber, 2010).

[9] Bernhard von Bülow, *Denkwürdigkeiten*, vol. 2 (Berlin: Ullstein Verlag, 1930), 20–1.

[10] Isabel V. Hull, *Absolute Destruction: Military Culture and the Practices of War in Imperial Germany* (Ithaca, NY: Cornell University Press, 2005), 135–6, 143–4; Wolfgang J. Mommsen, *War der Kaiser an allem Schuld? Wilhelm II und die preussisch-deutschen Machteliten* (Berlin: Ullstein, 2005), 103–4.

[11] Manfred Görtemaker, *Deutschland im 19. Jahrhundert: Entwicklungslinien* (Opladen: Leske & Budrich Verlag, 1996), 357.

[12] Hull, *Absolute Destruction*, 135–6.

[13] Sabine Dabringhaus, 'An Army on Vacation? The German War in China, 1900–1901', in Manfred Boemeke, Roger Chickering, and Stig Förster (eds), *Anticipating Total War: The German and American Experiences* (Cambridge: Cambridge University Press, 1999), 459–60. See also Yixu Lü, 'Germany's War in China: Media Coverage and Political Myth', *German Life and Letters* 61, no. 2 (2008), 202–14.

tone for war in China, but the punitive actions that were undertaken by the German occupying forces were largely improvised counterinsurgency operations which were the result of 'neither central military planning in Peking nor political guidelines from Berlin'.[14]

Wilhelm II was confronted by the seeming realization of his radically violent vision of colonial warfare, however, during the military campaign against the Herero and Nama nations in South West Africa four years later. During this war, Chancellor Bülow was forced to warn Wilhelm II that, unless the monarch intervened and used his sovereign prerogative to mitigate the genocidal conduct of Trotha, the violence perpetrated by German troops would see the cruel bloodlust of the Hun Speech and its refusal to countenance the acceptance of prisoners confirmed as official German military policy.[15] Confronted by this reality, and despite having no legal obligation to acquiesce to the overtures of his chancellor or deviate from what some assumed to be his preferred means of waging war, Wilhelm II submitted to Bülow's judgement and ordered Trotha to reverse his 'no prisoners' stance.

In 1904 South West Africa was still completing its transition from its origins in the mid-1880s as a chartered mining company colony on the Anglo-Dutch model augmented by the 'civilizing' efforts of the Rhenish Mission amongst the African population to a settler colony dedicated to the creation of a large, permanent German population transplanted to Africa.[16] The transition was predicated on an ever-accelerating process of accumulating territory undertaken by German settlers, a process that placed intense pressure upon the lands and herds of Herero pastoralists, at whose expense this expansion occurred.[17] The particular mechanism for this was often trade aimed at creating a situation of debt peonage, with merchants travelling throughout South West Africa seeking to push Herero

---

[14] Susanne Kuß, *German Colonial Wars and the Context of Military Violence* (Cambridge, MA: Harvard University Press, 2017), 5–36.

[15] Bülow, *Denkwürdigkeiten*, vol. 2, 20–1.

[16] On the course of settler colonialism in German South West Africa, see Dörte Lerp, 'Farmers to the Frontier: Settler Colonialism in the Eastern Prussian Provinces and German Southwest Africa', *Journal of Imperial and Commonwealth History* 41, no. 4 (2013), 567–83; Helmut Bley, *Namibia under German Rule* (Hamburg: Lit Verlag, 1996), 3–57; Jürgen Zimmerer, *Deutsche Herrschaft über Afrikaner: Staatlicher Machtanspruch und Wirklichkeit im kolonialen Namibia* (Münster: Lit Verlag, 2002), 13–21; Ulrich van der Heyden, 'Christian Missionary Societies in the German Colonies, 1884/1885–1914/1915', in Volker Max Langbehn and Mohammad Salama (eds), *German Colonialism: Race, the Holocaust, and Postwar Germany* (New York: Columbia University Press, 2011), 215–52; Adam A. Blackler, 'From Boondoggle to Settlement Colony: Hendrik Witbooi and the Evolution of Germany's Imperial Project in Southwest Africa, 1884–1894', *Central European History* 50, no. 4 (2017), 449–70.

[17] On the history of the Herero, see Jan-Bart Gewart, *Herero Heroes: A Socio-Political History of the Herero of Namibia, 1890–1923* (Athens, GA: Ohio University Press, 1995). For the effects of the Herero War on the Herero polity and people, see Zimmerer, *Deutsche Herrschaft über Afrikaner*, Jürgen Zimmerer and Joachim Zeller (eds), *Genocide in German South-West Africa: The Colonial War (1904–1908) in Namibia and Its Aftermath* (Berlin: Merlin Press, 2008); George Steinmetz, *The Devil's Handwriting: Precoloniality and the German Colonial State in Qindao, Samoa, and Southwest Africa* (Chicago: Chicago University Press, 2007), 179–216. By 1913, 15,000 European colonists had settled in the colony (of whom only 1,220 were adult German males.

communities into large debts that could only be discharged through the sale of land. According to German missionaries, the Herero had for years been 'ensnared, exploited, and embattled' by merchants seeking to dispossess them, with some reports of Herero also being shot by German settlers.[18]

That the war against the Germans was a reaction to the practices of German merchants was also argued by the Herero themselves in 1904. Among many others, Justus, a Herero man from Okahanja, informed the missionary August Kuhlmann that the Herero could simply no longer bear the oppression and beatings of German traders:

> The yoke of the Germans is too hard. If we all fall, write this to the Kaiser, to all the Germans, and to the great teachers: The troops are not to blame for the war. No, we have nothing against them. They can live in this land. The blame for the war lies with the merchants who harassed us with their trade. If we refused to be indebted to them, that led to trouble. If we became indebted to them through our purchases, that too led to trouble. They still mistreated us.[19]

So too the Herero translator Margaretha Getse reported to the Germans that 'the war came from the shop owners, the merchants, and the farmers.'[20] Even Governor Leutwein professed that he was inclined towards the view that the uprising had been fermenting for a long time as a result of 'the often violent manner of travelling merchants'.[21] With the land question becoming increasingly acute and the collapse of Herero cattle herds leading to high levels of Herero debt and dispossession, Herero–settler relations were increasingly strained before war broke out on 12 January 1904.[22] By 14 January, the seriousness of the uprising was apparent, with news reaching Wilhelm II in Berlin that the German naval vessel *Habicht* was requesting permission to land troops to help defend German settlements.[23] Chancellor Bülow made a statement to the Reichstag on 18 January 1904 informing deputies of the violence.[24]

---

[18] 'Die Rheinische Mission und der Herero-Aufstand'; Wilhelm Elger to Otto Forkel, 22 March 1904, in *BA Berlin* R1001/2114, 'Aufstand der Hereros 1904–1907', 9, 77–8.

[19] August Kuhlmann to Berner, 16 May 1904, in *BA Berlin* R1001/2114, 220–1. Bülow's own report to the Reichstag admitted that such abuses had occurred. See 'Denkschrift über Eingeborenen-Politik und Hereroaufstand in Deutsch-Südwestafrika', in BA Berlin, R1001/2117, 'Aufstand der Hereros 1904–1907', 7(21).

[20] Margaretha Getse to Otto Forkel, 23 March 1904, in in *BA Berlin* R1001/2114, 78–9.

[21] Theodor Leutwein, 'Der Herero-Aufstand in Deutsch Südwestafrika', *Deutsches Kolonialblatt* 15, no. 7 (1904), 206.

[22] For the immediate period prior to the war, see Leutwein, 'Der Herero-Aufstand in Deutsch Südwestafrika', 206–21.

[23] German Admiralty to Wilhelm II, 13 January 1904, in *BA Berlin*, R1001/2111, 'Aufstand der Hereros 1904–1907', 7.

[24] 'Erklärung des Herrn Reichskanzlers in der Reichstagssitzung vom 18 Januar 1904 über den Hereroaufstand', in BA Berlin R1001/2111, 53; Bülow, *Verhandlungen des Reichstages*, 18 January 1904, 329–30.

Cognizant of the Germans' military strength, in the first weeks of the war the Paramount Leader of the Herero, Samuel Maharero, attempted to form a broad military coalition of African nations in South West Africa, including their recent military opponents, the Nama. As his famous second letter to the Paramount Leader of the Nama, Hendrik Witbooi, declared, 'Let us die together, and not die through mistreatment, prison, or other such ways.'[25] As the conflict intensified, Maharero was also careful to delineate precisely against whom the Herero were fighting, namely German men of military age. In a letter to his people, Maharero had expressly forbidden the targeting of anyone who was not German—including the British, Boers, other Africans, and missionaries. As Governor Leutwein later confirmed, although 123 German settlers and soldiers were killed in the initial stages of the Herero War, women and children were deliberately spared in almost all cases.[26]

Once reinforcements were brought in from Germany, the early military successes of the Herero were brought to an end. Although no decisive military victory was achieved by Trotha, the Herero still paid an exceedingly high price for his command of the war in terms of casualties. Indeed, Trotha's genocidal conduct of the war saw their numbers plummet from as high as 80,000 before the war to around 15,000 after it, with most killed after the Battle of Waterberg during the flight across the Omaheke Desert. Compounding the Herero's plight, the conditions placed upon the post-war reintegration of the survivors into the colony also saw the remnant population reduced to a semi-free workforce suffering enormous mortality rates.[27]

The German Chain of Command

Although the colonial director, Dr Oskar Stübel, claimed to the Reichstag in mid-1905 that the German government had no information that suggested that reports from Africa about the brutal nature of Trotha's campaign were true,[28]

---

[25] Theodor Leutwein, *Elf Jahre Gouverneur in Deutsch-Südwestafrika* (Berlin: Ernst Siegfried Mittler und Sohn, 1906), 467–8. On the paramountcies of Samuel Maharero and Hendrik Witbooi, see Chapter 9.
[26] Leutwein, *Elf Jahre Gouverneur*, 466–7. On the dating of Maharero's letters, see Gewart, *Herero Heroes*, 156–61. For a list of Germans killed (including in later military action), see 'Verzeichnis der während des Hereroaufstandes ermordeten und im Gefecht gefallenen Personen', in *BA Berlin* R1001/2114, 227–31.
[27] For the war years, Caspar W Erichsen has argued that forced labour on the Lüderitz Bay to Keetmanshoop railway saw a mortality rate amongst African prisoner of 67%. See Casper W Erichsen, 'Zwangsarbeit im Konzentrationslager auf der Haifischinsel', in Jürgen Zimmerer and Joachim Zeller (eds) *Völkermord in Deutsch-Südwestafrika: Der Kolonialkrieg (1904–1908) in Namibia und seine Folgen* (Berlin: Ch. Links, 2003), 83. For later developments in the colony's post-war labour market, see Zimmerer, *Deutsche Herrschaft über Afrikaner*, 176–242.
[28] Oskar Stübel, *Verhandlungen des Reichstages*, 25 May 1905, 6161.

the chancellor had reported Trotha's genocidal military turn to Wilhelm II as early as October 1904.[29] At that time Bülow warned Wilhelm II that Trotha was waging war in a manner that was incompatible with both Germany's material interests and its international reputation. Crucially, the chancellor had to approach the emperor to recast the contours of German colonial warfare because it required the executive power of the monarch to countervail the orders of his nominated colonial representative.[30] Given this situation, two questions arise, namely how far Wilhelm II's prerogative power over the colony actually extended, and to what extent he sought to exert this power to its limits.

Despite Wilhelm II's own sense of himself as a seriously engaged military figure, he was often shielded from the full weight of his constitutional powers by others who understood his personal limitations only too well. As his long-time confidant Prince Philipp of Eulenburg-Hertefeld understood, managing Wilhelm II during a colonial war consisted of prompting all those surrounding him 'to regale the Kaiser with harmless stories and to avoid politics' while praying that 'nothing complicated approaches His Majesty.'[31] When Wilhelm II insisted, for example, during the Boxer War that, as supreme commander of the armed forces, he should personally receive the correspondence from the front and not the Foreign Office, the emperor's delusion that he was competent to deal with military matters was quietly circumvented by those, such as Eulenburg, Bülow, and Schlieffen, who knew that 'this standpoint is neither *politically nor militarily* feasible and *must* inevitably lead to a catastrophe.'[32]

This is not to say that the emperor was constitutionally or legally powerless in colonial matters. Indeed, the legal parameters of the royal prerogative in the German colonies were quite extensive.[33] This is because Articles 1 and 2 of the German Constitution, which stipulated to which territories the constitution extended, did not include South West Africa, or indeed anywhere else in Africa,

---

[29]   Bülow to Wilhelm II, 24 November 1904, in BA Berlin R1001/2089, 8–11.
[30]   In colonial affairs, the chancellor also carried what Ernst Rudolf Huber called the 'parliamentary accountability for countersigning actions of the colonial government' (Ernst Rudolf Huber, *Deutsche Verfassungsgeschichte seit 1789*, vol. 4: *Struktur und Krisen des Kaiserreichs* (Stuttgart: Kohlhammer Verlag, 1982), 630).
[31]   Eulenburg to Bülow, 14 July 1900, in John C. G. Röhl, *Philipp Eulenburgs politische Korrespondenz*, vol. 2: *Krisen, Krieg und Katastrophen, 1895–1921* (Boppard: Harald Boldt Verlag, 1983), 1983–4. See also Mombauer, 'Wilhelm, Waldersee and the Boxer Rebellion', 101.
[32]   Eulenburg to Bülow, 3 October 1900, in Röhl, *Philipp Eulenburgs politische Korrespondenz*, vol. 2, 2006. Emphasis in the original.
[33]   For a detailed discussion of the constitutional balance of powers and colonial affairs, see Matthew P. Fitzpatrick, *Purging the Empire: Mass Expulsions in Germany, 1871–1914* (Oxford: Oxford University Press, 2015), 230–5; Marc Grohmann, *Exotische Verfassung: Die Kompetenzen des Reichstags für die deutschen Kolonien in Gesetzgebung und Staatsrechtswissenschaft des Kaiserreichs (1884–1914)* (Tübingen: Mohr Siebeck, 2001); Ignacio Czeguhn, 'Die Mitwirkung von Bundesrat und Reichstag bei der Kolonialgesetzgebung', *Jahrbuch der Juristischen Zeitgeschichte* 8 (2006–7), 174–202. See also Huber, *Deutsche Verfassungsgeschichte seit 1789*, vol. 4, 604–34.

the Pacific, China, or even Alsace-Lorraine.[34] The colonies were territories outside the guarantees of the constitution and the concomitant regulatory role of German law.[35] Although sometimes contested,[36] most *Kaiserreich* legal experts agreed that the German colonies were territories external to the constitutional *Rechtsstaat* and, as such, were subject to the prerogative power of the emperor,[37] whose authority in the colonies was 'objectively unrestricted'.[38] Codifying this, Paragraph 1 of the 1886 Protectorate Law made it clear that in South West Africa, 'Sovereign power is exercised by the Kaiser in the name of the Reich'.[39] Given the apparently unlimited nature of the emperor's power over the colonies, one *Kaiserreich* jurist noted that Wilhelm II's power was that of a constitutional monarch domestically, but that the royal prerogative was clearly dominant in the colonies.[40]

This was an oversimplification, given that the 1886 Protectorate Law also offered the chancellor a significant degree of oversight. By 1904 the emperor's theoretically untrammelled colonial power had found some concrete limits in practice. Judicial affairs for German settlers had been placed under the purview of the colonial director, who was answerable to the chancellor.[41] The chancellor also had the power to offer German citizenship to foreigners and Africans living in the colony.[42] Perhaps most importantly, the chancellor was the legal co-signatory of the 'emperor's' colonial decrees and could technically decide to refuse to sign. In practice this never happened, because these decrees did not originate with Wilhelm II but rather came from the Colonial Department of the Foreign Office, often via the chancellor.[43] For its part, the Reichstag too had the constitutional power to refuse to pass the colonial budget, which allowed it not merely

[34] Ernst Rudolf Huber (ed), *Dokumente zur deutschen Verfassungsgeschichte*, vol. 2: *Deutsche Verfassungsdokumente, 1851–1900*, 3rd edn (Stuttgart: Kohlhammer Verlag, 1986), 64–5.

[35] Paul Laband, *Das Staatsrecht des Deutschen Reiches*, 3rd edn (Tübingen: J. C. B. Mohr, 1902), 146. On whether the colonies should be designated as 'Inland', 'Ausland', 'Reichsnebenland', 'Nebenstaat', or 'Außerdeutsche Reichslande', see Simon Reimer, *Die Freizügigkeit in den deutschen Schutzgebieten inbesondere die Ausweisung von Reichsangehörigen* (Münster: Verlag der Universitäts-Buchhandlung Franz Coppenrath, 1911), 8–12. For Wilhelmine attempts to argue for the jurisdiction of the Reichstag and the domestic constitution, see Friedrich Giese, 'Zur Geltung der Reichsverfassung in den deutschen Kolonien', in *Festgabe Bonner juristischen Fakultät für Paul Krüger zum Doktor Jubiläum* (Berlin: Weidmann Verlag, 1911), 417–46.

[36] Victor von Poser und Gross-Naedlitz, *Die rechtliche Stellung der deutschen Schutzgebiete* (Breslau: M. & H. Marcus, 1903), 45. On comparisons with Alsace-Lorraine, see Hermann Schreiber, 'Die rechtliche Stellung der Bewohner der deutschen Schutzgebiete', *Zeitschrift für Kolonialpolitik, Kolonialrecht und Kolonialwirtschaft* 6 (1904), 760–75, at 761; Herbert Hauschild, *Die Staatsangehörigkeit in den Kolonien* (Tübingen: J. C. B. Mohr, 1906), 27.

[37] Karl von Stengel, *Die Rechtsverhältnisse der deutschen Schutzgebiete* (Tübingen: J. C. B. Mohr, 1901), 33, 38ff.

[38] Laband, *Das Staatsrecht des Deutschen Reiches*, 147.

[39] 'Gesetz betreffend der Rechtsverhältnisse der deutschen Schutzgebieten', *Reichs-Gesetzblatt*, 17 April 1886.

[40] Giese, 'Zur Geltung der Reichsverfassung', 436.

[41] Egon Kruckow, *Ausweisungen aus den deutschen Schutzgebieten* (Berlin: Paul Greffin, 1913), 28; Laband, *Das Staatsrecht des Deutschen Reiches*, 147–9.

[42] Von Poser und Gross-Naedlitz, *Die rechtliche Stellung der deutschen Schutzgebiete*, 61.

[43] Laband, *Das Staatsrecht des Deutschen Reiches*, 148.

ex post facto power, but also a means of ensuring that colonial officials were ever mindful of how developments in the empire would be reported and discussed in the Reichstag. Nonetheless, an important role remained for the monarch. As Ignacio Czeguhn has remarked, 'With constitutional provisions unclear...the question of which organ of the empire and on what grounds had the competence to regulate colonization remained contested.'[44]

This contested and overlapping system of sovereign powers and legal competencies in South West Africa was tested by the events of the Herero War, and by Wilhelm II's disposition towards them. Despite the potential broader ramifications of the increasingly acute military crisis for Germany's sole African settler colony and for German imperialism more broadly, Wilhelm II intervened only twice in the conflict, once to choose a commander to replace Governor Leutwein selected from a list of options already decided by others and once to ratify a decision made by other arms of the state to disempower that commander once his methods proved too violent. In both instances, the emperor had to be prompted to fulfil his legally mandated role by others who were overseeing the war. From beginning to end, Wilhelm II absented himself from decision-making whenever he could avoid it.

Contradictory pressures surrounded the first decision the emperor was asked to make, which pertained to who would command the military force about to leave Germany to fight the Herero. Civilian authorities were keen to maintain the hitherto framing of the conflict as a problem of colonial law and order to be managed by the existing colonial protection force (*Schutztruppe*) under the continued command of Governor Theodor Leutwein, who, while technically the nominee of the emperor, was in practice subordinate to the Colonial Department of the Foreign Office. Against these civilian officials, however, were military authorities who wished to redefine the conflict as a formal war to be managed by Schlieffen, the chief of the German General Staff and a nominated military general.[45]

Up until this point, beyond assenting to the hastily assembled relief force of 500 men, Wilhelm II had steadfastly refused to intervene in the conflict, to the point that his inaction distressed some of his advisers. Remarkably, for the first half of 1904, when a successful military outcome for the Germans was far from certain, civil and military officials worried that, notwithstanding his clear limitations as a leader, the emperor was playing too modest a role, given his constitutional responsibilities. It was rumoured that, despite the urgent situation in the colony, he had avoided taking up an active role as supreme commander of the German army in the war because 'there was no glory or fame associated with it.'[46]

[44]   Czeguhn, 'Die Mitwirkung von Bundesrat und Reichstag', 175.
[45]   As per the law establishing the colonial armed forces of 9 June 1895. This law was supplemented by a series of provisions for the colonial armed forces which codified the role of the governor. See Laband, *Das Staatsrecht des Deutschen Reiches*, 149.
[46]   Vierhaus (ed), *Das Tagebuch der Baronin Spitzemberg*, 442.

Instead, Wilhelm II allowed the war to drift while he remained silent and absent, cruising aboard his royal yacht. Four months into the war, when the fate of the colony seemed to hang in the balance,[47] the *éminence grise* of the Foreign Office, Friedrich von Holstein, kept an anxious and deeply ambivalent watch on Wilhelm II's approach to colonial military matters, worried that if he actually decided to direct the African war, it would lead to a 'terrible catastrophe' because of his 'military ineptitude'.[48] Nonetheless, he was perplexed to see that Wilhelm II, when confronted with an acute military crisis in a German overseas territory, squandered his time obsessing about Russia's war with Japan instead, badgering Bülow with fantastic speculation that the Japanese could conquer Moscow in twenty years instead of involving himself in a real war that had already cost numerous German lives.[49] With the emperor stubbornly remaining at sea aboard his royal yacht, Holstein professed his suspicion that this absence was a deliberate shirking of his royal responsibilities:

> I regret that the Kaiser has remained away for so long. It is increasingly suspected of him that it is because of the Herero uprising. He is quite content with the blandishments offered on the subject. But the political rumour disseminated from here that the Kaiser is leading operations in South Africa from the *Hohenzollern* is a sham. He is directing nothing of the sort. It might not have been a bad thing if more troops had been sent over right at the beginning under the command of General von Trotha, who can be trusted with colonial situations, as the Kaiser had wanted.[50]

Instead of actively and personally directing the war according to his initial inclinations, which by law he clearly had the power to do, Wilhelm II had accepted, if not welcomed, the diminishment of his responsibility as commander-in-chief and left others to direct and prosecute the war. Other observers too were unsure whether this lack of royal engagement was a blessing or a curse. The German courtly diarist Baroness Hildegard von Spitzemberg noted that while some at court were complaining of Wilhelm II's 'constant overestimation of his political worth', others fretted that 'the indifference that he shows towards the Herero uprising is dreadful.'[51]

Eventually, in a May 1904 crisis meeting, where military officials and civil authorities met the Kaiser to discuss Leutwein's offer to resign his military command after what from Berlin appeared to be a series of military reversals, Wilhelm II

[47] Hull, *Absolute Destruction*, 22.

[48] Vierhaus (ed), *Das Tagebuch der Baronin Spitzemberg*, 440–1.

[49] Bülow, *Denkwürdigkeiten*, vol. 2, 64.

[50] Holstein to Stülpnagel, 23 April 1904, in Helmuth Rogge (ed), *Friedrich von Holstein, Lebensbekenntnis in Briefen an eine Frau* (Berlin: Ullstein Verlag, 1932), 232.

[51] Vierhaus (ed), *Das Tagebuch der Baronin Spitzemberg*, 442.

was informed that by law it was he who had to nominate the senior military figure who would lead the much larger military force about to leave for the colony.[52] Apart from Leutwein's deficiencies in the eyes of military planners, it was suggested to the emperor that, as an *Oberst* (colonel), the governor was not of sufficient rank to lead a major campaign of the German military undertaken by a force that could potentially include others of equal or higher rank.[53] Despite the protests of the Colonial Department, which wished to maintain civilian (that is to say, their) control over the war, the emperor's first major use of his imperial prerogative as head of the armed forces was to comply with the military's request to make a choice of commander.[54]

As Röhl has correctly argued, Lothar von Trotha was an unpopular choice among representatives of the civilian colonial bureaucracy.[55] Yet it is arguable that he was not the military's preferred choice either. In fact, precisely why Wilhelm II chose Trotha over other military colonial specialists is still the subject of some disagreement, although his reputation as a vigorous and brutal campaigner earned in both the Wahehe War and the Boxer War was well known. As Holstein had written a month earlier, from the beginning of the war the emperor had thought that Trotha should have been sent to South West Africa.[56]

Isabel Hull suggests that Trotha was strongly supported by the military's chief of the General Staff Schlieffen and the chief of the Military Cabinet, Dietrich von Hülsen-Häseler.[57] Bley argued, however, that while the director of the Colonial Department of the Foreign Office, Oskar Stübel, and other civilian officials such as Heinrich Schnee wished to keep Leutwein in command, the military was split between the Prussian Minister for War Karl von Einem, who suggested Georg von Gayl (Waldersee's subordinate in the Boxer Rebellion), and Schlieffen, who suggested to the Kaiser that he choose Trotha.[58] For Christopher Clark and Susanne Kuß, however, Trotha's appointment came against the advice of Chancellor Bülow, Stübel and, importantly, Schlieffen.[59] Katharine Anne Lerman has further argued that, in addition to Schlieffen, Wilhelm II's own

[52] Hull, *Absolute Destruction*, 22.

[53] Bülow in *Verhandlungen des Reichstags*, 9 May 1904, 2788; 5 December 1904, 3374–7. This was a lesson learned by the forced resignation of Hermann Wissmann as governor of German East Africa during the Wahehe War in 1896, when Trotha, who was leading the campaign, escaped the control of the governor by letting it be known that he outranked Wissmann. See Claudia Prinz, 'Hermann von Wissmann als "Kolonialpionier"', *Peripherie*, 118/119 no.30 (2010), 331–2.

[54] Bley, *Namibia under German Rule*, 155–60.

[55] Röhl, *Wilhelm II: Into the Abyss of War and Exile*, 298.

[56] Holstein to Stülpnagel, 23 April 1904, in Helmuth Rogge (ed), *Friedrich von Holstein Lebensbekenntnis*, 232.

[57] Hull, *Absolute Destruction*, 24–5.   [58] Bley, *Namibia under German Rule*, 158–9.

[59] Christopher Clark, *Kaiser Wilhelm II* (London and New York: Routledge, 2000), 103; Susanne Kuß, *Deutsche Militär auf kolonialen Kriegsschauplätzen: Eskalation von Gewalt zu Beginn des 20 Jahrhunderts* (Berlin: Ch. Links Verlag, 2010), 83.

military adviser, the chief of the Military Cabinet, Hülsen-Häseler, also opposed Trotha's appointment.[60]

According to two sources from May 1904, the emperor had chosen Trotha from this shortlist of three candidates against the advice of not only the civilian authorities but indeed against everyone else's advice. At the end of his report to the Bavarian War Ministry on 10 May 1904 detailing plans for the reinforcement of the colonial troops, Nikolaus Endres commented, 'The naming of Lieutenant General von Trotha as the leader of the Expedition Corps was done by His Majesty against the objections of the Imperial chancellor, the war minister, the chief of the General Staff and the colonial director.'[61] Two days later, Bavaria's representative in Berlin, Hugo Lerchenfeld-Köfering, also reported to Munich that 'the transfer of the leadership of the troops in South West Africa to Lieutenant General von Trotha has sprung utterly from the initiative of His Majesty the Kaiser.'

Interestingly, the report also argued that 'in the opinion of the responsible departments, the Colonial Division of the Foreign Office, the Prussian Ministry of War, and the General Staff, there were no grounds for relieving Leutwein of command.' The losses at the beginning of the uprising in South West Africa were not due to Leutwein's tactical failures, the report continued, but rather the 'lack of available troops and horses'. At the meeting with the emperor, most people in the room had believed that 'with the coming reinforcements Leutwein would fulfil his mission at least as successfully as his successor, who is inexperienced in South West African relations.' While he did not argue this to the Reichstag, this was also Chancellor Bülow's view, according to Lerchenfeld-Köfering.[62]

Yet, despite being an unpopular choice, Trotha's selection was not a total surprise. Trotha did have extensive military experience dating back to Prussia's campaigns against Austria in 1866 and against France in 1870–1. More pertinently, Wilhelm II had specifically chosen Trotha to command German forces in the Wahehe War in East Africa, selecting him above the more popular Hermann Wissmann. In this conflict Trotha had earned a name for himself as an uncompromising practitioner of colonial warfare, employing punitive terror tactics and 'collective punishment' against African villages, hanging inhabitants and burning the villages to the ground. Interestingly, upon his return, Trotha had written a memorandum recommending that colonial expansion by the German military be limited, so that it might be more effectively controlled by the limited resources of

[60] Katharine Anne Lerman, *The Chancellor as Courtier: Bernhard von Bülow and the Governance of Germany, 1900–1909* (Cambridge: Cambridge University Press, 2002), 96.

[61] 'Endres, Berlin, 10 May 1904, Betreff: Verstärkung für die südwestafrikanischen Schutztruppen', in BHStA München, Abt IV Kriegsarchiv MKr2657, 'Herero-Aufstand in Deutsch-SüdwestAfrika'.

[62] Lerchenfeld to Ministerium des Außern, 12 May 1904, in BHStA München Abt II MA 2682.

Germany's colonial military.[63] Thereafter Trotha also took part in the occupation of Peking during the Boxer Rebellion, albeit in the reconstruction rather than the fighting phase.[64] As the London *Times* later pointed out, 'Campaigning against the Hereros is a very different thing from promenading in China after all the serious fighting had been done by other people.'[65]

Given the options for colonial commander presented to him, Wilhelm II arguably chose the one best known to him by reputation, and one whom he had chosen before, with what passed for success in East Africa. Crucially, however, although the emperor had held the view that Trotha should have been put in charge of the campaign at its very beginning, and this was known by the Foreign Office for months prior to this meeting, Wilhelm II had left the prosecution of the war very firmly in the hands of the Colonial Department, to the extent that he began to be accused of allowing the war to drift out of control. It was only after attention had been drawn to the law demanding that the emperor, as head of the armed forces, name a new military leader that Wilhelm II chose the general he had long preferred to Leutwein, while also waving away Gayl, the other candidate offered by the military. Notwithstanding the legal opportunities for earlier direct intervention, Wilhelm II chose not intervene in the South West African War until it became clear that it was his direct and unavoidable responsibility.

Once formally brought into the process, Wilhelm II not only selected Trotha but also used his choice to boast that he had always had a better grasp of military necessity than both Schlieffen and Einem. Indeed, the crass manner in which he upbraided the two for their ostensible incompetence startled Robert von Zedlitz-Trützschler, the steward of the royal household, who quoted the monarch as berating them with the words, 'You old donkeys think you know better because you're older than me, but that's not the case.' Blaming his military leaders for the reversals Germany had faced in South West Africa, Wilhelm II declared, 'What I will order concerning South West Africa would have been the only solution, but you old donkeys of course thought you knew better, and now this stupidity has come back to haunt us.'[66]

Wilhelm II's selection of Trotha confirms that he agreed with the military that what was occurring in South West Africa was, as Susanne Kuß has recently argued, 'no longer the defeat of a "native revolt" but a veritable war'.[67] There would have been no ambiguity either about the marked difference between Leutwein's

[63] Christoph Kamissek, '"Ich kenne genug Stämme in Afrika": Lothar von Trotha: Eine imperiale Biographie im Offizierkorps des deutschen Kaiserreiches', *Geschichte und Gesellschaft*, 40, no.1, 2014, 81–7.

[64] Kamissek, '"Ich kenne genug Stämme in Afrika"', 88–90.

[65] *The Times*, 9 May 1904, in *BA Berlin* R1001/2114, 142.

[66] Robert von Zedlitz-Trützschler, *Zwölf Jahre am deutschen Kaiserhof* (Stuttgart: Deutsche Verlags-Anstalt, 1925), 68. Giving vent to his astonishment at the emperor's outburst, Zedlitz-Trützschler remarked: 'Difficile est satiram non scribere.'

[67] Kuß, *Deutsche Militär auf kolonialen Kriegsschauplätzen*, 83.

long-standing approach of mounting a punitive expedition before arriving at a negotiated settlement and the military record of Trotha, which suggested that he would settle for nothing less than complete capitulation by his military opponents. Given Trotha's unflinching use of violence in the past, Wilhelm II was no doubt fully aware that he had chosen the option of overwhelming violence and a full-scale military crackdown. This was certainly the result of his decision. While Leutwein remained committed to preserving the Herero polity as an important future workforce,[68] by October 1904, Trotha had declared himself in favour of destroying the independence and political agency of the Herero—'the nation as such'.[69]

Contrary to Jeremy Sarkin's assertion, however, Wilhelm II's choice of Trotha as commander does nothing to indicate that the Kaiser had gone beyond seeking a decisive military solution to demanding an explicitly genocidal one.[70] His strategy of the decisive military blow—a standard German military tactic shared in common with numerous other European states—was not predicated upon the physical extermination of the Herero.[71] Indeed, preparations had been made by Trotha to place up to 8,000 Herero soldiers in prisoner of war camps.[72] Rather, it was only upon the utter failure of the strategy of the 'battle of annihilation' in August 1904 that the war was radicalized to become an all-encompassing attempt to eradicate all Herero from the colony, to destroy the Herero nation as such. Intentionalist accounts that claim that either Wilhelm II or Trotha approached the war with a clear genocidal intent prior to the Battle of Waterberg miss the enormity and implications of Trotha's military failure at that battle and how his inability to conclusively engage with the Herero altered his strategic thinking. As Matthias Häußler has argued, this colonial intentionalism also sees the Herero 'eradicated and rendered invisible' as serious military opponents of the Germans and indeed as 'active participants' in the war.[73]

To make clear the path to genocide, Trotha's inability to defeat the Herero in the kind of decisive battle favoured by Schlieffen was laid bare at the Battle at Waterberg on 11 August 1904, after which the Herero (together with their cattle) slipped through his military cordon.[74] In the wake of this inconclusive encounter, Trotha mounted a chase through the Omaheke Desert in an attempt to bring

---

[68] Leutwein, *Elf Jahre Gouverneur*, 541–2.

[69] Dominik J. Schaller, '"Ich glaube, dass die nation als solche vernichtet werden muss": Kolonialkrieg und Völkermord in "Deutsch-Südwestafrika" 1904–1907', *Journal of Genocide Research*, 6, no.3 (2004), 395–430.

[70] Sarkin, *Germany's Genocide of the Herero*, 191.   [71] Fitzpatrick, *Purging the Empire*, 235–6.

[72] Matthias Häußler, 'From Destruction to Extermination: Genocidal Escalation in Germany's War against the Herero, 1904', *Journal of Namibian Studies* 10 (2011), 63.

[73] Häußler, 'From Destruction to Extermination', 60.

[74] Kriegsgeschichtliche Abteilung I des Großen Generalstabes, *Die Kämpfe der deutsche Truppen in Südwestafrika* (Berlin: Ernst Siegfried Mittler, 1906), 156–91, esp. 189.

about yet another 'decisive' battle. Failing to achieve this,[75] he wrote in his diary, 'We can or must now start from the beginning again; otherwise, it is over.'[76] As a result of this decision to start again, to employ a new strategy to win a war that had proved unwinnable by conventional tactics, Trotha shifted to a radicalized war of attrition characterized by denying the enemy access to waterholes and settlements, effectively ensuring that the Herero—including Herero women, children, and non-combatants—would die in the desert of hunger and thirst.[77] It was here, with Trotha's tactical innovation in the wake of his military failure rather than with a royal order, that the shift to genocide occurred, via a military cordon that would ensure widespread and indiscriminate starvation.[78]

Formal acknowledgement of this strategic shift came with Trotha's decree of 2 October 1904—almost two months after the Battle of Waterberg—which made it clear in addition that any Herero found returning to settled areas would be shot.[79] As he explained to Schlieffen two days later in his report, given his failure with orthodox military tactics, he had come to believe that 'The nation as such must be destroyed, or if this is not possible on tactical grounds...expelled from the territory.'[80] (See Figure 5.1.)

Thereafter, a small number of Herero led by Samuel Maharero reached the relative safety of British Bechuanaland, where Maharero petitioned the British for ammunition and military support to continue his campaign against the Germans. He also requested safe haven for child refugees and assistance in maintaining his control over dissident Herero, all on the basis of his family's past ostensibly close

---

[75] Kriegsgeschichtliche Abteilung I des Großen Generalstabes, *Die Kämpfe der deutsche Truppen in Südwestafrika*, 193–9.

[76] Lothar von Trotha, diary entry 13 August 1904, as quoted in Häußler, 'From Destruction to Extermination', p. 60.

[77] Kriegsgeschichtliche Abteilung I des Großen Generalstabes, *Die Kämpfe der deutsche Truppen in Südwestafrika*, 207. On the genocidal intent of the order, see Jan-Bart Gewald, 'The Great General of the Kaiser', *Botswana Notes and Records* 26 (1994), 67–76.

[78] Kuß, *Deutsche Militär auf kolonialen Kriegsschauplätzen*, 88. The Herero War was not the only occasion when starvation tactics were used by the Germans to win a colonial war. In East Africa in 1888 Consul General Michahelles had noted that 'Hunger was proving an increasingly effective means of pacification.' So too, in the war against Mangi Meli, Governor Gustav von Götzen had argued that:

As its last option, the *Schutztruppe* had to use the cooperation of hunger...Burning down villages, fields, and food supplies might seem barbaric to the distant observer. This method of warfare was not just the most promising one, but also the only practical one...According to me, military actions alone will be fruitless, only hunger and hardship will be able to force people into final submission.

(Michahelles to Bismarck, 22 October 1888 in *Verhandlungen des Reichstages*, Aktenstück 41, Nr 16, vol. 108, 1889, 405)

See also Damian Zane, 'The Search in Germany for the Lost Skull of Tanzania's Mangi Meli', BBC News, 13 November 2018, https://www.bbc.com/news/world-africa-45916150, accessed 18 October 2021.

[79] BA Berlin, R1001, No. 2089, 7.

[80] Trotha to Schlieffen, 4 October 1904, BA Berlin R1001/2089, 'Differenzen zwischen Generalleuntnant v Trotha und Gouverneur Leutwein bezgl. der Aufstande in DSWA im Jahre 1904', 5–6.

Figure 5.1 Lieutenant General Lothar von Trotha, commander of the armed forces in German South West Africa, with his staff during the Herero War
Source: Photo courtesy of the Bundesarchiv.

links to Queen Victoria and the British royal family.[81] The British authorities refused all of Maharero's requests beyond offering to allow Herero refugees to remain on British territory. Following the advice of the local Herero leader Sekgoma Letsholathebe, the British also refused to acknowledge Maharero's paramountcy and even his chiefly status, treating him strictly as a private person seeking refuge.[82] Despite the lack of any further British assistance, those who had reached Bechuanaland had certainly fared better than the majority of Maharero's people, many of whom had been killed in the war or during their desert exodus.

Unsurprisingly, Leutwein explicitly distanced himself from the expulsion order and its effects, arguing that the Herero had sent letters of surrender and that the military campaign to all intents and purposes had been won prior to its proclamation.[83] Trotha's response to Leutwein's attempt to have his order

---

[81] Matthias Häussler, Andreas Eckl, and Jekura Kavari, '"Hide My Children": Samuel Maharero's Letter to the Resident Magistrate, 28 September 1904', *Journal of Namibian Studies* 27 (2020), 125–33.

[82] See Jan-Bart Gewald, '"I Was Afraid of Samuel, Therefore I Came to Sekgoma": Herero Refugees and Patronage Politics in Ngamiland, Bechuanaland Protectorate, 1890–1914', *Journal of African History* 43, no. 2 (2002), 211–34.

[83] BA Berlin R1001/2089 46; Jörg Schildknecht, *Bismarck, Südwestafrika und die Kongokonferenz: Die völkerrechtlichen Grundlagen der effektiven Okkupation und ihre Nebenpflichten am Beispiel des Erwerbs der ersten deutschen Kolonie* (Hamburg: Lit Verlag, 2000), 260.

rescinded was blunt but technically correct in its assertion that only the German emperor had the authority to force Trotha to lift the genocidal cordon sanitaire:

> In such situations there is no parliamentarizing. I am happy to listen to your advice, but I cannot allow you an independent role in decision-making as long as the Kaiser retains me in my position, given the foundational differences in our views.[84]

Metropolitan Responses to Genocide

As Wilhelm II had given Trotha full military command over South West Africa, which was an extra-constitutional German colonial territory governed by royal prerogative, only the emperor had the executive power to force Trotha to rescind his *Vernichtungsbefehl*. Notwithstanding the fact that Trotha had been Wilhelm II's personal choice, this is precisely what happened. Having been authorized by Trotha—Germany's highest authority in South West Africa—by November 1904, the tactical shift to a genocidal war of attrition announced in October was reversed by the only person with the legal authority to do so, namely Wilhelm II.

The reversal of Trotha's genocidal expulsion proclamation in November 1904 was the emperor's second significant use of prerogative power during the conflict. Once again, however, this deployment of sovereign power was not an example of Wilhelm II's desire to play the active leadership role required of him by law. Rather, the emperor followed the strong advice of his civilian and military advisers, who had variously come to reject Trotha's approach on tactical and moral grounds. Recognizing that the military campaign had achieved everything it could, Schlieffen wrote to Bülow admitting that Trotha's attrition tactics were impractical and argued that they should be discontinued. In a letter sent to the chancellor on 23 November 1904, accompanied by a copy of Trotha's report,[85] Schlieffen cold-bloodedly stated that he agreed with Trotha that 'the burning race war will only be ended through the annihilation or the complete subjugation of one of the parties' and that he believed the eventual eradication of Africans was probably inevitable in the settler colony. Notwithstanding his professed personal sympathy for Trotha's desire to 'destroy the entire nation or drive them out of the country', however, he argued that the current conditions did not suggest that this could be achieved and that Herero prisoners must now be accepted on military

---

[84] Trotha to Leutwein, 5 November 1904, as cited in Schildknecht, *Bismarck, Südwestafrika und die Kongokonferenz*, 260.

[85] Schlieffen to Bülow, 23 November 1904, in BA Berlin R1001/2089, 'Differenzen zwischen Generalleutnant v Trotha und Gouverneur Leutwein bezgl. der Aufstande in DSWA im Jahre 1904', 3–4. For a recent reappraisal of Schlieffen's role, see Lukas Grawe, 'The Prusso-German General Staff and the Herero Genocide', *Central European History* 52, no. 4 (2019), 588–619.

grounds. Accordingly, the Herero should be approached for a negotiated surrender and, as Trotha's 'shoot on sight' proclamation had made this impossible, the annihilation order should be rescinded and a new one issued promising to spare those who surrendered.[86]

Having read both Trotha's report and Schlieffen's response to it, Bülow wasted no time in bluntly informing Wilhelm II that Trotha's conduct of the war was 'inconsistent with the principles of Christianity and humanity' and, paraphrasing ex-Governor Leutwein, that it undermined the economic basis of the colony which relied on Herero labour. On these grounds, Bülow wrote to Wilhelm II informing him that both he and Schlieffen agreed that Trotha's order had to be countermanded and that the monarch should order Trotha to embrace a tactical change that would allow the return of the remaining Herero from the desert.[87]

The chancellor also spoke to the emperor in person about Trotha's command. When he broached the matter of Trotha's radical violence, Bülow later recalled, Wilhelm II's 'eyes widened and he became greatly agitated', declaring that Christian values did not extend to 'heathens and barbarians'. Bülow parried this by arguing that he was not interested in a theological discussion but wanted to point out that Trotha's military conduct 'was worse than a crime; it was a mistake... Wars cannot be conducted purely militarily; politics requires a voice too.' At this, Wilhelm II left Bülow in a huff, but within hours the chancellor had received word that the emperor would submit to his judgement on the issue.[88] Preserving the constitutional chain of command even in the face of an unfolding genocidal crisis in South West Africa, Bülow had successfully convinced the emperor to countermand Trotha's order. In deference to his chancellor, Wilhelm II complied with this request on 29 November, ordering that any 'yielding Herero be granted mercy'. Thereafter, the monarch left it to Bülow and Schlieffen to negotiate precisely how this new policy would be carried out.[89]

On the same day, Bülow sent a detailed memorandum on 'native policy and the Herero uprising' to the Reichstag.[90] In it he offered the candid view that:

The transfer of native lands to white hands, the impoverishment of the middle and small cattle owners, the prevalence of indebtedness of many tribes, and the

[86] Schlieffen to Bülow, 23 November 1904, in BA Berlin R1001/2089, 3–4.
[87] Bülow to Wilhelm II, 24 November 1904, in BA Berlin R1001/2089, 8–11.
[88] Bülow, *Denkwürdigkeiten*, vol. 2, 20–1.
[89] Schoen to Bülow, 29 November 1904, BA Berlin R1001/2089, 13. After seeking Bülow's preferred wording of the telegram, which they received on 6 December, the General Staff sent the order on 8 December. It was received in Windhoek the following day. Schlieffen to Bülow, 30 November 1904; Bülow to Wilhelm II, 6 December 1904; General Staff to General Trotha, 8 December 1904, in BA Berlin R1001/2089, 14, 19–20, 48. Trotha resisted implementing a version of the order until 13 December. See, e.g., Trotha to Schlieffen, 11 December 1904, in BA Berlin R1001/2089, 63. For Trotha's full and formal acceptance of the order, see Trotha to Schlieffen, 1 January 1905, in BA Berlin R1001/2117, 57.
[90] 'Denkschrift über Eingeborenen-Politik und Hereroaufstand in Deutsch-Südwestafrica', in *BA Berlin*, R1001/2117, 'Aufstand der Hereros 1904–1907', 7.

brutality of many traders have obviously not improved the natives' experience of German rule. It is also no wonder that they have sought to excuse the uprising with these reasons...The fundamental cause of the uprising lies in the double fact that the Herero, as a traditionally freedom-loving, conquering, and bound-lessly proud people, on the one hand, found the expansion of German rule and their own repression increasingly burdensome and, on the other hand—and this is the decisive fact—had the impression of this German rule that they were in the final analysis stronger than it.[91]

The chancellor also spoke in the Reichstag a few days later, where he half-heartedly defended the military record of Trotha and, more enthusiastically, the German troops, and announced the reorganization of the Colonial Department so as to turn it into a ministry in its own right, as well as a drastic revamp of colonial rule in South West Africa that would move the colony towards self-government. In his speech, Bülow also made clear his own position on the con-duct of the war and publicly offered a formal and very public rejection of the logic of the *Vernichtungsbefehl* to the Reichstag (which was unaware of it), but more particularly to those such as Schlieffen and the emperor who were aware of the tactics employed by Trotha:

> There is one thing I wish to say explicitly. We are neither so cruel nor so unwise as to see the only possibility for the reconstruction of orderly conditions as being to shoot down mercilessly the half-starving and dying of thirst Herero bands that are streaming out of the wastelands of the desert. There can be no talk of that.[92]

Jeremy Sarkin has asserted that Wilhelm II's initial hesitation in agreeing to coun-termand Trotha stemmed from his desire to see through the genocide he had secretly ordered.[93] More coyly, Jan-Bart Gewald has argued that 'the personal involvement of the German Kaiser, Wilhelm II, in deciding how the war was to be fought in German South-West Africa, signalled the highest authorisation and endorsement for acts committed in the name of Imperial Germany.'[94] So too David Olusoga and Casper W. Erichsen's book *The Kaiser's Holocaust* suggests a direct congruence between the monarch's intentions and Trotha's genocidal com-mand.[95] While it seems clear that Schlieffen was opposed only tactically rather

[91] 'Denkschrift über Eingeborenen-Politik und Hereroaufstand in Deutsch-Südwestafrica', in *BA Berlin*, R1001/2117, 7(22).

[92] Bülow, *Verhandlungen des Reichstages*, 5 December 1904, 3375–8.

[93] Sarkin, *Germany's Genocide of the Herero*.

[94] Jan-Bart Gewald, 'Imperial Germany and the Herero of Southern Africa: Genocide and the Quest for Recompense', in A. Jones, *Genocide, War Crimes and the West: Ending the Culture of Impunity* (London: Zed Books, 2003), 60.

[95] Erichsen and Olusoga, *The Kaiser's Holocaust*, 138, 157–8.

than in principle to Trotha's genocidal innovation, there is no evidence to suggest that Wilhelm II ordered the complete annihilation of the Herero or had prior knowledge of Trotha's tactical shift, even if he was untroubled by its consequences. Not only is there simply no evidence for any 'secret' royal order, as Isabel Hull has made clear,[96] but to claim its existence is to misunderstand the cumulative radicalization of the colonial war from counterinsurgency under Leutwein, then a military 'battle of annihilation' under Trotha (which was expected to result in masses of prisoners of war), until finally it became a clearly enunciated policy of shooting and starving an entire nation, including women and children. The emperor, clearly comfortable with colonial atrocities, could not have foreseen that this particular form of radicalization would occur, much less ordered it. Crucially, irrespective of his personal views on Trotha's shift to genocidal attrition tactics (which suggest that he, like Schlieffen, was unmoved by humanitarian considerations), Wilhelm II's personal perspective on Trotha's conduct of the war proved to be a second-order consideration when it conflicted with the political assessment of Bülow. When asked by the chancellor to countermand a genocidal military order given by the emperor's hand-picked commander, Wilhelm II did so.

Domestic Consequences of Genocide

As almost all eyewitnesses from the time concur, the emperor was not in active command during the Herero-Nama Wars and contributed precisely nothing to the military campaign beyond what he was explicitly required to do by Schlieffen and Bülow, namely to empower a military leader of the expedition in May 1904 and then to reverse Trotha's genocidal October order in November 1904. The only sign of an independent line from Wilhelm II was the deeply unpopular naming of his favoured colonial war expert, Trotha, as the commander of the *Schutztruppe*, a decision he had ample reason to regret six months later. Given Wilhelm II's earlier rash claim that his military judgement was superior to that of his senior military staff, his prestige in political and military circles was severely damaged by the war in South West Africa, just as Zedlitz-Trützschler had predicted when Trotha was chosen.[97]

Although Trotha managed to hold onto his overall command for a further nine months, his military and moral disgrace was now an open secret. Increasing pressure was applied by the Social Democrats in the Reichstag, with Georg Ledebour quoting Trotha's 'shoot on sight' order once he found evidence of it in May 1905, declaring:

---

[96] Hull, *Absolute Destruction*, 28–30.
[97] Zedlitz-Trützschler, *Zwölf Jahre am deutschen Kaiserhof*, 66.

This decree that in itself bears witness to unbelievable brutality is in direct contradiction to the explanation that the colonial director gave here in the Reichstag, that the Imperial government does not want the extermination of the natives. General von Trotha has with the greatest recklessness defied this position of the Colonial Administration, which was no doubt brought to his attention, and simply announced the extermination of the natives, the so-called 'rebels' if they don't immediately surrender.

Ledebour demanded that the Colonial Department disavow Trotha's order and have him recalled immediately.[98] Few were confident, however, that this was a realistic demand, given the personal involvement of Wilhelm II in his selection. As Lerchenfeld reported back to Munich on 6 August 1905:

> Including amongst official circles, the view is well established that the choice of General Trotha as commander was not a good one. Even upon his announcement significant doubts about his ability had been raised, but since military victory eludes him and a number of poor decisions in civilian administration have been reported, he has been adjudged as sorely wanting. As he was appointed by His Majesty the Kaiser, no change in command can be expected soon. For the moment the loss of lives continues and the financial losses continue to grow. Already the costs of the uprising are in the vicinity of five hundred million [marks].[99]

Despite Lerchenfeld's pessimism, however, in the matter of Trotha's recall Bülow was also able to sway the emperor. By the end of the same month, he had convinced Wilhelm II to recall Trotha from South West Africa entirely.[100] The next time Ledebour had cause to mention Trotha in the Reichstag in December 1905, lambasting his 'cowardly brutality' and expressing his outrage at the 'unheard of infamy' of the *Vernichtungsbefehl* and its lethal effects, the Social Democrat was informed that the lieutenant general had already been recalled to Germany.[101] Tellingly, in South West Africa, the new governor, Friedrich von Lindequist, issued

---

[98] Ledebour, in *Verhandlungen des Reichstages*, 25 May 1905, 6159. The director of the Colonial Department, Dr Oskar Stübel, disingenuously denied the reports of Trotha's orders. See *Verhandlungen des Reichstages*, 25 May 1905, 6161. Ledebour fiercely attacked this lie in the Reichstag on 2 December 1905. As early as mid-March 1904 the Social Democrat August Bebel had protested in the Reichstag against what he claimed was Germany's 'bestial' policy under Leutwein of hanging or shooting Herero prisoners of war and attacking women and children, See August Bebel, *Verhandlungen des Reichstages*, 17 March 1904, 1891–3. Bebel's accusations had to be vigorously denied by Colonial Director Stübel and Chancellor Bülow. See *Verhandlungen des Reichstages*, 9 May 1904, 2787–9. On the claims and counterclaims of German atrocities during the early phases of the war, see Hull, *Absolute Destruction*, 13–21.
[99] Lerchenfeld to Staatsministerium des Außerns, 6 August 1905, in BHStA München Abt II, MA2683.
[100] Lerman, *The Chancellor as Courtier*, 136.
[101] Ledebour, *Verhandlungen des Reichstages*, 2 December 1905, 90–1.

a proclamation at the end of 1905 to the Herero that claimed that, with Trotha gone, the war could now end.[102]

The entire voting population of Germany too was eventually able to adjudicate on the war in German South West Africa. The so-called 'Hottentot election' of 1907 saw the German electorate cast their votes, if not on the isolated issue of the Herero-Nama Wars, then certainly on the empire's prevailing *Kolonialpolitik* and on the Reichstag's use of its power of fiscal review to challenge the military's role in colonial and military affairs by blocking military spending. With the parliament reaching an impasse, Bülow dissolved the Reichstag and sought a popular mandate for colonial spending.[103] As Erik Grimmer-Solem has argued, the election highlighted the participatory dimension of German colonial rule, offering 'a national referendum on the entire German colonial endeavour', wherein Reichstag deputies and candidates, civil society organizations, and voters took part in a public debate on the legitimacy of German colonial rule.[104]

Had the electorate voted for strongly anti-colonial parties, Germany's overseas empire might well have foundered for want of popular support and fiscal backing in the Reichstag. Far from hamstringing colonial endeavours, however, the German electorate spoke out strongly in support of empire and, indirectly, the war in German South West Africa, convinced that the anti-colonial Social Democratic position was tantamount to agreeing that the murdered German settlers in South West Africa had deserved their fate.[105] Instead of endorsing parties sceptical of *Weltpolitik* and *Kolonialpolitik*, power was firmly handed back to those advocating the continuation of German colonialism, irrespective of the price.

The order for colonial genocide in South West Africa was neither issued nor ratified by anyone above Lieutenant General Lothar von Trotha. Without question, Wilhelm II's decision to empower Trotha as the commander in the field was a necessary but certainly not sufficient precondition for the genocide, which was a product of Trotha's shift in military tactics to a war of attrition that sought to

---

[102] Bekanntmachung, in BA Berlin R1001/2119, 'Aufstand der Hereros 1904–1907', 13. Trotha's return to Germany did not, of course lead to the end of the war or the normalization of German–Herero relations. See Zimmerer, *Deutsche Herrschaft über Afrikaner*.

[103] G. D. Crothers, *The German Elections of 1907* (New York: Columbia University Press, 1941).

[104] Erik Grimmer-Solem, 'The Professors' Africa: Economists, the Elections of 1907, and the Legitimation of German Imperialism', *German History* 25, no. 3 (2007), 322. Crucially, Lowry has pointed to the fact that 'African actions' precipitated this colonial crisis within Germany, illustrating the multidirectional chains of causality between the colonies and the metropole. See John S. Lowry, 'African Resistance and Center Party Recalcitrance', 244–69. Matthias Häußler has argued that the election offered an electoral endorsement of 'the authoritarian state', a position which over-reads the breadth of the electoral message. See Matthias Häußler, '"Die Kommandogewalt hat geredet, der Reichstag hat zu schweigen." How the "Hottenototwahlen" of 1907 Shaped the Relationship between Parliament and Military Policy in Imperial Germany', *Journal of Namibian Studies* 15 (2014), 24.

[105] John Phillip Short, 'Colonialism, War, and the German Working Class: Popular Mobilization in the 1907 Reichstag Election', in Bradley Naranch and Geoff Eley (eds), *German Colonialism in a Global Age* (Durham, NC: Duke University Press, 2014), 211.

forcibly contain the Herero in the desert by threatening to shoot any who dared to return. This shift in tactics was neither discussed with nor condoned by Wilhelm II or Schlieffen and was disowned and reversed by the German state on the instruction of Chancellor Bülow.[106] While the genocide was a direct consequence of the actions of the royally empowered highest-ranking German officer in the colony (and was, therefore, an expression of German state power for which it bears full responsibility), it was not a consequence of a royal order, as Sarkin suggests, and was certainly not a direct consequence of the military leadership of the emperor, who was only sporadically involved, and then under the guidance of others.

As the executive representative of the state notionally possessing prerogative power over the colonies that approached the unbounded, Kaiser Wilhelm II was remarkably absent from decision-making. Despite his apparent enthusiasm for military affairs, the emperor avoided almost all comment on and responsibility for the colonial war beyond the unavoidable choices foisted upon him by the chancellor and the chief of the General Staff, Schlieffen. The apparently unconstrained royal prerogative, it seems, was limited by Wilhelm II's own unwillingness to become involved in South West African affairs unless explicitly called upon to do so by the law.

---

[106] Bley, *Namibia under German Rule*, 164–5.

6

Defending a Sovereign Sultan

On 31 March 1905 Kaiser Wilhelm II disembarked from his luxury yacht and rode into Tangier to announce Germany's support for Morocco's beleaguered Sultan Abdelaziz. Global newspaper reports recorded slightly differing accounts of his Tangier speech, but its point was unmistakable. The sultan was an independent, sovereign monarch and it was only with him that the German emperor would discuss matters pertaining to Morocco. The territorial integrity of Morocco was to be respected by all of Europe's powers, and trade with Morocco was to remain open to all. Wilhelm II had not only interrupted his 'recuperative cruise' in the Mediterranean to offer his personal support to a North African monarch but also offered the impression that he would assist the sultan in defending himself, at least diplomatically, against those who threatened the independence of his sultanate, namely France and Britain.[1]

Superficially, Wilhelm II's arrival as an emperor having come to assist a brother monarch against the republican French offers the impression that an earlier period of royal internationalism had been resurrected, with crowned heads of state guaranteeing the stability of the international monarchical order against radical change.[2] While in Morocco, however, the German emperor was far from the author of his own deeds. Indeed, Wilhelm II was interested neither in North African affairs nor in the personal fate of the Moroccan sultan. In fact, as this chapter shows, his brief landing took place despite his strong and repeatedly stated objections, while his bold articulation of Germany's support for the sultan's sovereign rights and the independence of Morocco was completely scripted for him by others more interested in the important global commercial principles at stake in Morocco.

Despite Wilhelm II's lack of interest in the particulars of the Moroccan question, the message of monarchical solidarity that he delivered sparked a major regional crisis. Much has been written about this crisis, usually in an attempt to divine what it reveals about the nature of European politics in the decade prior to the First World War. Firmly anchored in Europe, these accounts have presented the crisis as the product of a 'war party' within Germany that was attempting to

---

[1] For Wilhelm II's recollections of the visit, see Wilhelm II, *Ereignisse und Gestalten 1878–1918* (Leipzig: Koehler Verlag, 1922), 90–2. For German press responses to the Kaiser's visit to Tangier, see Otto Friedrich Ris, *Das Verhältnis der deutschen Presse zur offiziellen deutschen Politik während der ersten Marokkokrise* (Cologne: Verlag J. P. Backem, 1950), 80–9.
[2] Paulmann, 'Searching for a "Royal International"', 145–76.

The Kaiser and the Colonies: Monarchy in the Age of Empire. Matthew P. Fitzpatrick, Oxford University Press.
© Matthew P. Fitzpatrick 2022. DOI: 10.1093/oso/9780192897039.003.0007

manufacture a *casus belli* with France.[3] Other accounts, including that of Wilhelm II, have claimed that the crisis was masterminded by France's foreign minister, Théophile Delcassé, as a means of provoking a revanchist war with Germany.[4]

These explanations that focus on the crisis as a mere waystation on the road to 1914 overlook the Moroccan Crisis' position within the logic of imperial relations in Africa and how these affected the sovereign rights of African monarchs. The geostrategically important Sultanate of Morocco, bordering French Algeria and guarding the southern end of the Mediterranean Sea's access to the Atlantic, matters not so much because of its marginal role in the First World War a decade later as because it demonstrates the near disastrous effects of France's (in particular Delcassé's) determination to recalibrate and renew French colonial policy in North Africa after the twin blows of Fashoda and the consolidation of British control over Egypt.[5] Attention to this imperial context makes clear that Germany acted as it did not to provoke a pre-emptive war with France but to protect and expand its economic penetration of North Africa and to halt the expected imposition of monopolistic control over Moroccan trade by France, as had happened in Tunisia and Algeria. With its involvement in Moroccan affairs aimed at furthering its global open-door trade policy, Germany's intervention in Morocco was an expression of the economic underpinnings of *Weltpolitik*.[6]

The Erasure of Moroccan Sovereignty by Treaty

Wilhelm II's declaration of Germany's determination to defend Sultan Abdelaziz's sovereign rights was the culmination of the German reaction to the *Entente Cordiale* of April 1904. This treaty saw Britain deliver up Morocco to French control without reference to any other European power beyond Spain. In Berlin, it was noted that the treaty entirely ignored Germany's rapidly growing commercial

---

[3] Holstein in particular is often portrayed as seeking a preventative war. Norman Rich, *Friedrich von Holstein: Policy and Diplomacy in the Age of Bismarck and Wilhelm II*, vol. 2 (Cambridge: Cambridge University Press, 1965), 696–9. Compellingly arguing against this is Albrecht Moritz, *Das Problem des Präventivkrieges in der deutschen Politik während der ersten Marokkokrise* (Frankfurt am Main: Peter Lang, 1974).

[4] Wilhelm II, *Ereignisse und Gestalten*, 90–1. Writing to the Russian tsar in 1905, Kaiser Wilhelm II also believed that, were it not for the interference of Britain, the French would have realized that their future lay in working with the Germans, not against them. See Wilhelm II to Nicholas II, 26 September 1905, in Walter Goetz (ed), *Briefe Wilhelms II an den Zaren 1894–1914* (Berlin: Verlag Ullstein, 1920), 381.

[5] On the role of Delcassé, see Edmund Burke, III, *Prelude to Protectorate in Morocco: Precolonial Protest and Resistance, 1860–1912* (Chicago: University of Chicago Press, 1976), 68–70.

[6] Contra Martin Mayer, *Geheime Diplomatie und öffentliche Meinung: Die Parlamente in Frankreich, Deutschland und Großbritannien und die erste Marokkokrise 1904–1906* (Düsseldorf: Droste Verlag, 2002), 162. On the crisis and German commercial and financial interests, see also Heiner Raulff, *Zwischen Machtpolitik und Imperialismus: Die deutsche Frankreichpolitik 1904/06* (Düsseldorf: Droste Verlag, 1976).

interests in Morocco. While Britain's minister in Tangier, Arthur Nicolson, later claimed to have advised the French to come to an arrangement with Germany in the second half of 1904, the French either ignored his advice or never received it.[7] Having not been consulted about the effects of the *Entente Cordiale* on Morocco's sovereignty, the Germans declared that they were not bound by its terms.

While the *Entente Cordiale* was the immediate catalyst of the crisis, the Moroccan question had become steadily more acute since the French annexation of the Oasis of Touat in 1900–1, which had confirmed Morocco's inability to defend its territory militarily. The loss of Touat stripped the sultan of strategically and economically important territory and saw control over the trans-Saharan trade routes shift to France. The annexation also embittered Morocco's regional notables, who were disgusted by Abdelaziz's muted approach to France's preda-tions and pressured the sultan to declare war on the French.[8] In a kingdom in which the sultan's capacity to command the loyalty of regional notables (and suc-cessfully tax them) was a function of his ability to defend their territory militarily, the sultan's decision (at the prompting of Nicolson) to negotiate with the French instead of launching a campaign to dislodge them made him dangerous domestic enemies in the south-east who ignored the sultan's acquiescence and decided to fight against the French anyway.[9]

Prior to 1904, it had fallen to Britain to protect Morocco's independence, and it was due to fears of British resistance that France did not (as was expected) use the Touat campaign to provoke a broader war aimed at seizing the entire sultanate as a protectorate. Despite this 'restraint', however, by December 1900 the French were already deeply concerned that Germany was rapidly gaining in economic importance in Morocco:

> Germany has thought to find favourable ground for the development of its com-mercial enterprises. It has done so with remarkable tenacity and rare energy...if Germany is at present seeking to develop its commercial outlets in Morocco, its policy is closely linked to its own interests, and that, if possible, it would be quite willing to take a piece—and not the least good piece—of the Moroccan high-lands for itself.[10]

In Paris, the military had begun discussing how France might come to control the sultanate, speculating that, while the army of the sultan would be easily overcome,

---

[7] Harold Nicolson, *Lord Carnock: A Study in the Old Diplomacy* (London: Constable and Co., 1937), 159–60.

[8] Rose E. Dunn, *Resistance in the Desert: Moroccan Responses to French Imperialism, 1881–1912* (Madison, WI: University of Wisconsin Press, 1977), 176–203.

[9] Burke, *Prelude to Protectorate in Morocco*, 44–6; Nicolson, *Lord Carnock*, 129–30.

[10] États-Major de l'armée 2e Bureau, 'La Question marocaine' in *Archives diplomatiques* NS238, 'Maroc: Affaires Politiques: Établissement du protectorat, 1899–1905', 33–5.

French troops would face stiff opposition from battle-hardened forces loyal to provincial nobles, particularly in the mountains.[11] Accordingly, diplomatic avenues were pursued instead. These culminated in the signing of the *Entente Cordiale* as a vehicle for French attempts to move towards the 'Tunisification' of Morocco.

This new Anglo-French agreement, however, contradicted the existing international treaty framework regulating European relations with Morocco, namely the 1880 Madrid Agreement. Alongside its actual purpose of creating a small class of 'protected persons' enjoying extraterritorial rights, the Madrid Agreement had also offered an international confirmation of Moroccan sovereignty. Most importantly, Article 17 of the treaty guaranteed that 'The right to the treatment of the most favoured nation is recognised by Morocco as belonging to all the powers represented at the Madrid conference.'[12] Article 17, that is, saw Morocco grant all signatories equal status in Moroccan trade. Any change to this status would necessarily entail consultation with all of the affected parties, including Morocco and the treaty's other co-signatories. Crucially, the Sultan of Morocco was not merely the object of the Madrid Agreement, but a party to it, signing as a sovereign monarch regulating the relationship between his sultanate and the representatives of other states. *Ipso facto*, the treaty offered an internationally agreed-upon confirmation of the prerogative of the sultan to negotiate and enter into treaties pertaining to his own territory and relations with it.

The *Entente Cordiale* simply ignored this international framework. Far from preserving the sovereign status of the sultan and consulting other interested powers, the treaty effectively positioned Morocco as a French political and economic space equivalent to British-occupied Egypt. Sultan Abdelaziz was neither consulted on its terms nor was he a signatory to it. Despite the fiction that the treaty harboured 'no intention of altering the political status of Morocco', it was abundantly clear that Britain and France had decided between themselves that, as Article 2 declared, it fell 'to France...to preserve order in that country, and to provide assistance for the purpose of all administrative, economic, financial, and military reforms which it may require'. In clear contravention of the 1880 Madrid Agreement's clauses on trade relations, Article 4 of the *Entente Cordiale* expressly guaranteed France preference in road, railway, and port infrastructure contracts. More bluntly, Article 3 of the treaty's 'secret articles' also planned for the mutually beneficial territorial division of Morocco 'whenever the Sultan ceases to exercise authority over it'.[13] Precisely how the sultan would cease to rule his kingdom was left unsaid.

[11] 'Hypothèse d'une action militaire au Maroc', 20 March 1902 in *Archives diplomatiques* NS238, 68.
[12] Bevans (ed), *Treaties and Other International Agreements of the United States of America, 1776–1949*, vol. 1, 71–9.
[13] René Albrecht-Carrié (ed), *The Concert of Europe* (London: Palgrave Macmillan, 1968), 323–7.

Understandably, Abdelaziz was enraged by a treaty which the British fully understood would make French pre-eminence in Morocco permanent.[14] The sovereign rights of the sultan, however, were a price the British were prepared to pay in exchange for their security of tenure over Egypt. Given the quid pro quo French recognition of Britain's primacy in Egypt, British support for the French position and the tenets of the *Entente Cordiale* in Morocco thereafter was never open to doubt. France had effectively removed the largest single impediment to its desire to add Morocco to its North African holdings. A further treaty between France and Spain concerning Spanish rights to Ceuta and Melilla on the African side of the Straits of Gibraltar only confirmed France's intention to seize control over Morocco.[15]

The Moroccan View

With colonies of their own built on the back of overstretched interpretations of treaties with local rulers, the Germans were unlikely champions of Moroccan sovereignty. This rather surprising role was only possible, however, because it was mutually beneficial to both Morocco and Germany. The Germans were in no position to force their support upon the sultan, who might well have chosen either to allow the French to entrench their hegemony in exchange for his security as ruler or to take the more radical (but amongst Morocco's regional nobility very popular) step of expelling the Europeans and looking for support from the Ottoman Empire. The crisis rested upon the congruence of the sultan's desire (and that of his advisory council, the Makhzen) to fight for Morocco's sovereign rights with Germany's desire to preserve access to zones of investment and free markets in a region where they had no colonies. As Edmund Burke, III has argued, 'German intervention was predicated upon the fact of Moroccan resistance,'[16] and it is important to consider how the domestic political dynamics of Morocco saw a diplomatic space open up for Germany.

Relations between Abdelaziz and Wilhelm II did not begin suddenly in 1905. Rather, with the French thought to be on the verge of annexing Morocco in 1901, the sultan sent his adviser Si Mehdi el Menebhi to London and Berlin in search of diplomatic support. The Moroccan envoy had little luck in London, with Arthur Nicolson already having urged the British Foreign Office to back away from its traditional defence of the status quo in Morocco against the French:

---

[14]   Nicolson, *Lord Carnock*, 150.
[15]   'Treaty between France and Spain concerning Morocco', *American Journal of International Law* 6, no. 2 (Supplement: Official Documents) (1912), 116–20.
[16]   Burke, *Prelude to Protectorate in Morocco*, 81.

Personally I do not quite see what the Sultan can do alone and unsupported to resist the French advance. I doubt whether any Power would care to uphold the integrity of Morocco, and if the crash were in sight, the interested Powers would I presume content themselves with securing those portions of the Empire which they might think useful and which others would permit them to acquire.[17]

Menebhi's visit to Berlin was, by contrast, a friendly one. He visited the emperor and empress in Potsdam on 7 July 1901 and was also taken to inspect German troops, naval works, and, like many important visitors from abroad, the Krupp arms bazaar in Essen. In a stance consistent with Germany's earlier attitude towards King Chulalongkorn of Siam, however, Chancellor Bernhard von Bülow had strictly instructed Wilhelm II to maintain a 'reserved but not uninterested attitude' on the Moroccan question. This was in the hope that French predations in Morocco, like Siam, would alienate them from the British, who Bülow assumed would still defend the status quo in North Africa. As a result, Menebhi returned to Morocco without any diplomatic cover from Europe.[18] Preserving his links with Germany's royal house upon his return, Menebhi arranged for an ornamental rug and an ibex to be sent to Kaiserin Augusta Victoria in early 1902 as a gesture of thanks for the royal hospitality she had shown. Reciprocating, the German Foreign Office organized for a marble pendulum clock to be sent to Fez.[19]

More disastrously, however, the simultaneous trip to Paris undertaken by the Makhzen minister, Abdelkrim Ben Sliman, saw the French secure favourable conditions for their ongoing 'peaceful penetration' of Morocco via the Franco-Moroccan agreement of 20 July 1901.[20] The French refused to demarcate the border between Algeria and Morocco and insisted that they be given preferential status among the European powers in Morocco. In addition, Ben Sliman was warned that the Makhzen needed to choose whether it wanted the French to be 'the most reassuring of friends or the most formidable of enemies'.[21] The French also extracted the extraordinary promise from the hapless Moroccan envoy that any deal struck by Menebhi in London or Berlin would not be ratified in Fez without the explicit permission of France.[22] With Britain's support waning and the French successfully demanding significant political concessions, Morocco's independence was already in question well before 1904.

---

[17] Nicolson, *Lord Carnock*, 138–41.

[18] Pierre Guillen, *L'Allemagne et le Maroc de 1870 à 1905* (Paris: Presses Universitaires de France, 1967), 602–7.

[19] Mentzingen to Bülow, 27 February 1902; Mentzingen to Richthofen, 6 February 1902, in PAAA R 131412, 'Die außerordentliche Gesandtschaft des Sultans von Marocco' (unnumbered).

[20] Pierre Guillen, 'Les Milieux d'affaires français et le Maroc à l'aube du XXe siècle: La Fondation de la Compagnie marocaine', *Revue Historique* 229, no. 2 (1963), 419.

[21] Nicolson, *Lord Carnock*, 142–3.

[22] Gunther Mai, *Die Marokko-Deutschen 1873–1918* (Göttingen: Vandenhoeck & Ruprecht, 2014), 240.

Beyond the effects of the *Entente Cordiale*, the years 1904 and 1905 were politically difficult ones for Abdelaziz. The sultan was caught between the pressures caused by the demands of the European powers for radical political reforms and domestic rebellions in the south led by Jilali ben Idris al Yusufi Zarhouni (also known as Bu Himara or the Rogui) and, closer to Tangier, by the Jebala emir, Ahmed er Raisuni. In May 1904, the Makhzen's governor in Demnat, near Marrakesh, was murdered in the mosque during Friday prayers and the Jewish quarter was ransacked.[23] Anti-European feeling was growing and was often expressed as hostility to the sultan, who was perceived by nobles outside the cities as both weak and in thrall to European ideas and technology. In July 1904, Menebhi explained the sultan's position to the German envoy in Fez, Dr Philip Vassel:

> Dissatisfaction and bitterness reigns across the whole country. This sentiment does not, however, have anything to do with the Anglo-French agreement...as it is not yet generally known about. [Menebhi] believes in an imminent revolutionary movement if the sultan does not rule in an entirely different manner. If the sultan really wants to help his country, he must dismiss all of his current ministers.[24]

If Morocco's provincial nobles accused Abdelaziz of being a modernizing westernizer too closely aligned to the European powers, he was dismissed by European envoys as a backward Oriental monarch unaware of the realities confronting his kingdom (which European envoys saw as the inevitable Europeanization of Morocco). Early in his reign, the British envoy Nicolson belittled Abdelaziz as someone who 'amused himself with his picture books and mechanical toys' while the work of politics was done by his grand vizier.[25] Even in 1905, Vassel described him as someone for whom 'the realities of his kingdom and of life are as distant as they are uninteresting'.[26] Such caricatures, however, masked the otherwise remarked-upon thoughtful approach of Abdelaziz to internal reforms and his increasing confidence in affairs of state during a period of inordinate imperial pressure.[27] Even within a generally disparaging despatch, Vassel could also begrudgingly admit that the sultan's 'talents allowed him to intuit a great deal'.[28]

Irrespective of his personal traits, the contradictions of the sultan's political situation were irreconcilable with the responses required to quell domestic

---

[23] Mentzingen to Bülow, 21 May 1904, in R15489, 'Allgemeine Angelegenheiten Marokkos' (unnumbered).
[24] Mentzingen to German Foreign Office, 19 July 1904, in PAAA R15489.
[25] Nicolson, *Lord Carnock*, 118.
[26] Vassel to Kühlmann, 9 April 1905, in PAAA R15583, 'Die marokkanische Frage', 31.
[27] Burke, *Prelude to Protectorate in Morocco*, 47–9.
[28] Vassel to Kühlmann, 9 April 1905, in PAAA R15583, 31.

dissatisfaction and external pressure pulling in opposite directions. Moroccan provincial leaders were consistently enraged by Abdelaziz's reliance upon British and French advisers and demanded a shift towards a closer alignment with the Ottoman Empire. The European envoys, however, most notably the French, enjoined him to hasten the reorientation of the kingdom towards the economic, military, and political priorities of Europe. The increasingly bold encroachment of France into critical areas of Moroccan decision-making, particularly in the fields of economic and military affairs, steadily eroded the domestic authority of the Makhzen over its disillusioned provincial notables, who took resistance to the French into their own hands. In response Delcassé warned the sultan from Paris that the ostensible 'anarchy' of 'wild Moroccans' raiding French positions along the border with Algeria could see France intervene in Moroccan security matters.[29] In 1904, the French made good on this threat.

The entanglement of domestic and foreign woes also saw the Makhzen lose a sizable portion of its revenue, as the rebellions and uprisings that had broken out all over Morocco were increasingly accompanied by the refusal of regional nobles to collect or pay taxes. The state coffers were now only being partially recharged by the customs duties paid at the ports,[30] an income base so slender that the Makhzen was forced to seek foreign loans to keep the Moroccan government afloat. With Britain neutralized by the *Entente Cordiale*, the French delegation in Fez led by Georges Saint-René Taillandier was in an even stronger position to pressure Abdelaziz to accept loans exclusively from French financiers and insist upon French control over the collection of excises at Moroccan ports to pay for these loans. In early May 1904, less than a month after the *Entente Cordiale* had been signed, Vassel in Fez sent the German minister in Tangier, Friedrich von Mentzingen, a warning about the creeping French monopoly over Moroccan finances that was being abetted by pro-French Moroccan ministers:

> From those close to Hajj Omar Tazi [the Moroccan finance minister], I learn that the French...have warned senior government officials (probably Sheikh Tazi) against the Moroccan Treasury taking orders from others besides the French. I have stated that I did not believe that the French Government intended to restrict the freedom of trade of other Europeans in this way and that I would take note with interest of any official documents in which that view was expressed.[31]

[29] Radolin to Holstein, 1 April 1903, in Norman Rich and M. H. Fisher (eds), *The Holstein Papers*, vol. 4 (Cambridge: Cambridge University Press, 1963), 274.

[30] Ion Perdicaris, 'The General Situation in Morocco', *North American Review* 181, no. 588 (1905), 746.

[31] Vassel to Mentzingen, 6 May 1904, in PAAA R15489, (unnumbered).

Days later, the sultan made contact with the Germans via his senior military adviser, the Scot, Kaïd Harry Maclean, who informed Vassel in Fez that the sultan was upset about Britain's new unqualified support for the French. Abdelaziz had also complained to Maclean about Taillandier's insistence that the Makhzen only accept loans offered by French financiers and hand over its financial control of the harbours as collateral for any new loans.[32] Despite having agreed to investigate French financial assistance, now that the French were seeking to dictate their terms to the sultan, Abdelaziz had sent Maclean to Vassel to probe the German for support. In his report to Chancellor Bernhard von Bülow, Mentzingen professed to understand why, given that 'once the Moroccans have taken the money, the French will later know how to exploit the new situation the loan creates.'[33] A French loan, Mentzingen reasoned, although arranged with the consent of the sultan, meant 'a significant success for the French, and thus marks the first major step in their "*pénétration pacifique*"'.[34] This was also the fear of German traders and pro-colonial associations who, the French representative in Berlin, Georges Bihourd, warned Paris, were pressuring the German government to oppose France's attempt to control Morocco.[35]

When the loan of 50 million francs was finalized in May 1904, the French intention of using it to control the Moroccan economy and 'condition' the Moroccans to seek French assistance in all political and economic matters became clear.[36] For Delcassé, Abdelaziz's acceptance of the loan was a tacit admission that the sultan had 'in some degree ratified the declaration of 8 April which recognises our preponderance in Morocco.'[37] The French also moved in to control the customs houses at Moroccan ports, seizing the sultanate's excise duties as collateral. Significantly, this imposition of French control over the customs houses was resisted, albeit briefly, by those working in them. It was only after the intervention of a senior Moroccan official attached to the French consul general that the French gained control over these tax offices.[38]

Given his limited options for raising additional income to offset his new loans, the sultan proposed to the Europeans that the tariffs payable at Moroccan ports might be raised to compensate for Morocco's increased debt burden.[39] Despite understanding the sultan's inability to pay for the loans otherwise, his suggestion

---

[32] Vassel to Mentzingen, 11 May 1904, in PAAA R15489, (unnumbered).

[33] Mentzingen to Bülow 18 May 1904, in PAAA R15489, (unnumbered).

[34] Mentzingen to Bülow, 31 May 1904; Mentzingen to Bülow, 28 June 1904, in PAAA R15489, (unnumbered).

[35] Bihourd to Delcassé, 30 May 1904, in *Archives diplomatiques* NS 54, 'Maroc: Politique étrangère Relations avec l'Allemagne', 39–41.

[36] Burke, *Prelude to Protectorate in Morocco*, 69–71.

[37] Delcassé, quoted by Christopher Andrew, *Théophile Delcassé and the Making of the Entente Cordiale: A Reappraisal of French Foreign Policy 1898–1905* (London: Palgrave Macmillan, 1968), 265.

[38] Mentzingen to Bülow, 16 July 1904, in PAAA R15489.

[39] Mentzingen to German Foreign Office, 30 July 1904, in PAAA R15489.

was immediately opposed by France and Britain. Commenting on this resistance, Mentzingen argued that this was in line with Delcassé's plan to ensnare Morocco in a debt trap which would quickly deliver the Moroccan economy to its French financiers. Only once Morocco was French, Mentzingen predicted, would tariffs rise.[40]

Despite their opposition to any reforms suggested by the Moroccans, the French attempted to expand the definition of control over the customs houses to include a thoroughgoing reorganization of the ports themselves. They also asserted a 'responsibility' to patrol the Moroccan coastline with French cruisers, ostensibly to stop smugglers bypassing the customs houses or delivering arms to the sultan's domestic enemies. For Mentzingen, this revealed France's intention of keeping 'all other nations locked out' of Moroccan trade, a strategy that he suspected would become the rule rather than the exception 'if we allow it'.[41] The first two French naval vessels deployed under this plan, the *Kléber* and the *Galilée* were sent to Tangier in July 1904, with Taillandier confirming that 'in future there would always be French warships here', including ships sailing under the Moroccan flag, but worked by French sailors.[42] Effectively, France was confirming its ostensible right to control Moroccan trade, while creating the preconditions for any future naval blockade, should they deem one necessary.

Domestically, news of the French loan saw 400 rebels led by Emir Raisuni respond by kidnapping foreign residents (including the American Ion Perdicaris) in May 1904 and demanding both ransom money and a degree of regional autonomy from Abdelaziz, both of which were granted.[43] In the wake of some cross-border incursions by provincial Moroccan leaders that targeted French Algerian military commanders along the Moroccan-Algerian border in June 1904,[44] Taillandier also claimed that France required control over Morocco's internal security apparatus, in particular over the training and commanding of Moroccan troops, as well as over the Tangier police force. The French ambassador also argued that by seeding Moroccan barracks with Muslim Algerian non-commissioned officers, a more 'reliable' army under French control would gradually develop. More ominously, Taillandier warned that any disturbance to the peace in Tangier would lead to 'an armed intervention' by the French. All of this was applauded by the British press as a welcome corollary of the *Entente Cordiale*.[45]

[40] Mentzingen to Bülow, 3 August 1904.
[41] Mentzingen to Bülow, 18 August 1904, in PAAA R15489.
[42] Mentzingen to Bülow, 31 July 1904, in PAAA R15489.
[43] See Perdicaris, 'The General Situation in Morocco', 745–53. The kidnapping sparked a major international incident that arguably helped Theodore Roosevelt get elected in the United States. See Thomas H. Etzold, 'Protection or Politics? "Perdicaris Alive or Raisuli Dead"', *The Historian* 37, no. 2 (1975), 297–304; 'Le Maroc en 1904', 11 January 1905, in *Archives diplomatiques* NS 185, 'Maroc: Politique intérieure VI, juillet 1903–décembre 1905', 216–34.
[44] Burke, *Prelude to Protectorate in Morocco*, pp. 75–6.
[45] Mentzingen to Bülow, 1 July 1904; Mentzingen to Bülow, 14 July 1904, in R15489; *The Times*, 4 July 1904, in PAAA R15489.

These French inroads were resisted by the sultan, who did what he could to maintain control over his troops in the face of domestic rebellion and mounting French pressure. In late June 1904, Abdelaziz sent Hamza Ben Hima from Saffi to Tangier with 400 soldiers to reinstate civil peace. Troops from Casablanca were also sent to support Ben Hima. These measures too were opposed by Taillandier, who insisted upon the primacy of his plan for French control over the Moroccan military. Despite France's protests, however, by mid-July the sultan had formally refused French requests to place the police of Tangiers under French control,[46] agreeing only that one French captain, a lieutenant and three sergeants might work with the Moroccan police, a situation begrudgingly described by Taillandier as 'a satisfactory start'.[47]

The link between domestic rebellion and French penetration strengthened throughout 1904, particularly in Larache. Indicative was the local resistance mounted against the French trader Jennard, who obtained permission from Abdelaziz to transport goods between Larache and Fez. When Jennard attempted to make improvements to the road to ensure that it was passable by loaded wagons, he was challenged by 'a large contingent of native riders', who threatened him and let him know in no uncertain terms that 'wagon traffic and the improvement of the roads were not wanted' and that that he should return to Larache. Given this resistance, Jennard gave up his attempt to build the road that would have opened up the region to French commerce.[48] Not long afterwards, further anti-sultan and anti-European disturbances in Larache were met with French naval assistance, despite even Taillandier and the captain of the *Kléber* admitting that the threat to security there had been 'ridiculously exaggerated'.[49]

Elsewhere there were reports from Hajj Mohammed Torres in Fez that a protest meeting south of Tetuan, as well as one closer to Tangier under the leadership of Raisuni, had vowed to fight for the removal of French warships and the end to French control over the customs houses.[50] French intelligence in Morocco was blunt in its assessment:

The spirit of independence has penetrated so deeply into the tribes that the Makhzen cannot now count on their support, and the sultan will now require a real expedition to restore his authority in these deeply troubled regions. The Moroccan government is therefore being forced into a very difficult situation in which the most loyal provinces which have always been loyal to it and which

[46] Vassel to Mentzingen, 16 July 1904; Mentzingen to Bülow 30 June 1904, in PAAA R15489.
[47] Mentzingen to German Foreign Office, 27 July 1904, in PAAA R15489.
[48] Mentzingen to Bülow, 31 July 1904, in PAAA R15489.
[49] Delcassé to Taillandier, 25 October 1904; Taillandier to Delcassé, 26 October 1904; Taillandier to Delcasse, 31 October 1904, in *Archives diplomatiques* NS 185, 'Maroc: Politique intérieure VI juillet 1903-décembre 1905', 195–6, 200–5; Kühlmann to German Foreign Office, 29 October 1904, in PAAA R15506, 'Die Beziehungen Marokkos zu Deutschland', 37–9.
[50] Mentzingen to Bülow, 12 August 1904, in PAAA R15489.

have always provided it with the best troops are at present refusing to march with it.[51]

In Fez itself, Abdelaziz was presented with a list of demands by a group of highly honoured Islamic scholars led by Sherif Jafar al Kittani, who insisted that the sultan sever all ties with the French, replace European advisers with Ottoman ones, and fire any pro-French ministers in the Makhzen. As a result of this intervention, many European advisers were dismissed.[52] By the end of 1904, a French Foreign Office report noted that their capacity to coerce the sultan into supporting them was limited by the increasing fragmentation of political power, which was reverting to Morocco's independently minded provincial nobility. 'The spirit of insubordination is making steady progress among the tribes,' the report complained. 'The people have a visible tendency to ignore the Makhzen and to recognize no authority other than that of the notables of their tribes.'[53]

The German Intervention

Unable to leverage his state out from underneath French influence alone, the sultan's resistance to France also entailed a tactical shift towards the Germans. In mid-December 1904, the Moroccan minister Ben Sliman followed up Maclean's earlier meeting with Vassel, soliciting his help and asking him to what extent the sultan could count on German 'moral support' in his attempts to resist 'French impositions' upon his sovereignty. The German minister in Tangier (now Richard von Kühlmann) advised Bülow that a carefully worded statement hoping for the prosperity of Morocco might offer the sultan something that might pay dividends to German interests in Morocco.[54]

Unlike in 1901, the sultan's overtures fell on fertile ground, with the German Foreign Office already alarmed about the threat to German commerce represented by any coming French protectorate. Throughout 1904, reports had been reaching the Foreign Office that the French were already squeezing German firms out of Morocco, as they had elsewhere around the globe, and that they were likely to continue doing so:

The monopolizing economic policies of France in Algiers, Tunis, and Siam ... and the numerous rallies of colonial and press circles in Paris, justify the assumption that France, if it had a firm foothold in Morocco, would seek to displace other foreign

[51] Malpertuy to Taillandier, 10 December 1904, in *Archives diplomatiques* NS 185, 210–11.
[52] Guillen, *L'Allemagne et la Maroc de 1870 à 1905*, 826–7; Burke, *Prelude to Protectorate in Morocco*, 79–80.
[53] 'Le Maroc en 1904', 11 January 1905, in *Archives diplomatiques* NS 185, 216–34.
[54] Kühlmann to Bülow, 17 December 1904, in PAAA R15506, 90.

industry and trade there in favour of its own subjects as far as possible....Due to the looming French monopoly, the existence of large German companies operating in Morocco is threatened...The Imperial envoy in Tangier shares this view. He sees in the introduction of the French monopoly system, which is not doubted by him, a grave disadvantage for German interests that quite destroys their reasonable hopes.[55]

With these concerns in mind, by the beginning of January 1905 Bülow too was warming to the sultan's overtures. Initially a cautious political strategy to deal with France's hegemonic pretensions was devised, one that saw Germany deny French and Spanish reports that the sultan was facing pressure from the combined nations of Europe. Whenever confronted with the claim of 'unanimous action', Bülow argued, German diplomats should object that 'Germany, as well as various other great powers, have until now not been involved in the redrafting of the Moroccan question.'[56]

By the end of January 1905, however, Bülow had sent Kühlmann the details of a broader plan for closer relations between Morocco and Germany, in the hope that German support for the sultan might give France pause for thought. Not only were German and French interests not identical, Bülow argued, but Germany had received 'no official communication from France concerning the intended reconfiguration of Morocco'. Consequently, Germany had 'no reason to take notice of this reconfiguration'. Vassel should inform the sultan during his next audience that, while Germany could not declare war on France for the sake of Morocco, the gentle stoking of mistrust between France and Germany would ensure that the bellicose anti-German party in France remained opposed to a Moroccan war, because 'it would require a large army and necessitate the partial exposure of the German border'.[57]

At the same time, the sultan continued to stymie French attempts to seize control of the Moroccan military and economy. At the suggestion of the conservative Makhzen minister Si Feddoul Gharnit,[58] the sultan called together a council of Moroccan notables as a national assembly, ostensibly to discuss the reforms proposed by France. Given the implacable hostility towards the French throughout the Moroccan provincial nobility, Kühlmann saw in this an admirable 'anti-French manoeuvre'.[59] As he reported, the notables who had been sent to Fez for consultation were expected to reject French calls to place themselves under their tutelage:

[55] Kries, 22 October 1904, in PAAA R15506, 32–3.
[56] Bülow to Kühlmann, 2 January 1905, in PAAA R15506, 99.
[57] Bülow to Kühlmann, 30 January 1905, in PAAA R15506, 114–15.
[58] Burke, *Prelude to Protectorate in Morocco*, 77.
[59] Kühlmann to German Foreign Office, 29 January 1905, in PAAA R15506, 113.

The sultan has convened an emergency meeting at Fez, in order to generate strong moral support against the French demands... From Tangier, the mayor Si El-Arbi El Abarudi and Si Sadek Aharden have received the Sherifian order to go to Fez as soon as possible. Both are not principally anti-foreigner in outlook, but are of a conservative disposition and not in favour of French efforts to establish their hegemony. All conscripted notables, two from each city, are said to be of a similar political colour... The mission of the French mission has been made infinitely more difficult by this skilful move of the sultan. At the very least, it will be six weeks before the arrival of all the delegates, and before the meeting is complete it is unlikely that serious negotiations will take place. Then the sultan will have the strong backing of this assembly to reject all drastic demands by pointing to public opinion. At the French embassy, the measure would have been a most painful surprise.[60]

The assembly's discussions of the reforms proposed by France revealed the depth of feeling regarding France's encroachments on Moroccan sovereignty. It endorsed a strongly anti-French position, refusing the reforms on the grounds that they impinged upon the foundational principles of trade equality enshrined in the 1880 Madrid Agreement. Only the question of allowing French military assistance to secure the Algerian border was considered by the Moroccan assembly to be in any way reasonable.[61] When the sultan asked Islamic scholars to provide him with a ruling on the permissibility of European advisers, they offered the fatwa that 'The foreigners are the original cause of our misfortunes' and called for the dismissal of all European advisers and their replacement by Ottoman Muslims. In the aftermath of this national assembly, the pro-French Mohammed Torres was also replaced as representative to the foreign missions in Tangier by the anti-French Abd-al Salam Tazi.[62] Some leaders such as Muhammed bin Abd al-Kabir al-Kittani went so far as to advise Abdelaziz that the Moroccans were prepared to fight a holy war against the French.[63]

The principle of equality in the 1880 Madrid Agreement was also used by Germany to support the sultan, including against his domestic opponents. In March 1905, Vassel warned Ben Sliman that, while Germany had no wish to meddle in Moroccan domestic politics, any reforms 'needed to be implemented in such a way that during and after them no nation exercised primacy over the others'. Vassel also advised Ben Sliman against accepting reforms that that could later offer de facto support to French pretensions in Morocco.[64] In his discussions with

[60] Kühlmann to Bülow, 29 January 1905, in PAAA R15506, 117–18.
[61] Vassel to Kühlmann, 18 March 1905, in PAAA R 15577, 'Die marokkanische Frage', 247.
[62] Burke, Prelude to Protectorate in Morocco, 78.
[63] Vassel to Kühlmann, 17 March 1905, in PAAA R 15577, 245–6; C. Richard Pennell, Morocco: From Empire to Independence (London: Simon & Schuster, 2013), 132–4.
[64] Vassel to Kühlmann, 15 March 1905, in PAAA R 15577, 235–40.

Hajj Omar Tazi, Vassel also suggested that it was the French who had been supplying smuggled arms to the sultan's many domestic enemies, as a means of generating a false flag military crisis that would lend credence to France's claims that French control of the security forces was required to guarantee law and order.[65]

In his reply, Ben Sliman professed his furious agreement on the question of the Madrid Agreement, formally reassuring Bülow that he had no intention of eroding the principle of equal rights for the European powers, which had offered a bulwark against imperial penetration for decades: The sultan, he argued, would preserve the Madrid Agreement's 'equality clauses' and had no intention of altering their application:

> What Your Grace has heard about our intention to change the present political situation is without foundation, as the Makhzen has no interest in changing anything in its policy towards the powers, apart from those reforms necessary for the welfare of the domestic population and the subjects of friendly governments as well as the prosperity of the Sherifian government. The implementation of any reforms will take into account the equality of rights and maintain any existing agreements with friendly states.[66]

Outside Morocco, as Germany's protests grew louder, British and French newspapers and government officials accused Germany of deliberately creating trouble in Morocco where none had existed. They also accused Wilhelm II and Germany of being manipulated by Abdelaziz. London's *Daily News* reported that 'the Sultan's advisers are almost to a man anti-French, anti-European. If they can play off Germany against France, they will do it. They are beginning it now.'[67] In London, Germany's ambassador, Paul Wolff Metternich, warned that Britain's view was that the sultan was simply using Germany against France in a deceptive game of '*tertius gaudens*'.[68] Behind the scenes, the French scrambled to offer late assurances to Berlin that they would preserve free trade in Morocco.[69]

The Kaiser's Visit

Far from having set off from Germany intending to support the sultan, it was while he was on one of his many Mediterranean pleasure cruises that Wilhelm II

---

[65] Vassel to Kühlmann, 17 March 1905, in PAAA R 15577, 241–4.
[66] Ben Sliman to Bülow (via Kühlmann), March 1905, in PAAA R 15577, 218–21.
[67] 'The Friend of Sultans: Kaiser's Moroccan Trip: Where the Trouble Lies', *Daily News*, 23 March 1905, in PAAA R 15577, 13.
[68] Metternich to Bülow, in PAAA R 15577 *Frage*, 358.
[69] 'Note', Paris, 9 March 1905, in *Archives diplomatiques* NS14, 'Maroc: Politique étrangère: Relations internationales: Negociations secrètes relatives au Maroc III, juillet 1904–mai 1905', 103.

was called upon by Bülow to show Germany's resolve on the Moroccan question by landing at Tangier. The emperor's brief royal visit of a few short hours was made under extreme duress. After a shaky landing in a small launch, Wilhelm II was greeted by the venerable Mulai Abdelmalek, the great-uncle of Abdelaziz, who carried with him a handwritten letter from the sultan marking the occasion (see Figure 6.1).[70] From there the emperor rode into Tangier amidst a noisy storm of acclamation.[71] Wilhelm II then spoke to senior members of the German community in Morocco and to the representatives of the other European

Figure 6.1 Handwritten letter to Kaiser Wilhelm II from Sultan Abdelaziz of Morocco
Source: Photo courtesy of the Politisches Archiv des Auswärtigen Amts.

[70] Bülow to Wilhelm II, 26 March 1905, in PAAA R 15577, 41–3. Bülow's information on who would be greeting the Kaiser came from Kühlmann to German Foreign Office, 26 March 1905, in in PAAA R 15577, *Frage*, 124. For the original of the letter, see PAAA R15579, 'Die marokkanische Frage', 59–61.
[71] Mai, *Die Marokko-Deutschen, 1873–1918*, 277–88.

governments, including the French. In these conversations he reiterated Germany's support for an independent Morocco and for the sovereign rights of the sultan.

Wilhelm II's 1905 role in defending the sultan's sovereign rights was conspicuously at odds with Germany's own colonial record of abolishing the independence and sovereign rights of African, Asian, and Pacific kingdoms. The emperor's intervention was all the more surprising given that he had consistently opposed entering into the politically poisonous waters of the Moroccan question,[72] while his animosity towards potentially unwieldy colonial entanglements had only been heightened by the ongoing conflict in South West Africa which had led him to baulk at the idea of colonial entanglements in lands that were home to 'warlike peoples'.[73] Had Wilhelm II been actively directing German foreign and colonial policy, Germany's forthright intervention on behalf of Sultan Abdelaziz would never have happened.

Although there were claims from the French and the British that the visit was an expression of Germany's desire to annex part or all of Morocco, German diplomatic correspondence of April 1905—the high point of Germany's diplomatic defence of Morocco—rules this out. Indeed, German policymakers seemed at pains to emphasize that Moroccan sovereignty, not German hegemony, was the objective of their diplomatic efforts. When, for example, Germany's negotiator in Morocco, Christian von Tattenbach, contacted Chancellor Bülow offering to bypass the sultan and negotiate directly with the French to secure territory in exchange for dropping Germany's objections to French hegemony, Bülow replied that Germany could not countenance such a move, given the repeated assurances Germany had given that they were uninterested in increasing their own territory. Instead, Bülow argued, Germany's options were either to sacrifice Morocco to the French or 'extend the life of the Sherifian kingdom in the expectation of a beneficial shift in relations'.[74] Bülow remained committed to the latter course, mystifying several German diplomats, including Kühlmann, who had also received offers from the French of 'every desirable advantage in Morocco' as well as a 'large colonial area' elsewhere when he visited Paris. These offers, however, were simply ignored by the chancellor.[75]

This came as a surprise to many observers outside Germany. The Habsburg envoy to Berlin, László Szőgyény-Marich, for example, told the French that he

[72] Röhl, *Wilhelm II: Into the Abyss of War and Exile 1900–1941*, 334.

[73] Bülow to Tattenbach, 30 April 1905, in PAAA R15583, 213.

[74] Tattenbach to Bülow, 29 April 1905; Bülow to Tattenbach, 30 April 1905, in PAAA R15583, 213, 230–5. Wilhelm II was so far removed from discussions that he was surprised to hear of Tattenbach's suggestion when the tsar told him of it. See Wilhelm II to Nicholas II, 28 November 1905, in Goetz (ed), *Briefe Wilhelms II an den Zaren 1894–1914*, 384–5. Tattenbach's freelancing was also reported to the British foreign minister. See Frederick V. Parsons, *The Origins of the Morocco Question 1880–1900* (London: Duckworth, 1976), 528.

[75] Vierhaus, *Das Tagebuch der Baronin Spitzemberg*, 451–2.

assumed that Wilhelm II's visit to Morocco was as a direct representative of the commercial interests of Krupp or the Hamburg-America shipping line.[76] Inside Germany, however, the royal visit was met with interest but low expectations by the colonial lobby, which had witnessed the spectacular lack of colonial results stemming from Wilhelm II's visit to the Ottoman Empire in 1898. The pan-German organ the *Rheinisch-Westfälische Zeitung* bemoaned that 'there can hardly be any difference of opinion in Germany regarding the political value of the emperor's journeys. The history of the emperor's reign has taught us that they have rarely resulted in important consequences.' Referring to Wilhelm II's visit to Sultan Abdulhamid II in 1898, the paper concluded that:

> Seven years ago the emperor visited Palestine and it was thought that the whole of Asia Minor would be secured as a sphere for German commercial expansion. A German railway connecting the Bosphorus with the Persian Gulf was to strengthen Germany's grip on Asia Minor. German industry, however, has made little progress in Asia Minor, and the construction of the Baghdad railway cannot be begun. The emperor is now going to Morocco, and, in our opinion, diplomatic action in regard to this country could not be initiated in a more unsuitable manner.[77]

Territorial expansion was repeatedly ruled out by Bülow and the German Foreign Office. Instead, as Wilhelm II's visit made clear, the priority was the preservation of the economic open door when it came to trade, investment, and industry in Morocco. Support for the sultan was, for Bülow, a stance against France's monopoly-oriented imperialism, which threatened to lock German commerce out of North Africa. Nowhere did he make this clearer than in the Reichstag, where he confirmed that Wilhelm II would not be making any territorial claims in Tangiers:

> A year ago His Majesty the Kaiser explained to His Majesty the King of Spain, that Germany was not seeking territorial advantage in Morocco. Given this clear explanation, it is pointless to ascribe to the visit to Tangier of His Majesty any selfish intentions against the integrity or independence of Morocco…Quite apart from the visit, and independent from the territorial question there is the question of whether we have German economic interests to protect in Morocco. Indeed we do. Just as in China, we have a considerable interest in the maintenance of the open door, that is to say, the equal status of all trading nations…German economic interests in Morocco, as is known, are substantial,

[76] Bihourd to Delcassé, 9 April 1905, in *Archives diplomatiques* NS 14, 128.
[77] *The Standard*, 23 March 1905, quoting the *Rheinisch-Westfälische Zeitung*, in PAAA R 15577, 12.

and it is our task to ensure that they remain treated equally with those of all other nations.[78]

None of this was of interest to Wilhelm II. The initial suggestion for a royal visit came from the Tangier correspondent of the *Kölnische Zeitung*, August Hornung, and it was Bülow (following the advice of Kühlmann) who had set Wilhelm II in motion and choreographed the visit.[79] Afterwards the emperor would complain of having been used as a 'puppet' in Tangier.[80] The experience rankled with him. 'Never forget', he wrote to Bülow afterwards, 'that you personally used me against my will in Tangier, for the sake of the success of your Morocco policy.'[81] His 1922 account of the visit similarly preserves his bitterness about the Tangier visit. Although embellishing his political farsightedness, Wilhelm II's account offers an interesting glimpse of political decision-making during his reign:

> The very much *contre coeur* trip to Tangier occurred in 1905.... At the end of March I intended, as in the previous year, to take a recuperative cruise around the Mediterranean... As the time to depart approached, Bülow expressed the further wish that I should call into Tangier and, through this visit to the Moroccan harbour, strengthen the position of the sultan against the French. I refused this, because it appeared to me that the Moroccan question was too explosive and I feared that my visit would do more harm than good. Bülow, however, continued to insist on it, without ever really convincing me of the necessity or point of the visit. On the voyage I was accompanied by Baron von Schoen as a representative of the Foreign Office. Together we discussed several times the opportunities presented by the visit. We agreed that it was better to refrain from going. From Lisbon I shared this decision with the chancellor. Bülow answered with the emphatic demand that I must take into account the

---

[78] Bülow, in *Verhandlungen des Reichstags*, 29 March 1905, 5709.

[79] Pierre Guillen argues that Kühlmann had discussed a 'personal intervention by the Kaiser' with Taillandier in December 1904. Gunther Mai and Michael Mayer both argue that although Kühlmann claimed the credit, the real instigator was Hornung. Hornung's telegram to the *Kölnische Zeitung* read:

> Given the immense popularity enjoyed by the emperor among all Muslims since his trip to Palestine, the news of his arrival in the Mediterranean has aroused great interest among Moroccan notables. On several occasions, the hope was expressed here that the emperor could visit a Moroccan city. He would be sure of a warm welcome.

Characteristically, Röhl argues that the idea was actually Wilhelm II's, before he suddenly and inexplicably changed his mind. See Guillen, *L'Allemagne et le Maroc de 1870 à 1905*, 818, 838–9; Mayer, *Geheime Diplomatie und öffentliche Meinung*; Mai, *Die Marokko-Deutschen 1873–1918*, 272–3; Röhl, *Wilhelm II: Into the Abyss of War and Exile, 1900–1941*, 334–5.

[80] John C. G. Röhl, *Philipp Eulenburgs Politische Korrespondenz*, vol. 3 (Boppard am Rhein: Harald Boldt Verlag, 1976), 2115.

[81] Albrecht Moritz, *Das Problem des Präventivkrieges in der deutschen Politik während der ersten Marokkokrise* (Frankfurt am Main: Peter Lang, 1974), 113.

view of the German people and the Reichstag, which were in favour of this trip. It was necessary for me to travel to Tangier. With a heavy heart I relented.[82]

Wilhelm II certainly expressed his deep misgivings a number of times during the planning phase for the visit. Indeed, Bülow had to reassure and cajole the emperor right up until the day of the landing. Three days before the visit, Wilhelm II tried to call it off, claiming that 'Tangier is already in chaos, with an Englishman almost murdered yesterday.' He professed to see the whole affair as 'very dubious'. He also refused to get off the ship at all unless Tattenbach, who, the emperor said, had raised doubts about the landing, had disembarked and confirmed that it was safe.[83] Bülow immediately cabled Tattenbach to inform him that while 'the security of His Majesty was above all else', it was Tattenbach's duty to exercise his utmost influence over the emperor and remind him that if he did not land in Tangiers, 'the enemy press would naturally spread the story that His Majesty had wanted to cancel on the basis of a possible danger that would after the fact be represented as an imaginary one.'[84] Tattenbach acquiesced, replying that although 'around the Kaiser a strong current is against His Majesty landing in Tangier, in my opinion their expressed concerns and fears are not accurate'. Given the planning that had gone into it, Tattenbach admitted, the landing should proceed. Bülow replied that he was pleased to see that they were now all on the same page.[85]

With Tattenbach now working in accord with the chancellor's dramaturgical vision, Bülow wrote to Wilhelm II once again, feigning sympathy for the emperor's discomfort, but reminding him of the enormous strategic advantage that could be won by so resolutely defying the French:

> Delcassé is sweating blood, because Your Majesty will upset his well-crafted plans. He had announced in Fez that France was negotiating on behalf of all of the European Powers, which had all agreed to the subjugation of Morocco to France. If Your Majesty appears in Tangier, surrounded by the roaring jubilation of the Muslims, celebrated by the non-French Europeans, and without taking notice of the French, Delcassé is finished.[86]

The emperor remained deeply uneasy about the visit, however, and wrote to Bülow again on 29 March, this time pleading that his physical disability should preclude him from the visit:

---

[82]   Wilhelm II, *Ereignisse und Gestalten aus den Jahren 1878–1918*, 90–1.
[83]   Wilhelm II to Bülow, 28 March 1905, in PAAA R 15577, 289.
[84]   Bülow to Tattenbach, 28 March 1905, in PAAA R 15577, 296.
[85]   Tattenbach to Bülow, 29 March 1905; Bülow to Tattenbach, 29 March 1905, in PAAA R 15577, 351, 353.
[86]   Bülow to Wilhelm II, 29 March 1905, in PAAA R 15577, 314.

Figure 6.2 Street view of Kaiser Wilhelm II riding into Tangier, March 1905

To mount a Berber horse that has not been tested or ridden in by a groom, is, because of my left arm, dangerous in any case, and the horses there, which are already lively, will be even more excited than usual because of the enormous hubbub that will take place in Tangier. That leaves the gentle ones, which I believe only women ride there. To go by foot has been ruled out as absolutely impossible by Tattenbach.[87]

Again, Bülow reacted quickly, telling Kühlmann in Tangier to make sure that the Kaiser's horse had a good temperament.[88] Bülow then made it clear to Wilhelm II that the visit must go ahead, and that the German consul in Tangier was aware of the issue. Were the emperor to get an uncontrollable horse that in any way embarrassed him in the eyes of the world, the consul 'knows what awaits him'.[89] In the end, Wilhelm II enjoyed his triumphant horseback entry into Tangier amidst the 'indescribable cheering' of the Moroccans in what one of his companions enthusiastically described as a 'magnificent Oriental scene' (see Figure 6.2)[90]

Not only did Bülow force the very doubtful monarch to land in Tangier, but he also carefully scripted his responses to any questions he might encounter while

[87] Wilhelm II to Bülow, 29 March 1905, in PAAA R 15577, 368–73.
[88] German Foreign Office to Schoen, 23 March 1905, in PAAA R15578, 'Die marokkanische Frage', 62–3.
[89] Bülow to Kühlmann, 30 March 1905; Bülow to Wilhelm II, 30 March 1905, in PAAA R 15577, 374, 384–7.
[90] Schoen to Bülow, 31 March 1905, in R15578, 115–21.

there. All answers, Bülow insisted, were to foreground the protection of German trade in Morocco, which would be lost under French rule. Consequently, the emperor's role was to stress Germany's strong support for the status quo:

> Naturally it does not lie in German interests if the sultan were to impose the beginnings of a French Protectorate. To work against this, it is in my humble opinion to be recommended that ~~the independence of Morocco be defended or it will be immediately lost to France~~ Your Majesty greets the emissary of the sultan with honours and ostentatiously as the emissary of his sovereign, and offer your salutations to the sultan…it will depend on the words of Your Majesty whether the sultan continues to defend Morocco's independence or submits to France without further ado.[91]

The chancellor, nonetheless, pointed out that there were limits to German support. Under no circumstances should Wilhelm II imply that Germany would 'risk a war with France over Morocco', as that might encourage the Moroccans to start an ill-advised conflict in the expectation of German military support. On the other hand, Bülow reasoned, a strategic ambiguity on the question might prove advantageous. The position that 'Germany has no agreements that would hinder it being directed by its own best interests' might, he argued, plant seeds of doubt in the minds of the French 'but does not oblige us to do anything'.[92] Bülow's supposition proved correct, with the French ambassador in Berlin unsure how to read Germany's strategic silence:

> This silence is in line with the policy the chancellor proclaimed in the Reichstag and the emperor in Tangier: the Germans will not permit France any special treatment in Morocco and intend to ensure, through direct negotiations with the sultan, the protection of all its interests. Has she tried, by adopting this attitude, to intimidate us and to obtain, by the prospect of a conflict, concessions which she would not dare to conquer by force of arms? I do not think so…Wilhelm II is not, I am convinced, currently considering a war against France.[93]

Although a military alliance was out of the question, withdrawing Germany's 'moral support' for the sultan would also be tantamount to abandoning Germany's economic interests there. Accordingly, Bülow advised the emperor to adhere to a strict script that focused on these issues, and to say only:

---

[91] Bülow to Wilhelm II, 26 March 1905, in PAAA R 15577, 71–86. The draft section crossed out (by Bülow) offers a pithy summary of his thinking as he wrote the draft of his letter.
[92] Bülow to Wilhelm II, 26 March 1905, in PAAA R 15577, 71–86.
[93] Bilhourd to Delcassé, 28 April 1905, in *Archives diplomatiques* NS 14, 168.

It is well-known that I do not desire Moroccan territory, but I attach importance to remaining on an equal footing with other nations in commerce and communications with Morocco. Other trading nations have the same interest.... The interests of the sultan are identical with the interests of almost all seafaring and trading nations. If he preserves his independence, he preserves his freedom to grant equal rights to all in his kingdom.[94]

After a tricky landing in rolling swell, it was precisely this message that Wilhelm II delivered in person. The emperor's speeches echoed almost to the letter Bülow's scripted responses, firmly linking the question of the sultan's political and territorial sovereignty to the issue of free trade. Speaking to the Germans living and working in Morocco, Wilhelm II declared:

I am glad to meet the German pioneers in Morocco and to be able to say to you that you have done your duty. Germany has significant economic interests in Morocco. I will encourage and protect trade with Morocco, which is showing a satisfying growth, and thereby ensure the complete equality of treatment of all the powers, which is only possible with the sovereignty of the sultan and the independence of the country. Both of these are for Germany beyond all doubt, and I am always ready to advocate for both. I believe that my visit to Tangier expresses this and makes it clearly known. It most assuredly evokes the conviction that what Germany does in Morocco will be negotiated with the sovereign sultan.[95]

This was also the substance of the emperor's exchange with Mulai Abdelmalek, in which he assured the Moroccan prince that Germany considered the sultan to be 'the ruler of a free and independent realm, free from subjection to foreign suzerainty' (see Figure 6.3). On the question of trade, the emperor informed Abdelmalek that he expected that German trade and transport would continue to receive 'the same advantages enjoyed by all other trading nations'. Wilhelm II promised that he would always 'deal directly with the sultan' and that he expected the implementation of only those reforms that were 'in accordance with the views of the sultan and his people, and without injury to the precepts of the Qur'an'. To remove any doubt that this constituted opposition to French demands for reform, the visiting emperor insisted that 'European customs and methods are not to be transplanted automatically.'[96] While the sultan's handwritten letter to Wilhelm II

[94] Bülow to Wilhelm II, 26 March 1905, in PAAA R 15577, 71–86.

[95] Johannes Penzler, *Die Reden Kaiser Wilhelm II in den Jahren 1901–Ende 1905*, vol. 3 (Leipzig: Philipp Reclam, 1912), 247–8.

[96] Schoen to Bülow, 31 March 1905, in PAAA R15578, 115–21. The Kaiser repeated these sentiments to the Italians in April 1905, saying that 'We had no other intention in Morocco than to enforce the principle of the 'open door', to acknowledge no foreign sovereignty and to deal with the sultan

Marokko. Besuch des Kaisers in Tanger.
Begrüssung durch die Abgesandten des Sultans.

Figure 6.3 Wilhelm II meeting the emissaries of the Moroccan sultan in Tangier

was a politically 'colourless' document,[97] Wilhelm II's (Foreign Office-drafted) response was more striking, offering German assistance to Morocco for any future reforms to trade, shipping, and communications that would assist the sultan to remain 'a free, independent ruler of a free and independent land, strong in the unanimity of the nations that all enjoy the same rights in His country.'[98]

The French, who had kept a close eye on Wilhelm II's visit,[99] were forced to respond to Germany's defence of the sultan by mirroring the language used by the emperor in their attempts to defuse the issue. Speaking in the Chamber of Deputies on 8 April 1905, Delcassé sought to reassure Europe and Morocco that France too held the sovereign rights of Abdelaziz to be important. France's intervention was predicated, he disingenuously claimed, on its desire to strengthen the 'nominal sovereignty, the especially precarious authority of the sultan' at the same time as they improved the 'living conditions of the Moroccan people' whose customs and beliefs, he continued, the French respected.[100]

---

directly as a ruler of a free and independent state.' See Wilhelm II to Bülow, April 1905 in PAAA R15578, 152–6.

[97] The closest the Sultan came to a political gesture in the letter was a repeated reference to the 'friendship' between Morocco and Germany. See 'Uebersetzung des Handschreibens Seiner Scherifischen Majestät des Sultans' in PAAA, R15579, 59–61.

[98] Vassel to Kühlmann, 20 March 1905; Kühlmann to Bülow, 25 March 1905: Wilhelm II to Abd-elaziz, 31 March 1905 in PAAA R15578, 47–50, 106, 108–11.

[99] Bihourd to Delcassé, 3 April 1905; Bihourd to Delcassé, 4 April 1905; Bihourd to Delcassé, 5 April 1905, in *Archives diplomatiques*, NS14, 110, 111, 115.

[100] Delcassé, 8 April 1905, in *Archives diplomatiques*, NS14 Maroc, 124.

In Morocco, the Makhzen knew better, welcoming German support as offering some respite from French predations, if not a solution. Even before the royal visit Menebhi had observed, 'in Fez, Germany is considered as the best and most disinterested of friends. The eyes of Moroccan patriots are turned towards her.'[101] Ben Sliman similarly noted that 'the sultan wants to cultivate the friendship of Germany. It is the only thing offering Morocco salvation.'[102] Germany's intervention even had an effect on the domestic rebellions afflicting Moroccan politics, with Perdicaris noting that the effect of the German show of support 'seems to have been to tranquilize in some measure the hitherto rapidly increasing dislike to foreigners, and to modify the widespread disaffection of the subjects of the Sultan.'[103]

Wilhelm II's visit was also met with some guarded warmth by many provincial Moroccan nobles who felt that the Germans might assist them in the preservation of their independence, while the French military reported that, with Wilhelm II's arrival, previously friendly Moroccans had suddenly become hostile to them.[104] For some Moroccan nobles, the royal visit was an opportunity to mend fences with the sultan, on the proviso that Abdelaziz maintained his new anti-French trajectory, as a report from the *Times* made clear:

> The Emperor's visit is being made the occasion for a great demonstration by the Moors. Hundreds of tribesmen are collecting in the neighbouring districts and will pour into Tangier the day before his Majesty arrives. The tribesmen are in the best of humours, and no disorders need to be feared. The local authorities here are showing great energy. Buildings are everywhere being repaired and repainted, decorations prepared and the streets repaved. Bu Amama, the important and influential Shereef whose territories adjoin the Algerian frontier, and who for years has been antagonistic to France, has written to the Sultan promising to put down Bu Hamara's rebellion and kill or capture the leaders provided that the Sultan becomes more orthodox and refuses the demands of the French. Should the Sultan accept their demands Bu Amama threatens to raise a general rebellion. The Sultan has sent him a valuable ring as a pledge of good faith.[105]

In Tangiers, Kühlmann too repeatedly emphasized the enthusiasm of the entire population, from the Moroccans themselves to the usually fiercely anti-royal

[101] Guillen, *L'Allemagne et le Maroc de 1870 à 1905*, 829.
[102] Guillen, *L'Allemagne et le Maroc de 1870 à 1905*, 830.
[103] Perdicaris, 'The General Situation in Morocco', 750.
[104] Dunn, *Resistance in the Desert*, 217.
[105] Walter Harris, 'The Powers and Morocco', *The Times*, 27 March 1905, in PAAA R 15577, 338. On Walter Harris's reporting in Morocco, see George Joffé, 'Walter Harris and the Imperial Vision of Morocco', *Journal of North African Studies* 1, no. 3 (1996), 248–65.

settlement of Spanish anarchists. Even British traders, Kühlmann reported, were defying London to erect a triumphal arch under which the Kaiser could ride.[106]

The provincial nobility were, nonetheless, still wary, with one British news-paper reporting the clear-sighted pragmatism of one regional sherif from the Filali family who declared himself to be 'unmoved by his kinsman, the Sultan Mulai Abdelaziz' and his attempts 'to bring Western culture to the Moors'. When asked about Wilhelm II's visit he argued that:

> The German Emperor's action is useful just so far as it hampers the French rep-resentatives in Fez. Germany is no more to us than France, and we are not deceived into the belief or hope that the German Ruler has no other object in view than to hold this kingdom together. We know now that if one Power inter-feres with another in Morocco, it is not for the sake of the Moors. One and all seem to think that this land is something to be bought and sold...In this coun-try...there are neither roads nor bridges, as you have remarked already. There is no rich store of food to feed an army. But there are men who have lived uncon-quered since the Idreesi Dynasty was founded. The Filali Sherifs have ruled Morocco for more than two hundred years, and there are mountain tribes still unsubdued. We are a fighting nation.[107]

On the question of whether he saw any prospect for a diplomatic means of accom-modating the French, the sherif's response was even more bellicose:

> I do not know...whether in your Western countries even a Sultan may surren-der his kingdom...I who speak to you have but to call, and all the south will rise. And if Our Master be deceived by the Infidel, I will cry aloud to the people. I will lead them against the French. And the northern tribes that have felt the scourge of Spain will rise too, aye, all Islam, even over the border.[108]

As the eventual overthrow of Abdelaziz in 1908 demonstrates, threats of an upris-ing against a sultan deemed to have done too little to preserve Moroccan inde-pendence were not merely empty words.[109] Sultan Abdelaziz was, however, aware of the depth of feeling surrounding him and the extent that his rule depended on a clear rejection of French hegemony. When the sultan informed the French in the wake of Wilhelm II's visit that the French reforms would not be accepted by

---

[106] Kühlmann to German Foreign Office, 29 March 1905; Kühlmann to Bülow, 24 March 1905, in PAAA R 15577, 388, 411. The Kaiser too mentioned the enthusiastic participation of Spanish and Italian anarchists. See Wilhelm II, *Ereignisse und Gestalten aus den Jahren 1878–1918*, 91.

[107] 'Patriotism of the Moors: A Wazir on the Powers: The Spirit of Revolt: Resistance to Aggression', *The Standard*, 1 May 1905, in PAAA R 155584, 'Die marrokanische Frage', 163.

[108] 'Patriotism of the Moors', 163.

[109] On the overthrow of Abdelaziz, see James N. Sater, *Civil Society and Political Change in Morocco* (London: Routledge, 2007), 30–1.

the Makhzen, the sultan's grounds for refusal were stated as being that 'It has not been possible for His Majesty to oppose the people.'[110]

Wilhelm II's landing in Tangier briefly bolstered Sultan Abdelaziz's claims to sovereignty, angering the British and briefly throwing French plans for the sultanate into disarray.[111] Nonetheless, Bülow's royal puppetry only succeeded in postponing the absorption of Morocco into the French Empire until after Abdelaziz's overthrow. Ultimately, Bülow's strategic ambiguity translated into a lack of diplomatic clarity that was compounded by the erratic and intemperate behaviour of Germany's delegate, Tattenbach, at the Algeciras conference in early 1906.[112] Germany's diplomatic defeat at the conference, and the signing of the Act of Algeciras by the sultan, led to renewed resistance from Moroccan notables dismayed by the apparent capitulation to the French. Despite disagreement on who should lead the fight against the French, the Moroccan rebels settled on Abd al-Hafid, the sultan's brother, who found sufficient support to mount a bid for the throne on an anti-French platform.[113] Assumed to be a stronger monarch than his brother, the new sultan in fact found himself unable to resist the growing power of the French and found his own sovereign power quickly subordinated to the French.

In defending the sultan, the Germans had followed their own perceived interests: protecting German business interests, defending the principle of the open door, and attempting to halt the pace of France's 'peaceful penetration' of Morocco. The sultan too, however, had followed his interests. In Germany he found a replacement power to act as a protector of his sovereignty once France had convinced Britain to give it a free hand in Northwest Africa. At the same time, he also managed to convince many provincial Moroccan notables that he had found a way to escape the incorporation of Morocco into the French Empire without precipitating a war against a European power he could not defeat. The sultan's agency and that of the Makhzen are crucial to understanding the Moroccan crisis and how Germany was led towards a political cul-de-sac in North Africa. That Germany was convinced to take a stance on the issue of free trade in North Africa, an issue that Germany had assiduously avoided confronting elsewhere, most notably in Siam, illustrates the ability of Abdelaziz to harness, if only fleetingly, the shift in German foreign policy under Bülow for the benefit of Morocco.

---

[110] Burke, *Prelude to Protectorate in Morocco*, 85.   [111] Nicolson, *Lord Carnock*, 161.

[112] Harold Nicolson, *Lord Carnock*, 170–99. Tattenbach had been chosen by Bülow to demonstrate German resolve. See Holstein to Radolin, 11 April, 1905, in Rich and Fisher (eds), *The Holstein Papers*, vol. 4, 297–9.

[113] Dunn, *Resistance in the Desert*, 216–39.

PART II
MONARCHY BEYOND
THE METROPOLE

7

Company Rule and the Sultan of Zanzibar

On 19 July 1888, just one month after Kaiser Wilhelm II had ascended the throne,[1] Sultan Khalifa of Zanzibar informed his people that he had leased a large section of his coastal territories on the mainland of Africa to the German East Africa Company (Deutsch-Ostafrikanische Gesellschaft: DOAG). Although this territory remained under the nominal sovereignty of the sultan, the privileges and responsibilities of government in these lands had now been handed over to the German company.[2]

Despite its status as a private sector colony, the German state would quickly be called upon to secure the DOAG's new territory, after the German company attempted to implement a series of political measures there that insulted and disempowered local notables. The actions of the DOAG caused a great outcry amongst the sultan's historically powerful (and in many instances largely autonomous) coastal elites, who were the proximate rulers of important coastal centres such as Bagamoyo, Dar es Salaam, Kilwa, Lindi, and Pangani. The outrage of these regional governors, the walis, quickly turned into a large rebellion against the German company and, in some regions, the sultan. Woefully underprepared for rule across such a vast territory, let alone revolt, the company's leaders were forced to prevail upon the German navy, the Reichstag, and the Sultan of Zanzibar to help them try to restore the order that their company had shattered.

The company's destabilization of the sultan's claims to rule over a patchwork of coastal territories that were in reality governed by local notables revolutionized political relations within the sultanate, engendering new power dynamics and allegiances that neither the Germans nor the sultan could control. The uprising also had an important economic dimension, and it was assumed by many Germans that it was primarily Arab traders unhappy with the sudden imposition of an apparent German monopoly over trade who were behind the revolt. As one German naval commander declared, 'The Arabs, who had earlier controlled trade in the region, were dissatisfied with the new arrangements, and it was easy for them to stir up the native population against the under-resourced East Africa

---

[1] For his address upon acceding to the throne, see Wilhelm II, 'An Mein Volk!', *Neueste Mittheilungen* 19 June, 1888, 1.
[2] Heinz Schneppen, *Sansibar und die Deutschen: Ein besonderes Verhältnis 1844–1966* (Münster: Lit Verlag, 2003), 211–13.

The Kaiser and the Colonies: Monarchy in the Age of Empire. Matthew P. Fitzpatrick, Oxford University Press.
© Matthew P. Fitzpatrick 2022. DOI: 10.1093/oso/9780192897039.003.0008

Company.'[3] It was not, however, only Arab traders in the region who were unhappy with the sudden DOAG takeover of their territory. African nations of the hinterland also seized the opportunity to reassert themselves on the African coast at the expense of the Sultan of Zanzibar and his hitherto loyal walis.[4]

The East African revolt and the various responses to it reveal the complexity of the contest for sovereign power in East Africa and the effects of German colonial pressure on the standing of Zanzibar's sultan. While, according to the lease agreement, formal sovereignty was shared between the Sultan of Zanzibar and the German company, in practice this fiction was accepted by neither the DOAG nor the coastal walis, both of whom believed that, in signing the lease, the sultan had effectively forfeited his claims to rule. The crisis caused by the loss of the sultan's legitimacy saw an outbreak of violence that the German state was quickly drawn into, as the limitations of private sector imperialism in the domain of security became apparent. As the increasingly important role played by the Reichstag and the German navy illustrated, the claims to sovereignty over East Africans made by a German commercial entity relied in the final analysis on the military and political support of the state.

Negotiating the Lease

Territorial leases were not uncommon in areas where rulers under pressure from European powers were not willing to fully cede sovereignty but permitted, for a range of reasons, a temporary loss of control over a part of their territory in exchange for other tangible rewards (most notably guaranteed income and security assurances).[5] From the position of colonizing powers, such leases offered access to coveted colonial resources and control over lucrative markets and trading hubs in regions where outright dispossession was difficult to effect. Often it was assumed by the state and private entities leasing extra-European territories that the concessions they had gained were tantamount to dispossession, with the term of the lease viewed as a period in which formal imperial control could be consolidated.[6]

The nature of the bargain eventually struck by Sultan Khalifa bin Said of Zanzibar with the East African Company was spelled out in the so-called 'Coastal

---

[3] Carl Dick, *Das Kreuzergeschwader: Sein Werden, Sieg und Untergang* (Berlin: Ernst Siegfried Mittler und Sohn, 1917), 5–6.

[4] As the German envoy to Zanzibar, Gustav Michahelles, made clear in a report to Bismarck, the terms 'Arab' and 'African' were relatively loose designations for cultural milieus rather than strictly operational racial categories. See Michahelles to Bismarck, 3 November 1888, in *Verhandlungen des Reichstages*, Aktenstück 41, Nr 19, vol. 108, 1889, 406–7.

[5] Michael J. Strauss, *Territorial Leasing in Diplomacy and International Law* (Leiden: Brill Nijhoff, 2015).

[6] Strauss, *Territorial Leasing*, 70–89.

Treaty' of April 28, 1888, which made clear that, although the sovereignty of the sultan was to be preserved in name, effective political and economic control had been handed over to the German company:

> His Majesty the Sultan confers on the German East Africa Company all powers that appertain to him on the mainland and in His territories and dependencies south of the River Umba, and cedes and surrenders to the same complete administration of this region. Authority will be exercised in the name of His Majesty and under his flag, as well as with due regard to His sovereign rights.[7]

That such a shared sovereignty arrangement between the sultan and the German company would be struck was by no means self-evident. When the Germans had initially sought to claim East African territories, the then sultan, Barghash bin Said, had sent his troops into the proposed areas and had protested strenuously against their annexation, insisting that the regions were part of his sovereign domain and that 'any chief who offers to transfer the rights of sovereignty to agents of the company is not authorized to do so.'[8]

Bismarck had answered the sultan's protests by sending a flotilla of naval vessels to Zanzibar, threatening complete annexation of the sultanate and forcing the sultan (and the watching British) to accept the German claims. This display of naval power, however, had few long-term effects in terms of local power dynamics, although, internationally, it led to the conclusion of the London Treaty which established the limits of German and British territorial claims in the region.[9] Prior to the 1888 coastal treaty, the DOAG's stations exercised very limited influence in East Africa and had looked destined for insolvency. The company's representatives in East Africa were tolerated outsiders rather than rulers. Sultan Barghash, on the other hand, maintained his indirect rule over his subjects through the walis.[10] As the reach of the DOAG contracted, many of the coastal notables who had signed treaties with the company simply reverted to older local commercial and political arrangements, while inland communities became more expressly anti-European as a result of mistreatment by the company's employees.

---

[7] 'Küstenvertrag', in Bruno Kurtze, *Die Deutsch-Ostafrikanische Gesellschaft: Ein Beitrag zum Problem der Schutzbriefgesellschaften und zur Geschichte Deutsch-Ostafrikas* (Jena: Gustav Fischer Verlag, 1913), 183–7.

[8] Rochus Schmidt, *Geschichte des Araberaufstandes in Ostafrika: Seine Entstehung, seine Niederwerfung und seine Folgen* (Frankfurt an der Oder: Trowitsch & Sohn, 1892), 14.

[9] Schmidt, *Geschichte des Araberaufstandes in Ostafrika*, 17–18.

[10] Fritz Ferdinand Müller, *Deutschland—Zanzibar—Ostafrika: Geschichte einer deutschen Kolonialeroberung 1884–1890* (Berlin: Rütten & Loening, 1959), 268–70, 357. The German East African soldier Rochus Schmidt argued that the walis did not hold any influence over Africans of the interior, who were, he argued, ruled by local African leaders. See Schmidt, *Geschichte des Araberaufstandes in Ostafrika*, 16–17.

The prospects of the DOAG might have continued to diminish, had it not been for the increasing pressure placed upon Zanzibar's sultan by his lenders. Despite the precariousness of the DOAG's foothold in East Africa, the elderly Sultan Barghash offered the company a lease over the coastal strip between the River Umba in the north and the River Rovuma in the south on 19 July 1887. The proposed deal was similar to that which he had struck with the British earlier that year in order to improve his increasingly dire financial position vis-à-vis his European creditors.[11]

The realization of the plan for a lease was marked by a number of difficulties, most of them of the DOAG's own making. Despite the founder of the DOAG, Carl Peters, arrogantly insisting that the locals would undoubtedly celebrate their liberation from the 'unbearable yoke of Said Barghash', the actions of Peters and the DOAG during the negotiations made it clear that Africans had more to fear from the coercive tactics of the Germans than from the sultan. In June 1887, Barghash complained to Bismarck that 'Dr Peters and his party were forcing our sheiks to sign pretended conventions by threats and committing other acts of violence and injustice,' which caused Bismarck to offer an apology.[12] The apology did not, however, change the predatory behaviour of the DOAG, and by November 1887, unilateral alterations made to the initial draft of the treaty significantly reduced the income the sultan stood to receive, were he to agree to the lease. Outraged and holding Peters personally responsible, the sultan refused to have anything more to do with him and insisted that Bismarck remove Peters, which Bismarck duly did.[13] Thereafter, Barghash refused to speak to company representatives and dealt only with the envoy of the German state to Zanzibar, Gustav Michahelles.[14]

Pleading ill health and disillusioned with the unequal deal the Germans were attempting to foist upon him, Barghash backed away from the proposed lease agreement, avoiding as far as possible any discussion of the issue. In February 1888 he was able to avoid any further serious negotiations by taking a trip to Muscat. Bismarck, however, remained undeterred by the sultan's absence, pressing him on whether he would conduct negotiations with the German consul and the DOAG from Muscat or whether he would give full power to one of his

[11] Schmidt, *Geschichte des Araberaufstandes in Ostafrika*, 19–20; Jutta Bückendorf, '*Schwarz-Weiss-Rot über Ostafrika!' Deutsche Kolonialpläne und Afrikanische Realität* (Münster: Lit Verlag, 1997), 331–2; Müller, *Deutschland—Zanzibar—Ostafrika*, 271–3.

[12] Barghash to Bismarck, 5 June 1887; Bismarck to Barghash, 6 June 1887, in BA Berlin R1001/8917, 'Die Correspondenz des Herrn Reichskanzler mit dem Sultan von Zanzibar', 5–7.

[13] Barghash to Bismarck, 7 November 1887; Bismarck to Barghash, 27 December 1887, in BA Berlin R1001/8917, 70, 80–2.

[14] Bückendorf, '*Schwarz-Weiss-Rot über Ostafrika!*', 334; Müller, *Deutschland—Zanzibar—Ostafrika*, 276–81.

officials remaining in Zanzibar.[15] The sultan did not answer him. In fact, he would never write to Bismarck again.

Sultan Barghash died on 27 March 1888, one day after returning from his trip to Muscat.[16] Although rumours circulated that he had been poisoned,[17] he had in fact succumbed to late stage elephantiasis. His death had long been expected, and negotiations between the British and the Germans had already seen both powers conspire to agree on a favoured successor, namely Khalifa bin Said.[18] Despite these contingency plans, from the Germans' perspective the death of Sultan Barghash was seen as a blow to their chances in East Africa, with Consul General Michahelles writing to Bismarck shortly before the sultan's death, presciently arguing that:

> For German interests in East Africa it is my humble opinion that it would be most useful if the doctors are able to extend the life of the current sultan. Although it might be simpler and easier for the settlement of outstanding questions to require of a royal successor requiring our support the desired concessions simply as a condition for it, on the other hand any successor to Said Barghash will never be what His Highness represents, namely the most influential and most famous ruler of the entire east coast. The great authority of the sultan is primarily personal, it is extinguished with his death, and as soon as it can no longer be exploited and used for the interests of the German East African Company, the company will be forced to increase its use of force more than it has needed to up until now, so as to hold its ground.[19]

Barghash's death during negotiations over the coastal leases saw Bismarck follow Michahelles' suggestion that the sultan's successor be informed that Germany saw his signature on the coastal leases as a *sine qua non* for recognition. As soon as the new sultan, Khalifa, contacted Bismarck and Germany's (new and short-lived) Kaiser Friedrich III to thank them for Germany's support for his candidacy, Bismarck expressed his conviction that Khalifa would no doubt bring 'pending negotiations...to a conclusion favourable to both countries by acceptation [*sic*] of

---

[15] Barghash to Bismarck, 22 February 1888; Bismarck to Barghash, 23 February 1888, in BA Berlin, R1001/8918, 'Die Korrespondenz des Herrn Reichskanzler mit dem Sultan von Zanzibar', 3–4.

[16] Michahelles to German Foreign Office, 27 March 1888, in BA Berlin R1001/8909, 5.

[17] Paul Reichard, *Deutsch Ostafrika: Das Land und seine Bewohner, seine politische und wirtschaftliche Entwickelung* (Berlin: Springer Verlag, 1892), 115.

[18] On Sultan Barghash's health and European plans for the succession, see German Foreign Office to Bismarck, 4 February 1888; Michahelles to Bismarck, 5 February 1888; Michahelles to Foreign Office, 11 February 1888; Hatzfeldt to Bismarck, 15 February 1888; Malet to Bismarck, 24 February 1888; Malet to Bismarck, 23 March 1888, in BA Berlin R1001/8908, 'Acten betreffend den Sultan von Zanzibar', 21–33, 35, 45, 47–8, 64–6, 85; Michahelles to Bismarck, 11 March 1888, in BA Berlin R1001/8909, 15.

[19] Michahelles to Bismarck, 5 February 1888, in BA Berlin R1001/8908, 35.

treaty proposals'.[20] A few days later Bismarck wrote to Consul General Michahelles in Zanzibar, instructing him that Friedrich III had indeed agreed to withhold formal recognition of the new Sultan of Zanzibar until the latter brought the stalled Coastal Treaty talks to a conclusion that satisfied German interests.[21]

Initially Khalifa stalled for time, at first pleading that he was not privy to his brother's policy deliberations and would need time to come to grips with such important matters of state.[22] Michahelles then volunteered an overview of negotiations up to that moment from Germany's perspective, ending by threatening the new Sultan that 'official recognition by His Majesty the Kaiser and King would be withheld until the proposed treaty had been accepted.' Advisers to the sultan pleaded with the German consul general to give Khalifa another week to acquaint himself with the detail, but Michahelles refused, declaring that he would not be able to take part in the official welcome of the European envoys that the sultan had planned for the next day. Understandably, Khalifa viewed the Germans' intransigence as an ultimatum and threatened to break off relations with them, until British mediation saw Khalifa declare his support 'in principle' for the German agreement, which allowed Michahelles to introduce his German staff to the sultan. This was a relief to both the sultan and the German consul general, who had feared that refusing to attend the ceremony would have 'destroyed the standing of the new ruler in the eyes of the local population'. Thereafter, negotiations continued, although, as Michahelles freely admitted, the sultan was still unclear what was actually being negotiated.[23]

Upon this news reaching Berlin, Bismarck informed the German emperor that their plan to withhold recognition of Khalifa until he had signed the treaty had worked. The way was now clear for Friedrich III to send the new Sultan of Zanzibar a congratulatory message which included the pointed message that 'By concluding the treaty with German society Your Highness gave a proof of true confidence in Germany; this feeling is mutual and under God's protection will be justified by the friendship of both our countries and their sovereigns'.[24] The German Foreign Office's preferred version of the treaty, including the greatly reduced rental income, was duly signed by Sultan Khalifa, on 28 April 1888. The term of the lease agreement was fifty years.

[20] Khalifa to Bismarck, 29 March 1888; Bismarck to Khalifa, 30 March 1888, in BA Berlin R1001/8918, 6–7. Also in BA Berlin R1001/8909, 10–13.

[21] Bismarck to Michahelles, 3 April 1888; Bismarck to Friedrich III, 17 April 1888, in BA Berlin R1001/8909, 'Acten betreffend den Sultan von Zanzibar', 14, 16. The incident suggests that Friedrich III was no less amenable to supporting his chancellor on questions of German colonial interests at the expense of monarchs in the global south than either his father or his son.

[22] Michahelles to Bismarck, 4 April 1888, in BA Berlin R1001/8909, 24–5.

[23] Michahelles to Bismarck, 9 April 1888, in BA Berlin R1001/8909, 31–3.

[24] Bismarck to Friedrich III, 17 April 1888; Friedrich III to Khalifa, 18 April 1888, in BA Berlin R1001/8909, 16–18.

The treaty that the new sultan signed made it clear that the DOAG had the power to make laws, establish courts, and issue its own currency. It also had the power to regulate trade and urban development, control the harbours, and collect port tariffs. The company could also benefit from any proceeds from mining. In exchange, the sultan would receive a percentage amount linked to the company's profits.[25] The arrangement was to be symbolized by the raising of two flags on public buildings: that of the sultan and that of the East Africa Society (not the German state), with the former raised higher than the latter.[26] This visible concession to the authority of the sultan not only was a reminder that the arrangement was a lease and not a purchase but was also designed to assuage the sultan's Arab and African subjects, who had been given no opportunity to contribute to negotiations and who were simply expected to adjust to the sudden changes to the political and economic status quo.[27] Confirming the changes to the sovereign arrangements, the sultan also sent a number of letters to his mainland walis, instructing them to remain in their posts and not to defy the orders of the new German authorities.[28]

The expansive territory granted under the lease arrangement may have suited the Germans in principle. Almost immediately after signing, however, the DOAG began to worry that it had bitten off more than it could chew. Ernst Vohsen, the new head of the DOAG in Zanzibar after Peters' recall to Germany, began to express serious doubts about the company's actual capacity to secure their newly leased territory from a reluctant sultan. For Vohsen, there were lingering questions about the extent of the sultan's actual political authority and capacity to offer meaningful military assistance to the company. More alarming were his concerns about Khalifa's loyalty to the Germans and the unverified reports he had received claiming that the sultan's steamer had been spotted delivering large quantities of arms and ammunition to Lindi.[29]

The stripping away of the power of local leaders was a deliberate part of the new company administration's plans for the region. One official admitted to

[25] 'Küstenvertrag', 183–7. In a complicated formula, the sultan was offered the following remuneration for the lease:

In view of the concessions, powers, and privileges granted to the Society in the foregoing, it assures the Sultan the dividend of twenty shares of the DOAG per 10,000 marks, that is, the payment of the dividend of a capital sum of approximately £10,000. This guaranteed amount shall entitle him to the portion of the net profit attributable to such a share of the Company's assets as is evidenced by the books of the Company after interest of 8 percent has been paid on the paid-in capital of the unit-holders.

[26] Schneppen, *Sansibar und die Deutschen*, 212–13.

[27] Müller, *Deutschland—Zanzibar—Ostafrika*, 275; Reichard, *Deutsch-Ostafrika*, 116. Schmidt argues that the transferral of tariff rights to the Germans would have aroused no protest and that it was the transferral of sovereignty that provoked the uprising. See Schmidt, *Geschichte des Araberaufstandes in Ostafrika*, 22.

[28] Khalifa to the Walis, 3 August 1888, 14 August, in BA Berlin R1001/406, 'Die Thätigkeit der deutsch-ostafrikanischen Gesellschaft', 6,17.

[29] Vohsen to Michahelles, 10 August 1888, in BA Berlin R1001/406, 14.

relishing the proposition of 'seeing the formerly all-powerful walis, who had worked secretly and openly against the undertakings of the German East Africa Company, reduced to becoming its obedient servants'.[30] Vohsen, however, began to worry about how he was to manage his new colonial possessions with only commercial agents, most of whom knew very little about Africa, and a handful of askaris, should local notables mount any serious resistance. He admitted quite openly that, without the sultan's complete support, 'the company itself does not today possess the required dependable military power to guard against distur-bances'. Recognizing the danger, Vohsen and Michahelles requested that naval vessels be sent to the coastline that had been ceded to the Germans.[31] Berlin agreed and the ageing *Olga* and *Carola* were sent, with the more powerful *Möwe* and *Leipzig* waiting offshore.[32]

The Revolt against Company Rule

Word of the treaty and of their transfer to the sovereignty of the Germans did indeed deeply upset the sultan's walis, akidas, and inland majumbe (African vil-lage leaders or 'mayors', as the explorer Paul Reichard characterized them),[33] who not only feared the financial implications for their own positions but also saw the agreement as an expression of Germany's undue influence over the sultan and a breach of the sultan's responsibility towards them. In practical terms, implement-ing the treaty would mean not only the institutionalization of the hegemony of a European trading rival in their territories but also the sudden imposition of a new poll tax, as well as levies on transport, agriculture, and funerals. Most damaging of all to the DOAG's pretensions to rule was the stipulation that Africans had to prove ownership of their own property to a new German land registry or risk having it declared public land and expropriated by the company.[34]

Predictably, uprisings broke out as local notables realized that their carefully calibrated relationships with the central power of Sultan Barghash had unexpect-edly been overturned by Khalifa and the German East Africa Company. From the perspective of both hinterland majumbe and the coastal walis and akidas who suddenly found themselves under German company rule, the Coastal Treaty clearly overstepped the sultan's rights to dispose of their sovereign rights and eco-nomic agency. In their opinion, if the sultan renounced his rule, power could only

---

[30] Schneppen, *Sansibar und die Deutschen*, 213.
[31] Vohsen to Michahelles, 8 August 1888, in BA Berlin R1001/406, 11–12; Müller, *Deutschland—Zanzibar—Ostafrika*, 360–1.
[32] Michahelles to Vohsen, 10 August 1888, in BA Berlin R1001/406, 13; Schneppen, *Sansibar und die Deutschen*, 213–14.
[33] Reichard, *Deutsch Ostafrika*, 180–1.
[34] Müller, *Deutschland—Zanzibar—Ostafrika*, 362–4.

revert to them. Sovereignty, they argued, was not a transferable commodity, and they refused to allow their sovereign rights to be stripped from them without a fight.[35]

Resistance also broke out around the symbolic politics of flag-raising. In Bagamoyo, for example, the wali made no protest against the Germans until he was instructed to remove the flag of the sultan that was flying from his house—in clear contravention of Article 1 of the Coastal Treaty. Vohsen complained to Michahelles, who offered the DOAG the resources of the German navy to force compliance from the wali.[36] A detachment of marines from the *Möwe* not only forcibly removed the flag but also cut down the flagpole from which it had flown. When the *Leipzig* arrived, the wali was then removed from his house, which was handed over to the DOAG.[37] While the company broadcast their firm belief that the sultan had been behind this resistance,[38] Khalifa complained to Berlin that the treaty he had signed demanded continued respect for his flag and that his honour had been injured by the mistreatment of his ensign,[39] which led Bismarck to formally reprimand Michahelles in a letter reminding him that Article 1 of the Coastal Treaty stipulated that the DOAG's authority was 'in the name of and under the flag of the Sultan'.[40] In Bagamoyo itself, the situation deteriorated once the naval vessels left, with the DOAG's agents forced to barricade themselves in their building, as the wali lost control to local rebel leaders Fumbo Mbili and Mavara.[41]

Unrest broke out in Pangani too, where the wali was forced to flee after his protests against the raising of the company flag and the transfer of power were met by threats of violence from marines from both the *Möwe* and the *Carola*.[42] Usefully, the complaints of the anti-German insurgents in Pangani to the German consul general, Michahelles, have survived in a remarkable document describing what Steven Fabian has called 'Zelewski's rampage'.[43] According to the insurgents,

[35] Müller, *Deutschland—Zanzibar—Ostafrika*, 367–9.

[36] Vohsen to Michahelles, 17 August 1888; Michahelles to Vohsen, 18 August 1888, in BA Berlin R1101/406, 'Die Thätitgkeit der deutsch-ostafrikanischen Gesellschaft', 19–21. For the DOAG's policy on flags, see Vohsen to Michahelles, 3 August 1888, in BA Berlin R1101/406, 3–4.

[37] Michahelles to Bismarck, 26 August 1888, in *Verhandlungen des Reichstages*, Aktenstück 41, Nr 3, vol. 108, 1889, 396–7.

[38] Vohlsen to Michahelles, 20 August 1888, in BA Berlin R1101/406, 29–30.

[39] Vohsen to Bezirks-Chef, 31 August 1888, in BA Berlin R1001/406, 180–1.

[40] Bismarck to Michahelles, 6 October 1888, in *Verhandlungen des Reichstages*, Aktenstück 41, Nr 5, vol. 108, 1889, 398; Tanya Bührer, *Die Kaiserliche Schutztruppe für Deutsch-Ostafrika: Koloniale Sicherheitspolitik und transkulturelle Kriegführung 1885 bis 1918* (Munich: Oldenbourg Verlag, 2011), 42–3. Confusingly, Schneppen erroneously argues that the treaty made no reference to the Sultan's flag. See Schneppen, *Sansibar und die Deutschen*, 219.

[41] Reichard, *Deutsch Ostafrika*, 130–1.

[42] Michahelles to Vohsen, 15 August 1888; Zelewski to Vohsen, 20 August 1888, in BA Berlin R1001/406, 23, 31–2; Michahelles to Bismarck, 25 August 1888, in *Verhandlungen des Reichstages*, Aktenstück 41, Nr 2, vol. 108, 1889, 395–6.

[43] Steven Fabian, 'Locating the Local in the Coastal Rebellion of 1888–1890', *Journal of Eastern African Studies* 7, no. 3 (2013), 438.

not only did the Germans insist on the raising of the company flag and the lowering of the sultan's flag, but German soldiers, led by Emil von Zelewski, forced their way into the mosque at Pangani during prayer time to look for the wali, burnt down the local fort, and released all of the prisoners inside it. Zelewski further threatened the populace that anyone not submitting to the rule of the Germans would be taken prisoner and sent to Europe. The following day, the Germans cut down the flagpole, seized the women, and 'did with them what they wanted'. A few days later, the Germans returned and threatened to put the town leadership in shackles and deport them. The Zanzibari forces refused to cooperate in enforcing this measure, claiming that the order was unlawful and that their loyalties lay with the sultan, not the Germans. They were relieved of their duties, and Zelewski insisted that the territory no longer belonged to Sultan Khalifa, but to the Germans, whereupon the inhabitants of Pangani replied that they refused to accept German rule, claiming instead that they were the subjects of the sultan.[44] Zelewski was then taken prisoner by the locals and was only released through the intercession of the commander-in-chief of the sultan's military, Lloyd Mathews.

In the first week of September, two DOAG officials were also imprisoned, and German marines were attacked by armed locals in Tanga.[45] In the same week, Pangani flared up again, with villagers from the hinterland streaming into the town and joining with others to imprison the DOAG officials in their quarters and rip down their flag. When Vohsen took 200 of the sultan's troops to personally intervene, the authority of the DOAG and the sultan was repudiated and Vohsen was fired upon. Once more, only the intervention of Mathews could secure the safe departure of the German DOAG officials from Pangani, which was by now swollen with over 800 rebels.[46] The sultan furnished the DOAG with documents confirming his wish that coastal towns cooperate with the Germans,[47] but when Mathews returned to Pangani with the news, his attempts to intercede on behalf of Sultan Khalifa were blocked by the emerging leader of the uprising, Abushiri bin Salim, who was able to swing the mood of the assembled rebels against Mathews by pointing to his European origins and his Christianity.[48] As Mathews wrote to Vohsen:

---

[44] 'Denkschrift der von den Aufrührern in Pangani nach Zanzibar entsandten Deputation', 14 August 1888, in BA Berlin, R1001/406, 110–12. For Zelewski's refutation of these claims on 16 September 1888, see R1001/406, 112–13.

[45] Michahelles to Bismarck, 18 September 1888, in *Verhandlungen des Reichstages*, Aktenstück 41, Nr 7, vol. 108, 1889, 400–1; Schmidt, *Geschichte des Araberaufstandes in Ostafrika*, 27.

[46] Michahelles to Bismarck, 18 September 1888, 24 September 1888, in *Verhandlungen des Reichstages*, Aktenstück 41, Nr 6, 9 vol. 108, 1889, 398–402; Schmidt, *Geschichte des Araberaufstandes in Ostafrika*, 26, 29; Bührer, *Die Kaiserliche Schutztruppe für Deutsch-Ostafrika*, 44–5. Bührer gives the figure as 8,000 rebels, but without any reason for deviating from Schmidt's figure.

[47] 'Von Kalifa bin Said an alle, die es lesen', 22 September 1888, in BA Berlin R1001/406, 148.

[48] Michahelles to Bismarck, 24 September 1888, in *Verhandlungen des Reichstages*, Aktenstück 41, Nr 9, vol. 108, 1889, 401–2.

Pangani and Tanga are very unsettled and so much so that my life was in danger and if I had not had any askaris with me should most likely have been shot, as I am a Christian and the people stated that I had become a German spy.[49]

Two German explorers, Dr Meyer and Dr Baumann, who chose this moment to emerge from the African interior, were also severely beaten and imprisoned in Pangani before meeting Abushiri face to face and being released in mid-October. According to the two explorers, Abushiri overtly rejected the authority of Sultan Khalifa and was in firm control of the movement in Pangani, where he was in the process of building his own kingdom as a ruler in his own right, styling himself as a new Tippu Tib, the famous Afro-Arab slaver who had carved out a sizable commercial empire for himself in the interstices of Zanzibari and European territorial claims.[50]

Hostilities continued to build, with German marines freeing DOAG employees from their captivity in Bagamoyo on 23 September at the cost of 100 African casualties.[51] By the end of September 1888, only Dar es Salaam, and (after the battle on 23 September) Bagamoyo were held by the Germans, while elsewhere DOAG agents were forced to retreat. In Kilwa, where the inhabitants declared that they would 'kill all the whites' if the flag of the sultan was not restored to its proper place, an anti-German gun battle broke out in which one of the German employees of the DOAG, Gustav Krieger, and an Arab DOAG employee named Ahmed were shot dead, while a second German, Heinrich Hessel, apparently committed suicide as the African rebels broke into their house.[52] In the battle, twenty African insurgents were also killed. When, at the DOAG's insistence, troops of the sultan attempted to enter Kilwa, they too were driven back, with the rebels in Kilwa insisting that, having sold his authority to the Germans, Khalifa had forfeited any right to rule them.

According to Consul General Michahelles, 'The power of the sultan on the mainland has completely collapsed.' Only a strong and continuous naval presence could keep Dar es Salaam and Bagamoyo under German control.[53] Vohsen agreed, writing to the DOAG board in Berlin that it was impossible for the DOAG to enforce the terms of the treaty with the sultan and that the sultan would be of no assistance to them:

[49] Mathews to Vohsen, 23 September 1888, in BA Berlin R1001/406, 149.
[50] Michahelles to Bismarck, 22 October 1888, in *Verhandlungen des Reichstages*, Aktenstück 41, Nr 18, vol. 108, 1889, 406; BA Berlin, R1001/693, *Politische Zustände in Deutsch-Ostafrika*, 18–21; Michelle Decker, 'The "Autobiography" of Tippu Tip: Geography, Genre and the African Indian Ocean', *Interventions*, 17, no.5 (2015), 744–58.
[51] Michahelles to Bismarck, 24 September 1888, in *Verhandlungen des Reichstages*, Aktenstück 41, Nr 10, vol. 108, 1889, 402; Reichard, *Deutsch-Ostafrika*, 131.
[52] 'Aussage Abdallah bin Masa', 'Aussage Fundi Fuma', in BA Berlin R1001/406, 170–1; Vohsen to DOAG Berlin, 2 October 1888, in BA Berlin R1001/406, 157–8. For reports of Hessel's earlier brutality towards Africans, see Bamberger in *Verhandlungen des Reichstages* 26 January 1889, 610–11.
[53] Michahelles to German Foreign Office, 29 September 1888, in BA Berlin, R1001/8909, 37.

The assistance of the sultan is imaginary, and his impotence is evident in all of his dealings in the Pangani affair and in the forced retreat or, better said, the flight of General Mathews. The sultan will nevermore be in a position to assist the company with his forces or his authority in the assertion of the rights granted to it by the treaty against the will of the coastal population. That has already been demonstrated, and the sultan has declared himself incapable of meeting the responsibilities laid out for him in the treaty. The Reich must therefore intervene with assistance—and long-term assistance—if the venture is to be saved.[54]

In accordance with this vision of the German Empire as the military guarantor of the DOAG, Vohsen demanded that the commander of the German cruiser squadron Karl August Deinhard bombard and then reconquer the coastal towns. Deinhard refused, insisting that it was not the navy's job to guarantee the economic success of a German business. The ships, he argued in accordance with orders agreed to by both Bismarck and the German emperor, were there only to protect German lives.[55]

Deinhard also strongly criticized the behaviour of the DOAG in his report to Berlin, arguing that 'the East Africa Company does nothing to help itself.'[56] Michahelles, however, remained stubbornly blind to the role that the German company had played in creating its own problems and insisted instead that the fault lay with the new sultan. In his eyes, the 'uproar on the mainland, as well as the strong animosity towards the Germans' was a symptom of dissatisfaction with Khalifa, not with the imposition of German company rule.[57] Vohsen, who had long imagined that the sultan had not only encouraged but armed the anti-German forces, had long wanted to hold the sultan personally responsible for the loss of European lives and property.[58] Although he admitted that the sultan had simply not understood what he was agreeing to when he had signed the treaty with the company, by October Vohsen was complaining to the DOAG in Berlin that, instead of trying to calm the situation, the emissaries of Sultan Khalifa were further inflaming the anti-German mood. In addition, he argued, the sultan was taking advice from a coterie of advisers who were deeply hostile to the DOAG.[59] The sultan's support for German rule, he claimed, was 'equivocal', and his troops were 'completely untrustworthy'.[60] The station commander Albrecht von Bülow

[54] Vohsen to DOAG Berlin, 25 September 1888, in BA Berlin R1001/406, 150-1.
[55] Bührer, Die Kaiserliche Schutztruppe für Deutsch-Ostafrika, 43-5.
[56] Karl Deinhard, 3 November 1888, in BA Berlin, R1001/693, Politische Zustände in Deutsch-Ostafrika, 83.
[57] Michahelles to Bismarck, 3 October 1888, in BA Berlin R1001/8909, 38.
[58] Vohsen to DOAG Berlin, 25 August 1888; Vohsen to Bismarck, 11 September 1888, in BA Berlin R1001/406, 60, 105.
[59] Vohsen to DOAG Berlin, 21 October 1888, in BA Berlin R1001/406, 232-9; Vohsen to DOAG, 2 October 1888, in BA Berlin R1001/406, 157-8.
[60] Vohsen to DOAG, 2 October 1888, in BA Berlin R1001/406, 157-8.

too reported that the sultan's soldiers were reluctant to attack the rebels, given that they were flying the sultan's flag.[61] At best, the monarch had, Vohsen argued, 'lost all power'.[62]

Sovereignty, the Sultan, and his Walis

Having been relatively quiet, Mikindani and Lindi also broke out into rebellion in late September, with the German agents there withdrawn back to Zanzibar as thousands of African warriors streamed into the towns.[63] Indian traders reported that 4,000 Africans held Lindi and Kilwa and were not permitting any Europeans to land. Although the trade of some commodities was still being permitted, grain exports were halted by the Africans, who were using it for their own purposes during the conflict.[64] All thoughts of administering the coastal territories vanished as the Germans sought simply to maintain a foothold on the coast. Planning began to turn to how the rebellion might be ended militarily. Antedating Lothar von Trotha's 1904 approach to warfare in German South West Africa by sixteen years, in October 1888 Michahelles pondered the idea of waging a war of starvation, arguing that 'hunger was proving an increasingly effective means of pacification.'[65] His primary desire, however, was for a military force that would enter East Africa from Dar es Salaam before pushing the rebels out of the other coastal towns. This, he argued could be led by the explorer Hermann von Wissmann.[66] Politically, Michahelles was in favour of deposing the Sultan of Zanzibar, despite personally liking the man. In his opinion Sultan Khalifa had little influence over events, but was instead a 'plaything of his environment'.[67]

Rebellions such as this one were not without precedent, and the nominal leader of the anti-DOAG rebellion, Abushiri bin Salim, had also rebelled against Sultan Barghash when he had ascended to the throne.[68] That he would do so again when Khalifa became sultan was not entirely unexpected. For Abushiri and the walis of the East African coast, the German lease and the manner of its implementation had offered an opportunity for them to gain independence from all central

[61] Bülow to DOAG, 1 October 1888, in BA Berlin, R1001/406, 162–3.

[62] Vohsen, 27 September 1888, in BA Berlin R1001/406, 161.

[63] Michahelles to Bismarck, 3 October 1888, in *Verhandlungen des Reichstages*, Aktenstück 41, Nr 13, vol. 108, 1889, 403–4.

[64] Michahelles to Bismarck, 21 October 1888, in *Verhandlungen des Reichstages*, Aktenstück 41, Nr 15, vol. 108, 1889, 405.

[65] Michahelles to Bismarck, 22 October 1888, in *Verhandlungen des Reichstages*, Aktenstück 41, Nr 16, vol. 108, 1889, 405.

[66] Michahelles to Bismarck, 4 October 1888, in *Verhandlungen des Reichstages*, Aktenstück 41, Nr 14, vol. 108, 1889, 404–5.

[67] Michahelles to Krauel, 22 October 1888, in BA Berlin R1001/8909, 42.

[68] Reichard, *Deutsch-Ostafrika*, 122.

control, particularly given that the German administration meant the loss of the few privileges their nominal subordination to the sultan had offered.[69]

These walis, however, were also in danger of being pushed aside by events, with German reports claiming that, while Arab traders might have roused the rebellion in both Kilwa and Pangani, they had long since lost control. It was now the Africans of the hinterland who appeared to have seized control of the rebellion, returning to try and reclaim their old coastal towns from all those they considered to be external powers, including the Germans, the sultan, and the Arab walis.[70] What had seemed to the German company to be a straightforward transferral of territory and sovereign powers from the sultan had escalated into a multidirectional struggle between the company, the German navy, the troops of the Zanzibar-based regime of the sultan, Arab coastal elites, and African people of the hinterland.[71]

From the perspective of the German explorer of East Africa, Paul Reichard, the problem was twofold. On the one hand, it appeared that 'the entire population of German East Africa was from the very outset hostile to the company and the conditions of the treaty.'[72] On the other, he argued in Orientalist terms, the Germans had from the very beginning 'committed the fatal mistake of treating with the late Sultan, Seyid Barghash, as if he had been a monarch endowed with all the virtues of a European sovereign, instead of a victim to the moral and intellectual vices of the cunning and insincere East.' The German government, in his estimation, should have simply annexed the sultan's territory without reference to the interests of Zanzibar or its ruler.[73]

For his part, Michahelles also believed that there were some coastal elites who would never have submitted to the reign of Sultan Khalifa after the death of his brother Barghash. He was optimistic, however, that they might be won over for the Germans if it was made clear to them that Germany was there to stay and that they would never have to face the 'revenge of the sultan'.[74] Such unfounded optimism is difficult to square, however, with the breadth and scale of the coastal uprising and the sheer number of considerations motivating the various actors, primary among them being that, as much as local notables had chafed under the reign of Sultan Barghash, his rule had been far more respectful of their

---

[69] Bismarck, 26 November 1888, in BA Berlin, R1001/693, *Politische Zustände in Deutsch-Ostafrika*, 77–8.

[70] Michahelles to Bismarck, 25 September, 3 October 1888, in *Verhandlungen des Reichstages*, Aktenstück 41, Nr 12 & 13, vol. 108, 1889, 403–4.

[71] Michahelles to Bismarck, 4 October 1888, in *Verhandlungen des Reichstages*, Aktenstück 41, Nr 14, vol. 108, 1889, 404–5.

[72] Reichard, *Deutsch-Ostafrika*, 117.

[73] As quoted in C. D. Collet, 'The East African Negotiations, an Anglo-German Conspiracy against the Sultan of Zanzibar', *Diplomatic Fly-Sheets* 5 (1887–1888), 377.

[74] Michahelles to Bismarck, 3 November 1888, in BA Berlin, R1001/693, *Politische Zustände in Deutsch-Ostafrika*, 69–71.

authority and interests than the German company had proved itself to be in a few short months.

The role and position of the sultan in the uprising was also viewed by Michahelles with continued suspicion. On the one hand, he had heard that the Swahili-speaking notables 'did not want to know about the sultan, since he had handed over the country without a fight'.[75] On the other, rumours were also circulating that the sultan was covertly offering aid and weapons to the rebels. One report argued that some of the sultan's troops who had been sent to fight Abushiri had simply defected to the insurgent camp.[76] Several reports also claimed that weapons and gunpowder had been delivered to the rebels from the sultan via his slave Ismael. Even Deinhard, the commander of the German cruiser squadron in East Africa and a critic of the DOAG, was of the opinion that it was 'increasingly improbable' that the sultan was not offering covert assistance to the rebels.[77] The German envoy admitted that there was no way to know whether 'the name of the sultan was being misused' by those fighting the Germans, or whether the rumours of his assistance to the rebels were true. Nonetheless, he informed the chancellor that he was suspicious enough to order a search for evidence that would implicate the sultan in the uprising.[78] The investigation into the sultan would prove inconclusive. However, the German envoy warned that there were 'increasing signs of a secretly hostile course of action by His Majesty against the East Africa Company'.[79]

On the whole, Michahelles was deeply pessimistic about the long-term utility of 'this Oriental despot' for German interests. In October 1888 he mounted the argument that 'the authority of the sultan has collapsed to the point that he is of no use to us. His rule will not last much longer.'[80] By November, this view had hardened considerably. The sultan, he argued, would be of little help in establishing German control over the East African coast:

> If the sultan was now to be restored through the joint efforts of Germany and England, we would have to reckon with the conjecture that he is now too weak to restore his rule himself...I believe we can rule out any honest cooperation from him in our colonial endeavours...He hates the company much too intensely to suddenly want the best for it, even if it is in his own interests.[81]

---

[75] Michahelles to Bismarck, 22 October 1888, in BA Berlin, R1001/693, 13–17.

[76] Franz Stuhlmann, 'Berichte über die augenblicklichen politischen Verhältnisse an der Ost-Afrikanische Küste', in BA Berlin, R1001/693, 46.

[77] Karl Deinhard, 3 November 1888, in BA Berlin, R1001/693, 85–6. See also BA Berlin R1001/8909, 53.

[78] Michahelles to Bismarck, 22 October 1888, in BA Berlin, R1001/693, 13–17, 38; Stuhlmann, 'Berichte über die augenblicklichen politischen Verhältnisse', 50. See Michahelles to Bismarck, 3 December 1888, in BA Berlin, R1001/693, 65.

[79] Michahelles to Bismarck, 3 December 1888, in BA Berlin, R1001/693, 65–6.

[80] 'Auszuge aus einem Privatbriefe des Generalkonsuls Michahelles in Zanzibar vom 22 Oktober d. J.', in BA Berlin, R1001/693, 22–4.

[81] 'Abschrift eines Privatbriefes des G Konsuls Michahelles in Zanzibar an den Geheimen Legationsrath Herrn Krauel', 3 November 1888, in BA Berlin, R1001/693, 75–6. Reproduced in BA Berlin R1001/8909, 42, 46–7.

The German Foreign Office demurred, however, remaining convinced that it was in Germany's interests to 'use the remaining authority of the sultan to pacify the native population, assuming that the sultan possesses the will to offer his support'.[82] A report to the trading house O'Swald and Co. in Hamburg (which had long-standing historic ties with Zanzibar) was even more emphatic in its recommendation that the sultan be handed responsibility for restoring order on the East African coast and that the catastrophic efforts of the DOAG not be supported by the German navy.[83] For their part, the British informed the Germans that they were 'not inclined to believe the suspicions raised against the Sultan of Zanzibar, but rather held the strong opinion that the sultan had sent neither weapons nor gunpowder to the insurgent natives and that his name was being misused by the insurgents instead'.[84] The Germans responded by sending the British their evidence in an attempt to undermine their support for the sultan,[85] but ultimately baulked when the British suggested that they discuss possible successors and proposed using a recent round of executions undertaken by the sultan as grounds to remove Khalifa on the grounds of mental instability.[86] Even Michahelles was edging towards supporting the devil he knew rather than leaping towards an unknown entity that might take his place. By January of 1889, he was convinced that there were no easy options, despite the increasing disorder, because 'there is not a single person with the sultan who possesses any real understanding of political affairs'.[87] Although by March 1889 the British and the Germans were both in agreement that Sultan Khalifa had not proved to be a reliable regional client, there was no agreed-upon path forward. Although the British periodically questioned whether or not Khalifa might be declared psychologically unfit to rule and replaced, Michahelles was now firmly of the opinion that 'the fall of the current sultan ... is not in our interests'.[88]

The Reichstag Debates on the East African Revolts

Despite the clear evidence that the rebellion was largely a product of the shift in regional power caused first by the death of Sultan Barghash and thereafter by the

---

[82] Letter to Michahelles, 29 November 1888, in BA Berlin, R1001/693, 100.

[83] 'Bericht über die Unruhen an der Küste', 22 October 1888, in BA Berlin R1001/693, 107–17.

[84] Hatzfeldt to Bismarck, 28 November 1888, in BA Berlin, R1001/693, 121–2. See also BA Berlin R1001/8909, 54.

[85] Bismarck to Hatzfeldt, 1 December 1888, in BA Berlin R1001/8909, 56.

[86] Hatzfeldt to Bismarck, 21 December 1888; Michahelles to German Foreign Office, 24 December 1888, in BA Berlin R1001/8909, 78.

[87] Michahelles to Bismarck, 13 January 1889, in BA Berlin R1001/8909, 126–8.

[88] Hatzfeldt to Bismarck, 6 March 1889; Michahelles to Bismarck, 11 February 1889; Hatzfeldt to Bismarck, 22 March 1889, in BA Berlin R1001/8910 'Acten betreffend den Sultan von Zanzibar', 4, 6–7, 9.

signing over of coastal sovereignty to the unprepared and overbearing Germans by Khalifa, combating the 'Arab Uprising' was presented to the Reichstag as an important part of Germany's anti-slavery responsibilities under the Berlin-Africa treaty. Weaving together the uprisings and the history of anti-slavery, in October 1888 Bismarck sent a letter to Ambassador Hatzfeldt in London asking him to convey to the British government the argument of the German government that only a naval blockade of the East African coast could halt the import of weapons to the rebels and hinder the slave trade. The British agreed, as did the Portuguese and Italians.[89]

Although there was some discussion in the initial Reichstag debate about the unfolding situation, surprisingly little was said about the potential for military action to improve the parlous condition of the East Africa Company's coastal holdings. The deputies avoided having a discussion of the complicated dynamics between the sultan, the German company, the Arab walis, and the African majumbe of the hinterland that the briefing provided to them by Bismarck on 6 December 1888 clearly invited. Instead, the Reichstag concerned itself in its first debate with an East African simulacrum, in which German naval action was not being used to assert the position of the DOAG against uprisings by coastal elites, but rather was combating Arab slavers intent on protecting an unwholesome trade.[90] The pretext was a flimsy one. As the British colonial bishop, Charles Smythies, wrote in a letter to the *Times* in late November 1888, however, '*Everyone here knows the slave-trade has nothing to do with it*.'[91]

Ignoring the openly imperialist suggestion made by Michahelles that German military power might best be used directly to help the DOAG control East Africa's coastal trade, the earnest Reichstag discussion focused on the humanitarian justification for a naval blockade of the East African coast. In what one contemporary called an 'extraordinarily shrewd political measure' that saw the Catholic Centre Party's Ludwig von Windthorst given custody of the motion, the naval blockade which had been negotiated with Britain in November 1888 was represented by the government as a purely anti-slavery measure that would 'win Africa for Christian civilization'.[92] In introducing his motion, Windthorst sidestepped the clearly pertinent issue of the DOAG's lease of the Zanzibar coast altogether, warning the Reichstag not to become sidetracked discussing the precarious position of the company and instead focus on what he identified as the real issue, namely

[89] Holstein to Leyden, 5 October 1888; Bismarck to Hatzfeldt, 21 October 1888, 22 October 1888; Hatzfeldt to Salisbury, 3 November 1888; Salisbury to Hatzfeldt, 5 November 1888, in *Verhandlungen des Reichstages*, Aktenstück 41, Nr 26, 27, 28, 33, 34, vol. 108, 1889, 410–13.
[90] For a detailed discussion of the campaign, see Bührer, *Die Kaiserliche Schutztruppe für Deutsch-Ostafrika*, 35–79.
[91] Charles Smythies, 'The Position in East Africa', *The Times*, 27 November 1888, in BA Berlin, R1001/693, 87. Emphasis in original.
[92] Aktenstück Nr 27, 27 November 1888, in *Verhandlungen des Reichstages*, 182; Schmidt, *Geschichte des Araberaufstandes in Ostafrika*, 37.

Arab slavery.[93] The National Liberal Adolph Woermann, who alongside being a politician was also the director of one of Germany's largest trading and shipping companies with important interests in Africa, also emphasized the dire economic effects of the slave trade, again without alluding to the DOAG. The Hamburg merchant argued in the Reichstag that he saw German colonialism as a cultural mission that would develop Africa economically along European lines. Combating slavery, he opined, was part of this work, and Germany should not only combat it with its navy but should also take the struggle onto the mainland of Africa.[94]

Only the Conservative Otto von Helldorf directly discussed Windthorst's proposal with overt reference to an ostensible need for the Reichstag to assist with the 'successful protection of German interests' and the 'protection of the honour of the German flag' in East Africa. It was simply unavoidable, he argued, that the Reichstag discuss the plight of the DOAG and of German commerce in the region, which required military assistance from Germany:

> We cannot avoid this, because it is directly connected to the entire question. And I say quite openly, the question of the German East Africa Company that has so preoccupied the press cannot remain unmentioned here. For the existence and operation of this company offer the possibility of a successful intervention by us. The empire has a protectorate in this region, a large and powerful territory; it is, as far as I know, larger than Germany and offers the hope of future development. It is inaccessible, however, because of a lack of control over the coast. This company was successful in gaining rule over the coastline through a treaty with the Sultan of Zanzibar, and the necessary way forward is in the end by protecting the rights that this company has acquired from the sultan, which gives us the chance to suppress the slave trade there on sea and on land... via the occupation of the slavers' lair in this country.

Drawing parallels with what he characterized as the Reichstag's mistake in not supporting German interests in Samoa from the very beginning, Helldorf insisted that the issue of the East Africa Company was not merely a question of the interests of a private company, but of furthering the interests of the German Empire and of 'civilization'.[95] Following this, the secretary of the German Foreign Office, Herbert von Bismarck-Schönhausen, attempted to push the debate away from the suggestion that the German government should militarily protect the private sector imperialism of the DOAG. Instead, he returned to the less divisive question of combating slavery, putting forward the disingenuous argument that the uprisings

---

[93] Windthorst, 14 December 1888, in *Verhandlungen des Reichstages*, 303–5.
[94] Woermann, 14 December 1888, in *Verhandlungen des Reichstages*, 305–8.
[95] Helldorf, 14 December 1888, in *Verhandlungen des Reichstages*, 308–10.

in East Africa were in fact a 'reaction' by slave-trading Arab chiefs who wished to protect their trade against the 'cultural mission' of the DOAG.[96]

Refusing to accept this argument, Ludwig Bamberger accused those in favour of the notion of an 'anti-slavery' blockade of East Africa of trying to hide the fact that the Reichstag was actually voting on militarily and financially protecting a colony owned by a German company, something that his left-liberal Independent Party could not support.[97] Wilhelm von Kardorff of the German Imperial Party objected to Bamberger's line of argument, once again seeking to connect assistance to the German company with both Germany's colonial mission and the broader international struggle against slavery.[98] The left-liberal interpretation was supported by the Social Democrat Paul Singer, who professed that the Social Democrats were fervently anti-slavery, but saw in Windthorst's bill only political cover for Germany's 'policy of colonial adventures', which they were against on principle.[99]

Conditions continued to deteriorate for the Germans in late December 1888 and January 1889, with Dar es Salaam attacked by rebels on 31 December 1888 and again on 25 January 1889. The town was evacuated by the DOAG, with the loss of some German marines.[100] In Pugu, just south of Dar es Salaam, one rebel leader, Soliman bin Sef, slipped through the naval blockade and attacked a Catholic German mission on 13 January 1889 with around 150 rebels. Three missionaries were killed in the attack, with others held for ransom. The rebellion also intensified in the south.[101]

As it became evident that 'the total defeat of the uprising was too difficult for the navy alone',[102] a further debate in the Reichstag considered whether the naval blockade should be complemented by a punitive expedition force of around 1,000 African mercenaries led by Wissmann that would venture inland to capture Abushiri, who was viewed as the leader of the uprisings.[103] Unlike Windthorst's earlier motion, which was narrowly presented as an anti-slavery measure, the new bill overtly sought to fund 'measures for the suppression of slavery and the protection of German interests in East Africa'. It presented the DOAG as fulfilling Germany's commitment to combat 'elements implacably opposed to Christendom and European civilization in agreement with the other Christian powers'. According to the bill's explanatory prologue, the company was entitled by dint of

---

[96] Bismarck, 14 December 1888, in *Verhandlungen des Reichstages*, 310–11.
[97] Bamberger, 14 December 1888, in *Verhandlungen des Reichstages*, 312–16.
[98] Kardorff, 14 December 1888, in *Verhandlungen des Reichstages*, 316–19.
[99] Singer, 14 December 1888, in *Verhandlungen des Reichstages*, 319.
[100] Reichard, *Deutsch Ostafrika*, 144–8.
[101] Reichard, *Deutsch Ostafrika*, 145–7; Schmidt, *Geschichte des Araberaufstandes in Ostafrika*, 33–4.
[102] Dick, *Das Kreuzergeschwader*, 6.
[103] Gabriel A. Akinola, 'The East African Coastal Rising, 1888–1890', *Journal of the Historical Society of Nigeria* 7, no. 4 (1975), 609–30; Schneppen, *Sansibar und die Deutschen*, 211–316; Fabian, 'Locating the Local in the Coastal Rebellion of 1888–1890', 432–49.

its fifty-year lease with the Sultan of Zanzibar to rule in the sultan's name. That the DOAG had been unable to do so, it continued, was because the Sultan's power had been shown to be unable to provide the necessary security conditions for the DOAG to rule. Accordingly, the company now required German state assistance. Without it, Germany could no longer continue 'to take part in the cultural work of civilizing Africa'. To this end, it was claimed, the creation of an African-staffed police force to maintain peace was also required.[104]

The bill was recommended to the Reichstag by Foreign Secretary Bismarck-Schönhausen, who reported that since the last vote some six weeks earlier, conditions had only worsened with the lack of any effective countermeasures against the 'Arab slave traders'. Christian missionaries had been killed, he continued, while Germany's marines were at the point of exhaustion, overworked and operating in extremely difficult conditions. Accordingly, the foreign secretary continued, an indigenous police force under the direction of Wissmann, whom he now introduced to speak, was also required.[105]

Wissmann too sought to maintain the fiction that the Reichstag was voting on the question of how best to combat the slave trade:

> The East African coast from Witu in the north to Rowuma in the south is the most important part of the whole continent for combating the slave trade...It is for this purpose that the coastal points that belonged to German firms, or rather were occupied by them and were taken by the rebels in the recent uprisings, must be won back. The Sultan of Zanzibar, who was contractually obliged to maintain the peace in these places for the [German East African] Society, is not in a position to do so and the movement has grown out of control.[106]

While the ostensible goal of combating slavery was applauded by most in the Reichstag, critics of the action remained sceptical of the capacity of the German navy to carry out the task set for it. Bamberger, for example, argued that the crudely exploitative nature of German colonialism in East Africa made it impossible to support. Better to admit its utter failure, now that the East Africa Company's only success in the region was 'that a coastline where peaceful trade had been conducted has now been bombed and reduced to ashes, becoming a scene of death and destruction'. Behind the talk of high-minded idealism regarding the fight against slavery, Bamberger insisted, was the real aim of supporting an unsuccessful German company. Just as the naval blockade had proved

---

[104] 'Entwurf eines Gesetzes, betreffend Bekämpfung des Sklavenhandels und Schutz der deutschen Interessen in Ostafrika', in *Verhandlungen des Reichstages*, Aktenstück 71, 1889, 491–3.

[105] Bismarck-Schönhausen, 26 January 1889, in *Verhandlungen des Reichstages*, 603–4.

[106] Wissmann, 26 January 1889, in *Verhandlungen des Reichstages*, 604, 623.

ineffective, so too the highly dangerous guerrilla war to be led by Wissmann would also not improve Germany's position.[107]

After Bamberger's blast at the folly of German *Kolonialpolitik*, the Centre Party's Windthorst sought to steer the debate away from a discussion of the effects of colonialism on East Africa, declaring that if he thought the debate was simply about furthering German colonialism, he would vote against it. Instead, however, he presented the bill as a necessary addendum to that which he had brought to the Reichstag a few weeks earlier. Securing the East African coastline from slavers now meant securing it for German interests. Windthorst maintained, however, that when the bill spoke of protecting these interests, this meant not only the interests of the DOAG but also Germany's interests in civilizing Africa. For Windthorst, that meant ensuring that the power and prestige of Germany was sufficiently respected by African chiefs so as to enable the suppression of slavery in their lands.[108]

For his part, Chancellor Bismarck freely conceded the ineffectiveness of the naval blockade so far in stopping slavery but sought to make a virtue of it none-theless, by arguing that it was not the effectiveness of the blockade (or lack thereof) that mattered, but rather that Germany had undertaken it with Britain, demonstrating their unity of purpose in Africa to local leaders. The coastline of Africa, he maintained could not simply be abandoned to the rebels, because it was from the coast towards the inland that the process of civilizing Africa would take place. The benefits might take twenty or thirty years to realize, but, even so, Germany should not retreat from its East African lease.[109]

The long-term leader of German colonial politics and the leader of the National Liberal Party, Rudolf von Bennigsen, made it clear that his party would support the DOAG and German colonialism in East Africa against naysayers like Bamberger. Even if mistakes had been made, such as the removal of the sultan's flag and its replacement with the company's, the colonial enterprise in East Africa was, he argued, simply too important to allow it to fail:

> Gentlemen, that we have a duty to keep those regions of Africa that are in our possession, irrespective of the endeavours against slavers and slave traders, appears to me, given the facts of the matter…indubitable. I shall not examine closely whose flag is raised over the land, but Germany is certainly engaged and so too German honour as well in the battles of our marines with rebellious blacks led by Arabs on the coastal strip.[110]

---

[107] Bamberger, 26 January 1889, in *Verhandlungen des Reichstages*, 606–14.
[108] Windthorst, 26 January 1889, in *Verhandlungen des Reichstages*, 614–17.
[109] Bismarck, 26 January 1889, in *Verhandlungen des Reichstages*, 619.
[110] Bennigsen, 26 January 1889, in *Verhandlungen des Reichstages*, 627.

The Social Democrats' leader, August Bebel, was less impressed by the idea of Germany undertaking a historic civilizing mission in Africa, rejecting the idea that the German population was the least bit interested in paying millions of marks for 'such colonial adventures'. The revolts against the Germans in East Africa were a result of German mistreatment and reflected, he argued, the broader experience of colonialism which demonstrated that all the powers could only keep their colonial subjects under control through violent means. Bebel further doubted that a commercially oriented entity such as the DOAG would take very seriously its new-found moral duty to act to suppress the slave trade.[111]

Ignatius Simonis from the Alsace-Lorraine Protest Party, on the other hand, overlooked the experience of foreign rule in his own territory to laud the bringing of Christianity and civilization to Africa and to praise the government's desire to combat slavery in German East Africa. Simonis reminded the Reichstag that Alsatian missionaries, including Jesuits, had already been working in East Africa for more than forty-five years. His primary concern was that these 'civilization-bringing' Jesuit missionaries not be expelled from German East Africa as they had been from Germany.[112]

The second Reichstag debate had in some ways been a more honest debate and saw an acknowledgement that the call to fight slavery in East Africa offered respectable political cover for the construction of a military force that could defend the commercial interests of the East Africa Company from African rebels seeking to dislodge both the Europeans and the weakened sultan from the east coast of Africa. Critically, the admission that Germany's ostensible civilizing mission was predicated on militarily subduing colonized territory on behalf of German commercial interests in no way lessened the resolve of a majority of Reichstag deputies to support the bill. The bill passed, and subsequently Wissmann was given his military command.

Wissmann arrived in Zanzibar on 31 March 1889, where he was greeted by Sultan Khalifa. He took command of his army, which consisted mainly of several hundred African askaris. An uneasy ceasefire had been negotiated prior to his arrival, but when Abushiri raided the small coastal village of Kaule and hacked off the hands of an African who had worked for the Germans, as a 'greeting' to the new German commander, Wissmann declared the ceasefire broken and, matching atrocity for atrocity, hanged two Africans accused of spying for the rebels. He then commenced military operations against Abushiri, and a bloody guerrilla campaign ensued.[113]

---

[111] Bebel, 26 January 1889, in *Verhandlungen des Reichstages*, 627–31.
[112] Simonis, 26 January 1889, in *Verhandlungen des Reichstages*, 632–6.
[113] For a German eyewitness account of preparations and of the campaign, see Schmidt, *Geschichte des Araberaufstandes in Ostafrika*. For the precise composition of the German military contingent, see 53–5.

By May 1889, the sultan was resigned to the German presence, and asked
Bismarck whether he might send a personal envoy, Mohammed ben Seliman al
Mandri, to Germany to deliver a personal letter of friendship to Kaiser Wilhelm
II. Bismarck duly arranged for Seliman to meet the emperor at the New Palace in
Potsdam, at 12.30 p.m. on 30 September 1889, to deliver Sultan Khalifa's letter
expressing his hopes for enduring friendship between the two lands (see
Figure 7.1).[114] Privately, Wilhelm II shrugged off the African sultan's entreaty
with the remark that any improvement in Germany's relationship with the sultan
'was up to him'.[115] Officially, however, Wilhelm II offered Khalifa his own message, hoping that 'the good relationship that exists between us will become
increasingly warm'.[116] In addition, the sultan presented Germany with the gift of
sixteen Arabic books on Ibadi Islam, which were eventually given to the Oriental
Seminar in Berlin.[117] In return, Germany sent the Khalifa a silver tankard
inscribed with his name, coat of arms, and an Arabic dedication, to be presented
directly to him by Michahelles.[118]

The attempt to revitalize the relationship between the Sultanate of Zanzibar
and the German Empire, however, came to nothing. Sultan Khalifa died suddenly
in February 1890, having ruled for not quite two years. Alarmed by the prospect
that Germany might seize permanent control of Zanzibar in the wake of its military campaign, the British moved to sign the Heligoland-Zanzibar treaty with the
new German chancellor, Leo von Caprivi, in July 1890.[119] With this the scope for
an independent role for the new Zanzibari sultan evaporated as the sultanate
became a British protectorate. Zanzibar continued to have sultans, but their sovereign power was severely curtailed.

The signing of the Coastal Treaty between Sultan Khalifa and the German East
Africa Company was supposed to inaugurate a new era of German economic
hegemony and political rule on the East African coastline. What the Germans
failed to take into account, however, was that—even without the European
powers—sovereignty in the region was contested between local notables, both
Arab and African, and the sultan. Just as Sultan Barghash had only been able to
win support for his claim to the throne from coastal walis through both military
action and financial inducements, so too Sultan Khalifa had yet to find the

---

[114] PAAA R250857, 'Die außerordentliche Gesandtschaft des Sultans von Zanzibar', 6, 118–20;
R250858, 'Die außerordentliche Gesandtschaft des Sultans von Zanzibar', 11, 21–3; R131415, unnumbered (26 December 1899).
[115] Reuss to Bismarck, 14 October 1889, in PAAA R250859, 'Die außerordentliche Gesandtschaft
des Sultans von Zanzibar', 31.
[116] PAAA R250858, 23.   [117] Brauner to Beechem, 4 November 1889, in PAAA R250859, 90.
[118] Bismarck-Schönhausen to Brauer, 7 October 1889; Moritz to Bismarck-Schönhausen, in PAAA
R250859, 9, 100–2.
[119] D. R. Gillard, 'Salisbury's African Policy and the Heligoland Offer of 1890', English Historical
Review, 75, no. 297, (1960), 631–53; G. N. Sanderson, 'The Anglo-German Agreement of 1890 and the
Upper Nile', English Historical Review, 78, no. 306 (1963), 49–72.

Figure 7.1 Personal letter from the Sultan of Zanzibar to Kaiser Wilhelm II
Source: Photo courtesy of the Politisches Archiv des Auswärtigen Amts.

terms upon which his rule would have been accepted by his ostensible mainland subjects.

Khalifa's involuntary decision to hand over the mainland coastal territories to the Germans exacerbated this already complex situation. With the legitimacy of the new sultan open to question, his right to dispose of his sovereignty over the territory and suddenly renounce his rule in favour of the Germans drew predictable criticism. This crisis of legitimacy was compounded by the clumsy and brutal manner in which the DOAG tried to assert its rule over the East African coast. Under-resourced and understaffed, they were forced to rely on not only the German navy but also a pro-colonial Reichstag, as well as a sultan whose legitimacy was rejected by many of his regional notables and whose commitment to his lease agreement with the Germans was the subject of extreme doubts.

8

Swapping a Sultanate for an Island

In late March 1890, Germany's consul general to Zanzibar, Dr Gustav Michahelles, sailed to the East African mainland to visit the small Sultanate of Wituland. In oppressive heat, he left his ship on the coast and made his way a short distance inland from the East African shoreline to the town of Witu, where he met Sultan Fumo Bakari. Although the previous ruler of Wituland, Sultan Ahmed (or Ahmed Simba) had signed agreements with Germany in 1885 in the hope of gaining protection for his small sultanate from its predatory, British-dominated neighbour Zanzibar, the relationship between Wituland and the German Empire had never been formally laid out in a treaty. Now Michahelles came to offer Sultan Fumo Bakari exactly that.[1]

After conferring with his advisers overnight, Sultan Fumo Bakari informed Michahelles in Swahili that he was happy to accept in its entirety the agreement that the consul general had presented to him, and by 10 a.m. on 1 April 1890, a signing ceremony was underway. Once signed, the agreement was sealed with a gift to the sultan from Kaiser Wilhelm II of a hunting rifle and a portrait of the German emperor. Fumo Bakari immediately had the portrait placed above his throne, so that 'both he and his subjects would have daily proof before their eyes that they lived under the powerful protection of the German emperor'. Consul General Michahelles came away greatly impressed with the sultan, who had assured the Germans that he would see it as 'his duty to obey all of the decisions of the German government without delay, even those that required a painful sacrifice from him'. Moved by the apparent depth of his new client king's loyalty, Wilhelm II wrote in the margin of Michahelles's report, 'We cannot let this man fall or be abandoned.'[2]

Less than three months later, however, the Sultan of Wituland had been completely abandoned by the Germans, having been traded to Britain as part of Germany's deal to obtain the small, but strategically important North Sea island of Heligoland.[3] Unbeknownst to Fumo Bakari, by the time his letter thanking the German emperor for his gifts and protection had been sent on 4 July 1890, the Anglo-German agreement transferring his kingdom to British protection had

---

[1] Michahelles to German Foreign Office, 20 April, 1890, in BA Berlin R1001/8870, 'Allgemeine Angelegenheiten des Witulandes', 76–86.
[2] Michahelles to German Foreign Office, 20 April 1890, in BA Berlin R1001/8870, 76–86.
[3] On Witu's place in the broader Heligoland-Zanzibar Agreement, see Jan Rüger, *Heligoland: Britain, Germany and the Struggle for the North Sea* (Oxford: Oxford University Press, 2017), 104–7.

The Kaiser and the Colonies: Monarchy in the Age of Empire. Matthew P. Fitzpatrick, Oxford University Press.
© Matthew P. Fitzpatrick 2022. DOI: 10.1093/oso/9780192897039.003.0009

already been signed.[4] The sultan was now under the protection of the British Empire, which had long disputed the right of Wituland to exist. Six months later, Fumo Bakari was dead.

The Kaiser's Loyal Sultan in East Africa

Wituland was a small East African sultanate with ties to German colonial interests that reached back to the 1860s, when the Prussian adventurer Richard Brenner had investigated the possibility of turning it into a Prussian colony. The idea was cautiously welcomed by Witu's Sultan Ahmed, who sought a strong counterweight to the looming danger of neighbouring Sultanate of Zanzibar. Due to the lack of interest of the Prussian Foreign Ministry, however, these plans came to nothing. Despite the inaction of the state, colonial interest in Wituland and East Africa more generally remained strong, particularly amongst the pro-colonial faction of Germany's left liberals and the left wing of the German National Liberals.[5]

To these pro-colonial Germans, Wituland and its cooperative sultan offered the promise of a gateway to East and Central Africa. From the British perspective, however, Wituland was 'a colony of outlaws', illegally founded and rightfully belonging under the sovereignty of their regional ally, Sultan Barghash of Zanzibar. For Britain's later consul general to Zanzibar, Arthur H. Hardinge, Witu's sultan was little more than a renegade and his capital a 'last refuge' for 'criminals, runaway slaves and outlaws from justice of every description'. Sultan Ahmed, Hardinge argued, was no monarch, but rather a mere 'petty chief'.[6] In an attempt to rid themselves of this nuisance, the British continually encouraged Barghash to militarily incorporate the Sultanate of Wituland into his territories in the mid-1880s.

With Zanzibar threatening the existence of his kingdom and poised to invade, renewed overtures from a German consortium (the Tana Committee) to commence commercial operations in Wituland, bringing with them the protection of the German state, were responded to favourably by the elderly Sultan Ahmed, who by now was struggling with advanced elephantiasis. Once again, Ahmed quickly declared himself to be German-friendly, signing three treaties with the German explorer Clemens Denhardt. Crucially, one of these recognized Denhardt and his brother Gustav as the representatives of Sultan Ahmed in Europe and

---

[4] Michahelles to Caprivi, 4 July 1890, in BA Berlin R1001/8871 'Allgemeine Angelegenheiten des Witulandes', 14.
[5] Müller, *Deutschland—Zanzibar—Ostafrika*, 293–4. For a colonial-era description of Wituland, see Gustav Hörnecke, 'Deutsch Wituland', *Deutsche Kolonialzeitung* 3 (1886), 482–6.
[6] Arthur H. Hardinge, 'Legislative Methods in the Zanzibar and East Africa Protectorates', *Journal of the Society of Comparative Legislation* 1, no. 1 (1899), 2.

Zanzibar, essentially passing the sultanate's foreign policy into private sector German hands. By the end of May 1885, Wituland was (by virtue of its arrangement with the Denhardt brothers rather than any direct dealings with the German state) officially under de facto German protection. Although the new arrangement did not immediately halt Zanzibar's campaign against the small sultanate, once Bismarck formally complained to London about the treatment of a territory now under German protection, Zanzibar's invading army was withdrawn from its frontiers. German commercial interests in Wituland and the sovereign rights of Sultan Ahmed had been temporarily secured against Britain and Zanzibar.[7]

For the Sultan of Witu, the deal with the Denhardt brothers had paid swift dividends, and it was the security they offered in an environment in which Britain and Zanzibar both saw Wituland as an impediment to their interests in East Africa that explains Sultan Ahmed's willingness to attach himself to German protection. According to Rochus Schmidt, who worked extensively with the sultan during his time working for the German Witu Company, Sultan Ahmed expressed his transactional attitude towards his new protector, the German Kaiser, as an arrangement that obliged him to keep Germans inside his territory safe, in return for the German emperor keeping his kingdom safe:

> I am under the protection of the German Kaiser, to whom I am loyal. Your Kaiser will protect me against those who are stronger than I am, but he will also hold me accountable so that nothing happens to you and other Germans still to come to this land.[8]

The sultan's 'sense of responsibility', as Schmidt called it, extended to guaranteeing the safety of Germans travelling to other communities and towns loosely under his control but lying outside the capital Witu. To this end, Ahmed informed neighbouring anti-European Galla territories that Germans travelling in the region were under the sultan's personal protection. As Ahmed explained to Schmidt, 'I am under the protection of your Kaiser, but you are under mine.'[9]

Despite this seemingly mutually beneficial arrangement, German traders were not uniformly welcome to other inhabitants of Wituland, with local religious figures expressing their clear disapproval of the extent of the Germans' influence over Sultan Ahmed.[10] Beyond the sultanate, the existence of Wituland remained an irritation to both the British and the Sultan of Zanzibar. Nonetheless, as long as Germany claimed to have an interest in protecting Wituland, they could do

---

[7] Müller, *Deutschland—Zanzibar—Ostafrika*, 296–300; Marguerite Ylvisaker, 'The Origins and Development of the Witu Sultanate', *International Journal of African Historical Studies* 11, no. 4 (1978), 683–4.
[8] Rochus Schmidt, *Aus kolonialer Frühzeit* (Berlin: Safari Verlag, 1922), 60.
[9] Schmidt, *Aus kolonialer Frühzeit*, 61.   [10] Schmidt, *Aus kolonialer Frühzeit*, 60–1.

nothing without provoking a broader conflict with the rapidly globalizing German Empire. And as long as Wituland remained under the German emperor's protection, German merchants looking for a trading post in East Africa were assured of the protection of Sultan Ahmed within his territory.

Apart from the security Germany offered Wituland from its main regional threats, the most tangible material benefit accruing to the sultanate from German involvement in its affairs was the expansion of its borders, courtesy of negotiations headed by Clemens and Gustav Denhardt, who insisted that Sultan Ahmed had a right to not only the small area surrounding the town of Witu but also a 3,000 kilometre long stretch of East African coastline from the north bank of the River Tana, all the way up to Kiwayu Island.[11] Much to the chagrin of Sultan Barghash, this more expansive Wituland now included mainland African coastline hitherto controlled by the Sultan of Zanzibar, albeit not the strategically important Lamu Island. Offering an insight into the competing interests in the region, these inflated territorial claims secured by the German consortium had initially been disavowed by the German government and the German East Africa Company (DOAG), which were simultaneously seeking to expand German influence in Zanzibar as part of their plan to consolidate the future of the DOAG's holdings on the East African coastline.[12]

For its part the new Witu Company, largely represented in Wituland by their agent Rochus Schmidt, aspired to play the same role there that the DOAG sought to play in its territories. Schmidt established a rudimentary presence for the company in Kiongue, Kimbo, and Manda.[13] However, the company's ability to secure the territory with the capital available to it was minimal. Given the modest resources available to the Witu Company, its security forces consisted of 'the hunting weapons of a couple of company officials spread out across the territory'.[14] Further difficulties were experience when the company sought to expand its reach into other regions (such as Kau on the River Tana and Kiongue) that did not accept the rule of Witu's sultan or the authority of the Germans or that were loyal to Sultan Barghash of Zanzibar rather than Sultan Ahmed.[15] (See Figure 8.1.)

The resolve of the Witu Company was further tested by a serious raid conducted by Somalis in 1887, which made clear that the Denhardts' promises to protect the sultanate were not supported by any credible military capacity. Even worse from the perspective of the company, unlike in the case of the DOAG in Zanzibar, the German state made it clear that it considered the company to be solely responsible for security in Wituland, a responsibility it was in no position to shoulder.[16] While the town of Witu itself remained unmolested by the Somali

[11] Ylvisaker, 'The Origins and Development of the Witu Sultanate', 684–5.
[12] Müller, *Deutschland—Zanzibar—Ostafrika*, 301–7.
[13] Schmidt, *Aus kolonialer Frühzeit*, 72–5.   [14] Schmidt, *Aus kolonialer Frühzeit*, 57–9.
[15] Schmidt, *Aus kolonialer Frühzeit*, 69–73.
[16] Müller, *Deutschland—Zanzibar—Ostafrika*, 309–17.

Figure 8.1 The Sultanate of Wituland, as per the *Deutsche Kolonialzeitung*, 1 May 1887

raiding party, several other villages were devastated. Gustav Denhardt, who was travelling through the territory at the time, also found himself besieged by the Somali attack. Cognizant of his commitment to protect the Germans, Sultan Ahmed gave Schmidt 100 troops to deal with the invaders and Schmidt set off to search for Denhardt and the Somalis. With the help of neighbouring Wapokomo and Galla communities who supplied Schmidt's army with canoes and supplies, the Witu troops succeeded in engaging and routing the Somalis before returning to Witu. Having also driven the Somali raiders from their territory as well, the previously hostile Galla accepted the authority of the sultan and, as a consequence of this, tolerated Schmidt.[17]

After Sultan Ahmed died in 1888, his pro-German cousin Fumo Bakari ascended the throne. Schmidt, who knew him well, thought of him as an 'affable' ruler, with whom he regularly played skat while the two smoked Indian

[17] Schmidt, *Aus kolonialer Frühzeit*, 65–9, 74–5.

cigars—something that the more religious Ahmed had never done.[18] Nonetheless, despite the friendly environment provided to the Germans by Wituland's sultans, the financial position of the overstretched Witu Company did not improve. When the Denhardt brothers faded into insolvency, their interests in Wituland were effectively sold to the German Colonial Association (*Kolonialverein*), which lobbied German merchants, industrialists, and financiers to invest in a revitalized Witu Company (*Witugesellschaft*) to ensure that Wituland did not simply pass into the hands of the British. By 1889, however, responsibility for its holdings had passed to its rival, the DOAG. Despite the DOAG's attempts to consolidate their influence in Zanzibar, Fumo Bakari maintained his pro-German stance, and there were some suggestions in the German press that Wituland's sultan was on the verge of allowing German settlers in his kingdom.[19]

This was encouraging news for one colonial opportunist, Andreas Küntzel, a German traveller who decided to try his luck in the sultanate. Küntzel had been trying to raise money to organize an expedition to establish a plantation and sawmill there since June 1887, having visited the sultanate in 1886 with Gustav Denhardt as part of an official German party that met both Sultan Ahmed and Fumo Bakari. Indeed, Küntzel had written an approving article about Witu for the German colonial newspaper of record, the *Deutsche Kolonialzeitung*, noting that it was 'clean and orderly' and presenting Sultan Ahmed's claim that Zanzibar was a 'robber state' that had long preyed on Witu in a sympathetic light. He also noted Ahmed's emphatic loyalty to the German emperor and his desire to one day visit 'Sultan Wilhelm' in Germany.[20]

In an attempt to attract investors and expedition members, Küntzel announced his colonizing plans for Witu in a German newspaper in June 1887, lauding Witu as superior to all other colonizing sites around the world, boasting a hospitable climate, a fever-free environment, friendly locals, good access to global trade routes, fertile soil, and reliable rainfall. The possibilities for trade were enormous, he argued, and settlers there could expect to sell ivory, rubber, sesame, peanuts, cereal crops, tobacco, and cattle on the global market. Above all, Küntzel argued in defiance of the facts, because it was a German colony, any German settlers 'stood under the direct protection of our German warships'. After seven years of travel through 'America, North Africa, India, Sumatra, Australia, and East Africa', he concluded, he was convinced that East Africa 'offers the best conditions for German colonists'.[21]

[18] Schmidt, *Aus kolonialer Frühzeit*, 62–3.
[19] 'Sultan Fumo Bakari von Witu und seine Leute', October 1889, in BA Berlin R1001/8870 , 12.
[20] Andreas Küntzel, 'Die Expedition von SM Kreuzerfregatte *Gneisenau* zu Achmed, dem Sultan der Suaheli', *Deutsche Kolonialzeitung* 3 (1886), 486–91.
[21] Andreas Küntzel, 'Das Suahelisultanat, der Schlüssel Ostafrikas', *Beilage der Berliner Börsen-Zeitung*, 19 June 1887, in BA Berlin R1001/8875, 'Die Unternehmen Küntzel im Suaheli-Sultanat', 7.

In follow-up articles, Küntzel argued that, unlike East and Central Africa, other German colonies such as Cameroon, South West Africa, and New Guinea would only ever be trading outposts. He also criticized how the Germans had dealt with Wituland, leaving it in the hands of the amateurish Denhardts. To his mind, waiting for the state to establish a colony there was wasting precious time. Instead, Germans should model themselves on the enterprising British and Dutch who had already colonized in the tropics. They should rely on private enterprise and, above all, invest in his association, to the tune of 10,000 marks each, which would see a thriving coastal colony up and running within five or six years, assisted by the benevolent Sultan Fumo Bakari.[22]

In an attempt to garner political support, Küntzel also sent notice to the German Foreign Office of his impending departure to Wituland, declaring that he was certain of the support of the sultan and hoping that he could rely on the protection of the German government.[23] The Foreign Office let Michahelles in Zanzibar know of his plans, as well as the Colonial Association in Berlin. It also informed Küntzel of their agreement, warning him, however, not to interfere with the interests of the Witu Company.[24] To this, Küntzel offered the surly reply that the Witu Company had better not interfere with his interests.[25] Having only informed the Foreign Office of his plans, Küntzel immediately set about advertising his colonial investment opportunity as 'government-approved', prompting inquiries from the police about the veracity of these exaggerated claims and forcing the Foreign Office to distance itself from him publicly.[26]

In Zanzibar, Michahelles sounded the alarm once he caught wind of Küntzel's plans, warning the Foreign Office that the would-be colonist had earned an unsavoury reputation in the region as a 'far from trustworthy person' whose attempts to get people to invest in his Witu venture had seen him labelled a 'swindler'. Before travelling to Wituland, Michahelles reported, Küntzel had led an extremely colourful life and was rumoured to have joined the French Foreign Legion, to have been involved in a robbery that ended in a murder, and to have been shot and seriously wounded while jumping ship in Singapore. It was after this wild period that he went to East Africa, where he earned a 'less than positive reputation' as an embezzler, reputed to have taken as much as 120, 000 marks from would-be investors. Police information from Bavaria confirmed this portrait, although it admitted that the charge of murder against him was as yet 'unproved'. From Witu itself came the news that other Germans working there

---

[22] Andreas Küntzel, 'Fehler unserer Colonisation in Ostafrika', Beilage der Berliner Börsen-Zeitung, 26 June 1887; 'Die Expedition für Plantagenbau nach dem Suahelisultanate in Ostafrika', Beilage der Berliner Börsen-Zeitung, 29 June 1887, in BA Berlin R1001/8875, 7.
[23] Küntzel to H. Bismarck, 3 July 1887, in BA Berlin R1001/8875, 6–7.
[24] Foreign Office to Küntzel, 6 July 1887, in BA Berlin R1001/8875, 9–11.
[25] Küntzel to H. Bismarck, 7 July 1887, in BA Berlin R1001/8875, 13–15.
[26] Weser Zeitung, 13 July 1887, in BA Berlin R1001/8875, 16–20.

wanted nothing to do with him. As he was a German subject, however, the sultan was diplomatically offering him polite assistance in accordance with his responsibilities towards Germans as he understood them.[27]

A further blow to Küntzel's reputation came in January 1889 when a newspaper report in the *Deutsche Kolonialzeitung* publicly debunked Küntzel's claims to have begun a logging business in Witu's hinterland. Far from owning a sawmill and logging company, the paper wrote, Küntzel only had a *shamba*, a hut on a small piece of land.[28] In an attempt to combat the increasingly negative publicity surrounding his Witu scheme, Küntzel sent a personal petition recommending it to Kaiser Wilhelm II in December 1889 in the hope that the emperor would intercede on his behalf and support his colonizing endeavours. The letter never left the Foreign Office.[29] Not long after this, Consul General Michahelles used the opportunity of his visit to Wituland while signing the protection treaty in April 1890 to visit Küntzel's property. He later wrote about it to Chancellor Caprivi, confirming that Küntzel's hut and holdings were very small and that Sultan Fumo Bakari had no intention of allowing him to undertake logging in the pristine forest surrounding Witu.[30]

Notwithstanding his serious doubts about Küntzel's inflated claims that he was in the vanguard of German colonialism in Wituland, Michahelles nonetheless agreed with Küntzel's assessment of the prospects for German colonists there. Indeed, the sultanate struck Michahelles as a rare and welcome opportunity for the German Empire, its merchants, and colonists. Although he admitted that it did not possess an ocean harbour, there were some excellent river bays for German trading vessels. Fumo Bakari's pro-German stance also meant that strong and ongoing military support from Germany was probably unnecessary. So too, he wrote, Wituland's climate and position made it ideal for trade and colonization without the need for burdensome financial support from the German state.[31] A formal state treaty between Wituland and Germany was a step forward in encouraging German interests in East Africa.

The treaty that Consul General Michahelles and Sultan Fumo Bakari signed on 1 April 1890 resembled others that the Germans had signed with other African monarchs in other protectorates.[32] Its ostensible premise was the mutual desire of Kaiser Wilhelm II and Sultan Fumo Bakari to formalize their 'friendly relations'

---

[27] Michahelles to H. Bismarck, 7 April 1888; Behrendt to Michahelles, 18 April 1889, in BA Berlin R1001/8875, 39–52, 76–7. Caprivi would candidly discuss these details of Küntzel's chequered past in the Reichstag in February 1891. See Leo von Caprivi, 6 February 1891, *Verhandlungen des Reichstages*, 1355.

[28] 'Kolonisation in Witulande', *Kolonial-Zeitung*, 4 January 1889, in BA Berlin R1001/8875, 84.

[29] Küntzel to Wilhelm II, 23 December 1889; German Foreign Office to Küntzel, 11 January 1890, in BA Berlin R1001/8875, 78–83.

[30] Michahelles to Caprivi, 17 July 1890, in BA Berlin R1001/8875, 87.

[31] Michahelles to German Foreign Office, 21 April 1890, in R1001/8870, 104.

[32] Michahelles to German Foreign Office, 13 April 1890, in R1001/8870, 72.

with a 'protection and friendship treaty', but its underlying purpose was to move from indirect relations mediated by the Denhardts' Witu Company to a direct treaty relationship between the two states of Germany and Wituland. Article I effectively superseded the Denhardts' role in Wituland and stipulated that, at the request of the sultan, the German emperor assumed 'protective rule (*Schutzherrlichkeit*) over him and his people', assuring the sultan of 'His Majesty's protection'. In return, the sultan promised not to engage in negotiations or agreements with other powers that would lead him to cede territory to those powers without the permission of the German emperor. German subjects and their property were afforded protection by Article II, which allowed them to travel and trade within Wituland's borders, as well as to buy land and settle there. The tax status of German subjects in Wituland was regulated in Article III, while Articles IV and V offered Germans and their African employees in Wituland extraterritorial legal rights, limiting the capacity of the sultan to decide on legal matters pertaining to them. Article VI stipulated that although the treaty would be drawn up in both German and Arabic, in the case of disputes, the German copy would take precedence.[33]

Fearing for their freedom to act unilaterally in the region, the British had protested against the signing of any further treaties with Wituland, arguing that any such treaty would grant the Sultan of Wituland immunity from facing the consequences of any actions he undertook that disadvantaged the British East Africa Company.[34] Lurking behind this line of protest was the international legitimacy that Germany was affording what the British still considered to be a renegade province of Zanzibar.

Only months after the treaty was signed, however, British interests in East Africa were given a shot in the arm when Salisbury was successful in insisting that the protectorate be bundled into the Heligoland-Zanzibar Treaty and handed over to Britain.[35] Although Article II of this treaty obliged the British to 'acknowledge the sovereignty of the Sultan of Witu' and not dissolve Wituland into Zanzibar,[36] the Germans had effectively traded Sultan Fumo Bakari's kingdom to the hitherto hostile British just months after a large and formal ceremony had publicly announced Wilhelm II's role as Witu's sworn protector.

---

[33] 'Schutz- und Freundschaftsvertrag zwischen dem deutschen Reiche und dem Sultanate Witu', in BA Berlin R1001/8870, 91–6.

[34] Hatzfeldt to H. Bismarck, 5 November 1889, in BA Berlin R1001/8870, 17.

[35] Müller, *Deutschland—Zanzibar—Ostafrika*, 309–25. See in particular the list of investors in the *Witugesellschaft* on p. 311. See too Andreas Birken, *Das Sultanat Zanzibar im 19. Jahrhundert* (Tübingen: Barbara v. Spangenberg KG, 1971), 151–5; Jörg Duppler, *Der Junior-Partner: England und die Entwicklung der Deutschen Marine 1848–1890* (Herford: Mittler, 1985), 286; Rüger, *Heligoland*, 82, D. R. Gillard, 'Salisbury's African Policy and the Heligoland Offer of 1890', *English Historical Review* 75, no. 297 (1960), 631–53; G. N. Sanderson, 'The Anglo-German Agreement of 1890 and the Upper Nile', *English Historical Review* 78, no. 306 (1963), 49–72.

[36] Andreas Birken, 'Der Helgoland-Sansibar-Vertrag von 1890', *Internationales Jahrbuch für Geschichts- und Geographie-Unterricht* 15 (1974), 194–204.

German Impotence in 'British' Wituland

The German handover of his sultanate came as a great shock to Sultan Fumo Bakari. When in April of 1890 Micahelles had come to Witu with a fifty-man guard to formalize Germany's promise to protect Wituland from the predations of enemies such as Britain and Zanzibar, the sultan had received personal gifts from Wilhelm II, including a large portrait of the emperor and a rifle as symbols of the binding personal and diplomatic relationships between the two leaders. Yet, by July 1890, the Germans had discarded Wituland in favour of Heligoland, and the sultan suddenly found himself under British 'protection'. This insult from a fellow monarch was compounded by the fact that Fumo Bakari only found out about this transfer of sovereign power by accident rather than through formal German government channels. Understandably, Fumo Bakari complained bitterly of his treatment by the Germans, declaring that 'the German Kaiser has sold me and my land like a herd of sheep.'[37] Some inside the German Reichstag agreed, with German Imperial Party deputy and pan-German activist Traugott von Arnim-Muskau later remarking that Germany's shabby treatment of an African monarch could only tarnish the empire's reputation in Africa.[38]

Once Germany had signed the agreement to hand the sultanate over to the British, events there quickly deteriorated. Just after Fumo Bakari had found out that he was no longer under the protection of Kaiser Wilhelm II, but rather Britain's Queen Victoria, the sultan told Germans to leave his kingdom, arguing that he could no longer guarantee their safety.[39] More seriously, on 15 September, having ignored advice not to go to Wituland, nine German subjects—led by the colonial adventurer Andreas Küntzel—were killed in the capital, Witu.[40]

Reports from Wituland made it clear that, in the wake of the Anglo-German Agreement which had seen his sultanate simply given by the Germans to the British, Sultan Fumo Bakari had insisted that Küntzel's desire to establish a sawmill in Wituland be expressly authorized by the British consul, just as enterprises had been directed to seek permission from German authorities when Wituland was a German protectorate. When Küntzel refused and began work without authorization, the sultan had him brought to Witu, where his party was housed, given a sheep, and told to wait for word from the British consul in Lamu. Infuriated, Küntzel spent his time in the town screaming abuse at the sultan from the square outside the sultan's palace before trying to break out of the fortified town with his men. Accounts vary, but during their escape attempt, shots were fired by Küntzel, one of his companions, or (less probably) a Witu guard. This led

---

[37] Schmidt, *Aus kolonialer Frühzeit*, 75–7.
[38] Traugott Hermann von Arnim-Muskau in *Verhandlungen des Reichstages*, 6 February 1891, 1362.
[39] Simons to Euan-Smith, 23 September 1890, in 'Correspondence Respecting the Punitive Expedition against Witu of November 1890', in BA Berlin R1001/8877, 86.
[40] Rüger, *Heligoland*, 104–8.

to a more general outbreak of violence that saw a number of Witu guards and all but one of Küntzel's men and other European settlers attacked and killed.[41]

For his part, the sultan explained that he had neither wanted nor ordered the violence and had indeed warned his guards against attacking Europeans inside the city.[42] Immediately after the killings, Fumo Bakari sent a message to the British envoy in which he explained what had happened. His report tallied with the reports of others that highlighted that Küntzel had ignored the sultan's order to gain permission from the British consul in Zanzibar before commencing logging, that the sultan had him brought to Witu to enforce his decision, that Küntzel became abusive, and that he had then precipitated the violence at Witu's southern gate that ended with the deaths of his men.[43]

Lurking behind the killings was the issue of the sovereign rights of Sultan Fumo Bakari during and after the negotiation of the Heligoland-Zanzibar Treaty. In what might be considered a complete break of faith between the German Empire and the Sultan of Wituland, the sultan had not even been consulted about the fate of his kingdom. That Wituland had been simply handed over by the Germans to the very power from which the sultan had sought protection had shocked Fumo Bakari, who gave voice to his protests in several letters to the British. His dismay was not merely because of his presumed personal attachment to Germany, as some observers assumed, but because the deal between the two European powers effectively bound him, via Britain, to the Sultan of Zanzibar, his 'deadly enemy'.[44]

Perhaps unprecedented in the history of German colonialism, the news of German settlers having been killed by Africans was received by some important segments of the German press with surprising restraint, even reports sympathetic towards the Africans. Partly, this can be explained by the broader antipathy towards the Anglo-German Agreement on Heligoland in pro-colonial liberal circles in Germany, which pounced on the Witu killings as further proof of the damage it had caused to German interests in Africa. Beyond this, however, there was a remarkable amount of attention paid to the role the German colonial adventurists had played in their own deaths. In the prominent liberal newspaper the *Vossische Zeitung*, for example, it was argued that the thoroughly disrespectful conduct of the German colonists was in all probability the grounds for their deaths. According to the report, 'A strong provocation of the Africans by the expedition must have taken place. Without it, such an attack by natives on the coast, where the power of the Europeans is well known and has often been felt, is simply

---

[41] Redwitz to German Foreign Office, 23 September 1890; Michahelles to German Foreign Office, 4 October 1890; Michahelles to Caprivi, 3 October 1890, in BA Berlin R1001/959, 1,5, 11–13. See too BA Berlin R1001/959, 13–22.

[42] Toeppen, 19 September 1890, in BA Berlin R1001/959, 19–22.

[43] Fumo Bakari to Pigott, 19 September 1890, in BA Berlin R1001/959, 22–3.

[44] Müller, *Deutschland—Zanzibar—Ostafrika*, 325.

unthinkable.'[45] Other newspapers agreed, with the *Hamburger Nachrichten* mar-velling how a man of such ill repute as Küntzel had found people gullible enough to follow him to Africa. The newspaper wondered too 'how much damage could have been avoided if the complete unsuitability of these individuals for true col-onizing activity had been widely known'.[46] The more conservative *National-Zeitung* explicitly linked the killings to the handover of Witu to Britain, arguing that since then the sultan had lost all respect for the Germans and that the por-trait of Wilhelm II given to Fumo Bakari as a personal gift was being used for target practice.[47] Even in London *The Times* laid the blame squarely on Küntzel, who, the paper said, had abused the sultan and behaved violently, 'thus determin-ing the fate of the party'.[48]

One of the most forthright defences of Sultan Fumo Bakari came from the *Allgemeine Münchener Zeitung*, which argued that Germany was a strong enough nation to learn from its colonial mistakes, that as a colonial power Germany had responsibilities with regard to its protectorates and that the deeper cause of the deaths was Germany's betrayal of Sultan Fumo Bakari:

> Who can deny that the abandonment of the Sultan of Witu, which found its expression in the Anglo-German agreement, in the end offers the psychological explanation for the massacre of Küntzel and his comrades? The ruler, deceived in his hopes for Germany, wanted to but could not curb the bitterness of his people, and Küntzel—certainly not blamelessly—fell victim to them. But let us look at the genesis of the matter objectively. The Sultanate of Witu is by dint of its geographical position the natural enemy of Zanzibar, and as such also the enemy of England, whose influence on the coastline-ruling island inhibits the lively development of Witu. It is therefore understandable that the ruler of Witu sought out a counterbalance to England's dominance and, as early as 1859, approached Prussia for protection...If today the telegraph reported that Witu has been destroyed by the English, there may well be a sense of satisfaction for the German blood that has flowed, but it would not be equal to the moral sense among the natives of the injustice that Germany has done them.[49]

Kurt Toeppen, a Wituland old hand who had led the Witu Company until the sultan had advised Germans to leave the sultanate, agreed with this sentiment. Toeppen had returned to Witu the day after the killings and had earlier warned Küntzel that the mood in Witu had changed markedly after the Anglo-German

[45] *Vossische Zeitung*, 26 September 1890, in BA Berlin R1001/8875, 99.
[46] *Hamburger Nachrichten*, 27 September 1890, in BA Berlin R1001/8875, 112.
[47] *National-Zeitung*, 27 September 1890, in BA Berlin R1001/8875, 101.
[48] *The Times*, 3 October 1890, in BA Berlin R1001/8875, 123.
[49] *Allgemeine Münchener Zeitung* 31 October 1890 in BA Berlin R1001/8876, 'Die Unternehmen Küntzel im Suaheli-Sultanat. Die Ermordung von Küntzel und Genossen', 66–7.

Agreement had traded Witu away. His concerns had been dismissed by Küntzel, who felt he could trade on his presumed personal friendship with Fumo Bakari. If that did not work, Küntzel had boasted to Toeppen, then the sultan would find out that 'he would not stand for any nonsense.' Without excusing Küntzel's wilful blindness to new realities in the sultanate, Toeppen argued that the killings were firmly tied to Germany's betrayal of the sultan. 'The cause of the butchery in Witu', he argued, was to be sought 'in the embittered mood that was evoked by the sudden withdrawal of Germany's protectorate, particularly given that this transfer was announced in a, to put it mildly, unceremonious manner by the English consular agent Simons.' The 'brusque and inappropriate actions of Küntzel' were, he concluded, only the proximate catalyst.[50]

In its report of the Witu killings, the colonial newspaper for which Küntzel had once written, the *Deutsche Kolonialzeitung*, offered some surprisingly candid regrets about its earlier association with him. Its editor, Gustav Meinecke, admitted that Küntzel had increasingly become 'a man we did not wish to have much to do with'. He reminded his readers that the newspaper had issued a warning in January 1890 against becoming involved in Küntzel's Witu scheme, and opined that 'None of this might have happened if our warning had been heeded.' With regard to the broader political context of the killings, the newspaper also pointed to Germany's betrayal of the sultan, reporting that when Küntzel arrived in Wituland, Sultan Fumo Bakari 'had nothing good to say about the German-English agreement'. Nevertheless, the paper insisted that both the British and the German governments needed to take 'energetic steps' in response to the killings. In particular, as the newly responsible colonial power in Wituland, Meinecke argued, the British had a responsibility to ensure that such events never occurred in Witu again.[51]

Just what role Britain should play was a matter of some debate. From the perspective of Germany, the logistical problems associated with exacting retribution and compensation for the killings without the help of another power were insurmountable. Lacking in particular the naval resources to retaliate, the Germans were forced to request that the British navy mount a punitive expedition. The German Foreign Office reasoned that it could justify this request by arguing that, in the wake of the Anglo-German Agreement, the sultanate was now part of the British Empire.[52]

This was not the first time that the German navy had found itself inadequate to the task in East Africa. A joint Anglo-German 'anti-slavery' blockade along the coast of East Africa used to apply pressure to the Sultan of Zanzibar had also seen

[50] Toeppen in *Hannoverscher Kurier*, 24 January 1891, in BA Berlin, R1001/8877, 'Die Unternehmen Küntzel im Suaheli-Sultanat. Die Ermordung von Küntzel und Genossen', 136.
[51] 'Der Fall Küntzel', *Deutsche Kolonialzeitung*, 4 October 1890, 248.
[52] Redwitz to German Foreign Office, 23 September 1890, in BA Berlin R1001/8875, 'Die Unternehmen Küntzel im Suaheli-Sultanat', 89.

Germany require the assistance of an additional British cruiser and even an Italian naval vessel to maintain any semblance of effectiveness.[53] This was besides other parts of the world where Germany's naval weakness was apparent, such as Liberia and in particular Chile, where Britain had also loaned Germany the naval power it so clearly lacked.[54]

The situation in Wituland was complicated, however, by the fact that the British claimed that any expedition to punish the sultan should be a German affair.[55] Although the German envoy in Zanzibar had reported to the German Foreign Office that the British had initially offered to send a warship to Lamu, an offer Berlin accepted,[56] by the next day Salisbury was insisting that Germany send a formal request for a ship to go to Witu.[57]

Britain tried to distance itself from the incident further, when Salisbury's undersecretary of state, Thomas Villiers Lister, insisted that Britain had no responsibility to assist Germany in Wituland because the sultan had not been officially notified that Witu was now an imperial possession of Queen Victoria and not Kaiser Wilhelm II. This was strongly contested by Germany's ambassador in London, Paul Wolff Metternich, who insisted on the 'immediate punishment' of Witu by the Royal Navy.[58] Although Lister admitted that the final decision on the sovereign status of Witu would rest with Salisbury, he very much doubted that it was a British possession just yet. As Metternich wrote to Chancellor Caprivi:

> He supported himself with the claim that the transfer of protective rule would first be complete once the appropriate notification is sent to the Sultan of Witu from the governments of Germany and England. Only from that moment on does a duty fall to England under international law.[59]

The German response to this claim betrayed their indignation. Once the Heligoland agreement had been signed, the German Foreign Office reasoned, surely Germany had relinquished all of its responsibilities for the Sultan of Witu and Britain had assumed them. The notification of the sultan was, according to Berlin, 'a mere formality'. The German Foreign Office's disregard for Fumo Bakari continued, as it pointed out that during the negotiations preceding the

---

[53] Duppler, *Der Junior-Partner*, 287–91.
[54] On Liberia, see Duppler, *Der Junior-Partner*, 283–5. On Germany's perceived sluggishness in sending naval vessels to Chile, see Ekkehard Böhm, *Überseehandel und Flottenbau: Hanseatische Kaufmannschaft und deutsche Seerüstung 1879-1902* (Hamburg: Bertelsmann Universitätsverlag, 1972), 38–46.
[55] Michahelles to Caprivi, 3 October 1890, in BA Berlin R1001/8876, 22–9; Michahelles to German Foreign Office, 3 October 1890, in BA Berlin R1001/959, 4.
[56] Marschall to Redwitz, 23 September 1890, in BA Berlin R1001/959, 1.
[57] Hatzfeldt to German Foreign Office, 24 September 1890, in BA Berlin R1001/8875, 93.
[58] Metternich to German Foreign Office, 4 October 1890, in BA Berlin R1001/8875, 127.
[59] Metternich to Caprivi, 4 October 1890, in BA Berlin R1001/8875, 129–32.

Anglo-German Agreement the Sultan of Witu had not been consulted on the questions of who his preferred colonial sovereign was and 'whether he wanted to submit to English protective rule'. His views had been deemed simply irrelevant. In the same way, his views after the fact were similarly beneath consideration. The question of which empire the Sultanate of Wituland belonged to was, according to Germany, a product of 'an agreement between Berlin and London'. This agreement was, the Germans asserted, 'utterly independent of the possible views the Sultan of Witu may have in relation to it'.[60]

Salisbury, however, made it clear to the Germans that he too did not agree that the sultanate was a British protectorate at the time of the killings. Indeed, it was the British position that the formal transfer of Witu to British rule had not yet taken place even a month after the killings. That the British had 'every desire to co-operate in the measures which might be found necessary to punish the authors of the German murders' should not, Salisbury made clear, be confused with the British accepting 'the responsibility which was put on them by the German government'.[61] Any British action in Wituland was evidence of Britain's good will towards Germany, rather than the fulfilment of its duty as the sovereign power in Wituland or an admission of its culpability for not having adequately secured the region.

The British view was hotly contested in the German press, with the *National-Zeitung* publishing an account pointing out that the British had in fact informed Fumo Bakari of his absorption into their empire. According to this report, the British had told the sultan by letter that Wituland was a British protectorate in August 1890. When the sultan had protested that Britain did not have the right to declare Witu a British protectorate without his agreement or without consulting him, he had bluntly been informed that consultation was not required. Ignoring Germany's own dismissal of the sovereign rights of the sultan, the paper argued that Britain's peremptory and high-handed dismissal of the views of the sultan had led to an uproar in Witu; indeed, Britain's 'reckless actions', the report concluded, might have been the underlying cause of the killing of Küntzel and his companions while they were in the sultan's custody.[62]

This account was partially corroborated by the testimony of one of the survivors from Küntzel's expedition, Fritz Häßler, whose account of the colonizing party's reception in Witu confirmed that Sultan Fumo Bakari 'complained bitterly' about the Anglo-German Agreement and the fact that he had neither received formal notification of its impact from Germany nor been asked whether he agreed to be traded to the British. According to Häßler, the sultan had been visited by the British consul, who informed him of the new arrangements on

---

[60] Metternich to Caprivi, 4 October 1890, in BA Berlin R1001/8875, 129–32.
[61] Salisbury to Malet, 13 October 1890, in BA Berlin, R1001/8877, 69.
[62] *National-Zeitung* (undated), in BA Berlin R1001/8875, 137.

17 August 1890. By the time Küntzel's party stood before Fumo Bakari, Häßler reported, the portrait of the German Kaiser that had previously sat above the sultan's throne was nowhere to be seen.[63]

Although he was not present at the time of the killings, Häßler also gave further details of how the killings had come to pass, confirming initial suspicions that the sultan had not ordered them, but that they were a result of the actions of the Germans themselves. According to Häßler's account, Fumo Bakari had told Küntzel that, as the British now controlled the sultanate, he needed to get the permission of the British consul before commencing work there. The settlers returned to Küntzel's compound where they started working. When they met with resistance from locals in the vicinity of Küntzel's property, who argued that the sultan had told them to stop them, Häßler set off on 14 September to gain permission from the British for their work, while the rest of the party were taken to Witu to see the sultan once again. According to his information, the party was met in a friendly manner by Fumo Bakari in Witu, but when the party was detained, they attempted to leave the town by force, shooting several African guards dead in the process, before they were killed themselves.[64]

Häßler's source for events in Witu was in all probability the British consul, whose telegram account of the killings tallies almost exactly with the German's own:

> Küntzel, who with nine Germans came to cut timber in Witu although Fumo Bakari refused permission, insisted on proceeding with operation and when resistance was offered, took up arms. He and 7 others went to Witu wishing on 15th to leave town, gate keeper would not let them pass. Küntzel drew revolver shot him and others. Natives then turned on Europeans killing all party, then came to Mkonumbi, Küntzel's head-quarters, killed Carl Horn. Hassler is safe here. Toeppen now in Witu, was not there at time...I believe all true.[65]

The consul's account also confirmed that prior to trying to break out, Küntzel had stood in the square before the sultan's palace, screaming obscenities.[66] These details were also verified by Kurt Toeppen, who argued that the sultan had acted in a conciliatory fashion towards Küntzel, because 'the sultan knew Küntzel was like a mad man'. When the sultan told Küntzel that he had to stay in Witu until the British had approved his plans, the German colonist reacted badly:

---

[63] *Frankfurter Zeitung*, 6 October 1890; *Freisinnige Zeitung*, 7 September 1890, in BA Berlin R1001/8875, 138, 144.

[64] *Frankfurter Zeitung*, 6 October 1890; *Freisinnige Zeitung*, 7 September 1890, in BA Berlin R1001/8875, 138, 144.

[65] Michahelles to Caprivi, 3 October 1890, in R1001/8876, 22–9.   [66] Ibid.

going about in the street swearing at the sultan in Swahili, calling him a dog [and] saying that he was no one and that no one need ask his permission to do anything. He then said he was ready to fight and that [the sultan] better make himself ready, that his gun was equal to 100 of the sultan's.

He then confronted the town's gatekeeper, who told him he needed the sultan's permission to leave. 'Küntzel then took out his revolver and shot him at once.'[67]

Some of these details were disputed by the only German survivor of the actual attacks, the engineer August Meuschel, who escaped, despite being wounded, by hiding in long grass and then swimming across a crocodile-infested river. Meuschel admitted that when locals in the vicinity of Küntzel's property had refused to sell them food, the Germans had reacted by threatening to burn down their village. The rest of his account, however, was exculpatory. On the question of who shot first at the gates of Witu, he insisted that the first shot came from the crowd of angry Witu townsfolk chasing the German prisoners (see Figure 8.2). He also maintained that the gatekeeper alleged to have been shot dead by Küntzel was still alive.[68] According to Meuschel, the Germans decided that they needed to flee the city before they were killed by their guards. When they got to the city

Figure 8.2 The Flight from Witu, as per the account of August Meuschel, *Illustrirte Zeitung*, 29 November 1890

[67] Toeppen, 19 September 1890, in BA Berlin R1001/8876, 40–5.
[68] Valette to German Foreign Office, 31 October 1890; *Berliner Tageblatt*, 8 December 1890; *Augsburger Abendzeitung*, 17 December 1890, in BA Berlin R1001/8877, 38–45, 54, 138.

gate, they encountered an unarmed gatekeeper who removed the top bar of the gate when the Germans demanded he do so. Thereafter, Meuschel said, pandemonium ensued. As Küntzel got through the gate, the Africans chasing them began to fire on those still inside the city walls, killing several of them. With five of them remaining, they fled the city, but in about a quarter of an hour they again came under fire and returned fire. About half an hour into the flight from the city, Meuschel was shot through the leg and was unable to continue. He gave his revolver to Küntzel and hid in the long grass until the Africans had passed.[69]

Meuschel's account was completely at odds with that of Sultan Fumo Bakari, who sent a letter to the British to explain what had happened in his capital when Küntzel and his party had arrived in Witu and questioned the need for them to get British permission for his enterprise:

> I answered him, when I was under German protection I never did anything without their leave and now you go to Zanzibar to the English Consul and bring me a letter; if he gives you leave to build, you may come; there you may do what you want. Then he went back to Mkunumbi. My people wrote that he was building there, and I sent a letter to stop him; when they stopped him, he wanted to beat the people...Then I sent soldiers to bring the men to me. They came to the town, and I gave them a house to stay in...In the morning, when they awoke, he came up to my flagstaff; there he used abusive language; all the askaris wanted to make a row with him, but I stopped them and told them to leave him alone. They wanted leave to go to Mkonumbi; I told him I would write to the consul in Lamu and wait for his answer. Then he abused me still more, when I told him this...At 4 o'clock he went out by force. Then I sent Omari Madi. He went and talked to him, but he would not listen and abused me. Then he, Omari, talked and tried to get him in. He went out before I knew; he hit one man and knocked him down and hit another, and the askari would not remain still.[70]

When challenged by the British on his account, Fumo Bakari also sent another letter. The sultan's aggrieved tone in this second letter made clear that he had expected far more sympathy for his position than either Germany or Britain had showed him:

> Your honoured letter has reached me and I understand the contents thereof, that you say I am doing bad things. All that you mention was not done by me. During the time I enjoyed German protection, I looked after Europeans thoroughly, and also when I was put under your protection; I was even more careful to look well

---

[69] Testimony of Meuschel, in 'Correspondence respecting the Punitive Expedition against Witu of November 1890', in BA Berlin R1001/8877, 86.
[70] Fumo Bakari in BA Berlin R1001/8876, 46–7.

after any European that came to my place. And those [the murdered men], I took their arms because they came to interfere with me.

When I saw that they intended to behave badly, I took their arms in order to keep them quiet until I informed the English government, and their Somali interpreter was present. They refused to give up their arms, and they went to the gate, and they killed one of my doorkeepers. And there were some soldiers at the gate with whom the Germans fought. I told them [the Germans] that if they wished to work in Witu, they must obtain a letter from the consul in Zanzibar. They refused... And when the Europeans were going out, I sent my people to bring them back in order to keep them until I could inform your government, but when my men went to bring them, the Europeans killed some of them. And when my people saw this they could not restrain themselves, they did the same. This is how the thing happened.

And I have written to the Englishman who was at Lamu, to inform him that the Germans were behaving badly. He replied to me that there was no date to my letter: what kind of reply is this?

And we did not wish this [the murders] to happen in order to get their property. Their property remains where it was. I have not touched it.[71]

Dethroning the Sultan

Notwithstanding the fact that even German newspapers saw the German colon-ists in Witu as the authors of their own demise, in October 1890, Germany's new foreign secretary, Adolf Marschall von Bieberstein, was insisting to Ambassador Metternich in London that the British hold Fumo Bakari to account, arguing that if the sultan had not ordered the killings, he had at the least permitted them.[72] Marschall's position contradicted that of his man on the-spot, Michahelles, who saw Küntzel as the primary cause of the violence. Perhaps unsurprisingly, given Britain's long-held antagonism towards Wituland, Euan-Smith, the British com-mander of the proposed expedition, concurred with Marschall's view that the sultan was the cause of the violence. The British met the German proposal for a punitive expedition by suggesting that a joint action might be preferable, to which the Germans initially agreed.[73]

---

[71] Fumo Bakari to Fremantle and Euan-Smith, 20 October 1890, in *London Gazette*, 6 January 1891, 93. The correspondence between Fumo Bakari and Euan-Smith can also be found in 'Correspondence respecting the Punitive Expedition against Witu of November 1890 Presented to both Houses of Parliament Dec. 1890', in BA Berlin, R1001/8877, 86.

[72] Marschall to Metternich, 3 October 1890, in BA Berlin R1001/959, 4–5. Michahelle to Caprivi, BA Berlin R1001/959, 27–9.

[73] Metternich to German Foreign Office, 8 October 1890; Marschall to Michahelle,s 8 October 1890, in BA Berlin R1001/959, 5–6 (reproduced in BA Berlin R1001/8875, 145–6).

On 11 October, Salisbury sent a telegram to Germany's consul general, Michahelles, in Zanzibar, telling him that Admiral Fremantle had ordered Britain's consul general, Charles Euan-Smith, to go with Michahelles to Lamu in a man-of-war. Should the sultan refuse to offer them safe passage to Witu from there, Salisbury wrote, 'the British admiral is prepared to conduct a small expedition against the Sultan in concert with the British East Africa Company,' although he hoped that 'the presence of a man-of-war will have the desired effect and render such an expedition unnecessary.'[74] Michahelles decided to wait for the small German naval vessel *Schwalbe*, which took him there. On arriving in Lamu, however, he decided that, given the 'turmoil of the population', it was too dangerous for him to travel on to Witu, and both he and the British consul general decided to instruct Fumo Bakari to come to the coast to meet them instead.[75]

The British summons to the sultan was far from diplomatic. Rather than invite him to discuss the issue, the British peremptorily accused the sultan of having allowed 'shameful deeds' to have occurred in his town that resulted in the 'treacherous, foul and disgraceful murder of nine subjects of His Imperial Majesty the Emperor of Germany, and the causeless devastation and destruction of the plantations of other German subjects'. On this basis, the British navy insisted that Fumo Bakari immediately come to Lamu, warning of dire consequences, should he not come of his own will.[76] The sultan refused this demand, arguing that 'it is not the custom for the Sultan to leave his own place. If you have got anything more to say, you can say it, and I will send you a reply.'[77] Fumo Bakari also reiterated his point that it was Küntzel's party 'that began the fight, killing some of my people, consequently my people did the same'. In that sense, the Germans had reaped what they had sown. Although repeating that he had not ordered the killings, Fumo Bakari once again appealed to the British to understand his position and explain theirs better, arguing that 'if anyone goes to another person's place and beats and kills people, is it not your custom and law to punish the wrongdoers? Please let us know, so that we can learn.' Candidly, he also accused the British of wanting to 'come against us for nothing', that is, to use the matter as a pretext to attack Witu, which, as Admiral Fremantle freely admitted, had long been a geostrategic thorn in Britain's side in East Africa.[78]

---

[74] Memorandum, British Embassy Berlin, 11 October 1890, in BA Berlin R1001/959, 9. Also reproduced in BA Berlin R1001/8876, 9.

[75] Michahelles to German Foreign Office, 11 October 1890, in BA Berlin R1001/8876, 13.

[76] Euan-Smith and Fremantle to Fumo Bakari, 21 October 1890, in *London Gazette*, 6 January 1891 93 (also reproduced in 'Correspondence respecting the Punitive Expedition against Witu of November 1890', BA Berlin R1001/8877, 86; Euan-Smith to Salisbury, 22 October 1890, in 'Correspondence respecting the Punitive Expedition against Witu of November 1890', BA Berlin R1001/8877, 86.

[77] Fumo Bakari to Fremantle and Euan-Smith, 20 October 1890, in *London Gazette*, 6 January 1891, 93.

[78] Fumo Bakari to Fremantle and Euan-Smith, 23 October 1890, in *London Gazette*, 6 January 1891, 94; Edmund Robert Fremantle, *The Navy As I Have Known It* (London: Cassell, 1904), 376.

Before Fumo Bakari had even sent his reply, however, the British had already declared martial law over Wituland, satisfied that they had a clear *casus belli* that would justify their desire to remove Fumo Bakari from power.[79] Their professed assumption was that at least some of the killings had been 'directly ordered by the sultan'.[80] As the British consul general, Euan-Smith, would later write to Salisbury, his guiding assumption was that 'it has…been proved that no one was killed by the Germans until the people of Witu commenced to fire. The statement that Küntzel first shot the gatekeeper has been specially proved to be untrue.'[81]

Euan-Smith's communiqué to Salisbury and his account of the Küntzel outrage directly contradicted the testimonies of Michahelles, the Witu Company representative Toeppel, Küntzel's compatriot Häßler, the British consul at the time of the killings, and indeed the Sultan of Witu himself. Though Euan-Smith confidently asserted that the sultan's own testimony had been 'untrue', he offered the foreign secretary no proof of the allegation. Moreover, these allegations fell neatly and conveniently in line with British geostrategic designs in the region. Fumo Bakari and, before him, Sultan Ahmed had long frustrated British expansionist plans on the coast of East Africa. Even in the first weeks after the killings Euan-Smith openly expressed his hope than any coming campaign against the sultan would free the British East Africa Company from a 'dangerous enemy', indeed, that it would see Witu 'wiped from the face of the earth'.[82]

Given these imperial priorities, it is unsurprising that, in justifying the military campaign, Euan-Smith assumed that 'the massacre of the Germans, and the devastation of their estates were but the realization of a plan carefully considered, and ultimately sanctioned by the Sultan of Witu and his advisers'.[83] Equally unsurprisingly, upon defeating the sultan, the British intimated to the Germans that they no longer felt compelled to implement Article II of the Anglo-German Agreement that required the British to recognize the sovereignty of the Sultan of Witu over long-disputed coastal regions of East Africa. In light of their dependence on the British navy in the affair, the Germans indicated their willingness to concede the point and to renegotiate Article II, agreeing that 'the hostilities following the massacre render it out of date'.[84]

The Sultan of Wituland and the German consul general both blamed Küntzel and his band of colonizers for the troubles. The British blamed Fumo Bakari. It is worth considering, however, that other local forces at the grassroots were also at

---

[79] 'Declaration of Martial Law', 20 October 1890, in *London Gazette*, 6 January 1891, 94.

[80] Fremantle, *The Navy As I Have Known It*, 377.

[81] Euan-Smith to Salisbury, 30 October 1890, in 'Correspondence respecting the Punitive Expedition against Witu of November 1890', BA Berlin R1001/8877, 86.

[82] Michahelles to Caprivi, 3 October 1890, in BA Berlin R1001/8876, 22–9.

[83] Euan-Smith to Salisbury, 30 October 1890, in 'Correspondence respecting the Punitive Expedition against Witu of November 1890', BA Berlin R1001/8877, 86.

[84] Hatzfeldt to German Foreign Office, 12 November 1890; Marschall to Hatzfeldt, 12 November 1890, in BA Berlin, R1001/8876, 'Die Unternehmen Küntzel im Suaheli-Sultanat: Die Ermordung von Küntzel und Genossen', 92–4.

work, forces that point to the precariousness of the sultan's domestic position in the aftermath of the Anglo-German Agreement. Even prior to his arrival, Küntzel had been warned by other Europeans that Germans had been asked to leave Witu by the sultan, expressly because Fumo Bakari had admitted that 'he could not be answerable for their safety on account of the growing dislike evinced by his people towards Europeans and Christians generally, and towards Germans in particular.'[85] When German property in Witu was destroyed in the wake of the killings, the British took this as a telling sign that the sultan was 'unable to restrain his soldiers even in his own town, much less those in other places in his dominions'.[86] In his commentary on the British campaign, Michahelles told Chancellor Caprivi that he had never wavered from the view that 'it was not a premeditated and pre-planned malicious act of the sultan, but rather a sudden outbreak of the long-held animus of the local population,' a view that was carefully edited out of the version of his report that the Reichstag received.[87] Even Mueschel's first-hand account of the killings suggests that it was not so much the sultan as the local populace of Witu that had expressed their hostility towards the Germans. If this was the case, the bitterness unleashed by the Anglo-German Agreement did not only affect the sultan but had also galvanized anti-German opinion throughout Wituland and discredited the steadfastly pro-German Fumo Bakari in the eyes of his own people.

Convinced that Britain had sufficient grounds for military action, Fremantle commenced hostilities against Wituland and a small number of local allies on 24 October 1890, burning to the ground some coastal villages.[88] The expedition was a completely British affair but, as a courtesy, Michahelles was given advance knowledge of the details of the campaign.[89] On the same day that the British announced the beginning of their campaign in Wituland, Michahelles—the representative of the country on whose behalf it was being conducted—sailed back to Zanzibar, convinced that his presence in Wituland was superfluous, now that diplomacy had been abandoned.[90]

[85] Simons to Euan-Smith, 23 September 1890, in 'Correspondence respecting the Punitive Expedition against Witu of November 1890', BA Berlin R1001/8877, 86.

[86] Pigott to Euan-Smith, 29 September 1890, in 'Correspondence respecting the Punitive Expedition against Witu of November 1890', BA Berlin R1001/8877, 86.

[87] Michahelles to Caprivi, 2 November 1890, in BA Berlin, R1001/8876, 104–11. For the sanitized Reichstag version, see 160.

[88] British intelligence suggested that Fumo Bakari had asked for assistance from 'Mbaruk-bin-Rashid of Gazi, Salim-bin-Kamis of Takaungu, Sulieman-bin-Abdala of Mombrui, Dada Badada Galla, Avatula of Balo, Mze-bin-Saïf, and other Chiefs on the coast'. This was later modified by Euan-Smith: 'Suliman-bin-Abdullah has joined Fumo Bakari with 300 men, as has Avatula, chief of the Waboni…NO proof found of treasonous behaviour by Chiefs Salim-bin-Khamis or Mbaruk-bin-Rashid.' See Pigott to Euan-Smith, 21 September 1890; Euan-Smith to Salisbury, 30 October 1890, in 'Correspondence respecting the Punitive Expedition against Witu of November 1890', BA Berlin R1001/8877, 86.

[89] Michahelles to Caprivi, 18 October 1890, in BA Berlin R1001/959, 27–9.

[90] Michahelles to Caprivi, 2 November 1890, in BA Berlin R1001/959, 29–31.

After some light engagements en route, Witu was taken at 9 a.m. on 27 October by Fremantle's marines, Indian police troops, and (tellingly) forces provided by the Sultan of Zanzibar, the Lewali of Lamu, and the Lewali of Faza.[91] The one-sided nature of the campaign is revealed in the British report:

> The opposition was not vigorous, and the town was found to be evacuated. During the day the expedition was engaged in the work of thoroughly destroying the town and its defences. All the stone buildings and a large quantity of powder and ammunition were blown up, and the whole town utterly destroyed and burned to the ground…There were no lives lost on our side. The enemy's loss is estimated at between seventy and eighty killed and wounded.[92]

After the gifts given to Fumo Bakari by Kaiser Wilhelm II as a sign of his good faith had been retrieved from the sultan's palace, it was blown up, as was the armoury. The rest of the town was burnt to the ground. The destruction prompted Michahelles to criticize the British for displaying more interest in punishment than restoring security. Even Britain's Admiral Fremantle had his private doubts about a strategy that would intensify the hatred that locals felt towards Europeans—hardly the preconditions for successful future colonizing endeavours in the sultanate.[93] In a development not out of keeping with Britain's long-held views on the illegitimacy of the sultanate, the absolute destruction of its capital had been achieved.

With the news that Wituland had been cleared of forces loyal to the sultan, German colonial interests sought permission to be allowed back into the sultanate to continue their business. The British, however, declared the sultanate temporarily closed to Europeans on 6 November 1890.[94] When these German businesses sought compensation for the damage that the war against the sultan had done to their property, the British revived their earlier claim that, from a legal standpoint, the sultanate was still German at the time and that Germany and not Britain was liable for any losses they had incurred. When pressed, the British offered to make some confidential payments of up to £10,000 (which by March of 1891 had been reduced to £5,000), but insisted that these were *ex gratia* payments and represented neither an admission of liability nor a precedent for future claims.[95] A bounty of 10,000 rupees was also placed on Fumo Bakari's head by

---

[91] Fremantle, *The Navy As I Have Known It*, 378–9.

[92] Euan-Smith to Salisbury, 30 October 1890, in 'Correspondence respecting the Punitive Expedition against Witu of November 1890', BA Berlin R1001/8877, 86. For Fremantle's more detailed version of events, see Fremantle, *The Navy As I Have Known It*, 378–85.

[93] Michahelles to Caprivi, 2 November 1890, in BA Berlin, R1001/8876, 'Die Unternehmen Küntzel im Suaheli-Sultanat: Die Ermordung von Küntzel und Genossen', 104–11.

[94] Michahelles to Caprivi, 9 November 1890, in BA Berlin R1001/8877, 46.

[95] British Foreign Office to Hatzfeldt, May 1891, in BA Berlin R1001/1878, 'Die Unternehmen Küntzel im Suaheli-Sultanat. Die Ermordung von Küntzel und Genossen', 43; Hatzfeldt to Caprivi, 7

Fremantle for his role in the 'foul and shameful murders',[96] but by mid-January 1891, news had reached Europe that the Sultan of Wituland, hunted out of his kingdom, had died of a heart attack.[97] The British decided against a direct occupation of Wituland and instead looked to replace Fumo Bakari with a new, more pliable sultan.[98] A trial was also scheduled for twelve Africans suspected of being involved in the killings. Four of these trials were to take place under European 'supervision' to ensure a predetermined outcome, while the other eight were granted 'a fair and public trial...according to local law and custom'.[99]

Wituland and the Naval Question in the Reichstag

At the news that his April 1890 gifts to Fumo Bakari had been retrieved by the British, Kaiser Wilhelm II decided to give the sultan's rifle to Admiral Fremantle 'as a token of His Majesty's acknowledgement of the bravery displayed by the admiral and the troops under his command'.[100] Meanwhile, in London, wags joked that Salisbury had in effect become Germany's sergeant major.[101] Yet not all Germans were impressed by the way in which Germany had made itself so very obviously reliant upon the British navy to protect their interests in East Africa.

In the Reichstag, Chancellor Caprivi was closely questioned by the National Liberal deputy Dr Ludwig von Cuny on why the German Empire was unable to defend its own citizens abroad. Before the chancellor could respond, Cuny answered his own question, insisting that the problem was that Germany had no navy worth the name and that it had effectively outsourced its capacity to protect German citizens to Britain, whose navy had assisted the Germans not only in Wituland but elsewhere. Although Germany rightly cherished its friendship with

December 1890, in BA Berlin R1001/8877, 57–8. A formal public declaration of the transfer of sovereignty from Germany to Britain was made on 25 November 1890 in the *London Gazette*. See BA Berlin R1001/8872, 'Wituland', 8.

[96] Michahelles to German Foreign Office, 26 October 1890, 29 October 1890; Michahelles to Caprivi, 2 November 1890, in BA Berlin R1001/959, 23–4, 29–31; Hatzfeldt to Caprivi, 7 March 1891, in BA Berlin R1001/8877, 168; Michahelles to Caprivi, 2 November 1890, in BA Berlin R1001/8876, 122. For the detailed British account of the expedition, see Edmund Fremantle, *London Gazette*, 6 January 1891, 71–103, which makes no mention of the arrival and departure of Michahelles and the *Schwalbe*. Only the assistance of Meuschel and Häßler (both from Küntzel's original enterprise) were noted.

[97] 'East Africa', *The Times*, 19 January 1891, in BA Berlin R1001/8872, 'Wituland', 12; Redwitz to Caprivi, 3 February 1891, in BA Berlin R1001/8877, 153.

[98] Hatzfeldt to Caprivi, 7 December 1890, in BA Berlin, R1001/8877, 57–8.

[99] Malet to Marschall, 3 April 1891, in BA Berlin R1001/1878, 23–6.

[100] German Foreign Office to Malet, 3 January 1891, in BA Berlin R1001/8877, 72; Fremantle, *The Navy As I Have Known It*, 385. The looted rifle is held by the Royal Museum in Greenwich, while Fumo Bakari's looted throne is now held in the British Museum. See https://www.rmg.co.uk/collections/objects/rmgc-object-2539 and https://www.britishmuseum.org/collection/object/E_Af1992-05-1 (accessed 15 October 2021).

[101] Fremantle, *The Navy As I Have Known It*, 386.

Britain, Cuny continued, he believed he spoke for his political allies when he said that 'our wish is that German interests and German property be protected by German ships.' Without an effective German navy, the empire's citizens would be greatly disadvantaged abroad by the preponderance of the British on the world's oceans. This had already happened in Africa, Cuny maintained, where a blockade ostensibly aimed at ending the slave trade had in fact impeded Germans trying to enter an African port. Two years ago, Cuny continued, he had successfully argued for a proposal requesting that the government 'protect and seek compensation for German citizens overseas'—specifically for those who had been disadvantaged by British pre-eminence. Now that Germany had (mistakenly, to his mind) ceded sovereignty of Wituland to Britain in exchange for Heligoland, the need for a strong, globally competent German navy was even greater.[102] Critics such as Cuny who wished to see Germany's navy increase its global reach and shrug off its reliance on Britain were infuriated by Caprivi's seemingly tepid colonial engagement.

It is unsurprising that a National Liberal like Cuny would express himself so vehemently in favour of both German colonial endeavours in Africa and the need for the German navy to act to protect them. Since the 1840s, Germany's national-ist liberals had seen the combination of colonialism and naval power as central to Germany's attempts to globalize its economy, settle its people outside Europe, and move towards an economy built on trade and manufacturing rather than agriculture.[103] Much of this past history of liberal enthusiasm for a naval empire has been obscured, however, by the strong tendency to view the genesis of the German fleet as lying with the strong intervention of the Kaiser and the single-minded determination of his naval secretary, Alfred von Tirpitz.[104] The National Liberal disappointment at Germany's inability to play a meaningful role in the punitive naval expedition to Witu is a further illustration of the fact that Wilhelm II was but an enthusiastic latecomer to a half-century-old movement.[105]

For his part, Caprivi was very careful in his Reichstag discussion of the events in Witu. Unwilling to concede that the Heligoland-Zanzibar Agreement had played any role, he laid the lion's share of the blame on Küntzel. Over two days he gave the Reichstag a frank assessment of Küntzel's violent past and argued that, given Küntzel's temperament, the killing of him and his party would have in all likelihood occurred irrespective of whether Witu was a British or German pro-tectorate. He also conceded Cuny's point that Germany was simply not in a

---

[102] Ludwig von Cuny, 6 February 1891, *Verhandlungen des Reichstages*, 1352–3.

[103] Matthew P. Fitzpatrick, *Liberal Imperialism in Germany* (New York: Berghahn, 2008).

[104] Michael Epkenhans, *Tirpitz: Architect of the German High Seas Fleet*, (Washington DC: Potomac, 2008); Volker Berghahn, *Der Tirpitz-Plan: Genesis und Verfall einer innenpolitischen Krisenstrategie*. (Düsseldorf: Droste Verlag, 1971).

[105] Walter Nuhn, *Kolonialpolitik und Marine: Die Rolle der Kaiserlichen Marine bei der Gründung und Sicherung des deutschen Kolonialreiches 1884–1914* (Bonn: Bernard & Graefe Verlag, 2002).

position to respond in the way the British had, seeking to turn this reality into a blessing in disguise:

> Were we in the position to bring together such an expedition for the sake of a German, we would have needed resources of about the same scope as the concentration of ships off Zanzibar in 1885. By dint of the great number of ships the English have, just one of their numerous stations on different coasts has around as many ships as we have cruisers in service in the entire world. Consequently, had we had to bring together a landing party of nine hundred men, we would have had to bring together seven or eight cruisers. That means taking cruisers away from other stations, which would have taken an inordinate amount of time and led to a not inconsiderable expense... I mean to say, that is, that even from a purely financial perspective, history shows that we were correct [to give up Witu], because it shows just how expensive possessing an absolutely worthless land can be.[106]

Here Caprivi tried to lower the expectations that many had of Germany's navy, giving voice to his scepticism of naval colonialism and deflecting criticism of his 'new course'. The fledgling chancellor, whose foreign policy apparently followed the dictum that 'early next year there will be a two-front war' in Europe,[107] had tried as head of the Admiralty to curb the enthusiastic globalism that had characterized naval thinking in Germany when Albrecht von Stosch had been chief of the Imperial Admiralty. As Alfred von Tirpitz would later recollect, Stosch had been a fervent believer in the need for German colonies since the 1870s and had seen the navy as integral to Germany's attempts to catch up with the other global empires of Europe.[108] Under him, the navy had been calibrated to 'reinforce and protect Germandom and German endeavours in the world'.[109] Consequently, the navy had supported German *Weltpolitik* with its frigates and corvettes that rushed around the globe as a 'colonial police', or rather a 'global fire brigade', putting out the small spot fires sparked by empire.[110] Caprivi, on the other hand, believed that the navy was simply too overstretched for the kind of decisive global presence that Stosch, Cuny, and other pro-colonial figures desired, and under him the German navy was pushed to concentrate primarily on coastal defence.[111] As chancellor, Caprivi saw his task as being to maintain a navy that could successfully engage with proximate regional threats while also maintaining a

---

[106] Caprivi, 5–6 February 1891, *Verhandlungen des Reichstages*, 1331, 1355.

[107] Alfred von Tirpitz, *Erinnerungen*, (Leipzig: Koehler Verlag, 1919) 23, 26.

[108] Tirpitz, *Erinnerungen*, 21–2.   [109] Tirpitz, *Erinnerungen*, 12–14.

[110] Heiko Herold, *Reichsgewalt bedeutet Seegewalt: Die Kreuzergeschwader der Kaiserlichen Marine als Instrument der deutschen Kolonial- und Weltpolitik 1885 bis 1901*, (Munich: Oldenbourg Verlag, 2013), 7.

[111] Tirpitz, *Erinnerungen*, 12–14; Ernst zu Reventlow, *Deutschland zur See: Ein Buch von der deutschen Kriegsflotte*, (Berlin: Springer, 1914), 64–78.

credible but thinner global presence that would lend only modest assistance to *Auslandsdeutsche*.[112]

On Cuny's broader question of the capacity of Germany's navy to be called into action to support German interests and German citizens abroad, Caprivi freely conceded that it was currently impossible for the German navy to undertake the kind of global actions that the British navy could. If German ships could not respond to crises involving Germans all around the world, Caprivi admitted, it was because 'not enough German ships are stationed abroad to be there in time whenever disturbances break out and German interests might be damaged'. Caprivi pointed out that sending a German warship to a colonial trouble spot would mean taking it from their station elsewhere and leaving other colonies undefended. Additionally, had the German government decided to order a ship to attend an emergency, the delay in their arrival would doubtless be considerable, because 'the telegraph doesn't extend to everywhere'. It was pointless, Caprivi reasoned, to send German ships to places that had probably long ago returned to order. Far better to have German interests defended quickly by another imperial power on the spot, namely Britain.[113] Accordingly, Caprivi shaped his recount of the Küntzel killings to try and convince the Reichstag that the Anglo-German Agreement had made good financial and strategic sense. It had, he argued, already saved considerable German expense on a naval expedition to Wituland, and it would continue to make even more sense in the future as it secured a better relationship between Britain and Germany.

For liberal naval enthusiasts such as Cuny, however, Caprivi's description of the German position in East Africa did not offer any real justification for capitulating to the British in East Africa. Rather, it seemed to underline the need for a larger, more globally active navy. It was along these lines that the Reichstag deputy (and Vice President of the Pan-German League) Traugott Hermann von Arnim-Muskau argued against reliance on the British navy. Caprivi's imperial accountancy, he maintained, did not consider the possibility that, had Germany been in a position to lead a punitive expedition against the Sultan of Witu, Germany could then have placed the sultanate under direct German rule, just as Britain had done in Egypt. According to Arnim, this would have offered Germany a stepping stone for control not only of the East African coastline but also of the 'inner coastline of East Africa' and the Central African caravan routes, through the establishment of a series of stations in Central Africa in places such as Nyanza. For such enterprises, he argued, more—not less—colonial expenditure was required.[114]

---

[112] David H Olivier, *German Naval Strategy 1856–1888: Foreunners of Tirpitz*, (London: Frank Cass, 2004), 153–83.

[113] Leo von Caprivi, 6 February 1891, *Verhandlungen des Reichstages*, 1354–5.

[114] Traugott Hermann von Arnim-Muskau, 6 February 1891, *Verhandlungen des Reichstages*, 1362–3.

The protests of empire-minded Germans against the Anglo-German Agreement and its disregard for the sovereign rights of the sultan, as well as Germany's abdication of responsibility in Wituland and in naval affairs in East Africa more generally came too late for Fumo Bakari. Predictably, the British did not allow their newly chosen Sultan of Wituland any real independence, and in 1894 the British simply placed their newly acquired sultanate under the administration of the Sultan of Zanzibar, with a British officer acting as resident there.[115]

This final betrayal of Wituland's independence and of its dead sultan, hailed by pro-colonial Germans as 'this loyal colonial friend, this enthusiastic supporter of Germany',[116] and the betrayal of Wituland's original trust in Germany to protect it from the predations of its larger and more powerful neighbour were sharply criticized in the Reichstag. Once again it was the pan-German deputy Arnim who bemoaned the fact that 'sovereignty has been transferred to the Sultan of Zanzibar, and the Sultan of Witu has now been taken as a prisoner to Zanzibar.'[117] Arnim's regret might have been heartfelt, but it was also an expression of the frustration of colonially minded Germans who regretted that Fumo Bakari, an amenable African monarch loyal to the German emperor who saw it as his responsibility to help German traders and settlers, no longer ruled. With the loss of the Sultanate of Wituland, Germany had lost a potentially lucrative foothold facilitating further economic penetration of East and Central Africa.

The sudden abandonment of Fumo Bakari by the Germans in favour of closer treaty ties with Britain and the subsequent destruction of Witu by the British illustrate how the conditions informing the carefully calibrated decisions made by monarchs in Africa and elsewhere to enter into treaty or protectorate arrangements with Europeans could be undone by rapid changes in those conditions. The sovereign agency of the Sultan of Wituland existed in a geostrategic microclimate that was destroyed surprisingly quickly by imperial exigencies emanating from elsewhere. Given the threat posed by British-supported Zanzibar, the sultans of Wituland had little alternative but to embrace a large power such as Germany that had the capability to deter the immediate threat of their neighbour's predations. Ultimately, however, this alliance only deferred rather than averted the absorption of the sultanate into British-held territory.

---

[115] Hardinge, 'Legislative Methods in the Zanzibar and East African Protectorates', 3.
[116] Arnim, 18 March 1895, *Verhandlungen des Reichstages*, 1565–6.
[117] Arnim, 18 March 1895, *Verhandlungen des Reichstages*, 1565–6.

9

Paramountcy in German South West Africa

According to one account, upon learning that the wife of Germany's Crown Prince Friedrich was a daughter of Britain's Queen Victoria, the Paramount Leader of the Herero, Samuel Maharero, expressed the wish that he too should one day be married to one of the queen's daughters. After all, he explained to a missionary, as the ruler of Hereroland he should be held in the same esteem as Queen Victoria.[1]

Immediately prior to 1904, Samuel Maharero's position in South West Africa was indeed comparable to that of a monarch. As later oral testimony recalled, Maharero 'was actually what people called a king, the king of all Herero speaking people in South West Africa'.[2] Despite this elevated position, however, at no time did Maharero enjoy the same esteem as the royal heads of Europe (or indeed Asia or other African royals) in the eyes of Germans in the colony or in Berlin. Rather, his reign was both contested by his own people and treated by Germans colonial authorities as a means to a colonizing end.

Against the backdrop of the uneasy relations between the representatives of the German Empire and the two dominant paramount leaders in South West Africa prior to the wars of 1904, namely Samuel Maharero and the Paramount Chief of the Nama, Hendrik Witbooi, this chapter examines the extent to which the Paramount Leaders of the Herero and Nama were able to insinuate their own priorities and those of their people into the metropolitan project of rule in Germany's only settler colony.[3]

German 'Protection' and the Herero

When the Germans formally assumed control over South West Africa in the mid-1880s, the position of Paramount Leader of the Herero was still a relatively

---

[1] Hedwig Irle, *Unsere schwarzen Landsleute in Deutsch-Südwestafrika* (Gütersloh: C. Bertelsmann, 1911), 18–19.

[2] Kaputu, quoted in Gerhard Pool, *Samuel Maharero* (Windhoek: Macmillan, 1991), 338.

[3] On settler colonialism, see, e.g., Patrick Wolfe, 'Settler Colonialism and the Elimination of the Native', *Journal of Genocide Research* 8, no. 4 (2006), 387–409; Corey Snelgrove, Rita Kaur Dhamoon, and Jeff Corntassel, 'Unsettling Settler Colonialism: The Discourse and Politics of Settlers, and Solidarity with Indigenous Nations', *Decolonization, Indigeneity, Education and Society* 3, no. 2 (2014), 1–32.

The Kaiser and the Colonies: Monarchy in the Age of Empire. Matthew P. Fitzpatrick, Oxford University Press.
© Matthew P. Fitzpatrick 2022. DOI: 10.1093/oso/9780192897039.003.0010

new one. The transformation of the position from short-term wartime exigency to that of a continuous peacetime ruler was largely a product of political developments during the period of Samuel Maharero's grandfather Tjamuaha and, in particular, that of his father Maharero Tjamuaha. Primary amongst the new imperatives driving change was the need to develop a means for the various Herero *otuzo* (patrilineal clans) to deal effectively with the representatives of European companies and states. With Herero loyalties split by a succession crisis after Maharero Tjamuaha's death in 1890, the survival of the paramountcy as an institution was far from assured.[4] In the context of an ever-growing German presence, however, the strategic support lent by the German colonial authorities helped secure the paramountcy as a position of continued importance. For German governors, dealing with a single paramount leader of the Herero was seen as far more expeditious than attempting to deal with the numerous, largely autonomous leaders whose voices competed in the *otuzo* system.[5] Not only was it preferable for the Germans to have a single leader with whom they could do business, but it was also preferable for that leader to be reliably pro-German.

Prior to his death, and in his capacity as paramount leader, Samuel Maharero's father Maharero Tjamuaha had signed a protection treaty on behalf of the Herero with Imperial Commissioner Dr Heinrich Göring on 21 October 1885.[6] The terms of the treaty promised the German emperor's protection for the paramount leader's people in return for a promise that the Herero would not cede their lands to any other European power and that they would respect the lives and property of Germans within their territory. While the Herero would have jurisdiction over their own internal legal affairs, the Germans would be free to establish their own legal system. The paramount Herero leader was also obliged to maintain the peace in his lands on behalf of the Germans.[7]

While the precise extent of what had been conceded by the Herero and what the emperor's protection amounted to were the cause of ongoing Herero grievances with the German state, the treaty was taken seriously by Maharero Tjamuaha. It was not the case that African nations like the Herero were unaware of the implications of the treaties that were offered to them. In fact, in some ways the Herero took the treaty's terms more seriously than the Europeans who offered them did. The treaty was, for Maharero Tjamuaha, a carefully considered arrangement that traded a portion of the sovereignty of his people for the promise

[4] Jan-Bart Gewald, *Herero Heroes: A Socio-Political History of the Herero of Namibia 1890–1923* (Oxford: James Currey, 1999), 28, 49.

[5] F. Rudolf Lehmann, 'Die Häuptlings-Erbfolgeordnung der Herero', *Zeitschrift für Ethnologie* 76, no. 1 (1951), 98–9; Ngungaa Hangara, *Otuzo twOvaherero* (Windhoek: University of Namibia Press, 2017), v.

[6] For copies of the treaties signed in South West Africa, see 'Denkschrift über Eingeborenen-Politik und Hereroaufstand in Deutsch-Südwestafrica', in BA Berlin R1001/2117, 'Aufstand der Hereros 1904–1907', 7.

[7] Pool, *Samuel Maharero*, 67–71.

of the protection of the German emperor against the Herero's more proximate foes, namely the Nama and their paramount leader, Hendrik Witbooi, who had gone to war after the Herero had massacred some of his people (including two of his sons) in an ambush, despite assurances of safe passage, while they were travelling through Hereroland during peacetime in 1885.[8] Given that Hendrik Witbooi (who refused to sign a treaty with the Germans) was still able to attack the Herero with impunity despite the treaty's promise of protection, Maharero Tjamuaha became increasingly convinced that the German emperor and the small population of Germans in his territory had failed to live up to their agreed obligations. Accordingly, Maharero Tjamuaha declared the seemingly worthless 'protection' treaty null and void in 1888. With the Germans not living up to his expectations, Maharero Tjamuaha now saw the treaty as 'just a piece of paper' that clearly did not offer his people the protection it purported to guarantee.[9] Thereafter, Maharero Tjamuaha looked, via the English trader Robert Lewis, to the British for a more satisfactory protection treaty just months after Wilhelm II acceded to the throne.[10] Having failed to live up to the expectations of the Herero, German officials were unceremoniously bundled out of Hereroland and the German presence there was reduced to a few missionaries.[11]

The German response to this challenge to their colonizing endeavours was to send out a small contingent of twenty-one soldiers to the region in 1889, led by Captain Curt von François. François's instructions made clear that he was not there to fight the Herero, but rather to arrest the presumed British go-between Robert Lewis.[12] The pitifully small band of German troops was safely ignored by the Herero as a minor inconvenience until they managed to establish a munitions blockade over an arterial trade route just as the Herero were once again weakened by their ongoing conflict with Witbooi. With the military situation against the Nama becoming desperate by virtue of the nuisance blockade of his supply lines, Maharero Tjamuaha was hastily forced to come to terms with the Germans.[13]

The war against Witbooi was still raging when Maharero Tjamuaha died in October 1890. Following the intercession of his mother Katare, Samuel Maharero sought to follow his father into the paramountcy. In the process he sought to sideline the more popular heir apparent, Nicodemus Kavikunua, and another

---

[8] Witbooi believed that Samuel Maharero had led the ambush. See Witbooi to the English in Walvis Bay, 4 August 1892, in Hendrik Witbooi, *Afrika den Afrikanern! Aufzeichnungen eines Nama-Häuptlings aus der Zeit der deutschen Eroberung Südwestafrikas 1884 bis 1894*, ed. Wolfgang Reinhard (Berlin: Dietz Verlag, 1982), 145–6, Gewald, *Herero Heroes*, 50–1.

[9] Matthias Häußler, 'Warum die Herero mit den Deutschen kooperierten: Zur "Pazifierung" einer akephalen Gesellschaft', *Mittelweg 36* 24, no. 4 (2015), 89–90.

[10] Pool, *Samuel Maharero*, 71–3.

[11] Curt von François, *Deutsch Südwest-Afrika: Geschichte der Kolonisation bis zum Ausbruch des Krieges mit Witbooi April 1893* (Berlin: Dietrich Reimer, 1899), 27–30; Gewald, *Herero Heroes*, 32–5.

[12] François, *Deutsch Südwest-Afrika*, 35.

[13] Gewald, *Herero Heroes*, 34–7; François, *Deutsch Südwest-Afrika*, 50–5.

popular Herero notable, Assa Riarua.[14] This intra-family coup severely dented Samuel Maharero's authority among the Herero, the majority of whom wanted Nicodemus to become their paramount ruler in accordance with Herero law.[15] A concerted letter-writing campaign by Samuel Maharero aimed at Curt von François sought to persuade the Germans that, under the European practice of primogeniture, he had the strongest claim to the paramountcy as the eldest son of the deceased Maharero Tjamuaha. The tactic did not fool François, however, who informed Chancellor Caprivi in February 1891 that, according to local practices, Nicodemus was in fact the 'rightful ruler'.[16] Nevertheless, this acknowledgement did nothing to guide German attitudes on the question of succession in practice, and German support for Samuel Maharero was soon forthcoming.

Although François saw it as beneath his dignity to go and speak to Samuel Maharero personally, he sent his brother Lieutenant Hugo von François to meet with him on 3 August 1891. At the meeting, Samuel Maharero complained that his role as paramount leader had not been recognized by several other Herero notables, including 'Manasse from Omaruru, Zacharias, Nikodemus, and Kambasesembi'. Consequently, he asked for an explicit statement from the Germans confirming their recognition of his status in return for a commitment to keep order in Hereroland. This formal recognition was duly given at the meeting.[17] According to (now Imperial Commissioner) François, as a result of this German intervention, 'From this day on Samuel Maharero was recognized by the Herero as paramount chief'.[18] As Jan-Bart Gewald has argued, however, German recognition did not simply translate into automatic acceptance of Maharero's paramountcy by other Herero notables. Indeed, the German support that Samuel Maharero had sought and gained was not intended by him to resolve the matter definitively, but rather was a strategic step aimed at leveraging this external German support for domestic, intra-Herero purposes.[19]

The course of the succession dispute and Samuel Maharero's gradual shift towards an accommodation with the Germans had also been shaped by the ongoing war against Hendrik Witbooi.[20] With Herero lands still coming under attack, Herero leaders (including Maharero Tjamuaha just prior to his death) had sought reassurances from the Germans in May 1890 that if they reinstated the protection treaty, they would be protected from Witbooi's attack. Heinrich Göring assured them that they would be, before leaving Africa for a new position as

---

[14] Lehmann, 'Die Häuptlings-Erbfolgeordnung der Herero', 95–100. The most detailed treatments of the succession dispute are Gewald, *Herero Heroes*, 41–60, and Pool, *Samuel Maharero*, 84–96.

[15] Kaputu, quoted in Pool, *Samuel Maharero*, 342.

[16] François to Caprivi, 10 February 1891, in BA Berlin R1001/2100, 'Das Herero-Land', 70.

[17] Lehmann, 'Die Häuptlings-Erbfolgeordnung der Herero', 100; François, *Deutsch Südwest-Afrika*, 147; Gewald, *Herero Heroes*, 45–6.

[18] François, *Deutsch Südwest-Afrika*, 147.   [19] Gewald, *Herero Heroes*, 30.

[20] Witbooi to the British in Walvis Bay, 4 August 1892, in Witbooi, *Afrika den Afrikanern*, 145–6, Gewald, *Herero Heroes*, 50–1.

German consul in Haiti.[21] Once again, the Herero placed themselves under German protection.

In a letter, Witbooi reproached Maharero Tjamuaha for having done so, warning that the Herero had abandoned their sovereign rights in the vain hope that the untrustworthy Germans would help them:

> But dear Captain! You have accepted another government, and submitted yourself to that government, to be protected by a human government, from all dangers, the first and the nearest, against me, in this war...It appears to me, you did not consider enough what the implications were on your side, for your country, your people, and your descendants, and also not for your leadership rights, and you believe that you will retain all these things of your independent leadership, after you have destroyed me, if you succeed, as you believe you will, but dear captain! It will eventually cause you much remorse, and you shall eternally bear remorse, for having placed your land and government into the hands of the white people.[22]

Witbooi was correct. When he attacked one month later, the Germans withheld military assistance from the Herero, opting instead for a munitions embargo on the Nama. This measure proved ineffective, and the Nama drove the hapless Maharero back.[23] Not only did the Germans decide to remain aloof from 'native affairs' in contravention of their assurances; when the Herero and their herds vacated southern Hereroland in an attempt to escape the Nama the German authorities promptly helped European settlers move into the territory, some of which was sold to the authorities by an increasingly impoverished Samuel Maharero.[24] To add insult to injury, Windhoek was taken from the Herero and was converted into a German town. Upon being told about it by Hugo von François, Samuel Maharero protested vehemently, 'Why have you come into our country? You promised us protection against Hendrik Witbooi! Where is this protection? If you won't protect us, we don't need you!'[25] The anger displayed by Samuel Maharero in his exchange with the Germans led First Lieutenant Franz Josef von Bülow to reflect on the broader rights and wrongs of German colonization in South West Africa:

> I cannot say that I took away a comfortable impression from this discussion. I was plagued by the feeling that our presence in the protectorate had begun either with a lie, false impressions, or a broken promise. Or that for some other

[21] Gewald, *Herero Heroes*, 39–40.

[22] Witbooi to Maharero Tjamuaha, 30 May 1890, as translated by Gewald in, *Herero Heroes*, 39–40.

[23] François, *Deutsch Südwest-Afrika*, 148–50.   [24] Gewald, *Herero Heroes*, 40, 47–8.

[25] Franz Josef von Bülow, *Drei Jahre im Lande Hendrik Witbois: Schilderungen von Land und Leuten* (Berlin: Ernst Siegfried Mittler & Sohn, 1896), 124.

reason we were wrongfully there, that we had not been a blessing to these people so far, and that we would never be one.[26]

In an even greater betrayal, Herero troops retiring from the battlefield where they had fought the Nama were attacked by their supposed protectors, the Germans, in April 1892, less than a year after they had declared Samuel Maharero to be the legitimate leader of the Herero.[27] This incident, coupled with the seizure of Windhoek as a German centre, prompted a disillusioned Samuel Maharero to write a personal letter of complaint to Kaiser Wilhelm II, giving the names of the German killers and demanding action. Repudiating German claims of friendship and protection for the Herero, Samuel Maharero wrote that he now saw that 'the friendship that my father first heard about was no friendship but my father's and my death.' Samuel Maharero also asked Wilhelm II to write to him and tell him whether he had ordered the Germans to attack him and his people:

> I ask with my whole heart, that you, most noble Kaiser Wilhelm II receive and read well my letter of today, and that you answer me clearly, whether Your Majesty gave the people in Windhoek the right to murder me and to use every means to oppress me.

Summing up his mistreatment, he asked the emperor rhetorically, 'Is that friendship? I do not understand it.' Wilhelm II, he concluded, should not allow him to be treated so poorly 'out of friendship, as the people say; otherwise it will kill me'.[28] The letter never reached the palace, with the German Colonial Office instructing Governor François to respond.[29]

Months later, after years of warfare, during which time the Herero succession dispute had rumbled on, Witbooi saw an opportunity to weaken Herero solidarity by exploiting the dissension in Herero ranks between pro-Nicodemus and pro-Maharero forces. Writing to Maharero, Witbooi offered a ceasefire while he went to war with the pro-Nicodemus Eastern Herero.[30] Superficially the offer had its attractions, offering Maharero both peace with his most dangerous external enemy and the potential defeat of a Herero rival who rejected his dubious claim to the paramountcy. In addition, a united front with Witbooi offered the possibility of concerted action against the Germans.

Maharero was, nonetheless, firm in his response, claiming that he would not sue for peace and that he was prepared for war, understanding that having his

---

[26] Bülow, *Drei Jahre im Lande Hendrik Witboois*, 125.   [27] Gewald, *Herero Heroes*, 53.
[28] Samuel Maharero to Wilhelm II, 19 March 1893, in BA Berlin R1001/2081, 'Allgemeine Angelegenheiten in Deutsch-Südwestafrika', 82–5.
[29] Colonial Office to François, 12 June 1893, in BA Berlin R1001/2081, 86.
[30] Witbooi to Maharero, 13 June 1892, in Witbooi, *Afrika den Afrikanern!*, 136.

internal enemies defeated by the Nama would only leave him isolated should Witbooi come after him later:

> I also want to mention the war that you intend to wage against Nicodemus and Kahimemua and your view that I should not be influenced by it and that I should conclude peace with you...If you want to kill Nicodemus, that is for our people as if you are killing my brother. If you kill Kahimemua, it is as if you were killing myself, because he belongs to our people...Did you think that you would have a better chance to kill me if I was alone with my tribe?[31]

Witbooi's peace offer might have been designed to divide and conquer, but he was also conscious that he too was negotiating from an increasingly weak position. The German arms embargo, which initially had done little to stop the rout of the Herero at Nama hands, was now beginning to bite. Further, with a greater German military presence in the region, Witbooi was compelled to look for other avenues to conclude a peace with the Herero. This time, he met with some success. Witbooi was not the only one who recognized the weakness of his position. Governor François, apparently alarmed by the prospect of the two largest nations of South West Africa concluding a separate peace, now attempted to convince Maharero that the time was ripe for the Germans to join the Herero in a joint military campaign against the Nama. Instead, peace between Maharero and Witbooi was reached in November 1892.[32] While the peace terms did not include a formal alliance of the Herero and the Nama against the Germans,[33] it was with Witbooi now his ally that Maharero had felt sufficiently emboldened to write his March 1893 letter complaining about the treacherous conduct of the Germans directly to the German emperor.

The Challenge of Hendrik Witbooi

Witbooi had not only been a complicating factor for Maharero. For Governor François, Witbooi represented a serious military threat to German colonization. While Witbooi was engaged in a full-scale war with Maharero, François was relatively well insulated against the possibility of an attack by the Nama. With the Herero and Nama now at peace, François took seriously the report of the Rhenish missionary Heidmann, who had written that the weapons prohibition on Africans had stirred up anti-German sentiment and that 'Hendrik Witbooi is making use of this and is seeking via peace with the Herero to bring about an alliance with the

---

[31] Maharero to Witbooi, 28 July 1892, in Witbooi, *Afrika den Afrikanern!*, 138–40.
[32] François, *Deutsch Südwest-Afrika*, 155–6.   [33] Witbooi, *Afrika den Afrikanern!*, 148–70.

goal of resistance against the government.'[34] The missionary's report, François wrote, was in accordance with his own understanding of the situation and expectations of the future. He was already concerned about the future effects of his intended declaration that land disputed by the Herero and Nama would henceforth be deemed Crown land.[35] The peace between the Herero and the Nama would exacerbate the threat of any further moves in this direction. 'Now that the natives were no longer distracted by war, they could translate into action the sum of their thoughts about the dangers posed by the infiltration of the whites into their lands.'[36]

For his part, Witbooi had written to the British in South Africa in August 1892 to formally lodge his view that the Berlin Africa Conference of the mid-1880s guaranteed no paramount African leader would be forced to accept a protection treaty against their will. He also gave voice to his fears about the Germans' intentions regarding him and his people. 'They have undertaken to destroy me in battle', he complained, 'although I have no idea of what I am supposed to be guilty.' For the Nama, the Germans' colonizing conduct was intolerable and dishonoured their own 'protection' treaties:

> The Germans tell the captains that they will protect them from other powerful nations that would come into this land and use violence to take away from the chiefs their territory and power. The Germans, that is, claim to protect the captains from unjust and ignorant people that would strip the captains of this land of their territory and power without permission. Things appear to me, however, to be quite different. After what I have seen and heard since the Germans have arrived, it appears to me that the Germans want to be the powerful ones themselves, who come into our lands like the supposed 'others'. They come here with their tasks, rule in accordance with their laws without asking about rights or truth, without obtaining permission from the captains, and impose laws on our land at their discretion that are simply impossible, unworkable, and unacceptable.[37]

When 216 German reinforcements arrived in Walvis Bay on 21 March 1893,[38] François seized his opportunity. There were no orders from Berlin that explicitly ruled out war with Africans in the protectorate, he reasoned, and 'to bring to the natives an understanding of [German] rule and to consolidate that rule, they first had to be shown that the German Empire had the power to do it and that it would use that power.'[39] Unable to extract compliance from Witbooi through negotiations and concerned about the prospects of a united front of Nama and

---

[34] Heidmann, as quoted by François in François, *Deutsch Südwest-Afrika*, 160.
[35] François, *Deutsch Südwest-Afrika*, 132.   [36] François, *Deutsch Südwest-Afrika*, 160–1.
[37] Witbooi to the British in Walvis Bay, 4 August 1892, in Witbooi, *Afrika den Afrikanern!*, 142–3.
[38] François, *Deutsch Südwest-Afrika*, 164–5.   [39] François, *Deutsch Südwest-Afrika*, 167.

Herero, Curt von François made a decision on 6 April 1893 'to launch an attack against Witbooi as soon as possible'.[40] In accordance with this decision, on 12 April 1893, François took 250 soldiers and brutally massacred dozens of Nama men, women, and children in a surprise dawn attack on Hornkranz.[41]

The first report reaching the German Foreign Office stated that eighty Nama had been killed and 100 had been wounded (with one German soldier killed and another wounded),[42] while *The Times* in London reported that 'upwards of 70 women, ten men and boys and some infants' were killed for the loss of one German soldier.[43] A later letter from a German soldier taking part in the action reported the dead from the raid as forty-eight men, sixty women, and fifteen children.[44] The *Frankfurter Zeitung* quoted British sources on the atrocity to argue that the killing of so many unarmed women and children could only strengthen those voices who condemned 'colonization by gunpowder and lead', and explicitly cast doubts on François's capacity to bring peace to the colony,[45] while the *Vossische Zeitung* falsely claimed that the attack was a necessary step to protect the German-friendly Herero (despite the fact that Witbooi and Mahrero were then at peace).[46] For its part, the English-language *Cape Times* forthrightly called François's assault 'the Massacre at Hornkrantz' and published chilling eyewitness details:

The manner in which Horncrantz was taken has fortunately few parallels even in the guerrilla warfare of South Africa... The attack on Horncrantz was made at dawn, and Witbooi and his men being unarmed fled. They left behind them the old men, the women, and the children thinking that these would at least be spared. But they reckoned without their enemies. The German troops shot the old men, the women, and the children down like vermin, and before the disgraceful carnage ended eight old men and 78 women and children had been blown literally to pieces. The ferocity of the soldiery was terrible... Infants were shot from their mothers' breasts, and bodies were roasted; in one case a group of women huddled together when a squad of German soldiers advanced to within three paces and then deliberately shot all of them dead. In another case a woman

[40] François, *Deutsch Südwest-Afrika*, 170.

[41] Leutwein, *Elf Jahre Gouverneur*, 15; Adam A. Blackler, 'From Boondoggle to Settlement Colony: Hendrik Witbooi and the Evolution of Germany's Imperial Project in Southwest Africa, 1884–1894', *Central European History* 50 (2017), 464–7; Gewald, *Herero Heroes*, 54.

[42] Telegram to German Foreign Office, 15 May 1893, in BA Berlin R1001/1483, 'Militärisches Einschreiten der Schutztruppe', 9.

[43] 'Damaraland', *The Times*, 16 May 1893, 5.

[44] 'Afrika', *Kölnische Zeitung*, 16 June 1893, in BA Berlin R1001/1483, 84.

[45] *Frankfurter Zeitung*, 16 May 1893; *Frankfurter Zeitung*, 18 May 1893, in BA Berlin R1001/1483, 18, 24.

[46] *Vossische Zeitung*, 16 May 1893, in BA Berlin R1001/1483, 19.

was killed, and her child, witnessing the occurrence, ran towards the body, but the soldiers blew the child's head off as it was running along.[47]

Witbooi's own account, as well as those of his messengers to the British in South Africa, captured similar details of the massacre, verifying the newspaper reports of the time:

> I did not think that so great a power in men and ammunition and so mighty a man and so great a man and also a captain of a civilized power would make war with such small disesteemed people as mine. To steal upon me in my sleep. The little children and women and men he has murdered. Some of the people he shot he burnt the dead bodies of. So did the Captain destroy my werf. I could not think this of a white man. He killed 10 of my men and 75 women and children...thus have the Germans shed much innocent blood of women and children, and he says that he will not stop until my death.[48]

Instead of exploiting the German atrocity to demonstrate the superiority of British colonialism, the British aided the German cover-up, warning the Nama not to publicize the 'indiscriminate slaughter' they had survived, as 'the story of the women killing would excite indignation among all civilized people'. Warning too against reprisals against civilians, the British insisted of the Nama that 'They must in no wise blame the German people for what had taken place. That the guilt, if guilt there were, rested alone with the individual perpetrators of the massacre'. The Nama agreed not to attack civilians, but expressed their determination to wage war against François and his army. In light of the massacre, the Nama messengers vowed to the British that 'they would fight it out to the end, as it would be better to die with their guns in their hands than submit to be put to death in cold blood'.[49]

In the wake of the massacre, the tension between François and his subordinate Bülow became increasingly pronounced. Bülow's verdict on the efficacy of François's campaign against Witbooi was caustic:

---

[47] 'Massacre at Horncrantz: German Troops Butcher Women and Children', *Cape Times*, 22 May 1893, in BA Berlin R1001/1483, 79. See also the relay of this report to settler colonial Australia: 'Massacre at Horncrantz', *Newcastle Morning Herald and Miners' Advocate*, 24 June 1893, 12. The Colonial Office sought to discredit reports of 'supposed transgressions against the Hottentots' as 'greatly exaggerated'. See Colonial Office to Bray, 18 June 1893; Bray to Caprivi, 27 June 1893, in R1001/2081, 87–90.

[48] Witbooi to Cleverly, 20 April 1893, in BA Berlin R1001/1483, 59–60. For the reports of Hendrik Witbooi the Younger and Petrus Sefta to John Cleverly, see BA Berlin R1001/1483, 64–70.

[49] Cleverly to Undersecretary for Native Affairs, Capetown, 9 May 1893, 61–3. In the same letter, Cleverly noted that German reports were filtering in, with these insisting that forty Nama men were killed, 'and they attempt to palliate the killing of the women and children as unavoidable'. He also added that the Germans' African guides corroborated the Nama version of events.

When the "war of annihilation against the Hottentots" had begun on 12 April 1893 with the ambush of Hornkranz, Hendrik counted barely 250 armed men, around 100 rifles, and 120 horses; six months later his force was 600 men, 400 rifles, and 300 horses strong. The intended war of annihilation had become a protracted affair in which the element of morale grew with each event on the side of the Hottentots, while the conviction of the incapability and powerlessness of the German troops filled the mood of the whites with uneasiness.[50]

Foreshadowing the ultimately genocidal 1904 tactics of Lothar von Trotha, albeit on a smaller scale, François unsuccessfully resorted to pushing the Nama into the waterless desert in an attempt to trap them 'between the dunes and the German lines'. In this way, Bülow recorded, 'Major von François left Hendrik the choice between dying of thirst or the soldier's death.'[51]

Outraged by François's terror tactics, Witbooi remained a formidable opponent of German rule, and military difficulties beset the understrength German forces trying to defeat the Nama in a guerrilla colonial war where every settlement was a potential target for Nama raids. Externally, the Germans attempted to argue that the eyewitness reports of the massacre were 'tendentiously biased and distorted'.[52] Flying in the face of the international outcry, Wilhelm II's sole response to reports of the raid was to suggest military decorations for three of the German soldiers who had attracted the praise of their commander.[53]

At the level of practical decision-making, however, the radically violent military solution favoured by François was viewed by the German chancellor Leo von Caprivi as simply untenable. Just as serious questions about the fitness for command of the François brothers were being asked in the settler colonial press in Africa,[54] so too in Berlin opposition to François's strategy of waging an unwinnable war was growing. Without wishing to be seen to be taking a backward step, the Colonial Office began to look for another way to conquer the territory. Finally, in November 1893, Theodor Leutwein was sent to South West Africa by Caprivi, who declared that Governor François's limited communication with Berlin had made it virtually impossible for the chancellor to assess the success of his attempt to defeat the 'half-soldier, half-prophet' Hendrik Witbooi and his Nama people militarily. In addition, Caprivi was keen to see the more than 200 soldiers he had sent to the colony return soon to alleviate mounting pressure being placed upon him regarding the cost of the expedition by elements within the Reichstag.[55]

[50] Bülow, *Drei Jahre im Lande Hendrik Witboois*, 318.
[51] Bülow, *Drei Jahre im Lande Hendrik Witboois*, 331.
[52] German Foreign Office to Hatzfeldt, 10 June 1893, in BA Berlin R1001/1483, 71.
[53] François to German Colonial Office, 21 June 1893, in BA Berlin R1001/1483, 142–4. See especially Wilhelm II's margin note '*Dekorierung vorschlagen*' on p. 144.
[54] 'The Germans in Namaqualand', *Diamond Fields Advertiser*, 21 July 1893, in BA Berlin R1001/1483, 140.
[55] Caprivi, 1 March 1893, in *Verhandlungen des Reichstages*, 1359.

Chancellor Caprivi's orders to Leutwein made clear that upon arrival Leutwein's task was to assess the military and political situation on the ground and suggest the best way forward:

> You will take into consideration that you will inform yourself as much as is feasible through your interaction with Major v François, with Germans, and with natives, and report to me as soon as you have made a judgement and have an opportunity... Your next task will be to inform yourself about the relations of the whites to the natives in the middle part of the protectorate and in particular about the measures taken and yet to be taken against the Hottentot Chief Hendrik Witbooi. In doing so, you will have in mind the view that our position of power vis-à-vis the natives must be maintained and increasingly entrenched under all circumstances... A further object of your observations is the question of whether hostilities are to be expected from other natives after the eventual defeat of Witbooi, in particular the Herero, and whether the reduction of troops wished for here can occur in the foreseeable future.[56]

Caprivi was hopeful of being able to use the Herero as shock troops against Hendrik Witbooi and the Nama. His letter also made it clear that Leutwein's primary task, as Wilhelm II's new viceregal representative, was to prioritize and firmly ground German interests in the colony. Caprivi ruled out in advance any thought of capitulating to the demands of an African paramount leader like Witbooi and, despite the lack of success of François's military strategy, mandated an approach that dealt with the thorny and foundational issue of how to deal with continued African claims to sovereignty by presuming their subjugation—a task that Leutwein saw as difficult, given the limited military resources he had at his disposal.[57]

The Leutwein System

Upon his arrival, Leutwein discovered that German support had indeed assisted Samuel Maharero in the ongoing internal Herero dispute regarding the legitimacy of his claims to the paramountcy. Nonetheless, he also found that Maharero was not inclined to support him or any German official unequivocally. With German rule outside Windhoek an illusion and the campaign against Witbooi destroying what little credibility the German army had amongst Africans, Leutwein professed to be shocked to learn first-hand of the 'dark mistrust' that the Herero

---

[56] Caprivi to Leutwein, in Leutwein, *Elf Jahre Gouverneur*, 16–17.
[57] Caprivi to Leutwein, in Leutwein, *Elf Jahre Gouverneur*, 16–17; Helmut Bley, *South-West Africa under German Rule, 1894–1914* (London: Heinemann, 1971), 5.

harboured towards the Germans. The war against Witbooi was in the balance in February 1894, and Leutwein saw in Maharero 'an immense danger at the rear of the troops fighting Witbooi'. While François was away fighting the Nama, Leutwein took it upon himself to try and improve relations with Maharero.[58]

Their first meeting began inauspiciously, with the Paramount Leader of the Herero refusing to speak to Leutwein until he had all but given up and was about to leave. When, upon leaving, Leutwein suggested that they meet again later to speak, Maharero replied that they had nothing further to discuss. At this point Leutwein seized the moment and claimed that 'The German Kaiser has sent me to hear the words of you, the paramount chief.' Given the unfulfilled promises of German help prior to the war against Hendrik Witbooi, Maharero remained unimpressed by the invocation of the German emperor, replying that 'Many people have introduced themselves as having been sent from the German Kaiser, but the Herero have never gained anything by it.' Maharero had then launched into a litany of complaints against the Windhoek government, which led Leutwein to apologize for past difficulties and to promise better things for the future. Characteristically self-congratulatory, Leutwein's later memoir claims that his attempt to smooth the waters was successful and that the two, he claimed, left 'in best friendship'.[59]

Given Germany's dire military position in the colony, Leutwein's charm offensive was the first step in his strategy of divide and rule. He explicitly began seeking alliances with willing African rulers, who now included Maharero, and isolating and deposing those who resisted the Germans before they could organize their people for military struggle. This involved backing the leadership claims of sympathetic notables against other, more intransigent rivals. Although the attempt to win paramount African leaders over to German rule predated his arrival in South West Africa and to a certain extent had characterized some of the earlier work done by Göring, this approach somewhat misleadingly became known as the 'Leutwein system'.[60]

Amongst the first leaders to be deposed was Andreas Lambert, an anti-German Nama chief who was tried for murder and executed by Leutwein as virtually his first order of business in mid-March 1894. It was a clear signal to African leaders in the protectorate of how he meant to conduct business with those the Germans saw as recalcitrant. Andreas Lambert was replaced by his brother Eduard Lambert, who tellingly tried to refuse the 'honour' in favour of the son of an older brother. Reluctantly, he finally agreed and signed the 'protection' treaty placed in front of him.[61] Not far away in Gochas, Andreas Lambert's ally Simon Cooper, clearly terrified by what had happened to Lambert, was spared by Leutwein when

---

[58] Leutwein, *Elf Jahre Gouverneur*, 18–20.   [59] Leutwein, *Elf Jahre Gouverneur*, 20–1.
[60] Bley, *South-West Africa under German Rule, 1894–1914*, 3–72.
[61] Leutwein, *Elf Jahre Gouverneur*, 25–7; Bülow, *Drei Jahre im Lande Hendrik Witboois*, 328.

he also agreed to be 'protected' by the Germans. Signing the treaty, he asked Leutwein how long the treaty would last in the hope that his people might simply wait out the Germans. The entire process of extracting a treaty was, Leutwein admitted, 'highly uncomfortable' for Cooper.[62]

In contrast to his ally Lambert, and perhaps as a signal of recognition that Witbooi had not begun the war against the Germans, but had been drawn into it by François's massacre at Hornkrantz, Leutwein accepted Witbooi's peace over-tures in early September 1894. Telling of his own relationship with François, Leutwein's later account of the defeat of Witbooi offered ample space for Witbooi's complaints against the Germans who had massacred his people, printing Witbooi's letters of complaint, the contents of which thoroughly discredited the military behaviour of François, without any editorializing, offering a kind of Melian Dialogue which made it clear that it was François who had ignobly broken the peace between the Germans and the Nama:

> I lay quietly sleeping in my house; then came François, shooting me awake, and this not for the sake of peace or because of any misdeeds by which I might have made myself guilty in word or act, but rather because I had not given up some-thing that was solely mine and to which I had a right. I did not give up my inde-pendence, because I have a right to what is mine and can give it or not to whosoever should ask as I see fit. François started a war against me because I would not give up what was mine... Such deeds I had not expected from François, particularly when you white people are the most rational and educated people who teach us the truth and justice.[63]

Notwithstanding the brutal conduct of the war under François, this did not alter the new governor's desire to subjugate Witbooi in accordance with his orders. Leutwein's answer to the paramount chief's protestations was blunt. He held out the hope of 'favourable conditions', that is to say, remaining nominally in power as paramount leader, should he surrender, but insisted that 'You no longer have any other choice other than unconditional surrender to the will of His Majesty the German Kaiser or war unto extermination.'[64] Witbooi replied that these condi-tions were 'hard for a person who is used to an independent, free life' and he refused Leutwein's conditions.[65] Accordingly, Leutwein attacked the Nama,[66] suc-cessfully forcing Witbooi to capitulate by pushing the Nama forces into the desert and cutting them off from water. Leutwein once again offered Witbooi conces-sions if he would 'unconditionally submit to German rule'. Unable to continue

[62] Leutwein, *Elf Jahre Gouverneur*, 28–9.
[63] Witbooi to Leutwein, 4 May 1894, in Leutwein, *Elf Jahre Gouverneur*, 32–3.
[64] Leutwein to Witbooi, 5 May 1894, in Leutwein, *Elf Jahre Gouverneur*, 34–5.
[65] Witbooi to Leutwein, 7 Mai 1894, in Leutwein, *Elf Jahre Gouverneur*, 35–6.
[66] For details of the campaign, see Leutwein, *Elf Jahre Gouverneur*, 44–59.

fighting, Witbooi finally capitulated and, in stark contrast to the executed Lambert, was thereafter given 2,000 marks per year to maintain internal order amongst the Nama.[67]

In December 1894, the prominent colonial judge August Köhler wrote to Berlin urging that similar deal be struck for Samuel Maharero. Köhler reported that 'With patient handling and as far as possible open accommodation from our side, the Herero are without too many difficulties a pliable tribe.' German interests were, he argued, served by continuing to support Maharero's claims to the paramountcy and remaining involved in Herero intra-communal affairs. Samuel Maharero was 'from a political point of view of not to be undervalued worth'.[68]

Maharero's pretensions to the paramountcy, however, remained a point of internal dissension amongst Herero leaders aligned with Nicodemus, many of whom were outraged that Maharero had come to power courtesy of what they saw as an internal 'family intrigue'.[69] This was no mere idle grumbling, and the degree of mutual support between Leutwein and Maharero saw some disaffected Herero leaders actually decide to emigrate with their people out of Herero territory into Tswanaland.[70] Crucially, this was not necessarily a protest against Samuel Maharero's unequal alliance with the colonizing Germans, as if this had betrayed an earlier matter of principle among the Herero nation regarding tactical alliances with the colonizers. Not only had his father Maharero Tjamuaha twice viewed aligning himself with the Germans as being in his best interests, but in March 1894 Nicodemus too had approached Leutwein in search of German support for his claims as paramount chief. In return Nicodemus had promised not only to maintain order for the Germans but also to allow German settlers to live on Herero land and to negotiate with the Germans on territorial questions.[71] Nicodemus's overtures were rejected, however, because Maharero had already won the race for German recognition.

An alliance with the Germans might have been ruled out, but Nicodemus continued to press his claim to the paramountcy, while Leutwein and Maharero worked together to block his claim and systematically isolate him and his allies. Leutwein used a ceasefire during the war with Witbooi in June 1894 to corner Nicodemus (whom he called the 'pretender to the throne') and force him to acknowledge Samuel Maharero's claims,[72] despite the fact that he was still perfectly aware that Nicodemus had the stronger claim to the paramountcy. Indeed

---

[67] Bülow, *Drei Jahre im Lande Hendrik Witboois*, 345.
[68] Köhler to Caprivi, 24 December 1894, in R1001/2081, 173–4.
[69] Jan-Bart Gewald, *Towards Redemption: A Socio-Political History of the Herero of Namibia between 1890 and 1923* (Leiden: Research School CNWS, 1996), 86–91; Lehmann, 'Die Häuptlings-Erbfolgeordnung der Herero', 95–8.
[70] Lehmann, 'Die Häuptlings-Erbfolgeordnung der Herero', 95.
[71] Pool, *Samuel Maharero*, 109, 112.
[72] Lindequist to Caprivi, 24 July 1894, in BA Berlin R1001/2100, 73–87; Leutwein, *Elf Jahre Gouverneur*, 59–62; Pool, *Samuel Maharero*, 113–15.

Leutwein would write to Chancellor Caprivi in July 1894, admitting that 'Nicodemus is in fact according to Herero law the rightful successor to the old Maharero.'[73] Leutwein's support for Samuel Maharero's paramountcy nonetheless remained unwavering, and Nicodemus *ipso facto* came to be viewed as 'dangerous opponent' of the German government. Publicly, Leutwein offered Nicodemus the sham promise to act as intermediary between the two Herero leaders in the interests of 'political expediency'. His sole aim remained, however, to make the Herero as a whole more pliant (*nachgiebig*) in the long run by ensuring the paramountcy of Samuel Maharero, whom he considered a more malleable leader.[74]

After Witbooi was eventually defeated and Nicodemus seemingly sidelined, there remained for Leutwein the task of isolating the last remaining Herero leader of significant independent standing who had not accepted Samuel Maharero's claims to the paramountcy. In November 1894, Leutwein and Maharero once again worked together to secure the subjugation of the powerful Herero leader Manasse Tjisiseta of Omaruru to the authority of Samuel Maharero and, thus, to the rule of the Germans.[75] Manasse, who was seen by Leutwein as 'one of the most intelligent' of the colony's African leaders,[76] had maintained a degree of economic and security sovereignty over his territory, despite his nominal dual subjection to a protectorate treaty with the Germans and the imposed paramountcy of Samuel Maharero.[77] His views on the effects of German settler colonialism were also very clear and bluntly articulated when he met Franz Josef von Bülow. For Manasse, Bülow recorded, 'the Germans and only the Germans were the root of all evil':

> The Germans have no right to be here, and pretend to be our masters. They own no land but build fortresses; they allow more soldiers to come from Germany but claim that they do not want war. They prohibit the provision of ammunition and make laws without asking the chiefs of the country, as is required by the protection treaties. To what end is all of this?[78]

Leutwein's chance to confront Manasse came when a white farmer and accused murderer named Christie was shot by Manasse's soldiers as he resisted their attempts to apprehend him. In the wake of the incident, (now Governor) Leutwein pressured Manasse into handing his soldiers over to the Germans for a trial. For Leutwein, the Christie case offered him the opportunity to demand that Manasse waive his legal jurisdiction over his people and renounce his autonomy within his territory in favour of the Germans. In the process, Leutwein called upon Samuel

---

[73] Leutwein to Caprivi, 17 June 1894, in BA Berlin R1001/2100, 71.
[74] Leutwein to Caprivi, 17 June 1894, in BA Berlin R1001/2100, 71.
[75] Pool, *Samuel Maharero*, 116–18.   [76] Leutwein, *Elf Jahre Gouverneur*, 62.
[77] Gewald, *Towards Redemption*, 86–91.
[78] Bülow, *Drei Jahre im Lande Hendrik Witboois*, 264.

Maharero to act in concert with the Germans in his capacity as the Paramount Leader of the Herero, despite the fact that Manasse had never recognized his claims to the title.[79] Hearing that Manasse had amassed an army of 1,000 soldiers, Maharero prevaricated before agreeing with Leutwein's argument that the 'Christie affair' would offer him a definitive opportunity to consolidate his claims to the paramountcy.[80]

Fully cognizant of the fate of Lambert, Manasse was exceptionally cautious in his dealings with Leutwein. He agreed to the governor's demands that Omaruru be garrisoned by the Germans and that Okombahe be directly ruled by the Germans.[81] Manasse also handed over to Maharero (but not Leutwein) one of his soldiers who had sought sanctuary with him after the Germans had sentenced him to death *in absentia*. In this way Manasse indicated his grudging acceptance of Maharero's claim to the paramountcy, a step that was preferable to personally turning his own loyal followers over to the Germans. By dint of Manasse's acceptance of Maharero's claims and Maharero's role as an intermediary between Manasse and Leutwein, Maherero was made complicit in the ensuing execution of the soldier. Manasse, on the other hand, could maintain the fiction that he had deferred to the paramount ruler of the Herero, who held responsibility for the ultimate fate of his subjects.[82]

Intra-Herero rivalries and the question of territorial sovereignty once again came to a head in 1895, when the German assessor (and later governor) Friedrich von Lindequist took his border commission to the region of Otjihaenena, where they were taken into custody by troops loyal to Nicodemus. Unusually, the negotiations to have him returned saw the Germans agree to Nicodemus's demand to further his chiefly autonomy within his region. Thereafter, the relationship between Maharero and Nicodemus improved considerably for a time, and Nicodemus began to cooperate with the Germans and Maharero.[83] This cooperation did not last long. As early as October 1895, Leutwein had begun preparing the ground in Berlin by suggesting that 'the prospects for an enduring and peaceful cooperation with the Herero are not good.' While expressing a preference for peace, the Colonial Office offered the possibility of military reinforcements, should they become necessary, giving Leutwein the military resources he might need in the wake of the territorial shake-up he had planned.[84]

On 20 January 1896, Leutwein hosted a meeting of Herero notables to address the question of the southern limits of Hereroland. The assembly was attended not

---

[79] Leutwein, *Elf Jahre Gouverneur*, 61–5.

[80] Leutwein, *Elf Jahre Gouverneur*, 62; Pool, *Samuel Maharero*, 117. In the event, less than half the rumoured number of soldiers had assembled.

[81] Pool, *Samuel Maharero*, 117.

[82] Gewald, *Herero Heroes*, 72–7; Leutwein, *Elf Jahre Gouverneur*, 63–4.

[83] Leutwein to Hohenlohe, 29 January 1896, in BA Berlin R1001/2101, 'Das Herero-Land', 20; Gewald, *Herero Heroes*, 102–5.

[84] Colonial Office to Leutwein, 29 January 1896, in BA Berlin R1001/2100, 183–7.

only by Samuel Maharero and Herero notables loyal to him but also by Nicodemus and another rival, Riarua.[85] During the meeting, Maharero insisted to the Germans that they take strong action against those Herero who, by questioning his conciliatory approach to the question, appeared to be questioning his paramountcy.[86] Leutwein duly warned Nicodemus and Riarua, the latter of whom was viewed by Leutwein after Nicodemus's apparent change of heart as being the current 'leader of the opposition', to respect Maharero's authority and deal with the Germans on the question of land sovereignty,[87] stating coolly that by their attitude to the Germans the dissidents were risking the total destruction of their nation through war: 'And the Herero should imagine a war with us as quite different from a Hottentot war. Such a war could only end with the annihilation of one of the parties, and this party could only be the Herero.'[88]

The result of this warning was a stunned silence. Further goading Nicodemus and Riarua, Leutwein offered generous territorial concessions to the Maharero-loyal Western Herero, shifting the internal border for their cattle to include a river 8 kilometres into designated German land, at the same time as refusing similar concessions to those loyal to Nicodemus, who had requested that the strategically important town of Gobabis be included inside their territory.[89] In his memoirs, Leutwein explained how he had relished his ability to further split the Herero chiefs:

> Now I was given the perfect opportunity to bring the maxim '*divide et impera*' into force. The wishes of the Okahandja tribe were granted, while those of Nicodemus were rejected outright. The latter turned three months later to rebellion, whereas the Okahandja-Herero remained on our side.[90]

As an earlier meeting in Grootfontein in August 1895 to consolidate the northern border of Hereroland had already hinted (see Figure 9.1), Leutwein was uninterested in finding mutually acceptable terms on the questions of land rights and sovereignty with Nicodemus or indeed anyone else beyond those directly aligned with Maharero and Witbooi.[91] Writing to Chancellor Hohenlohe about the 'Herero question' after the January 1896 meeting, he reported that his strategy remained simply 'to shore up the position' of Maharero to the exclusion of any other contenders for the paramountcy.[92]

Bitterly disappointed by Leutwein's apparent one-sidedness, there was nothing that Nicodemus could do other than 'to give the external impression of being

---

[85] Leutwein, *Elf Jahre Gouverneur*, 94.   [86] Bley, *Southwest Africa under German Rule*, 61.
[87] Leutwein to Hohenlohe, 29 January 1896, in BA Berlin R1001/2101, 18.
[88] Leutwein, *Elf Jahre Gouverneur*, 94. The minutes from that day confirm that 'At this point Major Leutwein expressed his view that a war against the Herero could only end with their complete annihilation'. See 'Protokoll', 20 January 1896, in BA Berlin R1001/2101, 36.
[89] Leutwein to Hohenlohe, 29 January 1896, in BA Berlin R1001/2101, 20–1.
[90] Leutwein, *Elf Jahre Gouverneur*, 95–9.   [91] Leutwein, *Elf Jahre Gouverneur*, 82–7.
[92] Leutwein to Hohenlohe, 29 January 1896, in BA Berlin R1001/2101, 17.

Dr. Hartmann   Leutwein   Samuel Maharero

Vertragsschließung mit Oberhäuptling Samuel in Grootfontein 1895.

Figure 9.1 Treaty signing between Leutwein and Samuel Maharero in Grootfontein, August 1895

satisfied' with this rejection. The matter did not rest there, however, with Leutwein further preparing Chancellor Hohenlohe for a reckoning with Nicodemus in the near future, warning of a potential military 'catastrophe' and arguing that 'this chief is doubtlessly one of those to be least trusted and from whose side hostilities are to be expected when the opportunity should arise.'[93] Leutwein's provocations succeeded and, after some initially covert forms of resistance, Nicodemus launched a full-scale revolt against Maharero and the Germans in March 1896.[94] Nicodemus's revolt was calibrated to coincide with a rebellion that had broken out amongst a portion of the Nama nation, including those led by Eduard Lambert, the brother of Andreas Lambert who had been executed in 1894.[95] As Leutwein reported with apparent satisfaction, 'Nicodemus had not planned his rebellion for long, but rather only as a consequence of the dismissive answer in regards to Gobabis.' The conflict, he candidly admitted, was in essence an attempt by Nicodemus to regain territorial sovereignty over a region he considered to be his and was the conclusion, Leutwein wrote, of the Germans' 'battle for the borders.'[96]

---

[93] Leutwein to Hohenlohe, 29 January 1896, in BA Berlin R1001/2101, 21–3.

[94] Hans Emil Lenssen, *Chronik von Deutsch-Südwestafrika*, (Windhoek: Verlag der Namibia-Wissenschaftliche Gesellschaft, 1994), 75–6.

[95] John S. Lowry, *Big Swords, Jesuits and Bondelswarts* (Leiden: Koninklijke Brill, 2015), 63.

[96] Leutwein, *Elf Jahre Gouverneur*, 98–9.

Nicodemus and his allies were rapidly and soundly defeated by the Germans. In defeat, he was, however, treated vastly differently from Hendrik Witbooi. As Leutwein laconically recorded the outcome of the defeat in his memoirs, 'Leader of the Eastern Hereros as well as other prominent persons captured, with the former shot. The entire Khaua tribe interned in Windhoek. Duration two months.'[97] Alongside his ally Kahimema, Nicodemus had been tied to a tree and executed by German forces, with the full approval of his rival Samuel Maharero, who had, fought in the war with Leutwein—remarkably alongside Hendrik Witbooi (see Figure 9.2).[98]

Y   Y   Y
Hendrik Witbooi   Leutwein   Samuel Maharero

Nach dem Gefecht von Otjunda-Sturmfeld 1896.

Figure 9.2 Witbooi, Leutwein, and Maharero after the Battle of Otjunda, 1896

[97] Leutwein, *Elf Jahre Gouverneur*, 432.   [98] Gewald, *Herero Heroes*, 107–8.

The alliance between Leutwein and Maharero had translated Maharero's dubious claim to the paramountcy into reality. While Leutwein saw in Maharero's tactic of cultivating German support a sign of his 'political intelligence',[99] the arrangement overwhelmingly benefitted the German governor, who was able to transfer many of his governing responsibilities to a pliant local ruler who had become increasingly dependent on German support. Like Witbooi, Maharero was paid 2,000 marks a year by the German government to ensure that the Herero did not contest German rule. He flew the German flag over his werf while, in return, the Germans maintained their support for Maharero's paramountcy in his domestic struggles against other Herero leaders.[100] To some of the Herero this confirmed their view that Samuel Maharero was simply an African representative of the German government.[101] Yet, like the defeated Witbooi, Maharero might have been a subordinate ally, but he was not simply a puppet ruler. Rather, his relationship with the Germans was a carefully nurtured and calibrated one, intended to extract the maximum benefit for himself as a ruler whose legitimacy was contested by other Herero leaders. As Jan-Bart Gewald has argued, Mahaerero was able to harness the 'threat of German firepower' to extend his tenuous grip on power and to secure the unlikely result of becoming the Paramount Leader of Hereroland. The cost, however, was any real scope for independent political action for the Herero as a nation short of open insurrection.[102]

The Royal Visit to Berlin

With the death of Nicodemus, Samuel Maharero was firmly entrenched in the position of Paramount Leader of the Herero. It was not only within South West Africa, however, that Maharero sought to consolidate his ties with the Germans. Cognizant of the fact that colonial governors were liable to be recalled to Germany by the German emperor (in reality on the advice of the chancellor, as Göring and François both had been), Maharero and Witbooi looked to ensure the long-term stability of their positions by forging a direct connection to the metropolitan sovereign. Accordingly, in 1896, both Maharero and Witbooi insisted on sending Herero and Nama emissaries to Berlin for the inaugural Colonial Exhibition,[103] to which 103 indigenous people from the various German colonies were sent.

[99] Leutwein, *Elf Jahre Gouverneur*, 307.

[100] Leutwein, *Elf Jahre Gouverneur*, 60; Lindequist to Caprivi, 24 July 1894, in BA Berlin R1001/2100, 74–5.

[101] Gert Sudholt, *Die deutsche Eingeborenenpolitik in Südwestafrika: Von den Anfängen bis 1904* (Hildesheim: Georg Olms Verlag, 1975), 140–1.

[102] Gewald, *Towards Redemption*, 75.

[103] Lenssen, *Chronik von Deutsch-Südwestafrika*, 78.

After much jostling for position amongst the notables of the colony, those who travelled to Berlin from South West Africa included Friedrich Maharero, Samuel Maharero's 22-year-old son, as well as Ferdinand Demóndscha and Titus Huárakka, a nephew of Hendrik Witbooi and (possibly) the son of Nicodemus (who had been selected before his father's 1896 rebellion). Accompanying them were the translator Josaphat Kamatoto and his wife Martha Kamatoto.[104] As the missionary Hedwig Irle related, Friedrich, the 'crown prince' of the Herero, was at the exhibition 'not to see but to be seen', that is, as part of the South West African exhibit.[105]

Maharero had been pressing for his son to travel to Germany for an audience with Wilhelm II since the ceasefire with Hendrik Witbooi and the sidelining of Nicodemus and Riarua in 1894. At this time, Lindequist had requested permission for the trip from Berlin on Maharero's behalf, writing to the Colonial Office that Maharero had made clear his wish that his oldest son travel to Berlin. Now that he 'stood in such friendly relations with the Germans', Maharero had argued, 'his son should see Germany and give his regards to Kaiser Wilhelm'. Lindequest noted that Leutwein had nothing against the proposal and that Maharero was prepared to pay the roughly 3,000 marks that a one-month round trip would cost.[106] To this, Lindequist added the remark that:

> In my humble opinion, a voyage to Germany by the likely successor to the para-mount chieftaincy might not only be of considerable advantage in the future, but would also not fail to make an impression on the entire Herero nation right now and considerably strengthen the trust that they have recently placed in German rule and in particular in Major Leutwein.[107]

The reply from the Colonial Office in 1894 had been lukewarm. Although Berlin had decided to leave the decision to Leutwein and Lindequist, they were warned that a visit by the son of Maharero with 'the intention of being introduced to His Majesty the Kaiser has scarcely any prospect of being realized'. Maharero should know this, they concluded, before he planned to travel.[108]

The exhibition of 1896, however, offered another, more straightforward opportunity for the journey, although it came at the cost of the visiting party arriving not as honoured royal guests, but rather as part of a colonial exhibition. This

---

[104] Felix von Luschan, 'Völkerkunde', in Hermann von Schweinitz, Carl von Beck, and Franz Imberg (eds), *Deutschland und seine Kolonien im Jahre 1896* (Berlin: Dietrich Reimer, 1897), 226; Leutwein, *Elf Jahre Gouverneur*, 96; Joachim Zeller, 'Friedrich Maharero: Ein Herero in Berlin', in Ulrich van der Heyden and Joachim Zeller (eds), *Kolonialmetropole Berlin: Eine Spurensuche* (Berlin: Berlin Edition, 2002), 206–11.
[105] Irle, *Unsere schwarzen Landsleute in Deutsch-Südwestafrika*, 87.
[106] Lindequist to Colonial Office, 24 July 1894, in BA Berlin R1001/2100, 84–5.
[107] Lindequist to Colonial Office, 24 July 1894, in BA Berlin R1001/2100, 84–5.
[108] Colonial Office to Leutwein, 18 October 1894, in BA Berlin R1001/2100, 94.

Figure 9.3 Friedrich Maharero while in
Germany in 1896

meant that, during his visit, Friedrich Maharero found himself studied by anthropologists, playing a role in the exhibition in Treptow Park, as well as visiting the Kaiser. While the organizers of the exhibition had hoped that the Herero would fulfil German expectations by appearing in 'heathen Herero costume' at the 'black villages' constructed for the exhibition, they were disappointed by the impeccably dressed and mannered Maharero,[109] whose stylish appearance won the hearts of many German women, as one later account recalled (see Figure 9.3).[110] As the anthropologist Felix von Luschan wrote in the official commemorative book marking the exhibition, the 'gentleman-like' manner and 'handsome' appearance of the Herero made a 'strong impression' on the Germans who saw them.[111]

The refinement of the African visitors to Berlin, led the colonial explorer Karl Dove to explain to German readers of the *Deutsche Kolonialzeitung* that the European-style appearance of Friedrich Maharero and his four compatriots was a consequence of the 'spread of Christianity' in the colony. He described the Herero as discerning customers of European clothing with an eye for style and fashion. Unlike many Germans, Dove added, the visitors followed the highly laudable principle that 'expensive but good is better than cheap and poor quality'. Although the Herero way of war was brutal by German standards, Dove opined, the Herero were highly adept at diplomacy.[112]

---

[109] Gesine Krüger, *Kriegsbewältigung und Geschichtsbewußtsein: Realität, Deutung und Verarbeitung des deutschen Kolonialkriegs in Namibia 1904 bis 1907* (Göttingen: Vandenhoeck & Ruprecht, 1999), 75.

[110] 'Rassenfrage', *Deutsche Kolonialzeitung* 36, 4 September 1909, 593–4.

[111] Luschan, 'Völkerkunde', 221–3. For Luschan's anthropological description of Friedrich Maharero's body, see p. 224.

[112] Karl Dove, 'Die Deutsche Kolonial-Austellung', *Deutsche Kolonialzeitung*, 19 September 1896. Dove also wrote the chapter on South West Africa in Schweinitz, Beck, and Frnz Imberg (eds),

Arguably it was not merely this reputed adroitness in diplomatic matters that explains how Samuel Maharero's son came to meet with Wilhelm II. This part of the visit to Germany was also a product of the colonial administration's attempt to seize the initiative in an increasingly strained relationship between Maharero and Leutwein on one side, and metropolitan commentators who saw Leutwein as captive to African interests at the cost of German colonial endeavours on the other. Prior to the visit, Samuel Maharero had asked Lindequist to organize an audience with Wilhelm II for his son, in the hope of extracting an assurance from the emperor that he would respect the territorial arrangements arrived at with Leutwein in Hereroland in 1895. A letter that Franz Josef von Bülow wrote to the Colonial Office made clear Maharero's expectation that Wilhelm II would meet the delegation that he had sent and that the emperor would listen to and confirm the agreed compromise. Bülow also noted that such a meeting could ensure the continued loyalty of the Herero to the Germans during a difficult period:

The four men sent by the Paramount Chief of the Herero, Samuel Maharero, for the colonial section of the Berlin Trade Exhibition, namely the eldest son and heir of Maharero, Friedrich, plus two additional sons of chiefs as well as the German-speaking spokesman, Josef, have asked me to organize on behalf of their paramount chief an audience with His Majesty the Kaiser...The Herero, who have travelled here at their own costs on the condition that they would be granted an audience with His Majesty, are the carriers of a short letter which contains only an assurance of loyalty. Besides this, the spokesman, who had recently read in the newspaper that the Governor of South West Africa, Major Leutwein, has been accused of too much leniency towards the Herero, would like to assure His Majesty that the governor has their full confidence and that he understands their character well. The Herero expect an assurance that His Majesty is willing to maintain the peace with them. If it is added to this assurance that His Majesty would use all of his power if the Hereros were to resort to their weapons, this would not fail to make a deep impression. Your Highness can be assured that a few minutes of the Sovereign's time could halt a bloody and pointless war which might otherwise be caused by the loose talk of our

---

Deutschland und seine Kolonien im Jahre 1896, 156–65. On European-style Herero dress, Josch Lampe has argued that the sartorial elegance of the Herero was an example of what Homi Bhabha has called 'mimicry': Josch Lampe, "'Meine Tochter [...] soll alles lernen, was die weissen Mädchen lernen...'.": "Schwarze" Perspektiven auf Deutschland um 1900', *Textpraxis* 11, no. 2 (2015), 7. In some ways, it more closely resembles Bhabha's idea of 'sly civility', particularly in the Herero's polite but firm 'refusal to satisfy the colonizer's narrative demand' and their capacity to undermine the simplistic binary distinction between *Kulturvölker* and *Naturvölker* assumed by many metropolitan observers. See Homi Bhabha, *The Location of Culture*, (London: Routledge, 1994), 99.

compatriots in the colony that could provoke the mistrust of the unknowing amongst the Herero.[113]

The Colonial Office was convinced of the soundness of Bülow's reasoning, and Wilhelm II met the Herero contingent at 2.30 p.m. on Saturday 19 September 1896.[114] If any territorial assurances were given at the meeting, none was mentioned by Friedrich Maharero, who nonetheless stayed in Germany for some time to undertake some military training. On his time in Germany, he would later recall dismissively, 'I was taken to Germany with the others to be shown to the Kaiser because he did not know his black subjects and also to be taught... We were there one year. We were not taught anything. Only we rode about on horses and dressed and were drilled as soldiers.'[115] As Joachim Zeller has put it, 'What impression Friedrich Maharero, as the most prominent member of the Herero delegation, left on Kaiser Wilhelm II is not recorded.'[116]

As Chancellor Caprivi admitted to the Reichstag in 1893, without cultivating close relationships with the Herero under the German-sponsored paramount leadership of Samuel Maharero, the Germans might have found themselves defeated in their only settler colony by a Herero-Nama coalition led by the 'half-soldier, half-prophet' Hendrik Witbooi.[117] Despite the benefits that German rule brought Maharero in his personal consolidation of power over Nicodemus, his tactical decision to acquiesce to German rule was central to the process of moving South West Africa towards an integrated and centralized settler colonial state. This unitary settler state was designed to serve the economic, political, and military ends of the German state and 'challenged the whole basis' for the existence of independent African polities.[118] There was nothing necessary or predetermined about Maharero's partnership with the German colonial administration, which was seen by many other African chiefs as illegitimate or at the very least impinging on their continued sovereign rights. Nevertheless, this cooperation also followed a clear history of such partnerships.[119] In many ways, Maharero was a clear example of an ambitious but domestically vulnerable political leader who utilized

---

[113] Franz Josef von Bülow, 12 September 1896, in BA Berlin, R1001/6350, 'Ausstellungen', 26–7. See also Krüger, *Kriegsbewältigung und Geschichtsbewußtsein*, 75. Most accounts follow Zeller in misattributing the letter to the later foreign secretary and chancellor, Bernhard von Bülow. See Zeller, 'Friedrich Maharero', 208; Lampe, '"Meine Tochter"', 7.

[114] Lyncker to Colonial Office, 18 September 1896; Colonial Office to Schweinitz, 18 September 1896, in BA Berlin R1001/6350, 28–31.

[115] Friedrich Maherero, as quoted in Peter H. Katjavivi, *A History of Resistance in Namibia* (Addis Ababa: Unesco Press, 1968), 11.

[116] Joachim Zeller, 'Die Leiche im Keller: Eine Entdeckungsreise ins Innerste der Kolonialmetropole Berlin', in M. Bechhaus-Gerst, R. Klein-Arendt, and S. Michels (eds), *Encounters/Begegnungen: History and Present of the African-European Encounter/Geschichte und Gegenwart der afrikanisch-europäischen Begegnungen*, vol. 3 (Münster: Lit Verlag, 2004), 102.

[117] Caprivi, 1 March 1893, in *Verhandlungen des Reichstages*, 1359.

[118] Bley, *South-West Africa under German Rule*, 7.

[119] Bley, *South-West Africa under German Rule*, 6.

the changed political and military balance resulting from colonization to avail himself of German power to eliminate his domestic rivals.[120] Crucially, there was no underlying reason why the Germans could not have instead decided to back Nicodemus's stronger claims to the paramountcy, particularly given his offer to work with them. While Samuel Maharero's elevation above other Herero leaders was undoubtedly of benefit to his campaign to become their paramount leader, it also placed him in an invidious position. On the one hand, his military strength was inflated by his alliance with the Germans. On the other, in the eyes of his rivals and compatriots, his alliance made him complicit with the expansion of German rule over Herero territory and their eventual dispossession.

Yet it is important to remember that Maharero's decision to lead his nation towards an alliance with the Germans was not a move of idiosyncratic opportunism. Rather, it followed the policy guidelines established by his father, who had decided that alliances with outside actors could secure not only the position of the Herero but the power of his family over them.[121] Nicodemus too had actively sought out an alliance with the Germans, before realizing that Maharero had beaten him to it. Initially, it was Hendrik Witbooi and the Nama who represented a far more pressing danger to the Herero than the thinly spread German forces in the early 1890s. Indeed, the main complaint that both Samuel Maharero and Maharero Tjamuaha had prior to the German campaign against Witbooi was that German military power and the German emperor's promise of protection were too little in evidence to be of use to the Herero nation in their continuing war against the Nama.

Unlike the terroristic military tactics of François displayed at Hornkranz, the Leutwein system of divide and rule seemed to offer room for African agency and even rewards for those leaders able to reach an accommodation with the Germans. This agency was always limited, however, by the growing structural demands of German settler colonialism, which insisted, in Chancellor Caprivi's words, that German 'authority in relation to the natives be maintained under all circumstances and increasingly secured'.[122] The paramount leaders of South West Africa and those who wished to be paramount leaders were invariably treated by the Germans in accordance with the interests of the colonizing state, as the various governors and military figures of the colonial period saw it.

That the Germans would securely gain control of the colony was never a foregone conclusion. Until the defeat of Witbooi, the spectre of a joint campaign of the Herero and Nama against the Germans remained a real possibility, one that would re-emerge in 1904. Samuel Maharero's belief that he could tactically align

---

[120] Häußler, 'Warum die Herero mit den Deutschen kooperierten', 95–6, 105.
[121] Häußler, 'Warum die Herero mit den Deutschen kooperierten', 105–6.
[122] Caprivi to Leutwein, in Leutwein Elf Jahre Gouverenur, 17.

himself with the Germans and maintain his power proved to be an illusion, as he came to accept, but not one that was self-evidently implausible in the early 1890s, when some of the most important steps in this direction were made. While Hendrik Witbooi could claim with justification that he had foreseen a time when Samuel Maharero would regret his people's turn to the Germans as the easiest route to security, he too had found that his paramountcy was reliant upon the increasingly restrictive dictates of the 'Leutwein system'.

10

The Limits of Royal Reciprocity

From the beginning of the Germans' arrival in the Cameroon Grasslands, King Njoya of Bamum was central to providing support and security to the colonizers, despite the fact that his kingdom lay within the sphere of influence of the powerful Fulbe Lamido of Banyo (and by extension the Emir of Yola).[1] Njoya approached the arrival of the Germans apprehensively, with an eye to the military suppression of other African rulers in the region who had dared to refuse the Germans' overtures since the 1880s. With these punitive military operations in mind, Njoya counselled his warriors that the Germans should be allowed to come to Bamum's capital Fumban unmolested. Failing to do so, he warned, would see the destruction of his kingdom. As the king later recounted in his history of Bamum:

> One day the whites appeared in the country. The Bamum said to each other: 'Make war against them.' 'No', said Njoya, 'for I have seen in dreams that the whites have done no harm to the Bamum. If the Bamum make war it will be the end of their own race, the Bamum, and of me. There will be very few Bamum survivors, and it will not be good.' He, Njoya, tore arrows, spears, and guns from their hands. The Bamum obeyed. They did not oppose the arrival of the whites. He, Njoya, helped the Bamum, and they remained at peace.

> But the Bamum feared the whites; what had to be done to be good with them? He, Njoya said, 'I will go and watch them, so that I can see how they live.' He left for Buea and Duala. On his return, he reported to the Bamum the observations he had made on the whites.

> He said to the Bamum: 'If the soldiers come to the market and take something, if they are plundering villages, if they hit people without reason, do not get angry. If the whites tear apart what you have in your hands, if they destroy something, or if they accost me, Njoya, you, the Bamum, must not get angry. Let me, Njoya, take care of settling relations with the whites.' Thus, Njoya helped the Bamum, who remained in peace. The Germans did good to him, Njoya. They left him all

[1] Claude Tardits, 'Pursue to Attain: A Royal Religion', in Ian Fowler and David Zeitlyn (eds), *African Crossroads: Intersections between History and Anthropology in Cameroon* (New York: Berghahn, 1996), 144–5. Tardits dates the beginning of Banyo's hegemony to the mid-1890s. Jaap van Slageren, however, points to the role of Njoya's father, King Nsangu, in courting the powerful Muslim kingdoms of the north in the mid-1880s. See Jaap van Slagerern, *Les Origines de l'Église évangélique du Cameroun: Missions européennes et christianisme autochtone* (Leiden: Brill, 1972), 101.

The Kaiser and the Colonies: Monarchy in the Age of Empire. Matthew P. Fitzpatrick, Oxford University Press.
© Matthew P. Fitzpatrick 2022. DOI: 10.1093/oso/9780192897039.003.0011

the power to govern the entire Bamum country. As long as he ruled the country, there was no disorder either among the whites or the Bamum.[2]

If King Njoya's account is to be believed, the peace between Bamum and the Germans was based on his clear-eyed assessment of the insuperable power differential between the two. As the following makes clear, however, Njoya came to see in the Germans not only a threat but also a powerful European sponsor for his own shaky domestic and regional power. Without losing sight of the fact that the outer limits of Njoya's agency were set by the overarching colonial priorities of the Germans, this chapter examines the king's continual recalibration of Bamum's relationship with the Germans and its earlier Muslim hegemons. It also scrutinizes the way in which Njoya attempted to augment his relations with the Germans by cultivating a personal relationship with Kaiser Wilhelm II, albeit one mediated by the colonial government in Cameroon and colonial officials in Berlin, as well as by Basel missionaries operating in the region. It illustrates how, by incorporating the symbols of power employed by both the German Kaiser and the Islamic lamidos of Cameroon's north, Njoya developed a multifaceted semiotics of rule that expressed his place as a ruler situated between two hegemonic powers, one European and one African.[3]

Pushing beyond the notion that African monarchs such as Njoya were simply coerced by German colonial officials into maintaining loyalty at all costs, the following emphasizes the extent to which King Njoya responded creatively to the arrival of the Germans to carve out a space for autonomous politics beneath the structures of German imperialism. This was largely (although not universally) welcomed by the Germans themselves. Indeed, Njoya found himself the beneficiary of a German imperial policy that fostered pliant existing West African kings and elites as a means of combating the difficulties of ruling a colony that had only a rudimentary military capacity and communications network. This was seen by German colonial officials as being far preferable to the blunter and more expensive mechanisms of garrisoned direct rule, as Rudolf Asmis, a senior colonial official in German Togo, later explained:

In the use of the indirect system of rule, the colonizing and ruling power attempts to achieve its political objectives through the involvement and use of the pre-existing tribal or familial organizations. They employ the chiefs, the kings, the akiden, lamidos, family elders... and give them general guidelines for rule, leaving it to them to translate these guidelines into specifics... Indirect rule

---

[2] Ibrahim Njoya, *Histoire et coutumes des Bamum rédigées sous la direction du Sultan Njoya*, trans. Henri Martin (Douala: Institut Français d'Afrique Noire, Centre du Cameroun, 1952), 134. See also p. 43.

[3] Stefanie Michels, *Imagined Power Contested: Germans and Africans in the Upper Cross River Area of Cameroon, 1887–1915* (Münster: Lit Verlag, 2004).

has the advantage that the natives are left with their own traditions and, consequently, their self-respect.[4]

What should be noted here is the degree to which, under conditions of informal rule, German power was pliable, able to be made congruent with pre-existing and newly emerging local political practices. It could be surprisingly responsive to local imperatives. While the Cameroonian gateway kingdom of coastal Duala was moved towards increasingly direct forms of rule, and non-compliant kingdoms were ruthlessly subjected to military subjugation, Njoya and other 'friendly' kings of Cameroon were regularly consulted by the Germans on issues pertaining to their kingdom.[5] As Englebert Mveng has argued, indirect rule meant that 'the pyramid of powers in the German colonial system went from the local chief to the Reich chancellor and the emperor, passing through the district chiefs, the military authorities, and the governor of the colony.'[6]

The often-drawn portrait of Njoya as an unswervingly loyal king, however, obscures the fact that Njoya had to make continual complex assessments of how best to preserve both his domestic position and the safety of his subjects in the face of German predations. As one Cameroonian historian has recently pointed out, failure to accommodate German power saw many African kingdoms 'shattered'.[7] Even in Germany, Cameroon had a reputation as a colony in which Africans were treated exceedingly badly, particularly under Governor Jesko von Puttkamer.[8] In an attempt to avert the political and humanitarian disaster that invariably resulted from Germany's military campaigns in recalcitrant African territories, many rulers, including Njoya chose cooperation over open defiance.

At the same time, however, local kings such as Njoya who were able to come to an arrangement with German colonial officials were also able, as Ulrike Schaper has argued, to leverage this new hegemon to shape the scope and modes of power they might exercise over their region, using 'their new resources for power independently of the interests of the Germans'. In pursuing their own local hegemonic projects, 'they were anything other than passive instruments of colonial politics.'[9]

---

[4] Rudolf Asmis, *Kalamba Na M'putu: Koloniale Erfahrungen und Beobachtungen* (Berlin: E. S. Mittler & Sohn, 1942), 156–7.

[5] Harry R. Rudin, *Germans in the Cameroons 1884-1914: A Case Study in Modern Imperialism* (New Haven, CT: Yale University Press, 1938), 214.

[6] Englebert Mveng, *Histoire du Cameroun* (Paris: Présence Africaine, 1963), 314. See also Ulrike Schaper, 'Chieftaincy as a Political Resource in the German Colony of Cameroon, 1884–1916', in Tanja Bührer, Flavio Eichmann, Stig Förster, and Benedikt Stuchtey (eds), *Cooperation and Empire: Local Realities of Global Processes* (New York: Berghahn, 2017), 194–222.

[7] Mathew Basung Gwanfogbe, 'Resistance to European Penetration into Africa: The Case of the North West Region of Cameroon', *Journal of the Cameroon Academy of Sciences* 13, no. 3 (2017), 128.

[8] This mistreatment is apparent in the reports of the Basel Mission, which monitored the nature of Germany's treatment (and mistreatment) of Africans. See Erik Halldén, *The Cultural Policy of the Basel Mission in the Cameroons 1886-1905* (Lund: Berlingska Boktryckeriet, 1968).

[9] Ulrike Schaper, *Koloniale Verhandlungen: Gerichtsbarkeit, Verwaltung und Herrschaft in Kamerun 1884-1916* (Frankfurt am Main: Campus Verlag, 2012), 124.

This capacity for broader possibilities of local autonomy and hegemony nonetheless existed within clear limits which, if exceeded, would see the Germans forcibly intervene.[10] Any new avenues of royal African agency were structured and delineated by the threat (and regular deployment) of German *force majeure*.

Njoya's strategy for negotiating these limits was the active cultivation of a personal, monarch-to-monarch relationship with the German emperor, a strategy which, unlike elsewhere, met with some short-term success. Once this strategy seemed to offer diminishing returns, however, Njoya shifted his attention once again to the Islamic north, in a quiet attempt to reposition himself and spread his risk between the Germans and these locally hegemonic forces.

From Islamic Kingdom to German Ally

Royal power in Bamum was often violently contested, and Njoya's path to the throne had been an incredibly difficult one. Crucially, Germany was not the first large power that Njoya had relied upon to ensure the acceptance of his claim to rule. In fact, it was by aligning himself with the stronger Muslim powers to the north of Bamum that Njoya had begun his strategy of seeking alliances with large external powers to facilitate his own political ambitions. Upon his ascension to the throne in 1894, Njoya had faced a challenge from Gbetnkom Ndombuo, who had held the important palace office of *nji fonfon* during the earlier regency period, when Njoya could not rule because he had not yet had any children.[11] With Bamum engulfed by a civil war, Njoya entreated the Lamido of Banyo, Umaru, to assist him in 1894.[12] The Fulbe cavalry ensured a swift end to the war in Njoya's favour, with the rebel *nji fonfon* captured, tied to a stake, coated in palm oil and powder, and burned alive.[13]

Now secure on his throne and supported by his powerful and highly esteemed mother Njapdunke,[14] the grateful King Njoya declared Islam to be the source of Fulbe strength and quickly oriented himself and the royal court of Bamum

---

[10] See, for example, King Fonyonga II of Bali-Nyonga, who went from being seen as a pliant and loyal client ruler to finding himself sidelined when he was suspected of using his privileged status to pursue expansionist goals that were not congruent with the colonial administration's strategic designs for the region. See Florian Hoffmann, *Okkupation und Militärverwaltung in Kamerun: Etablierung und Institutionalisierung des kolonialen Gewaltmonopols*, vol. 1 (Göttingen: Cuvillier Verlag, 2007), 215–18; Andreas Merz, 'Die Politik Bali-Nyongas (Grasland von Kamerun) gegenüber der Basler Mission und der deutschen Kolonialmacht' (PhD diss., University of Basel, 1997).

[11] For Njoya's detailed history of the kings of Bamum prior to and including himself, see Ibrahim Njoya, 'Geschichte der Bamum-Könige aus Rifum: Nach den Aufzeichnungen des Bamumkönigs Ndschoya', trans. Christoph Geprägs (1911), Basel Mission Archives (BMA) E-10.1, 2.

[12] Martin Göhring, 13 May 1906, in BMA E-2, 22, 279, 10.

[13] For Njoya's accounts, see Njoya, 'Geschichte der Bamum-Könige aus Rifum', 11–12, and Njoya, *Histoire et coutumes des Bamum*, 35–6.

[14] Stolz to Komitee der Evangl. Missionsgesellschaft zu Basel, 22 January 1906, in BMA E-2,20b, 382.

towards Islamic practices that he considered to be the 'war medicine' that had delivered him victory. By the time the Germans arrived in Bamum's capital Fumban in 1902, it had a mosque and was a trading post for Muslim traders and religious scholars, whose white robes Njoya and his entourage had adopted, replacing earlier local modes of Bamum attire. To consolidate Njoya's ties to the Islamic north, reciprocal gift-giving between Bamum, Banyo, and Yola began in earnest.[15] As Galitzine-Loumpet argues, 'Islam and its material culture appeared then as the vectors of a new political power.'[16]

Clearly, prior to the arrival of the Germans, Njoya's Bamum was already a kingdom that had undergone considerable cultural change as it gravitated towards the culturally, politically, and militarily dominant orbit of Banyo, and towards the northwest Islamic region more broadly.[17] It was also evident to German missionaries that Bamum's reorientation towards the Islamic north was not only religious and military but also economic, with Fumban's market now integrated into Hausa trade routes. As the Basel missionary Karl Stolz reported in 1906, 'When we arrived in Bamum, it was market time. We saw that there were more than two hundred people. The core of these markets is naturally the Hausa.'[18]

The arrival of the Germans disrupted Njoya's gravitation towards the Islamic north, at least initially. Not only did the arrival of the German military upset the regional dynamics of power at the macro level, but the protection afforded by Germany to both the Basel missionaries and German traders affected the extent to which Bamum's religious and economic reorientation could continue. Instead, Njoya found himself having to respond to these European interlopers in a way that would preserve his own hard-won authority and protect his lands and people, while also showing due consideration to his protectors, the Fulbe.

From the colonizers' perspective, Njoya's adaptation to his new German visitors was viewed as a self-explanatory recognition by the king of Germany's higher civilizationary standing and his desire to emulate it. According to the racialized reasoning of the ethnographer Marie Thorbecke, the Kingdom of Bamum came to stand 'at the pinnacle of all of the tribes of the grasslands',[19] because of its embrace of European civilization. She went on to pay Njoya the racist compliment that he was, 'one of the very rare blacks that possess a pronounced spiritual

---

[15] Tardits, 'Pursue to Attain', 144–5; Christraud M. Geary, *Things of the Palace: A Catalogue of the Bamum Palace Museum in Foumban (Cameroon)* (Wiesbaden: Franz Steiner Verlag, 1983), 61–2.

[16] Alexandra Galitzine-Loumpet, 'Reconsidering Patrimonialization in the Bamun Kingdom: Heritage, Image, and Politics from 1906 to the Present', *African Arts* 49, no. 2 (2016), 69.

[17] For a longer history of Islam in Bamum, see Forka Leypey Mathew Fomine, 'A Concise Historical Survey of the Bamum Dynasty and the Influence of Islam in Foumban, Cameroon, 1390–Present', *African Anthropologist* 16, nos. 1&2 (2009), 69–92.

[18] Stolz to Komitee der Evangl. Missionsgesellschaft zu Basel, 22 January 1906, in BMA E-2,20b, 382. See also Christraud M. Geary, 'Political Dress: German-Style Military Attire and Colonial Politics in Bamum', in Fowler and Zeitlyn (eds), *African Crossroads*, 170.

[19] Marie Pauline Thorbecke, 'Bamum', in Franz Thorbecke (ed), *Im Hochland von Mittel-Kamerun* (Hamburg: L. Friedrichsen & Co., 1914), 15.

independence'.[20] Ruling over a 'culturally elevated population', Thorbecke argued, the king had from inner conviction eagerly embraced Western rule and westernization more broadly from the beginnings of the German period. Thereafter, she claimed, 'it was Njoya's greatest wish and most earnest endeavour to civilize himself and his entire people as quickly as possible according to the European model.'[21]

Njoya was also praised for his pro-German attitude by other German observers, who saw in him a modernizer and an exceptional personality. From their earliest contact with Bamum, German officials considered Njoya to be amongst the most dependable kings in the colony. In the initial reports of his visit to Bamum, the German officer Richard Hirtler described the king as a decidedly pro-German ruler, 'a man who fulfils all the hopes expected of him'. Njoya, he argued was 'a great friend of the German cause' who had 'proved his loyalty on more than one occasion'. Lapsing into racial typologies, he praised Njoya's 'relatively high cultural level and his intelligence', which 'elevate him far above the other chiefs of the district'. The way Njoya had treated him, Hirtler enthused, was 'simply grandiose, and what I saw made a positive impression.'[22] The Basel missionary Martin Göhring concurred, arguing that, 'Njoya is absolutely a rare African personality. He is interested in everything.' In light of Njoya's receptivity to Christian practices (monogamy notwithstanding), another missionary, Karl Stolz, would also praise him as a 'clever and farsighted king'.[23]

This sanguine version of the success of Germany's civilizing mission in Bamum, and Cameroon more broadly, has had some recent proponents, with Emmanuel Matateyou arguing that 'on balance it seems that German colonization had more positive sides to it for the Bamumian people...The German colonies are to be credited for several social and infrastructural achievements. Their presence allowed the Bamumian people to gain access to modern civilization without bloodshed.'[24] So too, Mveng has argued that the German colonizers offered much to Cameroon:

> Ports (Rio del Rey, Victoria, Tiko, Douala, Kribi...), maritime stations (Ukoko, Campo, Grand-Batanga...), modern cities (Douala, Yaounde, Ebolowa, Edea...), impressive military fortresses (Yoko, Mora...), a railway network,

---

[20] Thorbecke, 'Bamum', 20.   [21] Thorbecke, 'Bamum', 18.

[22] Richard Hirtler 'Bericht des Oberlieutenant Hirtler über seine Expedition nach Bamum', *Deutsches Kolonialblatt* 14 (1903), 493, also cited in Christraud Geary and Adamou Ndam Njoya, *Mandu Yenu: Bilder aus Bamum, einem westafrikanischen Königreich 1902-1915* (Munich: Trickster Verlag, 1985), 171.

[23] Göhring, 31 December 1907, in BMA E-2, 25, 61; Stolz, 'Ueberblick über den Stand unserer Arbeit und die sich ergebenden Aufgaben', 20 March 1908, in BMA E-2, 26, 90, 5.

[24] Emmanuel Matateyou, 'King Njoya and the Kingdom of Bamum', in David McBride, Leroy Hopkins, and Carol Blackshire-Belay (eds), *Crosscurrents: African Americans, Africa, and Germany in the Modern World* (Columbia, SC: Camden House, 1998), 157.

roads, huge plantations,...hospitals, schools, a well-structured administration, an African elite every day more numerous, none of these achievements which are the pride of colonizing peoples were missing on the honour roll of Germany. Germany created Cameroon, which did not exist before, a magnificent accomplishment. In the centuries to come, this African land, today proud to be independent, will not forget those who in the colonial melee have providentially shaped its destiny.[25]

Such *ex post facto* endorsements of the civilizing effects of German colonization contrast greatly with Njoya's own often repeated account, however, which foregrounded not enthusiasm, but rather his alarm, caution, and a sense of the greater military and social risks that would be posed if the Bamum massacred the Europeans who arrived in 1902:

The whites arrived. The Bamum said to the king, 'Let's make war on the whites.' 'No,' he replied. 'The whites are my friends!' Thus, the whites settled in the land of the blacks. All the kings who wanted to oppose the whites were defeated. 'Bamum,' said the king, 'you see, if I had acted stupidly, the whites would have conquered Bamum.' The Bamum said 'It is true what King Njoya says. If King Njoya says something, no one should doubt it. King Njoya's wisdom is superior to that of all other people.'[26]

This glimpse at the internal divisions in Fumban when the Germans arrived illustrates the extent to which German colonialism and Njoya's hold on power in Bamum were mutually constitutive. Indeed, as late as 1914, the Germans still saw the need to support Njoya, who, it was reported to Berlin, 'has to deal with a strong reactionary party in his lands, which sees his pro-European views and progressive perspective as a departure from ancestral ways and customs'.[27] As his memoir makes clear, Njoya was fully aware of both his domestic vulnerability and the earlier violent punitive expeditions launched elsewhere in the colony in the 1890s.[28] Given what Stefanie Michels has called the 'extremely brutal and sadistic

---

[25] Mveng, *Histoire du Cameroun*, 338.

[26] Njoya, 'Geschichte der Bamum-Könige aus Rifum', 11–12; Njoya, *Histoire et coutumes des Bamum*, 41. Njoya's repeated retelling of this incident illustrates its importance to him as an explanation for his seeming embrace of autocolonization.

[27] As quoted in Karin Hausen, *Deutsche Kolonialherrschaft in Afrika: Wirtschaftsinteressen und Kolonialverwaltung in Kamerun vor 1914* (Zurich: Atlantis Verlag, 1970), 167.

[28] For the wars fought for control of Cameroon, see Hans Dominik, *Kamerun: Sechs Kriegs- und Friedensjahre in deutschen Tropen* (Berlin: Ernst Siegfried Mittler und Sohn, 1901); Hans Dominik, *Vom Atlantik zum Tschadsee: Kriegs- und Forschungsfahrten in Kamerun* (Berlin: Ernst Siegrfried Mittler und Sohn, 1908). For Cameroonian oral histories of this period of warfare, see Albert-Pascal Temgoua, 'Souvenirs de l'époque coloniale allemande au Cameroun: Témoignages des Camerounais', in Stefanie Michels and Albert-Pascal Temgoua (eds), *La Politique de la mémoire coloniale en Allemagne et au Cameroun—The Politics of Colonial Memory in Germany and Cameroon* (Münster: Lit

nature of these wars,'[29] it is unsurprising that Njoya decided that the tempting short-term expediency of massacring a small and vulnerable party of whites who arrived in Fumban in 1902 might well have genocidal consequences for the Bamum in the longer term:

> After that, the whites appeared. 'Let's resist them; let's drive them out,' said the Bamum. 'No,' said Njoya, He saw in dreams what the whites would do to the Bamum. 'If we make war on the whites, all Bamum will be destroyed too. Only a few of you will remain, you will be unhappy.' And Njoya himself removed the Bamum arrows, spears, and rifles. The whites arrived and did not make war on them. Thus, Njoya contributed to the happiness of the Bamum.[30]

Notwithstanding the fact that Njoya's account dates to the late German period, there is no reason to doubt that the Bamum were split on the question of war or peace with the Germans, given that the same question had emerged and been answered differently across Cameroon. The king's account illustrates his firm understanding of what was happening all over Cameroon. Knowing the costs of resistance, he urged peace, even under the most trying of circumstances, in the interests of preserving the kingdom and his rule over it. Even when a second expedition of Germans directly assaulted the dignity of Njoya by walking on the king's royal carpet and by sitting on his throne, Njoya intervened to stop the angry crowd of thousands armed with rifles and spears from killing the disrespectful Germans.[31] Given the backdrop of colonial violence, German accounts of Njoya as a welcoming and instinctively pro-German ruler who was convinced of the superiority of European culture should be treated with deep suspicion.

The Nso War and King Nsangu's Head

Around the time of Hans Glauning's 1905–6 wars across Cameroon, Njoya signalled his desire to draw even closer to the Germans by joining German military operations. In particular, Njoya sent his troops to fight in a military campaign undertaken by German-led African forces against Bamum's local adversaries, the Nso of the Bamenda Grassfields. In early 1906, when Glauning led a large army on this military campaign, visiting Bamum on the way,[32] Njoya enthusiastically

---

Verlag, 2005), 25–35. See also Geary, *Things of the Palace*, 63; Monika Midel, *Fulbe und Deutsche in Adamaua (Nord-Kamerun) 1809–1916: Auswirkungen afrikanischer und kolonialer Eroberung*, (Bern: Peter Lang, 1990), 140.

[29] Michels, *Imagined Power Contested*, 373.
[30] Njoya, *Histoire et Coutumes des Bamum*, 42.
[31] Geary, *Things of the Palace*, 63.
[32] Martin Göhring, 13 May 1906, in BMA E-2, 22, 279, 4–5.

joined the campaign against this rival kingdom, adding 200 of his own warriors to Glauning's 190 African troops.[33]

From the German perspective, the war against the Nso was an outcome of a global tightening of their colonial security position in the wake of what the Germans still saw as the 'unprovoked' Herero uprising in German South West Africa. As the African expert August Seidel warned in 1906, 'Alongside a strong military force only continuous observation and extreme caution can protect us from catastrophes like the one that recently befell us in South West Africa.'[34] In Cameroon, it was decided that the loyalty of the Nso was doubtful and that such potential military risks could no longer be accepted.

The Basel missionary Göhring gave the reason for the German attack as being that the Nso had 'for a long time no longer subordinated themselves to the authority of the military station Bamenda,'[35] something also attested to by Nso oral tradition.[36] It is worth pointing out, however, that this security risk had been created by the behaviour of the Germans themselves. As Verkijika Fanso and Elizabeth Chilver have made clear, although the first contacts between the Germans and the Nso were largely harmonious from the German perspective, from the Nso point of view the Germans had signally failed in their diplomacy by neglecting to 'make presents: they treated the Nso like monkeys'.[37] It was not until the expedition of the notoriously violent Hans Houben in June 1902, however, that Nso attitudes towards the Germans hardened, after he burnt down the palace in Kumbo, ransacked the town, massacred the locals, tortured to death the king's chief servant, and shot one of his own guides whom he suspected of taking them in the wrong direction.[38]

From Njoya's point of view, however, the campaign was not merely an opportunity to demonstrate his loyalty to the Germans. Rather, it represented an opportunity for him to consolidate his domestic power through a successful military campaign and, crucially, offered him a chance to attack a rival regional power. Indeed, the Nso had not only defeated Bamum in a war in the late 1880s but in the course of this war had also decapitated Njoya's father, King Nsangu.[39] Nsangu's

---

[33] Hans Glauning, 'Kamerun: Bericht des Hauptmann Glauning in Bamenda über die Bansso-Expedition', *Deutsches Kolonialblatt* 17 (1906), 705; Gwanfogbe, 'Resistance to European Penetration into Africa', 125.

[34] August Seidel, *Deutsch-Kamerun. Wie es ist und was es verspricht* (Berlin: H. J. Meidinger, 1906), 35.

[35] Martin Göhring, 13 May 1906, in BMA E-2, 22, 279, 10.

[36] Verkijika G. Fanso and Bongfen Chem-Langhëë, 'Nso Military Organisation and Warfare in the Nineteenth and Twentieth Centuries', in Fowler and Zeitlyn (eds), *African Crossroads*, 102.

[37] Verkijika G. Fanso and Elizabeth M. Chilver, 'The Nso and the Germans: The First Encounters in Contemporary Documents and in Oral Tradition', in B. Chem-Langhëë and V. G. Fanso (eds), *Nso' and its Neighbours: Readings in the Social History of the Western Grassfields of Cameroon* (Oxford: African Books Collective, 2011), 119–24.

[38] Fanso and Chilver, 'The Nso and the Germans', 124–9; Hoffmann, *Okkupation und Militärverwaltung*, vol. 2, 114.

[39] For the Nso version of the campaign, see Fanso and Chilver, 'The Nso and the Germans', 119–51.

head had been kept as a war trophy and had become a humiliating symbol of the enduring regional dominance of the Nso.

Although Emmanuel Matateyou has suggested that Njoya's compliant attitude towards the Germans had been aimed more or less solely at cajoling them into just such a revanchist military campaign against the Nso, so that he could retrieve the head of his father for ceremonial purposes,[40] this seems to invert both the causality and the power relations between the Bamum and the Germans. Njoya may have, as the Basel missionary Göhring argued at the time, 'enthusiastically joined with Glauning against the Nso to take revenge',[41] but the decision to attack them was not his. Even Njoya's own less than modest account of the war does not claim that it had been his own idea:

> The Nso refused to receive the Germans. They [the Germans] went to wage war in their country, accompanied by King Njoya. The king fought with ardour, and the Nso nearly killed him. The Bamum killed 1,500 Nso. When King Njoya returned from the war, the Kaiser gave him a medal, supporting him and recognizing the help he had given to the Germans. Sometime later, the Kaiser again gave a medal to the king, in exchange for the services he had rendered. The Germans loved King Njoya, and they honoured him very much.[42]

By the end of the German colonial period, the awarding of medals and honours to Africans (alongside Europeans) who had served militarily on behalf of the Germans on the colonial frontier was not particularly rare. In 1913, for example, twenty-two African non-commissioned police officers (*Unteroffiziere*) and soldiers were awarded medals of the Order of the Crown for more than twenty years' service with the German colonial authorities in German East Africa.[43] In Cameroon, other African leaders besides Njoya were awarded service medals, with the Red Eagle medal being awarded by the Kaiser to Lamido Buba of Garua and Lamido Halide from Binder. Their advisers were also given the Crown medal.[44]

---

[40] Matateyou, 'King Njoya and the Kingdom of Bamum', 154–5.

[41] Martin Göhring, 13 May 1906, in BMA E-2, 22, 279, 10.

[42] Njoya, *Histoire et coutumes des Bamum*, 134.

[43] Conze to Valentini, 22 October 1913, in GStAPK, Rep 89 Rep 3279, 'Akten betr. Ordensverleihungen in den Schutzgebieten. Sammelberichte'. For an example of a European settler colonist being awarded the Crown medal see the case of Alexander Niet in German South West Africa in 1908: Derberg to Lucanus, Berlin, 3 March 1908, in GStAPK, IHA Rep 89 Nr 32478, 'Akten betr. Ordensverleihungen in den Schutzgebieten. Sammelberichte'.

[44] Conze to Valentini, 19 August 1913, in GStAPK Rep 89 Rep 3279, (unnumbered). Lamido Buba was awarded his medal for his 'unswerving friendliness to Europeans and unwavering loyalty' in the face of a Fulbe uprising in 1907. Lamido Halide was awarded for the 'outstanding loyalty' he showed to the Germans by moving his capital and bearing substantial territorial losses and dissent amongst his own people when the border between German and French territory was shifted in 1908.

In 1906/7, however, such awards were unheard of in Cameroon, and it is unsurprising that Njoya proudly displayed his medals to the missionary Göhring, who
wrote patronizingly of the incident:

> In recognition of his good service in the military sphere—he had supported the
> colonial army in the expedition against the Nso—he was awarded the Military
> Merit Medal in silver. For his achievements in regard to economics and agricul-
> ture he received the Crown Order Medal in gold. He is as proud as a king of both
> decorations.[45]

Quick to mention his decoration for service from Wilhelm II, what Njoya did not
mention was that the tactical freelancing and disorderly atrocities committed by
the steadily increasing numbers of Bamum soldiers invading Nso territory
became a military liability to the Germans. One oral Nso account of the Bamum
campaign suggests that 'women and children were killed so that Nso should die,
so that no women should be left to conceive Nso.'[46] After it became clear that
Njoya's troops were plundering conquered Nso lands and murdering the inhabitants without regard to their commanders or military imperatives, the Bamum
warriors and Njoya were escorted back home over the border on 3 May 1906.[47]

Although the Bamum held a great celebration to herald their victory and Njoya
proudly informed the Basel missionaries that he had personally killed two men in
the campaign,[48] it was German priorities that had counted in this expedition. As
Glauning's report of the 1906 war makes clear, beyond military imperatives, preparing the region and its people for the coming of European plantations and agriculture was also important. Indeed, Glauning ended his report of the campaign
with a careful description of the landscape, climate, and vegetation of the region
in which he had just waged war. He also reported that, once the Nso had surrendered, the African troops under German command were not permitted to destroy
the villages and towns they had just defeated 'on economic grounds'. The broader
economic background to this military push into a somewhat distant region was
made abundantly clear in the final paragraphs of the report:

> With the establishment of better transport routes to the coast, products such as
> rubber, cola, and ivory could come under consideration for export alongside
> cotton, tobacco, wax, goatskins, and corn, which is extensively cultivated. Given
> its elevated position and its climate, as well as the soil's suitability for agriculture
> and cattle ranging, the region would also suit settlement by European settlers.[49]

---

[45] Göhring, 31 December 1907, in BMA E-2, 25, 61, See also Geary and Njoya, *Mandu Yenu*, 174.
[46] Fanso and Chilver, 'The Nso and the Germans', 136.
[47] Glauning, 'Kamerun', 705; Hoffmann, *Okkupation und Militärverwaltung*, vol. 1, 211.
[48] Martin Göhring 13 May 1906, in BMA E-2, 22, 279, 10.   [49] Glauning, 'Kamerun', 706–7.

Glauning's military campaign against the Nso was no mere punitive raid. It also paved the way for new plans for the wholesale economic penetration of the Bamenda Grassfields, where, as in the rest of Cameroon, 'the idea of plantations was decisive from the very beginning of the colonial era.'[50] Although the expedition had been sparked by the hostility shown by the Nso towards the Germans after Houben's assault on the region, German military power also served to establish the requisite security conditions for planned new economic ventures, including plantations and settler outposts. Meanwhile, the Reichstag was offered the ever-successful rationale that the Nso had been attacked because they were 'much feared slavers'.[51]

Notwithstanding the German locus of the campaign, Njoya also profited from the defeat of the Nso. The only Nso village that was destroyed by German troops was a small one on the border of Bamum territory from which Nso raids had been launched. Destroying it was a fundamental step towards securing Njoya's territory.[52]

More importantly for Njoya, however, was the fact that the head of his father, King Nsangu, killed and decapitated while leading his troops against the Nso, was returned to Bamum. The German officer who returned it to him, Karl von Wenckstern, described the handover of the relic to Njoya in detail:

Two hours after my arrival in Batabi…I met the Chief Njoya, to whom I had earlier sent news of the delivery of the head and who was accompanied by many of his nobles and some of his soldiers.

After a heartfelt greeting, Njoya entreated me to give him the head of his father today. The delivery of the head was a truly touching scene…there was a certain mistrust to be read in the faces of Njoya and his nobles…In Njoya's face the question plainly stood "Is it really the right head?" It was a peculiar, endlessly expressive look with which Njoya considered the skull that I held before him.

Then the strong, large man broke down, sobbing like a child. Njoya was lifted up by his nobles, most of whom were violently weeping, and seated on a chair. It took a long time until he had calmed down; then he asked me to give him the head. He stroked it and cradled it in tears.[53]

For Njoya, the Nso campaign marked a qualitative shift in his relationship with the Germans. The return of King Nsangu's head was the beginning of the

---

[50] Halldén, *The Culture Policy of the Basel Mission in the Cameroons*, 94.
[51] Fanso and Chem-Langhëë, 'Nso Military Organisation and Warfare', 102.
[52] Glauning, 'Kamerun', 706.
[53] Karl von Wenckstern, 'Der Kopf des Bamum-Herrschers', *Deutsches Kolonialblatt* 18 (1907), 258–9. For Nso accounts of the return of Nsangu's head, see Fanso and Chilver, 'The Nso and the Germans', 139–41.

high-water mark of his goodwill towards the Germans, with Wenckstern over-whelmed by the effusive thanks that were showered on him by Njoya. The Basel missionary Göhring also commented that since then 'the king and the king's mother are extremely friendly and obliging towards us. The king visits us more often and stays interminably.' Hopes of an imminent mass conversion to Christianity were high.[54]

The return of Nsangu's head was not simply a moment of family sentimentality. Rather, in an environment in which royal power remained tied to public demon-strations of political and military success, the return of the war trophy to Fumban further consolidated Njoya's claims to kingship in the eyes of his people, signal-ling a homecoming for a fallen king and the renewed power of Bamum over the Nso.[55] It also validated Njoya's appeasement strategy towards the Germans. According to Njoya, the gift of Nsangu's head by the Germans would never be forgotten by him or his people. 'I tell you openly', he said to Wenckstern, 'it is only now that I really see, that the whites mean to do me good.' These were sentiments that he reinforced in a speech before his people when they had returned to Fumban.[56] In his own account, the king dwelt on German praise for the king-dom's loyalty during the war:

> The Bamum thought that they could not take vengeance for the death of their parents, their fathers, their king, whose heads had remained in the land of the Nso, but he, Njonga, avenged these dead by triumphing over the Nso. Hauptmann Glauning gave a medal to the king, saying that he was a brave man and so too were the Bamum. Sometime later, the Kaiser, through Governor Ebermaier, gave me, Njoya, a medal with a lot of congratulations.
>
> The Bamum were pleased to see that the king had avenged those who had fallen on the battlefield in the land of the Nso, and they were trying to satisfy the Germans for the decorations, the works, and the good they do for them.[57]

Mandu Yenu

It is within the context of the Nso campaign and Njoya's long-term strategy of preserving his autonomy by courting good relations with the two hegemonic powers in his region that his gift of his father's throne, Mandu Yenu, to Wilhelm II

[54] Martin Göhring, 13 May 1906, in BMA E-2, 22, 279, 7, 9–10.
[55] Steven Nelson, 'Collection and Context in a Cameroonian Village', *Museum International* 59, no. 3 (2007), 25.
[56] Wenckstern, 'Der Kopf des Bamum-Herrschers', 259.
[57] Njoya, *Histoire et coutumes des Bamum*, 135.

must be seen. The gift remains contentious, with Eugène Désiré Eloundou, amongst others, casting useful doubt on just how free this choice to send his throne to Germany was. Certainly, given the clear power differentials between Germany and Bamum, the balance between royal agency and colonial structures must be assessed carefully.[58] On the one hand, Njoya was unambiguous in his initial reluctance to part with the throne. On the other, in the end he did so seemingly willingly. His reasons for this apparent change of heart are complex and cannot be simply ascribed solely to German coercion.

Diplomatic gift exchanges between King Njoya and Kaiser Wilhelm II were not unusual, with Njoya having earlier sent the German emperor a royal pipe, a chiefly sword with an embroidered sheath, and a royal headdress.[59] Indeed, the gift of the throne had been preceded by a flurry of mutual exchanges of gifts between Njoya and Wilhelm II in 1904 and 1905. During this period, Njoya also sent five enormous and ornately decorated ivory tusks to the emperor, which were received with diplomatic gratitude.[60] In return, Njoya was given silk and damask, inscribed German flags, a portrait of the Kaiser, and several cuirassier helmets decorated with the imperial eagle and spike, swords, and pieces of armour.[61] It was these gifts which became the basis for Njoya's incorporation of German uniforms into his semiotics of rule, outfitting himself and his troops in German military attire on some ceremonial occasions.[62]

As the correspondence between the director of the African division of the Berlin ethnological museum, Felix von Luschan, and Glauning in Cameroon makes clear, Njoya had clearly and repeatedly been approached to make this particular gift. In December 1905, Luschan had asked Glauning to attempt via 'peaceful and legal means' to secure the throne, or if that was not possible, to obtain a copy of it. In March 1906, that is, one month before the campaign against the Nso began, Glauning reported back to Luschan that 'unfortunately he could not report anything encouraging,' because although Njoya was in favour of it, his nobles were firmly against it, because 'it was the throne of his father and they fear evil if they gave it up.'[63] At this time, Njoya seems to have felt that he was clearly

---

[58] Eugène Désiré Eloundou, *Le Sud-Kamerun face à l'hégémonie allemande 1884–1916* (Paris: L'Harmattan, 2016), 78. This accords with recent popular accounts that doubt the freedom of choice exercised by Njoya. See, for example, the perspective of the movement that has mobilized against the Humboldt Forum and its colonial artefacts in which the throne is described in the following terms: 'Its history is characteristic of the often denied unequal power relations as well as the questionable dealings of European museums with the numerous treasures from the once colonized parts of the world' (*No Humboldt21! Moratorium für das Humboldt-Forum im Berliner Schloss*, http://www.no-humboldt21.de/information/preussischer-kulturbesitz/#juni2013, June 2013, accessed 18 October 2021).

[59] Eloundou, *Le Sud-Kamerun face à l'hégémonie allemande 1884–1916*, 78.

[60] Puttkamer to German Foreign Office, 8 February 1904; Eulenberg to German Foreign Office, 16 April 1904; Puttkamer to German Foreign Office, 6 January 1905, in BA Berlin R1001/4102, 'Geschenke an Häuptlinge in Kamerun und in den Nachbarkolonien und Gegengeschenke', 75–9, 97.

[61] Tippelskirche to German Foreign Office, 21 March 1905, in BA Berlin R1001/4102, 103–4.

[62] Tippelskirche to German Foreign Office, 21 March 1905, in BA Berlin R1001/4102, 103–4.

[63] Luschan to Glauning, 15 December 1905; Glauning to Luschan, 24 March 1906, quoted in Geary and Njoya, *Mandu Yenu*, 180.

Figure 10.1 King Njoya's with his throne, Mandu Yenu, in 1906

within his rights to refuse to offer the throne, a remaining symbol of his father's authority, as a gift without fear of any repercussions for his refusal (Figure 10.1).

When Glauning approached Njoya again in 1906, however, this time after the Nso campaign, the king's reaction was, according to Glauning, very different:

One other piece of news! Chief Njoya of Bamum, whom I recently visited, said to me that he intends to visit the governor on the coast in a few months. I used the opportunity and prompted him, as I knew that he was unwilling to give away the famous throne of his father, and, given the attitude of his people he could not, that he should however create an exact copy of the throne and present it to the governor as a gift for His Majesty the Kaiser. I told him that the Kaiser is interested in such things and has a house in which all of these things are preserved. Njoya was very enthusiastic about this suggestion and promised me that he would commission a true copy of the original. He also promised me not to offer the original to anyone else.[64]

The gift of a copy of the royal throne of Bamum to the Kaiser was, according to the ex-governor, Puttkamer (who disingenuously represented himself as the pivotal figure in the entire operation), a gift specifically intended to convey thanks for the Germans' campaign against the Nso:

These objects are of an inestimable aesthetic value. That is why through Captain Ramsay's knowledge of the existence of the royal chair, I immediately tried to save it for the Berlin museum. Captain Glauning was in charge of negotiations. On 27 February 1908, when I had the honour to exhibit our recent acquisitions to show to his Majesty the Kaiser the writing invented by Njoya himself, it was possible for me to announce to him that the royal throne would be added, which this intelligent and loyal tribal chief wanted to give him in thanks for the military support that we brought him.[65]

In the event, however, it was not a copy but the original throne which was sent to the German emperor. In April 1908, Bernhard Ankermann informed Luschan that, because those crafting the copy of the throne had run out of time before Njoya was leaving for the coast, the king had been 'encouraged' by the Basel missionary Göhring to present the original throne to Governor Seitz as a gift to the Kaiser. From Njoya's perspective, his visit to the governor on the Cameroon coastline to deliver his throne was too important to be delayed, given that it was also a commercial voyage related to his attempts to consolidate direct trade with the Europeans in Duala. As Göhring later reported to the Basel Mission, 'Njoya wanted to profit somehow from his visit.'[66]

[64] Glauning to Luschan, 19 July 1907, quoted in Geary and Njoya, *Mandu Yenu*, 181.

[65] Puttkamer to Colonial Office, quoted in Eloundou, *Le Sud-Kamerun face à l'hégémonie allemande 1884–1916*, 78.

[66] Ankermann to Luschan, 26 April 1908, quoted in Geary and Njoya, *Mandu Yenu*, 181. For Göhrings report of Njoya's trip to the coast to offer his throne as a gift to the Kaiser, see Göhring, 'Jahresbericht', 27 January 1909, in BMA E-2, 28, 65. See Göhring, 'Quartalbericht', 2 October 1908, in BMA E-2, 28, 64.

In his report to the colonial office, Seitz reported back on the gift of the throne (accompanied by other presents such as a sword, headdress, and pipe), saying that Njoya had refused all other offers for it once he had heard that Wilhelm II was interested in such objects. Seitz patronizingly urged its acceptance as an expression of Njoya's 'repeatedly proven loyalty' and 'above all his childlike and certainly sincere devotion to the person of His Majesty the Kaiser', which, he argued, was an example to other rulers in Cameroon.[67]

If Seitz's characterization of Njoya's loyalty to the Kaiser is read in isolation, the provenance of the throne (which is still in Berlin) does seem to point to the exploitation of the goodwill of a subordinate and infantilized African monarch. Read together, however, with Njoya's firm sense that the Nso campaign marked a qualitative shift in the relationship between Bamum and Germany, as well as the last-minute decision of Njoya to keep the new throne and send off the old one to ensure that he would not have to cancel his important coastal venture, then the charge of cynical exploitation of a helpless African monarch appears less plausible.

It seems not unreasonable to suggest that, after the campaign against the Nso, Njoya wanted to make a large gift that would cement his position in the eyes of the Kaiser (see Figure 10.2). That the throne was a relic of his father's rule is also signifi-cant under the circumstances, given the centrality of the recovery of King Nsangu's head to Njoya's understanding of the Nso campaign. Ute Röschenthaler appears correct in arguing that Njoya's motives for the gift were a mix of practicality—namely that the copy of the throne that he had agreed to send was not yet ready and he wanted to present a gift at the birthday celebrations—and obligation, arising from the sense of personal and political debt that Njoya felt he had incurred after the Nso campaign and the return of King Nsangu's head.[68]

The Limits to Germanization

Prior to the Nso campaign, Njoya had already begun experimenting with the introduction of German artefacts, clothing, and symbols of power into his self-presentation as Bamum's king. He had also offered the German emperor (and the governor) gifts of his own, notably ivory, in an attempt to create a personal bond between the two monarchs. The gifts of clothing, armour, and weapons from Wilhelm II had also enabled Njoya to create German uniforms that were worn by himself and his soldiers on ceremonial occasions in a simulation of German

[67] Seitz to the Colonial Office, 7 February 1908, in BA Berlin R1001/4102, 116–18. Also quoted in Geary and Njoya, *Mandu Yenu*, 186.
[68] Ute Röschenthaler, 'Of Objects and Contexts: Biographies of Ethnographica', *Journal des Africanistes* 69, no. 1 (1999), 93–5.

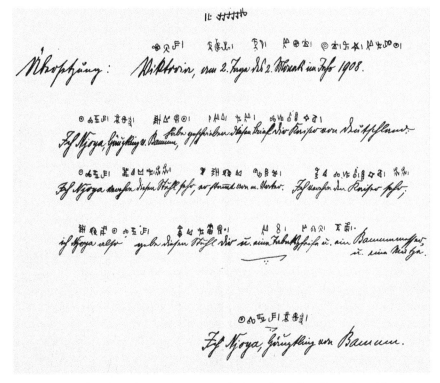

Figure 10.2 Sultan Njoya's 1908 letter to Wilhelm II formally offering him Mandu Yenu as a present, translated by Göhring

ceremonial forms that suggested Njoya's attachment and proximity to the German monarch.

Njoya's use of German uniforms was quite short-lived, however, certainly too short-lived to be 'the dominant visual symbol of the alliance between the Bamum and the Germans'.[69] Nor was the adoption of German dress a sign of Njoya's subjugation. Rather, Njoya's appropriation of German uniforms, particularly for the purpose of being photographed by German photographers, offered a visual expression of Njoya's claim to royal status, if not equality, with his German observers. Consequently, Geary is quite correct in arguing that 'The most prominent theme in the photographs was "Njoya, the powerful and intelligent king."'[70] As Michael Rowlands too has made clear, the photographs of Njoya taken in 1908 at the German emperor's birthday celebrations were intentionally calibrated for the impact they would make in Berlin. 'Njoya certainly knew', Rowlands has

---

[69] Christraud M. Geary, *Images from Bamum: German Colonial Photography at the Court of King Njoya, Cameroon, West Africa, 1902–1915* (Washington DC: Smithsonian Institute Press, 1988), 53–9.
[70] Geary, *Images from Bamum*, 50.

Figure 10.3 King Njoya in German-style uniform

argued, 'that the photograph would be taken back and shown to the German court' (see Figure 10.3).[71]

This modicum of *imitatio imperii* also held local significance, as an appropriation of German forms that offered a visual expression to the Bamum and other Africans of Njoya's close ties to German power.[72] His deliberately chosen German-style costumery was 'designed to reinforce the power of Njoya',[73] by appropriating and translating the semiotics of German courtly attire into a local 'indigenous idiom' endowed with meaning according to both African and European categories.[74] The same effect was achieved when the German national anthem was taught in Njoya's local school, where the original lyrics were

---

[71] Michael Rowlands, 'Of Substances, Palaces and Museums: The Visible and the Invisible in the Constitution of Cameroon', *Journal of the Royal Anthropological Institute* 17 (2011), s23–s38.

[72] On the concept of *imitatio imperii*, see Christian Scholl, 'Imitatio Imperii? Elements of Imperial Rule in the Barbarian Successor States of the Roman West', in Christian Scholl, Torben R. Gebhardt, and Jan Clauß (eds), *Transcultural Approaches to the Concept of Imperial Rule in the Middle Ages* (Frankfurt am Main: Peter Lang, 2017), 20–39.

[73] Rowlands, 'Of Substances, Palaces and Museums', s29.

[74] Geary, 'Political Dress', 180, 189.

seamlessly adapted into the local language to become the equivalent of 'Fumban Fumban *über alles*'.[75]

Neither ethnic drag nor burlesque, Njoya's rendering of Wilhelm II's sartorial language of power was an example of what Nicholas Thomas has described as a politically laden 'intercultural transaction' through which questions of power were self-consciously mediated through the retooling of foreign cultural artefacts.[76] This appropriation of European symbols of office to convey political status to both European and African constituencies mirrored Njoya's earlier foray into adopting Hausa dress as an expression of his political affiliation with them. In both instances, a delicate balance between the local and the new had to be struck.[77]

Between 1908 and 1910, however, Njoya's flirtation with German cultural forms as a way of signalling his identification with his German allies began to wane. It was replaced by a renewed interest in signalling his simultaneous attachment to the Islamic north. In religion and culture, Njoya became adept at code-switching between the European Christian forms of the Germans and the Islamic cultural forms of the Hausa and Fulbe as a way of reconciling the competing demands of maintaining his autonomy without alienating either of the hegemonic powers in his region.

Njoya's guarded preservation of his independence was signalled in his approach to religion and his balancing of Christianity, Islam, and local religious forms. Despite being seen by the Basel missionaries as outwardly 'amenable to everything',[78] Njoya never converted to Christianity and remained (at least nominally) a Muslim throughout the German period. Yet even this was not a simple expression of open solidarity with the Muslim Hausa traders who came to Fumban, for whom he had built a small mosque near his palace. Indeed, after Njoya had lost patience with the Hausa's apparently less than honest trading practices, he had this mosque demolished and moved to 'a newly built Hausa village' on the outskirts of town.[79] In place of the old mosque Njoya even allowed a small chapel to be built, sparking misplaced hope that he would soon Christianize his people.[80]

---

[75] Ernst Vollbehr, cited in Simon Dell, 'Yepap's Resources: Representation and the Arts of the Bamum in Cameroon and France, 1902–1935', in Daniel J. Rycroft, *World Art and the Legacies of Colonial Violence* (Farnham: Ashgate, 2013), 35.

[76] See Nicholas Thomas, *Entangled Objects: Exchange, Material Culture, and Colonialism in the Pacific* (Cambridge: Harvard University Press, 1991), 187. On ethnic drag, see Katrin Sieg, *Ethnic Drag: Performing Race, Nation, Sexuality in West Germany* (Ann Arbor, MI: University of Michigan Press, 2009).

[77] Galitzine-Loumpet, 'Reconsidering Patrimonialization in the Bamun Kingdom', 68.

[78] Göhring, 31 December 1907, in BMA E-2, 25, 61.

[79] Thorbecke, 'Bamum', 20; Schaper, *Koloniale Verhandlungen*, 352.

[80] Wilhelm Schlatter, *Geschichte der Basler Mission 1815–1915*, vol. 3 (Basel: Verlag der Basler Missionsbuchhandlung, 1916), 288–90. Following missionary reports, Schlatter explained Njoya's persistence with Islam as resulting from his commitment to polygamy. See for this reasoning, Stolz, 'Ueberblick über den Stand unserer Arbeit und die sich ergebenden Aufgaben', 20 March 1908, in BMA E-2, 26, 90, 5.

Beyond religion, the king's independence was also reflected in his management of his kingdom's commercial relations. Trade was critical to both his relations with the Islamic north and the German south. As Marie Thorbecke makes clear, the king was economically dependent 'on the whites on the one hand and the Hausa on the other'.[81] Notwithstanding the inordinate pressures of German colonialism, however, King Njoya appears to have negotiated his way through the multidirectional thicket of competing economic priorities created by the Hausa, the German colonial authorities, German missionaries, German traders, coastal Africans, and the various factions within the Bamum nation itself in a highly dexterous fashion.

Exemplifying this is Njoya's deft handling of a dispute with German rubber traders, who had been deliberately suppressing the price they paid him for the commodity by claiming it was of inferior quality. To circumvent their predatory behaviour, Njoya came to an arrangement with the Basel Mission to break the traders' monopoly and secure better prices. The traders complained about this sudden competition from Africans in what they had hoped would be a monopoly trade situation. To ensure that Njoya's goodwill towards the government continued, however, the colonial authorities found in his favour, particularly after he complained about the traders' insulting behaviour towards his mother in Bamum.[82] The language of the judgement is worth noting, in so far as it indicates just how successful Njoya's balancing act had been:

I would add here that the Chief Njoya of Bamum is one of the few great chiefs of Cameroon, who placed himself under German rule voluntarily. Well before colonial troops came to Bamum, he had sent numerous delegations to the governor, to express his recognition of German rule. In 1904 Governor Puttkamer received a number of gifts from Njoya for His Majesty the Kaiser, and in 1905 return gifts from His Majesty were solemnly given to Njoya by Chief Judge Dr Meyer. It is absolutely necessary to avoid the loyalty of such a chief being shattered by the improper actions of a few Europeans, even if this results in a certain hardship for them.[83]

Later, Governor Theodor Seitz too came to be impressed with Njoya's enterprise, stating in his memoirs that 'Njoya in particular knew how to adjust neatly to the new arrangements, and had an account with the Basel Mission in Duala that occasionally had several thousand marks in it.'[84] In his report to Berlin about the

[81] Thorbecke, 'Bamum', 19.

[82] 'Angelegenheit betreffend die Ausweisung des Agenten Schultz aus dem Bamendabezirk', 7 February 1907, in BA Lichterfelde R1001/4292, 'Allgemeine Angelegenheiten der inneren Verwaltung in Kamerun', 107–16; Hausen, Deutsche Kolonialherrschaft in Afrika, 151.

[83] 'An den Herrn Unterstaatssekretär', 30 November 1907, in BA Lichterfelde R1001/4292, 121.

[84] Theodor Seitz, Vom Aufstieg und Niederbruch deutscher Kolonialmacht, vol. 2 (Karlsruhe: Verlag C. F. Müller, 1929), 51.

gift of Njoya's throne, Seitz also expressed his support for Njoya's monopoly-busting economic initiative and restraint in the face of the provocations of German traders outraged by his economic success:

> Regarding the political side of the visit of the Chief of Bamum, I could not refuse the request of the chief to appear in Buea on the birthday of His Majesty, although the appearance of Njoya on the coast might not be in the interests of the companies based in Bamum. The latter have complained through the chamber of commerce in Duala that Njoya is collecting rubber by force with his soldiers, which he then sells to the Basel Mission, and further that he has forbidden his subjects to sell the rubber to the Hausa trading in his lands. Both complaints have been proven to be completely unfounded... Since he has been trading with the Basel Mission, he has regularly been paid well and now has an account with the mission that is 27 000 marks in credit... If one considers the actions of the white traders in Bamum—I need only mention the slander of Njoya's mother by the trader Schultz—it is no wonder that Njoya tries to avoid firms whose representatives often treat him in savage ways. That he continues to deal with whites with the requisite consideration demonstrates the innate tact of this child of nature, who puts to shame many of the ostensible carriers of modern civilization.[85]

Despite their admiration for his business acumen, however, Njoya's appropriation of elements of both European and Hausa culture was less well understood by German observers, and the king's propensity for code-switching puzzled some European observers. Thorbecke, for example, reached for a racialized theory of cultural hierarchy to explain Njoya's assimilation of European culture as merely an 'external mimicry [*Nachahmung*] of European cultural forms', an appropriation demonstrating that 'the African was and is absolutely not in a position to grasp and understand the intrinsic worth and composition of such an old, slowly evolving culture as ours.'[86] Lost to her was the fact that the king's 'mimicry of European forms' was central to what Itohan I. Osayimwese has called Njoya's 'autoethnography', a process of conscious self-fashioning that allowed him to deploy the semiotics of German and Islamic dress, architecture, deportment, and self-representation for political purposes.[87] As part of this process, particularly

---

[85] Seitz to the Colonial Office, 7 February 1908, BA Berlin R1001/4102, 116–18. Also quoted in Geary and Njoya, *Mandu Yenu*, 186–7. For further details of his commercial dealings with the Basel Mission (and the role of a gift and countergift dynamic within it), see Göhring, quoted in Geary and Njoya, *Mandu Yenu*, 204. See also Geary, *Things of the Palace*, 65–6.

[86] Thorbecke, 'Bamum', 18.

[87] Itohan I. Osayimwese, 'Architecture with a Mission: Bamum Autoethnography during the Period of German Colonialism', in Nina Berman, Klaus Mühlhahn, and Patrice Nganang (eds), *German Colonialism Revisited: African, Asian and Oceanic Experiences* (Ann Arbor, MI: University of Michigan Press, 2014), 31–49.

between 1906 and 1910, Njoya purposively grafted German cultural and economic practices onto Bamum, all the way down to attending mission Christmas
celebrations with his highly esteemed mother and incorporating German architectural forms into new buildings in his capital.[88] At the same time, however,
Njoya continued to orient himself towards the Muslim kingdoms to his north,
maintaining a careful middle road between the two regional hegemons.[89]
Thorbecke confessed that the continued cultural and religious inroads made by
Islam were of great concern to some German observers, admitting that:

> It is frequently expressed that through the donning of Fulbe attire and the
> absorption of many of the colourfully theatrical Fulbe customs Njoya could also
> be gradually drawn across to the religion of the Fulbe, to Islam, and thereby be
> pushed into opposition to German rule, under the protection of which the
> Christian mission works.[90]

Although Thorbecke registered Njoya's renewed engagement with the Islamic
north, she misunderstood how and why it had occurred. Njoya had shifted, she
claimed, 'partly on his own initiative, partly under the mild pressure of the government, from indiscriminately mimicking all things European'. It was largely as a
result of this pressure, she maintained, that 'he has returned to wearing African
attire; not the old indigenous Bamum attire that may have struck him as too hum-
ble, but rather the attire of the Hausa and Fulbe, whose splendour and rich materials better convey in his opinion the dignity of a great chief.'[91] Thorbecke sought
to reassure her German audience that 'in no way does this discarding of European
dress represent an inner disassociation from the Germans, an internal rejection of
their rule. Njoya reassures anyone who will listen that he sees in the whites his
friends and his mentors from whom he and his people can only learn.' Rather, she
insisted, it was a simple question of expense.[92]

---

[88] Göhring, 31 December 1907, in BMA E-2, 25, 61; Osayimwese, 'Architecture with a Mission';
Mark D. Delancey, 'The Spread of the Sooro: Symbols of Power in the Sokoto Caliphate', *Journal of the
Society of Architectural Historians* 71, no. 2 (2012), 177. On Njoya's intimate involvement in and oversight of Fumban's architecture, see Paul Jenkins, 'Bamum 1906–1915: A Royal Architect, His
Missionary Builder and a Historical Relationship in Need of a Substantial Present-Day Re-Assessment',
in Geert Castryck, Silke Strichrodt, and Katja Werthmann (eds), *Sources and Methods for African
History and Culture: Essays in Honour of Adam Jones* (Leipzig: Leipziger Universitätsverlag,
2016), 214–42.
[89] Alongside dress and architecture, perhaps the best indicator of Njoya's capacity to navigate the
tensions between European and African hegemons was his development of his own written script (as
exemplified by Figure 10.2) that was uniquely his and neither European nor North African. Kenneth J,
Orosz, 'Njoya's Alphabet: The Sultan of Bamum and French Colonial Reactions to the A ka u ku
Script', *Cahiers d'études africaines* 217 (2015), 45–66; Thorbecke, 'Bamum', 20; Martin Göhring, 'Der
König von Bamum und seine Schrift', *Evangelische Heidenbote* 80, no. 6 (June 1907), 41–2.
[90] Thorbecke, 'Bamum', 20.   [91] Thorbecke, 'Bamum', 18–19.
[92] Thorbecke, 'Bamum', 19.

That the German authorities had placed some pressure on Njoya not to dress his soldiers in the German style was true. In 1908, the colonial government felt that by dressing his men in German-style uniforms, Njoya might mislead other Africans into confusing Njoya's men with actual German soldiers, muddying the distinction between ruler and ruled (as Njoya may well have hoped to do).[93] Missionaries in the region, however, were not sure that Njoya's personal shift to Hausa dress around the same time was simply a case of Njoya following German advice on sartorial matters. Rather, the Basel missionaries were convinced that the king's change in attire signalled a renewed gravitation towards the Islamic north that was occurring as his alliance with the Germans began to impinge upon his autonomy.

Specifically, the sartorial change coincided with a shift in German policy that directly affected Njoya's regional security by forbidding his soldiers from having firearms. It was at this time that the king began renewing the earlier alliances with the Fulbe that had proved so profitable to him in the past. Having freely possessed firearms in previous years and being personally protected by an armed praetorian guard, Njoya rejected the spurious new German claim that the 'true' weapons of a Bamum warrior were the spear, the bow, and the arrow.[94]

The consequences of the armaments ban were clear to the missionary Göhring, who reported that after being confronted in 1908 with the new disarmament demands, 'Njoya disbanded his soldiers, bought nothing but Hausa garments, and put aside all things European.' Already witnessing an apparent resurgence in Islam in Bamum,[95] Göhring argued that the Basel missionaries now feared 'for our entire project here.'[96] Although complaints to the governor about the feared repercussions of the ban brought a short reprieve, the relationship between Bamum and Germany had been fundamentally altered.[97] The Bamum missionary station report from 1910 confirmed that the king's shift in attire had indeed indicated a reorientation back towards the Islamic north,[98] while another report regretted the renewed influence of Njoya's 'arch-conservative advisers' who were

---

[93] Geary, 'Political Dress', 186–7; Linda Ratschiller, 'Material Matters: The Basel Mission in West Africa and Commodity Culture around 1900', in *Verflochtene Mission: Perspektiven auf eine neue Missionsgeschichte* (Cologne: Böhlau, 2018), 136.

[94] Menzel, 13 January 1909, in Geary and Njoya, *Mandu Yenu*, 192. The ban was consistent with the new course of the post-Herero War period and was also in line with the Brussels Agreement of 22 July 1908 that saw most European powers agree to withhold weapons from Africans. See *Kolonial-Gesetzgebung* XII, documents 278, 375; Helmuth Stoecker, *Drang nach Afrika: Die deutsche koloniale Expansionspolitik und Herrschaft in Afrika von den Anfängen bis zum Verlust der Kolonien* (Berlin: Akademie Verlag, 1991), 145.

[95] Eugen Schwarz, 'Beschreibung a) erste Reisen nach Bamum b) Bamum in Friedens- und Kriegszeiten' in BMA E-10.3,13, 88–9.

[96] Göhring, 'Quartalbericht', 2 October 1908, in BMA E-28, 64.

[97] Geary, 'Political Dress', 190. On the relationship between the Basel missionaries and the German colonial authorities, see Halldén, *The Culture Policy of the Basel Mission in the Cameroons*.

[98] Schlatter, *Geschichte der Basler Mission 1815–1915*, vol. 3, 291–2.

believed to be trying to derail any Europeanizing plans.[99] As Geary has argued, 'From the Bamum point of view, King Njoya's decision to forgo German uniforms and wear only Hausa-style attire was a deliberate statement of new political alliances.'[100] Now clad in the signature clothing of an Islamic lamido, Njoya resumed his earlier exchange of diplomatic gifts with the Islamic north until another German ban ended these interactions.[101]

Njoya's throne made it safely to the Royal Anthropological Museum in June 1908.[102] However, the exchange of gifts with the German emperor halted almost immediately thereafter. To put it simply, the Germans failed to offer gifts of a suitable calibre to honour the political spirit of this exchange between brother monarchs. On the completely ill-judged advice of Governor Seitz, Wilhelm II sent the eagerly awaiting King of Bamum the disappointing gift of an orchestrion (replete with portraits of the emperor and empress on its doors), despite the fact that Njoya had already expressed his indifference to the gramophone he owned because there were no actual musicians.[103] The royal gift was played a couple of times before being placed in a hut where it mouldered and rusted during the rainy season. The portraits of the royal couple were relegated to the missionary school.[104] Later, Njoya remarked that he would have preferred to have been given a European stud farm.[105]

Eloundou has argued that the arrival of the Germans upset unfolding local forms of hegemony, removing Bamum from the orbit of local hegemons in Banyo and allowing Njoya to establish a degree of regional autonomy. The presence of the Germans, he has argued 'allowed the Sultan to escape this heavy vassalage'.[106] Yet, as this chapter has demonstrated, it was not a question of either the German Kaiser or the Lamido of Banyo for King Njoya. The King of Bamum was able to retain a remarkable degree of regional autonomy within the overarching edifice of the German Empire, accepting the benefits that flowed from this position while maintaining close contact with the Islamic north. As his initial wariness regarding the Germans demonstrates, Njoya was under no illusions that this autonomy was anything other than a product of the new regional aegis of the Germans. Nonetheless, Njoya was hardly fleeing from the weight of his vassalage to Banyo, particularly given that he freely chose to renew his ties with the north again after 1908. As the Basel missionary Hohner explained:

[99] Eugen Schwarz to Comitee, 25 June 1910, in BMA E-2, 32, 63.
[100] Geary, Images from Bamum, 59.
[101] Hohner, 16 January 1912, quoted in Geary, Things of the Palace, 62.
[102] Luschan to Colonial Office, 10 June 1908, in BA Berlin R1001/4102, 135.
[103] Seitz to Colonial Office, 25 February 1908; Dernburg to Seitz, 30 November 1908; Eulenberg to Dernburg, 24 July 1908, in BA Berlin R1001/4102, 123, 140, 144; Geary and Njoya, Mandu Yenu, 187–8.
[104] Martin Göhring, 'Jahresbericht für 1909', 12 January 1910, in BMA E-20,30, 63.
[105] Anna Rein-Wuhrmann, quoted in Geary and Njoya, Mandu Yenu, 188.
[106] Eloundou, Le Sud-Kamerun face à l'hégémonie allemande 1884–1916, 78–9.

The friendship between the Bamum chief Njoya and the great Fulbe lamidos in the north continues. Even the Lamido of Yola, which is situated in English territory, sent a delegation with gifts this past year to woo the friendship of the great Bamum Lamido 'Ibrahim'. The Bamum chief was quite flattered and immediately sent a delegation in return... He soon wanted to send another delegation to Yola with English money, but the latest government decree forbids the Bamum chief Njoya to have any further intercourse... with the Fulbe Lamidos for political and economic reasons.[107]

Recognizing that he was his own man, despite his appearance of amenability, the Basel missionaries quietly began separating their endeavours in Bamum from the fortunes of King Njoya by 1913, sensing that things had changed. Privately, they recognized his desire to balance his relations with the Germans against those with other regional hegemons and bitterly accused him of 'fickleness'.[108]

Despite his renewed gravitation towards the Islamic north, however, Njoya remained outwardly compliant towards the Germans, whose military power he knew not to underestimate. Crucially, not only did he refuse to support the rebels who apparently appealed to him from coastal Duala in 1914; he also exposed their plot to the Basel missionaries.[109] The resulting charge of treason against King Rudolf Duala Manga Bell would see the Dualan monarch hanged.

---

[107] Hohner, 16 January 1912, quoted in Geary, *Things of the Palace*, 62.
[108] 'Protokoll über die vom 5–8 Dezember 1913 in Bonaku stattgehabten Kleine Brüderkonferenz' in BMA E-2, 38, 91.
[109] Rudin, *Germans in the Cameroons*, 413.

11

The Kaiser's Birthday Present

On 27 January 1909, Germany celebrated the fiftieth birthday of Kaiser Wilhelm II. In schools all over Germany, special celebrations were held in his honour, while the front pages of newspapers offered thanks and praise for their king and emperor.[1] The liberal *Vossische Zeitung* proclaimed that, on the day of this royal celebration, 'wherever the German tongue is heard...the citizens of the newly unified empire think with pride on the House of Hohenzollern.'[2] The more conservative *Norddeutsche Allgemeine Zeitung* praised the large segment of the German nation that 'took an intimate part' in the celebrations and looked with 'love and loyalty' to the sovereign, cognizant of how in his over twenty years as monarch Kaiser Wilhelm II had shown that 'the good of the nation and the greatness and prosperity of the Fatherland' were his 'guiding star in all his efforts and actions.'[3]

The public festivities for the royal birthday were as ostentatious and effusive as ever. Wilhelm II was, however, far from the peak of his popularity at this time. Only a few months earlier the emperor's interview with the British *Daily Telegraph* newspaper had exposed his dilettantish approach to Germany's *Weltpolitik* to the broader German population, and the opprobrium that had followed had gone some way towards souring the public mood. As the *Berliner Volkszeitung* reported, the public embarrassment of the monarch's recently botched interview had 'cast a shadow' over the birthday celebrations.[4] For the *Vossische Zeitung* too, the emperor's birthday was being celebrated under the pall of the 'hard and shattering test' of the past few months.'[5] Even the usually loyal *Norddeutsche Allgemeine Zeitung* felt compelled to admit that Wilhelm II had not been spared a number of recent 'disappointments and bitter experiences.'[6]

Part of the scandal surrounding the *Daily Telegraph* interview stemmed from the substance of Wilhelm II's remarks and their effects on the British public. In comments displaying a signature lack of tact and understanding, the emperor had declared that the British were 'mad' and that his personal intervention had helped

---

[1] See, e.g., 'Zum 50. Geburtstag des Kaisers', *Berliner Tageblatt und Handels-Zeitung*, 27 January 1909; 'Unserm Kaiser Wilhelm II zu seinem 50. Geburtstage', *Pillauer Merkur*, 27 Januar 1909.
[2] 'Zu Kaisers Geburtstag', *Vossische Zeitung*, 27 January 1909.
[3] 'Dem Kaiser und König', *Norddeutsche Allgemeine Zeitung*, 27 January 1909.
[4] 'Fürst und Volk', *Berliner Volkszeitung*, 27 January 1909.
[5] 'Zu Kaisers Geburtstag', *Vossische Zeitung*, 27 January 1909.
[6] 'Dem Kaiser und König', *Norddeutsche Allgemeine Zeitung*, 27 January 1909.

The Kaiser and the Colonies: Monarchy in the Age of Empire. Matthew P. Fitzpatrick, Oxford University Press.
© Matthew P. Fitzpatrick 2022. DOI: 10.1093/oso/9780192897039.003.0012

save them in their war against the Boers.[7] Beyond the damage done to the Anglo-German relationship, however, the deeper domestic issue arising from the interview, as the emperor came to realize, was the fact that he had presumed to have 'a political discussion of that kind with a foreigner without the agreement of the Reich Chancellor'.[8] The monarch's overstepping of his subordinate role in foreign policy and his lapse into what one liberal politician called 'impetuous expressions of monarchical subjectivism' saw Wilhelm II exposed to scathing criticism by all sides of politics in the Reichstag and in the German press. The interview's suggestion that German foreign policy might in some way reflect the emperor's personal proclivities had even led some to call for his abdication.[9] Later, the monarch would admit that the ferocity of the public's repudiation of his actions had caused him great psychological distress.[10]

Those close to Wilhelm II professed to feel sorry for him during his tarnished birthday celebrations. Baroness Hildegard von Spitzemberg wrote in her diary, 'Never have I thought so intensively about my emperor on his birthday than today, with a heart full of compassion and sympathy for the man who has been so humiliated by fortune.'[11] Yet, despite the uproar over his unwelcome and ill-informed public discussion of foreign policy, the pomp and ceremony planned for his birthday went ahead. Germany's other royals travelled from their states to assemble before the emperor to wish him many happy returns,[12] while sycophantic commemorative works such as Adolf Stein's *Wilhelm II* sought to rehabilitate the wounded monarch with effusive praise.[13] Far from helping his emperor, however, Stein's exaggerated declaration of adoration was publicly mocked, with one cartoonist depicting Stein as an obsequious royal bootlicker.[14]

As Martin Kohlrausch has recently argued, royal birthday celebrations were not merely a celebration of the emperor, but also helped associate the monarchy with the success and vitality of the nation. This fusion of Germany's 'dynastic and nationalist programmes' positioned the emperor as a '*Reichsmonarch*', a figure that publicly personified the empire.[15] To celebrate the monarch's birthday was also to celebrate the life of the nation, its global renown, and the contribution of the monarchy to these. In the same way, royal birthday celebrations in Germany's colonial empire played an important part in normalizing German rule and linking

---

[7] *Daily Telegraph*, 28 October 1908.

[8] Röhl, *Wilhelm II: Into the Abyss of War and Exile 1900–1941*, 678.

[9] Röhl, *Wilhelm II: Into the Abyss of War and Exile 1900–1941*, 662–95.

[10] Wilhelm II, *Ereignisse und Gestalten 1878–1918*, 99.

[11] Vierhaus, *Das Tagebuch der Baronin Spitzemberg*, 498.

[12] 'Zum 50. Geburtstag des Kaisers', *Berliner Tageblatt und Handels-Zeitung*, 27 January 1909.

[13] Adolf Stein, *Wilhelm II*. (Leipzig: Dietrich'sche Verlagsbuchhandlung, 1909).

[14] *Simplicissimus* 13, no. 47 (22 February 1909), 807.

[15] Martin Kohlrausch, 'Loss of Control: Kaiser Wilhelm II, Mass Media, and the National Identity of the Second German Reich', in Milinda Banerjee, Charlotte Backerra, and Cathleen Sarti (eds), *Transnational Histories of the 'Royal Nation'* (New York: Palgrave, 2017), 90.

the colonies to metropolitan power. Whether in Africa, Asia, or the Pacific, the emperor's birthday was used as a means of fusing disparate parts of the conquered extra-European world to German political culture and of imposing metropolitan rhythms on colonized spaces via public celebrations that encouraged a sense of personal attachment to the monarch and the empire he personified.

Accordingly, at a safe distance from the domestic controversy surrounding the *Daily Telegraph* affair, the fiftieth birthday of the emperor was marked in the colonies with public festivities and a holiday. In the Marshall Islands, formally a German protectorate since 1885,[16] the royal birthday celebrations were marked most years with a large public celebration and a regatta, as well as dancing and feasting.[17] The celebrations in 1909, however, began somewhat differently from those of most years, with a pointed sermon delivered to the assembled Marshall Islanders on *Romans* 13:1 and its central message of the necessity of remaining obedient to governing authorities.[18] Only after this did boat races and dances follow, including some dances performed by the dependants of the Marshallese 'king' (*iroijlaplap*), Kabua. In another break with the practice of other years, once the royal birthday celebrations had ended, Kabua asked the governor whether he might send a drum and some of the spears and other equipment used in the dances to Kaiser Wilhelm II as gifts for his birthday.[19] Permission was granted and the gifts were duly sent.

When news of Kabua's gifts reached Bernhard Dernburg, the state secretary for the Colonial Office, he wrote to the chief of the Kaiser's Civil Cabinet, Rudolf von Valentini, to inform him that 'Paramount Chief Kabua' wanted to send the emperor 'for whom he has great admiration, some mats and other items [a drum and spear] used in festive dances, as a sign of his adoration'. In addition, Kabua had sent a 'self-written letter to the emperor'. By way of context, the colonial secretary also informed the palace that Kabua was 'presently the most influential chief of the natives of the Marshall Islands' and that Kabua's letter and gifts had already arrived in Germany. Prior to being delivered, however, the Colonial Office wanted to know how the monarch wished to proceed and whether he was inclined to accept Kabua's gifts.[20] On behalf of the palace, Valentini replied that the

---

[16] The Marshall Islands became part of German New Guinea in 1906. See 'Verordnung betreffend die anderweite Regelung der Verwaltung und der Rechtsverhältnisse im Schutzgebiet der Marshall-, Brown-, und Providence-Inseln', in BA Berlin R1001/2957, 'Organisation einer deutschen Verwaltung auf den Marshall-Inseln', 72.

[17] See, for example, the description of festivities in 1903, in BA Berlin R1001/3076, 161–7, and 1908, in BA Berlin R1001/3077, 'Allgemeine Verhältnisse auf den Marshall-Inseln', 34.

[18] Romans 13:1 states 'Let everyone be subject to the governing authorities, for there is no authority except that which God has established. The authorities that exist have been established by God' (NIV translation).

[19] GStAPK, I. HA, Rep. 89, Nr. 20492, 32–6.

[20] Dernburg to Valentini, 9 July 1909, in BA Berlin R1001/2781, 'Geschenke für den Kaiser und Gegengeschenke', 5. The correspondence between Dernburg and Valentini is reproduced in GStAPK, I. HA, Rep. 89, Nr. 20492, 'Geheimes Zivilkabinett', 36–8.

emperor would accept the gifts 'with interest' and that they would be transferred to the Royal Anthropological Museum. Wilhelm II also expressed his desire to offer a return present and to answer Kabua's letter with a short personal letter of his own, the precise contents of which he would leave to the Colonial Office.[21]

The Colonial Office replied a week later that, given Kabua had always expressed his admiration of the portrait of Wilhelm II in the governor's office in Jaluit, a fitting return present would be a similar portrait of the emperor.[22] Regarding the question of a personal letter, however, the Colonial Secretary was very clear:

> On the delivery at the same time of a handwritten royal letter, in my opinion it might be advisable to refrain from this, as Kabua, although he is the most influential chief of the Marshall Islands, is not of sufficient standing to honour him in such a way. Given too his level of education, he would not be in a position to sufficiently esteem the mark of distinction that such a handwritten letter would offer.[23]

In the face of this strongly worded advice, the emperor acquiesced, and steps were taken to send Kabua the royal gift of a custom-ordered colour portrait of Wilhelm II without the personal honour of an accompanying royal note.[24]

Just why Kabua was denied a personal letter from Wilhelm II thanking him for his birthday present has been the topic of some conjecture, with Andi Zimmerman arguing that the lopsided exchange coordinated by the Colonial Office was calibrated to 'suggest that Kabua was a lesser subject rather than an equal monarch'.[25] This is partly true, in the sense that the issue of rank and equality mattered greatly in Germany's colonial empire and all correspondence was carefully weighted to reflect metropolitan considerations of propriety. Nonetheless, as cases as varied as King Chulalongkorn of Siam, Sultan Abdelaziz of Morocco, Sultan Fumo Bakari of Witu, and King Njoya of Bamum show, the Colonial Office had rarely baulked at the idea of the German Kaiser sending reciprocal gifts and letters to non-European monarchs and had never felt that this offered anything beyond the courtesy of a notional equality that implied no enduring obligation.[26] So too, high German honours and orders had regularly been bestowed upon monarchs and paramount leaders all over the world, but never with the intention of signalling that these did or did not place limits on Germany's imperial penetration of the

[21] Valentini to Dernburg, 18 August 1909, in BA Berlin R1001/2781, 9.

[22] Dernburg to Valentini, 27 August 1909, in BA Berlin R1001/2781, 10.

[23] Dernburg to Valentini, 27 August 1909, in BA Berlin R1001/2781, 10.

[24] Valentini to Dernburg, 28 September 1909, in BA Berlin R1001/2781, 13.

[25] Andrew Zimmerman, *Anthropology and Antihumanism in Imperial Germany* (Chicago: University of Chicago Press, 2001), 151–2.

[26] For a detailed discussion of Marcel Mauss's theory of reciprocity and royal gifts, see Matthew P Fitzpatrick, ' The Kaiser's Likeness: German Colonialism and Royal Gift-Giving in the Age of Empire', *History Australia* 18(2), 2021, 322–341.

global south. Consequently, to understand why Kabua received a gift from Wilhelm II but not the customary honour of a personal handwritten letter, it is necessary to understand what was happening in the Marshall Islands at the time of the Kaiser's fiftieth birthday and assess just where Kabua stood in relation to German colonial rule in the Pacific, both prior to and during this period.

The Origins of Germany's Relationship with 'King' Kabua

In 1881 the German illustrated newspaper *Die Gartenlaube* published a scurril-ous article by the ethnographer Otto Finsch on what he called the 'pathetic ruler', King Kabua of the Marshall Islands. Unaware that Kabua would be integral to German rule in the Marshall Islands for the coming three decades, Finsch wrote:

> Kabua can only write his own name with great effort, can barely speak a few words of English, and has an indolent, dull-witted mind, whose only talent lies in lying and deception...Because Kabua owns very little land, he is poor, and for this reason is greedy. He takes the greater part of the earnings of his subjects for himself, and this has made him very unpopular. His influence is therefore unimportant.

Referring to a picture of Kabua and his supporters (see Figure 11.1), Finsch could only concede one positive attribute to Kabua, namely that his blue tattoos looked 'very becoming' on his brown skin.[27]

Despite Finsch's dismissive portrait, as a prominent leader of the people of the Marshall Islands' westerly Ralik Chain, Kabua had successfully maximized his domestic political influence through war and diplomacy, but also by leveraging German trader (and later German state) control over the Marshall Islands. Kabua was so successful in this enterprise that, although he was only one of several regional leaders, he was treated by German merchants, planters, and governors as the King of the Marshall Islands.

For many years prior to the consolidation of German rule, the close relation-ship between Marshallese notables (*iroij*) and overseas merchants had deeply affected the nature of politics and the distribution of wealth in the Marshall Islands.[28] On the one hand, European traders needed a local interlocutor with whom to conduct business and from whom they could acquire access to land for their plantations and stations. On the other, prominent Marshallese leaders

---

[27] Otto Finsch, 'Bilder aus dem Stillen Ocean. 1. Kriegsführung auf den Marshall-Inseln', *Die Gartenlaube* 42 (1881), 700–3.

[28] Julianne M. Walsh, 'Imagining the Marshalls: Chiefs, Tradition and the State on the Fringes of US Empire' (PhD diss, University of Hawai'i, 2003), 164.

Figure 11.1 King Kabua (third from right with a spear) and his supporters, as portrayed in *Die Gartenlaube*, 1881

sought domestic political and economic advantage by courting European support for their positions, which they hoped would translate into material, even armed assistance, should local rivalries turn to open conflict. In this, Kabua had proved himself particularly adept, to the extent that during a local war he had even managed to convince one prominent German trader, Adolph Capelle, to transport his war party aboard a company ship to fight a battle on another island.[29]

At the time of the arrival of Germany as a colonial power in the Marshall Islands, Kabua was in the midst of asserting his right to be recognized as paramount leader or king (*iroijlaplap*). Unlike the dismissive description offered by one later German observer of this position as one of 'patriarchal despotism',[30] the *iroijlaplap* acted more as *primus inter pares* among his *iroij* (who exercised very real political and economic power over their dependants) than as a divine-right monarch. One of the primary powers of the *iroijlaplap*, however, was a degree of control over how land was bestowed, a power that encouraged a heightened loyalty among locals and pragmatic support from land-hungry traders looking to establish plantations and commercial outposts in the region.

---

[29]   Francis X. Hezel, *The First Taint of Civilization: A History of the Caroline and Marshall Islands in Pre-Colonial Days, 1521–1885* (Honolulu: University of Hawaii Press, 1983), 220–2. The battle never eventuated.

[30]   Landeshauptmannschaft to Hohenlohe, 14 November 1897, in BA Berlin R1001/3076, 136.

While the Germans' main rivals to their claims to the Marshall Islands were the Spanish, British, and Americans,[31] Kabua's most serious challenge to his claims to the paramountcy came from his cousin and longstanding rival, Loiak. Not only did both Kabua and Loiak have competing claims to the paramountcy, but both had advanced rival claims to be the ruler of the entrepôt island of Ebon, a major regional site of commerce before trade moved to the island of Jaluit during the German period. Although Loiak's claim to the paramountcy was accepted by many Marshallese, Kabua also enjoyed domestic support, particularly after marrying Limokoa, the widow of the last paramount *iroijlaplap*, Kaibuke (who also happened to be the father of his rival Loiak). In the context of the matriarchal political and inheritance system of the Marshall Islands, the marriage significantly enhanced Kabua's status domestically.[32] Beyond this, Kabua could also count on the support of many of the (increasingly influential) foreign traders in the region.[33]

The fierce rivalry between Kabua and Loiak came to a head in September 1876, when Loiak led hundreds of his followers in an attack on Kabua. Although Kabua had enjoyed a strong local reputation as having been a fearless warrior in his youth, on seeing Loiak's superior forces approaching, Kabua retreated to the island of Jaluit. A counterattack from Kabua and his subjects was long expected, but failed to materialize.[34]

Kabua had decided not to chance his arm in open battle. Shortly thereafter, however, the overarching political landscape of the Ralik Chain was changed by the abrupt advent of formal German primacy over Jaluit. At the centre of this seismic shift was Kabua. When a German corvette, the *Ariadne*, arrived in the Marshall Islands on 26 November 1878 charged with gaining privileged trading rights and the right to establish a coaling station in Jaluit, it was with Kabua that its commander, Bartholomäus von Werner, negotiated.[35] As Werner revealed in his memoirs a decade later, beyond these publicly announced mercantile object- ives, the deeper purpose of the naval visit was to secure what could be taken of the Marshall Islands as a German colony and ensure that they did not become a colony of the British, Spanish, or Americans. In terms of his approach, Werner admitted that:

German trading interests are so important here that I felt myself compelled to use farther-reaching measures than I usually do to protect the islands from the

---

[31] Dominic Alessio, Katherine Arnold, and Patricia Ollé Tejero, 'Spain, Germany and the United States in the Marshall Islands: Re-imagining the Imperial in the Pacific', *Journal of New Zealand and Pacific Studies* 4, no. 2 (2016), 115–36.

[32] H. Seidel, 'Von den Marshall-Inseln', *Deutsche Kolonialzeitung*, 15 May 1902, 195; L. Sander, *Die deutsche Kolonien in Wort und Bild* (Leipzig: Verlag für Allgemeines Wissen, 1906), 655.

[33] Julianne Walsh, *Etto Nan Raan Kein: A Marshall Islands History* (Honolulu: Bess Press, 2012), 191.

[34] Hezel, *The First Taint of Civilization*, 221.

[35] Bartholomäus von Werner, *Ein deutsches Kriegsschiff in der Südsee* (Leipzig: F. A. Brockhaus, 1889), 360–78.

covetousness of other nations. I hope that what I have done leads to these islands being annexed by the German Empire.[36]

The 1878 negotiations between the German navy and the people of Jaluit were far from even-handed. While Kabua was initially welcoming to the Germans, treating them to a festive display of martial dancing on 27 November, the mood soured considerably when German troops reciprocated the next day by staging a 'mock' invasion of the town, which included a bayonet charge, rapid rifle fire, and the use of artillery firing blanks. The deliberately aggressive military display caused the alarmed Marshallese to flee in fright, leaving Kabua standing petrified, pale, and unable to speak. Thereafter, Werner wrote, the locals were 'far more mistrustful', and in the aftermath of the military demonstration Kabua refused to eat with the Germans.[37]

The military display by the German troops was deliberately calculated to soften the path to German control of the islands. As the commander of the *Ariadne* recorded in his memoirs, the mock invasion was designed 'to show the islanders, who had not seen anything like it before, the power of the Europeans'. The manoeuvres certainly had the desired effect of intimidating their Marshallese negotiating partners, but this had been at the cost of any mutual trust that might have otherwise developed. From the German perspective, however, they had succeeded in establishing a firm basis upon which to ground their lasting control over the Marshall Islands:

> The war dance of the German warship, which was not well received by our guests and which was by all accounts relayed to the other islands in even more exaggerated descriptions, will probably bear fruit for decades and guarantee the safe protection of German life and property.[38]

On the day after this shocking display of European military power, German preponderance was confirmed in a 'most favoured nation' treaty signed by Kabua and his adopted son, Nelu (who was also the son of the last king, Kaibuke) on board the *Ariadne*. The treaty allowed the Germans to establish a coaling station at Jaluit and offered German merchants on the Marshall Islands the enhanced rights that they sought.[39] With the treaty signed, Kabua stood on the deck of the corvette, 'dressed in a new black suit and wearing shoes and socks for the first

---

[36] Werner, *Ein deutsches Kriegsschiff in der Südsee*, 360. Parts of the colony would later be bought from Spain.

[37] Werner, *Ein deutsches Kriegsschiff in der Südsee*, 372–3.

[38] Werner, *Ein deutsches Kriegsschiff in der Südsee*, 373.

[39] Hermann Mückler, *Die Marshall-Inseln und Nauru in deutscher Kolonialzeit* (Berlin: Frank & Timme, 2016), 45; Seidel, 'Von den Marshall-Inseln', 194.

time in his life,[40] watching the raising of the new, conspicuously German-looking red, white, and black flag of the Ralik Islands.

The encounter did not, however, solely benefit the Germans. Two day later the German warship cruised over to Ebon, where, its captain had been led by Kabua to believe, US missionaries were trying to undermine his power in order to create a Marshallese republic under US control and Kabua's rival, Loiak, was ostensibly attempting 'to free himself from the reign' of 'King' Kabua. Within hours of arriving in Ebon with Nelu, Werner had assembled the notables of Ebon in front of a heavily armed party of German troops and extracted a promise from the assembled *iroij* not to resist the terms of the new treaty between Germany and Kabua.[41] With this blunt action to enforce the terms of the newly signed treaty, Werner arguably became the first representative of the German state to impose and defend Germany's claim to a colony—some six years before it would become a burning issue in Africa.[42] In doing so, Werner had also intervened, on partisan intelligence provided by Kabua, in the local dispute regarding the paramount position of *iroijlaplap*. The Germans' robust intervention in Marshallese politics had left Kabua in no doubt about the extent of German naval power in the Pacific. It also suggested to him new possibilities for what he, as an ally of the powerful Germans, stood to gain domestically in his dealings with Loiak.

Once Werner and the *Ariadne* had left the region, tensions between the two rivals for the paramountcy continued to simmer until 1880, when their conflict flared again, this time on Jaluit. Although both armies were armed with rifles, there were no deaths on either side, with menace rather than violence characterizing the confrontation.[43] Despite his new German connections, however, the showdown ended with yet another defeat for Kabua. This time he was exiled by Loiak to his home atoll of Ailinglaplap, where he stayed until he was later permitted to return to Jaluit.[44]

Kabua's subordination to Loiak seemed confirmed in the eyes of his people, but Germany's recognition of his status as king was revived in early 1885, when he requested that the Germans not ratify the sale of his lands to foreigners agreed to by lesser Marshallese nobles when they were drunk, as was becoming established practice.[45] The outcome of this request was that the foreign secretary, Herbert von

---

[40] Hezel, *The First Taint of Civilization*, 298–9.

[41] Werner, *Ein deutsches Kriegsschiff in der Südsee*, 377–8; Walsh, *Etto Nan Raan Kein*, 192; Hezel, *The First Taint of Civilization*, 301–2.

[42] Alessio, Arnold, and Tejero, 'Spain, Germany and the United States in the Marshall Islands', 115–36. For Germany's earlier history of private sector and civil society imperialism, see Fitzpatrick, *Liberal Imperialism in Germany*.

[43] Hezel, *The First Taint of Civilization*, 293, 297.

[44] Mückler, *Die Marshall-Inseln und Nauru in deutscher Kolonialzeit*, 45.

[45] Kabua, Lomoro, and Hernsheim to Bismarck, 26 March 1885; Hernsheim to Bismarck, 4 May 1885, in BA Berlin R1001/3071, 'Allgemeine Verhältnisse auf den Marshall-Inseln: Verwaltung, soziale, wirtschaftliche und politische Entwicklung, einheimische Bevölkerung, Expeditionen', 7–8.

Bismarck-Schönhausen, ordered the German cruiser *Nautilus* to visit the region to regulate and further formalize relations between Kabua and the Germans.[46] By late August 1885, the German Foreign Office had moved towards a plan to annex the Marshall Islands so that it should become a formal protectorate under the German flag and the interests of Hamburg firms trading in the region could be protected.[47] On 29 August, Chancellor Otto von Bismarck had authorized the annexation of the Marshall Islands as a German protectorate,[48] with the emperor's pro forma approval also sought on the same day.[49] Tellingly, the Admiralty's instructions spelled out that while the 'recognition of Germany's protective relations through a treaty with chiefs is desirable', it was 'not necessary if it is too time-consuming'. Up to 500 marks was allocated for diplomatic gifts to hasten the decisions of the *iroij*.[50]

When the *Nautilus* arrived in the Marshall Islands seeking another protection treaty in October 1885, the Germans revitalized Kabua's claims to the paramountcy. As one of the crew members of the *Nautilus* recounted in his diary, a chance meeting of the leaders of the Ralik Chain with Kabua that was under way when they arrived made the German task far easier than it might have been:

> On Jaluit resides the most powerful chief of the Marshall Islands—King Kabua. His Majesty is about 40 years old and knows a few scraps of English and German. He generally dresses in European style. The chiefs belonging to the Ralicks are much more powerful than those of the Radacks, and it happened that when the *Nautilus* arrived in Jaluit the most powerful chiefs, with the exception of the chief of Ebon, were on a visit to King Kabua. This incident saved a great deal of time and trouble, as it obviated the necessity for a visit to several islands.[51]

The official reports back to Germany from the Marshall Islands confirmed these details. They also made clear that the elevation of Kabua to the status of king was not an accident. The consul's report was assiduous in referring to Kabua as 'king', and commented on how convenient it was that the king was being visited by his fellow notables, instead of them being 'strewn across numerous islands'.[52] In particular, the report from the *Nautilus* to the Admiralty made it clear that 'It is

[46] Herbert von Bismarck, margin note in Hernsheim to Bismarck, 4 May 1885, in BA Berlin R1001/3071, 7.

[47] Hatzfeldt, 'Notiz betreffend die Marshall-Inseln', 27 August 1885; Kusserow to German Foreign Office, 28 August 1885, in BA Berlin R1001/3071, 12–18.

[48] Otto von Bismarck to Foreign Office, 29 August 1885, in BA Berlin R1001/3071, 26.

[49] Herbert von Bismarck to Wilhelm I, 29 August 1885, in BA Berlin R1001/3071, 37–40.

[50] Admiralty to Hatzfeldt, 31 August 1885, in BA Berlin R1001/3071, 47.

[51] 'The Annexation of the Marshall Islands by Germany', *Shanghai Mercury*, as reproduced in the *Brisbane Courier*, 17 February 1886, 3.

[52] Hernsheim to the German Foreign Office, 4 November 1885, in BA Berlin R1001/2606, 'Streitigkeiten mit den einheimischen Missionaren auf Ebon und Kusaie wegen Überschreitung des Handelsverbots mit Spirituosen', 9–10.

critical to German interests here to ensure the greatest respect for King Kabua among the natives and in Jaluit, as the seat of the German consulate, and to celebrate this ceremonially.'[53] To this end, Kabua and other Marshallese leaders were invited to pay the commander a visit on board the *Nautilus*, where Kabua was 'greeted and hosted in a distinguished fashion, and was given a twenty-one-gun salute upon his departure.'[54] After hosting Kabua and his 'subordinate chiefs', the matter of another treaty was broached:

> On the same day, the commandant returned the visit to Kabua, who had prepared an honourable reception for him and his officers. The purpose of the visit of His Majesty's cruiser *Nautilus* was explained to Kabua. As he showed himself to be fully inclined to sign an agreement, he was asked to come to the consulate the following day at 4 p.m. to sign the treaty. At the appointed hour, on 15 October, Kabua arrived at the consulate, accompanied by the chiefs Loiak, Nelu, Lagajime, and Launa…I then read aloud the agreement that was drafted in German and Marshallese, and after I had explained to the king and his chiefs the few paragraphs in the local language, the treaty was signed…In the name of His Majesty the Kaiser of Germany, the commandant then gave Kabua and his chiefs the gifts brought for this purpose, which were received with great satisfaction.[55]

The new treaty was marked by a curious linguistic double standard that may have misled many of the *iroij* signing it. Despite the fact that it was also a feature of the 1878 treaty, it is arguable that the *iroij* beyond Kabua were not aware of his elevation to kingly status courtesy of the treaty (or had refused to acknowledge it), because the Marshallese text of the treaty between the *iroij* and the German captain of the *Nautilus* that was read aloud placed all of the Marshallese signatories on the same footing, simply listing the leaders without any difference in rank as 'the *iroij* named Kabua, Lagajimi, Nelu, Loiak, Launa' (*Iroj roe tan Kabua, Lagajimi, Nelu, Loiak, Launa*).[56] The German text of the treaty, however, with its repeated mention of 'King Kabua', offered Kabua the paramountcy that he had sought but in actual fact twice failed to wrest from Loiak. Despite having defeated Kabua, in the German text of the treaty, Loiak was declared to be simply one of the four other 'chiefs'. Not only did the German text invert the actual power

---

[53] Rötger to Admiralty, 'Bericht über politische Lage und Thätigkeit SM Krz *Nautilus* während des Aufenthalts bei den Marshall-Inseln', 30 November 1885, in BA Berlin R1001/3072, 'Allgemeine Verhältnisse auf den Marshall-Inseln', 13–28.

[54] Rötger to Admiralty, 30 November 1885, in BA Berlin R1001/3072, 13–28; Hernsheim to the German Foreign Office, 4 November 1885, in BA Berlin R1001/2606, 9–10.

[55] Hernsheim to the German Foreign Office, 4 November 1885, in BA Berlin R1001/2606, 9–11.

[56] The treaty in both German and Marshallese can be found in Hernsheim to the German Foreign Office, 4 November 1885, in BA Berlin R1001/2606, 21–6. See also Ingrid A. Ahlgren, 'The Meaning of Mo: Place, Power and Taboo in the Marshall Islands' (PhD diss., Australian National University, 2016), 227–8; Walsh, *Etto Nan Raan Kein*, 195.

relations of the Marshall Islands (at the cost of Loiak), but Kabua's kingly status now seemed to be guaranteed by a protection treaty with Germany which offered the Germans primacy over the other European powers and a formal textual basis for their colonial claims in the region. As Julianne Walsh has argued, 'Kabua and German interests were mutually supported.'[57] Tellingly, perhaps, the only person described in the Marshallese text as *iroijlaplap* was Kaiser Wilhelm II: the *iroijlaplap* of Germany. This may also explain why Kabua was simply listed as one of several *iroij* in the Marshallese text, impressing upon them that, under the new arrangements, all of the Marshallese *iroij* would now be subordinate to the metropolitan *iroijlaplap*, Wilhelm II.[58] Nonetheless, in the German text, Kabua was singled out as King of the Marshall Islands, whose sovereign prerogative enabled him to sign a treaty with the viceregal representatives of the German emperor.

The treaty between Kabua and Germany was one of many such treaties that formed the shaky legal framework of Germany's global empire. Signed with the military might of the Germans not only in mind but often openly on display, these treaties were rarely an expression of a non-European ruler's uninhibited sovereign decision-making or agency. More often Germany's treaty-harvesting expeditions reflected the imperatives and anxieties of a European power in global completion with other imperial powers seeking to gain control of the world's few remaining independent territories. Nevertheless, local imperatives also informed the growing economic, social, political, and military entanglements between the Germans and the Marshallese, and while the treaty-signing tours of the German navy were supported by the might of the German imperial state, it was not only naval force but also a degree of mutual interest that brought Marshallese leaders like Kabua and Loiak to the negotiating table. Although earlier *iroijlaplap*, most notably Kaibuke, had resisted entering into formal relations with the global empires of the West, having experienced first-hand the danger they posed,[59] the new generation of *iroij*, including both Kabua and Loiak, saw some political and economic advantages in aligning themselves with the Germans.[60]

In the case of Kabua, the decision to sign a treaty with the Germans reflected a desire to take advantage of the arrival of a new ally possessing seemingly overwhelming power for the purposes of consolidating and enhancing an otherwise comparatively weak position in domestic political and military affairs. Part of the appeal, however, was financial, with planning for the colony in 1888 ensuring that the *iroij* received around one-third of tax revenue (which, after discussions with

[57] Walsh, 'Imagining the Marshalls', 168.

[58] Hernsheim to the German Foreign Office, 4 November 1885, in BA Berlin R1001/2606, 21–6; Monica C. LaBriola, 'Likiep Kapin Iep: Land Power and History on a Marshallese Atoll' (PhD diss.: University of Hawaii, 2013), 306.

[59] Hezel, *The First Taint of Civilization*, 200.

[60] There is of course no way that either could have known that it would be the beginning of 'a century of imperial rule...by three successive foreign powers' (LaBriola, 'Likiep Kapin Iep', 206).

German representatives, Kabua and other *iroij* had agreed to collect) from the colony. German colonial officials hoped that they could count on the goodwill of Marshallese notables (in an environment where the German navy might be stationed weeks away) by ensuring their continued—and in many cases enhanced—prosperity and by protecting their authority in the face of their dependent subjects.[61]

Not all *iroij* saw their interests as best served by supporting the Germans, however, with some electing to support rival powers in the region. As late as mid-1886, some pro-American *iroij* such as Lebomari of Nanorik still refused to recognize both Germany's claims and Kabua's right to accept German rule on their behalf. Only the threat of German naval action brought Lebomari to acquiesce and reluctantly accept Royal Commissioner Wilhelm Knappe's argument that 'beneficial results' would flow from placing himself under German protection. Even then Lebomari insisted on speaking personally with Kabua first.[62]

This use of the German navy to visit Marshallese notables and coerce them into accepting German rule led the commander of the Pacific cruiser squadron, Eduard von Knorr, to express his concern that relations had been prematurely soured on some islands and that the brevity of the punitive naval expedition against recalcitrant *iroij* might not have ended the difficulties being caused by pro-British and pro-US notables. Had he had more time, he argued, he might have had the opportunity 'to show the chiefs and the natives the benevolence of the new masters and the benign side of the warship'.[63] Precisely what he saw as the benign face of German naval power in the Pacific he did not say.

German-*Iroij* Cooperation

In broad terms, however, the attempt to control the Marshall Islands by preserving and co-opting the power of the *iroij* succeeded. By May 1894, there was sufficient acquiescence to allow Governor Georg Irmer to report to Chancellor Caprivi that 'The chiefs have in most cases accustomed themselves to the new arrangements and are satisfied with their comparatively large incomes.'[64] This was certainly the case for Kabua, who, according to Knappe, had faced debts of $6,000

---

[61] 'Bemerkungen der Vertreter der Jaluit Gesellschaft zum Budget Entwurf', in BA Berlin, R1001/2956, 'Organisation einer deutschen Verwaltung auf den Marshall-Inseln', 20; 'Bemerkungen zu dem Budget für die Marshall-Inseln', in BA Berlin R1001/2955, 20–1; Knappe to Bismarck, 16 June 1886, in BA Berlin R1001/2954, 'Organisation einer deutschen Verwaltung auf den Marshall-Inseln', 29–30.

[62] Knorr to Bismarck, 12 June 1886, in BA Berlin R1001/2954, 44–5.

[63] Knorr to Bismarck, 12 June 1886, in BA Berlin R1001/2954, 49.

[64] Irmer to Caprivi, 31 May 1894, in BA Berlin, R1001/2957, 46.

in April 1887.[65] Given too his domestic political and military weakness and the fact that he had been bested (if not outright defeated) and exiled twice by Loiak, Kabua's capacity to act as *iroijlaplap* would have otherwise been highly circumscribed, as the German anthropologist Augustin Krämer observed in the 1890s. 'Kabua is king', Krämer wrote, 'only by the grace of the Germans, and he only has a say over those islands that actually belong to him.'[66] Another Pacific-based writer for the *Deutsche Kolonialzeitung* similarly noted that 'The so-called King Kabua has not remotely earned this designation as an attribute of sovereign rule.' Instead, it was pointed out, Kabua only exercised 'a certain personal influence over a few islands' such as Jaluit and Ebon and that even this was contested. The only place that he had uncontested power was on his home island of Ailinglaplap.[67]

While the cooperation between some Marshallese elites and the Germans was initially mutually beneficial, on the German side it was clearly aimed at enhancing their economic and political penetration of the region. Central to this control was the question of land ownership. Prior to German rule, Marshallese *iroij* could offer parcels of land as gifts and rewards to those they considered had offered them exceptional service. It was this power to grant land beyond the usual matrilineal hereditary processes that had enabled European missions, merchants, and planters to access land in the Marshall Islands from *iroij* seeking out external alliance partners who in turn 'had the potential to bolster their cultural, political and economic capital and improve the lives of their constituents.'[68] As Monica La Briola makes clear, for Marshall Islanders, this was not a result of Marshallese notables having suddenly embraced European notions of exclusive, hereditary, and saleable land ownership rights, but rather was a product of the gradual extension of local practices of land distribution to cover European newcomers.[69] Such subtleties were, however, lost on Europeans eager to consolidate permanent control of the gifted land for copra plantations, missions, and trading posts and who saw themselves as having gained full, inalienable rights over the land they were given. Before long, the islands became dotted with signs that declared to locals that certain lands were now taboo (*mo*) to Marshall Islanders and that the coconuts on that land belonged exclusively to European copra traders. Alongside these German signs came German laws and German taxes. By the time Wilhelm II came to the throne in 1888, the *iroij* found themselves effectively usurped in their

---

[65] Knappe to Bismarck, 12 April 1887, in BA Berlin R1001/2955, 4. Debts such as Kabua's were often leveraged by European traders to control the extraction of copra from the *iroij*. The German administration sought to halt this practice, concerned that this debt peonage saw the economy of the Marshall Islands informally controlled by American and British traders. See BA Berlin R1001/2783, 'Regelung der Schulden der einheimischen Bevölkerung'.

[66] Augustin Krämer, *Hawaii, Ostmikronesien und Samoa: Meine zweite Südseereise (1897–1899) zum Studium der Atolle und ihrer Bewohner* (Stuttgart: Strecker & Schröder, 1906), 216.

[67] 'Die Verhältnisse auf den Marshall-Inseln', *Deutsche Kolonialzeitung* 23 (1886), 789–90.

[68] LaBriola, 'Likiep Kapin Iep', 142–3.   [69] LaBriola, 'Likiep Kapin Iep', 142–3.

rights by German commercial interests, which heavily restricted the ability of the Marshallese to transfer or dispose of their land.[70]

In January 1888, the two largest German firms operating in Jaluit, namely the *Deutsche Handels- und Plantagengesellschaft* (DHPG) and Robertson & Hernsheim, merged to become the Jaluit Company (*Jaluit Gesellschaft*), and it was this entity that governed the Marshall Islands on Germany's behalf until 1906, when it became part of the administrative territory of German New Guinea. On a shoestring budget funded by a poll tax, the Jaluit Company ruled the islands in conjunction with the *iroij*, with little oversight from Berlin. Concentrating on the production and sale of copra, the Jaluit Company jealously guarded Germany's (that is to say, the company's) monopoly rights in the region, forbidding the gifting or sale of land to any non-German outsiders, and imposing harbour tariffs that effectively stifled any competition from other nations. So successful were they in this that the Jaluit Company ran their operations at a profit—a rarity within the German Empire.[71]

Stability and general law and order were outsourced to the *iroij*, who received their third of the copra tax in return.[72] This was a modest price to pay, given that the company's profitability was greatly assisted by the continuation of the pre-German practice of corvée labour under which the *iroij* channelled periods of free labour from their dependants to plantation work. When this earlier aspect of Marshallese social relations was applied to planting, harvesting, and transporting work on the expanding coconut tree plantations, it kept labour costs for the production of copra artificially low.[73] This market advantage meant that the Jaluit Company was keen to ensure that their highly protected market was not jeopardized by Marshallese plantation workers finding out exactly how valuable their labour was. As Wolfgang Treue noted, by locking out foreign firms and sitting snugly behind enormous tariff walls, all the while monopolizing relations with the *iroij*, the company did everything it could to avoid a situation in which labourers 'learned the true worth of copra and raised the price'.[74]

Marshallese workers did not, however, remain entirely blind to the value of their copra or their labour and sought ways to negotiate directly with the company. When traders with the Jaluit Company briefly experimented with circumventing Marshallese notables by buying copra directly from workers in 1895, both

---

[70] LaBriola, 'Likiep Kapin Iep', 206–208, 298–301.

[71] Francis X. Hezel, *Strangers in Their Own Land: A Century of Colonial Rule in the Caroline and Marshall Islands* (Honolulu: University of Hawaii Press, 1995), 45–50.

[72] 'Bemerkungen der Vertreter der Jaluit Gesellschaft zum Budget Entwurf', in BA Berlin R1001/2956, 20; Knappe to Bismarck, 16 June 1886, in BA Berlin R1001/2954, 29–30; Walsh, *Etto Nan Raan Kein*, 198.

[73] P. A. Erdland, *Die Marshall-Insulaner: Leben und Sitte, Sinn und Religion eines Südsee-Volkes* (Münster: Aschendorffsche Verlagsbuchhandlung, 1914), 108–9, 111.

[74] Wolfgang Treue, 'Die Jaluit-Gesellschaft', *Tradition: Zeitschrift für Firmengeschichte und Unternehmerbiographie* 2/3 (1962), 115.

Kabua and Loiak expelled the Jaluit Company from Ailinglaplap rather than accept the financial ruin such innovations would have engendered. This protest from the two most powerful *iroij* in the region eventually forced the governor to travel to Ailinglaplap to mediate.[75]

Occasionally, tensions between the *iroij* and their dependent labourers split the Germans on the best course of action, as in 1897, when news of tension between Governor Irmer and his deputy Arno Senfft over the question of copra production and the exploitation of commoners by Marshallese elites reached Germany. Irmer had written to Berlin complaining that Senfft was seeking to erode the power that the *iroij*, who had hitherto been integral to Germany's position in the region, exercised over their dependants.[76] In his defence, Senfft argued that he had only attempted to alleviate draconian regulations regarding copra production that some *iroij* had imposed on their people. He was, he insisted, otherwise still unstinting in his efforts to maintain the authority of the *iroij*.[77] The German Colonial Department supported Irmer, ruling that it could not allow a weakening of the influence of the *iroij*, to whom 'we have to thank for the straightforwardness of our governance in the protectorate', in economic or political matters.[78]

Shortly after the turn of the century, the Jaluit Company also had to contend with a protracted strike by some islander workers that lasted three years and 'paralysed its operations'.[79] Another notable incident that nearly ended in violence came in 1901, when Marshallese workers on the island of Mejit struck for more pay. Earning two marks per day to carry sacks of copra across the reef to waiting ships, the labourers demanded four marks. When the governor and the commander of a German cruiser came ashore with some officers to deal with the situation, one of the officers was seen loading his revolver. Immediately according to one contemporaneous report, 'six natives with knives stood behind each white'. The Germans were disarmed, and events seemed to be on the verge of escalating, until a translator of mixed German-Marshallese heritage intervened. Although one source from the time suggested that the governor pardoned those involved,[80] collective punishment was not long in coming. Besides imprisoning the leaders of the strike, the then governor, Eugen Brandeis, imposed a collective punishment on the island of Mejit, ordering them to provide an additional 100,000 pounds of copra—almost an additional year's worth of production.[81]

---

[75] 'Protokoll über die am Freitag, den 21 Juni 1895 abgehaltenen Sitzung', in BA Berlin R1001/3075, 'Allgemeine Verhältnisse auf den Marshall-Inseln', 171; Irmer to Hohenlohe-Schillingsfürst, 19 July 1896, in BA Berlin R1001/3076, 59–61.

[76] Irmer, 'Jahresbericht', 1896, in BA Berlin R1001/2957, 52.

[77] Senfft to Colonial Department, 4 April 1898, 58–60. Any diminution of *iroij* authority, Senfft argued, should be attributed to the actions of the missionaries in the region.

[78] Colonial Department to Irmer, 26 November 1897, in BA Berlin R1001/2957, 56–7.

[79] Hezel, *Strangers in their Own Land*, 104.   [80] Erdland, *Die Marshall-Insulaner*, 94–5.

[81] Brandeis was known as the 'flogging governor' after using flogging as a punishment for the Marshallese. His behaviour led him to be severely criticized in the Reichstag. Dirk H. R. Spennemann,

Notwithstanding such incidents, it was acknowledged by both the Jaluit Company and Berlin that the skeleton crew of German officials in Jaluit could not rule the colony effectively without the assistance of Marshallese notables. This realization led to careful assessments of how far the authority of the *iroij* could be shaken by the Germans before they jeopardized their own authority. Despite, for example, the Jaluit Company having wrested from the Marshallese the right to become the owner of any 'uncontrolled or unused land' in the protectorate,[82] such was the precarious nature of German rule that any attempts to assume control of land in the name of the German Crown were not only discussed with the relevant *iroij* but also carefully weighed up by both the governor and metropolitan officials, including, on occasion, the chancellor.[83] As the Colonial Section of the Foreign Office bluntly advised Governor Friedrich Louis Max Biermann in 1890, any governing measures that restricted the sovereignty of the *iroij* could only be introduced if they did not endanger their authority amongst their own people and thereby jeopardize German rule, which was based on elite cooperation.[84]

The Land Question and the Kaiser's Birthday

Kabua's sense of his importance to the power of the Germans never wavered, leading him to insist upon his sovereign rights whenever he felt it necessary, particularly in relation to the politically sensitive topic of land ownership. In 1901, for example, Kabua was involved in a messy controversy with the Jaluit Company over land which the company viewed as unused (and therefore forfeited by the Marshallese to the company), but which Kabua declared to be his. In this instance, Kabua agreed to renounce his claim to the disputed land in return for territorial compensation elsewhere.[85] More serious, however, was Kabua's 1907 conflict over land with another *iroij*, which seriously threatened the peace and almost reignited the dormant conflict between his followers and those of his cousin Loiak. Not only was this conflict the final instalment in the life-long rivalry between Kabua and Loiak, but the land controversy also helps explain why Kabua suddenly felt moved to offer Kaiser Wilhelm II a birthday present in 1909.

An Officer, Yes, But a Gentleman...? Eugen Brandeis, Military Adviser, Imperial Judge and Administrator in the German Colonial Service in the South Pacific (Sydney: University of New South Wales Press, 1998), 25–6, 43–5; Bruno Ablaß, 15 December 1905, in *Verhandlungen des Reichstages*, 346–7; Ernst Müller, 4 December 1906, in *Verhandlungen des Reichstages*, 4131–2.

[82] 'Entwurf zum Vertrage mit der Jaluit-Gesellschaft', in BA Berlin, R1001/2956, 7.

[83] See, e.g., Landeshauptmannschaft to Hohenlohe, 14 November 1897, in BA Berlin 3076, 136–7.

[84] Letter to Biermann, 17 September 1890, in BA Berlin R1001/3074, 'Allgemeine Verhältnisse auf den Marshall-Inseln: Verwaltung, soziale, wirtschaftliche und politische Entwicklung, einheimische Bevölkerung, Expeditionen', 118–19.

[85] Jaluit Gesellschaft to Colonial Department, 14 May 1901, in BA Berlin R1001/2503, 'Jaluit-Gesellschaft—Kolonialgesellschaft für die Marshall-, Brown- und Providence-Inseln, 131–3; Hütter to Colonial Department, 19 June 1901, in BA Berlin R1001/2503, 139–44.

The acrimonious land dispute that threatened the peace of the colony came after the death of Loiak. Upon his death, Loiak's land was claimed by one of his subordinate notables, Litokua.[86] According to some, Kabua had in fact initially agreed that the property rightfully belonged to Litokua. Before long, however, Kabua had declared that, as the *iroijlaplap* of the Ralik Chain, Loiak's property rightfully belonged to him. A three-week-long court case presided over by a German magistrate scrutinized Kabua and Litokua's competing claims to the land. During this time, rumours of threatened violence abounded, as the translator at the trial, Father August Erdland, recounted:

> Kabua's subjects had buried thirty spears near the court to use to kill the judge, the court stenographer, and me, as the sworn translator, should the verdict favour the subordinate chief. Litokua, for his part, had hidden in the bush for his protection fifteen of his subjects, whom he had armed with machetes.[87]

When the verdict came out in favour of Kabua, the violence seemed to have been averted, despite the fact that Litokua insisted that the land in question was his according to Marshallese inheritance law and that the German trial had reached the wrong verdict.[88]

The matter did not end there, however, with both Litokua and Erdland, writing letters after the trial alleging that Kabua had tampered with witnesses. In confronting Kabua with these charges, the highest-ranking German official in the colony at the time, Acting District Officer Joseph Sigwanz, trod carefully so as to avoid a potentially explosive reaction:

> I immediately summoned Kabua and his entourage. The persons who had been summoned from Ailinglaplap appeared in Jaluit in mid-October. In order not to agitate them prematurely, I did not state the true reason for the summons in the writ. To avoid arguments between the parties and their followers at the start of the new trial, I waited for the arrival of the SMS *Condor*, which came into Jaluit on 20 October. I then examined Loiak's wife, Limoot, and she declared that the evidence she had previously given in court was based on falsehood.[89]

The claims of witness tampering by Kabua were upheld by the court, which heard that Loiak's wife and subjects had been coerced into falsifying their statements, while Loiak's nephew was adjudged to have given false testimony in order that he

---

[86] Sigwanz to Colonial Department, 1 June 1907, in BA Berlin R1001/3077, 26.

[87] Erdland, *Die Marshall-Insulaner*, 105.

[88] Kaiserlicher Bezirksamtmann to Colonial Department, 16 July 1907, in BA Berlin R1001/3077, 28.

[89] Sigwanz to Dernburg, 12 November 1907, in BA Berlin R1001/3077, 30–4. See also Walsh, *Etto Nan Raan Kein*, 215.

might marry Kabua's daughter.[90] Kabua was fined and, most significantly, in October 1908 the court rescinded its decision to grant him Loiak's land.[91]

Kabua's reaction was, according to Erdland, immediate and defiant. Kabua 'shook with rage and bluntly informed the judge that he would never give Loiak's land to the minor chief [Litokua], even if he was sent into exile with his family'. It was only the direct threat of German military intervention from the German cruiser anchored in the harbour that 'staved off scenes of bloodshed'.[92] The report on the incident to the Colonial Office in Berlin from Sigwanz offered the sense that the colony had only narrowly averted a civil war between the followers of Kabua and Litokua, once again through a show of German naval force. After the judgment had gone against him, Kabua asked Sigwanz where he could 'eat fish' with Litokua, a Marshallese expression for declaring war. Thereupon, Sigwanz warned Kabua that 'the times when natives fought wars were past and that I would send him with all his followers to New Guinea if it came to war'.[93]

With sentiments running very high among Kabua's people on the day of the judgment, Sigwanz asked the commander of the SMS *Condor* to patrol Jaluit at night. The commander agreed, and, according to the governor, these patrols 'had a powerful impact' on Kabua and his supporters, leading Kabua to ask Sigwanz to forgive him for his outburst, assuring him with a handshake that 'he would not lead a war against Litokua'.[94] As in 1878 and 1885–6, the intervention of the German navy had proved decisive.

Kabua, nonetheless, found other ways to circumvent the German court's order. When Litokua visited his new territories in late February 1908 to collect his tribute (paid in copra) from his new subjects, he found that Kabua had already been to them and collected the copra. After Litokua complained to Sigwanz, the acting district officer wrote to Kabua warning him against such actions. In response, Kabua responded that, despite his loyalty to the German Kaiser and his officials, he would not reimburse Litokua.[95]

In his report to Berlin, Sigwanz confided that he was helpless to do anything else because of the strong support Kabua enjoyed and the meagre police force at his disposal. In Sigwanz's estimation, 'an energetic crackdown' was 'absolutely necessary, if the standing of the government is not to suffer'. To that end, he requested that the SMS *Condor* return to assist in vigorous action against the 'greedy' Kabua.[96] Sigwanz's immediate superior, New Guinea's Governor Albert

[90] Erdland, *Die Marshall-Insulaner*, 105.
[91] Sigwanz to Dernburg, 12 November 1907, in BA Berlin R1001/3077, 30–4.
[92] Erdland, *Die Marshall-Insulaner*, 105–6.
[93] Sigwanz to Dernburg, 12 November 1907, in BA Berlin R1001/3077, 30–4. See also Walsh, *Etto Nan Raan Kein*, 215.
[94] Sigwanz to Dernburg, 12 November 1907, in BA Berlin R1001/3077, 30–4. See also Walsh, *Etto Nan Raan Kein*, 215.
[95] Schwabe to Dernburg, 21 May 1908, in BA Berlin R1001/3077, 39.
[96] Sigwanz to Dernburg, 20 March 1908, in BA Berlin R1001/3077, 35–6.

Hahl, demurred. Once Sigwanz's stint as acting district officer was over, Hahl recommended that his replacement, Wilhelm Stuckhardt, only use violence against Kabua if absolutely necessary.[97] The German government physician Gustav Schwabe agreed with Hahl, arguing that dislodging Kabua would be difficult, and that the (second) court decision which had arrived at a verdict against Kabua should be reviewed.[98]

German naval intervention against Kabua was only narrowly averted. By the time that the *Condor* arrived in Ailinglaplap in October 1908, his land case had already been placed under review by Stuckhardt and Hahl, a process which would last until early 1910.[99] Consequently, no military measures were undertaken and the (now seriously ill) Kabua was left in control. The *Condor*'s commander commented that Kabua's 'approaching end would not disadvantage the government... The influence of Kabua is so great that any measures against him by the government could lead to an uprising.'[100]

Kabua continued to dispute the judgment against him, and in Jaluit rumours were growing of a coming rebellion against the Germans, caused by the land dispute and the two conflicting judgments that it had produced, which had seen 'the trust of the natives in the government disappear'. When Stuckhardt sailed on board the *Condor* to visit Kabua in Ailinglaplap, Kabua was convinced that the district officer had come to take him to exile in New Guinea. Rumours were also mounting that a new, royal decision on the land affair would be announced on the occasion of the German emperor's birthday in January 1909.[101] It was recommended to Stuckhardt by a number of Europeans in the colony that both Kabua and Litokua be prevented from coming to Jaluit for the royal birthday celebrations, where it was said that the dances they would perform would signify 'war and taunt the other party with cowardice', thereby escalating the crisis.[102] The district officer decided, however, that this would seem like an admission of weakness. Both parties were warned against any demonstrations or violence, and the royal birthday festivities proceeded as planned, with Kabua playing a central role in them. In the event, they were violence-free.[103]

It was against this background of possible rebellion or civil war between rival Marshallese factions, a threat made known to Colonial Secretary Dernburg in Berlin by the governor,[104] that Kabua's offered his birthday gifts to Wilhelm II.

[97] Hahl to Stuckhardt, 23 June 1908, in BA Berlin R1001/3077, 38.
[98] Schwabe to Dernburg, 21 May 1908, in BA Berlin R1001/3077, 39.
[99] Erdland, *Die Marshall-Insulaner*, 106. See also Hezel, *Strangers in their Own Land*, 126–7.
[100] Ahlert to Wilhelm II, 27 October 1908, in BA Berlin R1001/3077, 45.
[101] Stuckhardt to Hahl, 22 February 1909, in BA Berlin R1001/3077, 48–52.
[102] J. de B. to Krümling, 15 February 1909; Krümling to Stuckhardt, 6 December 1908, in BA Berlin R1001/3077, 53–4.
[103] Stuckhardt to Hahl, 22 February 1909, in BA Berlin R1001/3077, 48–52.
[104] Hahl to Dernburg, 30 March 1909, in BA Berlin R1001/3077, 58–9. Hahl also requested funds for the establishment of a Melanesian police force of thirty men for the Marshall Islands.

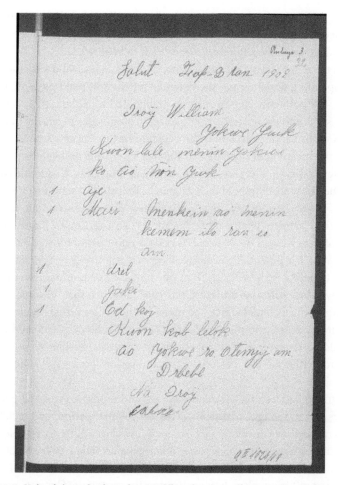

Figure 11.2 Kabua's list of gifts to 'Iroij William', personally signed by Kabua
Source: Courtesy of the Geheimes Staatsarchiv Preußischer Kulturbesitz.

The gifts, District Officer Stuckhardt wrote, had not been solicited, but rather 'were completely in accordance with Kabua's own decision'.[105] Also included was the personally signed letter addressed to the emperor, 'Iroij William' (see Figure 11.2). In it Kabua expressed his pleasure at being able to 'chat' with the German emperor. The letter also described the nature of the royal birthday celebrations held in Jaluit on 27 January 1909, noting the pointed homily on *Romans* 13:1.[106] The accompanying account of the celebrations also included a description

[105] Stuckhardt to Hahl, 22 February 1909, in BA Berlin R1001/3077, 48–52.
[106] 'Die Lehrer haben uns über das Wort Römer 13:1 belehrt', Kabua to Wilhelm II in GStAPK, I. HA, Rep. 89, Nr. 20492, 32–5; Zimmerman, *Anthropology and Anti-Humanism in Imperial Germany*, 151.

of the morning regatta, the toast to the emperor, a breakfast feast, and the dances performed in honour of the German emperor. The ceremonial objects used during the dance were, the letter said, Kabua's gift to Wilhelm II.[107]

Given the narrow avoidance of violence after the second land trial, the rumours of an impending uprising, and the potential for the still-pending verdict to spark violence, the pointedly chosen sermon highlighted by Kabua in his letter was a telling insight into the anxieties of the German authorities regarding the possibility of an outbreak of violence on the occasion of the emperor's birthday. In this context, the meaning of the gifts and Kabua's letter were ambiguous. On the one hand, they could be interpreted by the German officials as a sign of Kabua's loyalty to the German Empire and its monarch. Refusing to send them would have been an insult that might have exacerbated Kabua's increasing antagonism towards the Germans. On the other, the gift was an assertion by Kabua of his right to be treated as King of the Marshall Islands, a reminder of his status in the treaty of 1885. With the potentially explosive land case still under review, Kabua sought out direct contact with Wilhelm II, as one monarch to another. Issues of seemliness may have partially underwritten the concerns that Colonial Secretary Dernburg in the Colonial Office had about Wilhelm II sending Kabua a personal letter, but it was in the immediate context of the volatility engendered by the land trial and the strength of Kabua's reaction to it that German colonial officials sought to withhold the personal communication between Wilhelm II and 'King' Kabua.

Gift-giving between the German emperor and monarchs from all parts of the world was a routine part of diplomacy in the colonial period, and racial considerations, as well as considerations of hierarchy, played little to no role, even in colonial sites where undeniable power differences prevailed. Indeed, not only had gifts been bestowed upon Kabua and other *iroij* after the signing of the 1885 treaty in Jaluit, but gifts were also given again upon the visit of the German navy in May 1886.[108] Mutual gift-giving between the emperor and non-European monarchs was simply a normal part of conducting business in the colonies, one that neither suggested any underlying equivalency between the two nor had any meaningful effects on the broader dynamics of imperial power.

Rather than reflecting a general matter of principal aimed at avoiding an implied equivalency between the German monarch and a non-European counterpart, the withholding of a personal note to Kabua from Wilhelm II should be seen within the local context of Kabua's land claims and German concerns about the possibility of violence in the Marshall Islands. The Colonial Office was reluctant to facilitate Kabua's attempt to cultivate the personal patronage of the emperor, lest this prove embarrassing, should the German navy be called in to

---

[107] Kabua to Wilhelm II in GStAPK, I. HA, Rep. 89, Nr. 20492, 32–5.
[108] Knorr to Bismarck, 12 June 1886, in BA Berlin, R1001/2954, 40–4.

remove Kabua from power. In addition to this, it was increasingly well known in German circles in Jaluit by 1909 that Kabua's claim to be King of the Marshall Islands was an invented product of Germany's need for a local ally in the region in the 1870s and 1880s and Kabua's desire to win external support for his domestic political and military competition with Loiak. The decision to deny the *iroij* a royal letter, a decision ostensibly based on Dernburg's estimations of Kabua's powers of comprehension, in fact reflected a desire to avoid complicating any future action that might need to be taken to quell a potential rebellion by Kabua and his followers as they attempted to assert their land claims at the expense of local rivals.

The emperor's birthday in 1909 was a difficult occasion for both Wilhelm II and King Kabua. While the German monarch was still nursing the self-inflicted wounds of the *Daily Telegraph* affair, an ailing Kabua found himself struggling to realize his territorial claims in the face of a number of contradictory court decisions presided over by German officials. Adding to his difficulties were German suspicions that he was planning to launch a violent rebellion and his own suspicions that the Germans meant to send him into exile in New Guinea. Seeking a means to reassert both his status and his reputation as a reliable ally of the Germans, Kabua hit upon his royal gifts as a means of establishing a personal relationship with Wilhelm II and demonstrating his loyalty to the Crown.

Despite not being granted a personal letter of thanks from the German monarch, Kabua was content with the eventual outcome of the review of the land case. When the revised judgment was handed down in January 1910, less than a week before the Kaiser's next birthday, it argued that the earlier judgments had been insufficiently grounded in 'native law'. The new judgment, it asserted, now reflected the 'legal sensibilities of the natives' and moved past the alleged sectarian intrigues of Erdland,[109] proposing a compromise which satisfied Kabua but also offered some concessions to Litokua.[110]

According to a report to the German Colonial Office, the 1910 royal birthday celebrations saw 'the old enemies Kabua and Litokua reconciled' at a festive breakfast banquet.[111] A few months later, on 4 July 1910, Kabua died at the age of 90. He was officially hailed by the German district officer in Jaluit as someone who had always maintained his loyalty to the German emperor, and, pointedly, as someone who had never needed to be suppressed by force of arms during the twenty-six years of German rule he had endured. Significantly, Kabua's portrait of

---

[109] Berghausen to Dernburg, 12 February 1910, in BA Berlin R1001/3077, 85–8. The report also discusses the complications to local inheritance law by the emergence of a significant number of unrecognized children of white fathers.

[110] For the particulars of the decision, see Berghausen, 'Urteil in dem Erbstreit des burak—iroj Litokua gegen den iroj Kabua', in BA Berlin R1001/3077, 92–5. See also Erdland, *Die Marshall-Insulaner*, 106; Hezel, *Strangers in their Own Land*, 126–7.

[111] Berghausen to Dernburg, 31 January 1910, in BA Berlin R1001/3077, 84.

Wilhelm II had also reached him just prior to his death, upon the conclusion of his legal battle with Litokua.[112]

The title of king had meant a great deal to Kabua, both in terms of prestige among the Germans and in terms of its material importance to Marshallese politics. In distant Germany, his kingly status had always been taken for granted in newspaper reports about colonial affairs in the Pacific.[113] Not only had his status enabled him to enrich himself as an intermediary between his labouring subjects and the Germans, but it had also enabled him to seize the initiative against local rival *iroij*, most notably Loiak and Litokua, who had forthrightly questioned Kabua's claims to land and the titular role of *iroijlaplap*. Yet Kabua's claim to be king did not long outlive his lifetime. When District Officer Georg Merz came to Ailinglaplap to pay his respects two months later and saw that Kabua's tombstone had been engraved with the title of 'king', Merz ordered that it be altered from 'king' to '*iroij*'. With the former Marshallese 'king' now reduced in rank *post mortem*, Merz then haggled a deal with Kabua's successor to purchase some of Kabua's old lands.[114] To the relief of the German governor in New Guinea, the death of Kabua, unlike that of Loiak, did not upset the new 'land peace'. German control over the islands continued without significant local challenge. It was only with the arrival of their Japanese imperial rivals during the First World War that the Germans would be dislodged from the Marshall Islands.[115]

[112] Merz to Lindequist, 5 July 1910, in BA Berlin R1001/3077, 97; Merz to Hahl, 16 September 1910, in BA Berlin R1001/3077, 115–16.

[113] See, e.g., *Neueste Mittheilungen*, 8 January 1886, 3.

[114] Merz to Hahl, 6 September 1910, in BA Berlin R1001/3077, 100–5; Walsh, *Etto Nan Raan Kein*, 502.

[115] *Die deutschen Schutzgebiete in Afrika und der Südsee. Amtliche Jahresberichte, 1909/1910* (Berlin: Mittler, 1911), 176.

12

A Visit to the King of Samoa

In 1910, Tupua Tamasese Lealofi, widely tipped to be the next Paramount Chief of Samoa, travelled to Berlin to meet the titular King of Samoa, Kaiser Wilhelm II. According to one newspaper report, Tamasese was not unknown to the emperor, who confessed to having heard a great deal about his reputation as a 'great fighting man in the old troublous days of Samoa'. Now that Samoa was under German rule, however, those fighting days were gone forever, and there was, the emperor declared, only 'peace and happiness for your beautiful islands'. The message that Wilhelm II asked Tamasese to take back to the Samoans was that 'the emperor loves them and has no other wish than to see them happy, prosperous and contented.'[1] This seemingly innocuous offer of good wishes was part polite blandishment, but also part warning. Now that Samoa was firmly under German rule, there was no reason, the emperor implied, for Tamasese or any other Samoan to return to fighting. In particular, any violence surrounding the perennially thorny accession question needed to be averted.

Wilhelm II had assumed his Samoan royal title—*Tupu Sili o Samoa*—in the wake of Germany's annexation of Samoa in March 1900. The decision to offer the emperor the title Samoan king was part of Governor Wilhelm Solf's attempt to indigenize the appearance of German rule and was announced at an assembly in Apia on 11 April 1900. At the same time, Solf announced that the present leader of Samoa, Mata'afa Iosefo had been relegated to a position beneath the emperor and his viceregal representative, Governor Solf as *Ali'i Sili*, translated by the Germans as 'paramount chief'. The paramount Samoan leader now sat in a tertiary position intended to be 'the channel through which the wishes and orders of the administration would reach Samoans'.[2]

In coming to Germany, Tamasese addressed himself directly to these new power structures, as both a colonial subject visiting the metropolitan centre of the global German Empire and as a Samoan noble visiting his 'king'. Yet the expectation that Tamasese's visit to Berlin would help settle the question of who was to be German Samoa's next paramount leader was a cruel illusion. Unbeknownst to

---

[1] 'Tamasese Interviews the Kaiser', *Sydney Morning Herald*, 9 November 1911, in BA Berlin, R1001/3066, 187.
[2] Peter J. Hempenstall and Paula Tanaka Mochida, *The Lost Man: Wilhelm Solf in German History* (Wiesbaden: Harrassowitz, 2005), 61; George Steinmetz, *The Devil's Handwriting: Precoloniality and the German Colonial State in Qingdao, Samoa, and Southwest Africa* (Chicago: University of Chicago Press, 2007), 324–5.

The Kaiser and the Colonies: Monarchy in the Age of Empire. Matthew P. Fitzpatrick, Oxford University Press.

Tamasese and other noble Samoans, Wilhelm II had already authorized his governor in Samoa to abolish the Samoan paramountcy and replace it with a new advisory role to be shared by two Samoan nobles. Tamasese would never have the chance to claim Samoa's highest position.

Colonial Intrigues and Samoan Kings

The decision to abolish the paramountcy was not the first time that Samoa's rulers had been dislocated by imperial rivalries. During the nineteenth century, conflict over succession to Samoan titles had intensified as rival candidates were backed not only by opposing local factions but also by representatives of the different imperial powers, who sought to manipulate local rivalries to their advantage as they jostled for position in the Pacific. Intervention in Samoan political struggles by Germany, the US, and Britain became increasingly common as foreign companies backed by powerful political representatives able to summon gunboats in defence of their interests came to view the appointment of Samoa's leaders as something that could not be left to chance.

Their corrosive intervention distorted Samoan politics, weakening the capacity of any Samoan leader to gain and then maintain the level of political control necessary to ascend to the position of king or paramount ruler without violent intervention by one of the imperial powers. As Malama Meleisea has argued, Samoa's kings had historically emerged after one faction had been decisively overwhelmed by another, often by force. Consequently, kings relied at least partially on their military dominance to maintain their position, 'an impossible goal in Samoa since the 1860s when European gun boats had given the settlers a balance of power they could exercise to bring down any Samoan'.[3] As the British diplomat (and later Governor of Fiji) John Bates Thurston observed:

> In their original state it is probable that one of the two parties dividing Samoa would have conquered the other, and that after a struggle, with its attendant loss of life, permanent tranquillity might have been attained. But the effect of foreign intervention—too little for control but too much if control was not aimed at— has been to keep the dividing forces in equipoise.[4]

The 1873 solution to the dilemma had been a shared kingship leading two advisory councils. This local compromise decision was short-lived, however, with an

[3] Malama Meleisea, *The Making of Modern Samoa: Traditional Authority and Colonial Administration in the History of Western Samoa* (Suva: University of the South Pacific, 1987), 39.

[4] Thurston to Granville, 29 April 1885, in Edward Hertslet (ed), *British and Foreign State Papers, 1887–1888*, vol. 79 (London: Her Majesty's Stationery Office, 1888), 969.

American adventurer, Colonel Albert Steinburger, managing to insinuate himself into Samoan politics briefly as 'premier' in 1875. By 1876 Steinburger had been deported, but his deportation had polarized Samoans not only with regard to who should succeed him but also on the questions of the rights of non-Samoans to own property and trade in the region. These disagreements led to further violent conflict which, assisted by German gunboat diplomacy, strengthened German interests (represented by the Hamburg firm Godeffroy and Son's man on the spot, Theodor Weber), and boosted Germany's claims to primacy in the region.[5]

This did not end the rivalry between the imperial powers in the region. To German eyes, the two kings of the early 1880s, Malietoa Talavou and his successor Malietoa Laupepa favoured US and particularly British interests over German ones. Indeed, Malietoa Laupepa's ascendancy was confirmed in an agreement signed on board the USS *Lackawanna*. The vice king, Tupua Tamasese Titimaea, on the other hand, and his increasing number of adherents were seen as more sympathetic to Germans.[6] In late 1885 and early 1886, however, pro-British Samoans overreached their position by inviting the British to declare Samoa a British protectorate. At this, the German consul, Weber (supported by the man-of-war *Albatross* and a rival faction clustered around Tupua Tamasese), pushed Malietoa from power.[7] Unsurprisingly, Malietoa responded by requesting that the United States and Britain preserve his rule against any challenge from his German-backed rival Tupua Tamasese.[8] The stand-off resulted in an agreement between the three powers to host a meeting between King Malietoa and Vice King Tupua Tamasese on board the USS *Mohican* in June 1886. Despite the temporary truce that was brokered, by 1887 Germany became convinced that Tupua Tamasese (whom Salisbury referred to as 'the protégé of Germany') was held in higher esteem by the Samoans than Malietoa.[9] Accordingly, the German contingent in Samoa began to work for his accession to the kingship, arguing that the USS *Mohican* meeting had 'amounted to recognition of the *de facto* existence of Tamasese's party on the same footing as Malietoa's'.[10]

Surprising everyone with his own regional solution aimed at countering Tamasese and the Germans, Malietoa invited Hawaii's King Kalakaua to sign a pact with him in early 1887 that would create a Polynesian confederation and

---

[5] Paul M. Kennedy, *The Samoan Tangle: A Study in Anglo-German-American Relations, 1878–1900* (Dublin: Irish University Press, 1974), 8–13; Meleisea, *The Making of Modern Samoa*, 36–9.

[6] Kennedy, *The Samoan Tangle*, 25.

[7] Powell to Salisbury, 5 January 1886, in Hertslet (ed), *British and Foreign State Papers, 1887–1888*, vol. 79, 973.

[8] Malietoa to Greenebaum, 13 May 1886, in Hertslet (ed), *British and Foreign State Papers, 1887–1888*, vol. 79, 981.

[9] 'Agreement Made on Board United States' Ship Mohican at Apia Harbour, June 8, 1886'; Salisbury to Malet, 14 June 1887, in Hertslet (ed), *British and Foreign State Papers, 1887–1888*, vol. 79, 996.

[10] Malet to Salisbury (quoting Plessen), 19 February 1887, in Hertslet (ed), *British and Foreign State Papers, 1887–1888*, vol. 79, 991.

bring Samoa into the US orbit while bolstering the Malietoan party in Samoa. The astonishing agreement read as follows:

> By virtue of my inherent and recognized rights as King of the Samoan Islands by my own people and by Treaty with the three great Powers of America, England and Germany, and by and with the advice of my Government, and the consent of the Taimua and Faipule representing the legislative powers of my kingdom, I do hereby freely and voluntarily offer and agree and bind myself to enter into a political confederation with His Majesty Kalakaua, King of the Hawaiian Islands, and I do hereby give this solemn pledge that I will conform to whatever measures may hereafter be adopted by His Majesty Kalakaua, and be mutually agreed upon to promote and carry into effect this political confederation and to maintain it now and for ever.[11]

This attempt to form a Polynesian confederation upset both the Germans and the British,[12] who resolved to work in tandem to have it overturned. The Germans threatened war against Hawaii, while in the US even the secretary of state, Thomas Bayard, was against the proposal, which threatened to bring serious conflict between the European powers to the Pacific.[13] Britain's disapproval was made known in their cold assurance that King Malietoa would only be 'regarded as the lawful King of the Navigators Islands until he is lawfully deposed'.[14]

By August 1887, the Germans were ready to depose the king, lawfully or not, with the foreign secretary, Herbert von Bismarck-Schönhausen, telling the British that in light of the recent developments they were 'compelled...to declare war' against Malietoa 'and to refuse him our recognition as ruler', while offering military support to Tupua Tamasese.[15] By 25 August, the German consul, Becker, was ready to announce that 'My government has recognized Tamasese as King of Samoa.'[16] Emboldened, Tupua Tamasese formally declared his kingship on 25 August.[17] Far from taking the heat out of the situation, however, on the same day the British and American consuls in Samoa jointly declared that 'We...hereby

[11] Malietoa, 'Convention for Political Confederation with King Kalakaua', 17 February 1887, in Hertslet (ed), *British and Foreign State Papers, 1887–1888*, vol. 79, 992.

[12] Kennedy, *The Samoan Tangle*, 65.

[13] Kalakaua, 'Convention for Political Confederation with King Malietoa', 20 March 1887, in Hertslet (ed), *British and Foreign State Papers, 1887–1888*, vol. 79, 992–3.

[14] Salisbury to West, 31 May 1887, in Hertslet (ed), *British and Foreign State Papers, 1887–1888*, vol. 79, 994.

[15] Bismarck to Hatzfeldt, 7 August 1887, in Hertslet (ed), *British and Foreign State Papers, 1887–1888*, vol. 79, 997; Becker to Malietoa, 24 August 1887, in Hertslet (ed), *British and Foreign State Papers, 1887–1888*, vol. 79, 999.

[16] Becker to Wilson, 25 August 1887, in Hertslet (ed), *British and Foreign State Papers, 1887–1888*, vol. 79, 1004.

[17] Tamasese to Wilson, 25 August 1887, in Hertslet (ed), *British and Foreign State Papers, 1887–1888*, vol. 79, 1006.

give notice that we and our Governments do not, and never have, recognized Tamasese as King of Samoa, but continue as heretofore to recognize Malietoa.'[18]

With the British and the Americans united behind Malietoa, in spite of the difficulties he had caused, and the Germans rallying to Tamasese, the scene was set for a clash of the imperial powers over the question of the Samoan succession. Unexpectedly, these great power tensions were rendered largely moot by the Samoans themselves, who surprisingly declared their support for Tupua Tamasese. On 19 September 1887, the British consul reported that a majority of Samoan notables (*matai*) had, he felt, under the threat of a German invasion, offered their allegiance to Tupua Tamasese as 'King of all Samoa'. Finding himself bereft of support, Malietoa surrendered and was taken into exile aboard the *Adler* to Jaluit on the Marshall Islands,[19] leaving behind a message for his supporters:

> To all Samoa: On account of my great love to my country and my great affection to all Samoa, this is the reason I deliver up my body to the German government. That Government may do as they wish to me. The reason of this is because I do not desire that the blood of Samoa shall be spilled for me again, but I do not know what is my offence which has caused their anger to me and to my country.[20]

By October of 1887, the British had accepted the German fait accompli and agreed that 'Tamasese is *de facto* King of Samoa' and that the British would not support a US boycott of his governing institutions.[21]

Matters did not rest with the ascendancy of the Germans via Tupua Tamasese. With Malietoa having 'bequeathed the care of his native land to his kinsman, Mata'afa',[22] burgeoning anti-Tamasese sentiment crystallized around Tui Atua Mata'afa Iosefo, and this rivalry tipped into civil war in August 1888.[23] Although Tupua Tamasese was protected by German marines from the *Adler*, he was deserted by the Samoans, who now hailed Mata'afa as their king. Temperatures rose to the extent that the British and the Germans came close to being on opposite sides of a shooting war when in October 1888 German sailors fired on a canoe filled with Mata'afa's men, inadvertently hitting the houses of British subjects. The

---

[18] Wilson to Mitchell, 25 August 1887, in Hertslet (ed), *British and Foreign State Papers, 1887–1888*, vol. 79, 1005.

[19] On his exile in the Marshall Islands, see BA Berlin R1001/3078, 'König Malietoa von Samoa: Internierung auf den Marshall-Inseln, Begnadigung und Rückführung'; Wilson to Salisbury, 19 September 1887, in Hertslet (ed), *British and Foreign State Papers, 1887–1888*, vol. 79, 1011–12.

[20] Mata'afa, cited in Henry Clay Ide, 'The Imbroglio in Samoa', *North American Review* 168, no. 511 (1899), 680.

[21] Mitchell to Wilson, 28 October 1887, in Hertslet (ed), *British and Foreign State Papers, 1887–1888*, vol. 79, 1018.

[22] Ide, 'The Imbroglio in Samoa', 680.

[23] Meleisea, *The Making of Modern Samoa*, 40; Coëtlogon to Salisbury, 11 September 1888, in Hertslet (ed), *British and Foreign State Papers, 1887–1888*, vol. 79, 1038.

British responded by garrisoning their consulate and offering to protect British subjects aboard Her Majesty's ship *Lizard*.[24]

Not only did Mata'afa prove victorious, but, in a major military defeat, 56 of the 140 German marines supporting Tupua Tamasese were killed or wounded. Some of these soldiers were reported as having had their heads removed as war trophies, a turn of events that saw Germany later insist that Mata'afa was no longer an acceptable candidate for the Samoan kingship.[25] The surprise compromise candidate agreed to by the three powers was Malietoa Laupepa who, since going into exile, had been smuggled by the Germans first to German Cameroon and then to Hamburg before being returned to the Marshall Islands. After this round trip, his attitude towards the Germans had softened markedly.[26]

As a newly successful military leader, Mata'afa Iosefo refused to simply give up his paramount position. Instead he led a parallel government as a rival monarch to Malietoa until 1893, when Malietoa attacked and defeated him and turned him over to the British and Germans. It was now Mata'afa's turn to face exile in the Marshall Islands. It was only upon Malietoa's death in August 1898 that Mata'afa returned to Samoa and successfully fended off rival claimants to the throne, in particular Malietoa Tanus, the 17-year-old son of Malietoa Laupepa. With Mata'afa seemingly in the ascendancy, the American chief justice in Samoa, William Lea Chambers, suddenly announced that in his view Mata'afa was ineligible for the throne, and declared that Malietoa Tanus was the rightful king. This unilateral US intervention in the kingship was prevented by force of arms, with a Samoan-German force restoring Mata'afa to the throne and sending Malietoa (and Chambers) into hiding under British protection.[27]

The American Bombardment

The nadir of this great power proxy violence surrounding the Samoan throne came with the arrival of the USS *Philadelphia* in March 1899. Supported by the British, its commander, Rear Admiral Albert Kautz, bombarded the Samoan coastline and sent American and British troops into the interior in an attempt to dislodge the pro-German faction. In a conflict which once again saw rival Samoan factions supported by rival imperial powers, the situation was one where, as Henry Clay Ide wrote, 'a gentle, picturesque and kindly people are engaged, under the auspices of three great powers, in exterminating one another.'[28]

---

[24] Coëtlogon to Salisbury, 5 November 1888, in Hertslet (ed), *British and Foreign State Papers, 1887–1888*, vol. 79, 1041–2.

[25] Ide, 'The Imbroglio in Samoa', 680–1.   [26] BA Berlin R1001/3078.

[27] Ide, 'The Imbroglio in Samoa', 681–3.   [28] Ide, 'The Imbroglio in Samoa', 683–4.

The Germans had expected that the US naval bombardment would be disowned by both the British and American governments as an error of judgement by a rogue commander in the heat of the moment.[29] Even Cecil Rhodes declared the bombardment 'absolutely illegal and unfriendly to Germany'.[30] Surprisingly, however, Salisbury dug in, fending off German protests, and backing the US action. In the US itself, the *Washington Post* offered a glimpse of the gap between the US's diplomatic rhetoric and the personal views of Rear Admiral Kautz, reprinting his mocking letters that described Malietoa Laupepa (whose rights he was ostensibly championing) as a half-dressed, barefooted barbarian.[31]

While the Americans were privately disparaging their candidate for Samoan king, the German press was angrily criticizing its government's handling of the crisis, accusing it of being asleep at the wheel, with Chancellor Hohenlohe whiling away his time at a birthday party in Baden-Baden, while the foreign secretary, Bülow, was apparently off holidaying on Nordeney.[32] Behind the scenes, however, Bülow was vigorously stirring the pot, insisting that Britain offer Germany a deal in Samoa that took German interests into consideration.[33] Bülow also goaded Kaiser Wilhelm II into a fury by emphasizing the ostensibly perfidious role played by Britain as the true instigators of US military action. The Americans, Bülow argued, had been duped into being used as muscle for British interests, a charge that gained the furious agreement of the emperor. Bülow painted the British as the main impediment to Mata'afa's paramountcy and peace in Samoa, declaring that Britain's obstructionist attitude would have important consequences for Germany's relations with Britain:

The friendly relations that Your Majesty has observed since last summer in all parts of the world and in all questions regarding England cannot be continued, in light of the disappointment and agitation of German public opinion regarding the behaviour of the English in Samoa, if the English government in the Samoan question does not definitively and quickly take up a position that is considerate of us...If England were to break a sealed agreement with Germany, Your Majesty could, of course, not respond to this act of directly injuring our rights and public disregard with a declaration of war, but could well recall his representative from England, given that discussions about international law are pointless, if internationally legal agreements are not kept...The case of Samoa is proof that overseas policy can only be conducted with sufficient naval power.[34]

---

[29] *Frankfurter Zeitung*, 30 March 1899, in PAAA R19498, 'Samoa Inseln' (unnumbered).
[30] Hatzfeldt to Hohenlohe, 15 April 1899, in *Die Grosse Politik der Europäischen Kabinette 1871–1914*, vol. 14(2) (Berlin: Deutsche Verlagsgesellschaft für Politik und Geschichte, 1924), 610.
[31] *Washington Post*, 27 April 1899, in PAAA R19499, 'Samoa Inseln' (unnumbered).
[32] *Deutsche Zeitung*, 31 March 1899, in PAAA R19498 (unnumbered).
[33] See also Kennedy, *The Samoan Tangle*, 164–8.
[34] Bülow to Wilhelm II, 1 April 1899, in PAAA R19498 (unnumbered).

Wilhelm II applauded Bülow's anti-British, pro-naval stance, declaring that it was what he had 'been preaching to those Reichstag deputy oxen every day for ten years'.[35] So successful was Bülow at ratcheting up the emperor's anti-British stance, the monarch decided to pour some royal petrol onto the flames by sending a long and extremely ill-advised letter to his grandmother Queen Victoria, in which he attempted to blacken Salisbury's name as an enemy of German *Weltpolitik*. The letter was so intemperate that Queen Victoria felt compelled to defend Salisbury and rebuke her wayward grandson, exclaiming 'I doubt whether any Sovereign ever wrote in such terms to another Sovereign, and that Sovereign his own Grand Mother.'[36]

For their part, Wilhelm II's 'oxen' in the Reichstag showed that many of them were in full agreement on the question of who was to blame for the Samoan kingship dispute. The matter was discussed on 14 April 1899, after the National Liberal and Secretary of the Pan German League Adolf Lehr demanded (with the support of parties ranging from left liberals to arch-conservatives) that the chancellor report to the Reichstag on the current state of affairs.[37] Here too the tone was one of hot-headed attacks on the British as not only the instigators of the American bombardment of Samoa but also the chief impediment blocking Germany's colonial expansion.[38] The remedy to British obstructionism, Lehr argued, was for Germany to show the same nationalist egoism in foreign affairs as the British by building a strong fleet that could protect their economic interests around the world. Irrespective of its intrinsic value, Lehr argued, Samoa was a test of 'the maintenance of the great power status of the German Empire'.[39]

Despite Lehr's clear invitation to harangue the British, Bülow struck a much less combative tone in his reply to the Reichstag than in his correspondence with Germany's ambassador in London. After pointing out the strong interest in the matter among the German public, Bülow stuck closely to a script that emphasized the framework of international law in which the dispute was situated. Germany, he argued, had abided by the 1889 Treaty of Berlin, whereas the actions of London and Washington were, according to the treaty, illegal. On the question of the

---

[35] Bülow to Wilhelm II, 1 April 1899, in PAAA R19498 (unnumbered).

[36] Wilhelm II to Queen Victoria, 22 May 1899, in *Die Grosse Politik*, vol. 14(2), 615–19. Queen Victoria continued, 'I should never do such a thing and I never personally attacked or complained of Prince Bismarck, though I knew well what a bitter enemy he was to England, and all the harm he did' (Victoria to Wilhelm II, 12 June 1899, in *Die Grosse Politik*, vol. 14(2), 620–1).

[37] *Verhandlungen des Reichstages*, 14 April 1899, 1754.

[38] Hans Delbrück, 'Eine Berichtigung des H. K. T. Vereins und Weiteres zur Polenfrage. Samoa', 378–83. Delbrück complained that 'Such an embarrassment as this debate has scarcely been experienced by any parliament of a great people.' Delbrück's concerns were shared by the Swiss paper, *Der Bund*, which argued that pan-German hot-headedness unnecessarily raised the temperature of anti-German sentiment in the US, where one congressman had already argued that 'the Germans need a thrashing, just as the Spanish have been thrashed' (*Der Bund*, 18 April 1899, in PAAA R19499 (unnumbered)).

[39] Lehr, *Verhandlungen des Reichstages*, 14 April 1899, 1754–7.

Samoan kingship, Bülow simply lied, declaring that Germany had always remained neutral. Given, he continued, that all three consuls had approved the provisional government of Mata'afa, the German consul was obliged to consider it as the legal status quo until a unanimous resolution of the three powers appointed a new government. It was this strict neutrality with regard to the question of the internal processes of the Samoans, Bülow claimed with a straight face, that had prompted the Germans to neither approve nor participate in the intervention undertaken by the British and American navies. The significance of the dispute, he concluded, was not to be measured in the material worth of Samoa to Germany but in how it demonstrated how Britain would act towards its treaty obligations to Germany throughout the world.[40]

In fact, Bülow no longer had any need to whip up further anti-British sentiment in the Reichstag, as he was able to report that an agreement had been reached with the British government the previous day. On 13 April 1899, Salisbury had finally offered a proposal that averted a complete break in Anglo-German relations. The deal proposed that Samoa be ruled by committee, with each of the three powers offering a commissioner who only had the power to act when all three of them agreed to the action in question.[41] In addition, all contenders for the Samoan kingship were to be dissuaded from pressing their claims until a commission came up with a final settlement. At least briefly, it appeared as if Samoa would have no king, only a colonial administration. Despite a rumour in Switzerland's *Intelligenzblatt* that the Americans would call upon the Swiss to administer Samoa as a neutral power,[42] the question confronting the joint commission was whether Britain, Germany, the US, or a combination of the three would come to rule Samoa.

As the diplomatic tussle over the Samoan throne and imperial control over Samoa continued within the commission,[43] both global and regional considerations came to bear upon the powers. From Bülow's perspective, Germany needed to make it clear that Britain had no strategic or economic need for Samoa, given their control of Fiji, whereas for the German public, Samoa was the 'starting point of our colonial endeavours'. German public opinion would accept nothing other than Samoa as the anchor of the German Pacific.[44] In London, however, not only

[40] Bülow, *Verhandlungen des Reichstages*, 14 April 1899, 1757–8. This stance, that maintaining Germany's treaty-defined rights in Samoa was a broader matter of national honour, won Bülow a vote of thanks from the German Colonial Society. See Deutsche Kolonialgesellschaft to Hohenlohe, 8 June 1899, in PAAA19499 (unnumbered).

[41] Bülow to Hatzfeldt, 13 April 1899, in *Die Grosse Politik*, vol. 14(2), 605–6.

[42] *Intelligenzblatt*, 19 April 1899, in PAAA R19499 (unnunmbered).

[43] For a blow-by-blow account of these negotiations, see *Die Grosse Politik*, vol. 14(2), 627–75, and PAAA 19500, 'Die Samoa Inseln'.

[44] Bülow to Hatzfeldt, 6 May 1899, in *Die Grosse Politik*, vol. 14(2), 613–14; Hatzfeldt to Hohenlohe, 12 June 1899, in PAAA 19499; *Daily News*, 9 November 1899, in PAAA R 19508, 'Zustimmungsadressen und Pressäußerungen anläßlich des Abschlusses des Samoa-Abkommens zwischen Deutschland, England und Amerika' (unnumbered).

was Salisbury convinced that the Germans were using Britain's difficulties in South Africa as a bargaining chip in the Pacific,[45] but it leaked back to Berlin that British cabinet ministers were hesitant to come to terms with Germany because they were afraid that 'Australia would not permit the complete surrender of English claims to Samoa', a colonial consideration that Wilhelm II viewed as so minor as to be 'unbelievable'.[46]

In fact, there were many in Australia who supported the German rather than the British position. The Catholic Cardinal of Sydney, Patrick Francis Moran, led a vigorous protest movement against the US bombardment and in support of the kingship of the Catholic Mata'afa. The cardinal compared US military action in Samoa to the Armenian massacres and demanded that Samoan rights and traditions, as well as its monarchy, be preserved from the predations of the Americans. The Samoans, he claimed, had chosen Mata'afa as their king, but the US, 'bent on making the Pacific Ocean an American lake', had tried to usurp the rightful king. On the bombardment, the cardinal stated that he 'did not call it warfare' but rather 'deliberate murder'.[47] A Sydney newspaper also strongly condemned the British for becoming complicit in the jingoistic warfare of the Americans:

> It is a humiliating reflection on civilisation to see the two foremost nations of the world not only instigating native races to butcher each other, but taking an active part in the work…If the Samoans do not want Malietoa for their King, it is no business of freedom-loving Britons or Americans to force him upon them at the bayonet's point, as they are now doing. These people have the same right as we have to choose their own rulers, or they have not. If they have, except for the purposes of protecting their own subjects, no foreign Powers are justified in interfering with their recognised method of electing a King. If they have not, then the interference should not take the form of backing tribe against tribe.[48]

These Australian denunciations of American sailors as 'cowardly murderers' were heard in the United States. The *Boston Evening Transcript* protested indignantly against 'the idea that the vicious Americans have misled the virtuous Englishmen in Samoa'. The newspaper insisted that the real reason for these false claims were Australian concerns that the British were being displaced in the Pacific by the Americans.[49]

---

[45] Hatzfeldt to Hohenlohe, 3 October 1899, in PAAA R 19500 (unnumbered).

[46] Bülow to Wilhelm II, 29 May 1899, in PAAA R19499 (unnumbered). Bülow received this message via Frederick Holls on 15 May 1899. See Bülow to Hatzfeldt, 16 May 1899, *Die Grosse Politik*, vol. 14(2), 615. The claim was repeated numerous times by the British throughout the negotiations.

[47] 'Cardinal Moran Denounces the War: Murder of the Natives: America a Dangerous Nation', *Daily Telegraph*, 1 May 1899, in PAAA R19499 (unnumbered).

[48] 'The Fighting in Samoa', *Daily Telegraph*, 1 May 1899, in PAAA R19499 (unnumbered).

[49] *Boston Evening Transcript*, 9 June 1899, in PAAA R19499 (unnumbered).

Nonetheless, there were notes of disquiet in the US too about the rush to thrust a king on the Samoans by force, with the *New York Tribune* quoting Robert Louis Stevenson's stepson Lloyd Osbourne as saying that 'Mata'afa has a majority and the bombardment of natives was unwarranted.' On Rear Admiral Kautz, Osbourne caustically wrote, 'His only successful achievement has been the bombardment of villages full of women and children... He is killing Samoans because an overwhelming majority of them chose their king according to the laws and customs of Samoa.'[50] Other US newspapers also condemned the bombardments, reporting that 'the villages near the beach are populated only by women and children, old people and the sick' and that they were 'regularly being bombed without warning'.[51]

Of the domestic critics of the US war against Samoa, Henry Clay Ide was probably the most prominent. The ex-presidential commissioner and then later chief justice in Samoa wrote in support of Mata'afa and of the Samoan monarchy as an institution, criticizing the US for believing that they could successfully install an unpopular king:

> If a king is installed at the behest of the powers, and against the protest of the great mass of the Samoan people, he will have little more power than the President of a debating club. The natives will refuse to pay taxes or to obey the commands of the King, they will identify all foreign officials with the attempt to force upon them a native ruler whom they loathe, will commit depredations upon the plantations of foreigners and will decline to obey the summons of the Supreme Court. They will refuse to build roads, or to allow the King's adherents to come into the localities possessed by his opponents. The King will be a King of a few natives about Apia. The processes of the court will reach only through practically the same territory, while all the rest of Samoa will sit sullen, obstinate and disloyal. It will be a paper government and not an actual one. Of course it is in the power of the three great Governments to crush all native opposition, if they see fit to do so, and to kill, if need be, those who resent what they deem to be injustice; but that is an unworthy thing for three of the mightiest Governments on earth to set their hands to. The Samoans are an interesting, picturesque and kindly people, by nature and training; and it would be horrible, an act to be execrated by mankind, to see them trampled and crushed under the iron heel and torn and mangled by shells.[52]

---

[50] 'Lloyd Osbourne on Samoa', *New York Tribune*, 14 June 1899, in PAAA R19499 (unnumbered).
[51] *New Yorker Staats-Zeitung*, 21 June 1899; 'Blame the English', *St Louis Globe*, 21 June 1899, in PAAA R19499 (unnumbered).
[52] Ide, 'The Imbroglio in Samoa', 679–93.

The Abolition of Samoan Kingship

Despite the numerous voices around the world in support of the rights of the Samoans to decide who should be their king, one of the first decisions of the Samoa Commission of 1899 was to dismantle the Samoan monarchy. In place of a King of Samoa came territorial partition between Germany and the United States, with Britain renouncing its claims to Samoa in favour of primacy in Tonga. All pretence by the three powers of having only intervened to defend legitimate Samoan self-rule ended abruptly. As Bülow wrote to Wilhelm II's brother, Prince Heinrich, 'The preservation of the kingship had to be recognized as impractical for the peaceful development of Samoa,'[53] artfully neglecting to say that this was precisely because the kingship issue had been exploited by the three powers as a means of tightening their grip on Samoa. In Britain, the press rationalized the abolition of the Samoan throne as timely, given that in recent years 'The King had no authority or practical power.' This article too failed to mention the decades-long role played by the imperial powers in manipulating the Samoan throne, instead suggesting that the monarch had to be dethroned because 'the greater part of the population was, for all intents and purposes, in permanent rebellion against him.'[54]

The abolition of the Samoan monarchy was far from universally welcomed, even in Europe. Britain's *Morning Post* argued that the Samoans were 'attached to the institution of the monarchy'. Beyond this, the paper felt that abolishing the monarchy and entrusting government to a 'shadowy administrator' would simply drive underground 'the partisans of the rival ex-Kings', who would continue to upset Samoan politics.[55] No tears were shed for the Samoan kings by the German government, however, which revelled in what was interpreted as a personal triumph for the foreign secretary, Bülow. Tsar Nicholas II personally congratulated him on his success, while one Viennese newspaper opined that 'Count Bülow has become an expander of the empire.' Since he became foreign secretary, the paper continued, 'a great power has become a world power.' Ignoring the numerous local wars waged for control of the Samoan throne, the paper declared that 'in the art of bloodless conquest, Count Bülow is a master.'[56] Not content with simply gaining control of much of Samoa, the Germans went on to demand compensation from Britain and the US for the damage caused by the US naval bombardment of the Samoan coastline. The question of indemnity was settled by the

---

[53] Bülow to Prince Heinrich von Preußen, 15 August 1899, in *Die Grosse Politik*, vol. 14(2), 626.
[54] *Daily Telegraph*, 9 November 1899, in PAAA R 19500 (unnumbered).
[55] *Morning Post*, 12 October 1899, in PAAA R 19500 (unnumbered).
[56] 'Von Großmacht zur Weltmacht', *Wiener Allgemeine Zeitung*, 10 November 1899, in PAAA R 19508 (unnumbered).

appointment of the King of Sweden as an agreed-upon independent arbiter who could impartially assess the claims and counterclaims made by the three powers.[57]

For their part, the Samoans did not simply accept the agreement of the powers quietly. Undeterred by the new arrangements, Mata'afa Iosefo pushed his claim to be pronounced king (*Tupu Sili*) of the German segment of Samoa.[58] In the end, however, the new German governor, Wilhelm Solf, came up with a plan to defang permanently the question of kingship in Samoa by declaring that it was not Mata'afa, but Kaiser Wilhelm II who was the new *Tupu Sili*, with Solf as his viceregal proxy. Beneath the German layer of administration, Mata'afa was named '*Ali'i Sili*'—paramount leader—the local conduit for relations between the Germans and the Samoans, who would be advised by the *faipule*, an advisory body of Samoan nobles.[59] The compromise arrangement remained in place until 1912.

Exemplifying the enduring Samoan disquiet over the dismantlement of the Samoan monarchy was the 1908–9 rebellion known as the *Mau a Pule* (not to be confused with the later Mau rebellion under New Zealand's administration). The key figure here was Lauaki Namulau'ulu Mamoe, an orator chief who amplified the political and economic grievances of many Samoan notables who felt themselves to have been sidelined by Solf. Lauaki grafted these disparate grievances onto the question of who would be granted the title *Ali'i Sili* upon the death of the increasingly frail Mata'afa Iosefo.

From the German perspective, the answer was no one. Solf had already begun to consider a plan to abolish the paramount position of *Ali'i Sili* upon the death of Mata'afa. For Lauaki, however, reviving authentically Samoan decision-making bodies that included rival contenders for the throne from both the Sa Malietoa and Sa Tupua factions and placing them at the heart of the German administration was key to renewing and reinvigorating autonomous Samoan politics, precisely the opposite outcome desired by Solf.

Lauaki's machinations, if brought to fruition, would have posed a direct threat to German administration and a serious challenge to Solf. In the event, though, Solf and his deputy, Erich Schultz, sought to defuse the crisis before it had a chance to escalate. This they did in two ways. In the first instance, they struck at the edifice of unity that Lauaki had used to his advantage, hinting that the Samoan coalition was in fact being used by one of the factions to increase its power under the guise of representing a pan-Samoan movement. While this disinformation

---

[57] The idea originated in London. Bülow to Foreign Office, 18 July 1899, in PAAA R 19499 (unnumbered).

[58] Peter Hempenstall, *Pacific Islanders under German Rule: A Study in the Meaning of Colonial Resistance* (Canberra: ANU Review, 2016), 30–5.

[59] Hempenstall, *Pacific Islanders under German Rule*, 32–6; Steinmetz, *The Devil's Handwriting*, 324–7. For Samoan demands that the *Ali'i Sili* be treated as equal in dignity to the representative of the emperor to the Samoan people, see BA Berlin R1001/2950 'Errichtung einer deutschen Verwaltung in Samoa', 154–7.

campaign was under way, Solf also secured German naval support in order to convince the Samoans that any attempt to revolt would be futile. Four vessels, including the cruiser *Leipzig*, now steamed from their Chinese deployment to Apia. This was an expensive precaution, and 5,000 extra marks was granted to Solf for the purpose of hosting so many naval vessels.

In the event, Solf's courting of the navy almost backfired, however, with the corvette captain, Emsmann, insisting that the navy was the true instrument of the emperor's *Weltpolitik*, not the governor. Accordingly, Emsmann argued, he should exercise authority over German Samoa for the duration of his stay. Solf resisted the navy's attempt to wrest control of the colony, however, in a turn of events that one hagiographic biography described as 'a remarkable vindication of the laws of right of civilian power against the claims of the military'.[60] In the end, the threat of violence sufficed, and the navy was not needed to defeat Lauaki militarily. Instead, Lauaki accepted that his protest had been defeated and went into permanent exile on the island of Saipan. In the aftermath of the incident, Solf warned the remaining *matai* of Samoa 'to bear in mind that there was only one head in Samoa … His Majesty the Kaiser'.[61]

Tamasese's Visit to Germany

It was in the aftermath of the *Mau a Pule* crisis and the demand for the return of political rights and offices for Samoans that Tupua Tamasese Lealofi, the presumptive heir to the paramount position of *Ali'i Sili*, left for Germany. In some ways, Tamasese's trip to Germany to meet the emperor mirrored the visits of other non-European royals who had visited Wilhelm II as a means of shoring up their domestic position and enhancing their status, security, and visibility internationally. There were, however, some important differences. Although Tamasese was a likely candidate for the Samoan paramountcy, it was still assumed that the position would be contested by the supporters of other Samoans holding important noble titles. Also important was the fact Tamasese came to Germany as a royal living under German rule, with '*Tupu Sili*' Wilhelm II ostensibly his king. Accordingly, his visit was both a result of and had consequences for the internal workings of Germany's Pacific empire, bringing him face to face with both the King of Samoa and the Emperor of the German Empire, now combined in the person of Wilhelm II. In domestic terms, this personal audience offered him

[60] Eberhard von Vietsch, *Wilhelm Solf: Botschafter zwischen den Zeiten* (Tübingen: Rainer Wunderlich Verlag, 1961), 54.

[61] Solf, quoted by Meleisea in *The Making of Modern Samoa*, 82–3. On the *Mau a Pule* generally, see Hempenstall, *Pacific Islanders under German Rule*, 55–67. On the costs of the naval visits, see Reichsschatzamt to Kaiser, 1 July 1910, in GStAPK IHA Rep 89 Nr 32474, 'Akten betr die Gouverneure in den Schutzgebieten'.

the chance to consolidate his prestige amongst Samoans at a critical time and signal to German officials in Samoa and Germany that he understood Samoa's position within the German Empire more intimately than any other contender for the paramountcy.[62]

There was, however, another important factor structuring the circumstances in which Tamasese arrived in Germany to pay a visit to the German emperor, one far less likely to elicit the awe of his compatriots. Unlike other noble visitors to Germany such as King Chulalongkorn of Siam or Prince Zaifeng of China—but like Friedrich Maharero before him—Tamasese had come to Germany as a part of a travelling show that saw him and several other Samoans presented as exhibits in German zoos. Although the recruitment of indigenous peoples from the German colonies for human exhibits (*Völkerschauen*) had been banned in 1901, a troupe had been brought together by the Marquardt Brothers and had been permitted to leave Samoa in 1910 after Governor Wilhelm Solf interceded to allow it, citing the desire of the presumed claimant to the position of paramount chief, Tamasese, to come to Germany on a diplomatic mission to meet the emperor.[63] According to one newspaper report, Samoa's presumptive heir to the position of paramount chief had declared to Governor Solf, 'I am Tamasese. My heart is gladdened to travel to Germany to see the emperor and the princes of Germany.'[64] The extent to which he was made aware of how he might be treated whilst in Germany is unclear, but the Samoan noble was clearly shocked at the undignified treatment he was subjected to upon arriving in Germany.[65]

The restrictions placed upon Tamasese as an ethnographic curiosity housed in a zoo clashed with his status as a Samoan noble in all too apparent ways. Carl Marquardt attempted to control closely Tamasese's movements while on tour, but this did not stop him from looking up his old German friends, Otto and Bella Riedel, who had spent a great deal of time in Samoa working for the *Deutsche Handels- und Plantagengesellschaft* (DHPG). Tamasese's sudden and unexpected arrival on the Riedels' Hamburg doorstep surprised and delighted them, as Otto Riedel later recalled in his memoirs:

> One day…my wife and I heard a tumult at our front door. Our Hamburg maid shrieked loudly, and a dusky voice called through the house 'Bella! Bella!' My wife ran out. Outside stood Tamasese and his second wife Vaainga. The giant

[62] Christopher Balme, 'New Compatriots: Samoans on Display in Wihelminian Germany', *Journal of Pacific History* 42, no. 3 (2007), 342–3.

[63] Christopher B. Balme, *Pacific Performances: Theatricality and Cross-Cultural Encounter in the South Seas* (New York: Palgrave, 2007), 133–4.

[64] 'Der Empfang des Großhäuptlings Tamasese durch den deutschen Kaiser', *Australische Zeitung*, 19 July 1911, 10.

[65] On the tour, see Hilke Thode-Arora, 'A Diplomatic Visit? Tamasese in Germany and the Samoa Show of 1910–11', in Hilke Thode-Arora (ed), *From Samoa with Love? Samoan Travellers in Germany 1895–1911: Retracing the Footsteps* (Munich: Hirmer Verlag, 2014).

Samoan simply brushed our small maid aside as it became clear to him that the Riedels lived here and rushed over to my wife and me...Marquardt apparently didn't want him to come to see me. But Tamasese had simply got into a car with his wife and said to the Hamburg driver "Otto Riedel!" He couldn't imagine that there would be someone in Hamburg that didn't know me. The driver, with whom Tamasese could naturally only make himself understood with gestures, acted very sensibly. He looked in the telephone book, found my address and brought his exotic passenger exactly where he wanted to go...My wife was thrilled to be able to speak Samoan again to her heart's desire and I was amazed by the sureness with which these Samoans had found their way to us.[66]

Thereafter, Tamasese and Vaainga visited the Riedels frequently while they were in Hamburg, with the Riedels even putting on a Samoan-style feast in their honour, albeit one without the whole roasted pig that was 'usual in Tamasese's house'.[67]

The Riedels' pleasure at being reacquainted with Tamasese and Vaainga was tempered by the fact that the royal visit of their friend, one of the most important men in Samoa, had seen him being exhibited in German zoos, a reality that sat uncomfortably with them. At the zoo, Tamasese and his group were called upon to dance, box, canoe, play games, and prepare kava for German audiences wishing to see 'exotic' human specimens from the German colonies (See Figure 12.1). Witnessing what Tamasese and his companions were compelled to do at the zoo was even worse than reading about it in the newspapers, and Riedel admitted:

> For my wife and me, it was no real joy to see this. We had the feeling that a trust had been broken here...I was not very happy to see my old friend stared at behind bars in the zoological gardens, and I vigorously shared my opinion that the natives of our colonies should not be used for entertainment.[68]

The nature of the performances at the zoos, as well as the 'undignified' conditions in which the Marquardts kept the troupe, also deeply disappointed Tamasese, who noted to his Hamburg friend the marked discrepancy between his earlier high expectations and his experience of his trip to Germany.[69] At the prompting of Riedel, however, Solf intervened to ensure that the conditions for the Samoan party in Germany improved, and Tamasese was eventually treated with a modicum of the dignity he had initially expected. In Munich he was able to visit Prince

---

[66] Otto Riedel, *Der Kampf um Deutsch-Samoa: Erinnerungen eines Hamburger Kaufmanns* (Berlin: Deutscher Verlag, 1938), 218–20.

[67] Riedel, *Der Kampf um Deutsch-Samoa*, 218–20.

[68] Riedel, *Der Kampf um Deutsch-Samoa*, 218–20.

[69] Riedel, *Der Kampf um Deutsch-Samoa*, 218–20.

Figure 12.1 Postcard: 'Prince Tamasese with Wife Vaainga and Family'
Source: Courtesy of Archive Reinhold Mittersakschmöller, Vienna.

Ludwig, who accepted the Samoan fine mats that Tamasese had brought him as a present. In return, Ludwig gave Tamasese a gold ring.[70]

Solf also arranged for Tamasese to meet Wilhelm II. Should the emperor fail to meet this representative of Samoa's *matai*, Solf had warned, the 'political situation

---

[70] Riedel, *Der Kampf um Deutsch-Samoa*, 219–20; *Samoanische Zeitung*, 2 December 1911.

Figure 12.2 Tamasese and Colonial Secretary Wilhelm Solf in Berlin, 1911

in Samoa would be destabilized'. Preparations were thus made for three meetings: one at Kiel Castle, a second at the spring military parade in Tempelhof, and a third at the city palace.[71] At the Tempelhof Field, Tamasese and three of his warriors observed a military parade from the royal carriage (see Figure 12.2). Here he met Wilhelm II, 'who spoke to him in a friendly manner and later sent him a portrait of himself'.[72] The meeting and the military parade had a profound, long-term impact on Tamasese, according to Riedel, who commented that 'after he had experienced that, there was no doubt for him that the Germans were the most powerful nation on earth'.[73]

The third meeting with Wilhelm II, shortly after the parade, took place at the city palace. It too went off without a hitch, as newspaper reports make clear:

The High Chief Tamasese of Samoa [was] ... received by the emperor in the castle of Berlin following the spring review of the Guards Corps. Governor Dr Solf was present at the reception. The emperor expressed his satisfaction at seeing Tamasese, whom he had not believed he would have the opportunity to ever see in person. Tamasese presented the emperor with two of the famous fine mats of

[71] *Samoanische Zeitung*, 2 December 1911; Anne Dreesbach, *Gezähmte Wilde: Die Zurschaustellung 'exotischer' Menschen in Deutschland 1870–1940* (Frankfurt am Main: Campus, 2005), 275; Horst Gründer and Hermann Hiery, *Die Deutschen und ihre Kolonien* (Berlin: be.bra Verlag, 2017), 290.

[72] Riedel, *Der Kampf um Deutsch-Samoa*, 219–20.

[73] Riedel, *Der Kampf um Deutsch-Samoa*, 219–20.

Samoa. One was to be for the emperor, the other for the empress, who observed the reception from the balcony. The emperor thanked and offered the Samoan prince graciously his hand for farewell, which Tamasese kissed...In political regard, Tamasese is a person of greatest importance...If this title [*Ali'i Sili*] is bestowed once again after the death of Mataafa, who is already at a very advanced age, Tamasese will be the most distinguished candidate.[74]

Tamasese's own recollections of the royal audiences were also reported in great detail by the *Sydney Morning Herald* in November 1911, when the Samoan party stopped over in Sydney on their way back to Samoa. For Tamasese, the most memorable aspect of the trip was his audience with Wilhelm II, who apparently greeted him with the Samoan greeting 'Talofa' while shaking hands. The emperor, Tamasese reported, was 'neither big nor small', but the Samoan was certainly impressed by (or rather had impressed upon him) the size of the German army. The impression he brought back with him to the Pacific of the military parade on the Tempelhof Field was of 'miles of soldiers'. As a future paramount chief, Tamasese had noted the true extent of German military resources, commenting that he had 'thought of the bigness of Germany and the littleness of Samoa. We knew they had a big army but never did we dream that it was so big, big, big as that!'[75] The German-language press in Australia also remarked that 'Tamasese had multiple opportunities during his stay in Europe to become convinced of the power and greatness of the German Empire'. Given Tamasese's status and reputation as a warrior of some renown, it is likely that the impression that Germany was a great military nation was precisely that desired by Solf and the Colonial Office. Even once Samoa had been occupied by New Zealand during the First World War, Tamasese remained convinced that Germany would win the war.[76] The intended lesson had been learned, and, it seemed, Tamasese would 'doubtless have the best influence on the future relations of the Samoan people to their new Fatherland'.[77]

The Abolition of the Paramount Chieftaincy

That Tamasese was both an ethnographic exhibit in a zoo and the honoured guest of the German emperor shows how unclear the status and importance of the rulers of Samoa were to German authorities, and how precarious their position

[74] *Schlesische Zeitung*, 3 June 1911, in Arthur J. Knoll and Hermann J. Hiery (eds), *The German Colonial Experience: Select Documents on German Rule in Africa, China, and the Pacific 1884–1914* (Lanham, MD: University Press of America, 2010), 125–6; 'Tamasese Interviews the Kaiser', *Sydney Morning Herald*, 9 November 1911, in BA Berlin, R1001/3066, 187.
[75] 'Tamasese Interviews the Kaiser', *Sydney Morning Herald*, 9 November 1911, in BA Berlin R1001/3066, 187.
[76] Riedel, *Der Kampf um Deutsch-Samoa*, 219–20.
[77] 'Der Empfang des Großhäuptlings Tamasese durch den deutschen Kaiser', *Australische Zeitung*, 19 July 1911, 10.

within the German Empire was. Governor Solf was entirely correct in predicting that any royal snub to Tamasese would have had important consequences for the future of the Pacific colony. As many commentators at the time observed, Tamasese was 'next to Mataafa...the greatest of all the living Samoan chiefs'.[78] Some newspapers even speculated that his father, 'who was recognized as King by all the Samoan tribes' had taught Tamasese to regard the Germans well and 'keep true to the friendship with Germany and the treaties made with it'. In any case, it was seen as self-evident that, 'should the title be offered again after the death of the very elderly Mataafa', Tamasese was the Samoan noble most likely to be named paramount chief.[79] Had Wilhelm II, the 'King of Samoa', refused to meet him and had he returned home without having seen the military might of Germany or having only experienced the humiliation of having been exhibited in zoos, his future dealings with German colonial officials might well have been very different.

This is particularly the case, given Solf's radical plans for the paramount office of *Ali'i Sili* once Mata'afa died. In fact, these plans hint at the more complex background to Tamasese's trip to Germany. Given the law against recruiting performing troupes in the colonies, Solf's permission to the Marquardt brothers was highly irregular, particularly given the status of the intended performer. The context of this, however, was an impending long-planned shift in the political structure of Samoa, which had already been approved in Berlin, but which could only be implemented after the death of the current paramount chief, Mata'afa Iosefo. This shift was the abolition of the office of paramount chief and its replacement with two advisory roles, to be shared between Samoa's two main rival factions.[80] With Mata'afa ailing, Solf thought it opportune to have Tamasese as far from Samoa as possible when the position of paramount chief became vacant.[81] A tour of Germany, where Tamasese would be kept away from Samoan domestic politics while becoming acquainted with the full extent of German military power, was a well-timed opportunity.

The plan to abolish the paramount chieftaincy was the latest development in a long history of political changes brought about by the Germans through their desire to control Samoa.[82] It was also the final step after the imperial powers of Britain, Germany, and the United States had interfered in Samoa's domestic politics, partitioned the islands into a German and American zone, and then abolished

---

[78] 'Tamasese Interviews the Kaiser', *Sydney Morning Herald*, 9 November 1911 in BA Berlin R1001/3066, 187.

[79] 'Der Empfang des Großhäuptlings Tamasese durch den deutschen Kaiser', *Australische Zeitung*, 19 July 1911, 10.

[80] Hempenstall, *Pacific Islanders under German Rule*, 67.

[81] Gründer and Hiery, *Die Deutschen und ihre Kolonien*, 288–90. A slightly different understanding of Solf's reasoning is offered in Dreesbach, *Gezähmte Wilde*, 275.

[82] Kennedy, *The Samoan Tangle*.

the Samoan kingship. When the kingly title was revived by Solf, it was only in order to hand it to Kaiser Wilhelm II, while the Samoans were instructed to be content with the position of paramount leader. Now that too was to be abolished.

The abolition of the position of *Ali'i Sili* had long been in preparation. It was more than a year after Solf revealed to the Colonial Office his plan to abolish the paramount chieftaincy that Chancellor Theobald von Bethmann-Hollweg revealed it to Wilhelm II in a letter on 10 March 1910, a year before the emperor would meet Tamasese. The letter argued that the change was a necessary response to the *Mau a Pule* crisis, which the chancellor characterized as an outbreak of 'native discontent' caused by the early rumblings of a succession dispute.[83] The danger had not passed and the question, he said, of who would replace Paramount Chief Mata'afa upon his death 'continues to stir the passions to a large degree' in Samoa. Consequently, Governor Solf had advised authorizing the plan well in advance, so that when the current *Ali'i Sili* died, the Germans governor could 'avoid the outbreak of new unrest between the Samoans'. Only 'the complete abolition of the position of *Ali'i Sili*' could avoid a civil war in Samoa, the chancellor informed Wilhelm II, but such a move could not be done by the governor alone. Rather, the announcement had to be presented in a ceremonial form, in keeping with Samoan political practice. Additionally, a move as politically momentous as this could not be made by the governor alone. Instead, it required the formal intervention of the King of Samoa, Wilhelm II.

This royal intervention consisted of Wilhelm II approving the draft decree that Governor Solf had written and sent to Berlin. The decree was, according to Solf, a declaration of the emperor's will 'in a form appropriate to Samoan ways of thinking'.[84] Wilhelm II assented, and both he and the chancellor signed the decree to be read to the Samoans upon the death of Mata'afa, whenever that should occur. The royal decree that Solf had prepared after the challenge to German rule presented by the *Mau a Pule* movement addressed the social conflicts of Samoa by imposing a colonial version of the wisdom of Solomon. It read:

> In My great love for the Samoan people and in recognition of the equal status of both of the two High Families Sâ Tupua and Sâ Malietoa, I wish and order that after the passing of the honourable Paramount Chief Mata'afa an *Ali'i Sili* will no longer be appointed, so that through such an appointment one or other of the two High Families will not be degraded and aggrieved. I empower My representative in Samoa, the governor, to select one member from each of the Tupua and Malietoa families to be the governor's trusted friend and adviser, and as a

---

[83] On the events of 1909 and 1910, see BA Berlin R43/930, 'Samoa'.
[84] Bethmann-Hollweg to the Kaiser, 10 March 1910, in GStAPK IHA Rep 89 32471, 'Häuptlinge und Fürsten in den Schutzgebiet', 11.

342   THE KAISER AND THE COLONIES

sign of the dignity of the new position, the income of the former *Ali'i Sili* will be shared between these two chiefs.[85]

Unbeknownst to Tamasese, this plan to abolish the highest office held by a Samoan had all been settled before he arrived in Germany. If he had hoped that by establishing a personal connection with Wilhelm II he would improve his chances of ascending to the paramountcy, it was a mistaken hope. Governor Solf had ensured that no *Ali'i Sili* would emerge again under German rule.

The decree was eventually read to the Samoans upon the death of Mata'afa, but not by Solf. In the end, Mata'afa did not succumb until February 1912, well after Solf had left Samoa to become the colonial secretary in Berlin. Before dying, the *Ali'i Sili* had distributed his fine mats (*'ie toga*) in accordance with Samoan custom, with one sent to Wilhelm II as 'a final sign of his loyalty and respect'.[86] The rest were distributed to other Samoans. Although the division and acceptance of a chief's fine mats before death was ostensibly a personal affair, it was often highly political in nature, and even Tamasese's visit to Germany was reflected in this ceremony, with one pro-Tamasese village refusing to accept any after having heard about the shabby treatment of their candidate for the paramountcy while he was in Berlin.[87]

Unsure of the reception of the abolition decree, upon Mata'afa's death in 1912 the ex-governor and now colonial secretary, Solf, argued that the German government should send one or more naval cruisers to the region in case the reform was summarily rejected by the *matai*.[88] The precautionary measures proved unnecessary, however, with the decision to split the paramountcy between two advisers (called *Fautua Kaisalika*) representing the two leading families received quietly by the Samoans. The relieved new Samoan governor, Erich Schultz, reported back to Solf enthusiastically that 'During a native ceremonial assembly, the abolition of the rank of *Ali'i Sili* and the appointment of the two chiefs Tamasese and Tanu as his advisers...had been accepted by the natives with joy and thanks'.[89] Whether these thanks were conditioned by Tamasese's recent first-hand experience of the extent of German military power is not recorded.

The two *Fautua Kaisalika* swore an oath to the colonial regime binding them to be 'sincere and obedient to His Majesty the Kaiser and his representative in Samoa, the governor' and to 'do nothing of my own free will that might be

---

[85] GStAPK IHA Rep 89 32471, 13. This differed greatly from the 1873 shared kingship in that it was only an advisory role, not a leadership role. On 1873, see Meleisea, *The Making of Modern Samoa*, 36.

[86] Schultz to Solf, 24 August 1911, in BA Berlin R1001/2780, 'Geschenke für Kaiser Wilhelm II. und Gegengeschenke—Samoa', 54; Solf to Wilhelm II, 13 February 1912, in GStAPK IHA Rep 89 Nr 32471, 14.

[87] Schultz to Solf, 24 August 1911, in BA Berlin R1001/2780, 54–5.

[88] Solf to Kaiser, 30 March 1912, in GStAPK IHA Rep 89 32471, 15.

[89] Solf to Kaiser, 23 July 1913, in GStAPK IHA Rep 89 32471, 16. See 'Tamasese Interviews the Kaiser', *Sydney Morning Herald*, 9 November 1911, in BA Berlin R1001/3066, 187.

contrary to the laws of the Imperial government'. Alongside this, the official *fa'alupega* (Samoa's graded list of honours) was altered to reflect the new ladder of offices; 'the Kaiser, the governor, the *Fautua*, the *Faipule*, the various ranks of native officials'. As one Samoan historian has characterized the new arrangements, 'the sole authority in German Samoa was that legitimised by the German Emperor through the appointments made by his representative, the governor. There was to be no legitimate Samoan authority save that delegated to Samoans by the governor'.[90]

Notwithstanding the prophylactic effects of Tamasese's visit to Berlin and the muted response to the Solf reforms to the paramount chieftaincy, Governor Schultz and the Colonial Office remained alert to the potential for a Samoan backlash against the new political arrangements. Indeed, Schultz looked for a way to remind the *matai* of Germany's overarching political authority and military strength. In September 1913, Wilhelm II was informed that the governor had felt it necessary to make it clear once again to the *matai* that he was not compelled to solicit advice from his Samoan advisers on all issues, nor was he bound to accept their advice if it was given. Uncertain of the effects that this forceful reiteration of German power would have on the disempowered Samoans, Schultz had asked whether a 'squadron of cruisers' might visit Samoa sometime in the next year 'so that the Samoans can have it placed before their eyes that Your Majesty possesses the instruments of power to punish the disobedient and disloyal at any time, and to lead them back to their duty'.[91]

Alongside such military sticks, some modest carrots were also offered by the Germans, particularly in the shape of symbolic gifts that denoted a recognition of the status of the *Fautua Kaisalika*. Just before the First World War, Governor Schultz suggested that Wilhelm II should present highly prized orators' fly whisks (*fue*) as gifts from the emperor to his two Samoan paramount advisers, Tamasese and Tanu. Yet even these handcrafted royal gifts were not meant to be a sign of the emperor's generosity of spirit, but rather were calibrated as part of 'native policy' to reward them for their loyalty under the new system. The gifts also suggested that the emperor was watching and judging their efforts and could intercede with a 'special act of grace' to reward good behaviour. The royal gifts, that is, were used to ensure that stability and a proper sense of the imperial hierarchy prevailed in the colony.[92]

Tamasese and the First World War

When the First World War came to Samoa in the shape of a modest-sized invasion from New Zealand, Tamasese was viewed with suspicion as an enemy

---

[90] Meleisea, *The Making of Modern Samoa*, 86–7.
[91] Conze to Kaiser, 10 September 1913, in GStAPK IHA Rep 89 32471, 17.
[92] Solf to Kaiser, 23 May 1914, in GStAPK IHA Rep 89 32471, 19.

sympathizer who kept a portrait of the German Kaiser in his home and was prone to raising the German flag. Even under occupation, he boasted of having been to Berlin to visit Wilhelm II, 'the biggest and greatest man on earth'.[93] As his Hamburg friend Riedel wrote, 'After he had experienced that, there was no doubt for him that the Germans were the most powerful nation on earth. During the war he believed in our victory until the end'.[94] This view was corroborated by the German diarist Frieda Zieschank, who was convinced that Solf's intervention to secure Tamasese a place at the Templehof Field and a meeting with Wilhelm II had convinced the Samoan leader that the polished troops he had seen in Berlin would defeat the 'good-for-nothing' New Zealander troops he had seen.[95]

This was certainly the intelligence being received by the German Colonial Office during the war. According to a German still living under the occupation of the New Zealanders in Samoa in 1915, Tamasese was one of only two Samoan *matai* (the other being Tagaloa in Saluafata) who 'remained absolutely German'. Despite being forbidden to do so, Tamasese had also held a large celebration for the Kaiser's birthday.[96] The *Fautua Kaisalika* reassured his German friends in Samoa that he had not become pro-British. The German emperor was having a difficult time, he conceded, but he, Tamasese, would wait out the war in peace and trust. He was convinced that Germany would win the war.[97] Another German report from Samoa in 1915 explained the extent of Tamasese's loyalty:

> Colonel Logan did everything he could to coax Tamasese over to the side of those in favour of the English, but with little success. Logan once went with Roberts to Tamasese and sought to convince him to remove the portraits of the emperor and the empress from his house. Tamasese apparently said, however, that he would do that when the war was over and only if Samoa became English.[98]

That Tamasese had remained pro-German, the report continued, was evident in his defence of the German population in the colony after the policy of interning the Germans had been announced. In fact, when the head of New Zealand's occupation force, Colonel Logan, threatened to deport all Germans living in Samoa to

---

[93] Meleisea, *The Making of Modern Samoa*, 104.

[94] Riedel, *Der Kampf um Deutsch-Samoa*, 218–20.

[95] Frieda Zieschank, *Ein Jahrzehnt in Samoa 1906–1916*. (Leipzig: Haberland, 1918), 144–5. According to Zieschank, Tamasese's exact words were ,'Pele tania fita fita ele ni fita fita e tele valea—fita fita siamani tele lele!'

[96] Ludwig Geiger to Solf, 1 June 1915, in BA Berlin, R1001/2625, 'Akten betreffend den Krieg in Samoa', 49–52.

[97] 'Zweiter Bericht des Vermessungs-Assistenten Arendt über die Zustände in Samoa', 3 November 1915, in BA Berlin R1001/2626, 'Akten betreffend den Krieg in Samoa', 122–40.

[98] 'Bericht des Vermessungs-Assistenten Arendt über die Zustände in Samoa', in BA Berlin R1001/2626, 26–58.

New Zealand, and confided that some of the New Zealander troops could be moved to commit violence against the Germans in revenge attacks for German atrocities in Belgium, Tamasese informed Logan that the Samoans would not allow the Germans to be harmed.[99] Going further, Tamasese told Logan that 'Many German wives are of Samoan ancestry. They, and also the white women born in Samoa, are seen by the Samoans as part of their community, and the imprisonment of them would lead to bad blood with the Samoans.' When Logan argued that he might not be able to protect them, Tamasese responded that the Germans did not need the New Zealanders' protection, because they stood under his protection and the protection of the Samoans.[100] Refusing to use the car that Logan had put at his disposal and threatening anyone who sought to move the portrait of the German Kaiser that Wilhelm II had personally given him, Tamasese was the last man in Samoa to fly the black, white, and red flag of Imperial Germany in Samoa, well after the Germans had all had theirs confiscated.[101]

Dying on 13 October 1915 from an acute infection, Tamasese did not live to see the German emperor would lose the war and the Samoan people come to be ruled by their most recent invaders, the New Zealanders. As one last indignity, Tamasese was pestered on his deathbed by the New Zealanders into signing a statement (in Samoan) to the effect that he considered himself to be a subject of King George V and that he had pledged his loyalty to the British Crown. The notice was affixed to the wall in the room where his body lay in state before his funeral, but for Germans living in Samoa, the signed statement was simply beyond belief. Tamasese, had, they insisted, remained in favour of the Germans in his heart,[102] and, as Riedel wrote to the Colonial Office, his death represented 'a serious injury to the protection of German interests'.[103]

Despite his pro-German tendencies, Tamasese's life was honoured under the watchful eye of the New Zealanders with an enormous funeral procession of over 1,000 people. His whole village kept a mourning vigil for him, while government buildings and shops were closed as a mark of respect. Flags too were flown at half mast. His funeral oration was held by the *matai* Afamasaga and was even attended by Colonel Logan, his wife, and numerous other New Zealander officials, as well as other high-ranking Samoans.[104]

[99] Riedel to Solf, 6 December 1915, in BA Berlin R1001/2626, 14; Ludovica Schultze, 'Schulbericht über die Besetzung des deutschen Schutzgebietes Samoa', 20 March 1916, in BA Berlin R1001/2627, 'Akten betreffend den Krieg in Samoa', 4–8.

[100] 'Bericht des Vermessungs-Assistenten Arendt über die Zustände in Samoa', in BA Berlin R1001/2626, 26–58. See also Zieschank, *Ein Jahrzehnt in Samoa*, 145–6.

[101] Zieschank, *Ein Jahrzehnt in Samoa*, 145.

[102] 'Zweiter Bericht des Vermessungs-Assistenten Arendt über die Zustände in Samoa', 3 November 1915, in BA Berlin R1001/2626, 122–40.

[103] Riedel to Solf, 6 December 1915, in BA Berlin R1001/2626, 14.

[104] 'Zweiter Bericht des Vermessungs-Assistenten Arendt über die Zustände in Samoa', 122–40.

Seen from Berlin, the question of who should rule Samoa was a European one, not one for the Samoans themselves. The experience of the decades-long 'Samoan tangle' had confirmed that intra-Samoan contests for the paramountcy were in fact proxy conflicts for colonial powers seeking to dominate the Pacific. Under this view, preserving the sovereignty of the Samoans could only jeopardise German geostrategic and economic interests. The answer to this problem was to add the title of 'King of Samoa' to the titles already held by Wilhelm II.

For the Samoans, however, the kingship question offered evidence of just how far the imperial powers would go in breaking down their political and social structures before they had achieved what they wanted. There were, it seemed, no limits to how far these foreign powers would go to secure their interests. When taking sides in the various succession struggles failed to deliver the outcomes the powers required, they quickly moved to arming Samoa's rival factions. When this proved too dangerous, in the sense that it risked sparking a shooting war between the powers themselves, they struck an agreement to abolish the Samoan throne and partition Samoa into two protectorates, with Wilhelm II declared king of one of them. Finally, when in German Samoa the question of who should be named *Ali'i Sili* under the new Hohenzollern *Tupu Sili* proved too thorny, this position too was abolished.

Abolishing the paramountcy was the last step in a long history of German intervention in Samoan disputes over the throne for imperial purposes, of disempowering Samoans, and of gradually alienating them from control of their own territory. It confirmed that, despite the careful attempts to preserve the dignity of Samoa's nobility, there was no question that they were now a subject people. This relationship was neatly encapsulated by Tamasese's experiences in Germany, where he was treated both as an esteemed royal guest and an ethnological specimen offered up to the curious gaze of German onlookers.

13

Hanging a King

In July 1902, King August Manga Ndumbe Bell, his son Rudolf Duala Manga Bell, and other high-ranking Duala arrived in Germany. Alongside German citizenship for himself and his son, the King of Duala wanted to meet Wilhelm II and personally intercede to improve the conditions of his people in colonial Cameroon. Although he was not offered the citizenship he wished for, Manga Ndumbe Bell had the opportunity to meet (or, as it was phrased, 'pay homage to') the emperor, before outlining his people's complaints in a written petition which was laid before the Colonial Office. The two monarchs, Wilhelm II and Manga Ndumbe Bell, met at the Autumn Parade of the Guards Corps on the Templehof Field, an event which greatly enhanced Manga Ndumbe Bell's status amongst the Duala kings in Cameroon. This was particularly the case, given that when another Dualan, King Akwa, arrived in Berlin just months later, he was offered no such audience.[1] By 1914, however, relations between the Duala and the German authorities had deteriorated so badly that Manga Ndumbe Bell's son Rudolf Duala Manga Bell would be arrested on the orders of the colonial secretary, Wilhelm Solf, and hanged for high treason, an event that became so notorious that even Vladimir Lenin would note Rudolf Bell's death as an example of the iniquities of imperialism.[2]

From Treaty to Dispossession

Duala had shifted to German control when, on 12 and 13 July 1884, the economically and politically embattled kings of Cameroon's commercial coastal region signed treaties of protection offered to them by German traders.[3] The treaty, signed by

---

[1] Andreas Eckert, *Die Duala und die Kolonialmächte: Eine Untersuchung zu Widerstand, Protest und Protonationalismus in Kamerun vor dem Zweiten Weltkrieg* (Münster: Lit Verlag, 1991), 140–1; Stefan Gerbing, *Afrodeutscher Aktivismus: Interventionen von Kolonisierten am Wendepunkt der Dekolonisierung Deutschlands 1919* (Frankfurt am Main: Peter Lang, 2010), 71–3.

[2] Vladimir I. Lenin, 'Junius: Die Krise der Sozialdemokratie', in Vladimir I. Lenin, *Werke*, vol. 39 (Berlin: Dietz Verlag, 1965), 304. The note comes from his reading of Rosa Luxemburg's *Die Krise der Sozialdemokratie* (Bern: Unionsdruckerei, 1916), 52.

[3] Adolf Rüger, 'Die Duala und die Kolonialmacht 1884–1914: Eine Studie über die historischen Ursprünge des afrikanischen Antikolonialismus', in Helmuth Stoecker (ed), *Kamerun unter Deutscher Kolonialherrschaft* (Berlin: VEB Deutscher Verlag der Wissenschaften, 1968), 186. For the straitened circumstances of the Dualan kings, see Edwin Ardener, *Coastal Bantu of the Cameroons* (Oxford: Routledge, 2017), 18–20. On the European legal context of the treaty process, see Mieke van der Linden, *The Acquisition of Africa (1870–1914): The Nature of International Law* (Leiden: Brill Nijhoff, 2016), 174–214.

The Kaiser and the Colonies: Monarchy in the Age of Empire. Matthew P. Fitzpatrick, Oxford University Press.
© Matthew P. Fitzpatrick 2022. DOI: 10.1093/oso/9780192897039.003.0014

the representatives of Hamburg traders and (an earlier) King Bell, King Akwa, and King Dido, was a relic of the period of 'rogue empires' in which firms and individuals claimed to be capable of holding sovereignty over non-European lands and peoples.[4] To the extent that the treaty expressed the sovereign will of the African rulers who signed it-and later generations of Cameroonian kings (at least strategically) acted on this assumption-its text made clear the extent and limits of the renunciation of sovereignty, on terms that would become of crucial importance thirty years later:

> We the undersigned independent Kings and Chiefs of the country called 'Cameroons'...voluntarily concluded as follows:

> We give this day our rights of Sovereignty, the Legislation and Management of this our Country entirely up to Mr Eduard Schmidt acting for the firm C. Woermann and Mr Johannes Voss acting for Mssrs Jantzen & Thormählen , both in Hamburg, and for many years trading in this River.

> We have conveyed our rights of Sovereignty, the legislation and Management of this our Country to the firms mentioned above under the following reservations.

> 1. under reservation of the rights of third persons.

> 2. reserving that all friendship and commercial treaties made before with other foreign governments shall have full power.

> 3. that the land cultivated by us now and the places the towns are built on shall be the property of the present owners and their successors.

> 4. that the Coumie [commercial tax] shall be paid annually as it has been paid to the Kings and Chiefs as before.

> 5. that during the first time of establishing an administration here, our country fashions will be respected.

> Cameroons, the twelfth day of July one thousand eight hundred and eighty four.[5]

The importance attached by the Duala to control of the land and of their economic and juridical independence had also been confirmed in a separate document in 1884, a memorandum attached to the Protection Treaty that warned that 'Our cultivated ground must not be taken from us, for we are not able to buy and sell us other country.' To preserve the hitherto economic relations of the region, the coastal kings also insisted that 'White men should not go up and trade with the

---

[4] Press, *Rogue Empires*.
[5] 'Protektoratsvertrag vom 12./13. Juli 1884', in BA Berlin R1001/4447, 3, as cited in Rüger, 'Die Duala und die Kolonialmacht', 258.

Bushmen, nothing to do with our markets, they must stay here in this river and they give us trust so that we will trade with our Bushmen.'[6]

This last condition was quickly ignored. By the early 1890s, the Cameroon Hinterland Society had demanded the end of these arrangements and the 'direct linkage of the world of European commerce with inland producers'.[7] Indeed, the entire German colonial enterprise in Cameroon was predicated on ending the Duala's position as economic intermediaries between Europeans and the merchants of the Cameroonian hinterland in favour of German trading companies.[8] Aided by numerous military campaigns to subdue the interior, German traders soon enjoyed near monopoly trading conditions in the colony.

This rapid economic change caused widespread immiseration for the coastal Duala. Nonetheless, they attempted to reinvigorate their economic position by shifting to the farming of cash crops, successfully competing with European firms by establishing (particularly cocoa) plantations.[9] Despite these attempts to adjust to the new economic realities of German control, conditions on the coast remained notoriously bad for many, particularly during the governorship of Jesko von Puttkamer.

Notwithstanding these hardships, the Bell Duala kings had preferred to work closely with the Germans and thus had enjoyed the same kind of privileged association as King Njoya of Bamum. Royal relations in the region had followed the pattern of other territories in which relations had remained cordial, including periods of gift-giving between the King of the Duala and Kaiser Wilhelm II.[10] All signs pointed towards this relationship continuing under Rudolf Manga Bell (see Figure 13.1). As a ruler who had lived and studied in Germany, he was in many ways an unlikely candidate to become the figurehead of colonial resistance. His status and his political importance as a Europeanized African noble meant that upon his return to Cameroon in 1908 to take up his role as king, colonial officials in both Cameroon and Germany offered Manga Bell clear financial incentives to remain loyal.[11]

---

[6] 'Wünsche der Kamerun-Leute', in BA Berlin R1001/4202, 101, quoted in Rüger, 'Die Duala und die Kolonialmacht, 186.

[7] 'Prospekt der Kamerun-Hinterland-Gesellschaft', November 1893, in BMA E-10.22, 9.

[8] Ralph A. Austen, 'The Metamorphoses of Middlemen: The Duala, Europeans, and the Cameroon Hinterland, ca.1800–ca. 1960', *The International Journal of African Historical Studies* 16, no. 1 (1983), 12.

[9] Yvette D. Monga, 'The Emergence of Duala Cocoa Planters under German Rule in Cameroon: A Case Study of Entrepreneurship', in William Gervase Clarence-Smith (ed), *Cocoa Pioneer Fronts since 1800: The Role of Smallholders, Planters and Merchants* (London: Palgrave, 1996), 119–36; Andreas Eckert, 'African Rural Entrepreneurs and Labor in the Cameroon Littoral', *Journal of African History* 40 (1999), 114; Ralph A. Austen and Jonathan Derrick, *Middlemen of the Cameroons River: The Duala and their Hinterland, c.1600–c.1960* (Cambridge: Cambridge University Press, 1999), 108–20.

[10] Colonial Office to Eulenburg, 3 September 1902; Colonial Office to Eulenburg, 26 January 1903; Eulenburg to Colonial Office, 30 January 1903, in BA Berlin R1001/4102, 71–3.

[11] Rüger, 'Die Duala und die Kolonialmacht', 220.

Rudolf Bell   Manga Bell und seine Familie.
mit seiner Frau   Manga Bell

Figure 13.1 King Rudolf Duala Manga Bell with his wife and family

In 1910, a plan authored by the regional colonial official Hermann Röhm that proposed alienating the Duala from their land intervened. The plan would see a racially segregated European-only harbour town built on Duala land that had hitherto been a site of cohabitation between Europeans and Africans. In both scale and intent the plan was in clear violation of the third condition of the 1884 treaty governing ownership of the land and the towns. Apart from segregating the population of Duala racially, it would also push King Rudolf Duala Manga Bell's people well away from the shoreline and into the hinterland.[12] Although in his later memoirs, Governor Theodor Seitz claimed that he had always assured the Duala that any land expropriations would only occur via direct negotiations and that he 'had no intention of forcing them away from the river', which was 'vital' for them,[13] it was Seitz who authorized the plan. While relations had been occasionally rocky prior to this decision, as when railway building began to impinge upon Duala lands, and the Bell Duala had felt compelled to remind Seitz of the inalienability of their

[12] For the genesis of the plan, see Wilhelm Solf, 'Denkschrift über die Enteignung und Verlegung der Eingeborenen in Duala (Kamerun)', 1 May 1914, *Verhandlungen des Reichstages*, vol. 305, 3271–7.
[13] Theodor Seitz, *Vom Aufstieg und Niederbruch deutscher Kolonialmacht*, vol. 2 (Karlsruhe: C. F. Müller, 1929), 43.

land under the terms of the 1884 treaty, it was Röhm's plan, approved by Seitz, that pushed the young King Rudolf Manga Bell from cooperation to protest.

As Andreas Eckert has made clear, the plan to dispossess the Duala of their land was not merely politically objectionable to them in the sense that it sought to segregate the African population from the new European town. In economic terms, it also rested upon the expropriation of economically invaluable coastal land with no meaningful compensation.[14] Given the sweeping nature of the plan's evictions, just how the question of territorial sovereignty and intercommunal relations was to be reflected in the domains of law, economics, politics, and culture now shifted to become the central question of German colonialism in Cameroon.[15] A law facilitating the expropriation of African land in Germany's colonies for 'the public good' had existed since 1903, but the alienation of African land in Cameroon had generally occurred under the unjust but less confrontational terms of an 1896 law declaring all uncultivated land to be Crown land, irrespective of whether it was understood by local African nations as belonging to their extended territory.[16] Röhm's plan for coastal Duala went well beyond that, however, in its intention to expropriate lands that were integral to the political and economic life of the Duala and forcibly move them to a new, yet to be built inland settlement called New Bell (Neu-Bell).

Importantly, there was no real discussion of the incommensurability of Dualan and European property law at the heart of this dispute between Rudolf Manga Bell and the colonial administration, nor was the Dualans' protest expressed as a desire for complete decolonization. Throughout the entire dispute, Rudolf Duala Manga Bell at no time referred to any legal framework beyond that which the Germans themselves had erected. Far from legal pluralism or an appeal to precolonial Dualan law, Rudolf Manga Bell's protest engaged in a close and careful critique of the Germans' implementation of their own colonial laws, relying on the terms of the 1884 treaty between the Germans and the African kings of Cameroon as the basis for his objections.[17] By positioning the issue of territorial sovereignty as a question of whether Röhm's plan accorded with the principles of

[14] The proposed compensation was forty pfennigs per square metre—well below the market value of twenty marks per square metre. The offer would later be raised to (the still paltry) two marks, ten pfennigs. See Eckert, Die Duala und die Kolonialmächte, 165.
[15] Andreas Eckert, Grundbesitz, Landkonflikte und kolonialer Wandel: Douala 1880 bis 1960 (Stuttgart: Franz Steiner Verlag, 1999), 1–3.
[16] 'Kaiserliche Verordnung über die Enteignung von Grundeigentum in den Schutzgebieten Afrikas und der Südsee', 14 February 1903, and 'Allerhöchste Verordnung über die Schaffung, Besitzergreifung und Veräußerung von Kronland und über den Erwerb und die Veräußerung von Grundstücken im Schutzgebiete von Kamerun', 15 July 1896, in Julius Ruppel (ed), Die Landesgesetzgebung für das Schutzgebiet Kamerun (Berlin: E. S. Mittler und Sohn, 1912), 687–9, 727–34.
[17] On the question of legal pluralism in German Cameroon, see Andreas Eckert, 'Verwaltung, Recht und koloniale praxis in Kamerun 1884–1914', in Rüdiger Voigt and Peter Sack (eds), Kolonialisierung des Rechts: Zur kolonialen Rechts- und Verwaltungsordnung (Baden-Baden: Nomos Verlagsgesellschaft, 2001), 174.

the 1884 treaty, the Duala were able to situate the Reichstag, the colonial secretary, and the imperial chancellor as parties legally bound to uphold the terms of the treaty in their favour.[18] As Adolf Rüger argued, 'At the beginning they believed that factual objections would suffice to deflect the looming danger and that it was merely a question of law and justice.'[19] It was this appeal to the ostensibly contractual nature of German colonial claims that unwaveringly underpinned the Dualan king's approach to the issues of territorial sovereignty, land expropriations, and forced removals.

As Rudolf Manga Bell pointed out repeatedly in his petitions to German authorities, Röhm's plan to dispossess the Duala was in clear contravention of the 1884 stipulation that 'the land cultivated by us now and the places the towns are built on shall be the property of the present owners and their successors.' Given that the Duala had already stood by and watched as their original economic role as intermediaries between European traders and the populations of the Cameroonian hinterland had been deliberately eroded, this amounted to a second attack on the integrity of the 1884 treaty. With their earlier livelihoods lost, the Duala were now expected to willingly vacate their traditional lands and relocate to an inferior position outside the newly established German town.[20]

For their part, the Germans cited multiple grounds for the expropriations. One of the main attempts to build a case for them rested on the medical testimony of Dr Hans Ziemann, whose alarmist statistic that 72 per cent of the local population had malaria was frequently cited by the colonial secretary (and ex-Governor of Samoa), Wilhelm Solf, as unshakeable medical grounds for a radical programme of civic hygiene. In his study, Ziemann asserted that the use of quinine to treat the African population was 'simply impossible' and that razing part of the town, relocating the Duala people inland, and establishing a one-kilometre buffer zone between the black and white townships was in line with world's best medical practice, a solution predicated on the assumption that such a buffer would prevent mosquitoes from entering the new (apparently malaria-free) white zone. In addition, Ziemann added, the plan had the 'enormous advantage' that it would liberate colonial whites from the effects on their nervous system of living amongst 'the yelling and screaming, often unruly natives.'[21]

---

[18] Katrin Otremba, 'Stimmen der Auflehnung: Antikoloniale Haltungen in afrikanischen Petitionen an das Deutsche Reich', in Ingo H. Warnke (ed), *Deutsche Sprache und Kolonialismus: Aspekte der nationalen Kommunikation 1884–1919* (Berlin: Walter de Gruyter, 2009), 235–62.

[19] Adolf Rüger, 'Die Widerstandsbewegung des Rudolf Manga Bell in Kamerun', in Walter Markov (ed), *Études africaines/African Studies/Afrika-Studien* (Leipzig: Karl Marx University Press, 1967), 109.

[20] For literary treatments of Manga Bell's resistance, see Azanwi Nchami, *Foot Prints of Destiny* (Mankon: Langaa RPCIG, 2009); Christian Bommarius, *Der gute Deutsche: Die Ermordung Manga Bells in Kamerun 1914* (Berlin: Berenberg, 2015).

[21] 'Gutachten des Regierungsarztes Professor Dr Ziemann über die Notwendigkeit der Entfernung der Eingeborenen aus der Nähe der Europäer in Duala', 28 May 1910, in Solf, 'Denkschrift über die Enteignung und Verlegung der Eingeborenen in Duala (Kamerun)', 3306; see also 3272. Ziemann's conclusions were supported by two more German doctors on 31 December 1912. See Philalethes

Ziemann may have offered a useful pretext to Solf, but medicalizing the expropriation measures was seen as unnecessary by Röhm, who understood the plan as best justified on the grounds of the intrinsic necessity of racial segregation. Indeed, the language of Röhm's proposal displayed all the hallmarks of the post-1904 Herero War obsession of the Germans that prioritized the maintenance of a colonial hierarchy that distinguished clearly between rulers and the ruled.[22] Röhm argued that the expropriation plan was necessary, given:

> the significance and the opposition of the white race in relation to the blacks. From this point of view it must be authoritatively demanded, so as to avoid the danger before it is too late, or at least for as long as possible, that the English have encountered on the African West coast (see Lagos, Sierra Leone, Calabar) and that we are quite close to now here in Duala, namely the establishment and development of social and political equality with the natives.[23]

Once the German Colonial Office approved Röhm's plan, after listening to Ziemann's apparent health concerns, the Reichstag provided funding for the project. After Seitz left the colony, however, his temporary replacement Otto Gleim (who had lived in the colony for over a decade) began to express his doubts about its sense, both in practical and racial terms. Having discussed it with the Duala leadership, Gleim argued for important modifications, acknowledging that removing the Duala, who relied upon their fishing industry, from the river hardly made sense, and that the burgeoning African merchant class, as well as the Dualan royal family, should surely be allowed to remain in their newly built European-style houses in the region slated for German development (see Figure 13.2). The Colonial Office in Berlin disagreed strongly, however, and directed Gleim to stick to the original expropriation plan.[24]

Once Gleim was recalled to Germany, Acting Governor Wilhelm Hansen also did what he could to drag his feet on the project, despite also being directed by

Kuhn and Noetel, 'Gutachten über die Notwendigkeit der Verlegung der Eingeborenen von Duala', 31 December 1912, in Solf, 'Denkschrift über die Enteignung und Verlegung der Eingeborenen in Duala (Kamerun)', 3320–1. For a detailed discussion of Ziemann's claims, see Wolfgang U. Eckart, 'Malariaprävention und Rassentrennung: Die ärztliche Vorbereitung und Rechtfertigung der Duala-Enteignung 1912–14', *History and Philosophy of the Life Sciences* 10, no. 2 (1988), 363–78.

[22] Ulrike Hamann is in this regard correct to point to the Herero War in South West Africa as a caesura in Cameroonian race relations. See Ulrike Hamann, *Prekäre koloniale Ordnung: Rassistische Konjunkturen im Widerspruch. Deutsches Kolonialregime 1884–1914* (Bielefeld: transcript, 2016), 219.

[23] Röhm in BA Berlin R 1001/4427, 13. Also quoted in Rüger, 'Die Duala und die Kolonialmacht', 221. Hamann sees this planned city as a Foucauldian heterotopia. It is worth considering that the real heterotopia was the racially integrated city in which political and social equality was drawing ever nearer that Röhm feared. See Hamann, *Prekäre koloniale Ordnung*, 254–5.

[24] Rüger, 'Die Duala und die Kolonialmacht', 222. Rudolf Manga Bell would later recall this to argue that, after speaking with the Duala notables, Gleim 'no longer saw the point of carrying out the plan in its entirety'. See Rudolf Manga Bell to Solf, 13 September 1913, in Solf, 'Denkschrift über die Enteignung und Verlegung der Eingeborenen in Duala (Kamerun)', 3382.

Manga Bell's Palast in Duala (links Rudolf Bell's Haus).

Figure 13.2 King Rudolf Duala Manga Bell's palace in Duala, inside the expropriation zone

Undersecretary Peter Conze in the Colonial Office to ensure that the expropriations took place 'without delay'.[25] Even after the new governor, Karl Ebermaier, came to Cameroon with very clear instructions to move the Duala out of the town, Hansen deferred any action before finally also being sent back to Germany, where he remained a sharp and very public critic of the expropriation plan. The new governor proved a more faithful instrument of the Colonial Office and did what he could to hasten Röhm's dispossession plans, in the mistaken belief that once they had been presented with a fait accompli, the Duala would have no choice but to submit to their altered circumstances. Playing no small part in his decisiveness was the concern that a failure to act would be understood by the Duala as political weakness, suggesting that he might be overruled from Berlin if local monarchs directed their appeals to the colonial metropole.[26]

Royal Resistance and '*Petitionismus*'

King Rudolf Duala Manga Bell remained steadfast in his determination to resist the expropriation measures, not by force but through passive resistance. He aimed in

---

[25] Rüger, 'Die Duala und die Kolonialmacht', 223.
[26] Rüger, 'Die Duala und die Kolonialmacht', 225.

particular at generating interest in the Dualan cause inside Germany by petitioning the Reichstag.[27] In late 1911 Rudolf Manga Bell sent a telegram to the Reichstag asking for its assistance in convincing the Bundesrat and the imperial chancellor to reverse the expropriation measures, which he argued 'put in question the foundations of life of the entire nation'.[28] Rudolf Manga Bell did this in the belief that, as one historian has recently put it, 'a petition to the Reichstag, as a democratic institution within a constitutional monarchy, had a chance of undermining the interests of the colonial administration and the imperial government'.[29]

The telegram was supported in March 1912 by a longer, written defence, also sent to the Reichstag, which reiterated the Duala's right to possess their own land and outlined their fears of 'economic and cultural ruin'.[30] In Cameroon, however, German officials did what they could to dampen disquiet in a series of meetings with Duala's notables in November and December 1912. In these meetings, the officials insisted that they too were just following orders from their political masters in Berlin, with Governor Ebermaier arguing to Rudolf Manga Bell that 'the Kaiser, the Reichstag, the Colonial Office have already decided. I am the governor and I must obey them. You will receive no other answer; that I know'.[31]

Nonetheless, the 1903 colonial expropriation law offered some hope of success for the Duala's petitioning strategy by holding out the opportunity for government review of any decision to expropriate African land. In the law's original text, Paragraph 32 envisaged a situation not dissimilar to that afflicting the Duala:

> The imperial chancellor is empowered…to permit the reinstatement to natives of property that has passed out of the rule or possession of natives and into the possession of non-natives, in so far as the expropriation in the estimation of officials is necessary to secure for the natives the possibility for their economic existence and in particular their right to a homeland.[32]

Indeed, these were the grounds upon which Halpert, one of the German lawyers engaged by the Duala, sought to contest the expropriations in 1913.[33] This legal

---

[27] Hausen, *Deutsche Kolonialherrschaft in Afrika*, 157–9.

[28] Rudolf Duala Manga Bell to the Reichstag, 30 November 1911, in Solf, 'Denkschrift über die Enteignung und Verlegung der Eingeborenen in Duala (Kamerun)', 3307.

[29] Hamann, *Prekäre koloniale Ordnung*, 233–4.

[30] Duala Chiefs to the Reichstag, 8 March 1912, in Solf, 'Denkschrift über die Enteignung und Verlegung der Eingeborenen in Duala (Kamerun)', 3307–8.

[31] Minutes of meeting, Duala, 24 November 1912, in Solf, 'Denkschrift über die Enteignung und Verlegung der Eingeborenen in Duala (Kamerun)', 3315.

[32] 'Kaiserliche Verordnung über die Enteignung von Grundeigentum in den Schutzgebieten Afrikas und der Südsee', 14 February 1903, in Ruppel (ed), *Die Landesgesetzgebung für das Schutzgebiet Kamerun*, 733. The opinion of the Colonial Office that the paragraph related to the expropriation of European land to benefit Africans is not supported by the text of the law. See Solf, 'Denkschrift über die Enteignung und Verlegung der Eingeborenen in Duala (Kamerun)', 3337.

[33] Solf, 'Denkschrift über die Enteignung und Verlegung der Eingeborenen in Duala (Kamerun)', 3279. Solf claimed that §32 did not apply in this case, because the measure was not against the 'black

avenue, however, existed on paper only and was unlikely to gain much traction, given that, as a result of an outcry from Germans in the colonies, Chancellor von Bülow had quietly rescinded §32 in November 1903 with a regulation that stated that any such decision by the chancellor to rescind an expropriation measure was 'out of the question' and that his decision to this effect was 'incontestable'.[34]

Despite such a seemingly ironclad ban on appealing to an authority beyond the colonies, Rudolf Manga Bell's letter was (albeit belatedly) debated in the Reichstag's Petitions Committee on 5 December 1912. After six months, the result was disappointing for the Duala. The matter was simply handed back to the chancellor (and therefore the Colonial Office) to deal with internally.[35] Far from being discouraged, the Duala king lobbied even harder, both in Cameroon and in Germany, for the forced removals to be halted. In Cameroon, he met with the complete intransigence of Röhm and Ebermaier, while, in Germany, the determination of the colonial secretary, Solf, to support his governor was tempered only by the need to ensure the action did not lead to a public outcry that would attract the attention of the Reichstag. On the underlying issue of the necessity of expropriating Duala land and removing them from it, Ebermaier and Solf were in complete agreement.

This is not to say that the complaints of the Duala and the grounds for their dissent (namely the stipulations on territorial sovereignty at the heart of the 1884 treaty) were not understood. Rather, the legalistic arguments of Manga Bell and his people were parsed carefully by government officials in Cameroon, who offered their own interpretation of the concept of colonial sovereignty. In particular, the architect of the project, Röhm, disingenuously declared that any reference to the treaties of 1884 was 'erroneous' because the 'right of management' ceded to the Germans by the treaty overruled the stipulation that the Duala remain in possession of their land.[36] Evident in Röhm's argument was the desire to uphold the prestige of the governor and German officials against that of an African king who had sought to circumvent their power by appealing above their heads to the Reichstag.[37]

In early 1913, several petitions flowed to Berlin and to Cameroon's colonial government from Duala's African elites, pointing out their traditional and

race' to profit the 'white race', but rather was a measure designed to improve the lives of all, and instead of losing their home, the Duala were being provided with another.

[34] 'Verfügung des Reichskanzlers zur Ausführung des Abschnitts IX der kaiserlichen Verordnung über die Enteignung von Grundeigentum in den Schutzgebieten Afrikas und der Südsee, vom 14. Februar 1903', 12 November 1903, in Ruppel (ed), *Die Landesgesetzgebung für das Schutzgebiet Kamerun*, 734. See also Eckert, 'Verwaltung, Recht und koloniale Praxis in Kamerun 1884–1914', 174–7.

[35] 'Bericht der Kommission für die Petitionen', 19 February 1913, in Solf, 'Denkschrift über die Enteignung und Verlegung der Eingeborenen in Duala (Kamerun)', 3331–3.

[36] Madiba Essiben, 'Le Traité du 12 juillet 1884 comme source de l'antagonisme germano-douala à la veille de la Première Guerre mondiale', in Stefanie Michels and Albert-Pascal Temgoua (eds.), *La Politique de la mémoire coloniale en Allemagne et au Cameroun*, 15–24; Rüger, 'Die Duala und die Kolonialmacht', 225.

[37] BA Berlin R10001 4427, 136, in Rüger, 'Die Duala und die Kolonialmacht', 226.

ancestral connection to their coastal lands, as well as the economic hardship that would be caused by the expropriations.[38] Alarmingly for the Germans, rival Dualan nobles and other Cameroonian kings began to attach themselves to Manga Bell's cause.[39] The affair reached a point where Solf thought it advisable to speak to the naval secretary, Alfred von Tirpitz, who agreed to a naval demonstration off the coast of Cameroon by the light cruiser *Bremen*. In addition, he organized the landing of naval personnel in Duala in August 1913.[40]

The situation concerned Ebermaier enough that, in the same month, he unilaterally declared that Rudolf Duala Manga Bell had been stripped of his kingly position. Even this did not stop the Dualan king from assuming the role of representing his people. On 11 September 1913, he met Solf in person when the colonial secretary travelled to Cameroon to meet with the Duala. The day before, Solf had received an extensive petition from the (ostensibly now deposed) monarch that warned that forced removals were 'a great economic danger to the natives' which would 'restrict their cultural development'.[41] At this point, rather than engage in dialogue, Solf added his own stamp of authority to the actions of the governor and Röhm. In front of Rudolf Manga Bell (who the other African leaders insisted was their appropriate representative, notwithstanding his recent ostensible abdication) and other assembled high-ranking Duala, Solf insisted that:

The expropriation measures will not be overturned.... That is the decision that I have shared with your governor in the name of the Reichstag and of which you now have formal knowledge. With this, the matter is in the eyes of the government closed... My final word is, therefore, the decision has been made.[42]

[38] Duala Chiefs to the Reichstag, 15 January 1913; Duala Chiefs to the Reichstag, 7 February 1913; Duala Chiefs to the Imperial Government in Buea, 20 February 1913; Rudolf Manga Bell to the Imperial Government in Buea, 14 April 1913, in Solf, 'Denkschrift über die Enteignung und Verlegung der Eingeborenen in Duala (Kamerun)', 3321–31.

[39] Eckert argues that this stance was confirmed by the *Ngondo*, an assembly of Dualan notables. Ralph Austen argues that the *Ngondo* surfaced as a specific consultative organ in the 1930s, whereas as Jean-Pierre Félix Eyoum et al. maintain that the *Ngondo* was present as early as 1884. What is critical here, however, is that there was clearly a means by which colleective decisions were being taken or endorsed by leading Duala. See Eckert, *Die Duala und die Kolonialmächte*, 173; Ralph A. Austen, 'Inventing and Forgetting Traditions on the Cameroon Coast: The Ngondo Council and the Jeki Epic', *Passages* 7 (1994), 8; Jean-Pierre Félix Eyoum, Stefanie Michels, and Joachim Zeller, 'Bonamanga: Eine Familiengeschichte und die große Politik', *Deutschland Postkolonial* 2 (2011), 19.

[40] Rüger, 'Die Duala und die Kolonialmacht', 230; Eckert, *Die Duala und die Kolonialmächte*, 180.

[41] Rudolf Manga Bell to Solf, 10 September 1913, in Solf, 'Denkschrift über die Enteignung und Verlegung der Eingeborenen in Duala (Kamerun)', 3381–4.

[42] Solf, 'Denkschrift über die Enteignung und Verlegung der Eingeborenen in Duala (Kamerun)', 3274. Surprisingly hostile to Rudolf Manga Bell and the Duala is Colin Newbury, 'Partition, Development, Trusteeship: Colonial Secretary Wilhelm Solf's West African Journey, 1913', in Prosser Gifford and Wm. Roger Louis (eds), *Britain and Germany in Africa: Imperial Rivalry and Colonial Rule* (New Haven, CT: Yale University Press, 1967), 471. That Solf makes the declaration in the name of the Reichstag rather than the emperor is of significant interest.

The following day, Governor Ebermaier formally refused the petition of the Duala in a lengthy decision that questioned Rudolf Manga Bell's right to speak for the Duala, argued against the Duala's characterization of the new settlement of New Bell as a mosquito-infested swamp, and denied that the 1884 treaty in any way limited the colonial government's ability to make decisions curtailing African sovereignty over their lands.[43] At a subsequent meeting with Röhm, Dualan notables complained that Solf had shown them great disrespect, treating them like children and not discussing the matter with them properly. If the colonial secretary would not listen to them, they suggested, perhaps they should speak directly with the German emperor. To that end, the notables insisted that Rudolf Manga Bell be permitted to travel to Germany. Röhm categorically ruled out any such meeting between monarchs.[44]

Still the Duala refused to capitulate. By now some were beginning to contemplate a violent uprising, considering that legal avenues had led to nothing. Rudolf Manga Bell persuaded them instead to continue on with the tactic of 'Petitionismus', this time by sending a request directly to the chancellor asking for a personal audience, if not with him, then with his legal representative, Dr Halpert. He also sent a close associate, Ngoso Din, to Germany to argue the Dualan case personally.[45] There Ngoso Din collaborated with the journalist Hellmut von Gerlach and two lawyers, Dr Flemming in Hamburg and Dr Halpert in Berlin.[46]

Unlike the petitions of the Duala themselves, which concentrated on the legal question of their territorial sovereignty under the terms of the 1884 treaty, Halpert's letter to the colonial secretary, Solf, also attacked the faulty racial logic that underpinned the expropriation measures. Attacking the testimony of the medical expert Dr Philalethes Kuhn (who had verified the earlier opinion of Dr Hans Ziemann),[47] Halpert made the point that segregating blacks and whites in Africa was both impossible and nonsensical:

He sees the expropriations as necessary, because there are other irritations for the Europeans that are grounded in the customs and habits of the Africans, the

---

[43] Ebermaier, 'Beschluß' in Solf, 'Denkschrift über die Enteignung und Verlegung der Eingeborenen in Duala (Kamerun)', 3337–41.

[44] Minutes of meeting between Röhm and the Duala chiefs, 22 September 1913, in Solf, 'Denkschrift über die Enteignung und Verlegung der Eingeborenen in Duala (Kamerun)', 3341–3.

[45] Eckert, *Die Duala und die Kolonialmächte*, 184, 187–8.

[46] Engelbert Mveng, *Histoire du Cameroun* (Paris: Présence Africaine, 1963), 342. Flemming had written to Chancellor Bethmann Hollweg on the issue in August 1913, citing his power under §32 to intervene on behalf of the Duala. Halpert had written to Solf and the chancellor on 3 December 1913, focusing on the restrictions imposed by the Treaty of 1884. See Solf, 'Denkschrift über die Enteignung und Verlegung der Eingeborenen in Duala (Kamerun)', 3333–4, 3344–7.

[47] Kuhn also wrote an article reiterating the health and sociocultural grounds for the new policy of racial segregation. See Philalethes Kuhn, 'Die Sanierung von Duala', in *Das größere Deutschland*, reproduced in Solf, 'Denkschrift über die Enteignung und Verlegung der Eingeborenen in Duala (Kamerun)', 3364–6.

combating of which cannot be recommended, given that it is both futile and detrimental to the interests of the health and well-being of the blacks. He lists the followings as irritations: the constant smouldering of fires in their huts, the smells caused by them preparing their meals, the noise made from time to time when they are enjoying themselves, their loud conversations, their odour, that blacks are carriers of disease, the fact that white children learn about sexual relations earlier through their contact with black children. In examining these grounds offered by the expert for the necessity of the creation of a purely native town, it must be pointed out that the absolute separation of whites and coloureds is itself utopian! It only needs to be remembered that at all times whites in the tropical colonies must have black servants, that offices could not function without black clerks, that black children must be taught by white teachers, that blacks are the main customers of white merchants etc. Whites cannot manage without constantly being amongst blacks.[48]

Instead of the colonial government approving wholesale expropriations of land and forced removals of the Duala to a completely new town, Halpert suggested simply increasing police measures to minimize the disturbances described by Kuhn, which, he argued, hardly required the complete destruction of the town and the relocation of a coastal people to the hinterland.[49] Halpert also lodged a petition with the Reichstag on behalf of Rudolf Manga Bell in late 1913, a petition which accused the colonial government of everything from inflicting reckless damage on the lives of an entire African nation to tampering with the post so that telegrams from the Duala did not reach Germany when they were sent.[50]

By the time the expropriations were considered by the Reichstag in early 1914, the demolitions had already got under way in earnest, against a backdrop of Dualan passive resistance. Despite having lost their homes, the Duala refused to move to the new location set aside for them and camped instead on their recently cleared land.[51] The demolitions were temporarily halted in March, however, by the intervention of a Reichstag coalition, in particular the Social Democrats and the Polish Party, who offered support to Halpert's petition questioning the necessity and the drastic nature of the expropriations.[52] This led to a vitriolic conservative

[48] Halpert to Solf, 3 December 1913, in Solf, 'Denkschrift über die Enteignung und Verlegung der Eingeborenen in Duala (Kamerun)', 3345.

[49] Halpert to Solf, 3 December 1913, in Solf, 'Denkschrift über die Enteignung und Verlegung der Eingeborenen in Duala (Kamerun)', 3345.

[50] 'Petition gegen die Zwangsenteignung des Duala-Volkes', in Solf, 'Denkschrift über die Enteignung und Verlegung der Eingeborenen in Duala (Kamerun)', 3348–56.

[51] Solf, 'Denkschrift über die Enteignung und Verlegung der Eingeborenen in Duala (Kamerun)', 3276.

[52] On the Polish discussion of the expropriation of the Duala and its relationship to German rule in the Polish East, see Jawad Daheur, '"They Handle Negroes Just Like Us": German Colonialism in Cameroon in the Eyes of the Poles (1885–1914)' European Review 26 no.3 (2018), 492–502.

press campaign against the 'negrophilia of the Reichstag'.[53] Further pressure also came from the Association of West African Merchants in Hamburg, which insisted that the forced removals continue and argued that the Reichstag should not even consider the petition of the Duala, who it claimed were 'not German' and therefore had no right to such recourse.[54]

Refuting such claims in an interview with the *Berliner Tageblatt*, Rudolf Manga Bell's emissary Ngoso Din explained the predicament of the Duala, employing the tropes of the civilizationary discourse of the colonizers he was addressing. The Duala, he argued, were not like other Africans in that they were highly cultured merchants, civil servants, and farmers. The expropriation measures, which were, he argued, illegal, threatened not only their considerable cultural and economic progress (which itself relied on access to the coast) but indeed their capacity to live at all:

> In 1884 we entered into a contract with the government that secured the land that we own as our property for all eternity, and we believe that we are still secure for all time. Then came the expropriation process, which claims that our land should be taken from us for the public good. The territory offered to us lies two to three kilometres from the coast, in the middle of a swampy region that is unfit for cultivation...If we were now truly forced to move into this land, that would amount to our complete demise.[55]

The Role of Missionaries

As the crisis had unfolded Basel missionaries in Cameroon had also been writing to Europe looking for guidance on how to approach an issue they were finding difficult to negotiate. In January 1913, Johannes Vöhringer had written to the Mission Committee in Basel, laying out the colonial government's plans for expropriations and complaining about their impact:

> These plans will be carried out despite the protests of the blacks, who will be very greatly affected, and the firms and the missions who cannot see the purpose for the entire relocation and who will be greatly disadvantaged in trade and communications.[56]

---

[53] *Hamburger Nachrichten*, 19 March 1914, quoted in Rüger, 'Die Duala und die Kolonialmacht', 237.

[54] Verein Westafrikanische Kaufleute, Hamburg to the Reichstag, 23 March 1914, in Solf, 'Denkschrift über die Enteignung und Verlegung der Eingeborenen in Duala (Kamerun)', 3367.

[55] 'Der dualesische Gesandte: Unterredung mit dem geheimen Gesandten der Dualaneger', *Berliner Tageblatt*, 8 April 1914.

[56] Vöhringer to Komitee, 7 January 1913, in BMA E-2, 38, 4.

Vöhringer related how during negotiations with the colonial government the Duala had asked them to help overturn the plans, reporting that 'We did what we could,' but that the government was quite determined to proceed, irrespective of the protests. He continued, arguing that there was only 'the faintest hope of help' and that 'the only way is the Reichstag,' to which the Duala had appealed. He was, however, deeply pessimistic and presumed that the Duala would have to find a way to regroup in New Bell.[57] Another missionary, Friedrich Lutz, also wrote to Basel, complaining that while they had done their best not to become involved in the 'machinations of the natives behind the back of the government', the Catholic mission there was using the issue to 'gather the people around them'. Lutz reported that he continued to believe that their position of not going behind the back of the government was the right one and instead insisted that 'We want to be completely open,' by which he meant 'continue to reassure the natives, while continuing to talk to both Manga Bell and the colonial government to resolve the issue'. Although not wanting to take a public position or speak to Reichstag deputies, he suggested that the mission might try and get to the German chancellor to discuss the issue.[58] Two weeks later, Lutz declared that, with the Reichstag and Bundesrat offering seeming support for the plan, it was no longer of any use to discuss the morality of the expropriations, despite 'everyone admitting that it was a great hardship'. Completely underestimating the will of the Duala to continue to fight the measures, he resigned himself to reconciling the outraged Duala to the government's plan to demolish their homes.[59]

The determination of the Duala not to submit became evident to the missionaries, however, as rumours began to fly that the Duala were planning armed resistance to the measures. As Vöhringer noted, the Duala were 'deeply disappointed that the mission doesn't help'. There was not much talk about God's word, he added, 'when every conversation revolves around the land question'.[60] With the Reichstag having handed the question back to the Colonial Office, however, the prospects of a favourable outcome for the Duala seemed slight.[61] In September 1913, Lutz was recalled by Vöhringer to Duala, as the 'anger and bitterness' of the Duala became more pronounced.[62]

The Basel missionaries' stance was one of unhappy compliance with the measures ordered by the colonial government. As the December 1913 conference of the Basel missionaries in Cameroon succinctly put it:

On the expropriations issue, which has been unfavourably influenced by racial hatred and several unsuitable decisions of the government, the blacks had placed

[57] Vöhringer to Komitee, 7 January 1913, in BMA E-2, 38, 4.
[58] Lutz to Inspektor, 7 February 1913, in BMA E-2, 38, 9.
[59] Lutz to Inspektor, 5 April 1913, in BMA E-2, 38, 23.
[60] Vöhringer to Inspektor, 8 August 1913, in BMA E-2, 38, 47.
[61] Lutz to Inspektor, 22 August 1913, in BMA E-2, 38, 52.
[62] Lutz to Inspektor, 7 September 1913, in BMA E-2, 38, 58.

their hopes in us. We cannot help them, and now all missionaries are in disrepute with them, particularly we Basler, in whom they had placed the most trust. After they found no hearing with the colonial secretary, Solf, they placed their hope in the Reichstag deputy, Gerlach, and the Social Democrats. The Duala have been violated, and they do not know where to turn.[63]

Basel missionaries, in particular Vöhringer, reported in February 1914 that things were escalating towards a confrontation in Duala, with Rudolf Manga Bell's own house scheduled to be destroyed. Although colonial officials believed that the king was the key impediment to compliance, Vöhringer argued that 'the Duala are as one.' The missionary recounted how Rudolf Manga Bell feared for his life and complained that 'blacks are completely without rights,' and that he had expressed his hopes for some form of sensible legal intervention.[64] The work of the mission, he argued, risked destruction, as the forced removals alienated the Duala from both government and missionaries alike.[65] In April he repeated his judgement that the Duala were being treated unfairly by the colonial government as having no rights.[66] Other missionaries in Duala, however, such as Jakob Bührer, believed there was nothing the missionaries could do, arguing that 'as hard as the expropriations were and as much as they were felt by the affected to be an injustice, it did not lie in our power to prevent them.' Given their helplessness, Bührer opportunistically argued that the mission could purchase newly expropriated Duala land for its own purposes in good conscience.[67] So too Andreas Link offered his support for the demolition measures on the grounds of health and sanitation.[68]

For his part, the missionary Lutz entreated Governor Ebermaier to reconsider, arguing that his silence hitherto on the 'lack of rights for the natives' had caused him 'inner distress'. Lutz made clear his unease at the way in which Duala homes had been burned to the ground. Although he had counselled the Duala to comply with the colonial government's orders, he was greatly upset at what he called 'an injustice and a ravaging'. He urged the governor to compromise and only remove a small number of houses, allowing the Duala to remain.[69] His plea was answered by Röhm in mid-April 1914, who accused the Duala of having exaggerated their plight to the Reichstag.[70] Notwithstanding the search by many of the Basel missionaries for a compromise solution, they too were now treated with mistrust by

[63] 'Protokoll über die vom 5–8 Dezember 1913, in 'Bonaku stattgehabten Kleine Brüderkonferenz', in BMA E-2, 38, 91.
[64] Vöhringer, 9 February 1914, in BMA E-2, 41, 25, 2–5.
[65] Vöhringer, 23 February 1914, in BMA E-2, 41, 39.
[66] Vöhringer to Inspektor, 7 April 1914, in BMA E-2, 41, 61.
[67] Bührer to Inspektor, 5 May 1914, in BMA E-2, 42, 19.
[68] Link to Inspektor, 6 May 1914, in BMA E-2, 42, 20.
[69] Lutz to Ebermaier, 23 February 1914, in BMA E-2, 41, 36.
[70] Röhm to Lutz, 20 April 1914, in BMA E-2, 41, 69.

the Duala, who bluntly reminded one missionary's wife that 'you whites have taken our land.'[71]

In May 1914 the missionaries were finally given their instructions on how to respond before a Reichstag commission of inquiry that had arrived in Cameroon. Although thus far the mission had been keen to demonstrate its loyalty to the colonial government, it was now given more latitude:

> This case concerns the forcible dispossession of entire towns to the benefit of the ruling race, which is a one-sided privileging of the whites that, irrespective of what anyone might say, contravenes all given assurances. We should do what we can to ensure that a breach of law that in all circumstances would have utterly disastrous moral consequences be avoided.[72]

The missionaries were also empowered to make clear to the Reichstag representatives that the forced removals and destruction of Duala villages were also resulting in the splintering of their now embittered congregations. On the question of hygiene and racial separation, Basel instructed the missionaries to remain circumspect. 'It seems to us', the mission directors observed, 'the separation of natives and Europeans, irrespective of how desirable it might be in itself, is simply not achievable in practice.' The missionaries were also allowed to express their support for the good character and truthfulness of King Rudolf Duala Manga Bell. The message from Basel was clear: 'We encourage you to testify without timidity to what you see as right, even if it should not be to the liking of the government.'[73] Accordingly, when the delegation arrived in Cameroon, Lutz bluntly told them that 'we cannot support the expropriations in their current extent and form.'[74]

At the same time, the ex-governor, Hansen, was also trying to intervene against his erstwhile colleagues Solf, Ebermaier, and Röhm. Without completely discounting the underlying racial and health considerations that had driven the expropriation plan, Hansen argued that the plan had not so much been ill-conceived as poorly designed. In two major interventions in the *Berliner Tageblatt* in February and May 1914, Hansen spelt out precisely what had been at stake for the Duala ever since Röhm's plan had won the approval of Governor Seitz. In February 1914, he argued that the Duala were being displaced because of a 'fanciful understanding of the future growth of Duala as a European place'. He further argued that 'the

---

[71] Wilhelm Schlatter and Hermann Witschi, *Geschichte der Basler Mission 1815–1919*, vol. 4 (Basel: Baseleia Verlag, 1965), 107–8.

[72] Inspektor to Lutz, 4 April 1904, in BMA E-2, 41, 57.

[73] Inspektor to Lutz, 4 April 1904, in BMA E-2, 41, 57. Basel was also concerned about what might happen to the mission's African congregation if competing Catholic missionaries championed the cause of Manga Bell, while the Protestant missionaries allowed themselves to be associated with the colonial government's expropriation and demolition programme.

[74] Lutz to Inspektor, 7 May 1914, in BMA E-2, 41, 82, 4.

forced displacement is also an unwarranted hardship for the old indigenous population and will, should it actually be really undertaken, lead to serious difficulties for the government.' Hansen also offered what he saw as a realistic notion of race relations in Cameroon, declaring that 'whoever wants to work effectively in the tropics must immerse themselves in the life and perspective of the natives and should not fearfully avoid contact with them.'[75]

In May, he re-emphasized his position, making clear that the Duala feared for their very future. It was a misconception, he argued, that Africans were not attached to their homes or homeland: 'To the contrary, the natives have an exceptionally strong attachment to their country (*Heimatgefühl*).' Not only was the planned 'violent transplantation' politically dubious, he continued, but it also meant a radical transformation of the Dualan way of life, since they were being forcibly removed from the sea to the hinterland. 'Under these conditions', he argued, 'it is not surprising that the Duala are highly agitated by the threatened dispossession measures and are using all possible means to have them overturned.'[76] He also confirmed that the protests of the Duala fully conformed with the terms of the treaty that an earlier generation had signed with German treaty hunters, which had guaranteed them full sovereignty over their own land. Hansen finished with an expression of the Duala's desire to live on their ancestral lands, quoting the November 1912 words of Rudolf Manga Bell to Governor Ebermaier:

Our single wish is that we might live and die on the land that our fathers and grandfathers lived on and on which we grew up. We ask Your Excellency to grant this our sole wish. We do not want to leave the coast; we want to keep it in sight, as we have done since we were small.[77]

Claims of Treason

While Hansen and the Basel missionaries increased their pressure on German public opinion, the colonial secretary, Solf, continued both to argue away the petition of the Duala and to discredit Manga Bell. In the Reichstag, Solf swamped deputies with an enormous but carefully edited collection of documents relating to the expropriations.[78] Here he candidly declared that if the Germans were to acknowledge that the treaty of 1884 preserved the territorial sovereignty of the Duala, then 'It would best if [Germany] evacuated Duala immediately':

---

[75] Wilhelm Hansen, 'Der Etat des Schutzgebietes Kamerun', *Berliner Tageblatt*, 17 February 1914.
[76] Wilhelm Hansen, 'Die Denkschrift über die Verlegung der Dualas', *Berlin Tageblatt*, 9 May 1914.
[77] Hansen, 'Die Denkschrift über die Verlegung der Dualas'.
[78] Solf, 'Denkschrift über die Enteignung und Verlegung der Eingeborenen in Duala (Kamerun)', 3269–3388.

If their interpretation was correct, the Duala would practically be in a position to hinder every development in the locality of Duala. They could not be forced to hand over land for the construction of roads for the town, for the necessary government buildings, for the harbourside buildings, for train stations and train lines, for canalization and the supply of water... With that, the development of the protectorate of Cameroon would be brought to a halt.

Instead of acknowledging the Africans' interpretation of the 1884 treaty, he suggested that the treaty only obliged the Germans to offer 'appropriate compensation' for any land they expropriated, as was the custom in Europe.[79] In any case, Solf alleged, the entire premise of the petition was disingenuous and stemmed not from a fear of economic and social ruination, as the Duala claimed, but rather a desire by increasingly irrelevant Dualan elites such as King Rudolf Duala Manga Bell to profit from rising land prices in the central zone of the town. This attempt to preserve their ability to profit from land speculation, Solf claimed, came at the cost of the majority of Duala, who were happy to cooperate with the Germans and move to wherever they were directed.[80]

In spite of Solf's attempts at persuasion, the environment in the Reichstag was one of cautious goodwill towards the Duala. This changed, however, when Solf declared that he now had dramatic evidence that demonstrated that the loyal petitioning offered by Rudolf Manga Bell was simply a facade, covering a deeper, treasonous disloyalty. This evidence came courtesy of another king in Cameroon, namely King Njoya of Bamum, a steadfast ally of the Germans. Njoya claimed to have been approached by a Duala named Ndane, ostensibly a messenger from Rudolf Manga Bell, to join a conspiracy to end German abuses of power by inviting Britain to become their new colonial rulers. In light of the seriousness of the issue, Njoya had detained Ndane and consulted the missionary Christoph Geprägs, who advised him to report everything to the Germans before handing the messenger over to the colonial authorities. Njoya sent his report to Dr Krüger in Kuti on 28 April.[81]

---

[79] Solf, 'Denkschrift über die Enteignung und Verlegung der Eingeborenen in Duala (Kamerun)', 3278. For his part, Rudolf Manga Bell argued that expropriation ('Enteignung') was 'a German legal term that we will never understand here'. See Duala Chiefs to the Reichstag, 8 March 1912, in Solf, 'Denkschrift über die Enteignung und Verlegung der Eingeborenen in Duala (Kamerun)', 3308.

[80] Solf, 'Denkschrift über die Enteignung und Verlegung der Eingeborenen in Duala (Kamerun)', 3294–7. As Eckert has argued, 'There was hardly a single Duala who lived exclusively from land speculation' (Andreas Eckert, 'Afrikanisches Land—deutsches Recht: Landpolitik und Landkonflikte in Kamerun, 1884–1914', in Peter Heine and Ulrich van der Heyden (eds), Studien zur Geschichte des deutschen Kolonialismus in Afrika (Pfaffenweiler: Centaurus-Verlagsgesellschaft, 1995), 249).

[81] Walter Nuhn, Kamerun unter dem Kaiseradler: Geschichte der Erwerbung und Erschließung des ehemaligen deutschen Schutzgebietes Kamerun (Dessau: Wilhelm Herbst, 2000), 345–54. Claude Tardits argues that it was not Njoya but Geprägs that informed the authorities, however responsibility seems to lie with Njoya. See Claude Tardits, Le Royaume bamoum (Paris: Librairie Armand Colin, 1980), 234–8.

In his statement, Njoya made some extraordinary claims, chief among them being that Manga Bell intended to have his case against the German colonial government heard in Britain and, were he to be successful, he would 'place himself under the sovereignty of the English king', who would then take possession of Duala, Bali, and Bamum. Bali had, Ndane claimed, apparently already agreed to the plan, and Njoya was supposed to send a man to Duala so that Rudolf Manga Bell would know that he agreed to be part of the plan. The British were, Ndane claimed, already in Cameroonian waters, ready to claim the three Cameroonian kingdoms. Thereafter, 'all Germans would leave the land of the blacks.' The cause of the plot was apparent: 'The Germans want to take the homelands of the Duala.'[82]

In his accompanying letter to Lutz, Geprägs added that on 27 April, Njoya had come to the mission station and called the brothers together to inform them of the matter and to ask them for help by taking his letter to Kuti. The missionaries expressed their reluctance to get involved in the 'embarrassing' matter, but were convinced by the urgency Njoya expressed.[83] Crucially, Geprägs admitted that there was a lack of clarity on the question of whether Rudolf Manga Bell had sent Ndane or not. The missionary admitted that in questioning Ndane he had become less sure about who was behind the message:

> As Njoya wrote in his report, Ndane claimed at first that Duala Manga had sent him, but afterwards claimed that he was sent by a brother of his, and then that he had been sent without the knowledge of Manga! Whatever the truth may be, in any case, it is greatly regrettable that the Duala, in their limitless delusion, have been swept up in such an extremely reckless venture. And who is this Duala Manga? Surely not Rudolf Bell?...Such a course of action as that described seems to me doubly inconceivable from him, to provoke an utterly appalling disaster for his people and all those he sought to entangle.[84]

Upon his return to Fumban, the leader of the mission there, Martin Göhring wrote to his good friend Lutz, drawing on his wife's testimony to substantiate his fervent belief that Rudolf Manga Bell was innocent. Regretting that he had not been there to manage the affair, he wrote of the events of a follow-up investigation:

> Reviewing the notes from Geprägs—unfortunately I was not at home but travelling when events happened here—the people and the king were questioned again. Nothing new emerged from it; only I tried to confirm that the messenger belatedly said that it was not Duala Manga but his brother the tailor who sent

---

[82] Njoya to Krüger, 28 April 1914, in BMA E-2, 42, 212. See also Geprägs, Njoya to Krüger, 28 April 1914, in BA Berlin R10001/4430, 183–5.

[83] Geprägs to Lutz, 29 April 1914, in BMA E-2, 42, 213.

[84] Geprägs to Lutz, 29 April 1914, in BMA E-2, 42, 213.

him. Adametz supported me on this point, arguing that would be easy to explain, because the people always say that their chief sent them with something like this, when they were actually sent by someone else. In fact, my wife made a good point. The king came to my wife and explained the matter to her. She said to him that he should wait and wanted to send me a message to say that I should hurry home. The king decided, however, that he could not wait and that haste was required. He then went to Brother Geprägs who translated the report. During the discussion, the king had sent the Duala man to my wife. She asked him in Duala whether Rudolf had really sent him. He replied that no, he had not seen Rudolf, but the tailor had explained the matter to him, adding that he was acting on Rudolf's behalf. (Initially the man had claimed that Duala Manga had sent him.) Then the king and Geprägs asked the man again who had sent him— Duala Manga or the tailor? Then he said the same thing he had told my wife: the tailor had sent him and had claimed to be acting on behalf of Duala Manga. From here the assessor will go to Bagam, where there was supposed to have been a messenger, and then to Bali, where there was also supposed to be a message. Fonyonga [of Bali] denies the matter. I feel very sorry for Rudolf.[85]

Notwithstanding the central role being played in Rudolf Manga Bell's prosecution by the missionary Geprägs, none of the other missionaries in the region was convinced of the veracity of the report of the 'plot'. Vöhringer expressed his doubts on the basis of the king's hitherto 'clever and noble' character.[86] Despite the government's determination to convict him, Vöhringer was 'completely convinced that Duala Manga has nothing to do with the Bamum affair'. He saw it as an attempt to have Rudolf Manga Bell expelled from the colony and bitterly declared that 'there is a great deal of sin, dishonesty and injustice on the side of our government in this whole affair.'[87] Rudolf Manga Bell was, he maintained, a completely innocent party to a corrupt process that had seen the colonial government undermine the principles of justice.[88] Lutz also expressed his astonishment regarding the strange circumstances surrounding the 'Bamum letter',[89] while Philipp Hecklinger gave voice to his similar scepticism about the 'ostensible' mission to Njoya in Bamum from the Dualan king and stated his view that the 'interests of the government and of the mission are divergent'.[90] On the basis of this scepticism, at the same time as Ndane's confession was sent to the governor and then on to the Colonial Office, it was also accompanied by a letter from the Basel missionaries that

---

[85]   Göhring to Lutz, 16 July 1914, in BMA E-2, 42, 218. Manga Bell's brother, Mudute Bell, had also been arrested and placed in solitary confinement until his mental health gave way and he was released. See Vöhringer to Inspektor, 8 July 1914, in BMA E-2, 42, 28.

[86]   Vöhringer to Inspektor, 8 May 1914, in BMA E-2, 41, 85.

[87]   Vöhringer to Inspektor, 21 May 1914, in BMA E-2, 41, 92.

[88]   Vöhringer to Inspektor, 22 June 1914, in BMA E-2, 41, 108.

[89]   Lutz to Inspektor, 20 May 1914, in BMA E-2, 41, 91.

[90]   Hecklinger to Inspektor, 22 June 1914, in BMA E-2,41, 107.

confirmed that there was a great deal of doubt about whether it was Rudolf Manga Bell who had actually sent the message. While on 26 April Ndane had claimed he was a messenger from the king himself, they explained, on 28 April he had stated that 'It was not Rudolf Bell himself who had sent him, but a "brother" of Manga Bell.'[91]

The reasons for Njoya's unhesitating alignment with the Germans are difficult to explain definitively. For his part, Njoya explained it as a matter of honour. Having sworn an oath to the Germans and to the German Kaiser, he claimed that he could 'not hear anything about the Germans without passing it on to them'. Beyond that, he had seen first-hand in the Nso War, as well as in other German wars of 'pacification' in Cameroon, that the balance of military power clearly lay with the Germans and that any attempted revolt was unlikely to succeed. As Njoya remarked:

> The Germans are my rulers, and whether they treat me well or poorly, I remain loyal to them...I, Njoya, know that if I give my name to this matter and the Germans hear of it, they will attack and kill me along with Manga and Fonyonga, because we broke our oath to the Kaiser.[92]

More broadly, it is also not beyond the realms of possibility that Njoya saw some local advantage in destroying the last vestiges of the Duala's earlier hegemony over regional trade and politics. As early as 1903, Njoya had been insisting to the Germans upon the right to trade directly with the coast,[93] a trade that had led to Bamum and indeed Njoya himself becoming increasingly prosperous in the years since. In leftist circles in Germany, there were also arguments voiced in the social democratic newspaper *Vorwärts*, that Njoya's intervention was to be expected, given that Njoya was the 'favourite child' of the Germans and that Bamum had once been enslaved by the Duala and had ever since considered the coastal kingdom as an enemy.[94]

Notwithstanding the flimsy evidence linking Manga Bell to Ndane's message to Njoya, the King of Bamum's intervention had the electrifying result of virtually ending the Reichstag's resistance to Solf and allowing the colonial secretary to telegraph Cameroon with an order to arrest Manga Bell for high treason.[95] With the First World War having just broken out, Rudolf Manga Bell's position became even more parlous. Whereas in peacetime he might have expected his sentence to

---

[91] Ried, Geprägs, Mockler to Ebermaier, 29 April 1914, in BA Berlin R1001/4430, 186.

[92] Geprägs, Njoya to Krüger 28 April 1914, in BA Berlin R1001/4430, 184. See also Njoya to Krüger, 28 April 1914, in BMA E-2, 42, 212.

[93] 'Eine Gesandtschaft aus Bamum', *Deutsches Kolonialblatt* 14 (15 September 1903), 493.

[94] 'Immer neue Schachzüge in der Duala-Affäre', *Vorwärts*, 13 May 1914. By the time Bell was executed and the war had begun, the newspaper did not dispute the government line that he had committed high treason. See 'Manga Bell hingerichtet', *Vorwärts*, 20 October 1914.

[95] Rüger, 'Die Duala und die Kolonialmacht', 240–1, 248–9.

have been expulsion from the colony, with the sea lanes recently blocked, Rudolf Manga Bell and his close associate Ngoso Din (who had gone to Germany to lobby on behalf of his king) were sentenced to be hanged, despite the intercession of Catholic and Protestant missionaries in Duala. The terse account of the Basel missionary Hecklinger offers a sense of how quickly events moved in the first days of the First World War:

> *7 August*…From 2 p.m. the case against the High Chief Duala Manga and Ngoso Din for high treason with Assessor N. Dr E. served as defence. The court applied the death sentence. At 8.30 in the evening the verdict of the court case was related to me by the district office. At 10 p.m. the Pallotine missionary Father M., the head of the Baptist Mission, Missionary M., and I went to the governor to beg for the life of the condemned, Duala Bell. Arguments were exchanged in a serious mood. The governor will look at the case one more time. At 11.30 p.m. we departed from him; then I immediately went to the prisoners in the cell. It was lit by a weak kerosene lamp. Assessor D. committed the last will and testament of the High Chief to paper, and I served as a witness. At 1 a.m., he left the cell. Until 1.30 a.m. I stayed with them both and gave them both Holy Communion. I will never forget these night hours! At 2 a.m. I arrived home, but no sleep would come to me…

> *8 August.* From midday until 12.30 p.m. I was once again with the governor regarding the same matter as last night. Deporting the High Chief is not possible, given the current political situation. At 5 p.m. the two were hanged—God have mercy on their souls! That was my hardest day so far in Cameroon.

> *9 August.* Sunday. During Saturday night, a large number of the Duala people left for the interior with their belongings. Even at 5 a.m. I can still see a great number of people on the foreshore, preparing their canoes for departure…

> *13 August.* The governor held a meeting with the village elders of the Duala in which he discussed the matter of their high chief and discussed why he had to act as he did. He warned the hotheads amongst them and exhorted the better element to be reasonable.[96]

Although the public reason given by Ebermeier for their execution was 'high treason', internally the discussion revolved around the need for exemplary punishment of uncooperative African leaders during wartime.[97] The governor's justification to the Duala and to all Africans in the colony was telling in its call for

---

[96] Philipp Hecklinger, *Tagebuchblätter über Krieg und Kriegsgefangenschaft in Kamerun und England* (Stuttgart: Missionsagentur, 1915), 4–5.
[97] Uwe Schulte-Varendorff, *Krieg in Kamerun: Die deutsche Kolonie im Ersten Weltkrieg* (Berlin: Ch. Links, 2011), 76; Eyoum, Michels, and Zeller, 'Bonamanga', 29.

loyalty and its suggestion of spectral orchestrators of rebellion that needed to be cast out:

> You people of Duala! I appeal to you and proclaim to you: Manga (Rudolf) Bell has been hanged today because he had proven himself to be a traitor to the Kaiser and the empire. He had in his last moments accepted that he was spurred on by fear of the revenge of those of his people, whom you all know, who because of their fear sit secretly in the background, brewing poison and misleading their people. Manga's blood is on the hands of those who pushed him towards the path of crime. Those who do not wish to become criminals like Duala Manga and his assistant must tear themselves from every false leader who sits in the dark secretly brewing poison. Those who truly mean it are welcome. The government of the Kaiser will always be just and thankful to true servants and true subjects. What you are lamenting is the consequences of the activities of the shadow men who—as the government knows—were always in action, filling their people with hatred and keeping their people in terror with their poison, so as to oppress them. Shake yourselves free of them and you will be happier. Manga himself had bid his people in his last hour that through his death the Duala should return in their hearts to loyalty to the Kaiser and obedience to the government.[98]

According to the Basel missionaries, 'The execution of the judgment was seen by the locals as judicial murder.'[99] The missionary Stahl was bluntly told by a Duala woman that 'we are finished with the mission,'[100] while Hecklinger reported that scarcely any of the Duala returned to his church, a situation that, he said, 'was related to the death of the High Chief Duala Manga' (see Figure 13.3). Another missionary stationed in Sakbayeme reported the large number of refugees who had arrived from the coast. He also recorded how his Duala middle school teacher Bolanga 'wept like a child' upon hearing the news, while other chiefs from the region, frightened for their own fate under these new wartime conditions, came to him for an explanation of why Manga Bell had been hanged.[101] In March 1915, when the missionary Friedrich Ebding explained the reasons for the 'dissatisfaction of the Duala population with the German government' and why they had rejoiced at the coming of the British and the imprisonment of the Germans, primary

---

[98] Ebermaier, 8 August 1914, in Schulte-Varendorff, *Krieg in Kamerun*, 77. For further trials of Duala in the matter, see BA Berlin R 175-I/630, 'Vollstreckung der gegen die Genossen des Duala Manga Bell wegen Hochverrats verhängten Strafen'.

[99] Schlatter and Witschi, *Geschichte der Basler Mission 1815–1919*, vol. 4, 109.

[100] Schlatter and Witschi, *Geschichte der Basler Mission 1815–1919*, vol. 4, 109.

[101] Jakob Stutz, *Blätter aus den Kriegstagen der Basler Missionsstation Sakbayeme in Kamerun* (Stuttgart: Missionsagentur, 1918), 6.

Figure 13.3 The funeral of King Rudolf Duala Manga Bell, 1914

amongst them, he argued, were their wholesale dispossession and the hanging of Manga Bell.[102]

The legal protests of Manga Bell and the unswerving loyalty of Njoya were not forgotten by Germans who had been in Cameroon. In 1915, the former governor, Jesko von Puttkamer, slandered the Duala as a 'degenerate and mendacious rabble',[103] while praising the Bamum of Central Cameroon as 'loyal' and 'intelligent and untainted'. For Puttkamer, the consequences of the Duala's ostensible degeneracy for any future, post-war colonial rule in Cameroon were clear; namely the loss of their land and their expulsion from their lands.

> Without scruple, this useless and treacherous rabble must be done away with and replaced by civilized tribes from the interior. I believe the transfer of the entire nation to another less comfortable coastal region would be most suitable; the Spanish government might also decide to take the Duala as workers in Fernando Po.[104]

To be sure, part of this was Puttkamer's enduring fury at his own humiliating dismissal from Cameroon, as well as the news that the Duala had welcomed the

---

[102] Fridrich Ebding, 'Einiges über die Gründe der Unzufriedenheit der Dualabevölkerung mit der deutschen Regierung', 11 March 1915, in BMA E-4, 1 29a. Ebding also claimed that a list of Germans to be murdered during an uprising was found in Manga Bell's house. No other sources mention such a list.

[103] Jesko von Puttkamer, *12 Kriegs-Aufsätze* (Berlin: Verlag von Georg Stilke, 1915), 22–3.

[104] Puttkamer, *12 Kriegs-Aufsätze*, 22–3, 56–7, 63.

British as liberators from the Germans (news that King Njoya of Bamum had done the same had apparently not yet reached Puttkamer). Nonetheless, it also reflected the end point of the development of the German system of rule in Cameroon, which emphasized a choice between complete compliance or alternatively military suppression. The middle way, as endorsed by Rudolf Duala Manga Bell, of holding the Germans to account via the legal mechanisms of the *Rechtsstaat* had signally failed. This is not because the Reichstag lacked the power to delay and or even overturn the expropriation measures by squeezing the colonial budget, pressuring the chancellor, or by turning the glare of public opinion to the actions of colonial officials. Rather, in 1914, in the face of the seemingly irrefutable charge of high treason and having learnt the electoral lesson of 1907, the Reichstag decided against challenging the Colonial Office and Cameroon's governor.

The protests of the King of Duala demonstrated a strong belief in the rule of law and due political process. This belief was misplaced. Despite the foundational treaty which offered clear limits to the sovereign power of the Germans in the colony, these limits were ignored once they became inconvenient. An appeal to the Reichstag was a seemingly appropriate and legally correct way of attempting to hold the German Empire to account for its failings while arousing German public interest in the matter. In political terms, however, the resulting public pressure was insufficient to force the colonial authorities to back down of their own accord. In the final analysis, the requisite amount of public and political will to overturn an abuse of power was found to be lacking, particularly once what appeared to be a question of gubernatorial overreach was transformed into an allegation of high treason.

Rudolf Duala Manga Bell's execution occurred against a background of petitions, public discussion, protests to the Reichstag, ministerial briefings, and appeals to expert metropolitan and colonial opinion. Within the heightened context of the First World War, it offered not so much an illustration of the limits of the German *Rechtsstaat* in colonial matters as a demonstration of the cruel functioning of those norms in favour of the colonizing power.

Conclusion

The monarchs discussed in this book are far from the only ones whose rule intersected with German imperialism. Sultan Mkwawa of the Hehe, for example, was another East African ruler who, in the early years of Kaiser Wilhelm II's reign, found that his plans for regional dominance between Bagamoyo and Lake Tanganyika in East Africa clashed with Germany's colonial expansion in the area. With neither side willing to abandon their expansionist trajectory, a bitter war ensued in which Mkwawa decimated a large expeditionary force led by Emil von Zelewski in 1891 before finally succumbing to German starvation tactics.[1]

The intertwined history of Sultan Mkwawa and the Germans did not end with his death. When his body was found, Mkwawa was decapitated and his skull was delivered to Germany's imperial commissioner, Tom von Prince, and his wife Magdalene,[2] who kept it as a personal trophy. Thereafter it was presumed to have been returned to Germany,[3] where it was believed to have remained in a museum until Article 246 of the Versailles Treaty specifically demanded that Germany 'hand over to His Britannic Majesty's Government the skull of the Sultan Mkwawa'.[4] The Germans professed their ignorance of the skull's whereabouts until 1951, when the British Governor of Tanganyika, Edward Twining, claimed to have found a skull matching its description in the Bremen Anthropological Museum.[5] The skull was accepted by Mkwawa's grandson as authentic, and it was repatriated to Africa.[6] Unconcerned about whether the skull was actually that of the sultan, Twining emphasized that what mattered was that 'it has been accepted

---

[1] Jan-Bart Gewald, 'Colonial Warfare: Hehe and World War I, the Wars besides Maji Maji in South-Western Tanzania', *African Historical Review*, 40, no.2 (2008), 7–11; David Pizzo, '*To Devour the Land of Mkwawa': Colonial Violence and the German–Hehe War in East Africa, c.1884–1914* (Saarbrücken: Lambert Academic Publishing, 2010), 4.

[2] Magdalene von Prince, *Eine deutsche Frau im Innern Deutsch-Ostafrikas*, 179–83.

[3] Simon J. Harrison, 'Skulls and Scientific Collecting in the Victorian Military: Keeping the Enemy Dead in British Frontier Warfare', *Comparative Studies in Society and History* 50, no.1 (2008), 294–5; Jesse Bucher, 'The Skull of Mkwawa and the Politics of Indirect Rule in Tanganyika', *Journal of Eastern African Studies* 10, no.2 (2016), 284–302.

[4] Bucher, 'The Skull of Mkwawa', 299; Martin Baer and Olaf Schröter, *Eine Kopfjagd: Deutsche in Ostafrika: Spuren kolonialer Herrschaft* (Berlin: Ch. Links, 2001); Edgar V. Winans, 'The Head of the King: Museums and the Path to Resistance', *Comparative Studies in Society and History* 36, no.2 (1994), 221–41.

[5] Bettina Brockmeyer, Frank Edward, and Holger Stoecker, 'The Mkwawa Complex: A Tanzanian-European History about Provenance, Restitution, and Politics', *Journal of Modern European History* 18, no.2 (2020), 117–39; Rolleston to Gellately, 3 December 1952, in CO 822/566, as reproduced at https://blog.nationalarchives.gov.uk/the-skull-of-sultan-mkwawa/, accessed 18 September 2021.

[6] CO 822/566.

The Kaiser and the Colonies: Monarchy in the Age of Empire. Matthew P. Fitzpatrick, Oxford University Press.
© Matthew P. Fitzpatrick 2022. DOI: 10.1093/oso/9780192897039.003.0015

as such by the Hehe people.'[7] Recent research suggests that his cavalier approach to the repatriation of royal remains led to the wrong skull returning to Africa.[8]

Mkwawa was just one of many other monarchs and paramount rulers who were forced to respond to the challenge posed by Wilhelmine imperialism.[9] As the preceding chapters have demonstrated, each monarch (and those who exerted pressure upon them domestically) assessed and responded to the changed political environment engendered by German expansionism in a different way. Some decided to take up arms in defence of their sovereign rights and territories, while others chose the degree of accommodation and cooperation that best served their interests. Many of these monarchs shared the same fate as Sultan Mkwawa, with King Rudolf Duala Manga Bell of the Duala, Sultan Fumo Bakari of Wituland, and Paramount Leaders Samuel Maharero and Hendrik Witbooi of the Herero and Nama nations all failing to survive European attacks on their kingdoms.

Yet at the same time as some monarchs were hounded by European colonizers into an early grave, others engaged with the Germans in ways that paid political dividends, allowing them to maintain and even enhance their domestic standing (albeit often at the cost of their long-term sovereign power). The complex range of factors that informed such calculated pivots to the Germans and the political circumstances in which they occurred have been laid bare in this book, in the hope of moving German colonial history beyond a one-dimensional 'deficit framework' that devalues or ignores the expressions of agency and inventiveness of the colonized and presents non-European rulers as only ever hopelessly ensnared within metropolitan projects. Acknowledging and foregrounding the adaptations and inventiveness of non-European rulers, including their adaptation to new forms of global diplomacy under empire, reinstates the agency of the colonised where it was expressed and offers a valuable contrast to those numerous cases in which agency was not a part of the colonial encounter. Examining the different expressions of sovereign decision making and the exogenous and endogenous pressures and variables that informed it enables a more variegated understanding of the dynamics of Germany's global empire and its interactions with extra-European polities. While it is necessary to remain fully cognizant of the structural asymmetries of imperial power, the strategies used by African, Asian, and Pacific rulers to try and protect their interests and those of their

---

[7] Twining, 6 July 1954, in CO822/770.

[8] Brockmeyer, Edward, and Stoecker, 'The Mkwawa Complex', 117–39.

[9] Closely mirroring the fate of Mkwawa was that of Mangi Meli Kiusa bin Rindi Makindara, Paramount Chief of the Chaga in the Mount Kilimanjaro region, who, after having been defeated by the Germans in 1900, was hanged and had his head sent to Germany to become part of an ethnographical collection. See 'Die augenblickliche politische Lage am Kilimanjaro und Meru', *Deutsch-Ostafrikanische Zeitung*, 24 March 1900; Damian Zane, 'The Search in Germany for the Lost Skull of Tanzania's Mangi Meli', https://www.bbc.com/news/world-africa-45916150, accessed 18 September 2021; Jeremiah J. Garsha, 'Expanding Vergangenheitsbewältigung? German Repatriation of Colonial Artefacts and Human Remains', *Journal of Genocide Research*, 22, no.1 (2020), 60.

communities must be properly recognized if Germany's empire and its historical legacies are to be understood.[10]

Afterlives of Monarchy in Africa, Asia, and the Pacific

This agency-centred approach to decision-making cannot explain away the effects of empire. As the record of dispossession, disempowerment, and violence shows, the history of monarchy within the German Empire reveals just how misplaced and ahistorical colonial nostalgia is. While African, Asian, and Pacific rulers were indeed capable of making history, it was rarely under conditions of their own choosing. The organized efforts of German capital and the German state, backed by the German military, to externalize and globalize the German economy and population via the mercantile, political, and military penetration of the extra-European world threatened the sovereignty of all but a few of the monarchs they encountered. No historical account of global royal cosmopolitanism can ignore the structural forces that engendered territorial dispossession and the diminution (if not outright loss) of political sovereignty. Rather, the study of royal agency within empire highlights that it was underneath the macro-level material drivers of imperial expansion and alongside the routine, quotidian violence of colonialism,[11] that the thriving networks, ties, and entanglements were created and fostered by kings, queens, sultans, paramount leaders, emperors, and empresses who did their best to influence the operation, complexion, and effectiveness of these overarching structural dynamics.

Understanding the role of these extra-European monarchs in responding to and partially shaping the German Empire helps put paid to the assumption that Africa, Asia, and the Pacific have only a colonial past, while Europe alone has a political, military, and diplomatic history. The role played by monarchs and their domestic advisers, supporters, and detractors clearly dispels the enduring crypto-Hegelian myth of historic and non-historic peoples, and of the extra-European world as a static object of European imperialism and of a progressive historical *Weltgeist*.[12] These monarchs and their attempts to balance the demands of their domestic critics, their own elite interests and the predations of the Europeans show how those outside of Europe read their changing circumstances fluently and

---

[10] This critique is adopted from recent approaches to Indigenous health and education. See William Fogarty, Hannah Bulloch, Siobhan McDonnell, and Michael Davis, *Deficit Discourse and Indigenous Health: How Narrative Framings of Aboriginal and Torres Strait Islander People Are Reproduced in Policy* (Canberra: Lowitja Institute and National Centre for Indigenous Studies, 2018); Kerry McCallum and Lisa Waller, 'Un-Braiding Deficit Discourse in Indigenous Education News 2008–2018: Performance, Attendance and Mobility', *Critical Discourse Studies* (2020). doi: 10.1080/17405904.2020.1817115.

[11] Marie Muschalek, *Violence as Usual: Policing and the Colonial State in German Southwest Africa* (Ithaca, NY: Cornell University Press, 2019).

[12] Ranajit Guha, *History at the Limit of World History*, (New York: Columbia University Press, 2002).

prosecuted their own form of international politics and diplomacy with—and indeed from within—the German Empire. With this scope for adaptation and sovereign action in mind, it is clear that new histories of Europe and European imperialism are required that take seriously the diplomatic and political adroitness of those they encountered outside Europe and the complicated global negotiations of power that took place within and alongside imperial frameworks. Such new investigations are required to displace earlier histories that assumed the inevitability of global imperial clashes engendered by ostensibly immutable cultural differences and will serve to negate earlier framings of international history and international relations that, as Sam Okoth Opondo has argued, have reified 'Eurocentric constructions' of an unchanging global colonized alterity and an omnipotent Europe. New imperial histories in this vein would do much to reanimate 'the silenced or trivialized other' as it appears in European histories and interrupt Europe's 'self-scripting' as an all-powerful conqueror, without presuming to ventriloquize indigenous voices.[13] Indeed, such new histories are being written by historians who are pushing beyond the limits of area or national studies to revise the picture of European history and its connection with the histories of social and political change in Africa, Asia, and the Pacific.[14] For Europeanists and historians of the German Empire, however, the dimensions of the cleft between the totalizing claims to power of the colonizers and the complexity of imperial realities are still to be fully appreciated.[15]

As this book has shown, however, an attentiveness to how Europeans manipulated these extra-European monarchical expressions of sovereignty and agency remains indispensable. In the German Empire, there was a purposive unevenness in how the claims of parity made by non-European monarchs were treated. On the one hand, the relatively powerful monarchs of Siam, China, the Ottoman Empire, Zanzibar, and Morocco were treated, at least ceremonially, as royals enjoying a status not altogether dissimilar to that of the royal houses of Europe. Elsewhere, however, the leaders of smaller polities in Samoa, the Marshall Islands, Cameroon, Wituland, and South West Africa were often viewed by Germans as monarchs whose claims to legitimacy and sovereignty could be safely ignored unless they coincided with the imperatives of German rule. Even when members of noble families from these territories (such as Friedrich Maharero of the Herero

---

[13] Sam Okoth Opondo, 'Decolonizing Diplomacy: Reflections on African Estrangement and Exclusion', in Constas M. Constantinou and James Der Derian, *Sustainable Diplomacies* (New York: Palgrave, 2010), 109–27.

[14] See, e.g., Tracey Banivanua Mar, *Decolonisation and the Pacific: Indigenous Globalisation and the Ends of Empire* (Cambridge: Cambridge University Press, 2016); Sanjay Subrahmanyam, *Europe's India: Words, People, Empires, 1500–1800* (Cambridge: Harvard University Press, 2018).

[15] Notwithstanding the early efforts of works such as Jürgen Zimmerer, *Deutsche Herrschaft über Afrikaner: Staatlicher Machtanspruch und Wirklichkeit im kolonialen Namibia* (Münster, Lit Verlag, 2002) and Michelle Moyd, *Violent Intermediaries: African Soldiers, Conquest, and Everyday Colonialism in German East Africa* (Athens, OH: Ohio University Press, 2014).

or Tupua Tamasese Lealofi of Samoa) were able to reach Germany for audiences with Kaiser Wilhelm II, they did so partly as anthropological exhibits who were only briefly permitted to meet with the German emperor as leading representatives of their people. This contrasts greatly with the extraordinary levels of hospitality shown to the Siamese King Chulalongkorn or the Chinese Prince Zaifeng. Contrary to Cannadine's argument, questions of race and metropolitan assumptions regarding comparative civilizationary standings clearly played an important role in setting the tone of German *Weltpolitik*,[16] but so too did considerations regarding the size, power, and strategic importance of the various polities encountered by the Germans around the world.

Notwithstanding the clearly disparate treatment of monarchies, the institution of monarchy remained of the utmost importance to Wilhelmine Germany's global empire even when the sovereign rights of some royals were strategically ignored. Acknowledging the claims to primacy made by some non-European monarchs (but not others) and offering special rights and privileges to favoured rulers formed a key strategy used by the Germans to establish and maintain control over their territory. As the ascendance to power of Samuel Maharero in Hereroland and the recognition of Kabua as the 'King' of the Marshall Islands demonstrate, confirming, manipulating, or reforming existing hierarchical social structures that were already embedded and functioning in local political contexts was understood by German colonial authorities to be far more efficient than attempting to impose and defend an entirely new political structure. Where wholesale changes to prevailing political norms were deemed necessary by the colonizing power, as in Samoa, where the monarchy and then the paramountcy were both discarded, the military (particularly the navy) was often brought in to defend the abolition of these locally prized institutions. Elsewhere, as in German East Africa and Wituland, a lack of consultation with local elites or a clumsy attempt to implement changes to local political arrangements could easily result in a resort to devastating warfare.

Often, the challenges posed by German power to monarchs beyond Europe intersected with simultaneously occurring domestic dissent, itself often a product of social pressures engendered by new imperial conditions. Troublingly for such monarchies, preserving the conditions of internal accord that underpinned their domestic legitimacy often proved incompatible with the demands of the Europeans, so that the measures adopted by rulers to accommodate the European interlopers often risked provoking rebellion amongst their subjects. This was particularly the case in places like Morocco and Zanzibar, where disgruntled regional notables contested decisions made by their rulers to appease the European powers. Alternatively, when steps were taken to respond to internal discontent or

---

[16] Cannadine, *Ornamentalism*, 9.

forestall domestic instability by acceding to the demands of discontented subjects and rivals, such as in Duala and Boxer-era China, monarchs risked raising the ire of the Europeans and precipitating open conflict. In other places, such as Bamum and the Marshall Islands, rulers managed to straddle these contradictions and preserve their position under the Germans and at the apex of their local power matrix. In other sites such as Hereroland, the Germans facilitated the rise of apparently pliable rulers who would acquiesce and even assist as they applied violent pressure to recalcitrant neighbouring leaders and any of their own people who dared resist. As the case of Samuel Maharero demonstrates, however, the results of such interference were not always predictable. Elsewhere, as in Samoa, the Germans felt sufficiently powerful to dismantle monarchical structures and replace them with subordinate advisory positions in the hope of forestalling future expressions of destabilizing rivalry or dissent.

That some monarchies succeeded in provisionally solving the conundrum of domestic pressures and European demands is by no means proof of the benign nature or negligible effects of colonialism; nor is it an argument for monarchy as a uniquely resilient or stable form of government. Both colonialism and monarchy were forms of political control predicated on the maintenance of social and political inequality, and, as the preceding chapters have shown, both the Germans and the monarchs whose territories they colonized were often capable of leveraging their powerful positions (sometimes in mutually reinforcing ways) to preserve their relative dominance, albeit with varying results. While some monarchs (such as King Chulalongkorn) saw their best interests as being served by adapting their polities to European expectations and suppressing their domestic rivals and subordinates, others, including the sultans of Morocco or the last emperors of the Qing dynasty, ultimately found the contradictions between domestic and external imperial pressure too great to withstand.

This variegation is similarly evident in the period after Germany was forced to give up its global empire.[17] Some ex-German colonies retained their monarchies or elements of monarchical forms, including up to the present. Despite being a republic, the bicameral democracy of the Marshall Islands, for example, has maintained a Council of *Iroij*, which operates as an upper house and consists of those with the paramount title *iroijlaplap*.[18] A similar body, the House of Chiefs, appeared, disappeared, and recently reappeared in anglophone Cameroon.[19] The preservation of Samoa's *matai* system is guaranteed by Article 100 of the Samoan

---

[17] For the effects of decolonization on Germany, see Sean Andrew Wempe, *Revenants of the German Empire: Colonial Germans, Imperialism and the League of Nations* (New York: Oxford University Press, 2019).

[18] *Constitution of the Republic of the Marshall Islands*, https://wipolex.wipo.int/fr/text/201113, accessed 18 September 2021.

[19] Laura-Stella E. Enonchong, *The Constitution and Governance in Cameroon* (New York: Routledge, 2021), 191–2.

Constitution,[20] while, in Namibia, the powers of traditional leaders are recognized (but also strictly codified) by the Traditional Authorities Act of 2000.[21] In Thailand, the royal family who ruled Siam when Kaiser Wilhelm II reigned in Germany continues its unbroken reign up to the present under King Maha Vajiralongkorn.[22] Having endured and then been liberated from French control, the Alaouite sultans of Morocco (now kings) have also continued to reign over a gradually reforming but still recognizably monarchical state.[23]

Other monarchies, however, proved less long-lived. Zanzibar retained its sultans only until the revolution of 1964, which saw the sultanate join the Republic of Tanzania and the last sultan flee to Oman and then Britain.[24] For its part, China's Qing dynasty came to an end as early as 1912, when China shifted to become a republic after the Xinhai revolution. The extent to which the Qing fell victim to endogenous or exogenous pressures remains a subject of intense scholarly debate.[25]

Afterlives of Monarchy and Empire in Germany

The historical legacy of monarchy in Germany has recently emerged as a new front in German efforts to come to terms with the past. While debate has erupted most publicly over the role played by the House of Hohenzollern in the rise of the Nazis,[26] colonial legacies too have emerged as the subject of heated debate. As German and Namibian diplomats have sought agreement on what a suitable apology and level of reparations for Germany's genocidal colonial warfare might look like (with community representatives of the Herero and Nama nations effectively

[20] *Constitution of the Independent State of Samoa*, http://extwprlegs1.fao.org/docs/pdf/sam132838.pdf, accessed 18 September 2021. For a recent commentary on the system, see A. Morgan Tuimaeali'ifano, 'Matai Titles and Modern Corruption in Samoa: Costs, Expectations and Consequences for Families and Society', in Stewart Firth (ed.), *Globalisation and Governance in the Pacific Islands* (Canberra: ANU E-Press, 2019), 77–90.

[21] 'Traditional Authorities Act', 21 December 2000, in *Government Gazette of Namibia*, Nr. 2456, 22 December 2000.

[22] Pavin Chachavalpongpun, 'Constitutionalising the Monarchy: Uncompromising Demands of Thai Protesters', *Journal of International Affairs*, 73, no.2 (2020), 163–72.

[23] Yasmina Abouzzohour and Beatriz Tomé-Alonso, 'Moroccan Foreign Policy after the Arab Spring: A Turn for the Islamists or Persistence of Royal Leadership?', *Journal of North African Studies* 24, no.3 (2019), 444–67; Abdeslam Maghraoui, 'Monarchy and Political Reform in Morocco', *Journal of Democracy* 12, no.1 (2001), 73–86.

[24] Roman Loimeie, 'Memories of Revolution: Zur Deutungsgeschichte einer Revolution (Sansibar 1964)', *Africa Spectrum* 41, no.2 (2006), 175–97; James R. Brennan, 'Lowering the Sultan's Flag: Sovereignty and Decolonization in Coastal Kenya', *Comparative Studies in Society and History* 50, no.4 (2008), 831–61.

[25] James Leibold, 'Xinhai Remembered: From Han Racial Revolution to Great Revival of the Chinese Nation', *Asian Ethnicity* 15, no.1 (2013), 1–20.

[26] Karina Urbach, 'Useful Idiots: The Hohenzollerns and Hitler', *Historical Research* 93, no.261 (2020), 526–50; Stephan Malinowski, *Nazis and Nobles: The History of a Misalliance* (Oxford, Oxford University Press, 2020), 330.

sidelined from the discussion), the historic culpability of Kaiser Wilhelm II has also come into sharper focus, with the emperor viewed by some historians as the personal architect of colonial atrocities and, in the case of South West Africa, genocide.[27]

As this book has made clear, there is no question that military atrocities and indeed genocide were committed in Germany's colonies by armies led by Wilhelm II's viceregal military representatives. In the case of genocide in South West Africa, the commander-in-chief, Lothar von Trotha, was without doubt hand-picked by Wilhelm II from a provided shortlist of candidates. The atrocities of viceregal representatives like Trotha in South West Africa (and Curt von François at Hornkranz or Hans Dominik in Cameroon) were clearly committed in the name of the German state and Crown, as were the judicial or military regicides in Duala and German South West Africa and the banishment of paramount rulers that occurred in Samoa. While some of these crimes of the colonial state have crept into public discussion, many have fallen victim to the type of 'colonial amnesia' pointed to by Reinhart Kössler and Henning Melber.[28] Consequently, they are not only an appropriate site for a colonial *Vergangenheitsbewältigung* but also some commensurate form of *Wiedergutmachung*.

The narrower question of royal intent and Wilhelm II's personal responsibility for Germany's conduct in the colonies is a more complex one. Within Germany, the constitutional division of powers included an important role for Wilhelm II in colonial policy. Given that the colonies were not mentioned in Article One of the Constitution of the German Empire, these territories were technically extra-constitutional spaces that were legally under the direct rule of the emperor.[29] Except on very rare occasions, however, this was to all intents and purposes a legal fiction, given the clamour of the press and public opinion, the bully pulpit and budgetary oversight of the Reichstag, the raft of constraining legislation that governed life in the colonies, and the day-to-day management of colonial affairs by merchants, governors and officials in the colonies and in the Colonial Office, the Foreign Office, the *Kolonialrat*, and the chancellery in Berlin.

Kaiser Wilhelm II certainly played his constitutionally appointed role when called upon. Primarily, however, he served as a convenient synecdoche for German economic and state power. He was not remotely the initiator of German *Weltpolitik*, nor was he its sustained guiding voice. The economic drive to empire, all of the key decisions to embrace global imperialism as state policy, and the annexation of most of Germany's colonies clearly antedated his reign. For much

[27] Sarkin, *Germany's Genocide of the Herero*; Olusoga and Erichsen, *The Kaiser's Holocaust*.
[28] Reinhart Kössler and Henning Melber, 'Koloniale Amnesie. Zum Umgang mit der deutschen Kolonialvergangenheit'. *Standpunkt* 9 (2018), 1–4.
[29] Fitzpatrick, *Purging the Empire*, 16.

of his reign, Wilhelm II was slow—even reluctant—to become involved in colonial affairs. Far from exercising personal rule over the colonies, the emperor was willingly led in all but a handful of decisions by the Reichstag, his ministers and the colonial bureaucracy. While there is no question that Kaiser Wilhelm II (and indeed his father and grandfather) played a demonstrable role in supporting those creating and consolidating Germany's global empire, it is also clear that Wilhelm II was neither the instigator nor the impetus behind *Kolonialpolitik* or *Weltpolitik*.

With regard to South West Africa, it is true that Wilhelm II was initially unmoved by reports of Trotha's atrocities, however there is no evidence that Wilhelm II expressly ordered the genocidal starvation tactics adopted by his German commander, which had been used by other commanders in other colonial theatres of war. His indifference to the suffering of his colonial subjects is a telling insight into the emperor's personal belief that Christian principles and the rules of war did not extend to 'heathens and barbarians'.[30] Indeed, his cold-bloodedness in the face of genocide is also entirely consistent with the sentiments of his *Hunnenrede*, which was made before the embarkation of troops to the Boxer War but which had no effect on the prosecution of the war by the German forces.

That Kaiser Wilhelm II was personally ill-disposed towards many whom he saw as representatives of an inferior but nonetheless threatening alterity has long been known. Indeed, the chapters of this book have detailed his frequently expressed racist antipathy towards the many African, Chinese, Japanese, Pasifika, and Jewish people with whom he dealt as part of his duties. The impoverished state of Wilhelm's personal qualities, however, would only be of central historical importance if German *Weltpolitik* and *Kolonialpolitik* had been influenced or managed in accordance with the emperor's own pronounced predilections and prejudices. Given the absence of an absolutist kingship mechanism in Germany, this was not the case. Rather, at the macro level, colonial events, including atrocities and injustices, adhered to the structural logic of the drive to global empire, willed and supported by the globalizing liberal middle classes of the German nation and carefully directed by the empire's chancellors, bureaucrats, military, civil society associations, private sector entities, Reichstag deputies, and (as the 1907 election made clear) those who voted for them. At the micro level, colonial decision-making, particularly the decision of if, when, where, and how to engage with non-Europeans, emanated from Germans *in situ* who had been empowered by firms and by the state to make decisions in accordance with their estimation of Germany's national and economic interests. Reigning but rarely ruling, Kaiser

---

[30] Bülow, *Denkwürdigkeiten*, vol. 2, 20–1.

Wilhelm II was in most instances the emblematic embodiment rather than the sovereign locus of these dynamics. Offering his royal imprimatur to *Kolonialpolitik* and conducting himself as the highest representative of the German Empire was important and serious political work, but in most instances it was a role that supplemented the decision making processes that occurred elsewhere.

That the emperor was often incapable of successfully playing the role assigned to him is equally clear. In this study, only three colonial decisions of material importance have been identified as having been made by Wilhelm II. The first was the order to bring forward the long-planned seizure of Kiautschou Bay in response to the murder of German missionaries. The second was his ill-advised order to insist that the companions of Prince Zaifeng of China kowtow before him. The third was the decision to elevate Trotha to commander of the expeditionary force to wage war in South West Africa in 1904. All three were untrammelled disasters. Beyond this, however, the actual prosecution of Germany's military campaigns in German East Africa, Cameroon, Wituland, China, German South West Africa, and Samoa were all run without reference to the strategic thinking or professed military or political aims of the emperor. In most instances they were handled by military personnel at the behest of or under the command of Germany's colonial governors or other German authorities. In a few cases, such as the Boxer War, the naval blockade of East Africa, and the campaign against Sultan Fumo Bakari in Wituland, these campaigns were joint campaigns with other imperial powers, where the objectives of the different powers were not always congruent. In most cases, however, Germany's colonial military command was far more localized, so that colonial atrocities were often the result of a sudden change of tactics, often a shift to starvation tactics or civilian massacres, undertaken by the locally competent representative of the German state in the field, frequently after their military impotence had been exposed by the adroit military comportment of the local rulers they sought to subdue.

Most other critical decisions besides those of war and peace were also made independently of Wilhelm II. The decisions to discontinue Samoan kingship and then Samoa's paramountcy were made by Governor Wilhelm Solf. The decision to dispossess the Duala was made by Governor Theodor Seitz and confirmed by Governor Karl Ebermeier and Colonial Secretary Wilhelm Solf. The idea of using Wilhelm II to defend the Sultan of Morocco diplomatically against the French and the British originally came from Germans in Morocco and was then championed by Chancellor Bülow. In Ottoman affairs, the decision to pursue the construction of the Baghdad Railway lay with Siemens and other private sector parties, again with the assistance of Bülow. This does not mitigate Wilhelm II's constitutionally derived responsibility as German monarch. It remained the emperor's role to ensure that his viceregal representatives preserved the rule of law throughout the empire. To the extent that questions of direct culpability are of interest, Wilhelm II's 'guilt' lay with his dereliction of his duty of oversight, with his lack of interest in the fate of his colonial subjects, and with his clear indifference to the suffering engendered by the empire he reigned over and inflicted by those who ruled in his name.

Despite his clear lack of interest in directing events that occurred beyond Europe, Wilhelm II played an important diplomatic role in German colonial affairs and foreign policy in instances of summit diplomacy, which drew upon the architecture and symbolism of royal cosmopolitanism. Where imperialism called for pomp, splendour, and circumstance, Wilhelm II was available to play an important part whenever his journeys across Germany in his royal train or his sea voyages across Europe in his royal yacht permitted. In his role as the symbolic embodiment of the German state, Wilhelm II acted, particularly during instances of summit diplomacy, in accordance with the dictates and expectations of his government as the highest representative of the German Empire. In this way, he could, for example, play a role in kindling an enduring sense of loyalty to the German Empire in Tupua Tamasese Lealofi of Samoa, a loyalty which would prove to be a constant irritant to the occupying New Zealander forces in Samoa during the First World War. Wilhelm II could also help fulfil the formal conditions for peace after the Boxer War by accepting the apology of the Chinese emperor on behalf of the German nation, albeit not without placing the entire peace in jeopardy by insisting that the Chinese diplomats kowtow before him. The German Kaiser even made himself available—against his better judgement—to play the role of Bülow's puppet in Morocco, in an attempt to defend German economic interests there.

Fundamentally, and in line with Johannes Paulmann and Eva Giloi's understanding of the changing nature of monarchy in Europe, the role of Kaiser Wilhelm II in German colonialism must be read in terms of his capture and instrumentalization by others who promoted and implemented the policies and actions that constituted Germany's *Weltpolitik*. These interests, pursued politically as well as through the actions of private sector actors, were intrinsically material and reflected the perceived need to expand Germany's global reach through trade, diplomacy, warfare, and the annexation of territories. As this book has shown, the material prizes of *Weltpolitik* included gaining control over the copra plantations of Samoa and the Marshall Islands, underwriting loans and winning communications and railway infrastructure contracts in the Ottoman Empire and the Kingdom of Siam, establishing commercial and naval harbours in Langkawi and Kiautschou, gaining control of the regional trading hubs of East Africa and Cameroon, preserving the open door for German trade in Morocco and China, and restricting the ownership of productive land to German farmers in South West Africa. Achieving these ends demanded that the Germans develop a range of approaches when interacting with the rulers of these territories, who saw in the

Germans both a threat and an opportunity for them to pursue their own political and economic objectives. Far from directing these processes, however, Kaiser Wilhelm II responded as other nationalized European constitutional monarchs did, by following the foreign policy developed by his government, his bureaucrats, and his merchants.

Index